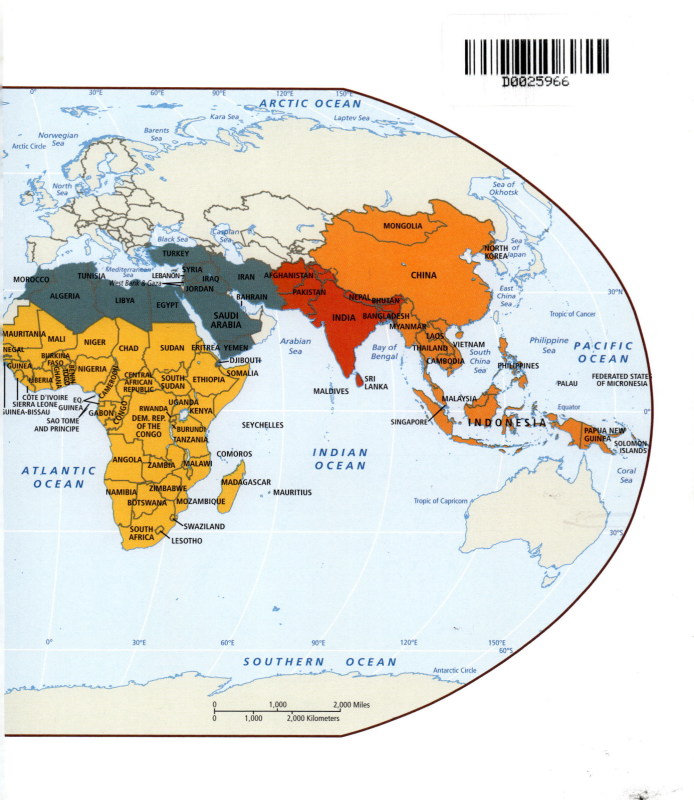

SHAPING THE DEVELOPING WORLD

The West, the South, and the Natural World

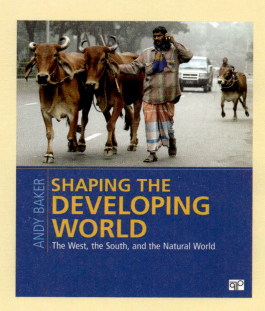

Why are some countries rich and others poor?

The consequences of colonialism, inadequate domestic institutions, gender inequality, and the effects of globalization, geography, and environmental degradation are just some of the factors at play in answering this complex question. Through a threefold framework of the West, the South, and the Natural World, Andy Baker provides a logical and intuitive structure for categorizing and assessing the factors that cause underdevelopment.

A series of well-designed features engages students in scholarship and helps them learn to think like social scientists.

- **Chapter-opening vignettes** paint scenarios that put a human face on underdevelopment and draw students into the material.

- **Country case studies** examine a country's development through the lens of the threefold framework and encourage students to think critically about scholarly explanations of the developing world.

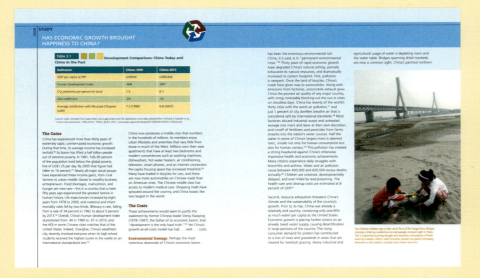

"I love the case studies. They cover different parts of the world, they cover various viewpoints, and they consistently weave together the strands of the threefold framework."

—Gina Yannitell Reinhardt, *Texas A&M University*

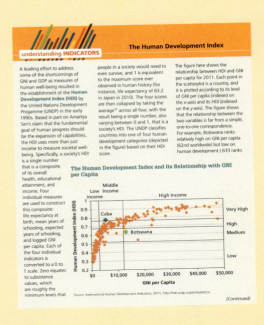

- **Understanding Indicators boxes** build students' data literacy through examination of how social scientists go about measuring concepts like prosperity, ethnic fragmentation, and gender equality, shining a light on how data can be used and its advantages and limitations.

- **Development in the Field boxes** spotlight different types of aid agencies and their work, such as microfinance institutions and democracy development efforts, so students see avenues for their professional aspirations.

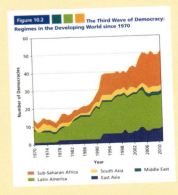

Figure 10.2 The Third Wave of Democracy: Regimes in the Developing World since 1970

Sub-Saharan Africa · South Asia · Middle East · Latin America · East Asia

- **Abundant graphics** illustrate concepts and contrast the disparities in countries' development and their sometimes rapid advancements, allowing students to apply the data literacy skills they've been building.

Other features that aid student comprehension

- **Bolded key terms** emphasize important concepts and are listed at the end of chapters to help with study and review.
- **Suggested Readings** and **Web Resources** point students to further resources for research and learning.
- A **glossary** defines key terms and concepts.

college.cqpress.com/sites/baker

Support for Instructors

A full set of **instructor ancillaries** saves time, eases class prep, and adds quality multimedia to your courses. Click on "Instructor's Resources" to register and download the materials you need.

- **Test bank**—approximately 400 questions, separated into multiple choice, short answer, and long essay, are available with test-generation Respondus software (compatible with most course management systems).
- **PowerPoint slides**—key concepts and instructor notes enhance lectures.
- **Downloadable graphics**—all of the book's tables, figures, and maps in PowerPoint, JPG, and PDF.

Support for Students

The open-access **student study website** combines valuable study materials that reinforce key concepts and offers opportunities to put knowledge to the test.

- **Study**—chapter summaries with review questions.
- **Quiz**—multiple-choice questions with automatic feedback.
- **Flashcards**—viewable by definition or by word, with marking and reshuffling.
- **Multimedia links**—connect to data and video resources on the web.

Shaping the Developing World

Shaping the Developing World

The West, The South, and the Natural World

Andy Baker
University of Colorado at Boulder

Los Angeles | London | New Delhi
Singapore | Washington DC

Los Angeles | London | New Delhi
Singapore | Washington DC

FOR INFORMATION:

CQ Press

An Imprint of SAGE Publications, Inc.

2455 Teller Road

Thousand Oaks, California 91320

E-mail: order@sagepub.com

SAGE Publications Ltd.

1 Oliver's Yard

55 City Road

London EC1Y 1SP

United Kingdom

SAGE Publications India Pvt. Ltd.

B 1/I 1 Mohan Cooperative Industrial Area

Mathura Road, New Delhi 110 044

India

SAGE Publications Asia-Pacific Pte. Ltd.

3 Church Street

#10-04 Samsung Hub

Singapore 049483

Printed in the United States of America

Library of Congress Cataloging-in-Publication Data

Baker, Andy, 1972–

Shaping the developing world: the West, the South, and the natural world / Andy Baker, University of Colorado at Boulder.

pages cm

Includes bibliographical references and index.

ISBN 978-1-60871-855-9 (pbk. : alk. paper)

1. Economic development—Developing countries. 2. Human security—Developing countries. 3. Developing countries—Politics and government. 4. Developing countries—Economic policy. 5. Developing countries—Social policy. I. Title.

HC59.7.B285 2014

338.9009172′4—dc23   2013012672

This book is printed on acid-free paper.

Acquisitions Editor: Elise Frasier

Development Editor: Nancy Matuszak

Production Editor: Laura Barrett

Copy Editor: Shannon Kelly

Typesetter: C&M Digitals (P) Ltd.

Proofreader: Eleni Georgiou

Indexer: Teddy Diggs

Cover Designer: Gail Buschman

Marketing Manager: Erica DeLuca

Permissions Editor: Jennifer Barron

SUSTAINABLE FORESTRY INITIATIVE

Certified Chain of Custody
Promoting Sustainable Forestry
www.sfiprogram.org
SFI-01268

SFI label applies to text stock

13 14 15 16 17 10 9 8 7 6 5 4 3 2 1

Brief Contents

PART IV | THE NATURAL WORLD: PHYSICAL GEOGRAPHY

Table of Contents

PART II | THE WEST: INTERNATIONAL CONTEXTS

PART III | THE SOUTH: DOMESTIC FACTORS

PART IV | THE NATURAL WORLD:
PHYSICAL GEOGRAPHY

Tables, Figures, and Maps

Tables

Figures

Maps

Preface

When I tell a roomful of students that "in the early twentieth century, 80 percent of Brazil's exports went to the West," indifference and glazed eyes reign. Alternatively, if I tell them, "According to some scholars, Brazil's trade with the West is what caused its underdevelopment," I instead find engaged students itching to argue and debate. It is theory—arguments about cause and effect—that makes data meaningful and interesting. This textbook on global development and underdevelopment takes this simple observation seriously. *Shaping the Developing World: The West, the South, and the Natural World* sees questions and answers about cause and effect as the best way for students to organize, understand, and remember topics and data on the societies of the developing world.

The book's layout and content are oriented around the vital causal question "why are some countries underdeveloped while some are developed?" Teaching students the various scholarly answers to this hotly debated question is a daunting task. The literature on this topic is vast, drawing from numerous disciplines, such as archaeology, anthropology, economics, geography, political science, and sociology. *Shaping the Developing World's* interdisciplinary approach brings order to this scholarly morass, making it easy for students to digest its complexity and weigh the merits of the many attempted answers to so important a question.

Organization and Approach of the Book

The book presents and is organized around a threefold framework—the West, the South,

and the natural world—for categorizing the various scholarly explanations for development and underdevelopment. Part I, Introduction (chapters 1–3) provides a basic foundation to development studies. It presents economic, political, and social characteristics of the developing world, describes various patterns and long-term trends in human development, and discusses the costs and benefits of economic development (a debate my students love to have). The threefold framework coverage starts with Part II, The West: International Contexts (chapters 4–6). These chapters consider theoretical explanations that attribute the causes of global poverty to the West, looking at factors such as colonialism, globalization, foreign aid, and the International Monetary Fund. Explanations that attribute causes of underdevelopment to the South—because of domestic economic and political institutions, culture, armed conflict, and gender roles—are explored in Part III, The South: Domestic Factors (chapters 7–12). Finally, Part IV, The Natural World: Physical Geography (chapters 13–14) covers explanations that attribute underdevelopment to the natural world, focusing on geography, climate, and environmental degradation.

Despite this orientation around theory, the book does not ignore description. Instead, it is through the central causal question and its potential theoretical answers that students learn important descriptive material on topics such as Western imperialism, the environment, democratization, international trade, the Washington Consensus, ethnic identity, political violence, female empowerment, and so on. Presenting information through the threefold scheme rather than as a series of randomly ordered thematic chapters provides instructors and students with a powerful road map for remembering and evaluating the information—one that is worthy of discussion and debate itself. This theoretical and explanatory approach is firmly within the new wave of social science pedagogy in which students learn social science logic as a way of thinking rather than acquiring only area-studies knowledge.

Shaping the Developing World also brings balance to what is often an ideologically charged debate. Arguments about what causes underdevelopment frequently morph into "who is to blame for global poverty?" and even some textbooks on less developed societies have overt ideological biases. *Shaping the Developing World* strives to convey explanatory material in a balanced way, giving the strengths and weaknesses of each scholarly theory. In particular, each presentation of a theoretical argument and its supporting evidence, which appear in sections labeled "Causes of Underdevelopment," are followed by "Critique" sections that raise shortcomings of the just-described theory. Moreover, end-of-chapter country case studies in chapters 1 and 4 through 14 illustrate three different theoretical arguments—at least one each from the West, the South, and the natural world triad—for why a country is underdeveloped. The case studies also encourage students through critical-thinking questions to think like social scientists and apply what they have learned to draw their own conclusions. By proceeding in this way, the textbook moves well beyond the defunct modernization-versus-dependency-theory dichotomy sometimes used to characterize the literature. It instead incorporates cutting-edge theory and research into the history of scholarly thought on development while still not completely ignoring the importance of these traditional approaches.

Special Features

Shaping the Developing World contains several special features that are pitched toward a wide array of student interests and needs. Each chapter opens with a fictionalized vignette that puts a human face on underdevelopment and the subsequent scholarly material. Recurring "Development in the Field" feature boxes are geared toward potential development practitioners. They describe aid agencies and opportunities for activism and employment that are relevant to the topic at hand, such as women's empowerment and microfinance institutions. These boxes also warn students of some of the precise limitations of these various humanitarian efforts. Another recurring box feature, "Understanding Indicators", builds data literacy by teaching students how social scientists have measured important concepts such as prosperity, democracy, economic informality, ethnic fragmentation, and environmental quality. Again, these boxes make students aware of the various drawbacks of existing measures. Each chapter concludes with suggested readings and web resources that students can access in their research.

Acknowledgements

I was lucky enough to finally find a permanent academic home in 2007 when I moved to the University of Colorado at Boulder. At the time, I had no idea that I would soon start writing an interdisciplinary textbook on global development. Fortuitously, CU ended up providing the perfect intellectual atmosphere for doing so. Through my affiliation with the Institutions group at the Institute of Behavioral Science, I was able to present several chapter drafts at our weekly brown bags. This group of ideologically and disciplinarily diverse political economy experts duly eviscerated each one, but I fought through the bruised ego and ended up with much better products as a result. Our group's leader, Lee Alston, wins the award for most chapters read, but I am equally appreciative of the other brown bag attendees who made comments: Jennifer Bair, David Bearce, Carew Boulding, David Brown, Ed Greenberg, Murat Iyigun,

Richard Jessor, Joseph Jupille, Moonhawk Kim, Tom Mayer, Isaac Reed, Jim Scarritt, Sarah Sokhey, and Jaroslav Tir. A few of my political science colleagues who were not members of this group were also kind enough to give me thorough comments on chapters in their areas of expertise: Krister Andersson, Aysegul Aydin, and Amy Liu. I am truly blessed to work at a place with world-renowned experts on so many development-related topics—the environment, globalization, democratization, Marxism, conflict, new institutionalism, development policy, cultural identity, economic history, and so on.

I am also appreciative of the staff at CQ Press for their assistance on the project. I will never forget when, after a passing conversation the day before with my CQ Press book rep about the threefold framework, acquisitions editor Elise Frasier called me and started talking about moving toward a contract. Elise's enthusiasm for the project kept me from doing what I originally planned: waiting another ten years before starting. Elise and my development editor Nancy Matuszak also provided excellent advice as I ironed out a number of issues big and small along the way, and my copy editor Shannon Kelly (among many other improvements) broke me of my habit of using too many quotation marks.

Thanks are also due to a few others. I owe an intellectual debt to Vikram Mukhija since the final product bears an imprint from the extensive advice he lent at the prospectus stage. I am also very grateful to Eve Rose, who gave me valuable advice and comments on the fictionalized vignettes. David Cupery, Alexandra Cutter, James Pripusich, and Sakif Khan provided research assistance. Finally, Ginna Fleming was kind enough to let us publish some of her beautiful and original photos.

I would also like to recognize the many helpful comments I received from colleagues across the country on the draft manuscript. Their time and thoughtful feedback was helpful to me during the revision process: John Bing, Heidelberg University; Kristin Edquist, Eastern Washington University; Zachary Elkins, University of Texas at Austin; Gustavo A. Flores-Macías, Cornell University; Barbara Deutch Lynch, Georgia Institute of Technology; Waltraud Q. Morales, University of Central Florida; David Penna, Gallaudet University; Jessica Peet, University of Southern California; Gina Yannitell Reinhardt, Texas A&M University; Richard Stahler-Sholk, Eastern Michigan University; Jessica C. Teets, Middlebury College; Anca Turcu, University of Central Florida; Lee D. Walker, University of South Carolina; and James Wunsch, Creighton University.

My immediate family deserves the most thanks. My wife Lila was extremely patient, supportive, and generous with her time during the two years it took to write this textbook. My daughter Della was also very forgiving of my occasional weekend absences, and I am proud to say that this book has taught her that flying toilets are not toilets with wings. I also remain grateful to my parents, Bob and Sue, for their long-standing support of my career. These four loved ones are all deeply deserving of this book's dedication.

To my family, Lila and Della.
To my parents, Robert and Susan.

Shaping the Developing World

A resident of Dharavi in Mumbai, India, checks his mobile phone in front of a small retail shop. Although debated, Dharavi is called Asia's largest slum, fitting a million people into an area the size of a few city blocks. Housing in Dharavi is dilapidated, and few of its residents formally own their homes. Despite this, the neighborhood teems with commercial and productive activity.

Underdevelopment and Diversity in the Global South

Nathalie of the Democratic Republic of Congo. Nathalie is an eight-year-old girl residing in the world's poorest country, the Democratic Republic of Congo. She lives in a remote rural village in the eastern province of South Kivu. Nathalie has five siblings, and another died in childbirth. Tragically, her mother also died during this stillborn birth. For the most part, Nathalie is now being raised by her aunts and a grandmother. Her family and fellow villagers grow their own food and thus have a precarious food supply. Nathalie, in particular, is malnourished. She is listless and undersized—given her height and weight, she would be mistaken for a six-year-old if in the United States.

food security

Nathalie goes to school in a small building with forty-six other children and one teacher. In a few years, Nathalie's schooling will be done. [Few girls are expected to be educated past thirteen, the age at which many of their fathers arrange for them to be married.] She is absent from school quite frequently. Twice a week she misses school to walk four miles round-trip to fetch clean drinking water. (Although she struggles to carry and balance three gallons of water on her head, Nathalie's brothers stay in school and are not expected to perform this task.) Nathalie also misses school quite frequently due to illness. She sleeps with her siblings under a mosquito net given to her family by a foreign humanitarian group, but every year Nathalie still suffers a few bouts of malaria sickness—chills, fever, vomiting, and headache. Even when in school, malnourishment complicates her ability to pay attention. Despite the schooling, Nathalie cannot read a simple text.

Patriarchy education

Nathalie's province has been troubled by war for years. Marauding bands of rebels, some of them from neighboring Rwanda, are known to sweep through the provinces' villages, stealing supplies, ransacking homes, and raping women and girls. Nathalie's village has been spared from the violence, yet she knows about the potential threat from adult

stability

villagers. They are debating whether to abandon the village and move to a refugee camp that would be a twelve-hour walk through thick forest and over muddy roads. The prospect terrifies Nathalie, as she has never been more than ten miles from her village. Despite the ongoing violence and potential threat in the province, Nathalie has never seen a Congolese soldier or police officer.

gov.

Priya of India. Dharavi, a neighborhood in the city of Mumbai (India), is considered by some to be Asia's largest slum. About the size of a large U.S. college campus, Dharavi has 1 million residents. Many of the homes in Dharavi are small wooden shacks with dirt floors that become muddy, like the unpaved streets outside, during the heavy rains of the summer monsoon. Few have toilets, so public restrooms are shared by hundreds of families. To avoid the wait at these latrines, some neighbors put their waste in a bag that is then hurled onto the street or nearby creek—so-called flying toilets. The neighborhood is seen by many as unsafe, and few parents allow their children to go outside after dark.

water

Priya is a twenty-eight-year-old Dalit woman who moved to Dharavi from a small rural village when she was six. Her parents had just died and her new caretakers, her aunt and uncle, moved with her to the city in search of better economic opportunities. Priya dropped out of school to marry around the age of sixteen and has since birthed three daughters. She works as a maid for a middle-class family and gets paid in cash the equivalent of US$22 per month. Her husband works a steadier manufacturing job, earning US$54 per month, but every day he endures an hour-long commute on crowded trains. Once off the train, he has to compete with hundreds of other commuters to hail an auto rickshaw to carry him the last two kilometers. On these combined wages, Priya's family rarely lacks for food, although their diet is not incredibly diverse or rich

in protein. Still, their income is not always sufficient to cover other expenses for items such as medicine, the family cell phone, train tickets, and entertainment for the girls. To supplement, Priya occasionally borrows money at about 15 percent monthly interest from a grocer who owns a small store down the street, and she remains indebted to him. She also keeps some extra savings in a bag under her bed, holding it for health emergencies or her daughters' weddings. *security*

Priya's house contains two rooms—one bedroom for Priya, her husband, and oldest daughter; and a second multipurpose room with a stove, dining table, TV, and couches where everyone else sleeps. This includes an unrelated single man who pays them US$11 per month in rent. The home does have electricity, but it draws from an illegal hookup that is potentially unsafe and not monitored by the utility company. Although Priya's home is meager, she is concerned about losing it. The Mumbai municipal government, which Priya voted against in the last election, would like to develop the area with modern housing, infrastructure, and amenities. If this development project occurs, a family like Priya's, which simply built its home without first securing ownership of the land beneath it, might have to leave Dharavi without receiving any compensation for its lost residence. While the government promises to give each dispossessed family a small flat (about 300 square feet) in the redeveloped neighborhood, Priya is doubtful. Without proof of ownership, there are no guarantees, and with no real sense of their future in Dharavi, Priya's family is hesitant to ever improve their home. *constant uncertainty*

Cheng of China. With a sense of foreboding, Cheng looks over his sixteen-year-old son's shoulder as he works on the family computer. His son is filling out applications for admission to some of the top universities in China. He is a talented student who attends an elite private prep school, but Cheng silently worries about his son's chances for admission. A year earlier, Cheng became an unlikely environmental activist and [critic of local officials in the Chinese Communist Party.] *too.* He thinks that, in having doing so, he may have derailed his son's educational aspirations. Cheng fears that the government could covertly keep the boy out of top schools. *education*

Cheng's entry into Chinese politics was sudden and unexpected. After all, he is a forty-two-year-old computer engineer whose salary affords his three-person family an apartment in a luxury high-rise complex, a car, a flat-screen television, a personal computer, and other modern amenities. Such comforts are not usually a recipe for political dissidence, but Cheng became a vocal critic of the ruling party when its environmental policy hit home. Cheng lives on the outskirts of the city of Wuxi near the shores of Lake Tai, long known as a haven for fishermen and, because of its natural beauty, tourists. Lake Tai in recent decades has become a hotbed of manufacturing activity. Local political officials encouraged industry as a means to raise the region's gross domestic product, and it dramatically boosted their tax revenues and the region's economic living standards. However, the boom around Lake Tai came with a dramatic cost, one that spurred Cheng's political activity: environmental degradation. Lake Tai is now heavily polluted. [The thousands of chemical factories on its shores dump toxic industrial waste into its waters. Most fish and many other aquatic species have died off along with the lake's attraction to potential tourists.] *environment* Most notoriously, the lake periodically experiences algal blooms, or overgrowths of toxic algae that literally turn the lake a fluorescent green color and emit a noxious odor that can be detected up to one mile away.

During one algal bloom, Wuxi's tap water turned yellowish-green and became undrinkable. Residents who showered in it smelled for the rest of the day. Cheng and other citizens queued for hours at shopping malls to buy bottled drinking water, which quickly became very expensive and was ultimately rationed by store owners. At nearly the same time, Cheng's mother died from cancer, a condition he suspected was caused by toxins in the city's water, food, and air. In response to both incidents, Cheng decided to organize small meetings with family and friends and even one street protest against pollution. He also investigated nearby factories to determine who was dumping waste, informing local political officials of his findings in the hopes that they might shut down or at least enforce regulations against polluting factories. His complaints were ignored and, in actuality, he has been followed and verbally intimidated by police. Cheng has kept his job, but he fears for his son's academic future.

Defining the Developing World

What do an African peasant girl, an Indian maid, and a Chinese software engineer have in common?[1] At first glance, seemingly very little. Nathalie and Priya are poor, yet Cheng leads a comfortable middle-class lifestyle. Nathalie is often hungry, but Priya and Cheng are not. Cheng resides in an authoritarian country, Priya lives in a democracy, and Nathalie lives in a place where the government has virtually no presence at all. Nathalie is rural, Priya is urban, and Cheng is suburban. Their very different life experiences would seem to undermine any attempt to lump them or the countries in which they live together, and yet [Nathalie, Priya, and Cheng are united in the fact they are all residents of the developing world. Not all of them are poor themselves, but their lives are shaped by the fact that they live in a less developed country.]

developing → shapes lives

Naming the Developing World

A developing or **less developed country** (LDC) is one in which a large share of the population cannot meet or experiences great difficulties in meeting basic material needs such as housing, food, water, health care, education, electricity, transport, communications, and physical security. For a society, the state of experiencing these deprivations is called **underdevelopment**, and the gradual process of shedding them is called development. Less developed countries are different from developed countries like the United States, since U.S. citizens have a relatively high average income and are largely able to meet basic needs. In sum, whether or not a country is defined as less developed depends on material factors of an economic and social nature.

The use of these terms and classification scheme is not always straightforward. The term "developing country" itself is imperfect because, as a descriptor, it is often inaccurate. Many poor countries are not developing. For example, Nathalie's DR Congo has become less prosperous, not more so, over the last fifty years. The notion of a less developed country is thus more accurate because it does not imply economic progress, yet even this seemingly innocuous term has its critics. In particular, the word "developed" offends some who see it as betraying a sense that rich countries and their peoples are more evolved, perfected, and superior to underdeveloped ones.

Other commonly used labels for poor countries also have shortcomings. Two are "global South" or just "the South." These terms make use of the geographical fact that the wealthiest countries are in the northern hemisphere with poorer countries to their south. Latin America is to the south of the United States, Africa and the Middle East are south of Europe, and the poorer regions of Asia are south of industrialized Russia. Like the others, these terms are imperfect. For example, wealthy Australia and New Zealand are among the southernmost countries of the world. Moreover, these terms obfuscate the classification issue by using a locational label for what is an economically and socially defined category of countries.

Another term frequently used is "Third World." French anthropologist Alfred Sauvy coined the term in 1952 to give identity to the many countries that, during the Cold War, were not formally allied with either the wealthy capitalist First World countries of the West (meaning the U.S. and Western Europe) or the Second World communist countries of the East. Thus, at its inception, the term Third World had a political and not an economic or social meaning. However, since the world's nonaligned countries also tended to be non-industrialized, the term eventually took on the economic meaning that has stuck to this day. Few users of the term today realize that some of today's so-called Third World nations, most notably China, were not originally classified as such. Because of this inaccuracy, along with the fact that many dislike the term because it implicitly ranks the quality of countries on a scale from one to three, "Third World" is largely avoided in this textbook. In the end, although each of the terms has its flaws and slightly divergent connotations, this textbook uses "less developed countries," "LDCs," "developing countries," "underdeveloped countries," "global South," and "South" interchangeably.

Delineating the Developing World

The map inside this book's front cover identifies the world's developing countries. Those classified as something other than less developed are shaded in gray. LDCs are colored by the five geographical regions that comprise the developing world: East Asia and the Pacific, Latin America and the Caribbean, the Middle East and North Africa, South Asia, and sub-Saharan Africa. To provide a point of contrast, information for the traditionally defined developed countries will often be described and summarized as the "High-income OECD" category. (The Organisation for Economic Co-operation and Development, or OECD, is an international organization that has included only rich countries since its inception in 1961.)[2] As is clear from the map, the vast majority of countries are less developed, and in fact about 80 percent of humanity resides in an LDC. Underdevelopment is thus much more prevalent than prosperity as a context of the human experience.

Furthermore, a large minority of humans are themselves impoverished. Many experts treat US$2 per day as the global poverty line, and anyone below US$1.25 per day is classified as extremely poor. In 2008, about 2.5 billion people, or 35 percent of the world's population, were below the poverty line, and 18 percent of humanity, or about 1.2 billion people, were below the extreme poverty line. As a region, South Asia has the largest number of these global poor, although sub-Saharan Africa stands as the world region with the highest share of its population below the extreme poverty line. Table 1.1 summarizes some of these economic and poverty statistics for each of the six world regions.[3]

The simple label "less developed" disguises a vast array of prosperity levels throughout the developing world. To better illustrate this diversity, Map 1.1 places LDCs into one of three categories based on the average economic living standards of their populations. The four categories are delineated by levels of gross national income (GNI) per capita. GNI per capita, along with the closely related gross domestic product (GDP) per-capita statistic, is the most commonly used measure of a country's overall economic prosperity. (See Understanding Indicators: Measuring Prosperity

with Gross Domestic Product.) For a given country, it can be thought of as the average citizen's income. According to the World Bank, low-income countries have an annual GNI per capita of US$995 or less. At this cutoff, the average citizen has an income of about US$3 per day. Lower-middle-income countries have average incomes between US$996 and US$3,945, or about US$3 and US$10 per day, respectively. Upper-middle-income countries are between US$3,946 and US$12,195. In contrast, high-income or developed countries are those with an average annual income greater than US$12,196. Map 1.1 makes it clear that less developed countries span everything from the many low-income countries of sub-Saharan Africa to numerous upper-middle income countries scattered throughout all five regions.

As indicated by these maps, this textbook does not include the countries of the former Soviet Union among its contents. These former members of the Second World have economic and social characteristics that are distinct from the traditionally defined less developed countries. In particular, they became independent countries in 1991 (much more recently than virtually all LDCs), with higher levels of industrialization, equality, educational attainment, and life

Table 1.1	**Poverty and Income Statistics in Six World Regions**		
Region	**Average Income**	**Percentage and Number Living in Poverty**	**Percentage and Number Living in Extreme Poverty**
East Asia and the Pacific	US$2,720	33 percent (640 million)	14 percent (270 million)
Latin America and the Caribbean	US$6,860	12 percent (68 million)	6 percent (34 million)
Middle East and North Africa	US$3,380	14 percent (45 million)	3 percent (10 million)
South Asia	US$964	71 percent (1.1 billion)	36 percent (575 million)
Sub-Saharan Africa	US$1,100	69 percent (560 million)	48 percent (390 million)
High-Income OECD	US$40,000	<1 percent	<1 percent

Source: Compiled from World Development Indicators, 2008, http://data.worldbank.org/data-catalog/world-development-indicators.

Notes: Average income is GNI per capita, Atlas method. Percentage and number living in poverty are those < US$2 per day. Percentage and number living in extreme poverty reflects those < US$1.25 per day.

Map 1.1 **Developing Countries by Average Economic Living Standards**

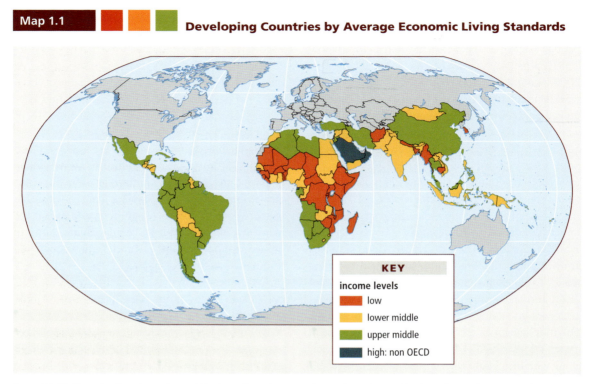

KEY

income levels
- low
- lower middle
- upper middle
- high: non OECD

Source: Modified by author from data at the World Bank, World Development Indicators, http://data.worldbank.org/data-catalog/world-development-indicators.

expectancy than standard LDCs. To be sure, many still have major pockets of poverty and social underdevelopment, giving them some shared characteristics with less developed countries. On most grounds, however, they are treated as a case apart. Throughout the book, readers will find data on LDCs and developed countries contrasted in tables and figures. In some figures, case study countries and some developed countries are labeled to make comparisons easier. A list of these country code labels is in the book's Appendix.

Economic, Social, and Political Characteristics

Given its diversity, the developing world defies simple summary. Few individuals in the developing world actually match the horrific images—such as the naked, starving child with the bloated belly or the illiterate child soldier—that are often seen in Western media and characterize many Westerners' notions of life in the developing world. Still, there are certain economic, social, and political commonalities that characterize most developing countries and that distinguish them from developed ones. All of these characteristics mentioned in this section are described in greater detail in subsequent chapters of this book.

Economic Characteristics

To say that LDCs tend to have relatively high rates of poverty or low per-capita GDPs is merely a starting point in describing their economies and economic characteristics. Another defining economic feature of the developing world is low productivity. In any given day, a typical person in the developing world produces fewer goods and services of value than does an average person in the developed world. Indeed, asking why a country is poor is nearly equivalent to asking why it is not productive: "Prosperity is the increase in the amount of goods and services you can earn with the same amount of work."[4] This is why gross domestic product is such a popular proxy for prosperity.

It is important to point out that, in describing people in the developing world as less productive, they are not being characterized as inherently lazy or deficient. It is not personal ability or effort but people's surroundings—the general characteristics of the economies in which they live—that largely determine how productive and thus how wealthy they are. The importance of economic context is most evident in the fact that, worldwide, a person's country of residence is more than three times as important for determining their income than are all of their individual characteristics, including innate ability and effort.[5] Rich countries have the technologies and institutions in place that make their citizens' efforts highly productive. For example, most of the things that make successful U.S. engineers rich are well beyond their making: the schools they attended, the banks that gave them loans for their education, the companies that hired them, the many customers rich enough to afford their services, the roads they use to get to work, the computer and telecommunications technologies they use at their work, the police force and legal system that protect their ownership of their earnings and home, and so on. In contrast, Nathalie and her family from this chapter's opening stories remain poor because, despite working hard to grow food and collect water, they toil in a context that does not provide them with these things. They lack modern farming equipment, roads and security to transport crops to markets, good schools, banks from which to borrow, a pool of well-off potential customers, and, of particular import to Nathalie's productivity, a clean water tap nearby.

Another feature of economies in the developing world is poor **infrastructure**, a term that refers to the facilities that make economic activity and economic exchange possible.[5] Infrastructure is generally divided into four sectors: transport, communications, energy, and water. Roads, telephones, electricity, and indoor plumbing are all examples of infrastructure. The opening vignettes to this chapter provide numerous examples of poor infrastructure in the developing world. Priya's husband wriggles onto a crowded train every morning and often cannot hail a rickshaw to complete his journey. Priya lives on muddy streets, has no toilet, and must use an illegal electricity hookup. Throughout India, only two-thirds of the population even has access to electricity. Nathalie lives far from any paved roads and has never seen a telephone. In her country, there are less than 2,000 miles of paved roads, and less than 20 percent of the population has a telephone.[6] Cheng is deeply affected by the polluted drinking water in his city, and China has some of world's most polluted freshwater sources.

As another economic characteristic, a large portion of economic activity in LDCs is concentrated in the primary sector, which is largely comprised of farming activities, and in unskilled labor. Less than 5 percent of the workforce in developed countries is in agriculture, yet in LDCs the amount is typically far greater than this. The vast majority of Nathalie's compatriots reside, like her, in rural areas and farm small plots of land for survival. The same applies to more than 40 percent of the Chinese and Indian populations. For those who do not work in agriculture, unskilled labor in the secondary (manufacturing) or tertiary (services) sectors is likely. As a maid, Priya provides manual labor in the services sector and her husband, as a factory worker, in the secondary sector. Skill-oriented jobs and economic activities that require a high degree of specialization and education are rarer in LDCs than in developed countries.

Finally, less developed economies have large informal sectors. The informal sector is comprised of economic activity that occurs outside the monitoring and legal purview of the government. Between 30 percent and 60 percent of all economic activity in most LDCs takes place in the informal sector. In developed countries, where this percentage ranges

Measuring Prosperity with Gross Domestic Product

A set of indicators all closely related to **gross domestic product (GDP)** contains the most widely used and recognized yardsticks of a country's prosperity. This includes the GNI per-capita figures used by the World Bank to classify countries into the groups reported in Map 1.1. Roughly speaking, a country's GDP for a given year is the total value added in the production of goods and services by all residents of that country, and the value of a good or service is determined by its price in the local currency. (GNI differs only in that it also includes income earned by citizens from assets or jobs they have abroad.) Dividing the total GDP by population size yields the GDP per-capita measure, which is the total value produced by the average citizen in the relevant year. GDP per capita is the most widely used measure of a country's average level of material well-being. Scholars convert GDP per-capita figures that are denominated in local currency to U.S. dollars (using the prevailing exchange rate) to make international comparisons of well-being more straightforward. In turn, a final adjustment that facilitates cross-national comparison of these dollar amounts is the purchasing

power parity (PPP) fix. A dollar goes farther in a country with a low cost of living, so, to better measure its average level of material prosperity, its raw GDP per capita figures can be adjusted upward to reflect the greater purchasing power of a dollar in its economy. In the end, of the various indicators within the GDP family, the GDP per capita at PPP measure allows for the most informative cross-national comparisons of citizens' well-being and will be frequently used in this book.

All that said, the heavy reliance on GDP-related measures to gauge human well-being has generated a number of criticisms. First, GDP equates the value of an economic activity or product to its price and thus does not accurately gauge its worth to quality of life. GDP excludes the many activities that contribute to a sense of fulfillment and purpose but that have no market price: volunteer activity, time spent with one's family, leisure activities, physical and mental wellness, intellectual fulfillment, political freedoms, happiness, cultural belonging, social connectedness, natural beauty, clean air, personal efficacy, and so on. Meanwhile, GDP gives value to many things

that do not enhance quality of life. For example, traffic jams (which increase the demand for gasoline), rising crime (which raises demand for lawyers and security personnel), threats to national security (military hardware), natural disasters (construction materials and services), unnecessary medical procedures (health equipment and doctors), and environmental catastrophes (cleanup services) all boost GDP.

Second, GDP overlooks the sustainability of production. For instance, politicians incentivized to grow short-term GDP figures have repeatedly created bubble economies driven by unsustainable debt that eventually implode in recession or depression. Similarly, it ignores what is destroyed in the production process. GDP makes no accounting for the depletion of natural resources used in production or for their availability to future generations. Environmental damage, greenhouse gas emissions (unless they are priced), and deaths caused by modern technologies are unaccounted for. As one example, the conversion of tropical rain forest to agricultural land by felling trees boosts a country's GDP since it makes the land more economically productive, yet this has devastating consequences for the local and global environment.

Finally, GDP per capita is indifferent to equality—that is, how dispersed the gains from production are around the average income. Decreases in inequality do not register as higher GDP, and GDP figures grow even when much of the newfound wealth accrues to the wealthy. Subsequent chapters in this book will introduce inequality measures and raise alternatives to GDP.

- Despite its shortcomings, why is GDP per capita so widely used as a measure of prosperity?

- What might be some better ways to measure human well-being than GDP?

from the single digits to the teens, governments register, regulate, and tax most businesses, workers, and major assets. In doing so, governments can provide a variety of benefits and services to citizens. Priya's story provides three examples of informality and its costs. First, she is paid at her maid job in cash, or under the table. This means that she receives none of the side benefits, such as an eventual retirement pension or unemployment insurance, that are typically offered workers in developed countries. Also, since her workplace is unregulated, there are no safety standards or rules against her dismissal in the event of illness or pregnancy. In India, an estimated 80 percent of nonagricultural jobs are informal.[7] Second, Priya's ownership of her home is neither recognized nor protected by the government. She thus has no means to protect this asset from theft, damage, or expropriation by other citizens or by the government itself. Third, Priya relies on informal channels to manage her cash flow. Priya stashes money in her house, making it susceptible to loss, theft, and depreciation through inflation. She also borrows from a nearby storekeeper at a very high interest rate. In India, less than 10 percent of the poor have formal bank accounts, and the average annual interest rates they pay on loans are more than five times the rates on offer in the developed world.[8]

Table 1.2 illustrates some of these features of less developed economies by summarizing information by world region about infrastructure (paved roads as a percentage of all roads), the primary sector (share of labor force working in agriculture), and informality (share of economic activity that is informal).

Social Characteristics

Underdevelopment is more than just an economic characteristic. Social underdevelopment is also a common feature in the global South. A society with poor social development fails to deliver educational and health amenities to large shares of its population. The systematic exclusion and disempowerment of major groups is also an aspect of social underdevelopment.

In the area of health, LDCs fall short of developed countries on a long list of indicators. Life expectancies are shorter, as deaths from diseases that are easily curable or preventable in the West are more common. Recall that both Nathalie and Priya had parents who died at a relatively young age. Moreover, Nathalie herself contracts malaria a few times year, a disease that children in the West almost never get. All told, average life expectancy is only in the high forties in DR Congo and the mid-sixties in India. Infant mortality rates are also higher. Again, the tragedy of Nathalie's sibling, who died at birth, attests to this. Nearly one in six children die before their fifth birthday in the DR Congo, and in India the figure is one in seventeen. Furthermore, nearly one woman in twenty dies in childbirth in the DR Congo. Even in China, where average life expectancies and infant mortality rates are closer to

Table 1.2 — Economic Characteristics in Six World Regions

Region	Paved Roads (as a percentage of all roads)	Share of Labor Force Working in Agriculture	Size of the Informal Sector (as a percentage of total economy)
East Asia and the Pacific	30.7 percent	39.6 percent	32.3 percent
Latin America and the Caribbean	22.5 percent	14.3 percent	41.2 percent
Middle East and North Africa	75.2 percent	27.2 percent	28.0 percent
South Asia	53.9 percent	53.5 percent	33.2 percent
Sub-Saharan Africa	18.8 percent	65.0 percent	40.8 percent
High-Income OECD	79.7 percent	3.3 percent	3.3 percent

Sources: Data on paved roads and labor force compiled from World Development Indicators, 2004–2009, http://data.worldbank.org/data-catalog/world-development-indicators; informal sector from Friedrich Schneider, Andreas Buehn, and Claudio E. Montenegro, "Shadow Economies All over the World," *World Bank Policy Research Working Paper*, no. 5326 (2010).

Western standards, the poor quality of the environment poses an ongoing health threat.

Moreover, in LDCs, levels of educational attainment and the quality of schooling tend to be lower, while literacy rates are often higher. Nathalie has little hope of being educated past primary school. What she is able to attain is of low quality, as she is in a classroom with more than forty children and can herself barely read. In DR Congo, only about one half of children complete primary education, and a third of adults are illiterate. Similarly, Priya did not complete secondary school in India, where only a minority of people do so. The same is true in China, Cheng's advanced degree notwithstanding.[9]

Social exclusion based on group status is also a common characteristic of underdevelopment in LDCs. Various forms of gender discrimination are particularly pernicious in many parts of the global South. Nathalie, not her brothers, is expected to fetch water and miss school because of it. She will also have a limited say over who her eventual marriage partner is. Cheng's only child is a son in a country where many parents strongly prefer sons to daughters and are willing to have sex-selective abortions to achieve this goal. Moreover, rural dwellers also tend to suffer higher degrees of exclusion than city dwellers

in LDCs. Worldwide, about 75 percent of those living in extreme poverty are residents of rural areas, even though less than 60 percent of LDC residents are rural.[10] Health and educational services, as well as infrastructure, are much less likely to reach rural areas than urban ones. Although urban slums such as Priya's Dharavi are often portrayed as the context for developing world poverty, Nathalie's rural reality is a much more common setting for the global poor.

Table 1.3 illustrates some of the social deficits that exist between rich and less developed countries. It reports regional averages for indicators of health (infant mortality), the social exclusion of rural populations (rural/urban gap in access to sanitation facilities), and gender discrimination (female/male gap in literacy).

Political Characteristics

Providing broad characterizations of the political systems of the less developed world is more difficult than describing its economic and social characteristics. After all, the very term "less developed" refers to an economic and social state of being, not a political one. Still, there are some tendencies that make political systems in LDCs different on average from

Table 1.3 Social Characteristics in Six World Regions

Region	Infant Mortality Rate	Rural Population with Improved Sanitation	Urban Population with Improved Sanitation	Female Literacy Rate	Male Literacy Rate
East Asia and the Pacific	17.0	57 percent	76 percent	91 percent	97 percent
Latin America and the Caribbean	16.2	59 percent	84 percent	91 percent	92 percent
Middle East and North Africa	26.1	59 percent	80 percent	68 percent	84 percent
South Asia	48.3	28 percent	59 percent	50 percent	73 percent
Sub-Saharan Africa	69.4	23 percent	42 percent	55 percent	72 percent
High-Income OECD	4.6	99 percent	99 percent	100 percent	100 percent

Source: Compiled from World Development Indicators, 2010, http://data.worldbank.org/data-catalog/world-development-indicators.

Notes: Infant mortality rate is deaths per 1,000 live births.

those in developed countries. The most important is that **political regimes**—that is, the set of rules that shape how a society is governed—tend to be more authoritarian and less democratic than regimes in developed countries. The developed countries of Europe and North America are democracies with free and fair elections, alternations in power among competing political parties, and legal protections of basic civil rights and liberties. In contrast, many of the top political leaders throughout the developing world are not selected through free and fair elections, nor do they uphold and respect their citizens' fundamental civil and political rights. All told, only about forty percent of LDCs are democracies, and virtually all of the political systems of the Middle East, as well as many in Africa and Asia, are authoritarian, including Cheng's China. Even in the LDCs where democracy does prevail, such as Priya's India, it is likely the case that the country became a democracy only in recent decades. By comparison, most Western countries have been democracies for nearly a century or more.

LDCs also experience more political instability than developed countries. Political instability exists when there is high uncertainty about the future existence of the current political regime. Wholesale changes in the political regime happen with some frequency in the developing world. Events that fall slightly short of this—widespread protest, political assassinations, terrorism, armed insurgencies, frequent turnover of the chief executive, failed efforts to change the government through illegal means (*coup d'état* attempts)—but that nonetheless indicate that the existing regime is under threat are also more prevalent in the developing world. The violence propagated by the armed bands in Nathalie's DR Congo is one indicator of political instability. By contrast, in the democracies of the developed world, alternations in power occur through election-based competition, and regime change and political violence are rare.

Another feature of LDC political systems is that they tend to have lower state capacity. State capacity is the degree to which a state is able to successfully and efficiently carry out its designated responsibilities and provide high-quality public goods and services. For example, many governments in LDCs are entirely ineffective at providing a safe environment for their citizens to live in. Recall that Nathalie has never seen a police officer or Congolese army soldier, despite the fact that she lives in a war-stricken province. Priya worries about safety because her city is deficient in preventing crime and lacks a legal system that can prosecute criminals. At the extreme, low state capacity can manifest as complete state failure, in which a state has no presence or ability to govern at all in most of its territory.

Finally, the vast majority of today's LDCs are former colonies. Colonialism is the governing of a territory by individuals and institutions from outside the territory, with the colony being the territory that is governed by foreigners. In the early 1500s, Spain and Portugal colonized much of Central and South America, commencing a five-hundred-year era of Western imperialism during which European powers took and held much of the non-Western world as their colonial possessions. Great Britain, France and the Netherlands were the other major Western colonizers during this era. Most of Africa, Asia, and the Western Hemisphere fell under Western colonial rule at various points during the era, which did not completely end until the decolonization of Africa in the 1960s and 1970s. For example, parts of Priya's India were colonized by various European powers—Netherlands, Denmark, France, Portugal, Great Britain—in the sixteenth and seventeenth centuries, and colonial rule of the entire Indian subcontinent was centralized under the British in the nineteenth century until Indian independence in 1947. Nathalie's DR Congo was colonized by King Leopold II of Belgium and then Belgium itself starting in the late 1800s, and European powers occupied many of the cities in Cheng's China during the nineteenth century.

Table 1.4 illustrates a number of these political features by contrasting regional averages on three political indicators: regime type (percentage of

Table 1.4 **Political Characteristics in Six World Regions**

Region	Democratic Countries	Failed and Successful Coups since 1946	Average Government Effectiveness Score*
East Asia and the Pacific	8 (of 16)	57	−.02
Latin America and the Caribbean	19 (of 24)	130	−.06
Middle East and North Africa	2 (of 18)	68	−.42
South Asia	3 (of 7)	29	−.23
Sub-Saharan Africa	19 (of 48)	226	−.82
High-Income OECD	30 (of 30)	13	1.33

Sources: Data on countries that are democratic is compiled from Polity IV Project: Political Regime Characteristics and Transitions, 1800–2010, www.systemicpeace.org/polity/polity4.htm; failed and successful coups, Monty Marshall and Donna Ramsey Marshall, "Coup D'État Events 1946–2011," Center for System Peace, http://www.systemicpeace.org/inscr/CSPoupsCodebook2011.pdf; government effectiveness, World Governance Indicators, 2011, http://info.worldbank.org/governance/wgi/index.asp.

*-2.5 is least effective and +2.5 is most effective

countries that are democracies), political instability (number of failed and successful coups), and state capacity (government effectiveness score assigned by the World Bank).

A Brief History of Economic Development

When looking at all of human history, the existence of less developed parts of the world is actually a rather recent occurrence, since modern economic growth and a set of more developed countries emerged just 250 years ago. A brief overview of this history helps put modern development and underdevelopment into context.

The Pre-Industrial Eras

Homo sapiens as a species has existed in its modern physiological form for about 200,000 years. For the first 190,000 (or 95 percent) of those years, humans lived as hunter-gatherers in small bands of a dozen to a few dozen people. Hunter-gatherers lived by foraging for edible plants, hunting live animals, and nomadically moving from place to place when food sources in one area became exhausted. The distribution of well-being across the human population was extremely equitable, as most food findings were shared within bands and there were no technologies or assets such as machinery or homes to make some bands wealthier than others.

Around 10,000 years ago, a variety of **agricultural revolutions**, defined as the invention and dissemination of farming, occurred in different pockets of the world and ushered in the Neolithic Era. The domestication of plants and animals enabled humans to exert greater control over the production of food. This increased food yields dramatically and freed up a minority of individuals in each society to take up professions—such as priest, merchant, engineer, inventor, soldier, politician, or artist—that did not directly involve food production. Farming also tied people to particular plots of land, removing the need for

nomadism and leading to sedentary societies. The first civilizations (Sumerian, Egyptian, Indus Valley) were stable settlements whose emergence was made possible by the agricultural revolution. The emergence of new specializations and the associated division of labor, along with variations in productivity across different farmers, introduced wealth inequalities into the human experience.

After the agricultural revolution spread to most human societies, economic experience remained defined by and fixed to agriculture for millennia. Up until the late 1700s, the vast majority of individuals worldwide were small-time farmers. Many were peasants engaged strictly in subsistence agriculture, growing themselves what they and their families ate and rarely, if ever, having a surplus to sell to others. Even in the most advanced civilizations of the 1700s, such as those of Europe and China, nonfarmers comprised at most 20 percent of the population. Average living standards, especially in comparison to modern ones, were very low. Famine was common, and even in times of plenty most people ate a nutrition-poor and undiversified diet. Most humans died of highly curable (by today's standards) infectious diseases or malnutrition in their thirties. Housing was primitive, with entire families sharing sleeping quarters and often, if fortunate enough to not sleep on a dirt floor, a single bed. Cities did not have underground sewage and indoor plumbing, so human waste ran everywhere in urban centers. Neither people nor information moved faster than horses could carry them, and individuals rarely travelled from their city or town. By the early 1700s, the ratio of average income in the world's richest societies to the world's poorest was a modest three to one. In a sense, everyone yet no one lived in the developing world. In other words, all humans lived in poor societies, yet because there was no developed world to speak of, there was no *less* developed world to speak of.

The Industrial Revolution

These conditions began to change very gradually in a few societies with the advent of the

Industrial Revolution in the late eighteenth century. The Industrial Revolution ushered in a new stage in economic history, the era of "modern economic growth," which has only been in existence for the last 0.1 percent of human history. This was not the first time that human economic activity grew more productive, but it was the first time that growth was so rapid and sustained. To illustrate, world GDP growth between 1500 and 1820 was .04 percent per year, but from 1820 to 1992 it was 1.21 percent per year.[12] Beginning first in Great Britain and then spreading to other parts of Western Europe and the United States, the Industrial Revolution rose out of a variety of inventions and small improvements to existing technologies that replaced human and animal labor with inanimate machine power. In other words, vast improvements in economic productivity were driven by the improvement and rapid accumulation of **physical capital**, the machines and factories that can be used to produce goods and services. Engines driven by steam and fossil fuels powered machines that could carry out menial tasks and create consumer products such as cotton clothing in a fraction of the time that it had taken previously. The advent of telegraph and railroad technology dramatically increased the speed of transport. Incremental technological advances in farming, such as better plows, seeding tools, and fertilizers, boosted annual crop yields and created surpluses that farmers could sell to others. These advances also freed up former farmers to move to cities and work in manufacturing or service jobs that were wholly unrelated to food production. Improvements in medical knowledge and the increasing availability of education for the masses led to dramatic improvements in **human capital**—the skill, knowledge, and health of the labor force.

Thus began a long and steady economic divergence between the West and the rest of the world. This divergence created the gap, still in existence today, between the rich countries that initially adopted the technologies and organizational features of the Industrial Revolution and the less developed countries that did not until much later. Figure 1.1 depicts an example of this divergence by showing the trend between 1800 and 1950 in GDP per capita of one of these early Western developers: the United States.[13] Its trend is shown in comparison to GDP per-capita trends in the three countries that were the subject of this chapter's opening vignettes: China, DR Congo, and India. The figure depicts quite clearly the severity of the divergence. The United States did have a tiny head start as of 1800, but by any modern standards it was a poor country, with roughly the GDP per capita that African countries Cameroon or Senegal have today. A US$1,000 gap between the United States and China in 1800 grew into a $6,000 one by 1900, and by 1950 it was a US$15,000 gap. The United States, along with a small number of other Western countries, left the rest of the world behind between 1800 and 1950. In doing so, the West created not just the developed world but a lagging less developed world. During these 150 years, the ratio of incomes in the richest to poorest countries had grown from about three to one to about forty to one.

This bifurcation between a wealthy developed world and a set of relatively poor less developed countries and colonies persisted until the 1950s. To be sure, some industrialization and catching up did occur among non-Western nations before then. After 1870, Eastern Europe (including Russia/Soviet Union), parts of Latin America (Argentina, Brazil, and Mexico), parts of the Middle East, and Japan began developing a manufacturing base. Given their late starts, however, they still lagged well behind Western living standards in 1950, with average incomes typically less than US$2,500 per year. Economically speaking, it is only a slight oversimplification to say that the world featured two camps in 1950: a wealthy West comprising just 20 percent of the world's population, and the very poor rest of the world.

Modern Economic Growth in the Developing World

After 1950, modern economic growth finally occurred in many of the countries that had been left behind by the Industrial Revolution. Many have grown as fast as or even faster than the West during this era, complicating the simple distinction between developed and developing world. This wave of progress has been much more widespread in its geographical scope than the Industrial Revolution, reaching most of the non-Western 80 percent of humanity that had been left behind. Countries throughout Latin America, the Middle East, Southeast Asia, and East Asia have experienced dramatic increases in GDP per capita and average livelihoods. Most began the 1950s mired in desperate poverty, yet the vast majority of countries in these regions today have developed at least a minimal industrial base, lowered their rates of extreme poverty, and seen average incomes rise well past US$2,500 per person. As one scholar puts it, "Never in the history of the world have the incomes of so many people risen by so much over such a prolonged period of time."[14] The fraction of humanity living in extreme poverty fell from well over 50 percent in the 1950s to around 18 percent by early 2013,[15] and world GDP per capita rose from US$2113 in 1950 to over US$10,000.[16] The size of the middle class, defined as people who have enough income to meet basic needs and afford at least some luxuries, has risen in every world region. By some measures, it has more than tripled in size in Asia and almost doubled in Africa since 1990.[17] Today, according to public

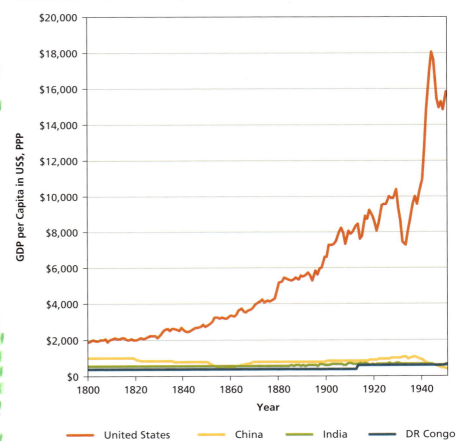

Figure 1.1 **The Economic Divergence between the West and the Global South, 1800–1950**

Source: Data compiled from Gapminder, www.gapminder.org/.

health expert Hans Rosling, "There is no such thing as a 'we' and a 'they,' with a gap in between. The majority of people are living in the middle."[18]

To be sure, this wave of modern economic growth has been extremely uneven in its timing throughout the developing world. It ranges from the East Asian "Tigers" of Hong Kong, Singapore, South Korea, and Taiwan, which skyrocketed from extreme poverty in 1950 to developed world status by 1980, to much of sub-Saharan Africa, where most economies have shown signs of life only in the last decade. In between these two extremes lies a myriad of patterns. For example, Latin America and much of the Middle East enjoyed rapid industrial growth in the first three decades following World War II, only to collapse into economic stagnation for two decades before re-emerging in the new millennium. In sharp contrast, giants China and India were late bloomers, beginning their dramatic and ongoing economic expansions in the late 1970s and early 1980s. As a result of this unevenness, the developing world now features a much more diverse array of living standards than it did in the 1950s. Figure 1.2 exemplifies this diversity and some of these regional patterns by showing the post-1950 trends in prosperity levels for the four countries of Figure 1.1 plus two more, Brazil and South Korea.

Figure 1.2 demonstrates that living standards have improved outside the West since 1950, but it also exemplifies the large and ongoing gap between the West and the South. The West itself continued to grow during this time period, and its head start as of 1950 was vast, accrued over nearly two centuries.

Figure 1.2 depicts how far China, even after three decades of blazing economic growth, would have to go to ever catch up with the per-person incomes of the United States. Moreover, as exemplified by the DR Congo case, some LDCs have experienced little to no growth since 1950. Extremely poor countries, which economist Paul Collier categorizes as the "bottom billion," [19] are almost exclusively in Africa, although they also include Afghanistan, Haiti, Myanmar, and North Korea. Because of these laggards, the ratio in incomes of the richest and poorest countries has ballooned to more than one hundred to one.

Goals and Organization: Who or What Causes Global Poverty?

This textbook has two primary goals. The first is to provide readers with a rich description of political, economic, and social life in the developing world. **Description** means the narration of a piece

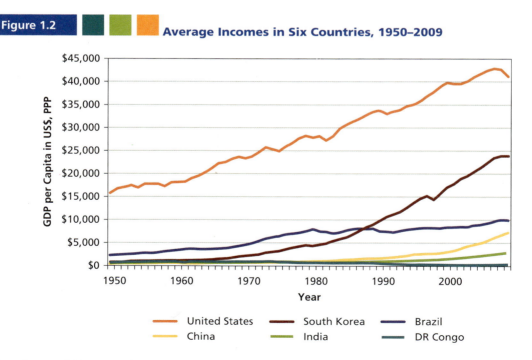

Figure 1.2 ■ ■ ■ Average Incomes in Six Countries, 1950–2009

Source: Data compiled from Gapminder, www.gapminder.org/.

of reality to create an image and understanding of it in the reader's or listener's mind. To that end, this book defines and portrays various features of the global South that distinguish it from the developed world, giving empirical data—that is, facts, histories, summaries, and other observable information—that capture many important aspects of less developed countries. The second goal is to lay out the various explanations for why global income inequalities exist. Stated differently, the book focuses on the following question: Who or what caused less developed countries to be poor? This is thus a goal of **explanation**, meaning argumentation about how one factor causes or influences another one. Any well-reasoned argument about why and how a particular factor causes another one is called a **theory**.

Causes of Underdevelopment: A Framework

Many readers might consider social science theories to be overly complicated and abstract. In fact, however, people engage in theoretical thinking about cause and effect all the time. Consider the following example. In 1948, its year of independence from Japanese occupation, Korea had a GDP per capita of just US$660. In 1960, its year of independence, Nathalie's DR Congo had a higher GDP per capita of US$870. By 2009, however, South Korea had a GDP per capita that was sixty-seven times that of DR Congo's. Why did this reversal of economic fortunes occur? Even if they know little about South Korea and DR Congo, most people can surely think of some plausible possibilities to answer this "why" question. Perhaps there is something about the countries' natural resources, leadership, climate, culture, or treatment by foreign powers that caused the difference in average wealth to emerge. The many plausible answers to this question about cause and effect are examples of theory.

The West, the South, or the Natural World?

Decades of scholarship on economic growth and global poverty have yielded a huge number of theories about why global poverty and inequalities between wealthy and poor nations exist and persist. Scholars from numerous disciplines—economics, sociology, anthropology, political science, geography, history, genetics, archaeology, physiology—have weighed in on this important question, blaming poverty on everything from tropical diseases to the International Monetary Fund. To give readers some means to navigate this complex scholarly terrain, this book provides an easy-to-remember, threefold scheme for categorizing and understanding the various theoretical answers to the question "who causes global poverty?": the West, the South, and the natural world. This categorization is evident in the parts of this book and throughout most of the end-of-chapter case studies.

Did the West cause today's LDCs to be poor? This category attributes underdevelopment in the developing world to international factors, namely those originating in foreign lands and particularly in Western Europe and the United States. Through the international slave trade, colonialism, globalization, and foreign aid, the West may have created disadvantageous contexts for development or even directly impoverished other parts of the world. Alternatively, are factors indigenous to the South itself the cause of global wealth disparities? This category attributes underdevelopment to origins that are internal to LDCs. A large body of scholarship indicts the domestic factors that are part of an LDC's own leadership, institutions, or culture, such as economic policy, laws and customs, and degree of internal harmony. Scholarship within this tradition attributes underdevelopment to factors such as undemocratic rule, corruption, weak property rights, a failure to embrace free markets, poor treatment of women and girls, civil conflict and violence, state failure, and rigid identities. Finally, do factors in the natural world that are beyond human design explain global poverty? This third and final category attributes economic underdevelopment to various aspects of geography and the physical environment, such as climate, topographical terrain, land productivity, and disease burdens.

Thinking about Theory. In thinking about theory and the threefold classification scheme, several points are in order. First, readers should reject the temptation to conclude that a single theory could successfully explain why some countries are rich and why some are poor. Reality is far too complex to be monocausal. For example, the brief history of economic development given in the preceding section might indicate that the question of why some countries are poor today may need two answers. A country is an LDC today because (1) it was left behind by the rise of the West during the first Industrial Revolution and (2) it has failed to rise as quickly as South Korea in the post-1950 world. The causes behind the relative distancing in livelihoods between European and non-European countries in the nineteenth century may be different from those behind the failure of so many countries to replicate the South Korean skyrocket since 1950.

Second, readers must understand that no amount of logic, empirical observation, or sophisticated statistical manipulation will ever prove a theory to be accurate or inaccurate. There are always overlooked theories and factors that could be the source of the true impact on development. For example, one could attribute the differences in prosperity levels between DR Congo and Great Britain to the fact that one was colonized and the other was a colonizer. But the differences between the two do not stop there. Great Britain is far from the equator while DR Congo is on it. Great Britain is a democracy while DR Congo is not. Great Britain has a relatively unified national identity while DR Congo does not. In fact, the list of differences between the two is infinite, so isolating the one or ones exerting the causal effect is impossible. For this reason, readers should remember the adage that "correlation does not mean causation." That said, readers can certainly use their own logical and observational faculties to arrive at conclusions about which theories are more or less useful for understanding the causes of underdevelopment.

Third, as with any categorization, the threefold classification has oversimplifying imperfections. For example, one explanation for Africa's underdevelopment is that many of its countries have numerous ethnic groups that struggle to cooperate and get along. This seemingly attributes the cause of underdevelopment to the South, meaning a domestic factor. However, African countries' high levels of ethnic diversity are partly due to the West, an international factor. European colonizers drew the national borders for much of the continent and, in doing so, grouped together many ethnic groups that had little in common. Rather than getting overly hung up on whether the theory attributes ultimate cause to the South or the West, readers should simply think of the classification as a useful, albeit imperfect, tool that helps them more easily understand and remember the various theories.

Finally, this textbook will avoid the emotion and ideology that often accompanies debates over the causes of underdevelopment. In practice, millions find there to be much at stake in considering what causes global poverty, since the answer allows one to assign blame for impoverishment. For example, Zimbabwe's president Robert Mugabe repeatedly deflects blame for his leadership of a country in economic decline by retorting that the roots of its plight lie in the past sins of Western colonialism and white-minority rule. *Shaping the Developing World* stays away from explicitly making moral judgments or casting blame for global inequality, although readers will surely see the ethical implications of many of the theories discussed within.

Organization of the Book

The threefold classification scheme provides the organizing framework for this textbook. This chapter and the following two comprise Part I, which provides an introduction to human development and the costs of development. Part II: The West: International Contexts contains three chapters on the various arguments that claim that Western factors are the cause of global poverty. Part III: The South: Domestic Factors contains six chapters on the various aspects of the South that might be the cause of LDCs' plight. Part IV: The Natural World: Physical Geography contains two chapters on nature and the possible geographical and environmental sources of underdevelopment.

Each chapter is organized to first provide readers with important descriptive material about the topic at hand. Subsequently, in sections called "Causes of Underdevelopment," they convey theoretical arguments about how the just-described factor might have caused underdevelopment. Since every theory has its limitations, each chapter then presents challenges to these theories in sections entitled "Critiques." A concluding case study presents information on a single developing country to illustrate how the main theoretical arguments presented in the chapter might explain its underdevelopment. The case study introduces alternative theoretical explanations for the country's less developed status, providing one example each from the South, the West, and the natural world framework. The next section of this chapter illustrates this case study approach, although it is not until Part II of the book that case studies with this approach return. Since Chapters 2 and 3 provide more descriptive, not theoretical, material, their case studies do not present the threefold framework.

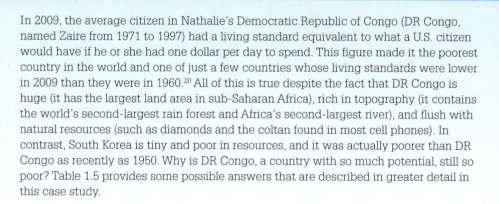

case | **STUDY**

WHY IS THE DEMOCRATIC REPUBLIC OF CONGO THE POOREST COUNTRY ON EARTH?

In 2009, the average citizen in Nathalie's Democratic Republic of Congo (DR Congo, named Zaire from 1971 to 1997) had a living standard equivalent to what a U.S. citizen would have if he or she had one dollar per day to spend. This figure made it the poorest country in the world and one of just a few countries whose living standards were lower in 2009 than they were in 1960.[20] All of this is true despite the fact that DR Congo is huge (it has the largest land area in sub-Saharan Africa), rich in topography (it contains the world's second-largest rain forest and Africa's second-largest river), and flush with natural resources (such as diamonds and the coltan found in most cell phones). In contrast, South Korea is tiny and poor in resources, and it was actually poorer than DR Congo as recently as 1950. Why is DR Congo, a country with so much potential, still so poor? Table 1.5 provides some possible answers that are described in greater detail in this case study.

WHY IS THE DEMOCRATIC REPUBLIC OF CONGO THE POOREST COUNTRY ON EARTH?

Table 1.5 **Development Comparison: DR Congo and South Korea**

Indicator	DR Congo	South Korea
GDP per capita at PPP	US$329	US$27,541
Population in poverty	73 percent	<1 percent
Human Development Index	.286 (187th of 187)	.897 (15th of 187)
Number of languages spoken	216	1
Persons removed through Atlantic slave trade	~1,000,000	0
Malaria cases per 100,000 people, 2008	37,400	8

Source: Data compiled from the World Bank,World Development Indicators, 2011 and 2008, http://data.worldbank.org/sites/default/files/wdi-final.pdf; United Nations Development Programme, "Human Development Report 2010," http://hdr.undp.org/en/reports/global/hdr2010/, 161; Human Development Index; Ethnologue.com; and Nathan Nunn, "The Long-Term Effects of Africa's Slave Trades," *Quarterly Journal of Economics* 123, no. 1 (2008): 139–176.

The South: Kleptocracy and Cultural Fragmentation

One set of possible answers lies in DR Congo's political leadership and the makeup of its society. Five years after achieving independence from Belgium in 1960, a young army officer named Joseph Mobutu staged a successful coup d'état, installed himself as president, and remained in that post for thirty-two authoritarian years. In office, Mobutu, who later renamed himself Mobuto Sese Seko, established one of history's most corrupt regimes. Telling his state employees to "go ahead and steal, as long as you don't take too much,"[21] Mobutu himself followed only the first half of this advice. Mobutu treated state funds as his own, amassing numerous palaces and mansions, many of them in Europe and some containing 14,000-bottle wine cellars, discotheques, private zoos, and doors so large they required two men to open.[22] Mobutu also allowed his political allies and even opponents

to participate in the plundering, keeping them quiescent to his otherwise ineffective rule. The means to wealth were not talent and hard work, but theft of taxpayers. Under Mobutu, DR Congo was considered the paradigmatic kleptocracy: government by those who steal.

In the interest of Zaireanizing (based on his own renaming of the country) the economy and redistributing wealth from rich Europeans to Zairian citizens, Mobutu expropriated most of Zaire's foreign-owned firms and farms. He kept some of the assets for himself and handed the rest over to Zairian public officials and other elites. In doing so, he gave agricultural land and factories to individuals not because they were good farmers or industrial managers, but because they were his cronies or leaders of important ethnic groups. Economic collapse ensued. Prices rose and store shelves emptied because the new Zairian owners of many businesses were not knowledgeable or motivated enough to produce goods and services as productively as the previous owners. The experience of expropriation discouraged future investment by both foreigners and Zairians. Between 1973 and Mobutu's departure from power in 1997, the average income in Zaire declined by two-thirds.[23]

Another possible answer resides in the fact that Congolese citizens have little cultural unity. Congolese identify more with their ethnolinguistic group, of which there are more than 200, than they do with the DR Congo as a nation. There is little sense of national identity, with one set of scholars characterizing this reality by saying that "there is no Congo."[24] This lack of national unity has erupted on multiple occasions into violent conflict that has had major economic costs. For example, in its first year of independence in 1960, the Congo nearly disintegrated into four separate countries as three different regions declared their desire to secede based largely around ethnic nationalist claims. The Congolese military eventually reunified the country, but only after years of violently repressing secessionist movements. More recently, the Great War of Africa (1998–2003), the deadliest war in the continent's history, occurred on Congolese soil when militias claiming to represent disillusioned ethnic groups in the far eastern corner of the country attempted to march all the way to Kinshasa in the west to overthrow the incumbent government. The conflict killed an estimated 5.4 million people and cost billions of dollars in lost economic activity.[25]

The West: Stolen Aid, Colonial Abuse, and Slavery

Mobutu didn't act alone. The West was complicit in his kleptomania. Soon after independence, Belgian and American intelligence agencies intervened in Congolese politics to place Mobutu in power

U.S. president Ronald Reagan (1981-1989) shakes hands with Zairian president Mobutu Sese Seku (1965-1997). Despite years of inept and corrupt rule that impoverished his country, Mobutu received millions of dollars of aid from the United States and other Western countries simply because he was seen as a reliable bulwark against communism in Africa.

over other leaders they saw as overly friendly with the Soviet Union. In the interest of keeping him in power, the United States, France, and Belgium granted Mobutu $1 billion in foreign aid over his thirty-two-year reign. Much of the aid ended up in the Swiss bank accounts of Mobutu and his cronies, and little was actually used to build schools, health clinics, or roads. The International Monetary Fund also extended eleven different bailout packages to Mobutu despite knowing that the funds were misused and ineffective in stabilizing the economy. Amidst all of the theft, U.S. president Ronald Reagan still called one of the world's most prolific thieves a "voice of good sense and goodwill"[26] because of his anticommunist credentials.

The West's complicity in the plundering of the Congo did not begin with the rise of Mobutu.

WHY IS THE DEMOCRATIC REPUBLIC OF CONGO THE POOREST COUNTRY ON EARTH?

Nearly a century earlier, King Leopold II of Belgium initiated his own reign of terror in pursuit of what he called "a slice of this magnificent African cake,"[27] a reign that stripped the Congo of natural and human resources. Leopold, who from 1885 to 1908 was the sole proprietor of the Congo Free State, implemented a brutal system of forced labor and looting that contemporary Arthur Conan Doyle called "the greatest crime which has ever been committed in the history of the world."[28] Leopold's armed security apparatus, the Force Publique, required native villagers to periodically collect quotas of ivory or rubber that were to be exported to Europe. These quotas grew increasingly difficult to fill as nearby reserves became exhausted, and when villagers failed to deliver a sufficient amount, they were whipped with strips of dried hippopotamus hide, had their hands chopped off, or were shot. Under Leopold, the population loss in the Congo Free State was an estimated 10 million people, and countless hours of labor and troves of natural resources were taken with no compensation in return.[29] Leopold and other Western powers even bear some responsibility for DR Congo's deep cultural divisions, since it was they who arbitrarily drew the colony's and eventual country's borders. In drawing the borders at a conference in Berlin in 1884 and 1885, they consulted no Congolese citizens and paid no heed to the fact that they were uniting more than 200 different ethnic groups into a single political territory.

Leopold's colonization of the Congo actually occurred relatively recently in the history of Western contact with Africa. As early as the sixteenth century, men and women residing in the territory that is today the DR Congo were being captured and shipped across the Atlantic Ocean to become slaves in the New World. Slavery was devastating not just to the slaves themselves, but also to the African economies they left behind. Between 1400 and 1900, almost 1 million people were forcibly removed from DR Congo territory.[30] This dramatic loss of human capital, often in exchange for destructive or unproductive imports such as guns, clothing, and seashells, kept the Congo's population growth and density low in a time when other continents were developing urban centers that were hotbeds of productivity and innovation.

The Natural World: Geography and the Resource Curse

Clearly, Congolese leaders and Western personnel have ravaged both the human and natural richness of the Congo for centuries. Is it possible, however, that all of this exploitation has been just a sideshow to the ultimate cause of DR Congo's poverty: geography? Beneath its flashy mineral wealth and its superlative river and rain forest lies a natural context that is quite detrimental to economic growth. First, DR Congo is wet—too wet: The country has more thunderstorms than any other in the world. This leeches its soils of their minerals and makes it impossible to grow all but a few crops.[31] Second, DR Congo has the largest number of malaria cases in the world, and the disease is the country's top killer. Like Nathalie, the average Congolese child suffers six to ten bouts *every year*, and 200,000 Congolese children die from malaria annually.[32] At best, children heal in a few days, yet during that time they have missed out on some schooling, may have drawn an adult caregiver away from work, and have probably experienced stunted brain development.

Nature also may have cursed the DR Congo in a more paradoxical way: by endowing it with a vast quantity of valuable natural resources. Although perhaps done with some hyperbole, one source estimated DR Congo's underground mineral wealth to be worth $24 trillion, more than the GDP of the United States or Europe.[33] DR Congo has the world's largest deposits of cobalt and coltan, and it also contains rich underground stores of copper, diamonds, and gold. Yet instead of making it rich, this mineral wealth fuels DR Congo's recurring political violence and conflict. For example, some of the violent domestic and foreign militias that marauded DR Congo during the Great War looted mines and used their booty to finance themselves. Moreover, few investors care to build up DR Congo's industrial base since its minerals sector remains so attractive.

All told, this long list of explanations for DR Congo's underdevelopment would seem to suggest that the odds are stacked heavily against the world's poorest country. But are all of these explanations equally plausible, and is the picture this one-sided? This textbook will give readers the tools to answer these questions in an informed way.

Thinking Critically about Development

- Some of these explanations for the Congo's poverty focus on individual people, such as Mobutu and Leopold, while others stress broader and less ephemeral factors, such as culture and climate. Generally speaking, which approach is more convincing? In other words, if the Congo had had better-intentioned colonial and post-colonial leaders, would it be wealthier today, or would this not have mattered?

- Is it possible that some of the factors listed as sources of Congolese underdevelopment, such as deaths from malaria and number of languages spoken, are more a *result* of underdevelopment than its cause?

- Is the comparison between DR Congo and South Korea useful for deciphering cause and effect, or are the countries too different from one another?

Key Terms

agricultural revolution, p. 15

description, p. 18

explanation, p. 19

gross domestic product, p. 10

human capital, p. 16

Industrial Revolution, p. 16

infrastructure, p. 9

less developed country (LDC), p. 5

physical capital, p. 16

political regime, p. 13

theory, p. 19

underdevelopment, p. 6

Suggested Readings

Banerjee, Abhijit Vinayak, Roland Benabou, and Dilip Mookherjee, eds. *Understanding Poverty.* New York: Oxford University Press, 2006.

Cameron, Rondo, and Larry Neal. *A Concise Economic History of the World: From Paleolithic Times to the Present.* New York: Oxford University Press, 2002.

Hochschild, Adam. *King Leopold's Ghost: A Story of Greed, Terror, and Heroism in Colonial Africa*. Boston: Mariner Books, 1998.

Smith, Dan. *The Penguin State of the World Atlas*. 9th ed. New York: Penguin Books, 2012.

Wrong, Michela. *In the Footsteps of Mr. Kurtz: Living on the Brink of Disaster in Mobutu's Congo*. New York: Harper Collins, 2001.

World Bank. *Atlas of Global Development*. 3rd ed. Washington, D.C.: World Bank Publications, 2011.

 ## Web Resources

Gapminder, www.gapminder.org

World Development Indicators, http://data.worldbank.org/sites/default/files/wdi-final.pdf

World Bank e-Atlas, http://data.worldbank.org/products/data-visualization-tools/eatlas

An Indian woman of the Bondo Poroja ethnic group winnows rice that has just been harvested. Rice is a staple throughout much of Asia, but if it is the primary source of calories in a person's diet, it can lead to malnutrition. In India, millions of children are malnourished not because they lack enough calories to eat, but because they eat an undiversified diet that is devoid of some crucial nutrients.

Human Development and Underdevelopment

Education

Ram, a forty-five-year-old husband and father of three, lives in a rural village in India's most populous state, Uttar Pradesh. He is a shoemaker with just a second-grade education, and he can barely read. Ram is diminutive, having been malnourished for years as a child, but at least he is alive. Two of his eight siblings did not see their fifth birthdays, one of them dying of diarrhea in the 1970s and the other of measles in the early 1980s. Unsanitary conditions and the lack of trained health professionals in his village contributed to both calamities.

Child mortality

Fortunately, Ram's three teenage children have had a better lot. All three of them have completed primary school, and one is finishing up secondary schooling in a nearby town with dreams of landing a plum government job. They have also avoided major health catastrophes, and Ram never experienced the misfortune his parents did of losing a child, in part because the village now has piped water and a health clinic. Still, struggles remain. Ram's children, although seemingly well fed, ate a diet in their youth that lacked in protein. As a result, they, like their father, are undersized. Moreover, while Ram is proud of his children's educational achievements, he is the first to express frustration at the quality of the education they received in the village. Teachers frequently did not show, and Ram is convinced that they discriminated against his kids for being members of a scheduled "lower" caste.

Social disparity shows development

Ram's family embodies the recent development tragedies and triumphs of not just India but of much of the less developed world. Quality of life is improving, as evidenced by the better health and educational outcomes of Ram's children in comparison to those of himself and his siblings. Yet it remains far below that of high-income countries on a number of grounds, as evidenced by their malnourishment and low-quality education.

This chapter describes the nature of health and education in the developing world. In doing so, it introduces and illustrates the concept of human development, a notion that envisions development not just as economic progress and income gains, but also as improvements in health, education, and other forms of social development. The chapter conducts two kinds of comparisons in describing health and educational outcomes in the global South. One is a snapshot or cross-sectional comparison that contrasts today's South with today's West. This approach portrays the clear social deficits between the developing and less developed worlds that are so visible and, to many, so discouraging in the contemporary global scene. The "snapshot" sections also point out how disparities within countries, particularly between urban and rural areas, are sharper in LDCs than in high-income countries. The other type of comparison appears in the "trends" sections, which conduct longitudinal comparisons to assess changes within the developing world through time. This perspective paints a far more optimistic picture, one of major improvement in human development within the global South over the past fifty years.

Defining Human Development

Underdevelopment is more than an economic status. For example, being poor entails more than just the inability to procure the modern amenities that a high income affords, such as personal computers, automobiles, and spacious houses. Economic underdevelopment also accompanies poor health, undereducation, and a frustrating lack of self-fulfillment. These are the fundamental aspects of human development.

The Human Development Approach

A leading body of scholarly thought on the noneconomic aspects of underdevelopment is the human development approach, also called the capabilities approach. Pioneered by philosopher Martha Nussbaum and economist Amartya Sen, the human

development approach holds that low-income or economic poverty is important because it is a source of the broader and more important problem of capability deprivation. **Capabilities** are substantive freedoms—that is, a set of opportunities that persons can choose that allows them to be who they want to be and do what they want to do. Capabilities include the opportunities to live, to be educated formally, to have nourishment, and to be professionally treated when sick or disabled. **Capability deprivation** (sometimes called human poverty) exists when one faces a lack of freedom to pursue these fundamental opportunities and, thus, to live the kind of life one has reason to value. To Nussbuam and Sen, the goal of social and economic progress should be to advance **human development**, which is the process of removing substantive unfreedoms,[1] such as the inability to eat healthy food, to pursue an education, or to see a qualified doctor or nurse when sick.

Central capabilities are those that are considered particularly important for human fulfillment, in part because they are fertile in building capabilities in multiple areas of life.[2] While advocates of the capabilities approach do not universally agree on what the list of central capabilities should be, there is consensus that healthiness and formal education are among the most fundamental capabilities for achieving human potential—hence the focus of this chapter. Premature death is the antithesis of human fulfillment, but nonfatal health problems such as chronic pain, preventable disabilities, recurring sickness, and malnourishment also hinder the ability of humans to live fulfilled and creative lives. Health problems are also detrimental to earning power and financial livelihood. An unexpected sickness can be devastating to a family's budget, and maladies such as malaria and chronic malnutrition stunt a person's productivity and brain development. Formal education is also a fertile capability as it creates a broader array of employment opportunities and career choices, as well as personal economic independence. Education also grants the ability to communicate and participate more effectively in one's society, and it improves health outcomes by making people more knowledgeable about modern medicine. Other capabilities that are central to most conceptualizations of human development include group equality, gender equity, and political rights, all of which are discussed in later chapters.

The Complex Relationship between Economic and Human Development

In general, rich countries have contexts that provide wider options for human fulfillment than LDCs. To Sen, "The process of development . . . is not essentially different from the history of overcoming . . . unfreedoms."[3] Economic development contributes substantially to enhancing capabilities since low personal and societal incomes are associated with restricted opportunities and limited potential for human fulfillment. On average, rich countries have better health and education outcomes, as well as greater political freedom and gender equality, than poor ones.

That said, human development and economic development are conceptually and empirically distinct. On a conceptual level, human development values education, health, social equality, and political freedoms for their own right, not just as a means to greater material wealth. The approach flips standard economics on its head: "Improvements in health, education, and security are what we *want* from development, while income is just a tool to help achieve them."[4] On an empirical level, economic and human development, although correlated with one another, do not always march hand in hand. Major advances in human development have often occurred in lieu of economic growth. Most telling is the fact that, over the last forty years, health and education outcomes have improved throughout the developing world, and, on average, they have improved just as rapidly in countries with slow-growing economies as in those with fast-growing ones.[5] Indeed, whereas Chapter 1 painted a picture of material divergence around the globe during the era of modern economic growth, a focus on human development reveals a far more

optimistic pattern. Due to gradual improvements in health and education, much of the developing world is converging toward rich-world qualities of life, leading some observers to conclude that "global development is succeeding."[6] Some of the evidence for this is presented below.

Health Snapshot: Description and Causes of the Developing World's Deficit

Good health is the most important aspect of human development. This section introduces some indicators of health and uses them to illustrate differences in health quality across world regions. The comparisons reveal one of the major human development deficits between LDCs and the West, although the size of the deficit varies by region. The section then describes the precise nature and immediate causes of various health problems.

Key Health Indicators: Life Expectancy and Child Mortality

Perhaps the most important overall measure of a society's health is its **life expectancy at birth**, which is the average number of years that newborns are expected to live if current mortality patterns prevail for their entire lives. Longer life expectancies mean fewer premature deaths are occurring, with more people living into old age and dying of natural causes. For the globe as a whole, life expectancy at birth is around seventy years, and in the developed world, average life expectancies are seventy-five or above. In contrast, they are quite a bit lower in South Asia and Southeast Asia, where they typically lie between the high fifties and mid-sixties, and they are a good deal lower in sub-Saharan Africa, where most countries have life expectancies in the forties or low fifties. That said, many countries classified as less developed have life expectancies that are in the low seventies and thus quite close to those enjoyed in the developed world. In China and most nations

DEVELOPMENT in the FIELD

Humanitarian Groups in Health and Education

Aid agencies that provide humanitarian assistance to improve health and education outcomes in less developed countries are legion. They range from major international governmental organizations affiliated with the United Nations (UN) to small groups run by a single director. The premier health organization worldwide is the World Health Organization (WHO), a specialized agency of the UN that coordinates major health initiatives. For example, the WHO plays a leading role in overseeing efforts to combat communicable diseases such as malaria, HIV/AIDS, and polio. UNAIDS plays a more focused role to achieve its declared goal of zero new HIV infections and AIDS-related deaths. The UN Educational, Scientific, and Cultural Organization (UNESCO) administers a multi-organization effort called Education for All (EFA) to make major improvements in educational access and quality, as well as literacy, by 2015. Finally, the UN Development Programme (UNDP) is the agency most associated with the capabilities approach, as it promotes a wide array of development goals and publishes an annual report that tracks human development worldwide.

Private organizations are also plentiful and range greatly in size. The Bill and Melinda Gates Foundation has a multibillion-dollar endowment from which it makes grants to humanitarian groups that are often (although not exclusively) involved in improving LDC health. Among other things, the Gates Foundation funds research and dissemination of vaccines. On a much smaller scale, philanthropist Greg Mortenson founded the Central Asia Institute to build schools in remote mountain communities of Afghanistan and Pakistan.[7] Other small humanitarian groups devoted to health and education number in the thousands.

Although they engage in philanthropic and humanitarian work, these groups are not beyond criticism. Some are accused of having excessive administrative costs, meaning a high share of their revenues (which largely come from charitable donations) goes toward employee salaries, marketing, and other operating costs rather than toward the advertised humanitarian purposes. For example, one study alleged that fully half of all the UNDP's revenue went toward employee salaries.[8] Lack of transparency and accountability are other commonly cited problems, as many of these organizations do not keep or publicize financial records about how donations are used. For instance, Mortenson has faced heated allegations of mismanaging donations, including the charge that he used them to promote book sales for personal gain.[9]

---

of the Middle East and Latin America, the life expectancy gap with the developed world is less than ten years. In 2010, Brazil's was 72.9, China's was 73.5, and Egypt's was 70.5, all within a decade of that in the United States (79.6).[10] Map 2.1 reports life expectancies for every country.

Two other leading indicators of a society's health are its child and infant mortality rates. **Child mortality**, or under-five mortality, is the death of a child before her or his fifth birthday. Every year, around 10 million children die before their fifth birthdays; more than 1,000 child deaths occur worldwide every hour. Almost all of these deaths are considered to be preventable in the sense that they would not have occurred had the child been born in a high-income country. Seventy percent of these deaths are cases of **infant mortality**, in which the fatality occurs before the child's first birthday. Experts define a country's child

Map 2.1 **Life Expectancy at Birth around the World, 2010**

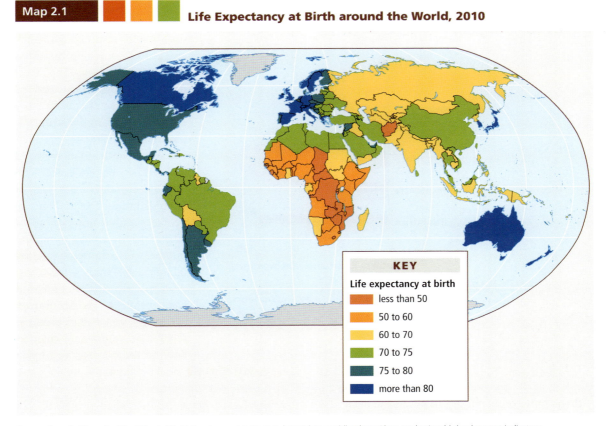

KEY

Life expectancy at birth

less than 50
50 to 60
60 to 70
70 to 75
75 to 80
more than 80

Source: Compiled from the World Bank, World Development Indicators, http://data.worldbank.org/data-catalog/world-development-indicators.

and infant mortality rates as the number of deaths that occur per 1,000 live births. Across the developing world, the child mortality rate averages around 75 deaths per 1,000 live births, whereas in the developed world it is just seven.[11] Sub-Saharan Africa has the world's most severe rates of child mortality, as fully half of all instances of child mortality occur there despite its having less than 15 percent of the world's population. Africa has thirty countries where more than 10 percent of children die before they turn five. Figure 2.1 reports child and infant mortality rates by world region.

Another characteristic of LDCs is that urban-rural disparities in human development are sharp. Rural residents tend to have shorter lives and run a higher risk of experiencing child mortality than their compatriots in the cities. For example, in

Cambodia's capital city, Phnom Penh, the infant mortality rate is thirteen deaths per 1,000 births, on par with that prevailing throughout much wealthier countries such as Thailand and Uruguay. In contrast, rates range from fifty to ninety deaths in its rural provinces.[12]

Life expectancy and child mortality indicators capture life-and-death matters, yet disparities between rich and poor countries also exist across a wide array of other health problems. One example is stunting, which is a severely slowed rate of body and brain development in children. In a variety of countries throughout sub-Saharan Africa and South Asia, between 15 percent and 25 percent of children have stunted development and are thus much shorter, thinner, and cognitively delayed than are healthy children. By some measures,

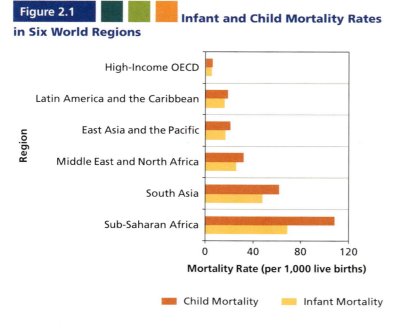

Figure 2.1   **Infant and Child Mortality Rates in Six World Regions**

Mortality Rate (per 1,000 live births)

Region:
- High-Income OECD
- Latin America and the Caribbean
- East Asia and the Pacific
- Middle East and North Africa
- South Asia
- Sub-Saharan Africa

■ Child Mortality   ■ Infant Mortality

Source: Compiled from the World Bank, World Development Indicators, 2011, http://data.worldbank.org/data-catalog/world-development-indicators.

Pakistan has the highest rate of stunting in the world at 30 percent.[13] Moreover, many less life-threatening problems are more prevalent in LDCs than in developed countries. Life without modern dental care, corrective eyewear, anesthesia, pain relief, the setting of fractured bones, prosthetic limbs, orthopedic surgery, and so on is an important reality for many in the global South.

The Immediate Causes of Poor Health Outcomes

What are the immediate causes of the shorter life spans, higher rates of child mortality, and other health problems in the less developed world? This section gives biological, social, and economic answers to this question, looking at the higher prevalence of malnutrition and infectious diseases and then moving to the lack of funding for and information about modern health techniques.

Malnutrition. Malnutrition is a condition in which the body does not receive enough nutrients. In LDCs, malnutrition has two major causes. The most obvious is insufficient caloric intake, estimated to be the cause of malnutrition in a billion people. Full-scale famines are mercifully rare in the modern world and tend to be associated with extreme events such as war or natural disaster. Yet millions of people simply cannot afford or access the necessary minimum number of calories. Another billion suffer from a less obvious form of malnutrition called hidden hunger. Hidden hunger occurs in a person that consumes a sufficient number of calories, but the calories are lacking in necessary nutrients such as vitamin A, iodine, iron, or protein.[14] In this sense, the person is eating the wrong foods. Many malnourished people do not even know of their condition since they are eating regular meals. For example, although malnutrition is widespread in India, just 2 percent of the population says it lacks enough food.[15] A contributing factor to hidden hunger can also be a body's failure to properly utilize nutrients once they are consumed, with diarrhea and intestinal worms being the most common causes of this nutrient malabsorption.

The World Health Organization (WHO) sees malnutrition as the single greatest threat to global public health because of the large number of complications that go with it. Indeed, Jean Drèze and Sen call it a "many-headed monster."[16] Most dramatically, malnutrition is present in at least 35 percent of child mortality cases.[17] Moreover, half a million children worldwide are blind because of vitamin A deficiency.[18] Iron deficiency can cause anemia, which is life threatening in pregnant women and can cause mental retardation. On top of these specific ailments, malnutrition weakens the immune system, making individuals susceptible to infectious diseases. It causes lethargy, which makes children less attentive in school and workers less efficient. Malnutrition is also the main source of stunting, causing irreversible damage if experienced in the first 1,000 days of life.[19] It can even affect children through their mothers since malnourishment in pregnant women can lead to low birth weight, stunting, or infant mortality. For all of these reasons, some experts see malnutrition as the cause of a poverty trap in LDCs: poverty causes malnourishment, which in turn makes the poor less productive, which in turn keeps them impoverished.

Infectious Diseases and Poor Water Infrastructure. Developing world populations suffer from a high burden of **infectious diseases** (also communicable diseases), which for this reason are sometimes called diseases of poverty. An infectious disease is one resulting from the presence in the body of a harmful microorganism. Examples include malaria, tuberculosis, cholera, AIDS, measles, and influenza. Infectious diseases are the primary cause of premature death in LDCs. Indeed, four of the five main causes of child mortality are infectious diseases: diarrhea, acute respiratory infections (mainly influenza and pneumonia), measles, and malaria.[20] In contrast, the vast majority of citizens in the developed world die from **noncommunicable diseases** such as heart disease, cancer, and diabetes, and these diseases are thus called diseases of affluence. To illustrate, only 28 percent of sub-Saharan Africans die of noncommunicable diseases, compared to 87 percent of Westerners.[21]

A primary reason for the greater incidence of infectious disease in LDCs is the suboptimal water infrastructure. In particular, LDCs have shortages of improved water sources that provide clean drinking water and improved sanitation systems that reliably separate people from their bodily waste. Many contagious diseases, such as cholera and rotavirus, are waterborne or passed among persons through contact with feces. Water that is soiled by human waste or other contaminants and then used for drinking, bathing, cooking, or swimming is a leading means of contracting harmful communicable diseases. Most of the time, the person with the disease suffers a few days of diarrhea and survives, but in some cases the diarrhea causes dehydration, electrolyte imbalance, and death. Diarrhea from these and other infectious diseases are involved in 20 percent of child mortality cases, killing around 1.5 million children per year.[22] Besides diarrhea, a similar family of infectious diseases caused by intestinal worms (hookworm, roundworm) is also common where water quality and sanitation are poor. Intestinal worms infect millions of children throughout rural Africa. Although they are rarely fatal, they cause health problems such as abdominal pain and malnutrition that keep children from attending school and workers from going to their jobs.

Worldwide, an estimated 1 billion people do not have even remotely clean freshwater within one kilometer of their residence, and another 2 billion have it within one kilometer but not through a household tap.[23] Both sets of persons must use untreated water fetched from streams, ponds, wells, rainwater collectors, or other sources, and they thus risk exposure to harmful pathogens. The inability to easily access an improved water source is a more widespread problem in rural than in urban parts of LDCs. That said, even in the cities of many middle-income countries where household connections are common, tap water is not sufficiently treated by utility providers to be trusted to drink. Instead, users rely on expensive bottled water.

Proper sanitation is even scarcer than clean drinking water in the developing world. It has been said that "the toilet has saved more lives than any other health device,"[24] since its primary function is to immediately distance humans from the dangerous microbes in their waste. Despite this, a majority of the world's people lack access to Western sanitation standards, defined as a flush toilet that dumps excreta into a sewer system that in turn treats the wastewater. Instead, fully 1 billion people worldwide defecate outdoors in a nearby field, ditch, forest, or body of water, risking the exposure of themselves and others to the pathogens in their feces. People in urban slums who use "flying toilets," in which one defecates into a bag and simply leaves it or tosses it in the street, are also part of this category. Another 1 to 2 billion people use various types of latrines—communal bathrooms that store the waste underground in a pit or a tank. Latrines are a notch up in safety from open-field defecation since they collect and hold waste in a central location that individuals naturally avoid. By some estimates, they reduce diarrheal illness by as much as 50 percent. Still, because they can allow waste to contaminate groundwater that may ultimately be drunk by humans, latrines are not as safe as the flush toilet. Of course, billions of developing world residents do have access to flush toilets that dump into public sewers, but even here exposure to feces can occur since utility companies in most LDCs do not treat wastewater before dumping it into rivers, lakes, and oceans.[25] For all of these cases, where open-field, latrine, or toilet defecation occurs, waterborne diarrheal diseases can still be contracted if users do not have a nearby place to wash their hands.

Figure 2.2 shows the share of populations in each world region that lack improved water and sanitation. The figure reports percentages for both urban and rural populations, highlighting the degree to which the latter in LDCs lag in this health-related factor. By one estimate, extending modern water infrastructure to the millions that do not have it would reduce the incidence of diarrhea by an estimated 95 percent and save billions of dollars spent on treating the ailment.[26]

Other Causes of Infectious Disease. Another reason for the prevalence of infectious disease in LDCs is the more limited dissemination of **vaccines** (also called vaccinations or immunizations), which are treatments that make one immune to a certain disease. For example, two leading killers of children worldwide are measles and tuberculosis, both infections of the respiratory system. Measles and tuberculosis are highly contagious because they can be communicated through salivary drops that travel through the air. Death from either is extremely rare in developed countries because more than 90 percent of children are immunized via injections they receive from a health professional in infancy. In contrast, in many LDCs, only 60 to 80 percent of children are immunized against measles, leaving millions vulnerable.[27]

Infectious diseases are also particularly problematic in the developing world because a host of maladies called tropical diseases exist in warm climates, where poor countries tend to be located, but not in temperate ones, where rich countries are usually found. The most widespread tropical disease is malaria. Certain species of mosquito carry the malaria parasite and pass it to human hosts by biting them. In most of the 200 million cases of malaria that occur worldwide each year, the human host has a debilitating fever for several days and then recovers. In well over half a million of these cases, however, recovery never occurs and death results. Around 90 percent of these fatal cases occur in sub-Saharan Africa. Even when recovery does occur, the disease can stunt physical and cognitive development in children if contracted multiple times in youth, as is often the case. A number of other tropical diseases, such as river blindness and dengue fever, also pose severe health risks.

A final contributor to the wider prevalence of infectious diseases in LDCs is the relative lack of information in the population about how they are contracted. To the untrained person, the notion that sickness is caused by living things that are invisible to the naked eye is not self-evident. The behaviors one should employ for prevention—such as washing one's hands frequently, avoiding swampy places where mosquitoes breed, and not letting children play where people have defecated—are also not readily obvious.

Figure 2.2 **Percentage of Individuals with Access to an Improved Water Source and Improved Sanitation: Urban-Rural Divides in Six World Regions**

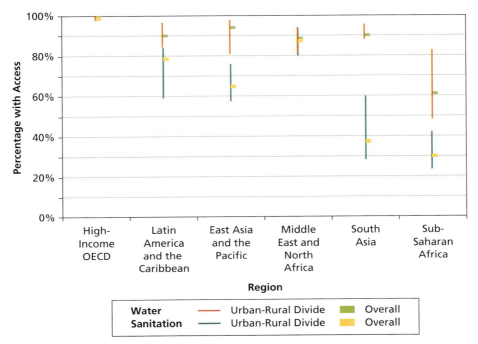

Source: Compiled from the World Bank, World Development Indicators, 2010, http://data.worldbank.org/data-catalog/world-development-indicators.

Note: Tops of red and blue lines are urban percentages, bottoms are rural percentages.

A particularly notorious example of the power of poor information to contribute to disease and premature death is the **HIV/AIDS epidemic** in Africa. Acquired immunodeficiency syndrome (AIDS) is an infectious disease that is caused by the human immunodeficiency virus (HIV). AIDS, along with tuberculosis, is the leading infectious killer of adults worldwide.[28] HIV is transmitted through bodily fluids that are capable of carrying the virus, namely blood, semen, vaginal fluid, and breast milk. The vast majority of transmissions occur through heterosexual intercourse, although women often transmit the virus to their children during birth or breastfeeding. Left untreated, HIV causes a person to develop AIDS, a condition that destroys his or her immune system and, in turn, leads to death over the course

of about ten years. The developing world carries a disproportionate burden of the global AIDS epidemic: 95 percent of the world's 33 million HIV-positive individuals reside in the developing world, and fully 60 percent of these are in sub-Saharan Africa.[29] At the epidemic's peak around 2000, more than 15 percent of the adult population of several African countries was HIV-positive.

Misinformation and a lack of correct information played and still play a role in exacerbating Africa's AIDS epidemic. During the 1980s and 1990s, the prevalence of the disease spiraled upward and became an epidemic, yet at the time relatively few Africans knew about the disease and about how to avoid contracting it. Most who died from AIDS did not even know they had it. Africa's societies at the time were predominately rural, poorly educated, and relatively unconnected to modern mass media, so transmitting information about the disease and prevention behaviors was difficult. To worsen matters further, many politicians avoided discussing the issue in public, and some even propagated false information, as was the case when South African president Thabo Mbeki's (1999–2008) made his famous assertion that HIV did not cause AIDS. This situation has improved in recent years as HIV testing and public awareness campaigns have proliferated, but these corrections came too late for millions.

Poorly Functioning Health-Care Sectors.

Throughout the developing world, large-scale shortcomings in health-care provision exacerbate the suffering and death rates caused by all kinds of health ailments. Virtually all governments in the South provide some health care to their populations, with these public services being free or highly discounted to users. This makes health-care provision an important part of the broader **welfare state**, which is the part of government that seeks to promote or protect the well-being of its citizens by providing such social services as education, housing, water, and retirement pensions. However, an underlying reason for shoddy health-care systems in poor countries stems from the fact that the governments are themselves poor. Governments rely on their citizenries through taxation to supply much of their revenues, yet poor citizenries cannot pay much in taxes. Overall, per-person public health expenditures are a fraction in LDCs what they are in the developed world. In 2007, average public spending on health per person per year in highly developed countries was around US$4,000. In very low-income countries, it was US$66.[30]

To fill the gap, the private sector often provides a large share of health-care services in LDCs, ranging from 20 percent to 80 percent in most cases, yet reliance on the private sector brings its own

problems. Typically, users must pay out of pocket for services, putting the poor on the constant brink of economic ruin should one of their family members get sick. Moreover, the quality of care is not necessarily higher in the private sector since the sector is only as well funded as its customer base. It is also less regulated, and research shows that private-sector care in LDCs is prone to overtreatment, in which prescription-happy health professionals provide unnecessary procedures and medicines because they profit from them. For example, in Brazil, birth by caesarean section is more common in the private than the public sector.[31]

The lack of funding for both the private and public health sectors manifests as a number of problems for patient care. First, many countries have a severe shortage of trained and qualified health-care personnel (physicians, nurses, and midwives). In high-income Western countries, there is an average of one doctor for every 350 people. In the developing countries of East Asia, the figure is one doctor per 850 people. In South Asia, it is one per 1,600 people, and in sub-Saharan Africa it is a mere one per 6,000 people. Some low-income countries have fewer than one physician per 10,000 people.[32] The consequences are severe. Because of the shortage of qualified personnel, the few available doctors and nurses are often in high demand. This inclines many of them to provide suboptimal patient care because they are rushed during their workday and have little fear of being out of work if they perform poorly. Moreover, millions in need simply do not see a health expert. For example, influenza is a leading cause of child mortality in LDCs, yet experts estimate that half of all children with flu and other acute respiratory infections do not see a health professional.[33]

Due to the relative lack of trained health professionals, false and underqualified ones often emerge to fill the void. Throughout the developing world, many individuals without medical degrees advertise themselves as doctors or nurses and attract a patient base. Without proper training, they end up missing easy diagnoses or mistreating common illnesses, with sometimes fatal results for their patients. Many patients cope with the shortage of qualified doctors by instead visiting traditional healers (herbal clinicians or medicine men). Traditional healers do not feign expertise in modern medical techniques, but they are visited nonetheless when they are closer, more quickly available, or less expensive than the nearest doctor or nurse.

Second, the lack of properly trained health professionals is exacerbated by widespread absenteeism. Many doctors and nurses fail to show up at their clinics or hospitals because of low pay and weak incentives to report in. One study of six LDCs in 2002–2003 found that doctors and nurses were absent from their posts 35 percent of the time.[34] This can be particularly devastating to rural individuals who may have walked long distances feeling miserable or with a sick child just to reach a health clinic that is, with no explanation, not staffed for the day.

Finally, health-care systems in LDCs are often characterized by deep inequalities. Public spending on health is often regressive, meaning the wealthy benefit more than the poor. Again, the urban-rural divide in access to professional care tends to be deep. High-quality doctors typically prefer living in cities where support staff, supplies, and pay tend to be better. As one illustration of this, virtually all urban households in Africa are within an hour's travel of a health center, while less than 50 percent of rural residents are that close to one.[35] Moreover, many medical treatments are hard to carry out without electricity and clean water. For example, vaccinations can be difficult to administer in rural areas because they require refrigeration.

Poor Decisions by Health Consumers. To be fair to the doctors and governments of the developing world, problems of a more bottom-up variety also exist in patient care. Many citizens of the global South fail to properly take advantage of health services even when they are available. Some do not get themselves or their children immunized simply out of procrastination. Many immunization courses require multiple visits over several months to a clinic, making them inconvenient. Also, immunizations' positive effects are largely invisible, so they seem less pressing to adults. As another example, patients themselves are often complicit in doctors overprescribing medications. After all, patients want to feel as if they have been treated for their illness, especially if they have walked a few kilometers while feeling downright miserable to reach a health clinic. On top of this, more times than not, they *will* feel better soon after the visit by virtue not of the medicine but of their bodies naturally defeating the illnesses. Either way, it hardens patients' resolve to be treated with something the next time around. A final example is a lack of breastfeeding, which is a powerful combatant against malnutrition at a most crucial time in a person's life. Worldwide, less than 40 percent of infants are breastfed exclusively for the first six months of life because mothers are too busy working in the fields or are unaware of the health benefits.[36] Of course, suboptimal consumer behaviors are also common in the developed world, but, given the more precarious health environment, their consequences can be more severe in poor countries.

Health Trends: Tracking Improvements in LDCs

Compared to the developed world, in LDCs infectious diseases and infant mortality are more prevalent, lives are shorter, and health-care systems are shoddier. Viewed from a longitudinal perspective, however, health in the developing world can be seen as a major success story. Comparing the contemporary South to itself a mere fifty years ago paints a picture of impressive progress.

Longer Lives

As a whole, life expectancies in the less developed world have increased by more than twenty years over the past half-century—the most rapid advance in human history. This has shrunk the gap between the high-income countries and all the others, as improvements in life expectancy have been more than twice as rapid in low-income countries as those in the wealthiest. Figure 2.3 illustrates this vividly by showing trends in life expectancy in six world regions since 1960. Improvements have been most dramatic in the Middle East and East Asia, where life expectancies rose by over twenty-five years in each. Improvements in Latin America (eighteen years) and South Asia (twenty-two years) were almost as impressive. Africa, despite the noteworthy headwind of the AIDS epidemic, also saw a net improvement of fourteen years, as the AIDS epidemic stalled an upward trend that reemerged in the 2000s. Although a gap between rich and poor countries remains, it was visibly smaller for all world regions in 2010 than it was in 1960.

Part of the driving force behind better life expectancies is that infant and child mortality rates have fallen. In 1960, the number of children under the age of five that died was around 20 million, fully twice the number in 2010 despite there being only half as many people in the world.[37] Stated differently, in 1960 the infant mortality rate averaged 200 deaths per 1,000 live births throughout the developing world; today, the number of countries with rates at or above that could be counted on one hand. The fall was most dramatic in the Middle East and North Africa. Under-five mortality rates of 250, meaning that fully one-quarter of children died before their fifth birthday, were reduced to the thirties by 2011. In sub-Saharan Africa, child mortality fell from 250 deaths per 1,000 live births in the mid-1960s to around 110 by early 2013. In South Asia, it fell from 240 to 60, and in Latin America it fell from 160 to less than 20. In short, tens of millions of young people in the developing world are alive today who would not have been alive had they been born just a few decades earlier.

Causes of Convergence: The Declining Cost of Good Health

Why and how did this stunning recent success in prolonging lives and saving children occur? The most important reason is that it has gotten less expensive over time to

Figure 2.3 **Life Expectancy at Birth: Trends in Six World Regions, 1960–2010**

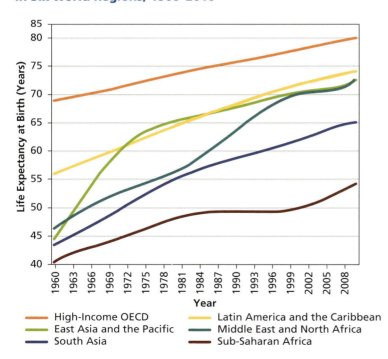

Source: Compiled from the World Bank, World Development Indicators, http://data.worldbank.org/data-catalog/world-development-indicators.

achieve better health outcomes. Constructing toilets, piping clean water, administering vaccines, treating diarrhea, curing infectious diseases, growing crops, adding precious micronutrients to food, and doing other things that are beneficial for health have become dramatically cheaper in recent decades. To give one example, Vietnam had a GDP per capita in 2000 that was similar to that of the UK 200 years ago, yet Vietnam's life expectancy was sixty-nine years, compared to a life expectancy in the UK in the early 1800s of forty-one years. As another example, between 1950 and 2002, per-capita income in Haiti fell by 25 percent, but infant mortality also fell—by 66 percent![38]

The worldwide spread of ideas and technologies has contributed to the declining cost of good health outcomes. Far and away the most important example of this is success in the discovery and dissemination of accurate scientific knowledge about infectious diseases, along with the distribution of effective preventions and treatments for these diseases. For instance, awareness campaigns regarding the importance of hand washing and rehydration solutions for diarrhea spells have yielded lifesaving results. A six-vaccine package distributed by international health organizations costs less than US$1,[39] and a de-worming pill that kills 99 percent of harmful intestinal worms in a body costs twenty cents.[40] Through the dissemination of vaccines, smallpox has been eradicated and polio and guinea worm disease nearly eradicated. The share of the world's children who are immunized against measles has ballooned from 2 percent to 80 percent in just fifty years.[41] Progress in combating even malaria, one the most intractable diseases because it has no vaccine, has also been rapid, as aid groups and domestic governments have distributed bed nets that protect sleeping children from mosquito bites and drained swampy areas where mosquitoes breed. Finally, through the combined efforts of governments, international aid organizations, private sectors, and community groups, billions of people have gained newfound access to safe water

and clean sanitation through investments in water infrastructure. All told, because infectious diseases have become less of a threat, the main causes of death in the developing world are increasingly becoming the diseases of affluence, such as cancer and heart disease.

The spread of technology and ideas has also mitigated the severity of hunger and malnutrition. As population sizes have continually swelled in the developing world, food production per capita has grown even more quickly, making it possible for humanity to more than keep pace in feeding its fast-growing population. Since 1960, the amount of food the world produces has more than doubled while the number of acres harvested has largely remained constant.[42] Technological innovations such as fertilizers, irrigation, and pesticides have increased farmer and land productivity. These adoptions have made food cheaper, resulting in rarer famines and less malnutrition. For example, China and India used to experience recurring famines, and in fact the most deadly famine in world history occurred just over fifty years ago in China (1958–1961). Today, however, a famine in either country would be almost unthinkable. Moreover, the world's citizens are eating more meat and protein-rich foods, so malnourishment has declined from an average of 25 percent of the developing world's population to about 16 percent in 2005.[43]

Education Snapshot: The Nature and Causes of the Developing World's Deficit

Formal education is instruction provided by trained individuals in a structured and certified schooling organization. Besides good health, access to formal education is widely regarded as the most important central capability, since it not only creates life and job-market skills, but also turns people into more empowered members of their community. This section describes the nature and causes of the educational deficits in the developing world.

Key Education Indicators: Attainment and Achievement

Indicators of education are often divided into quantity, which measures attainment or access, and quality, which gauges achievement or learning. The purpose is to distinguish between mere exposure to formal education and actual knowledge and skill acquisition. A number of markers exist to gauge quantity, or the number of people who are attaining formal education. A commonly used one is the **net enrollment ratio** at the primary and secondary levels. Net enrollment is the percentage of people of the relevant age group (ages six to eleven/twelve for primary, eleven/twelve

to seventeen/eighteen for secondary) that are enrolled in school.[44] Figure 2.4 shows these ratios for six world regions in 2007. In developed countries, primary school attendance is virtually universal, typically 97 percent or above. Primary enrollment ratios are also nearly universal in Latin America, East Asia, and the Middle East, all of which have percentages above 90 percent. The gap opens up, however, in looking at the percentages for South Asia (86 percent) and sub-Saharan Africa (74 percent). Worldwide, around 70 million primary-school-aged children are not in school, and nearly all of them reside in these two regions.

Figure 2.4 shows that the gap between the developed and developing world is even greater when considering enrollment ratios at the secondary level. In the developed fworld, more than 90 percent of children remain enrolled in school after completing their primary studies. Percentages are far lower across the developing world: 48 percent in South Asia and 26 percent in sub-Saharan Africa. In Latin America, East Asia, and the Middle East, secondary enrollment ratios are higher but still range only between 65 percent and 75 percent. Gaps in tertiary (college, university, or postsecondary vocational training) enrollments are even more yawning, as less than one African in twenty receives some postsecondary education, whereas two-thirds of Westerners do.

Two other indicators of educational attainment are mean years of schooling and the adult literacy rate. Mean years of schooling is the average number of years of formal education per adult (defined as those aged twenty-five and up). Adults in the developed world average 11.4 years of schooling, but that number drops to just eight in Latin America,

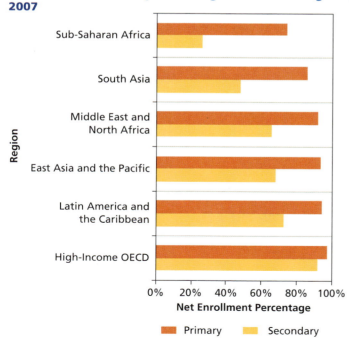

Figure 2.4   **Net Enrollment Ratios for Primary and Secondary Schooling in Six World Regions, 2007**

Source: Compiled from the World Bank, World Development Indicators, 2007, http://data.worldbank.org/data-catalog/world-development-indicators.

5.7 in the Middle East, and 4.5 in South Asia and sub-Saharan Africa. The adult literacy rate is the percentage of adults (persons older than fifteen) who can read and write. In practice, the bar for literacy in most statistical datasets is quite low, merely testing whether individuals can read and write a short text. Again, literacy rates in the developed world are typically 99 percent. In contrast, in the Middle East they are just 72 percent, and in South Asia and sub-Saharan Africa they are around 63 percent. Worldwide, around 900 million adults, about one in six—are illiterate. As with health outcomes, rural areas tend to have lower rates than urban ones on these measures: in low- and lower-middle-income countries, adult literacy rates are anywhere from ten to forty percentage points lower in the countryside than in the cities.[45]

These attainment indicators are relatively easy to gather, since they are the rough equivalent of counting heads. They fail to capture, however, the amount of actual learning and skill acquisition that takes place in formal educational settings. Measures of quality can fill this gap, but they are harder to collect. The evidence that does exist shows that students in developing countries learn less per year of schooling than those in developed ones. One rough but widely available proxy for quality is the average number of students per instructor, or the pupil-teacher ratio. In 2010 in the developed world, the pupil-teacher ratio in primary schooling was 12.1, and it was 14.2 at the secondary level. In contrast, ratios in the developing world were notably higher. In South Asia and sub-Saharan Africa, they were more than thrice as high at the primary level—in the low forties. A few countries, such as Rwanda, even have ratios in the sixties. At the secondary level, classrooms in South Asia and sub-Saharan Africa were nearly twice as crowded as those in high-income countries, with ratios in the mid-twenties. In other less developed regions, ratios are a good deal smaller than those prevailing in these two, but they still fall short of those in the

developed world.[46] Another more direct indicator of quality lies in internationally comparable math and reading test scores, but these are available for only a small subset of LDCs. One study of twenty countries found that eighth graders in developing countries scored only as well, on average, as developed-country fifth graders.[47]

The Immediate Causes of Poor Educational Outcomes

All told, education systems in LDCs pose a dual disadvantage to their citizens: students attain less formal schooling and learn less while they are in school. Scholars cite at least three immediate causes for this.

Low Funding. As with health, an overriding cause of poor education is a relative lack of funding. At the primary and secondary levels, the vast majority of children attend public schools funded by government expenditures. In fact, privately funded schools are much rarer than privately funded clinics and hospitals in LDCs. Not surprisingly, the funding gap between developed and less developed countries is vast. In developed countries, spending per primary student averages US$3,760, but it is one-eighteenth that amount (US$202) in low-income countries and one-eleventh that amount (US$338) throughout sub-Saharan Africa.[48] Even in middle-income countries such as many of those found in Latin America, the Middle East, and East Asia, spending per primary student is only one-fourth that of the developed countries.

Lack of funding also results in an absence of schools where they are needed. Many areas, especially rural ones, face an undersupply of schools. In the millions of villages that lack a primary school, children may have to walk long distances just to attend classes. Low funding can also mean decrepit or inadequate facilities. Many girls drop out of school upon reaching puberty because of a lack of private and sanitary bathrooms. Finally, limited government support means that many public schools in the developing world charge user fees, even of primary students. In Africa, an estimated 30 percent of educational funding comes from these fees.[49] Mandatory uniforms, school supplies, and lunch money are also costs that deter many parents from keeping a child in school.

Poor Instruction. Concerns related to poor instruction are also prevalent. First, in LDCs, 10 percent of primary teachers and 30 percent of secondary teachers are not formally trained as such.[50] Second, many schools are lacking in basic equipment such as blackboards, chalk, textbooks, or even an actual building. Third, school days are, on average, shorter in the developing world. Many schools, even in medium-income countries such as Brazil, operate on double shifts, in which children attend for just a half day (either in the morning or afternoon) with one teacher covering both shifts. Fourth, because of bad or no incentives, absenteeism among teachers is common. One study of seven developing countries found that teachers were absent an average of one out of every five days.[51]

Even when trained teachers are present, the curriculum and quality of instruction are often highly inadequate. Instruction in LDCs tends to be by rote memorization, with teachers reading or copying directly from a book onto a blackboard. Moreover, teaching often carries an elite bias that is allegedly a carryover from colonial days. For starters, millions of children in LDCs are taught in a nonnative language. Countries throughout Africa and South Asia teach in the official (often colonial) language, such as English, French, or Hindi, which a majority of children do not speak or understand prior to enrolling in school. Similarly, many instructors teach to the top of the class to prepare talented students for secondary and university entrance exams, a remnant of the pre-independence era when schools were meant to create a colonial elite.[52] Students that are average or below receive little remedial instruction and are simply left behind by this approach.

Parental Decisions. Bottom-up decisions, particularly those by parents, also shape school enrollment. In most instances, children fail to attend school or drop out early by choice of their parents, who have a variety of good reasons for making such a decision. Most importantly, when parents are poor, the opportunity cost of keeping their able-bodied children in school is high, especially since the benefits of schooling are not reaped until the future. Children can provide valuable assistance around the house or in the fields, and they can even hold wage-paying jobs that contribute to family income. Foregoing this help or income is too much for many needy parents. For this reason, the prevalence of **child labor**, when a child under the age of fifteen engages in sustained full- or part-time work (rather than just occasional household chores) tends to be high where educational enrollments are low. In sub-Saharan Africa, about 20 percent of children below fifteen are at work, the vast majority in agriculture on family or village plots. Even in middle-income countries such as those in Latin America, the figure is around 5 percent.[53]

Parents' perceptions of opportunity costs can seem particularly high when the eventual payoff from education is low. Many economies do not reward formal education, so parents see little value in keeping their kids in school. Without a well-developed industrial base or modern service economy, some LDCs simply have little demand for trained labor or do not provide wages to workers with secondary or college educations that are sufficiently higher than those paid to untrained workers. Similarly, when schooling is of low quality or when a child appears to be lost in her or his studies, it is natural for parents to conclude that it is a waste of time, especially when opportunity costs are high. Indeed, many poor families with multiple children invest in the child that they think has the best academic prowess by removing all but that child from school and encouraging her or him to be the one to pursue secondary and tertiary studies.

Bottom-up reasons also exist for low achievement, even in the absence of a child fully dropping out. Absenteeism among students, like that among teachers, runs high, ranging from an average of 14 percent of days in some countries to nearly 50 percent in others.[54] Many days are lost to illness and to parents' wish that their children do episodic work around the house fetching water, harvesting food, or watching a younger sibling. Finally, even when present, students who are malnourished learn less than well-fed ones.

Education Trends: Tracking Improvements in LDCs through Time

As with health outcomes, educational quantity and quality seem dire relative to those of the developed world. Again, however, a look back into recent history reveals dramatic improvements over a relatively short period of time.

Higher Enrollments and Better Quality

Since 1960, the mean years of schooling throughout the developing world has more than tripled, rising from 1.9 years to 6.4. Partly as a result, the literacy rate of the entire developing world jumped from 50 percent to 81 percent between 1970 and 2010. It nearly tripled (from 23 percent to 65 percent) in sub-Saharan Africa, and in South Asia it more than doubled (from 31 percent to 66 percent).[55] Not a single country has seen a decline in its basic education indicators since 1970. In short, the developing world is educating a higher share of its youth than ever before, and widespread illiteracy is gradually becoming a problem of the past. Figure 2.5 depicts these improvements and the global convergence by plotting average net primary enrollments in six world regions through time.

As further indication of these encouraging patterns, some experts point to promising trends in another statistic, the expected years of schooling. This is the average number of years that children of school-entering age can expect to receive if contemporary patterns of enrollment prevail throughout their lives. In countries where enrollment rates are improving quickly, the expected years of schooling can be a much larger figure than the mean years of schooling and a much better indicator of a society's current commitment to educating its children. That is because mean years of schooling can be pulled down by older adults who received little education because they were children in more austere times. For example, sub-Saharan Africa's expected years of schooling is 9.0, fully twice its current mean years of 4.5. South Asia's expected years (10.0) is more than twice its current mean (4.6), and in every other developing world region the expected mean is at least 60 percent higher than the current one.[56] In short, the educational attainment of less developed societies will continue to improve over the next several decades.

The quality of education has also improved, at least according to available indicators. Pupil-teacher ratios have declined from a developing-world average of thirty-two in 1970 to twenty-seven in 2010. The pace of this change, however, has been uneven across world regions, with only East Asia, Latin America, and the Middle East seeing improvements.

Causes of Convergence: Better Funding and Parental Commitment

The causes of these improvements lie in two developments. First, the developing world's governments are devoting more funds to education. Because education is almost universally seen as an important element of nation-building and economic success, most governments have ramped up their efforts to construct schools, especially in rural areas where distance is such a barrier to attendance. The spread of democracy to many formerly dictatorial countries also precipitated an increase in public expenditures on social services, including education. As part of their efforts, many governments have also tried to entice parents to keep their children in schools. One

Figure 2.5 Primary School Net Enrollment Ratio: Trends in Six World Regions, 1970–2010

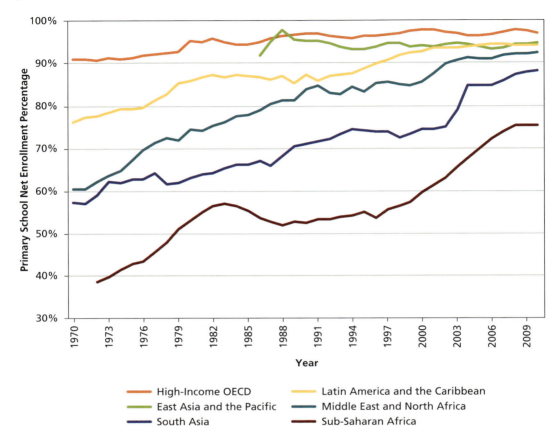

Source: Compiled from the World Bank, World Development Indicators, http://data.worldbank.org/data-catalog/world-development-indicators.

set of government programs that appears to have been successful in doing so is called conditional cash transfer (CCT) programs, forms of which have been enacted in more than thirty countries worldwide in the last fifteen years. Governments give cash grants to poor families that can demonstrate their compliance with certain behavior requirements, which almost always include school attendance for children. As another means to encourage parental commitment, several LDCs, such as Ethiopia, Kenya, and Malawi, recently abandoned user fees for primary schooling.

The calculus of whether to keep their children in school may also be changing for parents. Economic growth has transformed economies in the developing world. Globalization, industrialization, technological dissemination, urbanization, and the emergence of a modern service sector have all increased the demand for specialized skills and education. Formal education is thus increasingly rewarded with high-wage jobs that are ever more prevalent. In other words, education increasingly pays. It boosts eventual earning power, so parents are more willing to absorb the immediate sacrifices of keeping their children in school.

understanding **INDICATORS**

The Human Development Index

A leading effort to address some of the shortcomings of GNI and GDP as measures of human well-being resulted in the establishment of the **Human Development Index (HDI)** by the United Nations Development Progamme (UNDP) in the early 1990s. Based in part on Amartya Sen's claim that the fundamental goal of human progress should be the expansion of capabilities, the HDI uses more than just income to measure societal well-being. Specifically, a society's HDI is a single number that is a composite of its overall health, educational attainment, and income. Four individual measures are used to construct this composite: life expectancy at birth, mean years of schooling, expected years of schooling, and logged GNI per capita. Each of the four individual indicators is converted to a 0 to 1 scale. Zero equates to subsistence values, which are roughly the minimum levels that people in a society

would need to even survive, and 1 is equivalent to the maximum score ever observed in human history (for instance, life expectancy of 83.2 in Japan in 2010). The four scores are then collapsed by taking the average[57] across all four, with the result being a single number, also varying between 0 and 1, that is a society's HDI. The UNDP classifies countries into one of four human development categories (depicted in the figure) based on their HDI score.

The figure here shows the relationship between HDI and GNI per capita for 2011. Each point in the scatterplot is a country, and it is plotted according to its level of GNI per capita (indexed on the x-axis) and its HDI (indexed on the y-axis). The figure shows that the relationship between the two variables is far from a simple, one-to-one correspondence. For example, Botswana ranks relatively high on GNI per capita

The Human Development Index and Its Relationship with GNI per Capita

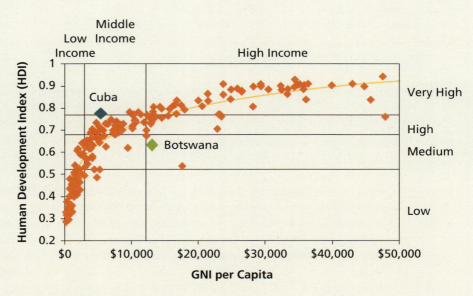

Source: International Human Development Indicators, 2011, http://hdr.undp.org/en/statistics/.

(Continued)

(Continued)

(62nd worldwide) but low on human development (.633 ranks 118th). This indicates that it, like all countries below the trend line, does a relatively poor job of converting its income into good health and educational outcomes. By comparison, Cuba's HDI rank (.776 ranks 51st) is much better than its GNI per-capita rank (103rd), which, as is the case with the countries above the line, means Cuba does an efficient job in buying good health and educational outcomes with relatively limited income. More generally, increased GNI improves HDI in low-income countries, but its impact declines considerably in middle- and high-income ones. In other words, upper-middle-income countries are much closer to high-income countries in terms of health and educational

outcomes than they are to low-income countries. This is a classic case of a logarithmic relationship.

Users of the HDI should keep in mind that this nonlinear relationship between HDI and GNI is partly by design, since GNI per capita in logged form is one of the four variables that goes into the composite. Furthermore, by incorporating GNI, HDI is partially subject to the standard criticisms (discussed in Chapter 1) of this measure. This is especially so since most countries have HDI scores that are close to what their GNIs would predict, as evidenced by how closely most of the points are to the yellow line in the figure. More generally, some critics of the HDI doubt that it adds much beyond the individual indicators that comprise it. The decision to

average the four indicators to create a final composite score is largely arbitrary, so one might be better served, if interested in studying human development, by analyzing mean years of schooling or life expectancy at birth on their own.

- What are the advantages and disadvantages of an index such as the HDI that summarizes multiple and very different indicators of a country's development with a single number?

- What would you conclude about the well-being of a population in a country that has a high HDI but a relatively low GNI? What about the reverse situation—a low HDI but a relatively high GNI?

STUDY

WHAT ARE INDIA'S CHALLENGES AND SUCCESSES IN HUMAN DEVELOPMENT?

The world's second-largest country is underdeveloped. Fully 70 percent of India's 1 billion citizens live below the global poverty line of US$2.00 per day, giving it nearly half of the world's poor.[58] But does economic underdevelopment limit capabilities and human development in India? In 2010, India had an HDI index of .52, placing it in the "medium human development" category. This middling score leaves plenty of leeway for interpretation. It is far short of that prevailing in the "very high human development" countries (average of .88) but a good deal higher than the mostly "low human development" countries of sub-Saharan Africa (average of .39). Moreover, India's HDI is up from .32 just thirty years earlier. Thus, depending on how one looks at it, India could be viewed as a human development nightmare or a success. This case study reviews evidence from both perspectives. (Recall that the South/West/natural world format for case studies is not presented until Chapter 4.)

Indian children sit on the floor in a primary school as they do their lessons. Many of India's schools are poorly equipped, and studies show that teachers often fail to show up for class. The share of children who are enrolled in primary and secondary school, however, has been steadily increasing in India for decades.

Health and Education Challenges

The challenges and shortfalls of human development in India are particularly severe in the arena of health. India's child mortality rate of sixty-three per 1,000 live births is more than ten times that prevailing in developed countries, and its life expectancy of sixty-five falls short by fifteen years.[59] India struggles mightily with malnutrition. Stunningly, over 45 percent of children under five (60 million in total) are malnourished, a figure that is more than five times greater than that prevailing in China and that remains stubbornly high even after two decades of booming economic growth.[60] India also lags in providing sanitation and clean water, so infectious diseases are common. Just 35 percent of Indians have access to a latrine or toilet.[61] In major cities, water is available through pipes just a few hours per day, and many of the faucets are publicly shared and thus long queues result. In rural areas, much of the population lacks access to piped water entirely. Regardless of location, piped water cannot be safely drunk straight from the tap.

Not surprisingly, basic medical care is also poor. India is sorely lacking in trained health professionals and equipment. On a per-capita basis, it has one-fifth the trained physicians and less than one-eighth the nurses of high-income countries.[62] Less than 40 percent of self-proclaimed "doctors" in the slums of Delhi have a formal medical degree, and the numbers are even lower in rural areas. Many individuals set up a doctor's office not because they have completed medical school, but simply because they think they would be good at it. Furthermore, public medical clinics have high absentee rates, with health professionals showing up only 57 percent of the time.[63] Even when present, doctors spend little time with patients and often recommend wrong or excessive medicines. One research team that observed patient-provider interactions in India coined the term "3-3-3 rule": the typical interaction lasted three minutes, the provider asked three questions, and the patient was offered three medicines.[64]

Internationally, India is near the bottom in terms of how much money its government spends on health care. In 2003, public-sector spending on health was just 1.2 percent of GDP, and even this was distributed inequitably. The poorest quintile of citizens (20 percent) was targeted by just 10 percent

WHAT ARE INDIA'S CHALLENGES AND SUCCESSES IN HUMAN DEVELOPMENT?

of this spending, while 30 percent of it benefited the wealthiest quintile. The private sector partially fills the gap, providing around 80 percent of all health services, but it is lightly regulated and expensive.[65] Unlike the public sector, its doctors do not need to be formally trained, and patients pay out of pocket.

Educational outcomes also lag in India. In terms of attainment, India has more than 30 million (mostly rural) children of primary school age who are not enrolled in school. This figure represents more than 10 percent of its age-eligible population and a third of the world's unenrolled children.[66] Fewer than two in three Indian adults can read.[67] Moreover, even students who are in school receive a low-quality education. One study found that half of fifth graders could not read a simple story, and less than one in three could do simple division.[68] At the primary level, there are forty students per teacher. A shocking study by the World Bank found that Indian primary teachers in public schools did not show up an average of one out of every four days and, when present, they often did not bother to teach, instead spending hours per day socializing with other teachers or reading the newspaper.[69] Despite this, as unionized public school teachers, they were almost never fired.

The Indian government devotes about 2 percent of GDP to spending on primary education, a figure that comes out to less than US$50 per student per year. India's public schools thus have high pupil-teacher ratios and high dropout rates. Moreover, public school teachers, who must be formally trained and thus often come from urban areas where training facilities are located, are often loathe to teach in remote rural areas. Because of these shortcomings in public education, there is widespread demand in India for private elementary schools, and private schools do have lower absenteeism and higher test scores.[70] Somewhat surprisingly, they are also within financial reach for many poor families, as some cost as little as US$1.50 per month.[71] But they have their own drawbacks. Aside from the fees, private school teachers are less likely to be formally trained. Indeed, private schools are often established in rural villages by a local citizen who is motivated to fulfill pent-up demand for schooling.

Health and Education Successes

These facts and figures on health and education seem dire, yet they look far less so when tracked over India's recent history. India's HDI was

| **Table 2.1** | **Development Comparison: India Today and India in the Past** |

Indicator	India 1980	India 2011
GDP per capita at PPP	US$844	US$3,163
Human Development Index	.344	.547
Life expectancy at birth	55	65.4
Mean years of schooling	1.9	4.4
Expected years of schooling	6.5	10.3

Sources: Data on GDP per capita at PPP compiled from Gapminder, www.gapminder.com; all other data compiled from United Nations Development Programme, International Human Development Indicators, http://hdr.undp.org/en/statistics/.

.20 lower just thirty years ago, and it graduated from low human development to medium human development around 2005. Table 2.1 summarizes some of these human development trends.

In the area of health, the signs of improvement are overwhelming. At independence in 1947, child mortality in India was 253, nearly four times its 2010 rate and higher than even the worst country's rate today. Life expectancy at birth has nearly doubled over that time, rising from thirty-six to sixty-five.[72] Today, the leading cause of death is not diarrhea or malaria, but the very rich-country-sounding heart disease. Malnutrition remains today's plague, yet India used to have recurring famines that killed millions. It has not had a major one since 1943. Access to clean water and sanitation have also been trending upward, both increasing by around twenty percentage points since 1990. Finally, the quality of medical care is improving since the number of certified health professionals per person has more than tripled since 1960.[73]

Improvements have also been massive in education. The literacy rate is up by twenty-five percentage points since 1981. The mean years of schooling doubled in the three decades following 1980, and the average child born in India today can expect to complete ten years of schooling, reaching well into secondary school.[74] India is now "within striking distance of universal elementary education,"[75] and public spending per elementary student nearly doubled in the 1990s. Today's Indian children will be far more literate

and far better educated than any generation that preceded them.

***

This data on human development in India conveys the nuance with which well-informed Westerners should view the developing world. As is widely assumed, educational and health systems do leave much to be desired in LDCs. The social deficits between rich and poor countries, however, are often smaller than many think, and these gaps are shrinking at an impressive speed that leaves plenty of room for optimism.

Thinking Critically about Development

- Since 1980, India's GDP per capita has tripled. What are some ways in which economic growth has caused the country's advances in human development, and what are some ways in which human development caused this economic growth?

- Is the human development approach sufficient for prioritizing what is important for well-being in India, or are there other criteria by which its progress should be judged?

- Will India's remaining problems in health and education simply disappear as its economy continues to grow, or will the government need to take direct action to improve the welfare state in order to better human development?

Key Terms

capabilities, p. 30

capability deprivation, p. 30

child labor, p. 44

child mortality, p. 32

HIV/AIDS epidemic, p. 37

human development, p. 30

Human Development Index (HDI), p. 47

infant mortality, p. 32

infectious disease, p. 35

life expectancy at birth, p. 31

malnutrition, p. 34

net enrollment ratio, p. 42

noncommunicable disease, p. 35

vaccine, p. 36

welfare state, p. 38

 # Suggested Readings

Banerjee, Abhijit V., and Esther Duflo. *Poor Economics: A Radical Rethinking of the Way to Fight Global Poverty.* New York: Public Affairs, 2011. Chapters 2–5.

Kenny, Charles. *Getting Better: Why Global Development Is Succeeding—and How We Can Improve the World Even More.* New York: Basic Books, 2011.

Nussbaum, Martha. *Creating Capabilities: The Human Development Approach.* Cambridge: Harvard University Press, 2011.

Sen, Amartya. *Development as Freedom.* New York: Alfred Knopf, 1999.

United Nations Development Programme. *Human Development Report: The Real Wealth of Nations.* New York: Palgrave MacMillan, 2010.

 # Web Resources

Demographic and Health Survey, www.measuredhs.com/

Global Hunger Index, www.ifpri.org/ghi/2012

Health Nutrition and Population Statistics, World Bank, http://data.worldbank.org/data-catalog/health-nutrition-population-statistics

Barro-Lee Educational Attainment Dataset, www.barrolee.com/

International Human Development Indicators, http://hdr.undp.org/en/statistics/

World Health Global Health Observatory, www.who.int/gho/en/

A youth from the Maasai ethnic group in East Africa proudly holds up his smartphone. Fifty percent of Africans own a mobile phone. Economic development can bring these new technologies to people of the developing world; however, some experts fear that economic growth threatens the existence of many distinct ways of life, leading to a Westernization in the cultures of many non-Western peoples.

The Benefits and Costs of Economic Development

L i is bored today, as usual. She works on an assembly line in a huge Chinese factory putting screws into a consumer electronic device. Her work is agonizingly repetitive and no longer engages her, even though the twenty-year-old has been working at the factory for only a year. Twelve months ago she moved by herself from her small rural village in Anhui province to the huge industrial city of Shenzen to take this job. She earns enough to have a mobile phone, buy some stylish clothing, and send some money back home to her parents and siblings. But she is homesick and often wonders if the move to the city was worth it.

migration based on resource scarcity + economic opportunity

The city's prodigious air pollution aggravates Li's asthma. While she has made some friends, she finds factory life (she literally lives in a dormitory on the factory site) impersonal and city dwellers to be rude and distant. Moreover, because she now sits all day instead of working around the house and fields, she has struggled with weight gain, and she's even somewhat embarrassed to go back home for her first annual trip to see her family. These issues notwithstanding, Li knows that there are no options for her back in Anhui except to eventually marry, have children, and be a homemaker, a lifestyle for which she fancies herself too intelligent and ambitious. Besides, her sick father needs the money she sends home to pay his medical bills. In short, Li is conflicted and unhappy . . . and bored.

Does economic growth yield merely superficial benefits that contribute little to human happiness and are outweighed by environmental, psychological, and social costs? It is common for Americans and Europeans to feel pity and compassion for poverty-stricken peoples and countries around the world, especially since the desire for development and economic growth is as close as humanity comes to a "universal religion."[1] Yet development is not an unequivocally beneficial good, as exemplified not just by Li's story but also by episodic rejections of technological advances in the developed world: organic food, homeopathic medicine, home births, caps on carbon emissions, eco-tourist vacations, and bike-to-work days. This chapter describes some of the costs and intellectual criticisms of economic development in subsections titled "The Cost." These are followed by subsections titled "The Response" that report defenses of development given by its advocates.

The Cultural Costs of Development

Modern economic growth dramatically changes the way that humans work, dress, eat, play, celebrate, interact, and transact. Many observers bemoan this as a loss of traditional ways of life.

The Cost: The Westernization and Homogenization of Cultures

A body of scholarly thought known as **post-development theory** denotes development as a Western invention that the West is now, out of an ethnocentric sense of superiority, imposing on non-Western cultures and peoples. According to anthropologist Arturo Escobar, the very notion that the less developed world is "poor" was contrived by the West after it became rich.[2] Many traditional peoples and less developed countries never considered themselves to be poor and underdeveloped until the West promoted the idea of its own affluence and superiority. As yardsticks of prosperity and well-being, Western thinkers use criteria that are specific to their own cultural and consumption-oriented preferences. To the extent that residents of the developing world yearn for Western amenities and standards of living, they themselves have absorbed alien notions of how to live and what to desire.

Post-development theorists see economic development as inducing a catastrophic **Westernization** or homogenization of the world's cultures.[3] Pre-development societies, both those from the past and those that still exist in today's LDCs, engaged or engage in their own distinctive cultural behaviors. This huge variety in lived habits—in clothing, in marital customs, in music and dance, in beliefs about the supernatural, in diet, in language, and in the organization of authority—provides a colorful diversity to the human experience, not to mention a means of identity and security to those that practice them. Economic development, however, often causes a disappearance of unique cultural practices and a convergence on a common, Westernized lifestyle.

Consider how different the following cultural habits of the Maasai peoples in Kenya and Tanzania are from anything practiced in the West. Women wear multicolored sarongs, stretch their earlobes with elaborate jewelry, and shave their heads. Boys are initiated into much-anticipated warriorhood status at adolescence in a days-long ritual that involves feasting, dancing, and call-and-response music with a unique syncopation. First marriages occur in the early teens and require the man's family to offer cows, sheep, and goats to the bride's family. Polygamy is common and divorce rare. A tradition of oral law arbitrated by a council of elders reigns, and many disputes are peacefully settled with apologies and an exchange of livestock.

Many practices such as these disappear as economic development occurs. Economic growth in non-Western countries tends to push individuals to cities and suburbs where they often adopt Western notions of fashion. Many pass their free time by watching television and consuming (often foreign) popular music and films. Instead of practicing subsistence agriculture or frequenting small street markets, people shop in oversized grocery stores. Foreign corporations such as McDonalds and Walmart become parts of these cities and shape what people eat and buy, and English or some other European language increasingly peppers signage and is spoken as a second language. Relationships take on a Western tone, with marriages occurring later in life and less at the discretion of parents, and divorce becomes more common. Forms of political organization and authority are much more distant and impersonal, as individuals only rarely know their leaders personally.

The Cost: Deteriorations in Social Connectedness and Personal Character

Some thinkers have attributed other negative changes in societies and persons to economic development. Development seemingly has the paradoxical effect of making individuals less socially connected while simultaneously making them more economically reliant on one another in a way that increases personal helplessness. From one perspective, development weakens interpersonal bonding and connectedness. Factory jobs and other forms of nonagricultural work separate individuals from their families for hours at a time, whereas farm work was a chore carried out collectively by most family members over the course of a working day. With modernity, economic forms of interaction replace more genuine and sincere forms of interpersonal exchange because people are turned into objects of economic gain or competitive threat. Individuals become increasingly distant from one another in large, impersonal urban areas that feature excessive hustle and bustle and little time to savor friendships and family.

From another perspective, development increases individuals' economic reliance on others, which has the negative effect of decreasing their independence and autonomy. Specialization is inherent to economic progress, yet specializing in one craft makes a person narrower and less well rounded. Philosopher Adam Smith feared that "the man whose life is spent performing a few simple operations . . . becomes as stupid and ignorant as it is possible for a human creature to become."[4] Moreover, by specializing in producing one thing and trading that for their necessities, development makes individuals helpless

to perform crucial economic tasks. For example, in developed economies, less than 5 percent of the workforce is engaged in farming, so few people are trained or skilled in how to raise food. In other words, the vast majority of the population is completely dependent on others for its survival.

Another common theme of development that critics blast is **consumerism**, the insatiable obsession with acquiring goods and services. To some, the consumerist impulse that is so prevalent in advanced economies makes people vapid and superficial, ultimately uninterested in deeper concerns such as spirituality, empathy, and interpersonal connectedness. Many individuals are motivated merely by "conspicuous consumption," a term coined by economic sociologist Thorstein Veblen to refer to visible acquisitions that are made merely to show off status.[5] In recoiling against consumerism, anthropologist Marshall Sahlins famously labeled hunter-gatherer living as the "original affluent society." Hunter-gatherers, he wrote, "have few possessions *but they are not poor*"[6] because material possessions and wealth were unavailable and even undesired. (Their acquisition would only limit nomadic mobility.) Moreover, Sahlins argued that hunter-gatherer societies were paradoxically affluent because they were based on sharing and reciprocity, not self-interested acquisition.[7]

The Response: Prosperity as a Universal Desire

Advocates of development respond to these charges about cultural change in a variety of ways. Responses to post-development theory see its view that modern economic growth is a Western invention imposed on an unwilling or easily duped global South as an anachronistic carryover from a distant past when only the West was developed. As of 2010, only about half of the world's fifty-three high-income countries (as classified by the

World Bank) were Western, and the list included decidedly non-Western countries such as Japan, Saudi Arabia, and Singapore. More generally, a wide array of evidence suggests that most people, not just Westerners, prefer more goods, greater comfort, and increased wealth to less of these. In other words, most of the items on any list of development's benefits are surely not just Western desires but universal human desires. These run from the merely life-enhancing (indoor heat and air conditioning, eyeglasses, treatment of nagging injuries, faster transport, sufficient living space, dental care, variety in food, electric light) to the life-saving (accessible clean water, sturdy shelter, cures to treatable diseases, sufficient nourishment, safe birthing facilities). As just one example, nearly 50 percent of Africans own a cellular phone, an indication not that Africans want to be more Western, but that they simply desire to communicate over greater distances.[8] Given this seemingly widespread preference for prosperity, economist Tyler Cowen says that to restrict development in the name of maintaining pre-development cultural traditions would turn the poor into the world's "diversity slaves."[9]

The Response: Minimal or Beneficial Cultural Change

Critics of post-development thought also contend that it exaggerates the degree to which economic growth homogenizes global cultures. Most countries that have experienced some degree of economic development maintain many distinctive aspects of their national character and culture. Many Indian women still wear the traditional and colorful *sari*. Saudi Arabia legislates and practices conservative social norms such as a prohibition against women driving. Mexicans and Thais still eat their distinctive, spicy cuisines. Nigerians watch "Nollywood" movies that were filmed on their home soil. In most countries that are in the process of developing, corporations that are potent Western symbols

constitute only a small share of their respective markets. For example, there remain countless food options in Indonesia aside from McDonalds.

Moreover, many scholars and thinkers have argued that economic prosperity, instead of deteriorating social connectedness and corrupting personal character, actually strengthens them. The philosopher Voltaire argued that commerce and specialization bring individuals together in mutually beneficial exchange, encouraging people to be gentler to one another. Discrimination is discouraged because individuals who choose not to engage in commerce with potential partners because of their race or creed forego the gains from exchange. A lack of need also frees up individuals to be charitable and empathic. To philosopher John Millar, "Men, being less oppressed with their own wants, are more at liberty to cultivate the feelings of humanity."[10] Wealth can also afford societies the luxury of educating their citizens. In turn, education can overcome the perils that specialization and repetitive tasks hold for intellect and self-reliance.

Advocates of development point to an array of empirical evidence to support these claims. Racism, sexism, torture, rape, political tyranny, and child molestation are far less accepted in developed countries today than they were in the past.[11] Furthermore, wealthy countries tend to have fewer internal divisions and civil wars than poor countries, and social trust and charitable giving increase with a country's average income.[12] The modern welfare state, which is the most extensive infrastructure for redistributing material resources to the less fortunate that humans have ever devised, provides education and health care much more widely and effectively in wealthy countries. Finally, rich countries feature greater gender equity and are more likely to uphold human rights and political freedoms than are countries in the developing world.

In contrast, the traditional ways of life that wither away with economic modernization often feature undesirable elements. Consider what some might see as the more troubling aspects of the

Maasai community's way of life. One of the Maasai's coming-of-age rituals is female genital mutilation (FGM), whereby a portion of a girl's or young woman's genitals are surgically removed without anesthesia or modern medical equipment. The procedure itself is excruciating and often leads to painful complications for the rest of the girl's life. Similarly, boys seeking warriorhood undergo circumcision, and they do so in a semipublic ceremony in which expressions of pain, including flinching or wincing, are interpreted as signs of weakness and unworthiness. Marriages are typically arranged by the fathers of the marrying couple, with the bride's father negotiating her away—to marry a man she may not know and who is typically much her elder—in what is seen as an equal exchange for livestock. Councils of elders are strictly male, unelected, and have been known to mandate whippings of young people just for moving to the city. In sum, many of the cultures which critics of development would seek to preserve in the name of diversity are themselves not celebrants of diversity and tolerance. To be sure, wealthy countries have not rid themselves of morally revolting practices such as gender violence and discrimination. Yet advocates of development point out that they *tend* to have fewer troubling cultural practices and violations of personal freedoms than they did in the past and than do many contemporary cultures in LDCs.

The Equity Costs of Development

Many critics of development argue that it creates and worsens inequities in the distribution of income within the entire human population and within designated societies.

The Cost: Deepening Global Inequality

It is beyond refute that modern economic development, precisely because it has not occurred

everywhere, has increased the degree to which income is concentrated in the hands of a relatively small and prosperous share of the global population. A few statistics illustrate vividly the degree of concentration in the **global income distribution**, a concept that captures how evenly spread world income is across its 7 billion citizens. Worldwide, the richest 10 percent of humans earn half of the world's income.[13] The richest 1 percent earns the equivalent of that of the bottom 57 percent, and the wealthiest 10 percent of the U.S. population earns as much as the world's 2 billion poorest people.[14] All told, levels of global inequality are far greater than inequality levels within even the world's most unequal countries.

To better understand the cause of this state of the world, it is important to know that global income inequality can be divided into two contributing components. The first component is the inequality that is due to the difference in countries' average incomes—for instance, the income of the average American citizen versus that of the average Congolese citizen. This is called **intercountry inequality**, or between-country inequality, and it refers to income differences that are largely due to one's location. The second component is **domestic inequality** or within-country inequality, which captures differences in incomes across individuals who reside in the same country—for example, the income of a wealthy American versus that of a poor American. In other words, this component picks up class differences.[15]

The primary creator of the current maldistribution of global income has been the upward spiral in intercountry inequality, a process of cross-national divergence that was described in Chapter 1. The modern economic growth that occurred in the nineteenth century raised prosperity levels almost exclusively in the West, and the West then continued to grow during the twentieth century. Overall, Europe's average incomes grew from two or three times those of African countries in 1800 to, by the twenty-first century, nearly one hundred times those in the

Measures of Income Inequality

The most commonly used metric for income inequality is the **Gini coefficient**, which is an index that ranges between 0 and 1 and varies positively with inequality—that is, it conveys greater inequality with higher values. A Gini coefficient of 0 represents a hypothetical case of perfect income equality, where every person (or country) has exactly the same income. A coefficient of 1 is a hypothetical case of the most extreme inequality, where one person (or country) has all of the income. Observed cases all fall somewhere in the middle. For example, the Gini coefficient for domestic income distribution in South Africa, one of the world's most unequal countries, is .65, whereas in Afghanistan, one of the world's most equal, it is .29.

A country's Gini coefficient is derived from its Lorenz curve. To draw a Lorenz curve, one lays out a two-dimensional graph, like the one in the figure, with the cumulative percentage of people from lowest to highest income on the horizontal (*x*) axis and the cumulative percentage of the country's total income on the vertical (*y*) axis. A man at 25 percent on the *x*-axis is in the 25th percentile rank of income earners in his country: he is richer than exactly 25 percent of

his compatriots. His placement on the *y*-axis then reveals the share of total country income that he and everyone poorer than him has. If at 5 percent on the *y*-axis, then that man and everyone poorer than him earns 5 percent of the country's income. A 45-degree line is drawn to depict the ideal of perfectly equal income distribution. (In this hypothetical country, everyone poorer than the person at the 25th percentile collectively has 25 percent of the country's income, everyone poorer than the person at the 75th percentile collectively has 75 percent, and so on.) The Lorenz curve for a given country is then drawn based on income information collected in surveys of the country's households.

Since all countries depart from the perfectly equal ideal, the Lorenz curve always falls below the 45-degree line. Countries that are highly unequal have a Lorenz curve (like B) that droops well below the 45-degree line, since people in the low and moderately low percentile ranks collectively have little cumulative income.

Two Lorenz Curves

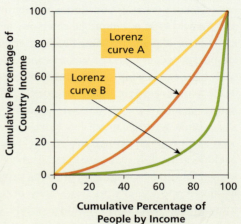

Countries that are more equal have a curve (like A) that hugs more closely to the 45-degree line. The Gini coefficient is the amount of area between the curve and the 45-degree line, expressed as a proportion of the entire area underneath the 45-degree line. The area between the curve and the 45-degree line is smaller for A than B. More area means greater inequality and a Gini coefficient closer to 1.

- What does a country's Gini coefficient reveal about it that its GDP per capita does not?

- What are some other possible measures of a country's degree of income inequality?

poorest African countries. To indicate just how important intercountry inequality is, economist Branko Milanovic points out that "in many cases practically *all* people living in a richer country are better off than *all* people living in a poorer country."[16] For example, just 3 percent of India's population has incomes greater than the poorest Americans.

Using the Gini coefficient measure of inequality, Figure 3.1 shows rather clearly how ballooning intercountry inequality created today's high rates of global inequality. The Gini varies between 0 and 1, with higher values meaning greater concentration of income in the hands of a few, and lower values meaning greater equity. (See Understanding Indicators: Measures of Income Inequality for details.) In 1820, the Gini for global inequality was around .45, but the between-country Gini was just .15. A person's country of residence determined just a third of the income level he or she was at. Most countries had very similar (and very low) average incomes, and most global inequality was thus due to income differences within countries. Over the course of almost two centuries of economic development, the global inequality Gini coefficient increased by .20 to .30 points, sitting by early 2013 between .65 and .70. This increase was *entirely* due to the explosion in between-country differences. The intercountry Gini rose from .15 to .55, a whopping forty-point rise. Today, about 65 percent of global inequality is attributed to these intercountry differences, meaning country of origin accounts for two-thirds of a person's income level.

The moral consequences of this rise in global inequality are, in the words of some critics of development, grotesque. Such inequalities tie livelihood to sheer luck—where one is born—rather than merit and effort. In this sense, "citizenship is fate,"[17] a fact that violates basic norms of fairness and equity that are rooted in most of humanity's cultural traditions.[18] They also build severe power imbalances into global political and economic configurations, as wealthy countries dominate international institutions and construct the most deadly military capacities. Poor countries may

Figure 3.1   Between-Country and Global Inequality, 1820–2000

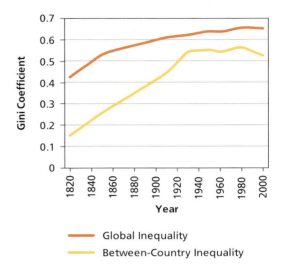

Sources: Data compiled from François Bourguignon and Christian Morrisson, "Inequality among World Citizens: 1820–1992," *American Economic Review* 92, no. 4 (2002): 727–744; Branko Milanovic, "Global Inequality and the Global Inequality Extraction Ratio: The Story of the Past Two Centuries," Policy Research Working Paper (Washington D.C.: World Bank, 2009).

also be disadvantaged in international economic exchange, having to export relatively inexpensive natural resource commodities in exchange for more expensive manufactured goods and services imported from high-income countries. Finally, the relative lack of buying power in the developing world means that the world economy undersupplies basic necessities. For example, of the 1,400 new drugs approved between 1975 and 1999, only 1 percent of them were for tropical diseases. Research on beauty products is better funded than that on many diseases of poverty.[19]

The Cost: Deepening Domestic Inequalities

To many observers, of equal or even greater concern is the notion that economic development seemingly tends to increase domestic inequalities. Thinkers as varied as Karl Marx and Thomas Jefferson believed that industrialization in mostly agrarian societies exacerbates domestic income inequalities. Marx alleged capitalist development to be immiserating the working class to the benefit of a small capitalist class, and Jefferson preferred a United States peopled by farmers who harvested small plots of land with traditional technologies. Philosopher Jean Jacques Rousseau also famously admired pre-agricultural societies for their lack of possessions and economic hierarchy.

Empirically, the beginning of industrialization in a country does tend to reward those who have investments or jobs in manufacturing because industrial machinery makes these workers more productive than farmers. Moreover, the manufacturing sector's advance further enriches those who are wealthy enough to have savings, since savings fuel the accumulation of capital.[20] A middle class with employment either in industry or in the government (which benefits from the taxation of industry) sprouts, and it can further widen its income gap with farmers and agricultural workers by paying for better schooling and medical care. This process occurred in Great Britain during its Industrial Revolution, when the Gini coefficient increased from .400 in 1823 to .627 in 1871,[21] and inequality has dramatically worsened in current fast-growing countries such as China (from .28 in 1984 to .42 in 2005).[22]

As with global inequalities, the alleged costs and moral consequences of within-country income inequalities are manifold. Smith noted that inequality, even in wealthy societies where the poor have their basic necessities met, raises the specter of social exclusion, as the poor cannot "appear in public without shame" and participate fully in community life.[23] More recently, experts have shown domestic inequality to retard economic growth, as it distorts markets, foments discrimination, stokes societal conflict and distrust, and wastes human potential. Some research shows inequality to be self-perpetuating because it restricts opportunities for the poor and entrenches political power in the hands of a wealthy few, who in turn use their power

to resist redistribution.[24] Domestic inequality is also bad for a society's subjective sense of well-being, as individuals, even many who are comfortably middle class, feel poorer than they actually are because they are comparing themselves to the rich. Neurological research even suggests a pernicious biochemical effect in the bodies of those who are forced to constantly compare themselves to richer people. This effect makes them more prone to a host of problems such as anxiety, mental illness, criminal violence, obesity, and drug use.[25] To be sure, some domestic inequality can be good, since it motivates people to become educated so they can earn higher wages, and the wealthy provide savings to fuel investment. In general, however, research seems to suggest that these positives are outweighed by the negatives.

The Response: The Complex Relationship between Development and Inequality

These claims about economic development and the exacerbation of income inequality are contested on a number of fronts. Responses largely have one of three themes: (1) nearly everyone is better off despite the rising global inequality of the past 200 years, (2) future economic development will actually improve global equality, or (3) development does not necessarily sharpen domestic inequalities. These are each described in turn.

Improvements in Absolute Well-Being. It is true that, since the dawn of the Industrial Revolution, the world's poorest areas have undergone massive increases in **relative poverty**—that is, deprivation compared to the wealthiest members of the global community. Advocates of development point out, however, that during this time few have experienced increases in **absolute poverty**, which is the inability to meet basic material needs. In other words, the West left the less developed countries behind, but this did not necessarily make the LDCs less able to meet their material needs. Throughout the twentieth century, most LDCs got richer, even if it was not enough to substantially reduce relative poverty. Moreover, as documented in Chapter 2, human development outcomes have dramatically improved in LDCs since 1950, even though for most of them relative poverty has not declined. In sum, it is crucial to not confuse rising global inequality with more material deprivation.

Shrinking the Global Income Gap. According to quite a bit of evidence and informed speculation, future economic development will not continue to widen the global income gap. If anything, it will probably reduce global inequality. Figure 3.1 above shows why. Global inequality worsened most intensely during the first 150 years of modern economic growth, during which rapid industrialization was confined largely to the West. Between 1820 and 1950, the global Gini coefficient grew by around .20. However, since 1950, as economic growth has occurred in much of the developing world, the global Gini coefficient has stopped growing and has remained rather stable. Moreover, since 1980, global inequality has even showed signs of decline. The primary driver of this has been rapid economic growth in the world's two largest countries, China and India, where hundreds of millions of people have been lifted out of poverty.[26] If China and India continue to grow relatively quickly over the next few decades, then 1980 may be remembered as the year of peak inequality.[27]

Domestic Income Inequality and the Kuznets Curve. The claim that economic development worsens domestic or within-country inequalities is also hotly contested. Arguments against it take two forms. First, for some time, the conventional wisdom among many economists was not that prosperity increased inequality, but that the relationship between economic prosperity and income inequality was a nonlinear one in the shape of an inverted "U." This shape, depicted in Figure 3.2, is known as the **Kuznets curve** after the economist Simon Kuznets. Kuznets argued that inequality worsens

as very poor countries industrialize, but, upon reaching middle-income status, further growth actually reduces inequalities.[28] In middle-income countries, growth and individual incomes are based less on industry and physical capital and more on services and human capital. Human capital is more evenly distributed across a population than physical capital, and governments of middle-income societies have some capacity and will to provide progressive taxation and mass education.

To the extent that the Kuznets curve is an accurate depiction of reality, it is a strong refutation of the argument that economic development is undesirable because it increases inequalities. After all, it suggests that rich countries can have the equality of poor agricultural societies yet with none of the poverty. There is some evidence to suggest that the Kuznets curve accurately summarizes the relationship between development and inequality in the real world. For example, Britain's Gini coefficient did increase from .400 in 1823 to .627 in 1871, but it fell back to .443 in 1901 and was around .360 by early 2013. Moreover, the world's most unequal societies tend to be middle-income countries such as Botswana, Brazil, Colombia, and South Africa.

The second line of argumentation reflects the current conventional wisdom, which is based on empirical findings that show little support for a positive relationship between growth and inequality (not

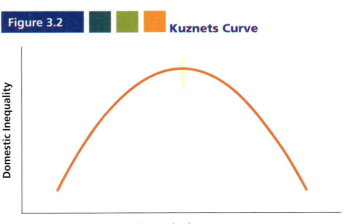

Figure 3.2 **Kuznets Curve**

Domestic Inequality

Per-capita income

to mention for a Kuznets curve). Many contemporary poor countries, such as Haiti, Paraguay, and Sierra Leone, have high rates of inequality, and many contemporary rich ones, such as Norway and Sweden, have low rates. In the second half of the twentieth century, Eastern European and East Asian countries such as Japan and South Korea experienced distribution-neutral progress by achieving rapid economic growth while maintaining a high degree of equity. Meanwhile, countries with high rates of inequality, most notably those in sub-Saharan Africa and Latin America, have seen only minor changes to their Gini coefficients even as they have experienced modest economic growth over the past half century. To give a more systematic view, Figure 3.3 plots 155 countries by their average income (on the *x*-axis) and domestic Gini coefficient (on the *y*-axis). The axes are the same as those in Figure 3.2, so if Kuznets was right, the trendline generated by the central pattern in the data

in Figure 3.3 should look like the Kuznets curve. If development increases inequality (as critics of development say), then the trendline should move from lower left to upper right in the figure. In actuality, neither pattern holds. Instead, inequality declines with a society's average income, although the relationship is not a strong one. Regardless, the objection to development on the grounds that it systematically increases inequality within societies has virtually no empirical foundation.

The Environmental Costs of Development

Much economic activity involves transforming and harnessing nature for human use. Economic growth thus almost inevitably entails costs for the natural world, and indeed perhaps the most

---

Figure 3.3 **The Relationship between GDP per Capita and the Domestic Gini Coefficient**

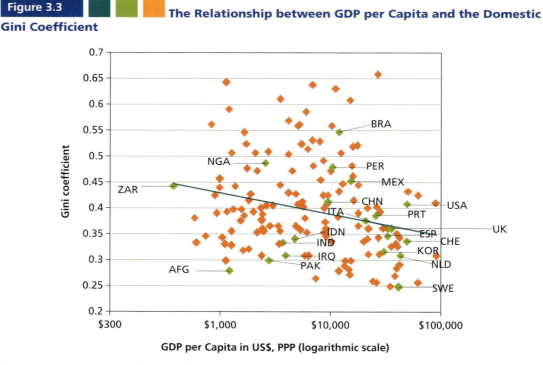

Source: Data compiled from the World Bank, World Development Indicators, most recent year available for each country, http://data.worldbank.org/data-catalog/world-development-indicators.

frequently cited cost of economic development is its effect on the environment.

The Cost: Environmental Degradation

These effects fall into three overlapping categories. The first is pollution, the second is natural resource depletion, and the third is climate change.

Pollution. Modern economic activity can dramatically increase pollution, which is the introduction of contaminants into the natural habitat. Factories produce waste that is often ejected into the air, dumped into bodies of water, or buried underground. Automobiles emit their waste directly into the air. Mines can leak acid and other waste into nearby soils and bodies of water. The pesticides and fertilizers used in high-tech farming techniques can leech into soils, rivers, and groundwater. Animal species can go extinct as industrialization and new patterns of land usage change their natural habitat. Highways and power lines create visual pollution by changing landscapes, and factories and automobiles add noise pollution to the urban experience.

These forms of pollution cause a loss of natural beauty. Pollution can make air smoggy with carbon monoxide, sulfur dioxide, and particulate matter. Rivers can become excessively odorous and unsightly as they run with ammonia from industrial waste, gasoline from urban runoff, synthetic fertilizers from agricultural runoff, and plastic garbage. Pollution can also create human health problems. Dirty air causes respiratory issues and skin irritations, polluted water can cause nausea and sometimes fatal diarrhea, and both can cause cancer. Exposure to heavy metals such as mercury and lead in air and water can cause developmental problems in children.

Natural Resource Depletion. Modern economic growth can also cause natural resource depletion and thus sow the seeds of its own unsustainability. History is replete with civilizations that disintegrated because of overuse and eventual exhaustion of natural resources.[29] For example, traditional civilizations such

as the Vikings, Maya, and Easter Island collapsed due to, in part, deforestation. While a resource-driven societal collapse has yet to happen to any modern society, the resources that underlie and drive modern growth are finite. For instance, much industrial activity is powered by fossil fuels, namely coal, oil, and natural gas, which are not in limitless supply. Growth can also cause land exhaustion as pristine lands are cleared for the construction of factories, commercial centers, landfills, and ever-bigger homes. Meanwhile, the need for farmland rises with the increasing consumer demand for meat, and forests throughout the world have been felled to turn them into ranches and cropland. Some areas can even turn to desert (desertification) when semi-arid land is cleared for agriculture, resulting in soil erosion. Furthermore, economic growth can diminish the supply of freshwater. Greater agricultural output and more farmland can exhaust groundwater and other water supplies when farmers employ irrigation techniques, and many factories consume water as part of their production processes.

Climate Change. Modern economic growth is also the primary source of **anthropogenic climate change**, which refers to changes to the climate caused by human activities. To power the machines and devices that have made the global economy so much more productive since the advent of the Industrial Revolution, humans burn fossil fuels that they have removed from below the ground and seas. Unfortunately, the burning of fossil fuels leads to a release of carbon dioxide into the atmosphere, which adds to the greenhouse gases that trap heat. Deforestation exacerbates the problem, as it means there are fewer trees and plants to absorb carbon dioxide and remove it from the atmosphere. Global average temperatures have risen by 1°C since 1880, with more than half of that increase occurring since 1970.

The eventual consequences of anthropogenic climate change are uncertain, but among the most plausible predictions are the following: ever-warmer temperatures and thus hotter summers, a loss of polar glaciers and a resulting rise in ocean levels, an increased frequency and worsening of extreme weather events such as floods and droughts, and an increased acidification and deoxygenation of oceans resulting in loss of some sea species. These consequences will weigh particularly heavy in the world's poorest countries and on the world's poorest people. Hotter growing seasons and more floods and droughts will mean lower crop yields and thus greater risks for hunger and malnutrition. Warmer temperatures may expand the geographical scope of the infectious diseases that thrive in the tropical climates where most LDCs lie. Scarcer drinking water and other natural resources could spur violent conflict and forced migration. One study estimates that developing countries will absorb 80 percent of the economic costs of climate change, with Africa and Asia suffering losses of 4 percent to 5 percent of their GDPs.[30] Additional annual deaths from climate change have already been estimated at 150,000.[31]

The Response: The Benefits of Development for the Environment

This list of environmental consequences seems a damning blot on the record of economic development. Not surprisingly, advocates of development have a series of responses.

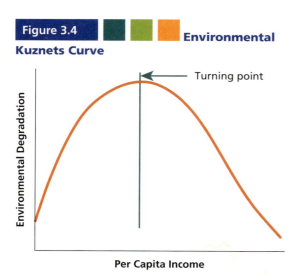

Figure 3.4 **Environmental Kuznets Curve**

Environmental Degradation (y-axis)

Turning point

Per Capita Income (x-axis)

Environmental Kuznets Curve. Most forms of environmental degradation, they are quick to point out, do not necessarily worsen with increased prosperity. Instead, environmental cleanliness and sustainability may actually improve once societies have the wealth to afford (1) the luxuries of cleaner technologies and environmental cleanup and (2) the kind of governments that can effectively enforce environmental regulations. If true, the worsening environmental damage caused by industrialization in countries moving from poor to middle-income status would be reversed as middle-income countries grow wealthier. This scenario bears a close resemblance to the Kuznets curve introduced above, and in fact scholars have developed the concept of the **environmental Kuznets curve (EKC)** to describe it. Figure 3.4 shows its purported nonlinear relationship between societal wealth and environmental cleanliness.

Evidence suggests the EKC to be an accurate depiction of the relationship between global development and many forms of environmental degradation. Scholarship in demonstration of the EKC has even been able to identify the location of the turning point for many pollutants, and most lie in the US$6,000 to US$13,000 per-capita GDP range.[32] Anecdotally, it is clear that the dirtiest countries in the world, and those in which many of the worst environmental catastrophes exist, are middle-income countries that have some industrial presence but have not yet reached developed world status. For example, middle-income China and India feature some of the world's dirtiest rivers and air. A 2007 study listed the world's ten most polluted places, and all were located in middle-income countries: Azerbaijan, China, India, Peru, Russia, Ukraine, and Zambia.[33]

In contrast, countries with the greatest affluence also tend to be those with the highest environmental standards. Wealthy countries such as Switzerland, Sweden, and Norway sit atop country rankings of environmental performance.[34] Evidence of a decline in pollutants after middle-income status is reached is also widespread. In the United States, most automobile emission pollutants are down by 50 percent from their 1970s peak due to higher emissions standards and improved exhaust technologies.[35] Economic development can also have a variety of land-preserving effects. The adoption of farming technologies, including genetically modified foods, can boost per-acre crop yields; the United States produced twice as much grain in 2005 as it did from the same acreage in 1968.[36] The use of underground fossil fuel deposits to power economic activity uses far less surface area than do more traditional means of fuel generation such as clear-cutting timber and growing biofuels. Fossil fuels may prevent the kinds of collapses that plagued unwitting premodern societies who engaged in deforestation.

Furthermore, wealthier countries have slower population growth. Population growth is a leading contributor to environmental strains. It is often said that "development is the best contraceptive,"[37] as the world's poorest countries still feature today's highest fertility rates. (Europe has the lowest fertility rates and sub-Saharan Africa the highest.) Moreover, fertility rates have declined from more than six children per woman in many developing countries to less than three in just the last few decades as these countries have experienced some economic growth. More growth in subsequent decades is projected to make further progress in quelling population increase.

Coping with Climate Change. Still, carbon dioxide emissions are the one nasty pollutant that seems not to follow the EKC pattern, since their per-person volumes currently grow linearly with per-capita GDP. Richer countries emit more carbon per person than middle-income countries, which in turn emit more than poor countries. For example, the average American emits seventeen metric tons of carbon per year, the average Argentinean five, and the average African less than one. Even so, advocates of development continue to defend against charges that development should be stalled or reversed in the name of preventing anthropogenic climate change.

One defense is well summarized by the observation that "the best protection against global warming is global prosperity."[38] Further economic development in the developing world, even as it contributes to carbon emissions, will prepare the poor and other residents of developing countries for the harmful effects of global climate change. Greater wealth will enable citizens to migrate or to afford better housing to protect them against extreme weather events. The adoption and further development of farming technologies, including drought-resistant seed types, can boost agricultural productivity gains at a much faster rate than climate change will slow them. Development will also bring better health systems in affected countries, providing residents with better defenses against a potentially more threatening disease environment.

Stated differently, the argument holds that resisting future advances in prosperity to prevent further climate change would be penny wise and pound foolish. The aforementioned statistic—that Africa and Asia will suffer GDP losses of about 4 percent to 5 percent from climate change—illustrates this point. Many countries on these two continents are adding this much or more to their economies each year. To forego further economic growth in the name of avoiding this mild headwind, advocates of development say, is simply bad mathematics. It may even be unethical. Restricting development to achieve cooler temperatures tomorrow places a heavy burden on today's poor, despite the fact that the vast majority of carbon emissions thus far have come from the rich.

Finally, some thinkers even allege that there may actually be an EKC when it comes to carbon dioxide emissions, but that it has not emerged yet because the GDP per-capita turning point is particularly high, upwards of US$30,000 or US$40,000. Wealthy countries will be the first to widely deploy cleaner power-generating technologies such as sun, wind, tidal, and hydrogen power simply because they will be more able to afford them. Developed countries have already been moving from more (wood and coal) to less (oil and natural gas) carbon-emitting technologies for a century, and they are likely to continue in that direction.

The Psychological Costs of Development

Even in the face of all these costs, many would argue that development is still worthwhile. Reasonable people could surely believe that less variety in global culture, dirtier air, rising global inequality, and a dose of shallow hedonism are a small price to pay for longer lives, greater comfort and convenience, and more enjoyable leisure activities. Yet what if development incurs a long list of costs without even increasing humanity's general sense of life satisfaction and well-being? In other words, what if money doesn't buy happiness?

The Cost: Insecurity, Alienation, and Unhappiness

Three sets of arguments question the assumption that development promotes human happiness and psychological satisfaction.

Economic Insecurity. Development can foment economic anxiety and insecurity. Modern economic growth requires a constant process of what economist Joseph Schumpeter called **creative destruction**,[39] whereby innovation leads to the adoption of new technologies that replace less productive, older ones. Creative destruction generates an ongoing displacement of workers and businesses, since jobs and firms that build or rely on old technologies disappear as they are out-competed by new ones. The high rates of destruction of jobs and business can thus generate elevated levels of economic insecurity. Those who are displaced from their traditional livelihoods and methods of producing face financial uncertainty and a variety of often unsavory options: adopt the new technology themselves, search for another job, try to start a new business, ask family members for financial help, learn a new trade, or move.

One example that has played out repeatedly but quietly throughout the era of modern economic growth is the displacement and urbanization of relatively unproductive rural farmers as technologically advances adopted by other farmers' increase agricultural productivity. This process begins when a few farmers adopt innovations—for example, tractors, irrigation systems, new fertilizers, pesticides—that boost their yields, making it possible for the country as a whole to produce the same or even a greater amount of food with fewer farmers. The new technologies make less productive farmers uncompetitive and impoverished, and many make the painful choice to abandon their farms and seek employment in cities. This process is why urbanization is a constitutive part of development: 90 percent of the workforce in the United States in 1790 was engaged in farming, compared with just 2 percent in early 2013.[40]

Alienation. Modern society may create various forms of what philosopher Karl Marx called **alienation**, a term he used to refer to any kind of disruption that occurs in the naturally harmonious relationships between humans and their surroundings. These disruptions can occur along a number of lines, such as between workers and nature, between workers and the process of creating and using a product, and between workers and other workers. For example, Marx claimed that, since they are premised on interpersonal competition for jobs and higher wages, modern capitalist societies sever otherwise healthy relationships among workers. Similarly, he saw specialization as divorcing workers from the intellectually fulfilling process of creating a product from start to finish and then deciding how to use it.

A host of subsequent thinkers have expanded on the notion of alienation in alleging different ways in which modernity and development deepen psychological malaise. For one, the consumerist impulse creates a self-perpetuating sense of unfulfillment since wealthy societies are constantly producing new goods and services that create new consumer tastes and thus a problem of "unlimited wants."[41] True satisfaction is unachievable since there is always something new that is not owned. Moreover, research on the "paradox of choice"[42] reveals that excessive consumer choice provokes anxiety about making just the right acquisition and constant regret about the option not chosen. Modernity also yields numerous concrete side effects that introduce new complications and threats to daily life. Traffic noise, congestion, and accidents are a byproduct of greater prosperity. Crimes such as thievery, substance abuse, and murder allegedly increase in cities, where life is more impersonal and communities less tightly knit. A bevy of new health problems emerge. Obesity and heart disease increase because food, automobiles, and sedentary office jobs are more readily available; industrial accidents occur in factories and mines; eating disorders rise along with the consumerist obsession with celebrity; city life boosts anxiety and depression; and cancer rates balloon as a result of environmental toxins. Finally, development brings new fears of physical insecurity since humans funnel a large share of the windfall from economic advance into building more devastating weaponry and other means of war.

The Easterlin Paradox. Some findings on the economics of happiness give yet another reason to doubt the presumed positive link between high income and life satisfaction. In a 1974 study of fourteen countries, economist Richard Easterlin introduced the **Easterlin paradox** by demonstrating that there was virtually no relationship between a country's GDP per capita and its average level of happiness. Rich people, he found, tend to be happier than their poor compatriots, yet wealthy countries do not necessarily have happier citizens than less wealthy ones.[43] In Easterlin's study, happiness was measured with public opinion survey questions in which respondents gave a self-rating of how happy they were. For example, despite huge gaps in average national income, Nigerian citizens were just as happy as West German ones, and Cubans were just as happy as Americans. He also showed that rapid economic growth in the United States from the 1940s through 1970 did not increase the country's average level of happiness. If anything, average happiness in the United States declined rather dramatically during the 1960s.

To explain this paradox, Easterlin argued that people's happiness was driven by relative income, or how wealthy they are in comparison to others in their country, and not by absolute income, which is the raw amount of earnings they have and consumption they do. The logic underlying this argument is succinctly captured in the following quote by philosopher John Stuart Mill: "Men do not desire merely to be *rich*, but to be *richer* than other men."[44] According to the paradox, the fact that most lower-class Americans possess and have access to amenities such as stable shelter, sufficient food, and a decent national infrastructure that make them richer in an absolute sense than billions of poor foreigners does not make them happier than these billions. This is because poor Americans are evaluating their livelihoods and deriving their desires by comparing themselves to other citizens of their own country, not of the world. In the Easterlin paradox, it is this "neighbor effect" that makes lower-class residents of wealthy societies no happier than the global poor, even though they are objectively richer. It also means that, even as they gain higher absolute incomes through time as their societies develop, those lower-class residents who remain on the underside of their country's income ladder do not get happier.

The implications of the Easterlin paradox and its underlying argument for the merits of development are profound. If economic growth and development do not increase human happiness, then it becomes much harder to argue convincingly that the benefits of development outweigh its costs. The rising tide of economic growth may lift all boats in a country, including those of its poorest, but the neighbor effect dictates that "raising the incomes of all does not increase the happiness of all."[45]

The Response: Revisiting the Ethics and Evidence on Happiness

Development proponents have responded to these critiques of the psychological consequences of economic growth with three central claims. ·

The Ethics of Insecurity. Advocates of development claim that a certain degree of societal economic insecurity is a small price to pay for the greater good of advancing societal prosperity. Change that induces displacement and insecurity does not necessarily make that change inherently bad or undesirable. For example, the signing of the U.S. Emancipation Proclamation in 1865 eventually brought upheaval to the lives of many freed slaves. Tens of thousands left their plantations and thus had no employment, land, or housing, yet few today would conclude that emancipation was wrong because it caused this insecurity.

Moreover, restricting economic growth and technological advance to protect those who would be hurt by them favors a minority at the expense of a majority. For most instances in which adoption of a more productive technology would cause displacement, the people facing the new challenge are a relatively small group of producers and workers. In contrast, all consumers would benefit from the new technology since it would typically produce goods of higher quality and lower price. Future generations would also benefit from the general boost to productivity. Thus, to the extent that a producing group can restrict technological adoption in the name of sheltering itself from insecurity, it has gained at the expense of a much larger number of present and future people. For example, the introduction of automated looms in nineteenth-century Britain dramatically lowered the price and boosted the availability to consumers of cotton clothing, which was much cooler and less itchy than the wool clothing widely used to that point. A group of clothing manufacturers known as the Luddites, who used the more traditional and slower hand loom, unsuccessfully attempted to destroy all automated looms. Had they succeeded, only they would have benefited at the expense of all British consumers, who would have continued to pay higher prices for uncomfortable clothing. In sum, advocates of modern economic growth claim that the gains of development reaped by most are worth the inevitable costs of displacement and insecurity experienced by a few. This is especially so since many who are displaced do find new economic opportunities after their period of displacement.

Adaptive Preferences. One response to the Easterlin paradox is that using a people's self-evaluation to capture their degree of happiness and subjective well-being is problematic. An argument popularized by scholars in the human development tradition (described in Chapter 2) points out the problem of **adaptive preferences** in human beings, which is akin to sour grapes thinking. In particular, the destitute often adopt a "psychological adjustment to persistent deprivation."[46] As a means of coping, they come to terms with their plight, adjusting their expectations downward and even accepting their situation as deserved: "When society has put some things out of reach for some people, they typically learn not to want those things."[47] For example, many women and girls in LDCs internalize the belief that they should not be formally educated or that their victimization by gender-based violence is deserved. One eye-opening cross-national study revealed that 70 percent of women in India and 94 percent in Egypt believed that beatings of wives by intimate partners were justifiable for one reason or another.[48] The deprived in these instances might not express extreme levels of unhappiness, yet their situation is surely not compatible with any plausible notion of human fulfillment or fairness. In the end, an excessive focus on subjective state of mind as the measure of development's success blinds one to the more objective standards of human livelihood that development often improves.

New Evidence on Societal Wealth and Happiness. The adaptive preferences critique of happiness measures notwithstanding, new empirical evidence on the relationship between development and happiness is more mixed than Easterlin and other skeptics claim. Most compellingly, recent findings from many more countries than Easterlin's original fourteen show a rather strong relationship between a country's average income and its average level of happiness. This casts doubt not only on Easterlin's neighbor effect critique of development but also on the allegation that development boosts alienation. Figure 3.5 summarizes the results of a global public opinion survey conducted in more than 130 countries between 2006 and 2012. The figure shows each country's average level of life satisfaction (on the *y*-axis) and each country's GDP per capita (on the *x*-axis). The upward slope (from lower left to upper right) to the points and the curve that summarizes the central relationship indicates a positive and rather strong relationship between wealth and happiness. The pattern is an uncharacteristically tight one with relatively little departure from the overall trend. Citizens in rich countries tend to be happier than those in middle-income countries, who in turn tend to be happier than those in poor countries.

Figure 3.5 **The Relationship between GDP per Capita and Happiness, 2006–2012**

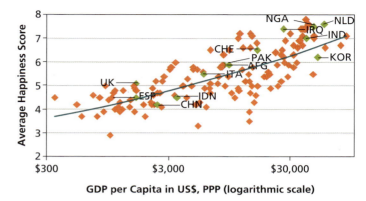

GDP per Capita in US$, PPP (logarithmic scale)

Sources: Data compiled from the World Bank, World Development Indicators, http://data.worldbank.org/data-catalog/world-development-indicators; and Gallup World Poll, http://www.gallup.com/strategicconsulting/worldpoll.aspx.

Note: Gallup World Poll question wording: "Please imagine a ladder with steps numbered from 0 at the bottom to 10 at the top. Suppose we say that the top of the ladder represents the best possible life for you, and the bottom of the ladder represents the worst possible life for you. On which step of the ladder would you say you personally feel you stand at this time, assuming that the higher the step the better you feel about your life, and the lower the step the worse you feel about it? Which step comes closest to the way you feel?"

case | **STUDY**

HAS ECONOMIC GROWTH BROUGHT HAPPINESS TO CHINA?

In 2004, Chinese premier Wen Jiabao called his country's twenty-plus-year economic boom "one of the most remarkable feats in human history,"[49] and the list of China's achievements in improving its citizens' economic livelihoods is indeed unprecedented. Yet China's boom has levied heavy costs in terms of environmental quality, rates of inequality, and degrees of societal happiness. What is the balance sheet of China's thirty-year miracle? Table 3.1 provides a preliminary assessment by comparing a variety of indicators from China's past to those prevailing in more recent times.

STUDY
case

HAS ECONOMIC GROWTH BROUGHT HAPPINESS TO CHINA?

Table 3.1 **Development Comparison: China Today and China in the Past**

Indicator	China 1980	China 2011
GDP per capita at PPP	US$934	US$8,848
Human Development Index	.404	.687
CO_2 emissions per person (in tons)	1.5	6.1
Gini coefficient	.29	.45
Average satisfaction with life score (10-point scale)	7.3 (1990)	6.8 (2007)

Sources: Data compiled from Gapminder, www.gapminder.com; life satisfaction score data compiled from Richard A. Easterlin et al., "China's Life Satisfaction, 1990–2010," PNAS, April 6, 2012, www.pnas.org/content/early/2012/05/09/1205672109.full.pdf.

The Gains

China has experienced more than thirty years of extremely rapid, uninterrupted economic growth. During that time, its average income has increased tenfold.[50] Its boom has lifted a half billion people out of extreme poverty. In 1981, fully 85 percent of the population lived below the global poverty line of US$1.25 per day. By 2005 that figure had fallen to 16 percent.[51] Nearly all major social groups have experienced these income gains, from rural farmers to urban middle classes to wealthy business entrepreneurs. Food shortages, malnutrition, and hunger are now rare—this in a country that a mere fifty years ago experienced the greatest famine in human history. Life expectancies increased by eight years from 1978 to 2009, and maternal and infant mortality rates fell by two-thirds. Illiteracy is rare, falling from a rate of 34 percent in 1982 to about 5 percent by 2013.[52] Overall, China's human development index skyrocketed from .40 in 1980 to .67 in 2010, and the HDI in some Chinese cities matches that of the United States. Indeed, Shanghai, China's wealthiest city, recently shocked everyone when its high school students received the highest scores in the world on an international standardized test.[53]

China now possesses a middle class that numbers in the hundreds of millions. Its members enjoy urban lifestyles and amenities that vary little from those in much of the West. Millions own their own apartments that have at least two bedrooms and modern conveniences such as washing machines, dishwashers, hot water heaters, air conditioning, television, smart phones, and an internet connection. Per-capita housing space has increased threefold.[54] Many have traded in bicycles for cars, and there are now more automobiles on Chinese roads than on American ones. The Chinese middle class has access to modern medical care. Shopping malls have sprouted around the country, and China boasts the two largest in the world.

The Costs

These achievements would seem to justify the statement by former Chinese leader Deng Xiaoping (1978–1997), the father of its economic boom, that "development is the only hard truth."[55] Yet China's growth-at-all-costs model has had . . . well . . . costs.

Environmental Damage. Perhaps the most notorious downside of China's economic boom has been the enormous environmental toll. China, it is said, is in "permanent environmental crisis."[56] Thirty years of rapid economic growth have degraded China's natural setting, partially exhausted its natural resources, and dramatically increased its carbon footprint. First, pollution is rampant. Once the land of bicycles, China's roads have given way to automobiles. Along with emissions from factories, automobile exhaust gives China the poorest air quality of any major country, with smog noticeably blocking out the sun in cities on cloudless days. China has twenty of the world's thirty cities with the worst air pollution,[57] and just 1 percent of city dwellers breathe air that is considered safe by international standards.[58] Most factories discard industrial waste and untreated sewage into rivers and lakes at their own discretion, and runoff of fertilizers and pesticides from farms streams into the nation's water sources. Half the water in some of China's largest rivers is deemed toxic, unsafe not only for human consumption but also for human contact.[59] This pollution has created a strong headwind against China's otherwise impressive health and economic achievements. Many citizens experience daily struggles with bronchitis and asthma. Water and air pollution cause between 400,000 and 600,000 excess deaths annually.[60] Children are sickened, developmentally delayed, and even killed by lead poisoning. The health-care and cleanup costs are estimated at 8 percent of GDP.[61]

Second, resource exhaustion threatens China's climate and the sustainability of the country's growth. Prior to its rise, China was already a relatively arid country, containing only one-fifth as much water per capita as the United States. Economic growth is placing further strains on an already taxed water supply, causing desertification in large portions of the country. The rising consumer demand for protein has contributed to a loss of trees and grasslands in areas that are cleared for livestock grazing. Heavy industrial and

agricultural usage of water is depleting rivers and the water table. Bridges spanning dried riverbeds are now a common sight. China's parched northern

Two Chinese children play on the sandy floor of the Yangzi River. Bridges crossing a dried up riverbed are an increasingly common sight in China. This is caused by recurring drought and excessive consumption of fresh water by humans. China's rapid economic growth has placed increasing demands on the country's already scarce water resources.

HAS ECONOMIC GROWTH BROUGHT HAPPINESS TO CHINA?

region, where 50 percent of the population lives, could eventually become the world's largest desert, and industry, agriculture, and residential consumers will all face water shortages in China's near future.[62]

Finally, China's rise has dramatically expanded its carbon footprint. Per capita carbon dioxide emissions have quadrupled since 1980, and the country is now the world's leading emitter, having surpassed the United States around 2006.[63] Much of the problem stems from China's dependence on coal as its primary generator of electricity. Of the fossil fuels, coal produces the most carbon emissions per unit of electricity generated, and China's huge coal reserves indicate it will not be weaning itself anytime soon.

Inequality and Insecurity. Another negative implication of China's development is a nearly unprecedented increase in inequality. Under the socialist command economy of leader Mao Zedong (1949–1976), China had one of the most equal income distributions in the world, with a Gini coefficient in the .20s. By 2013, inequality had ballooned to .45, making China one of the most unequal countries in Asia.[64] The income gains of the last thirty years have accrued much more rapidly in cities, where most factories have been built, and coastal provinces, which are close to global trading routes. Residents of inland provinces and the countryside have experienced income gains at much slower rates. Incomes in coastal cities now exceed those in the rural interior by a factor of six, one of the largest such gaps in the world.[65]

Modern economic development in China has also come at the cost of many individuals' sense of economic insecurity, as it has frequently resulted in physical displacements and unemployment. Hundreds of millions of formerly rural residents

have moved to cities to take factory jobs and seek out urban prosperity in what is probably the most massive human migration in history. While most migrants do see income gains, their moves often split families and represent a wrenching decision for villagers whose families have farmed for generations. Moreover, China's transformation to more modern and capitalistic economic growth has also caused a large number of layoffs, introducing the experience of unemployment to a country whose socialist government once guaranteed work for all who wanted it. Since 1990, state-owned enterprises have laid off an estimated 50 million employees in the interest of becoming more efficient and competitive.[66]

Psychological Impact. Finally, growth has also brought a number of distinctly modern frustrations and anxieties to the Chinese way of life. Traffic congestion is a near constant in cities. While admittedly an extreme example, in 2010 a traffic jam on an artery into Beijing stalled traffic over a seventy-five-mile stretch for *eleven days*! Industrial and mining accidents are common. Famine is no longer a worry, but eating disorders and skyrocketing obesity rates are. And middle-class parents and their teenagers stress about highly competitive college entrance exams and private school fees.

For these and other reasons, experts and its own leaders have diagnosed China with a happiness deficit. According to poll results, almost half of all Chinese citizens report themselves to be "unhappy" and less than 10 percent self-describe as "very happy." The world's fastest-growing major economy and rising superpower ranks only eighty-sixth worldwide in terms of the happiness of its citizens.[67] Rather than looking back at their pasts and feeling satisfied with their higher standards of living, Chinese citizens seem anxious about employment insecurity, increasing income inequality, traffic, and pollution. The buzzword among China's leadership is to create a "harmonious society" and move away from the growth-at-all-costs model by being more attentive to the environmental and social impacts of development. Yet it remains to be seen whether such measures will have an impact.

In sum, China is an unfolding example of the costs and benefits of development. The country's experience of the last thirty years provides fodder for both critics and advocates of rapid economic growth.

Thinking Critically about Development

- Given this list of pros and cons, do you think the Chinese were better off in 1980 than they are today? What criteria should be used in evaluating whether the Chinese are "better off" or not?

- Is China betraying its cultural heritage by pursuing economic progress, and thus possibly Westernization, so vehemently?

- Will China soon reach the peak of its EKC, such that future growth actually improves its environmental standards? Or will its environmental situation only worsen in the future?

 ## Key Terms

absolute poverty, p. 62

adaptive preferences, p. 70

alienation, p. 68

anthropogenic climate change, p. 65

consumerism, p. 57

creative destruction, p. 68

domestic inequality, p. 59

Easterlin paradox, p. 69

environmental Kuznets curve (EKC), p. 66

Gini coefficient, p. 60

global income distribution, p. 59

intercountry inequality, p. 59

Kuznets curve, p. 63

post-development theory, p. 56

relative poverty, p. 62

Westernization, p. 56

Suggested Readings

Cowen, Tyler. *Creative Destruction: How Globalization Is Changing the World's Cultures.* Princeton, NJ: Princeton University Press, 2002.

Diamond, Jared. *Collapse: How Societies Choose to Fail or Succeed.* New York: Viking Press, 2005.

Easterlin, Richard A. "Does Economic Growth Improve the Human Lot? Some Empirical Evidence." In *Nations and Households in Economic Growth,* edited by Paul A. David and Melvin Reder. New York: Academic Press, 1974.

Escobar, Arturo. *Encountering Development: The Making and Unmaking of the Third World.* Princeton, NJ: Princeton University Press, 1994.

Friedman, Benjamin M. *The Moral Consequences of Economic Growth.* New York: Vintage Books, 2006.

Milanovic, Branko. *The Haves and the Have-Nots: A Brief and Idiosyncratic History of Global Inequality.* New York: Basic Books, 2011.

Ridley, Matthew. *The Rational Optimist: How Prosperity Evolves.* New York: Harper, 2010.

 ## Web Resources

University of Texas Inequality Project, http://utip.gov.utexas.edu/data.html

World Bank, Poverty and Inequality around the World, http://go.worldbank.org/2PYY9EMYI0

World Database of Happiness, www1.eur.nl/fsw/happiness/

A mural in Mozambique depicts the violence and coercion committed against Africans under European colonial rule. Mozambique was colonized by the Portuguese, and the country achieved independence in 1975 only after years of violent struggle.

Slavery and Colonialism

I n June of 1992, a group of twelve people commissioned by the Organization of African Unity and calling itself The Group of Eminent Persons on Reparations met in Abuja, Nigeria. The group put together a short plan of action to guide efforts to demand that Africans and members of the African diaspora receive reparations (financial compensation meant to repair a past wrong) from the mostly Western countries that had benefited from the enslavement and colonization of Africa and Africans. The Nigerian president of the time pledged $500,000 to the cause, and at a follow-up conference occurring in Abuja just a year later, members proclaimed "that the damage sustained by the African peoples is not a 'thing of the past' but is painfully manifest . . . in the damaged economies of the Black World from Guinea to Guyana, from Somalia to Surinam."[1] While the group did not put a dollar figure on their demand, a subsequent reparations-seeking organization did in 1999, calling for US$777 trillion, nearly eighty times the United States' annual GDP.

That these events played out in Nigeria is fitting. Nigeria's reality suggests a number of ways in which economic and social damage caused by Western meddling may be more than just a thing of the past. Nigerian territory lost over 1 million people to the four-hundred-year Atlantic slave trade, and the advent of the trade precipitated the collapse on Nigeria's soil of one of Africa's most advanced civilizations. As if this were not enough, the British followed up the formal abolition of slavery by colonizing Nigerian territory for eighty years, stripping the colony of natural resources and abusing its workers in the process. Today, even after abolition and independence, Nigeria remains poor, seemingly unable to shake the weight of its exploited past.

The activists in the Group of Eminent Persons are not the only people who believe that slavery and colonialism are the root causes of underdevelopment in Nigeria, the rest of Africa, and the other continents of the developing world. This chapter explores arguments made by scholars to the same effect. It describes the history of the Atlantic slave trade and the era of Western colonialism, and it considers arguments for and against these institutions as the cause of contemporary poverty in the affected world regions.

The Atlantic Slave Trade

Slavery refers to a system of labor in which a person is both owned by and forced to work for another person. The first systematic and wide-scale exploitation by the West of peoples of what is today the developing world occurred through the **Atlantic slave trade**. The Atlantic slave trade began in the 1440s and lasted in an illegal form for several decades past its formal abolition by European powers in the early 1800s. Over this time, an estimated 12 million Africans were involuntarily taken from their continent and enslaved in the Western Hemisphere, and huge swaths of the New World had their demographics reshaped through the forcible resettlement of black Africans. The imprint of the Atlantic slave trade on the contemporary world is thus huge, and it may even provide an explanation for why so many countries remain poor.

The Triangular Trade

The Atlantic slave trade began in 1441 when a Portuguese sea captain named Antão Gonçalves captured twelve Africans while exploring the coast of West Africa in what is today Mauritania. He returned with his human cargo to Portugal and presented the slaves to his royal sponsor, Prince Henry the Navigator. Pleased, Prince Henry authorized further expeditions to import slaves from sub-Saharan Africa, and the four-century Atlantic slave trade began. For its first sixty years, slaves were simply shipped northward from Africa to Europe. However, a much longer and more transformative stage began with the first shipment of Africans across the Atlantic Ocean around 1502. For the subsequent three centuries, Portuguese,

Dutch, British, French, and other European traders shipped millions of slaves from Africa to their colonies in the New World. The trade peaked in the eighteenth century with an estimated 60,000 Africans crossing the Atlantic each year.[2]

The system of international exchange underlying the Atlantic slave trade is known as the triangular trade pattern, and it is depicted in Map 4.1. In the first leg of the triangle, European ships traveled to the western coast of Africa carrying manufactured goods such as cloth textiles, firearms, and ammunition, or decorative items such as sea shells, beads, silver coins, and porcelain. Once there, they would dock at ports and exchange their cargo for African captives incarcerated in barracks located at coastal trading outposts. The second leg was the infamous Middle Passage, in which the soon-to-be slaves were shipped across the Atlantic to the Americas to be sold at slave auctions. Captives were housed below deck and chained to one another with virtually no room to stretch out or roll over. Allowed no access to sanitary facilities, fatal diseases often flourished in such close quarters, and many others succumbed to dehydration. The third leg of the triangle provided the fundamental motivation for Europe's orchestration of the Atlantic slave trade: imports from the New World of plantation crops, most of which were the luxury commodities sugar and tobacco.

Features of the Trade in Africa

Europeans rarely went further than the African coast to collect slaves. In fact, no European even penetrated the interior of central Africa until the nineteenth century because of the continent's impassable rivers and disease threat. Instead, European slave traders relied on African slave merchants that brought detainees to the coast for sale. African merchants themselves were the ones who traversed Africa's interior and purchased captives from chiefs, kings, and other merchants. Captives were typically captured in slave raids or battles that took place among competing villages, tribes, and kingdoms. Moreover,

Map 4.1   The Triangular Trade

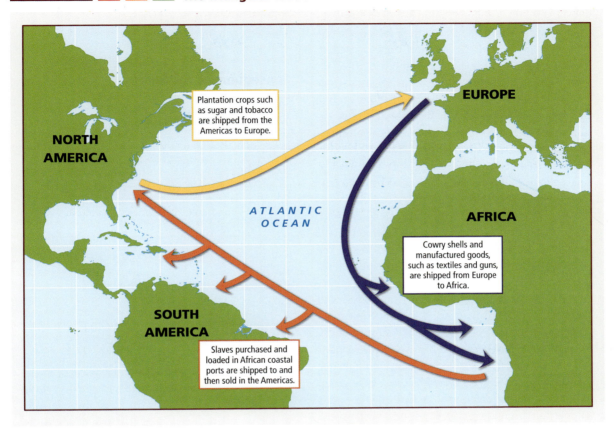

Plantation crops such as sugar and tobacco are shipped from the Americas to Europe.

NORTH AMERICA

EUROPE

ATLANTIC OCEAN

AFRICA

Cowry shells and manufactured goods, such as textiles and guns, are shipped from Europe to Africa.

SOUTH AMERICA

Slaves purchased and loaded in African coastal ports are shipped to and then sold in the Americas.

slavery within Africa—that is, ownership of Africans by Africans—was commonplace at the time. Slavery had been practiced in Africa for thousands of years, and anywhere from 30 to 60 percent of all Africans were enslaved to another African at any given time. The advent of the Atlantic slave trade was thus "an extension of the internal market."[3]

It is also important to add that Europe's was not the only or even the first foreign-imposed slave market in Africa. For centuries before the advent of the Atlantic trade, Middle Eastern merchants orchestrated a pattern of slave trading in which African slaves from south of the Sahara were transported across the Sahara to the Mediterranean basin, across the Red Sea to the Arabian peninsula, and across the Indian Ocean to the Asian mainland. From 800 to 1900, nearly 12 million Africans were enslaved in these Asian and Arab slave trades, matching the number of those shipped across the Atlantic from 1500 to 1900.[4]

Features of the Trade in Latin America

The vast majority of African slaves exported to the New World ended up in the tropics, namely the Caribbean basin and northern Brazil. Students of the United States are well aware of the Atlantic slave trade's impact on the country's history: it eventually contributed to secession and the Civil War, segregation and the civil rights movement, and a long-standing political division over race in society. Despite this profound influence, just 5 percent of all slaves who made the Middle Passage in the 400-year history of the Atlantic trade settled in U.S. territory. The largest share, about 60 percent, ended up in the Caribbean basin (in islands such as Cuba, Hispaniola, and Jamaica and in surrounding mainland territories such as Venezuela). Brazil was the single largest recipient, receiving 35 percent of African slaves who survived the Atlantic crossing, an estimated seven times the number that went to the United States. By 1800, 61 percent of Brazil's entire population was of African descent, compared to just 19 percent in the United States.[5] All told, the Atlantic slave trade had a much more profound influence on the demography and societies of the Western Hemisphere's tropical colonies and countries than on those of North America.

In the New World, most Africans lived and worked on large plantations that grew crops amenable to a tropical climate, namely sugar, cotton, tobacco, and rice. These types of crops were conducive to cultivation via a system of gang labor on large plantations, whereby slaves worked in a large group whose members repetitively carried out the same, simple task. In contrast, slavery was never widespread in areas with more temperate climates, such as the northern United States and southern South America, because cultivation of the grains and livestock common to these areas required greater attention and care from individual farmworkers. In this geographic context, there was a proliferation of small farms worked by cultivators with greater skill than slavery allowed, and the demand for slaves was more limited.

Causes of Underdevelopment: The Long-Term Damage of Slavery

Numerous scholars have blamed underdevelopment in both the slave-exporting continent of Africa and the slave-importing regions of the New World for the persistence of poverty in these parts of the developing world. They have pointed out a number of mechanisms by which slavery may have retarded economic growth.

Consequences for Africa

Some initial evidence that slavery has had a dramatic impact on African development is provided in Figure 4.1. The figure plots the GDP per capita in 2000 (y-axis) for each African country by a measure of the number of slaves that were removed from its territory through the Atlantic, Asian, and Arab slaves trades.[6] The figure shows a sharp negative relationship between a country's modern GDP per capita and the number of slaves extracted from its territory. In other words, countries whose territory was highly affected by the slave trade are worse off today—hundreds of years later—than those that were only weakly affected by it.

This evidence is suggestive, but what might have caused this link between poverty today and slavery so long ago? First, according to historian Patrick Manning, the slave trade may have dramatically slowed Africa's population growth, keeping its population density low. In turn, the relatively sparse population hindered its people's ability to trade among themselves and to construct cities in which economic development could flourish. Manning notes that the population effect of the slave trade goes beyond the loss of the 12 million Africans that survived the Middle Passage. By some estimates, another 12 million died en route, either in the Middle Passage or after capture. On top of this, another 12 million Africans were enslaved and exported as part of the Asian and Arab slave trades.[7] In sum, Africa lost well over 30 million people as casualties of the slave trade and, when considering that the continent lost not just the extracted slaves but also their offspring, the demographic consequences were enormous. One estimate holds that, if not for the slave trade, sub-Saharan Africa's population in 1850 would have been 100 million people. In actuality, it was 50 million, and Africa was the only continent to not experience population growth during the eighteenth century.[8]

Second, the economic logic behind the exchange of slaves for imports was particularly irrational from an African standpoint. According to historian Walter Rodney, Africa lost human resources through the slave trade while receiving virtually nothing in return that could enhance its economic productivity.[9] By exporting humans, Africa lost the labor and know-how of millions of people, a majority of whom were young (how plantation owners in the New World preferred them) and thus near the beginning of their productive and reproductive lives. It also made slave raiding and slave trading profitable, encouraging many Africans to divert their labor energies to a profession that was inherently counterproductive.

Moreover, Africa received items in return for its human exports that were at best useless and at worst destructive. Consider first the cowrie seashell, a particularly valued import that some Africans used as currency. Although colorful and beautifully patterned, "it would be difficult to find anything more useless than the cowrie shell."[10] Yet Africans imported some 10 billion of them during the eighteenth century alone.[11] More destructively, firearms and ammunition were other common imports, with the Europeans introducing some 20 million guns into the continent during the era of the slave trade.[12] These weapons were subsequently used in Africa's internal conflicts, making them all the more deadly. Modern weaponry also made African slave raiders more effective in capturing humans for eventual sale, creating a self-reinforcing guns-slave cycle. In the end, Africa received virtually nothing that could

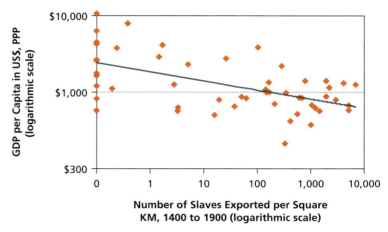

Figure 4.1 **The Relationship between GDP per Capita in 2000 and Total Slave Exports: Evidence from Fifty-Three African Countries**

Source: Nathan Nunn, "The Long-Term Effects of Africa's Slave Trades," *Quarterly Journal of Economics* 123, no. 1 (2008): 139–176.

make it more productive in exchange for its voluminous and precious "exports."

Third and finally, the slave trade created and deepened many of Africa's internal divisions, planting the seeds of a seemingly permanent mistrust that is inimical to economic prosperity. In creating a demand for captives, the Europeans who orchestrated the Atlantic slave trade encouraged Africans to carry out kidnappings against fellow Africans. Villages would raid nearby villages, so structures and sentiments that could unite villages into larger communities did not develop. Moreover, instances of individuals being captured and sold by fellow villagers or by citizens of the same kingdom were widespread. Many African kings and chiefs, allured by foreign imports, unwittingly sowed internal divisions within their fiefdoms by giving slave merchants and raiders access and ownership rights to some of their subjects.

The modern-day consequences of this increased internal discord are manifold. Numerous African kingdoms collapsed under the weight of the divisions caused in their societies by the slave trade, so emergent civilizations that could have

DEVELOPMENT in the FIELD

Anti-Trafficking Organizations

Slavery is now illegal virtually everywhere, but the practice is far from abolished. Human trafficking, the trade in persons who perform coerced labor for the profit of a trafficker, is also called modern-day slavery. Given its criminality and covertness, estimates of the global number of human-trafficking victims (modern slaves) vary wildly, ranging from 700,000 to 30 million. If the latter figure is even remotely close, then the total number of slaves today is greater than the number that existed at any previous point in human history, including at the peak of the Atlantic slave trade.

Worldwide, victims work in a wide array of labor sectors, such as domestic work and mining, but probably the most common is the sex trade. The vast majority (by some estimates 98 percent) of sex-trafficking victims are female, and sex traffickers tend to recruit victims from among vulnerable female populations, targeting teenage girls who are runaways, drug addicts, ethnic minorities, and/or in desperate need of employment.[14] Victims are typically lured by a fake job offer, a promise of emigration to a high-income country, or free drugs. Sex-trafficking detainees are often held in brothels and, although physical conditions alone can make escape difficult, brothel managers often employ other mechanisms to ensure compliance. These can include threatening violence against the girl's family should she escape or getting the girls hooked on drugs, which makes them dependent on the trafficker to feed their addictive cravings. For most victims, the enslavement ends after a years-long spell in a brothel when they reach an age (often in their twenties or thirties) at which they are considered to be less attractive to potential customers than newfound girls and younger women.[15]

A number of anti-trafficking organizations exist, including Not for Sale and Anti-Slavery International, which was actually founded in 1839 as an abolitionist group and claims to be the world's oldest international human rights group. But advocacy in this area is tricky. Most anti-trafficking activists frown on purchasing a victim's freedom from the trafficker. This is seen as a form of participating in the illicit trade itself, and often the trafficker will simply fill the vacancy with a new slave purchased with the proceeds from the sale. As a result, anti-trafficking organizations are largely limited to more incremental measures, such as encouraging law enforcement agencies to bring traffickers to justice, lobbying businesses and consumers to not purchase slave-produced commodities, and providing former trafficking victims with posttraumatic counseling and health services.

formed the building blocks of today's cities and unified nation-states disappeared. Today, Africa has the most severe levels of ethnic fragmentation in the world, and its postcolonial history is littered with violent conflict among competing ethnic groups. Even in peaceful locales, mutual fear and mistrust among ethnic groups runs high and, interestingly, is highest in areas where slave raids and kidnappings were most rampant.[13] This ethnic friction complicates economic exchange and the provision of public services that are meant to provide benefits across multiple groups. (Chapter 7 provides more details on the possible role of ethnic fragmentation in causing underdevelopment.)

Consequences for Latin America and the Caribbean

The permanent settlement of millions of Africans via the largest involuntary migration in world history may have also laid the roots of underdevelopment in the Caribbean basin and Brazil. Agricultural economist George Beckford developed the plantations economy thesis in the early 1970s to argue that slavery in the Caribbean created the region's "persistent poverty."[16] The creation of so many slave plantations—defined as a large tract of land operated by a white slaveholder and landowner—built in a structural rigidity to Caribbean economies that was hard to shake even after emancipation. Plantations produced a single crop for export, almost always sugar or cotton. The white landowning elites that profited from slave exploitation rejected new technologies, especially laborsaving ones that would have replaced their slaves. In doing so, they prevented industrialization, instead keeping the Caribbean economies largely tied to one agricultural commodity that held little promise for long-term development.

Subsequent scholars have made similar claims about slavery's negative legacy for development in Latin America. New institutional economists Stanley Engerman and Kenneth Sokoloff argue that, in the tropical climates where demand for slaves was at its highest, the importation of large numbers of Africans and their enslavement on large plantations created a long-term legacy of inequality and slow growth.[17] In societies such as Brazil and Jamaica, a white minority held most of the wealth and power over a black and enslaved majority. After abolition, this inequality remained, enabling landowning elites to block political and economic changes such as democratization, mass education, and extension of property rights for freed slaves that would have chipped away at their privileges and promoted economic growth. The lack of reform to these institutions only reinforced material inequality, leaving Latin America's tropical countries as some of the world's most unequal societies even to this day. Nonwhite populations are more likely to be landless, and they have lacked a legal system that encourages or harnesses their efforts.

Critique: Questioning the Magnitude of Slavery's Legacy

Few people today question the moral repugnance of the Atlantic slave trade, but the argument that Africa is still poor because of it has its scholarly detractors. Some scholars question whether the slave trade was extensive enough to cause the demographic effects attributed to it. At its peak, the Atlantic slave trade deprived Africa of an extra 6 of each 1,000 people per year. By way of comparison, deaths from disease and other natural causes cost the continent 50 per 1,000 people every year.[18] Western Europe lost a far greater share of its population to emigration during the eighteenth and nineteenth centuries, but it still industrialized at this time. Moreover, while the Atlantic slave trade did precipitate the collapse of several African kingdoms, it created many new African states as well. Africa's coast became dotted with city-states that popped up in response to the slave trade, yet these did not become the basis of modern, wealthy civilizations. In other words, the presence of high population density and nascent civilizational life was not a precursor to eventual economic development. Finally, some argue that, since Africans themselves already practiced forms of slavery, the advent of European demand drew on an already existing institution rather than radically transforming the continent's societies. It thus could not be responsible for the massive economic and social effects often attributed to it.

Arguments about the near-fatal consequences of slavery for economic progress in Latin America also have their critics. Both the plantation economies and the Engerman and Sokoloff versions of the argument see political, economic, and social arrangements as overly static or unchanging. For example, Beckford largely assumed that the plantation economy structure of the Caribbean had remained unchanged for over four hundred years. This viewpoint, however, ignores the effects of the emergence of a peasantry and free-wage labor after abolition. Similarly, Engerman and Sokoloff seem to overlook the inconvenient fact that inequality levels have not been constant throughout Latin American history. Latin America's severe rates of inequality did not emerge until the late 1800s, after emancipation and once some industrial growth began to occur. Prior to that point, some evidence suggests that Latin America was no more unequal than North America.[19]

Western Colonialism

Like the Atlantic slave trade, Western colonialism was a defining institution for the developing world, and many observers cite it as a cause of underdevelopment in today's global South. **Colonialism** is the governing of a territory by individuals and institutions from outside the territory. (The term "imperialism" is sometimes used as a synonym for colonialism, although imperialism often has broader uses that refer to any relationship in which one political entity has extensive influence or control over another.) Under colonialism, the governing entity is called the **metropole**, which has authority over the **colony**. Under a colonial arrangement, the colony lacks sovereignty, or supreme governing authority over its own territory. Sovereignty is instead claimed and exercised by the metropole.

The Importance of the Western Colonial Era for the Contemporary South

This chapter focuses on the era of Western colonialism, which corresponds to the 500-year period from 1450 to the mid-twentieth century. This era of Western colonialism is far from the only instance of colonialism in world history. Colonialism has a long history. It dates back to early expansionist civilizations such as those of ancient Egypt and Assyria and includes classical empires such as the Han Chinese, Greeks, and Romans. However, Western colonialism in the second half of the second millennium is the focus here because it transformed politics, economics, demography, and culture in the colonized societies that comprise today's less developed world. This subsection lists some of the ways in which Western colonialism was so transformative.

Transforming the Map and the Institutions of the Global South. Nearly all of the countries that are considered less developed today were colonized by a European country at some point during this era. A map showing the countries that were colonized by Europe during these 500 years bears a striking resemblance to the map of today's less developed countries. Exceptions exist, most notably former colonies such as Australia and the United States. In general, however, it is nearly constitutive of today's LDCs to have been a colonial possession of a European metropole at some point between 1450 and the 1970s. Moreover, this era literally drew the map of today's developing world. Most of today's less developed countries began life as administrative units under colonial rule, with their borders drawn by European imperialists. Before Europeans arrived, there was no such thing as, say, Argentina, India, or Guinea, yet when Europeans relinquished these colonial possessions, they left behind the sovereign nation-states that exist today.

Colonization also dramatically altered the ways in which non-Western societies were governed. The conquest of colonial territories often overthrew political and economic institutions that existed among native populations, such as the Aztec and Inca empires of the New World. In turn, the West often imposed European notions of bureaucracy and leadership that were alien to native societies. Moreover, economic production in colonies was reshaped to become tethered to the needs of the metropole and its settlers, with examples ranging from the benign, such as the construction of railroads running from inland to coast, to the reprehensible, such as the forced labor of natives. For Europeans, the primary motivation for 500 years of colonial conquest and rule was commercial: to secure access to precious metals such as gold and silver, consumer goods such as silk and sugar, and raw materials such as rubber and ivory. Most metropoles imposed a monopoly of commerce on their colonial possessions, meaning residents of the colony could only trade with agents of the metropole.

The Distinction of Difference between Metropole and Colony.

The imperialism of the post-1450 Western colonial era was distinctive from previous incarnations of colonialism because of the large distances between metropole and colony. Historically, colonialism occurred through the annexation of nearby territories. This is how, for example, the Roman Empire in the classical era and the Russian and Soviet empires in modern times expanded. The proximity between rulers and ruled tended to limit the cultural and biological differences between the two peoples. In contrast, in the age of Western colonialism, metropoles and colonies were on different continents, which made for dramatic differences between natives in the colonies and their white rulers. Europeans were almost completely alien to the colonial possessions they governed, and they often imposed upon them previously unknown technologies such as guns and biological realities such as horses and smallpox.

As one important result of these differences, white Europeans transformed demography, race, and race relations in **settler colonies**, defined as those to which whites emigrated from Europe and established permanent settlements with no intention of returning home. For example, Spain's conquests in the Western Hemisphere led to the creation of a new *mestizo* race of European–Native American mixture that today constitutes a majority in most Latin American countries. White settlement also transformed race and race relations in other settler colonies, such as Algeria, Argentina, South Africa,

and Zimbabwe. The demographic effect was more limited in **nonsettler colonies**, where the Europeans who lived in the colony were largely government officials and bureaucrats who did not intend to permanently settle and left at the time of independence. India and most of the colonies of Southeast Asia and sub-Saharan Africa were of the nonsettler variety.

Another crucial result of the massive differences between colony and metropole was that the Western colonial period reshaped the cultural life of the South, especially with regard to language and religion. Colonial conquest and rule flowed from an ideology of white racial superiority over the non-white natives, so colonizers held little regard for the natives' long-standing cultural practices. Indeed, a secondary motivation of Western imperialism was to "civilize" and proselytize to non-Christian peoples viewed as "primitive." In Latin America, the language (Portuguese and Spanish) and religion (Roman Catholicism) of the colonial masters were eventually adopted almost wholesale. Pockets of indigenous language and spirituality remain but are relatively rare in today's Latin America. Throughout Africa, the language of the European colonizer is commonly spoken as a second tongue, and the Christian religion is also widely practiced. That said, colonialism varied in its cultural influence. For example, most Indians still practice Hinduism and speak a native tongue as their first language.

A Brief History of the Western Colonial Era

The age of Western colonialism is best summarized by dividing it into three separate waves of expansion, and these correspond very roughly to the colonization of the three different continents that constitute much of today's developing world. First was the Iberian expansion of the early 1500s, which resulted in three centuries of colonial rule in Central and South America. Second was the era of the chartered trading companies throughout the seventeenth and eighteenth centuries, when parts of Asia were colonized. The final wave corresponds to the Scramble for Africa in the 1880s. These designations should be seen as a rough guide to complex historical trends rather than an exhaustive characterization of Western imperialism. Some exceptions are mentioned below. Table 4.1 provides a brief summary of the three eras.

The Iberian Expansion. The **Iberian expansion** refers to the period in the early 1500s when Portugal and Spain acquired colonial possessions following their newfound ability to navigate by sea to faraway places during the Age of Discovery. This colonization occurred as the two Iberian states (Portugal and Spain) made westward discoveries and conquests across the Atlantic Ocean in the forty-year period following Columbus's first voyage in 1492. In colonizing most of the New World, Portugal's and Spain's primary motivation was pursuit of the mercantilist imperative of accumulating as much precious metal (mostly silver and gold) in their metropoles as possible.

In 1500, Portuguese sailor Pedro Cabral discovered Brazil. Confronting minimal resistance from a sparse native population, the Portuguese initially established a series of coastal outposts up and down Brazil's Atlantic shores. While staying clear of Brazil's interior for over two centuries, the Portuguese constructed a colonial state along the coast that oversaw a small population of white settlers, coastal natives, and eventually African slaves.

In contrast to the Portuguese maritime empire, Spain had fewer qualms about constructing a colonial state that encompassed coastal and interior territories and that exerted complete political authority over the indigenous populations residing therein. Spain's most famous conquistadores, Hernán Cortés and Francisco Pizarro, conquered two of the world's most advanced civilizations at the time, the Aztec (1521) and Inca (1532), respectively. Over the subsequent three centuries of colonial rule, the Spanish crown laid claim to a landmass that extended from what is today the southwestern United States down to the southern tip of South America (with the only large exception being that of Brazil) and included several of the Caribbean islands. Spanish control over its colonies was extensive. The crown assumed ownership over all land and granted it to victorious conquistadores and other settlers. The metropole also granted Spanish settlers the right to extract taxation and labor by force from indigenous populations. Tragically, colonization reduced the indigenous population under Spain's control by 90 percent since the Spanish arrival exposed the native

Table 4.1 **Three Eras of Colonial Expansion**

Era	Regions Colonized	Period of Expansion and Colonization	Primary Colonizers	Period of Decolonization
The Iberian expansion	Latin America	1492 to 1530s	Portugal and Spain	1810s and 1820s
Era of the chartered trading companies	South Asia, Southeast Asia, parts of African coast	1600 to 1770s	Dutch East India Company, British East India Company	1940s (companies yield sovereignty to metropole states in 1800s)
The Scramble for Africa	Sub-Saharan Africa	1880 to 1914	Great Britain, France, Germany, and Belgium	1957 through 1970s

Source: Compiled by the author.

community to smallpox and other diseases to which they had no natural biological resistance.

The Era of the Chartered Trading Corporations.

Colonial expansion in the second era, roughly 1600 to the 1770s, was dominated by two **chartered trading corporations**: the Dutch East India Company (VOC, its acronym in Dutch) and the British East India Company (EIC). The respective metropole governments of the VOC and EIC conferred powers on the corporations (in legal documents called charters) to establish trading relations with native Asians throughout the East Indies (the lands surrounding the Indian Ocean) and East Asia. Metropole governments' primary goal was to secure the import of consumer commodities from Asia that were not native to Europe, such as certain spices, teas, and silk.

Although technically companies, the chartered trading corporations were endowed by their respective metropole governments with most of the powers of a functioning state. They operated by setting up trading outposts throughout the coasts of the Indian Ocean and East Asia. To ensure the success of their trading mission, the corporations' charters empowered them to "take suitable measures"[20] to secure trading arrangements with the native Asians living in and around the outposts, a measure tantamount to granting them full political authority. They thus assumed a number of statelike powers, including the power to tax and extract labor from nearby native peoples; to hold standing armies and fight wars; to pass laws and dispense justice through courts, prisons, and security personnel; to settle and own land; to negotiate and sign treaties with native rulers; and to provide public goods such as transport infrastructure. Corporations such as EIC and VOC even had their own flags and at times issued their own currencies.

The Dutch VOC dominated the seventeenth century and the British EIC dominated the eighteenth. By the 1660s, the VOC's outposts, although not penetrating very far inland, dotted the shores of

modern-day Bangladesh, India, Indonesia, Malaysia, Sri Lanka, and Taiwan. They also included one set up in 1652 near the Cape of Good Hope at the southern tip of Africa, where Dutch settlers had begun to establish permanent residency in what would eventually become South Africa. The VOC's power declined throughout the eighteenth century when it lost some of its major holdings, namely those in India and Malaysia, to its ascendant competitor, the EIC. At its peak in the mid-1700s, the EIC controlled almost the entirety of the Indian coast, as well as Sri Lanka and Malaysia. As the era of the chartered trading corporations closed, the declining companies handed over their possessions to their metropoles. When the VOC folded in 1800, sovereignty and operation of its remaining outposts in the Dutch East Indies (Indonesia) and the Cape Colony (South Africa) were transferred to the Dutch state. A similar process occurred as the EIC demised in the 1800s, as the Indian subcontinent was transitioned to British rule in 1857.

The Scramble for Africa.

The third era is the **Scramble for Africa**, which roughly spans 1880 to 1914. As its name implies, the era saw various European states and players rush into the continent to colonize and lay claim to its precious natural resources and agricultural potential. Natural resources such as gold, rubber, and ivory, along with crops such as peanuts, cocoa, and palm oil, were the main commercial goals of Western colonizers. By the end of the scramble, Africa went from being a continent whose interior had been largely untouched by Western imperialism to one that had been carved up into colonial territories that were wholly alien to the native communities living on the continent.

Although various European beachheads had existed along Africa's coast for centuries, the continent avoided full-scale Western colonization until the late nineteenth century because of its difficult terrain. As late as the 1840s, no European had successfully penetrated the heart of central Africa because it has no rivers that provide navigable passage from ocean to interior and because Europeans who had attempted to do so almost always succumbed to tropical disease. However, successful forays into the interior by explorers such as David Livingstone, Henry Morton Stanley, and Pierre de Brazza between 1850 and 1880 enabled Europeans to map Africa's previously unknown redoubts and even to begin signing treaties with African chiefs to secure their tribal lands. For several weeks in 1884 and 1885, leaders from a dozen European states met at the infamous Berlin Conference to lay down rules dictating how African territory would be divided and distributed to the various metropoles. At the conference and over the subsequent three decades, the United Kingdom, France, Germany, Portugal, Italy, Spain, and King Leopold II (then Belgium's monarch) each acquired a portion of African territory. As in earlier colonial occupations, Europeans forced natives to labor in order to extract natural resources and agricultural commodities for export to the metropoles.

Exceptions. Not all episodes of colonial expansion fit neatly into these three eras and categories. Four are particularly noteworthy. First, much of the Middle East did not come under Western rule until after World War I, and the colonial interlude in this region was relatively brief. Most of today's Middle Eastern countries were part of a separate imperial system, the Ottoman Empire (1453–1922), whose political capital was housed in modern-day Turkey. After the empire's defeat in World War I, some of its provinces were handed to World War I victors France (Lebanon and Syria) and Britain (Iraq, Jordan, and Palestine) until their independence just twenty to thirty years later. Second, the biggest prize, China, was never fully colonized by the West, although various European powers did establish governing enclaves in dozens of Chinese cities during the nineteenth century. Third, France acquired territories when it colonized parts of North Africa (Algeria) in the 1840s and Southeast Asia, namely

French Indochina (eventually Cambodia, Laos, and Vietnam) between 1885 and 1893. Finally, Europeans were not the only Westerners to colonize. The United States entered the colonial fray as a metropole by acquiring the Philippines from the Spanish in 1898 and occupying nearby Latin American territories such as Cuba and the Dominican Republic for some short-lived periods in the twentieth century. Map 4.2 depicts who was the most important colonizer of today's developing countries.

Decolonization and Independence. Decolonization and the attaining of independence refers to the restoration of sovereignty and autonomy (self-rule) to the peoples of a colony. Independence from Western imperialism occurred in two waves. The first major wave was the era of Latin American independence in the early 1800s, which reversed the Iberian expansion that had occurred 300 years earlier. Aside from the United States in 1776, the first country to achieve independence from Western colonialism was Haiti, which experienced a slave revolt in 1791 and finally declared itself a sovereign republic in 1804. Around this time, wars for independence also occurred in the various administrative regions delineated by Spain and Portugal throughout Central America, Mexico, and South America. Between 1810 and 1825, fifteen new countries achieved independence, turning most of Latin American territory into sovereign nation-states.

The second major wave of decolonization occurred around 150 years later in the two decades following World War II, and it nearly tripled the number of independent countries in the world. India and various colonies in Southeast Asia, most notably Indonesia, the Philippines, and Myanmar, acquired independence in the latter half of the 1940s, and independence for Vietnam and Malaysia followed soon thereafter. Parts of the Middle East and North Africa also achieved independence in the decade following the end of World War II. Decolonization in sub-Saharan Africa began in the 1950s

Map 4.2   **Developing Countries by Primary Western Colonizer**

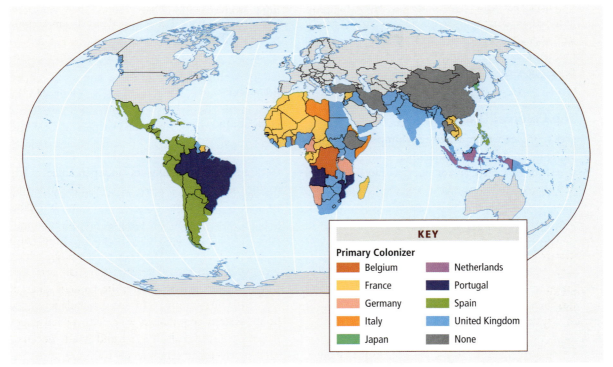

KEY

Primary Colonizer

Belgium		Netherlands	
France		Portugal	
Germany		Spain	
Italy		United Kingdom	
Japan		None	

Source: The United Nations and Decolonization, Trust and Non-Self-Governing Territories (1945–1999), www.un.org/en/decolonization/nonselfgov.shtml.

with the declaration of independence by Ghana in 1957. Within the space of just a decade, more than thirty new nation-states were created, and the African set of independent countries was further filled out with a small wave of transitions to sovereignty in the 1970s among former Portuguese colonies.

There was no one model for successful decolonization, as some countries achieved independence through violence and others more peacefully. In some instances, foreign occupying forces were defeated through prolonged and violent revolutions. In Spanish America, revolutions were led by Criollo elites against forces loyal to the Spanish crown. Revolutions had more mass involvement in Indonesia and some of the settler colonies of Africa (such as Algeria and Zimbabwe), where revolutionary

armies combined tactics of conventional and guerrilla warfare to ultimately overthrow their colonizers. In other instances, independence was achieved through more peaceful means. Mohandas Gandhi famously led a mass movement of nonviolent resistance against British rule in India. Most nonsettler colonies in Africa achieved independence through peaceful negotiations among African and (admittedly begrudging) metropole elites.

Causes of Underdevelopment: Western Colonialism's Consequences

The coincidence between the map of today's less developed countries and that of yesterday's

Western colonies is certainly suggestive of a cause-and-effect relationship between colonization and underdevelopment. But simply observing this coincidence is not evidence enough. What are the possible means and mechanisms by which colonialism impoverished and continues to contribute to the impoverishment of the less developed world?

The Colonial Drain

Colonialism involved theft and plunder in a variety of forms, all of which resulted in what scholars have called the **colonial drain**, or transfer of wealth from colony to metropole. Colonial drains were made possible by the West's political dominance, itself borne of superior military and technological power, and this central storyline was recurrent over five centuries and four continents of imperialism. According to many scholars, this theft and plunder accounts for why the era of colonialism translated into lost centuries of economic growth for colonized territories, all while Western Europe's economies gradually progressed.

Europeans enacted numerous practices that enabled them to extract natural resources and other forms of wealth from their colonies without giving fair compensation to colonial subjects in return. The widespread practice of forced labor, even when it fell short of formal slavery, is the most obvious and egregious example of this. For example, in King Leopold's Congo Free State, natives were forced, on threat of maiming or death, to collect rubber from trees for colonial officials. Even in contexts of "free" labor, colonial masters kept commodity prices and wages low through their enforced monopolies on commerce. As one piece of evidence, major colonies such as India and Indonesia had huge trade surpluses with their metropoles, meaning they exported more of value to them than they imported from them.[21] Moreover, colonizers also assumed the power to tax, and in some instances, otherwise free colonial subjects lost 60 percent of their income and labor to taxation.[22] As another practice, metropole

governments effectively stole financial capital from their territorial possessions by transferring treasury funds from the colony back home. These transfers, called home charges in British India, were justified on the grounds that colonial administration was costly and required compensation. Finally, European administrators and settlers time and again helped themselves to colonial lands. For example, the Portuguese and Spanish crowns, after conquering New World territory, assumed ownership of it and granted parcels of land to European conquistadores and settlers.

Scholars working within a Marxist tradition see the plunder and theft of Western colonialism as the primary cause of the long-standing divergence in living standards between West and South. Vladimir Lenin himself, main organizer of the Russian Revolution and first leader of the Soviet Union, laid some of this intellectual groundwork in his 1917 pamphlet *Imperialism, the Highest Stage of Capitalism*. Lenin saw imperialism as the means by which Western powers enabled the capitalist class (the *bourgeoisie*) to spread to and exploit less developed societies. To Lenin, the search by Western capitalists for new areas of growth and high rates of profit within their own societies had become exhausted. As a result, capital sought to expand abroad to largely agrarian societies. The resulting manifestation of this impulse was the political domination by Western states of undeveloped societies and the introduction to these societies of the exploitive capitalist mode of production.

Subsequent Marxist theorists provided more detail about how impoverishment of the colonies through this capitalist expansion took place. Ernest Mandel argued that due to the colonial state's backing of low wages, forced labor, limited social legislation, and high unemployment, Western-based capitalists could easily earn super-profits in the colonies by extracting income that rightfully belonged to workers.[23] Besides initiating this exploitation, the entry of the foreign *bourgeoisie* had long-term negative consequences for economic development. To Mandel, the metropole-based capitalist class found super-profits to be highest in the colonies' primary sectors, so they invested in agriculture and mining to the neglect of manufacturing. In doing so, they often wiped out colonies' nascent industrial sectors, stripping them of what could have become the basis of rapid capital accumulation and productivity gains. Moreover, in re-orienting their colonies around the production and export of primary products, metropoles effectively prevented the reemergence of industry. As an example, Mandel showed that India once exported finished clothing, but the colony reverted to exporting cotton after the influx of British capital in the late 1800s and early 1900s. In short, British India never developed a domestic *bourgeoisie*, a prerequisite for industrial growth in Marxist thought.[24]

Colonialism's Institutional Legacy

According to scholars within a variety of traditions, the effects of colonialism in Africa, Latin America, and much of Asia outlived the moment of independence by laying down long-lasting institutions that were detrimental to development. New institutional economists Daron Acemoglu, Simon Johnson, and James Robinson argue that Western colonialism created rules that centralized political power in a colonial and native elite.[25] Members of this elite used this political power to enrich themselves at the expense of the broader masses, concentrating wealth in their own hands through the various forms of economic exploitation and extraction listed above. In turn, their wealth enabled them to maintain their political dominance and rig rules about economic activity to their own benefit. Forced labor and a lack of land-ownership rights for the masses are just two examples of such economic institutions. In shaping rules to their favor, elites inhibited overall economic growth by discouraging investment and productivity gains among the masses. After all, the masses knew that they could not keep any hard-won wealth they generated, as most of it would be extracted by pilfering elites. To Acemoglu, Johnson, and Robinson,

postcolonial societies inherited this institutional arrangement of mutually reinforcing political and economic inequalities. Even after decolonization, elites were loathe to relinquish their privileges, and they used their political power to block institutional changes such as property rights for the masses that would have threatened these privileges. In doing so, however, they kept their societies mired in poverty by keeping in place institutions that discouraged productivity and investment on the part of the broader population. Figure 4.2 provides a visual summary of this argument.

As a paradigmatic example, these authors point to the *encomienda* and *repartimiento* systems established in the 1500s by the Spanish crown in its New World colonies. These were legal institutions in which the metropole granted to select Spaniards living in the New World the right to extract tribute and forced labor from the indigenous population living within a certain loosely defined tract of land. The crown also allowed these select few to use violence and coercion to protect their rights to land ownership, while the rights of the indigenous to own land were ignored and even disdained. These biased legal institutions created a small Spanish and Criollo elite and impoverished the indigenous masses during 300 years of colonial dominance. Although the *encomienda* and *repartimiento* systems were formally dissolved long before the successful independence movements of the 1810s and 1820s, they had created an economic legacy of inequality, with a white elite controlling most of the newly independent countries' land and wealth. After independence, members of this elite used the political power that their wealth afforded them to resist the emergence of new institutions (such as land redistribution, progressive taxation, universal suffrage, and state-sponsored education and health care) that would have redistributed wealth to the wider masses and incentivized productivity enhancements and growth. As evidence, Latin America's independent states were much later to arrive at democratizing and redistributive reforms than were Western Europe's.

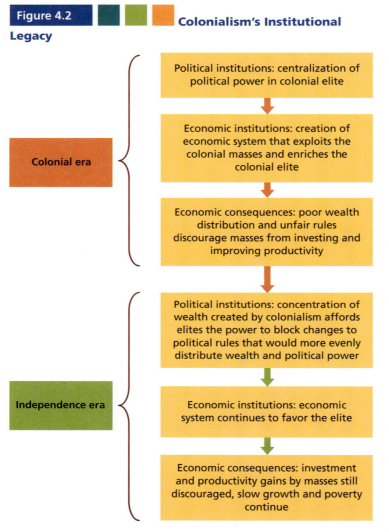

Figure 4.2 Colonialism's Institutional Legacy

Colonial era

Political institutions: centralization of political power in colonial elite

Economic institutions: creation of economic system that exploits the colonial masses and enriches the colonial elite

Economic consequences: poor wealth distribution and unfair rules discourage masses from investing and improving productivity

Independence era

Political institutions: concentration of wealth created by colonialism affords elites the power to block changes to political rules that would more evenly distribute wealth and political power

Economic institutions: economic system continues to favor the elite

Economic consequences: investment and productivity gains by masses still discouraged, slow growth and poverty continue

and grounded in ruthless extraction and dominance of civil society. Hamstrung with this political system, Africa's postindependence leaders were unable to implement new forms of governance that enjoyed legitimacy among the population and were grounded in free political competition and economic fairness. Instead, they adopted the oppressive elements of colonialism to impose forms of one-party or personalistic rule that fostered dysfunctional economies and poor social development.

Colonialism's Cultural Legacy

The era of Western colonialism also bequeathed many newly independent states with severe identity crises, leading in many cases to years of costly strife among ethnic and religious groups. In most instances, European occupiers drew the borders that delineated their colonial possessions with little regard for whether these borders were suitable to the physical and human geography on the ground. For many LDCs, the arbitrariness of the borders they inherited from colonial masters created problems after independence. Borders often united ethnic or religious groups with mutual animosities into the same country and divided peoples with a long-standing kinship into separate countries. This laid the groundwork for various postindependence conflicts and civil wars. Most notoriously, the British India colony contained modern-day India, Pakistan, and Bangladesh. It split into Hindu-majority India and Muslim Pakistan soon after

Political scientist Crawford Young agrees that the consequences of colonialism outlasted its formal demise. He says of Africa, "Although we commonly described the independent polities as 'new states,' in reality they were successors to the colonial regime, inheriting its structure, its quotidian routines and practices, and its more hidden normative theories of governance."[26] To Young, Africa's newly independent states inherited a colonial governing apparatus that was alien to the native population independence, but not before 1 million people died in the war over partition. In Africa, whose countries' shapes resemble (according to one scholar's quip) "drunken parallelograms,"[27] borders split more than 170 ethnic groups between adjacent nation-states, and the continent has had recurrent secessionist and ethnic violence in its fifty-year postcolonial history.

Furthermore, rule by Europeans may have actually sharpened ethnic divisions among colonial subjects who were later expected to live united in an independent nation-state. According to anthropologist Mahmood Mamdani, colonial administrators were known to engage in divide-and-rule tactics by playing one local ethnic group off of another. Famously, in the African colony of Rwanda, Belgian officials elevated the Tutsi ethnic minority into a position of dominance over the Hutu majority. According to Mamdani, this created the resentment that eventually fueled the genocide of Tutsis by Hutus, which occurred three decades after Rwandan independence.[28] Mamdani also argues that the British form of colonial governance known as indirect rule, whereby colonial officials designated various administrative powers to tribal chiefs, also set African against African. Through their acquired powers, chiefs and other African members of the British-labeled native authority exercised a repressive "decentralized despotism" over their African subjects before decolonization that laid the groundwork for predatory and autocratic rule after it.[29]

Critique of Colonial Legacy Arguments

Today, most scholars view Western colonialism as an immoral and shameful institution. Despite this, some do raise plausible questions about the extent to which Africa's, Asia's, and Latin America's underdevelopment can be attributed to Western imperialism.

Non-Western societies had severe technological and prosperity disadvantages relative to the West even before the Europeans arrived. Indeed, these disadvantages are what made Western conquest so easy across so many different times and places. Therefore, the case could be made that the reason LDCs are poorer than the West today is not colonialism, but rather the same set of factors—such as culture, geography or bad leadership—that made non-Western nations poorer and easily overcome at the time of conquest.

Stated differently, to pin the blame for non-Western underdevelopment on Western colonialism, one must be able to confidently answer the following counterfactual question with an unqualified "yes": Would much of the developing world be developed today if Europeans had never colonized it? Some forms of historical evidence make it difficult to give this positive answer. A handful of countries remain less developed today despite not being colonized or only being colonized briefly by the West. These include Ethiopia, Iran, Nepal, Thailand, and Turkey. For example, Europeans (Italians) occupied Ethiopia for a mere five years, and Thailand was never colonized. All of these countries were poor when the age of Western colonialism ended, despite the fact that European powers had little direct imprint on their economies, societies, and polities.

Other evidence suggests that critics may exaggerate colonialism's impact. European occupiers wanted colonies to pay for themselves because they did not want to transfer financial resources from metropole to colony. As a result, they often ruled colonies on the cheap, with small governing bureaucracies that were only large enough to maintain economic and social order. According to economist Peter Bauer, such a small European presence left vast parts of native territory and society untouched, limiting the impact of colonial institutions.[30] For example, much of Africa was governed by a "thin white line"[31] of European civil servants, often with just one colonial official for

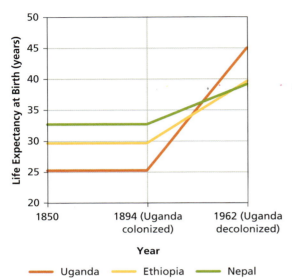

Figure 4.3   Life Expectancy at Birth in Ethiopia, Nepal, and Uganda, 1850–1962

Source: Data compiled from Gapminder, www.gapminder.org.

every 100,000 natives. Similarly, one picture often painted of colonialism's legacy is of a newly independent state that has been stripped of its most valuable natural resources and left to find a path to modern economic growth without them, yet the volumes of resources that were expropriated and exported under colonialism were a drop in the bucket compared to the resources that remain in most developing countries today.

Some observers, such as historian Niall Ferguson, even go so far as to say that colonialism helped the eventual developing world become better off.[32] After all, many precolonial native societies lacked writing (for example, much of sub-Saharan Africa and South America), rudimentary technologies (the Americas had no wheel), modern economic institutions and commerce (Islamic law governed property rights in the Middle East), and political and cultural unity (India had the caste system and hundreds of languages). Europeans brought things such as literacy, formal education, vaccinations, and railroad transport to Africa; conceptions of modern bureaucracy and rule of law to India; capitalist institutions such as the corporation to the Middle East;[33] and draft animals such as the horse and cow to Latin America. By the 1800s, Westerners brought scientific notions of medicine that helped combat preventable diseases. The arrival of Westerners also occasionally brought peace to formerly warring native societies. According to economist George Ayittey, the colonial era was a relatively peaceful one among Africa's various peoples and civilizations.[34] All told, it is true that some indicators of well-being, such as life expectancy and literacy rates, began to climb under colonial occupation. Figure 4.3 contrasts life expectancy improvements in Uganda under British rule with those in never-colonized Nepal and briefly colonized Ethiopia. Despite starting at a lower base, improvements in the twentieth century were more rapid in Uganda.

Arguments that attribute underdevelopment to Western colonialism also cannot account for change in postcolonial nation-states. Recent history contains numerous examples of less developed postcolonial countries that have dramatically transformed their societies' economic and political trajectories. For example, South Korea showed that postcolonial change of a rapid variety is possible. It emerged from a brutal colonial occupation by the Japanese (1910–1945) to become the less developed world's leading success story in the second half of the twentieth century. Similarly, other success stories, such as fast-growing Botswana and Chile, have seemingly shed the weight of their colonial pasts to implement prosperity-promoting political and economic institutions. The new institutional economics tools used by Acemoglu, Johnson, and Robinson often struggle to explain instances of abrupt social change such as these.

DO SLAVERY AND COLONIALISM EXPLAIN NIGERIA'S DEVELOPMENT FAILURE?

Nigeria has long aspired to be a regional and even a world leader. "Africa's Giant" is far and away the continent's biggest country by population, with around 160 million people. It has the world's twelfth-largest oil reserves, and by the 1980s it had a burgeoning industrial sector. Yet after more than fifty years of existence as an independent nation-state, Nigeria's postcolonial hopes of prosperity and global leadership have never been realized. It remains poor: 85 percent of Nigerian citizens live on less than US$2 per day, and only China and India have more poor people.[35] Its postcolonial political history has been a study in instability. Is the West, which exploited the territory's peoples and resources through slavery and colonialism for over 500 years, responsible for Nigeria's ongoing plight? As a point of comparison, Table 4.2 compares some of Nigeria's development causes and outcomes with those of its former colonizer, the United Kingdom.

The West: Slavery and Colonialism's Consequences

Nigerians are divided into more than 250 distinct ethnic groups and speak 420 different languages—some 7 percent of the world's total![36] This diversity has had severe societal consequences that include 2 million deaths[37] from ethnic-based violence since independence (including a three-year civil war) and a society and economy fragmented by mutual suspicion. By some measures, Nigerians are the most mistrusting people in the world, expressing an extreme degree of wariness toward their compatriots in public opinion surveys.[38] On top of this, Nigeria has never been able to get its industrial feet under itself, as its economy is still heavily grounded in agriculture and mining. Scholarship has attributed both problems, disunity and deindustrialization, to Great Britain's colonization of Nigeria (1886–1960) and the nearly 400 years of slave trading that preceded it.

Table 4.2 **Development Comparison: Nigeria and the United Kingdom**

Indicator	Nigeria	United Kingdom
GDP per capita at PPP	US$2,397	US$31,330
Human Development Index	.459	.863
Persons removed through the Atlantic slave trade	~1,000,000	0
Coups d'état since 1960	8	0
Number of ethnic groups	>250	~15
Malaria cases per 100,000 people	38,000	0

Sources: Data on GDP per capita at PPP compiled from Gapminder, www.gapminder.org; Human Development Index, http://hdr.undp.org/en/statistics/hdi/; Atlantic slave trade numbers, Nathan Nunn, "The Long-Term Effects of Africa's Slave Trades," *Quarterly Journal of Economics* 123, no. 1 (2008): 139–176; coups, Center for Systemic Peace, *Coups d'Etat, 1946–2011*, www.systemicpeace.org/inscr/CSPCoupsCodebook2011.pdf; ethnic groups, Oladimeji Aborisade and Robert J. Mundt, *Politics in Nigeria*, 2nd ed. (New York: Longman Publishers, 2001) and Office of National Statistics, 2011 Census for England and Wales, www.ons.gov.uk/ons/guide-method/census/2011/index.html; malaria cases, World Bank, World Development Indicators, 2008, http://data.worldbank.org/data-catalog/world-development-indicators.

DO SLAVERY AND COLONIALISM EXPLAIN NIGERIA'S DEVELOPMENT FAILURE?

Crafting Nigerian Disunity. The Atlantic slave trade led to the forced emigration of over 1 million people from what would eventually be Nigerian territory. The advent of this intercontinental trade precipitated the collapse of the Oyo Empire, a kingdom that emerged in the 1300s and had a population of 50,000 on the eve of the European arrival. If left undisturbed, Oyo could have formed the basis for a prosperous and unified nation-state on Nigerian soil today. At its peak, it encompassed most of modern-day southwestern Nigeria and was West Africa's most advanced civilization, but in their thirst for European imports, the empire's rulers and merchants became a key supplier of slaves to the coast for two centuries. To gather captives for export, Oyo conquered and raided nearby peoples. The slave trade thus pitted residents of eventual Nigerian territory against one another for centuries as Africans sought out fellow Africans for capture and export. The kingdom's territorial aspirations ultimately became unsustainable, and it collapsed in the early 1800s.

Moreover, the creation of Nigerian borders by Great Britain, which colonized much of Africa in the late nineteenth century, sowed the roots of ethnic discord. The British governed the Nigerian colony as three distinct territories, with each one corresponding roughly to the territory of Nigeria's three major ethno-religious groups: Hausa-Fulani (North), Yoruba (Southwest), and Ibo (Southeast). As a result, when these three entities merged into a singular sovereign Nigeria at independence in 1960, the state and society underlying the newly united territory was fractured and incoherent. Independence glommed together peoples and societies that, at best, shared no sense of shared identity and, at worst, were mutual enemies.

Crushing Economic Growth. The colonial experience was detrimental to Nigeria in other ways as well. The British wanted their colonial possession to pay for itself, wishing to not devote metropole funds to their faraway venture. As a result, in 1886 they effectively subcontracted out the process of governing to the

Royal Niger Company, a trading company charged with monopolizing foreign trade in the territory and taxing it to fund the colonial state. Britons back home benefited from the imports of cotton, cocoa, peanuts, and other natural resources. For example, the British extracted millions of tons of palm oil, a product that had long been used by native Africans in their cooking, and exported it back home to make soap and lubricant for industrial equipment. In return, Great Britain sent manufactured goods to Nigeria. In doing so, however, the metropole prevented the development of Nigerian industry, which could not compete with the inflow of British goods. Britain actively discouraged the production of locally made manufactured goods by charging fees for the internal transport of goods made by Africans but not those made by British industry. At independence, just 3 percent of Nigeria's GDP was in manufacturing.[39]

Colonial authorities also created suboptimal legal and institutional realities for the Nigerian masses by not establishing land-ownership rights, giving the peasant majority no incentive to enhance its productivity. For example, the colony experienced a fivefold increase in its production of cash crops between 1880 and 1960, but this increase came through a massive expansion in the amount of land and local labor devoted to growing commodities for export, not through the application of more productive cultivating technologies.[40] The era thus ended as it had begun, with an economy dominated by peasants using hand hoes on small plots of land that they did not formally own. Colonial institutions overtaxed and underincentivized Nigeria's peasantry.

* * *

This partial listing seems a convincing indictment of the West's responsibility for Nigerian underdevelopment, yet not everyone agrees that the Atlantic slave trade and colonialism were so transformative. One criticism lies in the observation that the sheer number of people removed from Oyo and the surrounding territory

Queen Elizabeth II (1952–present) inspects members of a Nigerian army regiment in 1956, four years before the West African colony gained independence. The regiment, fittingly known as the "Queen's Own Nigeria Regiment," followed British orders while Nigeria was under colonial rule.

through the Atlantic slave trade was a small share of the population. Removals from Nigerian territory averaged 300 people per month over the trade's 400-year history, all in a land with a population in the six digits. The effects of eighty years of colonization may also be exaggerated. The colonies that would eventually comprise the Nigerian nation-state had one colonial administrator per 100,000 people. This would be the equivalent of running modern-day New York City, a city with 40,000 police officers alone, with just 100 government officials. All told, critics find it implausible that the West knocked Nigeria off of a successful development path with such minor interventions. Rather, Nigeria was and is on an unsuccessful development path for other reasons.

The South: Domestic Problems in Independent Nigeria

Among these other reasons is a series of purportedly homegrown Nigerian problems. For one, Nigeria is notoriously corrupt. In a 2000 study, Nigeria ranked first out of ninety countries in terms of corruption levels, and in 2010 it scored just a 2.4 on a ten-point scale of transparency.[41] Corruption pervades everything from daily life to politics. Police demand small bribes from foreigners when they arrive at

the airport. Government officials stole millions of dollars from a program meant to fund houses for the poor. Individuals orchestrate what are known as 419 scams, in which (as American Internet users are all too familiar with) they falsely promise to make people rich in exchange for a cash advance. Governors demand fees just to provide their required signature on property sales. One former president is believed to have stolen US$12 billion over eight years in office. Elections are riddled with fraud. Corruption is so rampant that some politicians are open about it. In one case, a former head of the Central Bank admitted to taking money.[42] Perhaps it is this corruption, and not the white man's legacy, that makes mistrust so rampant among Nigerians.

Moreover, Nigeria's political system has been highly unstable and authoritarian. In its first twenty-five years of sovereignty, the military attempted more than half a dozen coups, some of which were successful. It ruled the country for twenty-nine of its first forty years, and during this time a patchwork of election attempts were postponed and annulled. Since 1999, Nigeria has had civilian government, national elections, and two changes in the head of state. However, all three presidents have come from

DO SLAVERY AND COLONIALISM EXPLAIN NIGERIA'S DEVELOPMENT FAILURE?

the same party, suggesting that the country is settling into an undemocratic system of one-party rule. The country's recent history of political instability and authoritarianism makes for a precarious business environment and harms economic growth since potential investors are highly uncertain of the future.

Finally, Nigeria's huge population places a heavy burden on its factors of economic production, and this stems from the high fertility rates that are often constitutive of cultures that marginalize women. The average Nigerian woman births 5.5 children during her reproductive years, a rate that, if sustained, will lead to a population of 300 million people by 2100. This would be the equivalent of today's U.S. population crammed into a territory the size of Arizona.[43] Its booming population places severe strains on the economy, as Nigeria must continually construct roads, schools, power stations, and water treatment plants just to keep up with the prevailing living standard. One of the reasons the manufacturing sector is so small is because the electricity sector cannot keep up with surging residential demand, much less industrial demand. In a patriarchal culture like Nigeria's, where females have only limited economic and educational opportunities, many women have little choice but to follow through on their husbands' preference for large families, which are considered a sign of virility and male strength.

The Natural World: The Burden of Geography and the Paradox of Oil Wealth

For all of these arguments about humanity's wrongdoing in Nigeria, it is possible that the fundamental cause of the country's poverty is not humanity at all. For example, arguments that attribute Nigerian underdevelopment to the West fail to explain why the West was able to colonize Nigerian territory in the first place. Geography may provide an answer: at the time of European expansion into Africa, nature had been granting the British access to large mammals such as horses, cows, pigs, and sheep for millennia, whereas the Oyo and surrounding cultures had none of these.

These animals provided Britons with a source of labor and high-protein food, both of which were crucial in allowing them to be more productive and technologically advanced than West Africa.

Another geographical reason for Nigeria's disadvantage may lie in its high tropical disease burden. West Africa was called the "White Man's Grave" by colonial officials because of the high mortality rates from tropical diseases experienced by Europeans in the region. One estimate holds that 60 percent of Europeans died within their first year of residence in West Africa.[44] Today, Nigeria experiences more than 1 million cases of malaria per year, and it has the world's highest incidence of guinea worm sickness.[45] Neither disease is automatically fatal, but both are responsible for countless days of lost work and school.

Aside from these obvious geographical disadvantages, nature may have cursed Nigeria in a more paradoxical way by giving it so much oil. The world's twelfth-largest reserves would seem to be a lucrative bounty. In actuality, Nigeria's petroleum industry creates few jobs, as it takes little labor to extract petroleum from underground since wells and pumps do most of the work mechanically. Moreover, the international demand for Nigeria's petroleum drives up the price of its currency, which makes its potential industrial exports more expensive on global markets. As a result, oil, and not colonialism or a lack of electricity, could be the reason behind Nigeria's weak manufacturing sector.

* * *

In sum, there is no shortage of factors that might lie behind Nigeria's poverty. The 2000s, however, have seen some improvement in the stability and openness of the country's political system. Moreover, defying the predictions of the resource curse, its economy has responded well to the global increase in petroleum prices. Per-capita income has grown by 50 percent in the new millennium. Time will tell if Nigeria is able to overcome the weight of its past and continue a steady process of economic and human development.

Thinking Critically about Development

- Aside from the precise reasons listed above, what other ways might Western colonialism and the Atlantic slave trade have led to an underdeveloped Nigeria?

- Is it plausible to attribute Nigeria's underdevelopment to Western exploitation when the people living in its territory were already poorer than the West prior to the Atlantic slave trade and colonization?

- Nigerian politician M. K. O. Abiola once said, "Who knows what path Africa's social development would have taken if our great centers of civilization had not been razed in search of human cargo? Who knows how our economies would have developed?"[46] What might be an educated guess at the answers to these questions? What would Nigeria's economy and society look like today if the West had never intervened in the territory after 1450?

Key Terms

Suggested Readings

Acemoglu, Daron, Simon Johnson, and James A. Robinson. "The Colonial Origins of Comparative Development: An Empirical Investigation." *The American Economic Review* 91, no. 5 (2001): 1369–1401.

Engerman, Stanley L., and Kenneth L. Sokoloff. *Economic Development in the Americas since 1500: Endowments and Institutions*. New York: Cambridge University Press, 2011.

Ferguson, Niall. *Empire: The Rise and Demise of the British World Order and the Lessons of Global Power*. New York: Basic Books, 2003.

Manning, Patrick. *Slavery and African Life*. New York: Cambridge University Press, 1990.

Nunn, Nathan. "The Long-Term Effects of Africa's Slave Trades." *Quarterly Journal of Economics* 123, no. 1 (2008): 139–176.

Rodney, Walter. *How Europe Underdeveloped Africa*. Washington, D.C.: Howard University Press, 1972.

Young, Crawford. *The African Colonial State in Comparative Perspective*. New Haven, CT: Yale University Press, 1994.

Web Resources

The Transatlantic Slave Trade Database, http://slavevoyages.org/tast/index.faces

Containers pile up and cargo ships dock at a port. The containers, each the size of a semitruck trailer, are loaded with internationally traded goods, many of them made for export in LDC factories. The widespread adoption of container shipping technology since the 1950s has dramatically lowered the costs of trade between countries. To critics of globalization, however, the resulting boom in international trade has only increased the exploitation of workers in less developed countries.

Globalization and Neocolonialism

C arlos has witnessed a lot of economic change in his eighty-plus years. For decades, the retired Brazilian's financial fortunes have ebbed and flowed with the economies of his country and world. He was born in the late 1920s in a rural village, one whose economic health depended on the harvests and sales of nearby coffee plantations. When foreign demand for coffee collapsed with the Great Depression in the 1930s, so did the standard of living for young Carlos and his family. They moved to São Paulo in the hopes of finding a better life in the city. A burgeoning industrial sector was growing there in the 1930s, in part because the Brazilian government was gradually abandoning a century-old economic philosophy of importing manufactured goods and paying for them with coffee exports. The national government enacted measures to limit imports and thus promote homegrown industry that could fulfill domestic consumers' demands. When he was in his late teens, Carlos found a unionized assembly line job in one of these São Paulo industries, and he remained an industrial employee with a steady income for four decades.

All that started to change, however, in the early 1980s. An international financial crisis spread to Brazil in 1982, precipitating a decade of high inflation and sluggish economic growth. The daily price increases exacted an economic toll on Carlos, but he was at least able to maintain factory employment. Even that was lost, however, when Brazil's leaders decided to reintegrate into the global economy in the late 1980s. Millions of industrial jobs disappeared, as many of Brazil's firms were unable to compete in world markets, and Carlos was one of those who lost his job. Although at retirement age, he still needed to work, so he took up informal work at lower pay for ten more years. To this day, Carlos remains bitter and confused about Brazil's decision to expose its economy to global activity. After all, it caused hardship for him the first time as well.

Carlos's story is one of a life deeply influenced by **economic globalization** (also global economic integration), which is the international movement of goods, services, capital, and people. Broadly speaking, economic globalization has three different forms. The first is **international trade**, the cross-border exchange of goods and services. The second is **capital mobility** or international financial flows, which refers to the movement of savings and investment among countries. The third is **international migration**, the changing of a person's residence from one country to another.

This chapter focuses on globalization from 1800 to the present, a period collectively known as the era of modern globalization. Various forms of globalization involving the global South existed before 1800. For example, ancient Sumer traded commodities with the Indus Valley civilization during the third millennium BCE, and, as discussed in the previous chapter, the 350 years following the advent of the Atlantic slave trade in the mid-fifteenth century featured various forms of exchange between the West and the South. However, the current era that began in 1800 is distinctive and important for two reasons. First, it is characterized by large amounts of voluntary economic exchange among agents (such as individuals, firms, and states) in sovereign countries. This contrasts with the preceding 350 years, during which most of the long-distance exchange involving the global South occurred under coercion by the West. Second, despite some ebbs and flows, the depth and scope of globalization has been greater in the current era. For this reason, globalization has dramatically shaped the social, political, and economic realities of the global South, and scholars have devoted a lot of attention to the topic. This chapter gives a brief history of the modern era of globalization and presents various scholarly interpretations that relate economic globalization to development and underdevelopment.

Table 5.1		The Modern Era of Globalization in the Developing World: Three Phases
Phase	**Period**	**Development**
The first global century	1800–1914	Steady increase in trade with and capital flows from the West
The ISI phase	1930–1980	Strict limits against most manufactured imports and capital inflows to foster industrialization
Reintegration	1980–present	Trade and capital market liberalization to reinvigorate exposure to the global economy

Source: Compiled by the author.

The era of modern globalization can be subdivided into three distinct phases (summarized in Table 5.1) for understanding the global South's role in the international economy. Phase one, known as the first global century, corresponds roughly to the period from 1800 to 1914, a time that was characterized by a steady increase in international trade flows. The second phase is that of import substitution industrialization (ISI). Running from about 1930 to 1980, the ISI phase was one in which governments throughout the developing world enacted measures to restrict various forms of engagement with global markets. The third and current phase is one of reintegration and is marked by a reinsertion of LDCs into the international economy over the past three decades. The first half of this chapter considers the first two phases while the second half takes up the contemporary phase.

From the First Global Century to Import Substitution

The 180 years following 1800 were transformative for the world economy and the global South. The LDCs that were independent as of the

1820s, especially those in Latin America, gradually grew more tied to the world economy over the course of the nineteenth century. Yet many of these ties were abruptly broken in the early twentieth century, especially in the 1930s and 1940s. The developing world turned inward at this time and remained so until the 1980s. What created this rise and then fall of globalization?

The First Global Century

Figure 5.1 depicts the increase in the volume of trade, capital, and migration flows that some have called the nineteenth-century globalization revolution. Five factors chipped away at the various barriers to cross-border exchange, creating humanity's first genuine period of liberal or **free trade**. First, new technologies made international trade more rapid and less expensive. Among these were the construction of railroads and telegraph lines, along with advances in shipping and refrigeration. Second, the West needed raw materials such as cotton, coal, iron ore, rubber, tin, and wool for its industrial revolutions, and many of these were available in abundance abroad. The West's newfound wealth also intensified its tastes for luxury food items such as beef, coffee, sugar, and tea, which were often produced more cheaply in foreign lands. Third, many governments reformed their **protectionist** policies, which are measures designed to block the entry of imports into the domestic market, by lowering barriers to trade in the mid-1800s. A preferred impediment to imports was a high **tariff**, a tax that local buyers were required to pay when purchasing a foreign-made good. Throughout the decades of the mid-nineteenth century, governments around the world shifted policy in a more liberal or open direction by lowering their tariffs while also relaxing rules against immigration and inflows of foreign capital. Fourth,

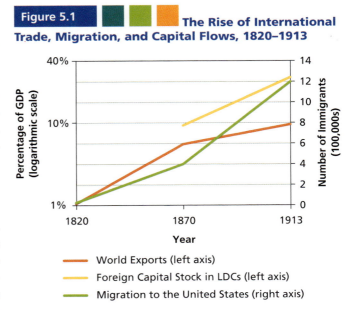

Figure 5.1 **The Rise of International Trade, Migration, and Capital Flows, 1820–1913**

— World Exports (left axis)
— Foreign Capital Stock in LDCs (left axis)
— Migration to the United States (right axis)

Source: Compiled from Angus Maddison, *Monitoring the World Economy* (Paris: OECD, 1995); Angus Maddison, *The World Economy: Volume 1, A Millennial Perspective* (Paris: OECD, 2006), 128; United States Department of Homeland Security, *Yearbook of Immigration Statistics: 2011* (Washington, D.C.: U.S. Department of Homeland Security, Office of Immigration Statistics, 2012), table 1.

many governments linked their currency **exchange rates** to the price of gold (the gold standard). This brought predictability to the prices of internationally exchanged goods, services, and capital, thereby facilitating their flow between countries.

The fifth contributing factor was the emergence of an intellectual climate that was favorable toward free trade. Prior to the nineteenth century, mercantilist ideas dominated European intellectual thought on global trade. **Mercantilism** defined a country's strength in terms of its ability to stockpile precious metals such as gold and silver. Since internationally traded goods were paid for with these metals, a primary way for a country to acquire them was to export more than it imported, a goal that mandated (among other things) protectionist policies. The first major intellectual broadside against mercantilist thought came from philosopher Adam Smith in his 1776 book *The Wealth of Nations*, in which he argued that the true wealth of a nation lay not in the quality and quantity of its virtually useless precious metals, but in those of its consumable goods, lands, and homes.[1]

An even more damning criticism of mercantilism was that of British banker David Ricardo, whose writings on the concept of **comparative advantage** in the early nineteenth century provided a founding plank of liberal trade theory.[2] Ricardo showed that a country gains in aggregate economic welfare if it specializes in making the good that it produces at the lowest opportunity cost—that is, the good in which it has a comparative advantage. Rather than diversifying to produce a variety of goods, a country can maximize consumption by making units of this good and exporting some of them in exchange for imports of the goods in which it does not have a comparative advantage. Comparative advantage is different from absolute advantage, which simply refers to which country produces a good more efficiently. To illustrate using Ricardo's original example, imagine that Portugal is more efficient at making cloth and wine than England, meaning Portugal has an absolute advantage over England in both goods. Imagine also that Portugal's efficiency advantage over England is greater for wine than for cloth, meaning Portugal has a comparative advantage in wine and England has one in cloth. With some simple math, Ricardo showed that, by specializing in making wine and exporting it to England in exchange for cloth, Portugal would consume more wine and cloth than if it balanced production between both. For its part, England consumes more of both if it specializes in producing and exporting cloth in exchange for wine, even though it is less efficient than Portugal in making cloth. All told, every country has a comparative advantage in some good, even if it has an absolute advantage in nothing, since (by definition) every country has something it produces with the lowest opportunity cost. In other words, all countries can gain from trade.

As a result of these five trends, the non-Western world became deeply involved in the global economy during this era, exporting its minerals and agricultural products to the West. Independent Latin America sent coffee, copper, silver, beef, sugar, and other commodities. African and Asian colonies were also involved, exporting (often under imperial coercion) cocoa, coconuts, gold, ivory, peanuts, palm oil, rice, rubber, and tea. In return, these continents imported cotton textiles and other manufactured goods, and foreign capital also flowed in. Indeed, the era saw the proliferation of major **multinational corporations (MNCs)**, defined as companies with assets and operations in two or more countries. For example, Mexico's dictator of the late 1800s, Porfirio Díaz, allowed American-based firms to participate in the extraction of his country's silver and copper reserves. Parts of the global South were also touched by global movements of people as millions of Europeans migrated to places such as South America and southern Africa.

This period of steadily increasing openness ended rather abruptly with the onset of World War I in 1914, and an era of economic nationalism and in some cases near **autarky** (when a country is completely closed to trade with foreigners) prevailed worldwide for decades. This downturn in the volume of international economic exchange lasted until 1945, spanning both world wars and the Great Depression. For the developing world, the West's wars and massive economic slump dried up global demand for its commodities. The countries of the South turned inward.

The ISI Phase

After World War II, the world's wealthy countries reopened to trade flows among themselves, but the inward turn in the developing world lasted a good deal longer. China and other socialist governments stuck to near autarky, restricting or controlling their citizens' ability to exchange with the outside world. Elsewhere, developing countries, including the many newly independent states of Africa and Asia, followed a less autarkic but still protectionist strategy known as **import substitution industrialization (ISI)**. Although pursued with varying flavors, degrees, and durations, most LDCs practiced ISI between 1930 and 1980. Under ISI, states erected barriers to imports of finished consumer goods so that homegrown industries could outcompete them in the domestic market.

Through a variety of protectionist measures, states sought to replace foreign-made goods with domestically made ones in the consumer market, hence the term "import substitution." In Latin America, the Middle East, and South Asia, tariffs that doubled or even tripled the original price of imports were common in pursuit of this purpose. To block certain imports, governments also used nontariff barriers such as ceilings on the number of imports of a certain good (quotas) and requirements that importers secure a license. The long-term goal of ISI was to spur the local manufacturing sector to move up the value chain, becoming more sophisticated and productive with time. Under protectionism, local industry was expected to first produce light manufactures (nondurable consumer goods such as processed food and clothing) in what is termed the easy stage of ISI. The manufacturing sector was then expected to develop durable consumer goods (such as automobiles and home appliances) and capital and high-technology goods (such as heavy machinery and computers) in what is called the hard stage. All told, policymakers believed that protectionism would foster modern manufacturing sectors, allowing their countries to diversify away from agriculture and creating jobs for an industrial middle class.

These protectionist measures notwithstanding, LDCs could not be completely autarkic under ISI. As relatively poor countries, most were completely bereft of the capital machinery and information technology needed to build manufacturing sectors, so they needed to acquire these from abroad. Two other strategies were thus part of the ISI package. To keep the costs of procuring these items low, a common strategy in Latin America was to maintain an overvalued currency. This lowered prices for imports, making foreign capital goods cheaper to acquire. This worked at slight cross-purposes with the high tariff and non-tariff barriers that were erected to block imports, but political leaders balanced out this undesirable effect of overvaluation by making barriers all the higher on the finished manufactured goods they wanted to see produced by domestic firms. The secondary strategy was to allow in small amounts of **foreign direct investment (FDI)**, which is the ownership and managerial control of a productive asset by a foreigner (and typically an MNC). For example, both Argentina and Brazil allowed Italian car manufacturer Fiat to build factories for vehicle assembly on their soil during the ISI era. That said, for the most part, foreign investment was heavily restricted by capital controls, which are rules complicating the entry of foreign capital. LDC governments prohibited or limited foreign ownership in many economic sectors.

In many LDCs, ISI seemingly achieved its stated purpose of industrialization. Economic output and employment in industry grew throughout Latin America and the Middle East. For example, under its first five years of ISI (1960–1965), Egypt generated 1 million new jobs and 6 percent GDP growth every year.[3] In Latin America, GDP per capita doubled between 1950 and 1980.[4] Countries such as Brazil, Indonesia, Mexico, Turkey, and Egypt had "economic miracles" and even began exporting some manufactured goods by the 1970s. As discussed below, however, the model also had various failings.

Export Promotion

Although ISI was the dominant approach throughout most of the developing world in the five decades after 1930, a few countries turned to an alternative in the 1960s and 1970s known as **export promotion** (also export-oriented industrialization, or EOI). These were largely Southeast Asian (Malaysia, Philippines, Thailand) and East Asian (Singapore,

South Korea, and Taiwan) countries and territories. These governments abandoned ISI at this time in pursuit of a package of policies meant to promote light manufacturing enterprises that could successfully produce for foreign markets, not just for domestic ones. Average tariffs were a good deal lower under export promotion than ISI, in part to make imported supplies such as capital equipment and raw materials more affordable to export-oriented firms. Export promotion also differed from ISI in that governments aided sales abroad by maintaining an undervalued currency, which made their countries' exports cheaper to foreign buyers. Governments also promoted export-oriented firms by providing them with subsidized credit and rebates on their supplies. As did some countries under ISI, many of those that adopted export promotion experienced economic miracles.

Causes of Underdevelopment: Dependency and Other Early Theories of Global Exploitation

Three bodies of scholarly theory, each heavily influenced by Marxist and other critiques of capitalism, emerged in the decades following World War II to heap most of the blame for underdevelopment in the South on the economic exchange that it carried out with the developed world both before and during the first global century and the ISI phase. Latin American structuralism, dependency theory, and world systems theory shared several central notions. Most importantly, they conceived of the world economy as an integrated capitalist system containing a core (or center), comprised of the technologically advanced wealthy countries, and a periphery, comprised of the largely agricultural poor countries. The economic dominance of the core was established via the abuses of Europe's colonial expansion. It was then perpetuated after decolonization by economic globalization and its inherent forms of unequal exchange between core

and periphery. Postcolonial arrangements took on a **neocolonial** tone, meaning that global power relations changed rather little from the era of Western imperialism, and exploitation of poor countries by rich ones continued. According to scholars within these traditions, the periphery did not receive fair returns for the primary products (raw materials and agricultural products) it exported to the core, and this imbalance resulted in a rapid process of technological accumulation in the center that occurred at the expense of the periphery. In other words, it was the core that had underdeveloped the periphery, and development in the periphery through engagement with the core was believed to be impossible. How, according to each line of thought, did globalization and unequal exchange undermine development in the periphery?

Latin American Structuralism

Working in the late 1940s and 1950s, Argentine economist Raúl Prebisch, the father of the **Latin American structuralism** school, took issue with Ricardo in arguing that free trade did not benefit all parties. Instead, peripheral countries experience declining terms of trade through time that gradually impoverish them. A country's **terms of trade** is the value it gets in imports for what it exports. More technically, it is the ratio of the average price on world markets of the country's exports to the average world price of its imports:

$$\frac{\textit{terms of trade}}{\textit{for country } x} = \frac{\textit{world price of exports from } x}{\textit{world price of imports into } x}$$

A high terms of trade for a country means that it can buy a lot of imports for a given quantity of its exports. A lower terms of trade means that it can only buy a small number of imports for that same quantity of exports. If the global price of a country's main export suddenly declines, it has, in a sense, grown poorer relative to the rest of the world since it cannot buy as much from the world as it used to. Prebisch argued that the global prices of primary products gradually decline relative to those of manufactured goods, leaving primary-product exporters (the periphery) with constantly declining terms of trade relative to the core. Over time, peripheral countries must export more and more just to be able to consume the same amount of imports from the core. Figure 5.2 shows the trend at which Prebisch was looking. The terms of trade in the global periphery declined from the late 1800s to the mid-1900s.

To Prebisch, the reason for the periphery's declining terms of trade lay in the greater levels of worker and business organi-

Figure 5.2 **Terms of Trade for the Global Periphery, 1865–1940**

Source: Christopher Blattman, Jason Hwang, Jeffrey G. Williamson, "Winners and Losers in the Commodity Lottery: The Impact of Terms of Trade Growth and Volatility in the Periphery, 1870–1939: Volatility and Secular Change," *Journal of Development Economics* 82, no. 1 (January 2007): 156–179.

zation in the core. In the core, active labor unions organized against wage declines, and this kept the prices of manufactured goods from falling sharply during recessions. By contrast, most agricultural and mining workers in the periphery were unorganized, so their wages and thus the prices of the commodities they produced could fall rather easily. Moreover, the number of firms in each of the core's manufacturing sectors tended to be low. For example, a very finite number of automobile companies exist in the West. The small number of companies keeps the severity of interfirm competition low, allowing them to sell their products at artificially inflated prices. In contrast, the number of entrepreneurs in the periphery's primary-product sectors (such as coffee farmers and sugar plantation owners) is enormous. Competition is fierce, so producers have to keep their prices low.[5]

Working independently of Prebisch, economist Hans Singer derived another reason why the periphery's terms of trade would decline over time. As persons and countries grow richer, their demand for luxury items grows while their demand for primary products tends to remain steady. After all, one can only consume so much food, so newfound wealth gets devoted to nonnecessities such as consumer electronic goods that are manufactured. This means that, as the core and the world as a whole grow richer, the international demand and prices for the agricultural products that the periphery exports will decline, while the demand and prices for the core's manufactured exports will increase.[6]

For this and other reasons, structuralists were convinced that market forces would not spontaneously lead to the emergence of a capitalist class and technological accumulation in the periphery. Guided by this conviction, Prebisch and others advocated a policy of inward-oriented development, of which ISI was the most prominent example. In the 1950s and 1960s, Prebisch became the developing world's paramount intellectual advocate of ISI and assumed for some time a post in the United Nations to promote it.

Dependency Theory

Latin American structuralism was a primary intellectual antecedent of **dependency theory**, a neo-Marxist body of thought that emerged in the late 1950s and flourished for thirty years. At its peak, dependency theory had scholarly adherents and contributors throughout every world region, and in many intellectual disciplines it was the dominant way of thinking about politics and economics in LDCs. Dependency theory was so named because its adherents saw the relationship between the core and periphery as one of dependence, with peripheral economies being heavily conditioned and ultimately exploited by the decisions and development prerogatives of the core. In other words, dependence stripped the periphery of its ability to shape its own economic and political fate.

As part of this dependence, the core actively underdeveloped the periphery by extracting surplus from it. Economic surplus is the difference between the value of a commodity and the necessary costs of producing it. To Marxists and neo-Marxists, the capitalist class expropriates much of this surplus by selling commodities at prices higher than the labor costs (the wages paid to workers) of producing them and withholding this difference from its rightful owners, the workers. In traditional Marxist thought, it is the domestic capitalist class, or *bourgeoisie*, that carries out this expropriation. By contrast, according to dependency theorists, it is carried out by an international *bourgeoisie* based in the core, one that first established its exploitive foothold in the periphery through colonialism and then maintained it in independence via economic globalization. Most dependency theorists favored autarky and socialist revolution to end the international extraction of surplus.

Dependency theorists identified a number of ways through which the transfer of surplus from periphery to core took place. According to economist Paul Baran, MNCs based in the core provided a crucial means.[7] Baran argued, similar to Prebisch, that capital in the core tends to be concentrated in

the hands of a small number of corporations, a situation he called monopoly capital. Through globalization, MNCs used the advantages of monopoly capital to keep the prices of their products high while simultaneously paying low wages to their employees in periphery or collecting rent from land they owned there. This created a large surplus in the periphery that MNCs sent back home (as funds called profit remittances) rather than reinvesting the surplus in the poor countries in which it was earned.[8] Dependency theorists were also critical of how MNC affiliates in the periphery often acted as isolated enclaves that created few beneficial linkages within their host economies. MNCs often paid little in taxes to their host government, and they tended to bring their own capital equipment from their home country rather than creating demand for it in the periphery.

Economists Arghiri Emmanuel and Samir Amin alleged a way in which surplus extraction occurred through international trade.[9] Capital is internationally mobile, which creates a unified global market and keeps the rate of profit equivalent in both core and periphery. In contrast, labor is immobile due to heavy restrictions on international migration. Stripped of the ability to conduct a global search for decent pay, workers in the periphery are consigned to earn wages that are perpetually lower than those earned by workers in the core. At such low wages, a greater share of the economic value produced by periphery workers is extracted as surplus. This surplus is transferred to the core when the core pays low prices for the periphery's exports because of the low wages its workers receive.

Dependency theorists also saw surplus extraction in how dependency structured social and political arrangements in the periphery. According to historian Andre Gunder Frank, dependency created in each peripheral country a small *comprador* ruling class that was enriched and politically empowered by the country's role in the global economy.[10] Much of this ruling class was comprised of landowning elites who benefited from agricultural and mineral exports. This ruling class acted as an intermediary, effectively managing the exploitation of peasants and workers on behalf of the international *bourgeoisie*. It paid low wages and backed politicians who repressed popular demands for higher pay and greater redistribution. The *comprador* class transmitted the surplus earned via these low wages to the core by purchasing imported luxury items from Europe.

In a similar vein, many later dependency theorists saw the hand of the international *bourgeoisie* in the installation of authoritarian regimes throughout Latin America in the 1960s, an indication of the periphery's inability to determine its own political fate. Foreign capital, the argument went, created alliances with local capital and the military to overturn democratic regimes and keep labor costs low through political repression. In some instances, core governments themselves are seen as instruments of foreign capital's wishes to shape politics in LDCs to its advantage. For example, in 1954 the United States carried out a coup against Guatemala's democratically elected president, Jacobo Árbenz, partially at the behest of the Boston-based United Fruit Company (UFC). Árbenz had proposed a reform of land ownership that threatened to expropriate some 40 percent of UFC's land in Guatemala.[11] After the UFC's hard lobbying of the Eisenhower administration, the U.S. Central Intelligence Agency overthrew Árbenz in an illegal coup. Guatemala's nascent democracy unraveled: Árbenz was replaced by a military junta and thirty years of civil war ensued.

World Systems Theory

World systems theory (WST) was initially developed by sociologist Immanuel Wallerstein in the 1970s and 1980s.[12] WST views the modern world economy as a monolithic capitalist world system with a fully integrated division of labor and commodity chain. WST downplays national borders and loyalties. In their place, it posits the core as a set of geographical areas that have high levels of capital accumulation, are well administered, and produce capital-intensive goods. The periphery is a set of areas that have little capital, are poorly governed, and produce primary products. WST thinkers also see semi-peripheral areas that produce labor-intensive manufactured goods. With the exception of some external areas of subsistence agriculture, all regions are linked into the global commodity chain that transforms raw materials into purchased consumer goods through a series of production stages. The process entails surplus extraction at each stage via familiar mechanisms: excessively low wages in the periphery, low prices paid for the periphery's exports, the concentration and superior organizational capacity of producers in the core, and the high profits on the core's capital investments. Capital accumulates in the core at the expense of the periphery because of this integrated system. Some WST thinkers add that the extraction of surplus stokes conflict within the periphery. The core is able to use the surplus it has extracted from the periphery to redistribute wealth within its societies to the poor and thus smooth over conflicts among social classes. Stripped of much of its surplus, the periphery does not have this luxury.[13]

Falling Behind in the First Global Century

These three schools of thought, all of them associated with the political left, are not the only arguments that attribute underdevelopment during the first global century to international exchange. Neoclassical economist Jeffrey Williamson argues that it was not coincidence that the first global century was the one in which the developing world fell behind.[14] He points out that, for much of the second half of the nineteenth century, the global prices of primary products were high because the West needed these raw materials to fuel the Industrial Revolution. High prices for its exports could have helped the South, since this meant its terms of trade were high. Instead, the lucrative gains in primary sectors drew investment away from burgeoning industrial ones, thereby maintaining the South's specialization "in sectors with little potential for learning and productivity improvement."[15] Moreover, Williamson adds, in concentrating so much productive activity in just one or two primary products (as Ricardian thought advises), the economies of the developing world were volatile. In the late nineteenth century, each Latin American country had a pattern where anywhere from 60 percent to 90 percent of its exports were a single commodity, such as sugar in Cuba or coffee in Brazil. As a result, the economic fates of these countries hinged largely on the foreign demand and supply of a single item. As it is, prices on primary products are historically more volatile than those on finished goods, so concentrating so much in one product made these less developed economies all the more exposed to risk.[16] This volatility was bad for long-term economic progress. It made potential investors more hesitant to take chances and forced states to cut social services during downturns. Recessions also pushed children out of schooling and into the labor market so families could get by.[17]

Critiques of Structuralism, Dependency Theory, and WST

Structuralism, dependency theory, and WST have largely fallen out of favor in most academic circles, although newer criticisms of globalization still flourish (and are discussed in the second half of this chapter). Part of the reason for the decline of these theories lies in their internal contradictions and conceptual problems. For example, Baran's monopoly capital critique of globalization ignores the role of demand in setting prices, and it underestimates the importance of price competition among firms even in concentrated markets. Similarly, dependency and WST exaggerate the extent to which the global market is a fully integrated system. Even today, most commodities and services are not traded across borders, so these arguments probably overstate the influence of international forces on a country's

well-being. Instead of walking through all of these theoretical problems, this subsection focuses on a few empirical shortcomings, meaning real-world patterns that these theories fail to explain.

The evidence of declining terms of trade in the periphery, so central to Prebisch's and some dependency theorists' critiques of international trade, is mixed. Whether a decline is observed depends on when one starts observing. As shown in Figure 5.2, Prebisch's work tracked primary-product prices from 1870 to 1940, meaning his series started amidst the commodities boom of the latter half of the nineteenth century. In contrast, studies such as Williamson's that track terms of trade from before to during this boom (1800–1870) show that the periphery's terms of trade actually rose.[18]

This finding is doubly bad for Prebisch's argument. Not only did terms of trade not decline in the periphery, but their general rise suggests that the level of a country's terms of trade is neither a cause nor even indicative of its overall well-being. The nineteenth century was the one in which the divergence between core and periphery was most rapid, yet it was a time of rising terms of trade for the latter. Overall, the declining terms of trade argument, whether the long-run trend is empirically true or not, falls short of being a general explanation for underdevelopment.

Structuralists were leading intellectual advocates of ISI, so as a critique of the approach it is worth pointing out that ISI often ended in disappointment. It is true that the 1950s, 1960s, and 1970s saw rapid economic growth under ISI in many developing countries, but sustaining this growth pattern proved to be difficult, as many of these countries experienced economic stagnation in the 1980s. A number of problems were inherent to ISI. First, the businesses that sprouted in ISI economies were highly inefficient, which hurt productivity and consumers. Unexposed to international competition, standards, and pricing, manufacturing firms made shoddy goods at relatively high prices. For example, in Chile, bicycles, heaters, and radios were two to four times more expensive than they were in high-income countries at the time, putting them out of reach of most of the lower and lower-middle classes. Consumer goods such as these also fell apart more easily.[19] Firms were also walled off in small markets, so they could not achieve the efficiency gains that come with size.

Second, ISI created deep new inequalities between rural and urban residents, as well as between formal and informal sector workers. ISI had an urban bias, since it protected manufacturing firms (which were mostly located in and around cities) from international competition and disadvantaged rural areas by making primary-product exports expensive through overvaluation. Urban capitalists and workers with formal-sector industrial jobs did well under this scenario, but landowners and other rural residents did not. Crop production often declined and rural incomes fell, so millions of peasants and other rural dwellers migrated to cities in search of more lucrative work. Unfortunately, there were not enough good industrial jobs to go around, so the urban informal sector ballooned in size. All told, ISI hastened urbanization throughout Latin America, as well as parts of the Middle East and Asia, but in doing so it created a large urban underclass.

Third, countries practicing ISI were victims of recurring balance of payments and even debt crises. A balance of payments crisis occurs when a country is running low on the foreign currency it needs to buy imported goods. As mentioned above, ISI practitioners could not completely wall themselves off from imports since they had to purchase from abroad the capital equipment needed to make manufactured goods at home. However, the overvaluation of the currency, the discrimination against rural and primary-product sectors, and the low quality of their manufactured goods made it difficult for ISI countries to export and thus earn the foreign currency they needed to pay for imports. To fill the gap, governments often had to borrow from foreign commercial banks and other international lenders, a pattern that increased the developing world's **foreign debt** (money owed to foreigners). During the 1970s, the less developed world's foreign debt increased by an order of magnitude, from US$70 billion to US$700 billion.[20]

To many observers, the death knell of ISI was the Latin American debt crisis of 1982. In August of 1982, Mexico informed its foreign creditors that it could no longer stay current on its monthly debt repayments. Foreign banks and other investors immediately stopped lending to Latin American and many other LDCs out of fear that they would not be repaid. The event precipitated a lost decade in Latin America of economic recession, high inflation, and declining real wages. It also cast doubt in the minds of many developing world politicians and policymakers on the merits of ISI, since part of the need to borrow from foreigners in the first place was due to a lack of export earnings.

Perhaps the most dooming evidence against the various early theoretical critiques of globalization was the dramatic economic rise between 1960 and 1980 of the East Asian Tigers, a class of countries frequently called the newly industrialized countries (NICs). In contrast to the economic collapses that followed some of the ephemeral ISI miracles in Latin America and the Middle East, the Asian countries that pursued export promotion enjoyed sustained growth despite, and by many accounts *because of*, their engagement with the global economy. In following an export-promotion strategy, businesses in Hong Kong, Singapore, and South Korea were forced to meet the more exacting quality and price standards of developed world consumers. Although the Asian Tigers began the 1960s as low-income countries, their manufacturing sectors were able to move up the global commodity chain by reinvesting revenues from export sales into capital equipment, which allowed them to gradually increase the technological sophistication of their exports. Today, South Korea's comparative advantage lies in capital-intensive manufactured goods (such as semiconductors, consumer electronics, cars, and steel) that require a well-educated labor force, and the country has long since graduated to high-income status. Some of the Southeast Asian countries that adopted export promotion policies, such as Malaysia, the Philippines, and Thailand, also enjoyed rapid and relatively sustained industrialization. The experience of the NICs belies an assumption of dependency theory that international trade relations are largely static, with the periphery perpetually paying low wages and exporting only primary products. Instead, peripheral countries can move up the global commodity chain through engagement with global markets, and wages and prosperity will increase as productivity rises.

Reintegrating the Globe

Starting in the 1980s, most LDCs abandoned their protectionist and ISI philosophies in favor of greater openness to the global economy. For many, this was a return to the liberal trade regime and heavy trade flows of a century earlier. Capital

and people also flowed to and from the South at increasing rates. These changes occurred because of a combination of policy and technological changes. The second half of this chapter recounts how this occurred and relates some of the arguments regarding the pros and cons of the new era of globalization for developing countries.

Trade Liberalization

Figure 5.3 shows the rise in trade flows in the developing world, depicting the trend in trade as a percentage of the developing world's GDP between 1970 and 2011. The percentage tripled over this forty-year period, rising most quickly after the mid-1980s. A primary driver was policy change. Most important were unilateral trade liberalization measures in which domestic political leaders decided to lower their countries' tariff and nontariff barriers to goods and services in the absence of international

Figure 5.3 Trade and FDI as a Percentage of GDP in the Developing World, 1970–2011

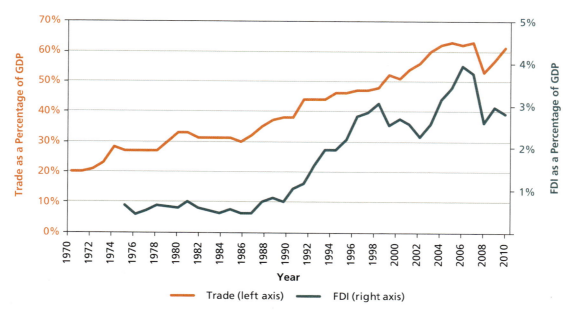

Source: Data compiled from the World Bank, World Development Indicators, http://data.worldbank.org/data-catalog/world-development-indicators.

agreement. For example, China began a steady trade liberalization process in 1978 at the discretion of its own leaders and without corresponding international negotiations. Similarly, in Latin America, average tariffs, which were 40 percent in 1980, had fallen to 11 percent by 2000, mostly as a unilateral choice by the region's politicians.[21]

At the same time, multilateral trade liberalization in a variety of forms accompanied and reinforced these unilateral embraces of greater openness. First, the developing world saw a proliferation of preferential (or regional) trade agreements, which are agreements reached among two or more countries to charge low or no tariffs on goods exported from each other. The Association of Southeast Asian Nations (ASEAN), the North American Free Trade Agreement (NAFTA), and the Southern Common Market (Mercosur) were among the ones that included at least one LDC. Second, the World Trade Organization (WTO) was inaugurated in 1995, replacing the General Agreement on Trade and Tariffs (GATT), to provide a multilateral negotiating forum and legal framework for lowering trade barriers. The members of the WTO (today 157 states) meet in periodic rounds of talks to negotiate over trade barrier reductions with agreed-upon exceptions. The WTO also has established rules against tariffs that vary by a product's country of origin, and violations of its provisions are adjudicated by a tribunal. Finally, multilateral liberalization has occurred through country dealings with the International Monetary Fund and World Bank (discussed in Chapter 6). These Bretton Woods institutions made hundreds of loans and grants to LDCs and, in doing so, often required recipient countries to adopt policies such as trade liberalization.

Technological change has also been behind the expansion of global integration. Telecommunications, computer, and Internet innovations dramatically eased communication between suppliers and customers across borders. Containerization technology, first invented in the 1950s and gradually improved upon over subsequent decades, markedly lowered the cost and duration of transporting goods over land and sea. Today, flat-decked cargo ships can carry semitruck-sized container boxes by the thousands, and these boxes can be unloaded by cranes in just a few hours and hauled away by trucks to their ultimate destination. Infrastructural improvements to ports and highways in many LDCs have also made trade more rapid and less costly.

Capital Market Liberalization

Most LDCs also grew more open to inflows of foreign capital by enacting capital market liberalization measures. Many countries lifted restrictions against FDI. As a result, MNCs such as British Petroleum, Starbucks, and Toyota established affiliates (such as retail outlets, factories, management offices, and mineral extraction sites) throughout the developing world. Between 1980 and 1997, the developing world's share of FDI worldwide nearly doubled,[22] and Figure 5.3 shows that, as a share of the developing world's GDP, FDI inflows quadrupled between 1990 and 2006.

LDCs also experienced a boom in **foreign portfolio investment**, which is a transaction in which a foreign investor lends money to a borrower (through means such as stock and bond purchases or bank deposits) without taking direct managerial control over the loaned funds. In contrast to FDI, in which foreigners typically establish and manage brick-and-mortar assets, foreign portfolio inflows entail relatively liquid funds and a hands-off approach by investors. As a result, foreign portfolio investors can more easily and quickly withdraw their investments, by doing things such as selling stocks or pulling their bank deposits, than can foreign direct investors. Throughout the 1990s, foreign lenders entered developing-world capital markets in droves, encouraged by signs of growth and high returns in countries that used to be quite poor. They also occasionally exited in droves, sparking global financial crises such as the 1995 peso crisis in Mexico and the 1997 East Asian financial crisis.

Changing Migration Flows

The international movement of people has also changed in important ways during the current era of economic globalization. In actuality, the share of humans that are international migrants (about 3 percent) has remained rather steady for fifty years. However, two important changes to the nature of these flows have occurred. First, the rate of South-North migration, or migration from developing to developed countries, has increased. Whereas in 1960 only about 14 million migrants (16 percent of all migrants) had moved from a less developed to a developed country, by 2000 that figure was 60 million, nearly 40 percent of the total. Second, migrants are sending increasing volumes of money back to their native countries. **Remittances**, which are transfers of money made by expatriates to their family and friends in their country of origin, have increased dramatically in volume, contributing substantially to international capital flows and even to global redistribution from rich to poor countries. Between 1990 and 2010, annual remittances sent to recipients in developing countries rose from US$30 billion to US$325 billion.[23]

Remaining Barriers. Although the volume of trade, capital flows, and migration has expanded in recent decades, many barriers to economic globalization still remain. In other words, statements that the world is "flat" or that there is a "death of distance" are highly exaggerated.[24] Many countries in the developing and developed world have important barriers to international exchange in place. For instance, rich countries still find ways to limit agricultural imports, and they subsidize their own farmers to the tune of US$300 billion per year. For their part, many LDCs maintain relatively high tariffs on manufactured goods. The stated purpose of the ongoing Doha round of WTO trade talks, which started in 2001, was for both sides to relax these restrictions, but the talks have repeatedly failed due to the hesitance of rich and poor countries alike to make such concessions. As another example, investment continues to carry a heavy home bias, as most people prefer to invest their savings in domestic opportunities. More broadly, due to the natural barriers of distance and difference, humans still do the vast majority of their communicating, purchasing, studying, working, and living in their country of birth.

Causes of Underdevelopment: Newer Concerns about Globalization

Although dependency theory and its cousins have fallen out of academic favor, criticisms of economic globalization have not. The legacy of dependency theory lives on in numerous arguments that continue to attribute many economic and social problems in LDCs to international forces.

Deindustrialization

Globalization critics claim that the trade and capital market liberalization measures of recent decades have reversed the industrialization that occurred in some LDCs under ISI, with negative social consequences. Soon after their economies were opened to foreign imports, thousands of industrial firms in LDCs folded. By global standards, they were inefficient and thus unable to survive against the newfound competition.

Cutthroat competition also came from the new MNC affiliates, which were more technologically advanced than local firms. Millions of formal-sector manufacturing jobs disappeared, and in many developing countries the number of jobs created by globalization opportunities, such as those in new export-oriented firms and MNC affiliates, was insufficient to fill the void. For example, whereas the establishment of Walmart and Carrefour supermarket branches does create some obvious employment opportunities, it may result in net job losses because these branches bankrupt small mom-and-pop retailers, which are less capital intensive and thus collectively employ a lot of people. Figure 5.4 shows industry's share of GDP during the late ISI and reintegration eras for all upper-middle-income countries, the very countries (such as Brazil and Turkey) that achieved some successes with industrialization under ISI. Industry declined throughout the 1990s.

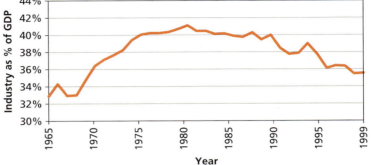

Figure 5.4 **Industry as a Share of GDP in Upper-Middle-Income Countries, 1965–2000**

Source: Data compiled from the World Bank, World Development Indicators, http://data.worldbank.org/data-catalog/world-development-indicators.

Sweatshops and the Race to the Bottom

A particularly controversial issue as LDCs have entered international markets in recent decades is the existence of **sweatshop** labor. A substantial share of the manufactured goods that consumers of any country purchase are made and exported by developing world factories that, to critics, have sweatshop conditions. Such conditions often include long work hours (sometimes as much as sixteen hours per day for six or seven days a week), poor pay that is below a purported living wage, mistreatment by supervisors (such as no bathroom breaks), unsafe working conditions, repression of efforts to unionize, and child labor. For example, Foxconn is a Taiwanese MNC that owns and operates factories in several developing countries, and in China it is actually the largest private employer. The company makes many electronic products with which Western consumers are intimately familiar, such as iPhones, iPads, Kindles, and Wii. Foxconn has come under sharp criticism for how it treats its 1 million Chinese employees. Pay is just US$2 per hour to most of its assembly line

workers. Sixty-hour workweeks with uncompensated overtime are common, as are ten-day stretches without a day off. Almost half of workers have experienced or witnessed an accident, and most workers carry out tedious and repetitive tasks, an aspect of the job that may have contributed to depression and numerous high-profile suicides by workers.[25] Critics see sweatshop conditions such as those at Foxconn as evidence of worker exploitation by global markets.

The existence of sweatshop labor is indicative of a broader threat from globalization: the race to the bottom. The **race to the bottom** refers to the alleged competition that occurs among LDCs as they seek to attract foreign investment. MNCs and other global investors are internationally mobile, able to shop around in search of the most attractive bidder for their capital. To attract this roving capital, the government of a developing country may reform its rules and institutions to be friendlier to business. If every government thinks in this way, it creates a competitive race to the bottom among LDCs, who try to outdo one another in making their workers' wages low, their laborers unorganized, their corporate taxes and

DEVELOPMENT in the FIELD

Promoting Fair Trade

The fair trade movement has sought to address some of the perceived social and environmental problems that are associated with international trade. Fair trade groups establish trading relationships between developed world consumers and developing world producers who adhere to certain ethical standards. The most important fair trade nonprofit organization is Fairtrade Labeling Organizations International (FLO), an umbrella organization that oversees a multinational certification process. Goods (most of them agricultural products) that are produced by farmers and workers in the developing world under conditions that meet FLO's standards receive a fairtrade label that is visible to potential consumers. The standards include a minimum price plus a fair trade premium paid to the farmers and workers, safe working conditions, no child labor, freedom of association

for workers, and organic forms of food cultivation. FLO and its various associated groups also seek out and train producers who want to be certified, and they conduct occasional inspections of their certified producers. Because of the high standards, fair trade products are virtually always more expensive than conventional ones, but many consumers in the developed world buy them nonetheless for the ethical satisfaction they get from it.

Although concerned with its consequences, the fair trade movement is clearly not a rejection of international trade. Many globalization proponents, however, criticize the movement nonetheless. One common criticism is that the higher price paid to certified producers encourages them to produce more output, which leads to a global oversupply of the commodity. This results in a decline in the price paid to noncertified producers, which

lowers their income. Another criticism is that, in practice, fair trade-certified producers do not receive all or even a majority of the added costs that consumers pay. Others involved in the process of moving goods from LDC producer to consumer in the developed world, such as the certification groups and retailers, also accept compensation. Finally, while the consumer demand for fair trade has grown rapidly in recent years, questions remain about whether it will ever be great enough to make a noticeable difference in developing-world livelihoods. Fair trade-certified goods still comprise a small fraction of the product markets in which they are active, and the nonprofit organizations have struggled to move their certification programs into manufactured products. Their success also depends on consumers' altruism, which usually takes a back seat to frugality.

worker benefits minimal, and their environmental and safety regulations lax. Governments may also cut social spending to convince foreign investors of their fiscal discipline and ability to repay loans, and they may keep bond yields and interest rates high (two growth-slowing measures) to attract portfolio investors.

Volatile Capital Flows

Another issue of intense debate surrounds the newfound volumes and volatility of international portfolio investment flows. Critics allege that, because foreign portfolio flows can enter and exit a country so quickly, they expose LDC economies to greater risk, higher volatility, and deeper recessions. In particular, the 1990s saw a wave of financial crises in LDCs that were triggered by **sudden stops**, or episodes of **capital flight** in which foreign lenders quickly withdrew their assets from an LDC in response to something that evoked fear for the profitability and security of their investments. These fears were often activated by herd behavior on the part of lenders rather than anything fundamentally wrong with the borrowing country's economics. In other words, lenders fled simply because they interpreted an initial wave of capital flight as a signal that agents in the borrowing country were not going to be able to repay their foreign lenders. This herd behavior and signaling effect often worked across borders, whereby an initial wave of capital flight from Thailand convinced investors that something was also wrong in nearby Indonesia. This gives financial crises elements of international contagion, spreading quickly through neighboring or similar countries and causing painful recessions. Finally, currency speculation and speculative attacks are often contributing factors to sudden stops and financial crises. Currency speculators bet on future movements of a country's exchange rate. If a wave of speculators bets against a poor country's currency by selling their holdings of that currency in a speculative attack, they can create a self-fulfilling prophecy, causing a sharp depreciation of the country's currency and a financial crisis with lasting effects.

The East Asian financial crisis of 1997 exemplifies these problems. After stringing together thirty years of impressive economic growth, by the 1990s experts were touting the East Asian miracle, which reached not just the obvious superstars Singapore, South Korea, and Taiwan, but also fast-growing Indonesia, Malaysia, the Philippines, and Thailand. In July of 1997, however, the Thai currency (*baht*) came under speculative attack and a major devaluation ensued. The contagion quickly spread to Thailand's neighbors elsewhere in Asia, all of whom devalued and faced

deep economic recessions. Malaysia's prime minister at the time, Mahathir bin Mohamad, famously lashed out at international financiers, saying their "wealth must come from impoverishing others, from taking what others have in order to enrich themselves . . . Society must be protected from unscrupulous profiteers. I am saying that currency trading is unnecessary, unproductive, and immoral. It should be stopped. It should be made illegal."[26] Other financial crises suffered by LDCs in the 1990s and 2000s, such as Mexico's in 1995, Brazil's in 1999, and Argentina's in 2001, bear the imprint of rapid capital outflows.

Foreign Debt

Even during more normal and stable times, international capital mobility can increase foreign debt. As loans, foreign portfolio inflows to a less developed country are tantamount to an acquisition of debt by some agent (and often the state) in the LDC. With time, the accumulation of debt can become a major drag on fiscal sustainability and economic growth, especially if the projects and investments that the loans funded either did not pay off or pay off only in the long run. Many states in LDCs end up servicing their foreign debts in perpetuity, making huge monthly payments that pay down the principal of a loan only slowly. These debt payments can exhaust a significant portion of states' budgets in the developing world and are themselves a form of capital flight. Figure 5.5 shows the increasing burden of foreign debt payments in LDCs after 1975.

International debt obligations are also problematic because they are usually denominated in a foreign currency. This means they are granted in foreign currency and thus must be paid back in foreign currency. For an LDC, repayment can deplete foreign exchange holdings (most of which are earned through exports) that could be better spent on imports of capital equipment or consumption goods. Moreover, the denomination of debts in a foreign currency exposes debtors

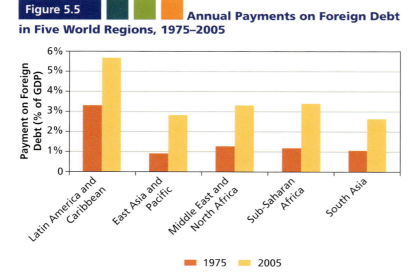

Figure 5.5 **Annual Payments on Foreign Debt in Five World Regions, 1975–2005**

■ 1975 ■ 2005

Source: Data compiled from the World Bank, World Development Indicators, http://data.worldbank.org/data-catalog/world-development-indicators.

and indebted states to exchange rate risk, meaning the amount they must devote to repayment could increase all the more if their own currency is devalued.

Brain Drain

A final set of criticisms of the new economic globalization is levied at international migration. **Brain drain**, also known as human capital flight, is the migration of skilled citizens away from a country, often to a wealthier one where they typically enjoy higher wages and better living standards. Well-educated people are often the most likely to emigrate from LDCs. For example, 75 percent of migrants from India to the United States have some college education, a total that far exceeds the rate of tertiary education among Indians that do not emigrate.[27]

Brain drain is often economically beneficial for the migrants themselves, but it can be hard on the less developed countries they leave. Through public schooling, the formal education of emigrants was typically funded by the taxpayers of their native countries. As a result, the application of emigrants' skills elsewhere is a waste of these resources and can even discourage governments in especially poor LDCs from investing in their secondary and tertiary education systems. More importantly, brain drain deprives LDCs of their emigrants' labor and know-how, a problem that is particularly acute given that most developing countries are starved for the engineers, educators, health professionals, and other skilled individuals that help an economy function and grow. For example, in Ghana, more than two-thirds of all trained health professionals emigrated between 1995 and 2002, causing significant damage to the country's health-care system.[28]

Critique: Defending Globalization

These concerns notwithstanding, most economists and political economists support economic globalization and find the current reintegration trends to be, on balance, favorable for the developing world. Their arguments are of both an empirical and theoretical nature.

The Benefits of Free Trade

It is the case that a few middle-income countries, such as Brazil and Turkey, did experience some loss of industry upon lowering their protectionist barriers, but the demand for exports has created millions of firms and jobs elsewhere in the developing world. China's openness has made it the world's leading exporter, a process that has been central in driving its rising wages and prosperity levels. Mexico has also become a manufacturing hub, due in part to its proximity to the United States. Much of sub-Saharan Africa has enjoyed solid economic growth since 2000 because of rising global prices for its mineral commodities. Even Brazil, despite undergoing some industrial decline, has experienced recent gains because of high global demand for its agricultural products. All told, while trade liberalization can certainly cause employment loss and bankruptcy for some people and sectors, it also creates jobs in export-oriented sectors. Systematic evidence suggests that the net benefits of trade are positive, as there is a strong empirical association between trade openness and economic growth.[29]

Moreover, while critics portray imports as a threat to many jobs, sectors, and livelihoods, imports are the basis of the dramatic gains that consumers enjoy from trade. After all, increased consumption was the basis of Ricardo's argument in favor of liberal trade. In the wake of trade liberalization, the quality, variety, and price of tradable goods improved dramatically in most LDCs. Consumers were no longer a captive audience to the inefficiently produced goods that their domestic industrial sectors produced under ISI. They could instead turn to imports made by the world's leading firms, and the newfound competition from imports made the surviving domestic firms more likely to produce higher quality and more cost-competitive goods.[30] In sum, consumers suffered the most under attempts at self-sufficiency, so they also gained the most when imports were allowed to enter more freely.

Labor Exploitation or Enrichment?

Globalization advocates respond to the sweatshop accusations by arguing that it is not globalization itself that has created such conditions. MNCs, their affiliates, and other suppliers to the global market that rely on sweatshop labor may appear to be brutal economic exploiters, but globalization proponents argue that Western standards are not the proper points of comparison for judging things such as pay and working conditions in factories in LDCs. The proper comparison, say globalization advocates, should be to the quality of employment that sweatshop workers would have if the export-oriented factories were not present. Here, the evidence is rather overwhelming. Outside these factories, wages and labor standards in the developing world are nowhere near those of the West. Indeed, MNC-affiliated and other export-oriented firms pay higher wages than domestically owned equivalents.[31] In other words, globally oriented firms pay well by local standards, and many workers in the developing world seek out jobs in these factories because they are better than the alternatives in rural subsistence or the urban informal sector.

Wages are low, the rebuttal goes on, in MNC-affiliated and other export-oriented factories not because of abuse by ruthless globalization interests, but because workers in LDCs are less productive than those in the West. As mentioned in Chapter 1, this low labor productivity is largely a function of the domestic context: poor schools, undeveloped infrastructure, weak property rights, rampant corruption, low technological acquisition, and so on. In other words, MNCs and sweatshops are not causing low societal productivity and poverty by paying workers low wages. Rather, it is the domestic contexts that cause low productivity and poverty, and this in turn is the reason why MNCs and affiliates pay what are, by Western standards, low wages.

Furthermore, globalization advocates argue that the evidence to support the race-to-the-bottom argument in LDCs is weak.[32] Governments are not progressively lowering labor and environmental standards to attract foreign capital, in part because foreign investors consider much more than just these two factors when they decide on where to invest. The size of the domestic consumer market is one relevant factor, and one that explains why China is the second-largest recipient of FDI in the world.

MNCs also prefer to invest in countries with a viable physical and legal infrastructure. Even with regard to wages, foreign investors do not simply seek out the world's most poorly paid workers. They are also attentive to training and educational backgrounds, and they are willing to pay more for workers that promise higher productivity. For example, the leading recipient of FDI in the world is not the country with the lowest wages, but the United States.

If anything, say their proponents, MNCs bring in capital equipment and business practices that make workers more productive. This lays the groundwork for greater prosperity and higher wages, not a race to the bottom. Again, China serves as a compelling example. In the 1980s, foreign investors set up factories on China's eastern coast, lured by the country's low wages and huge internal consumer market. With time, wages on the coast gradually rose because of booms in worker productivity. Investors are now moving inland, where wages are lower, to construct new factories. Presumably, the same process of rising productivity and wages will play out inland as well.

The Nature of Foreign Debt

Advocates of international capital flows argue that criticisms of foreign debt are based on a misunderstanding of the concept. Much of the foreign debt accumulated by LDCs is the result of their governments borrowing to cover a budget deficit. In other words, the accrual of debt to foreigners starts not as an imposition by external predators seeking to impoverish the developing world, but as a decision by developing world governments to spend more than they have in revenues. In many instances, the alternative for the borrowing governments would

be budget cuts and economic hardship. Developing world entrepreneurs also borrow from foreigners to fund investment projects, so their alternative would be a foregone business opportunity. Domestic banks and financial markets in many LDCs do not have sufficient capital to cover their country's borrowing needs. Stated differently, for many LDCs the choice is not foreign capital versus domestic capital, but foreign capital versus no capital. All told, the acquisition of capital from foreigners seems an obvious way to help fill the developing world's financing needs.

Brain Gain

Many advocates of international immigration argue that South-North migration provides a brain gain for the poor countries that send emigrants abroad. Expatriates rarely sever ties completely with their country of origin, instead periodically sending remittances to them. The volume of remittances that are destined for LDCs is more than thrice the annual volumes of foreign aid given by wealthy countries, and in some countries, such as El Salvador and Liberia, they total more than 10 percent of GDP. Nearly 10 percent of the world's population receives remittances periodically from someone living abroad, and many of these recipients depend on them to meet their basic consumption needs or pay down debts.[33] Given their volume, scope, and destination, remittances are easily the world's largest poverty alleviation effort and the most important way in which wealth is distributed from rich countries to poor ones. To critics of brain drain arguments, migrants often, through remittances, more than compensate their birth countries for the formal training they received there.

IS NEOCOLONIALISM WHY BRAZIL IS ALWAYS THE "COUNTRY OF THE FUTURE?"

Gifted with vast mineral resources, the world's biggest rainforest, a large and creative population, and nearly 200 years of independence and relative peace, Brazil seemingly has all the ingredients of a wealthy country. However, Brazil has largely failed to live up to its tremendous economic promise. Its per-capita income is one-quarter that of the United States. Twenty-five million Brazilians survive on less than US$2 per day, and the poorest 20 percent of its citizens receives only 3 percent of the nation's income.[34] Why has Brazil fallen so short? One common answer to this question is that Brazil has been underdeveloped by the West, first via colonialism by the Portuguese and then through neocolonial trade and investment relations after independence in 1822. This case study discusses and critiques some of the ways that neocolonialism may have made Brazil, as its residents joke, "always the country of the future." Table 5.2 compares Brazil's level of development to that of Portugal and also contrasts some of the variables that might be causes of the divergent development outcomes between the two.

Table 5.2   **Development Comparison: Brazil and Portugal**

Indicator	Brazil	Portugal
GDP per capita at PPP	US$10,373	US$19,906
Human Development Index	.718	.809
Primary products as percentage of total exports	49 percent	15 percent
Gini coefficient (inequality index)	.55	.38
Arable land (percentage of total land)	7 percent	18 percent

Sources: Data on GDP per capita at PPP compiled from Gapminder, www.gapminder.org; Human Development Index, http://hdr.undp.org/en/statistics/hdi/; total exports, "World Exports by Country and Product," Index Mundi, www.indexmundi.com/trade/exports/; Gini coefficient and arable land, the World Bank, World Development Indicators, http://data.worldbank.org/data-catalog/world-development-indicators.

The West: Failures of Openness

Brazil's engagement with the global economy has ebbed and flowed over its two centuries of independence. It exported agricultural products to the West during the first global century, and then turned inward during the middle of the next. More recently, it has reentered global markets. Given these changes, Brazil provides a nice test case for gauging the effect of globalization on development.

Structuralist and Dependency Interpretations of the Nineteenth Century. Brazil was very much a part of the first global century. During its first century of independence, Brazil pursued a liberal trade policy. It exported primary products, especially coffee, in exchange for manufactured goods and capital equipment made in the global core, most often in Britain. However, despite the promises of Ricardian thought, Brazil failed to thrive. By 1900, its average income was virtually

IS NEOCOLONIALISM WHY BRAZIL IS ALWAYS THE "COUNTRY OF THE FUTURE?"

the same as that at independence.[35] It remained a predominantly agricultural economy and a poor rural society while Europe and the United States left it behind.

What might explain the failure of Brazil's liberal trade policies to produce economic growth during this time? One possible explanation is Brazil's declining terms of trade. After 1870, the world price of coffee declined gradually and then collapsed quite dramatically in the 1930s. Brazil thus had to export increasing amounts of coffee to import the same amount of machinery and manufactured consumer goods from the core. Moreover, during this time the economy was heavily reliant on coffee exports. Coffee comprised almost two-thirds of Brazil's exports in 1890, exposing the country to a high degree of risk.[36] Between 1865 and 1939, Brazil's terms of trade had the highest rate of volatility of any country on record—thrice the average rate of the core—so economic crises were recurrent.[37]

According to economist Celso Furtado, Brazil's export orientation also enriched and empowered coffee plantation owners and other large landowners, who used their political power to extract resources from the state and resist modernizing reforms. These landed classes successfully pressured the Brazilian government to buy and even destroy coffee when world prices fell, diverting state funds from more profitable uses.[38] They also successfully lobbied the state to resist reforms such as land redistribution and democratization. Rich landowners connived with government to repress the wages of rural workers, who comprised the vast majority of the labor force. In selling the fruits of workers' labor on to the West, landed classes essentially catalyzed the transfer of surplus from periphery to core. Moreover, they used their export earnings largely to buy European luxury commodities that did little to make Brazil's economy more productive.

Successes of the ISI Phase. As if to demonstrate the validity of these critiques of globalization, Brazil turned inward in the 1930s and its economy proceeded to grow, finally commencing a process of rapid industrialization that weakened the political power of the rural landowners and that lasted through the 1970s. Brazil first increased

Antiglobalization protestors demonstrate at the World Social Forum in Brazil. The annual gathering attracts thousands of people from social movements around the world that are critical of global capitalism. Throughout its 200-year history, Brazil's economy has had very mixed success when engaging with the global economy.

protectionist barriers during the Great Depression in 1930 as the core's demand for its primary product exports collapsed. The positive results were almost immediate. Protected from global competitors, Brazilian industry flourished. The production of light manufactures grew at a rate faster than 5 percent per year through 1945. Encouraged by the early signs of success, Brazil's leadership became even more committed to a comprehensive ISI strategy in the 1950s, hoping it could soon produce capital-intensive goods such as automobiles and industrial machinery. Average tariffs on manufactured imports were raised to nearly 200 percent, and in thirty years Brazil's manufacturing sector grew eightfold. Domestic companies were supplying 99 percent of manufactured consumer goods to the Brazilian market, including cars, as had been hoped.[39] During one seven-year stretch (1968–1974) touted as the "Brazilian miracle," the overall economy grew at a rate exceeding 10 percent per year. All told, during the fifty years in which it was walled off from the core (1930–1980), Brazil's GDP per capita grew from US$1,000 to US$7,000.[40]

The Pains of Liberalization. Finally, trade and capital market liberalization reforms stung Brazil badly after their implementation in the early 1990s. The trade opening was followed by the scrapping of the country's industrial sector. Exposed to global competition, thousands of industrial firms failed, and hundreds of thousands of layoffs occurred. Economic growth rates fell below 5 percent per year. Moreover, in late 1998, Brazil's currency was subject to a speculative attack by international investors, and the country suffered a severe financial crisis. With their fears stoked by the Russian *rouble* crisis, many investors bet against the Brazilian currency (the *real*) in the expectation that its value would soon decline. Investors pulled their capital out of Brazil and in January 1999 their hunch provided to be self-fulfilling: Brazil was forced to devalue its

currency. The devaluation boosted inflation, and the capital flight raised unemployment as Brazil suffered a recession.

***

Many observers would criticize this summary of globalization's effects as a one-sided account. Regarding the alleged successes of ISI, these proved ephemeral. Brazil entered the 1970s with an industrial sector that, although growing, was inefficient because it faced virtually no international competition. This prohibited it from achieving sustained economic growth through export-oriented industrialization, as was occurring in the Asian Tigers at the time. Moreover, the lack of export earnings turned the Brazilian state and investors on to a borrowing spree in the 1970s that ballooned the country's foreign debt by a factor of ten.[41] The debt-fueled bubble burst in 1982, initiating more than a decade of hyperinflation and economic stagnation. To ISI's critics, this unraveling was the result not of too much globalization, but of too little. Finally, the short economic downtick in 1999 notwithstanding, Brazil's economy has been doing well under liberal trade policy ever since. Average incomes have grown by a third since the short-lived financial crisis, fueled in part by the country's (contra Prebisch) rising terms of trade. Global demand for its agricultural and mineral exports has boomed.

The South: Shortcomings of Domestic Institutions

Another critique of the theories that attribute Brazil's long-term economic travails to globalization comes from new institutional economics. This school of thought interprets Brazil's stagnation in the nineteenth century not as a failing of liberal trade policy, but as a result of its flawed domestic economic and political rules. For the first seventy years of its independent existence, Brazil was governed by an authoritarian monarchy that served

IS NEOCOLONIALISM WHY BRAZIL IS ALWAYS THE "COUNTRY OF THE FUTURE?"

to reinforce the status quo inherited from the abusive colonial era. For example, slavery was legal in Brazil throughout most of the first global century (until 1888), systematically repressing wages and internal market size by denying rights to its large Afro-Brazilian population. Moreover, government did little to redistribute land to the rural poor. Formal property rights were not even established until 1850, and even thereafter the state merely reinforced the ownership patterns, inherited from the colonial era, that concentrated large tracts in the hands of a relatively small landed elite.[42] Inequality in land ownership and political power translated into some of the world's worst income inequalities, and they stifled growth by discouraging the productive energies of the masses.[43]

Although Brazil's monarchy fell in 1889, the subsequent 100 years saw only fitful attempts to make its political institutions more democratic and inclusive. Various types of authoritarian regimes were sandwiched around an ill-fated experiment with democracy mid-century (1945–1964) that fell to a military coup. Although the urban bias of ISI actually weakened the rural elite during the middle half of the twentieth century, an industrialist class emerged to merely take its place in blocking progressive reforms that would have expanded and entrenched broader political and economic rights.[44] Not until 1985 did democratization seem to have some staying power. Brazil's "New Republic" has featured universal suffrage and regular elections ever since, and the economy has responded. The level of inequality has declined, in part because politicians have increased spending on the poor in search of their votes.

The Natural World: The Illusion of Abundance

Given Brazil's rich natural endowment, it would seem at first glance that its two centuries of relative economic disappointment can only be attributed

to human agency, be it by Westerners or Brazilians themselves. However, its natural context is less conducive to modern economic growth than this view suggests, hinting at a possible role for nature in its underdevelopment.

Most of Brazilian territory lies in the tropics, meaning it faces the alleged tropical disadvantage to development. Until very recently in its history, Brazil struggled with tropical disease. During the first half of the twentieth century, malaria afflicted 5 million Brazilians per year, and it was even more widespread in the nineteenth century when Brazil fell behind.[45] Mercifully, it was down to just 300,000 cases per year in Brazil by early 2013.

Furthermore, although Brazil has become something of an agro-exporting powerhouse in the last decade, it has long faced the challenge of having unproductive tropical soils. Half its territory is the Amazon rainforest in the north, which is too wet, canopied, and pest-ridden for agriculture. Another 10 percent is the dry and drought-prone *sertão* of the northeast. A further 20 percent is the semi-arid savannah lands of the *cerrado* in the center of the country, which did not start producing reasonable agricultural yields until very recently. Only in the country's south and southeast regions are there temperate climates with high-nutrient, moist soils. Lest one think modern technology has allowed Brazil to overcome this land constraint, it remains the case today that average incomes in Brazil's five wealthiest states, all of them in the south and southeast, are more than thrice those in its five poorest states, all of which are in the dry northeast.

* * *

All told, humans (both foreign and domestic), as well as nature itself, have provided plausible reasons for Brazil's underdevelopment, but recent decades have seen a transformation. Given its size and stability, Brazil is now a leader of Latin America in world affairs and is seen as an important player in international issues. Poverty and inequality have declined since the 1990s and, although far from perfect, a democratic political system finally seems to be well entrenched. The once and always "country of the future" may finally see its future arrive.

Thinking Critically about Development

- On balance, what does the evidence from Brazil indicate regarding the wisdom of a protectionist versus a liberal approach to development?

- To Prebisch, declining terms of trade were bad for the periphery, whereas for Williamson, it was rising terms of trade that underdeveloped the periphery in the nineteenth century. Does the Brazil case help to adjudicate between these contradictory arguments?

- Brazil's economic miracle actually occurred under a military dictatorship, but its recent economic success has been occurring under a democracy. Does this mean that political institutions and regimes do not matter for economic success?

 ## Key Terms

autarky, p. 106

brain drain, p. 120

capital flight, p. 119

capital mobility, p. 104

comparative advantage, p. 106

dependency theory, p. 110

economic globalization, p. 104

exchange rates, p. 105

export promotion, p. 107

foreign debt, p. 113

foreign direct investment (FDI), p. 107

foreign portfolio investment, p. 115

free trade, p. 105

import substitution industrialization (ISI), p. 107

international migration, p. 104

international trade, p. 104

Latin American structuralism, p. 108

mercantilism, p. 105

multinational corporation (MNC), p. 106

protectionist, p. 105

race to the bottom, p. 117

remittances, p. 116

sudden stop, p. 119

sweatshop, p. 117

tariff, p. 105

terms of trade, p. 108

world systems theory (WST), p. 111

Suggested Readings

Bhagwati, Jagdish. *In Defense of Globalization*. Oxford: Oxford University Press, 2004.

Dos Santos, Theotonio. "The Structure of Dependence." *American Economic Review* 60, no. 2 (1970): 231–236.

Frieden, Jeffrey A. *Global Capitalism: Its Fall and Rise in the Twentieth Century*. New York: W. W. Norton and Company, 2006.

Prebisch, Raul. *The Economic Development of Latin America and Its Principal Problems*. New York: Economic Commission for Latin America, 1950.

Rodrik, Dani. *Has Globalization Gone Too Far?* Washington D.C.: Institute for International Economics, 1997.

Williamson, Jeffrey G. *Trade and Poverty: When the Third World Fell Behind*. Cambridge: MIT Press, 2011.

 ## Web Resources

KOF Index of Globalization, http://globalization.kof.ethz.ch/

OECD International Investment Statistics, www.oecd.org/daf/internationalinvestment/

UN Comtrade International Merchandise Trade Statistics, http://comtrade.un.org/

World Trade Organization, www.wto.org/index.htm

A Haitian couple loads their car with humanitarian food aid given by the United States. Over several decades, Haiti has received billions of dollars in aid from the United States and other rich donor countries, but it remains the poorest country in the Western Hemisphere.

Foreign Aid and the Bretton Woods Institutions

Asiya is a thirty-eight-year-old Pakistani nurse . . . or at least she *could* be a nurse. Asiya successfully completed a nurse training program administered and funded by foreign aid and, more specifically, the World Bank. The program had good intentions. Pakistan has a severe shortage of nurses. There is just one nurse per 2,000 people, in comparison to twenty per 2,000 in the United Kingdom.[1] To address this problem, the World Bank, along with the Pakistani government, has funded a variety of nurse training programs over the course of the last few decades. Asiya enrolled in one in the early 2000s with high hopes.

Alas, things did not work out. When Asiya completed the program, there were no jobs in Pakistan's health sector to be found. The government did not have enough money to hire more nurses at a decent wage. Moreover, it turns out that being a nurse in Pakistan is not a desirable line of work. Nursing is widely considered a disrespectful profession, and many nurses are verbally harassed by patients, doctors, and even family members. As a result of the poor job prospects and the low prestige, many of Asiya's peers who completed the training program actually moved abroad, plying their trade elsewhere. Pakistan thus has little to show from the World Bank program except more debt, since the program was funded by a low-cost loan. As for Asiya, she eventually married, had children, and now rarely leaves the house. Pakistanis in need of a nurse's care go without her services.

Foreign aid is big business. Aside from the sheer volumes of money behind it—US$100 billion every year in public funds—aid to the less developed world permeates pop culture. Hit songs raise money for famine and earthquake relief, movie stars adopt African children to send a humanitarian message, and rock singers report that the end of global poverty is "up to us" in the West.[2] Yet foreign aid can be ineffective or even counterproductive, as Asiya's story illustrates. Is aid a cause of the ongoing gap between the world's rich and poor nations?

This chapter describes the modern foreign aid regime and includes a detailed discussion of two of the most controversial financial institutions in the world, the International Monetary Fund and the World Bank. It gives arguments for and against aid and these two Bretton Woods institutions, and then it illustrates the various arguments by further exploring the Pakistani case.

Foreign Aid

Foreign aid, also called official development assistance (ODA), refers to public (state-controlled) resources that are loaned at lenient terms or given by a government to (1) another government, (2) a nongovernmental organization (NGO), or (3) an international organization (such as the World Bank) and whose ultimate purpose is to enhance development within the developing world. Stated more succinctly, aid is government monies that are sent overseas to improve human livelihood in poor countries. Aid goes toward a wide variety of activities, including social development projects (building schools and hospitals), natural disaster and war relief, and support for transitions to democracy and free markets.[3] Wealthy governments that grant aid monies are called donors, and the countries in which the funds are received and used are called recipients.

Understanding Key Concepts and Players in the Aid Regime

The modern foreign aid regime is complex. It involves thousands of organizations, employs millions of people, and distributes tens of billions of dollars each year. This section summarizes some of its main elements.

Types of Foreign Aid. Foreign aid takes three primary forms. Grants, by far the most frequent form, are funds or in-kind goods and services that are given without expectation of repayment.

Soft loans (also called concessional loans) are aid given to a recipient with the expectation that it will be repaid, but with terms for the loan that are lenient to the borrower (such as a lower interest rate or longer pay-off period). Finally, **debt relief** is aid in the form of forgiveness of part of an LDC's debt to foreign investors.

Another crucial distinction lies in how aid is channeled to its ultimate recipients. **Bilateral aid** is aid that a government gives directly to a foreign government or to an NGO or private citizen in an LDC. For example, the United States Agency for International Development (USAID) is a U.S. federal agency that is the main distributor of U.S. bilateral aid to LDCs. USAID follows the dictates of Congress, the president, and executive agencies such as the departments of state and defense in sending U.S. government funds directly overseas for development purposes. Worldwide, about three-quarters of all aid flows are bilateral. In contrast, **multilateral aid** is monies that a government gives to an international organization such as the United Nations Development Programme, the European Union, or the World Bank that in turn distributes the funds to recipient governments, NGOs, or private citizens in LDCs. Figure 6.1 contrasts the flow of these two different types of aid.

Types of Aid Agencies. An **aid agency** is any organization that administers and distributes aid. These can be bilateral government organizations such as USAID, development NGOs such as Save the Children, or multilateral government organizations such as the World Bank. Official bilateral aid agencies are government bodies that are a part of a donor country's executive branch and receive their funding approvals from the legislature and their funds from taxpayers. Many donor countries have a primary agency that is in charge of distributing much of its bilateral aid. Aside from USAID, others examples are Great Britain's Department for International Development (DfID) and the Swedish International Development Cooperation

Agency (Sida). Wealthy donor countries often have vastly different priorities that determine how they distribute aid. For example, the United States has long tended to use aid as a foreign policy tool to achieve strategic geopolitical goals such as the containment of communism or terrorism. In contrast, Japan is well known for pursuing commercial goals, using aid to create business opportunities overseas for Japanese entrepreneurs.[4]

Development NGOs are organizations that are neither profit oriented nor part of the public sector and that are devoted to improving at least one aspect of human welfare somewhere in the developing world. NGOs can be based either in a wealthy donor country or the recipient country. For instance, Doctors Without Borders is based in Switzerland, while the Bangladesh Rural Advancement Committee is in Bangladesh. NGOs actually play multiple roles in the international aid regime. They raise funds, promote public awareness, create ideas and conduct research, lobby public officials, and provide technical assistance and delivery of services in the recipient country. Oxfam is a development NGO that carries out all of these roles, but many specialize in just a few. For example, the Jubilee 2000 coalition has largely focused on raising knowledge about and pressuring public officials on LDC debt relief. Perhaps the most crucial role played by NGOs is service delivery in the recipient nation. As indicated in Figure 6.1, bilateral and multilateral public agencies often give funds to NGOs (15 percent of all aid, by some estimates) instead of governments and rely on them to provide the intended service.[5]

Finally, multilateral aid agencies are international organizations that receive most of their funding from their member states' periodic dues and, in

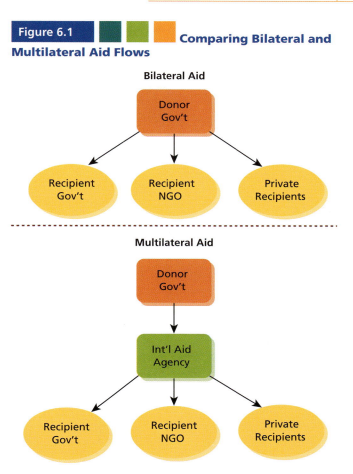

Figure 6.1 **Comparing Bilateral and Multilateral Aid Flows**

Bilateral Aid

Donor Gov't → Recipient Gov't, Recipient NGO, Private Recipients

Multilateral Aid

Donor Gov't → Int'l Aid Agency → Recipient Gov't, Recipient NGO, Private Recipients

turn, disburse aid largely at their own discretion. A number of United Nations (UN) specialized agencies, such as the World Health Organization (WHO) and the United Nations Children's Fund (UNICEF), fit this model, although both also raise private contributions. The World Bank and the regional development banks, such as the Inter-American Development Bank and the Asian Development Bank, also operate by collecting public funds from member states and redistributing them, typically in the form of soft loans for specific projects. (Given its size and importance, the World Bank is discussed in greater detail below under the topic of the two Bretton Woods institutions.)

A Brief History of Foreign Aid

The modern foreign aid regime has evolved through various stages since its beginnings in the 1940s. What began largely as an extra tool in the West's anticommunist toolkit eventually emerged into a US$100 billion industry with designs on eradicating global poverty.

Cold War Realist Beginnings, 1945–1970. Foreign aid began in the immediate post–World War II era as "a child of hardheaded, diplomatic realism."[6] Aid was borne of Cold War geopolitical self-interest, not of an altruistic concern for the foreign poor. By 1947, the Soviet Union had absorbed much of Eastern Europe into its sphere of influence, and fears abounded that it would move westward, deeper into Europe. A communist-backed insurgency existed in Greece, and the Soviets had intentions on expansion into Turkey as well. The United States president of the time, Harry S. Truman, announced a plan (part of the Truman Doctrine) to disburse bilateral aid to the Greek and Turkish governments to shore up their incumbent regimes in their efforts against communist incursion. The United States followed up by enacting the Marshall Plan later that year, committing US$13 billion in aid to Europe to help the continent reconstruct itself and, it was believed, to make communism less alluring to Europeans.

Following the Chinese Communist Party's takeover of the Chinese mainland in 1949, the United States introduced aid programs to a variety of Asian countries, and by the close of the 1950s it was spreading its aid benevolence throughout the developing world to provide a bulwark against the spread of communism. Aid to anticommunist Latin American governments took off with particular speed in the 1960s after the Cuban Revolution of 1959 stoked fears of spreading communism in the United States' backyard. With their economies on firm footing, Western European countries also entered the donor fray in the 1950s and 1960s, as several established aid ministries and sharply boosted their aid outflows to former colonies and noncommunist allies.

The primary strategy of donors was to give aid directly to Western-friendly, anticommunist governments to keep them in the allied camp. To be sure, inklings of a more altruistic component to aid were evident in the era. In 1949, Truman implemented the Point Four Program to disseminate scientific advances in agriculture and industry to LDCs. Also, over a decade later, John F. Kennedy founded the Peace Corps, the Alliance for Progress (an aid program to Latin America), and USAID, noting that the creation of the latter in 1961 was "not to contain the spread of communism . . . but because it [was] right."[7] Ultimately, however, these commitments to altruism were largely subservient to the anticommunist drive.

Aid for Development in the Era of Détente, 1970–1989. The 1970s and 1980s were transformative decades for the foreign aid regime, as aid from wealthy donor countries took on a more altruistic look. The era of *détente* relaxed Cold War rivalries, and economic and food crises hit numerous LDCs. Early in the 1970s at a UN meeting, wealthy countries pledged (but have never complied) to boost their aid-giving to 0.7 percent of GDP from the then-current level of about 0.25 percent. Development NGOs also proliferated and became more professional and organized, pressuring governments to address underdevelopment and not just strategic self-interest.

As a result, the nature of aid-giving changed in crucial ways. Aid flows ballooned, more than doubling between 1970 and 1989. Foreign aid was much more likely to end up in needy countries, not just in the hands of Cold War allies. Aid for famine relief, family planning, health and educational infrastructure, rural and agricultural development, and other humanitarian projects increased at the expense of direct transfers to friendly governments. Moreover, multilateral aid organizations, most notably the World Bank, gained a weightier presence in the global development assistance system. In delegating more funds to multilateral aid organizations, wealthy donor countries were effectively yielding part of their decision-making power about where to allocate aid to international institutions, entities that would presumably not have the narrow interests of a single donor in mind. By 1980, the share of all aid that was channeled through international institutions was up to one-third, an increase from an average of one-tenth in the previous era. (Understanding Indicators: Classifying Official Development Assistance illustrates some of these trends in aid-flow volumes through time.) Finally, both bilateral and multilateral donors began using their leverage to encourage recipient nations to adopt policy and institutional changes, most notably market-oriented economic reforms and democratization.

Donor Fatigue, 1990–1999. The 1990s was a decade of donor fatigue, as these years witnessed a decline in funding and enthusiasm for aid. The Cold War had ended, sapping aid advocacy of this realist motive. Moreover, the West experienced economic recession at the beginning of the decade, so donor governments decided that their tax revenues were better spent at home. Aid-giving dropped by 20 percent worldwide in the two years after 1995, and as a share of the West's GDP, ODA fell from 0.32 percent to 0.22 percent.

Still, donors did find new purposes for aid amidst the tightening budgetary constraints. Western countries poured money into postcommunist countries such as Russia to support their transitions to capitalism and democracy. There was also an increase in postconflict aid, meaning funds to support societies that were emerging from war, such as the former Yugoslavia and several in Africa. Aid for global environmental problems also surged as Western donors sought to address such problems as species preservation and ozone depletion.

Finally, activists placed the issue of debt relief for the developing world on the global agenda, arguing that debt owed mostly to Western lenders hamstrung the developing world's ability to improve the livelihoods of the poor. In 1996, the World Bank launched the **Heavily Indebted Poor Countries (HIPC) initiative** to enact debt relief for poor countries that had demonstrated a commitment to implementing poverty-reducing policies. Debt forgiveness more than quintupled between 1990 and 2004.[9]

Development Revitalized? 2000–Present. In terms of the global aid regime's commitment to development, the new millennium has been the best of times and the worst of times. On the one hand, the altruistic purposes of aid reached an unprecedented prominence. The millennium began with a flourish of rhetorical commitment to development. In 2000, at a meeting organized by the United Nations, nearly 150 heads of state and heads of government signed the UN Millennium Declaration, which committed them to achieving the **Millennium Development Goals (MDGs)**. In seeking to achieve eight development goals by the agreed-upon year of 2015, wealthy nations reaffirmed their long-ignored promise to raise aid levels to 0.7 percent of their GDPs. (See Development in the Field: The Millennium Development Goals.) Aid-giving rebounded from its 1990s trough, almost doubling in the fifteen years before 2010. For its part, the United States boosted its aid outflows by a greater percentage than it had in forty years.[10] George W. Bush introduced the President's Emergency Plan for AIDS Relief (PEPFAR), a US$15 billion initiative to combat the HIV/AIDS epidemic in Africa, and the Millennium Challenge Account, a proposed US$8.5 billion plan devoted to a wide array of development goals. British prime minister Tony Blair, calling "the state of Africa a scar on the conscience of the world,"[11] founded the Commission for Africa and called for an immediate US$25 billion increase in aid to the continent. Other Western donors upped

understanding INDICATORS

Classifying Official Development Assistance

Deciding what is and what is not foreign aid entails more than a few judgment calls. Consider foreign assistance to a poor country's defense and military. This should seemingly not be considered foreign aid, since defense is not necessarily a development purpose. But if physical security in the nation receiving military assistance could be immediately enhanced by stronger defense, why should military assistance, but not foreign-funded health projects, be excluded from aid tallies? Another grey area lies in private charitable donations by foreigners to LDCs, such as a U.S. citizen's monthly donation to Save the Children. These have a clear development purpose, so should they not be considered foreign aid simply because they are not public funds? Finally, what about aid funds that must be repaid, even if at lenient terms? Does it make sense to consider loans, even soft loans, aid?

The Organisation for Economic Co-operation and Development compiles the most widely used data on foreign aid. It defines official development assistance (ODA) as "grants and loans . . . that are undertaken by the official sector, with promotion of economic development and welfare as the main objective, at concessional financial terms (if a loan, having a grant element of at least 25 percent)."[8] OECD statistics on ODA thus exclude military assistance (since it is not economic development and welfare), private donations (since they are not official, meaning public), and soft loans that have no grant element. The figure here shows the volume of foreign aid, according to the OECD's definition and data, since 1960. The amount of ODA has increased nearly fourfold since then, with the amounts channeled through multilateral organizations growing at an even faster rate.

Official Development Assistance Flows, 1960–2011

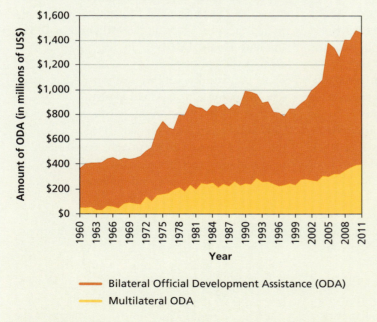

— Bilateral Official Development Assistance (ODA)
— Multilateral ODA

Source: The Organisation for Economic Co-operation and Development, International Development Statistics, www.oecd.org/dac/stats/idsonline.

- Should military assistance and private contributions be included in foreign aid data?

- What accounts for the steep increases in ODA in the early 1970s and early 2000s?

their debt forgiveness efforts, granting billions of dollars in debt relief to many of the world's poorest countries.

On the other hand, it is too soon to pronounce the modern aid regime as entirely successful and development focused. Elements of calculated geopolitical strategy have crept back into the logic of aid-giving. Most telling, the United States, while no longer needing to use aid as a Cold War tool, now uses it as a tool in its war against terrorism. After September 11, 2001, Afghanistan, Iraq, and Pakistan became leading recipients of aid because of their perceived centrality to the West's strategic interests. Even the increase in development assistance was partially motivated on the belief that poverty breeds terrorism. Moreover, despite boosts in aid outflows over the 1990s low point, Western countries remained far from the magic 0.7 percent goal they had been promising for forty years. As of 2011, aid was less than half this amount, and all indications were that many developing countries would fall short of achieving the MDGs.

Causes of Underdevelopment: The Case for Aid Skepticism

Since the dawn of the modern aid regime in the 1940s, the West has devoted about US$2.5 trillion to foreign aid, and it continues to do so at a rate of nearly US$100 billion per year. Foreign aid is seemingly a way for the West to put forward an altruistic face, to right the past wrongs it has committed against the global South, and to close the global gap between the haves and the have-nots. Yet could foreign aid be a means by which the West, either intentionally or unintentionally, causes and prolongs underdevelopment? Despite its seemingly altruistic purposes, there is widespread criticism of foreign aid. At best, scholars and other observers who are aid skeptics argue that there is a failure of **aid effectiveness**, which is the ability of aid to deliver tangible improvements in development outcomes. At worst, some argue that aid bears a primary responsibility for keeping poor countries poor.

Donor Motives

One reason why aid may not advance development is that, as stressed in the history given above, donors often have self-interested motives for granting aid that have little to do with the goal of improving livelihoods in LDCs. The realist purposes of aid can distort its effectiveness in a variety of ways. During the Cold War, Western governments often granted aid to ostensibly anticommunist and pro-Western leaders without regard to how the monies were used or to the leader's commitment to internal democracy. For example, over the course of three decades, Belgium, France, and the United States granted more than US$1 billion in aid to Zaire's government when it was led by Mobuto Sese Seko. Rather than using it to build schools and hospitals for his country's indigent people, Mobuto squandered much of it on palaces and other luxurious indulgences for himself. Grants from the West during the Cold War also propped up brutal authoritarian governments just because they were waging civil wars against communist insurgencies (such as those in El Salvador and Liberia).

Other realist purposes divert funds away from the world's neediest. Most famously, Israel and Egypt were long the two leading recipients of U.S. bilateral aid, commanding around 25 percent of all U.S. aid for decades, which both received as enticements for signing the Camp David peace agreement with one another in 1978.[12] Israel continued to receive the aid long after graduating to high-income status, and Egypt was wealthier than the vast majority of its African neighbors. Colombia, an upper-middle-income country, is another leading recipient of financial assistance from the United States, receiving support for its efforts to combat cocaine production and trafficking. All told, less than half of all foreign aid goes to the poorest sixty-five countries, and fully 10 percent goes to countries that are classified as upper income.[13]

DEVELOPMENT in the FIELD

The Millennium Development Goals

At the 2000 Millennium Summit of the United Nations, the 193 member states approved the Millennium Development Goals (MDGs). Each developing country is meant to achieve a set of eight goals. Most are targeted improvements to be reached by 2015 in one or a few of the country's development indicators. The eight goals are as follows:

(1) Halve the 1990 proportion of people living in extreme poverty and in hunger.

(2) Enroll all primary-school-aged children in formal education.

(3) Eliminate gender gaps in primary and secondary school enrollment.

(4) Reduce the under-five mortality rate by two-thirds its 1990 level.

(5) Reduce the maternal mortality rate by two-thirds its 1990 level and achieve universal access to reproductive health services.

(6) Halt the spread of HIV/AIDS and reduce the incidence of malaria and other tropical diseases.

(7) Reverse the loss of environmental resources and natural diversity and halve the proportion of people living without safe drinking water and sanitation.

(8) Develop a global partnership on problems such as LDC debt, trade restrictions, dissemination of pharmaceuticals, and the spread of information and communications technologies.

In response to the MDGs, a number of aid agencies sprang up to promote awareness and achievement of the goals, including the United Nations Millennium Campaign and the Micah Challenge. The Millennium Villages (MV) project is one initiative organized and sponsored by the Millennium Promise, the United Nations Development Programme, and the Earth Institute (which is directed by Jeffrey Sachs). The MV project picked around a dozen villages in Africa to be recipients of aid. The project takes a comprehensive or integrated approach to aid and rural development, as it funds initiatives to improve all of the following within each village: education, health, gender equity, agricultural productivity, infrastructure, and environmental sustainability.

Despite their altruistic intentions, criticisms of the MDGs exist.

Most obviously, the MDG pronouncement says little about *how* these goals will be achieved. Politicians and members of the aid community enjoy making flamboyant promises about what aid can accomplish, largely because that seems to be what donors and taxpayers want to hear. In doing so, they promote the widespread tendency to overlook the more realistic but therefore more mundane and incremental changes that aid can accomplish, such as a refurbished rural road or a few more teachers trained. The MDGs also ignore the obvious trade-offs among all of the goals. Toward which area should the marginal aid dollar be given to produce the most effective development outcomes? Merely saying "all of them" disregards the reality of resource limitations and runs the risk of wasting money on ineffective means. Finally, the MDGs perpetuate the problems of poor accountability and weak incentives. There is no provision in the UN Millennium Declaration to fire aid bureaucrats or close down ineffective aid agencies if goals are not reached by 2015. With so many aid agencies and such grandiose targets across so many countries, it is not even clear who one would punish for failing to meet the goals.

Another damaging self-interested goal that donor states pursue with aid donations is seeking to deepen commercial ties with a recipient, benefiting their own exporters or guaranteeing their access to crucial imports in doing so. On the export side, around half of all bilateral aid flows are **tied aid**, which is aid granted to an LDC on the condition that the recipient uses it to purchase goods or services produced by the donor country. For instance, much Japanese aid is given with stipulations that recipients use it to purchase equipment from Japanese firms. The problem with tied aid is that it subjects the recipient to a monopolistic arrangement. Rather than being able to shop around for the highest-quality materials at the lowest price, recipients are constrained to make their purchase from one country's producers, who can charge above-market prices or provide low-quality products. Some estimates suggest that tied aid increases costs to recipients by 20 percent.[14] On the import side, donor countries often use aid to secure access to a recipient country's natural resources. For example, the recent rise of China as an aid donor to Africa is often a means for China to secure access to some of Africa's natural resources. As a result, African exporters may fail to receive a fair price for their sales.

Donor Paternalism and Lack of Accountability

Even when a donor gives aid with good intentions, it can fail to produce the desired effect on development. The ringleader of aid skepticism, economist William Easterly, accuses donors and agencies of giving aid with a failed bureaucratic "planner's" mentality—one that harbors a thinly veiled arrogance and paternalism toward people in the developing world.[15] To Easterly, Westerners swoop into poor countries convinced that it is up to them and their superior financial resources to save and develop the global South. In doing so, these Western aid "experts" often hatch one-size-fits-all plans that present a single idea as the panacea for global poverty: debt relief, market reforms, microfinance, democratization,

birth control, and so on.[16] This mentality makes aid bureaucrats blind to the nuances and realities of the local context. Rather than asking people in recipient countries about their wants and needs, donors adopt the paternalistic attitude that they know better than the poor themselves what is best for the poor. The negative consequences can be concrete. For example, donors once constructed a fish farm in some Malian canals that happened to be dry for half the year. Local residents knew this but simply were not asked about it.[17]

Easterly also argues that, as part of this paternalism, Western donors and aid agencies operate in a world without feedback and accountability for their performance. For the most part, aid groups are incentivized to keep the money flowing: raise as much as possible and then, to please their funders, move these funds out to some visible development project. They have few incentives to then monitor and evaluate the effectiveness of their projects, since monitoring costs money itself, is not flashy to humanitarian givers, and could reveal embarrassing failures and wastefulness. As a result, aid projects are rarely driven by systematic knowledge about what will and will not be effective.

Moreover, even if aid workers and donors knew what worked in development, they often have little incentive to implement it because they operate under a perverse system of accountability. Aid workers and agencies are ultimately accountable to their donors, upon whom they rely for funds. So long as donor funds keep flowing, the aid community has no real mechanism for sanctioning (such as with job dismissal or pay cuts) its workers and agencies when their development efforts are ineffective. In other words, agencies' real incentives are to market themselves to wealthy philanthropists and to donor governments, not to be effective in alleviating poverty.

Donor Fragmentation and Aid Volatility

Two other shortcomings on the donors' end can complicate the ability of recipients to use aid profitably. First, donors cause problems by failing to coordinate their aid-giving and development project efforts among themselves. This is the problem of **donor fragmentation**, as evidenced by the fact that LDCs receive foreign aid from, on average, twenty-five different official donors and fifty NGOs funding hundreds of projects.[18] Recipients thus have to deal with the bureaucratic nightmare of complying with a vast array of uncoordinated donor requirements and conditions. Furthermore, fragmentation means that donors and aid agencies often duplicate services. For example, in the wake of natural disasters, international humanitarian organizations often flood in to the same affected sites rather than coordinating to spread their efforts out geographically.

Second, aid flows from the West can be volatile and unpredictable, making it difficult for recipient governments to plan ahead. In the West, aid amounts are often approved by executives and legislators on an annual basis, so they can ebb and flow with domestic idiosyncrasies such as public sentiment, political will, economic health, interest group demands, and perceived foreign policy needs. In some of the world's poorest countries, foreign aid can constitute as much as 25 percent to 50 percent of the government's budget, so sharp drops in aid can have major effects on a government's ability to provide services. Figure 6.2 illustrates this volatility by showing annual aid flows since 1980 to Mozambique as a share of that country's GDP.

Recipient Absorptive Capacity and Governance

Even if donors and aid agencies have good intentions, good incentives, awareness of best practices, and proper coordination, further challenges to aid effectiveness come from the receiving end. Many aid projects fail because of less developed countries' lack of **absorptive capacity**—that is, the economic, social, and political context to use aid effectively. For example, increased capital (meaning buildings and machinery) is a necessary ingredient of economic growth, but this does not mean that a boost in aid to fund capital accumulation automatically translates into more growth. After all, machines need skilled individuals to operate and maintain them, and buildings need educated people to work in them. Many aid-receiving countries, however, lack workforces that have the requisite skills to take advantage of the potential gains from aid-funded capital inflows. This problem can also work in the opposite direction. As with Asiya in this chapter's opening vignette, aid can be used to train more doctors, nurses, and teachers, but if the country cannot afford to hire them or to provide well-supplied clinics and schools for them, then the efforts are largely wasted. For these reasons, the original aid skeptic, economist Peter Bauer, pointed out a fundamental paradox of aid: if the conditions for the effective use of aid are in place in a country, then that country is probably wealthy enough to not need aid.[19]

Similarly, many aid projects fail because of bad government in the

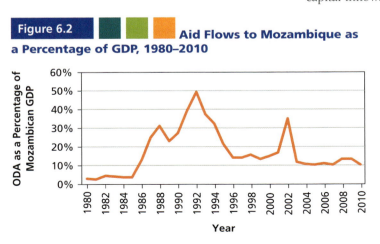

Figure 6.2 **Aid Flows to Mozambique as a Percentage of GDP, 1980–2010**

Source: Compiled from the Organisation for Economic Co-operation and Development, International Development Statistics, www.oecd.org/dac/stats/idsonline.

receiving country.[20] Famously, Bauer saw aid as a wasteful subsidy of corrupt governments by rich-country taxpayers. Low-income countries tend to have poor governance, which means they are corrupt, authoritarian, and fail to provide the public services and legal frameworks that are needed to make aid projects work. In other words, domestic governments struggle to police the highways, pay the teachers, regulate the medical care, and sanitize the water supplies that are funded by foreign aid. In its worst form, bad governance can result in outright theft of aid inflows. For example, food aid to Somalia often falls into the hands of politicians and warlords who horde it or sell it.[21] The problem of poor governance in the developing world thus creates another paradox for the foreign aid regime: since the poorest countries tend also be the most poorly governed, the world's neediest reside in places where aid is most likely to be squandered.

Some aid skeptics even go so far as to claim that aid worsens governance, and thus material well-being, in recipient countries. Economist Dambisa Moyo indicts development assistance for breeding addiction and **aid dependency** in Africa.[22] Aid constitutes about 15 percent of GDP in the typical African country and provides more than 20 percent of public services in over sixty countries worldwide.[23] It thus can engender laziness on the part of recipient governments who, rather than making the effort to provide high-quality public goods themselves, simply continue to accept aid inflows that keep their economies and meager public services inching along. In other words, recipient governments look outward for their development mainsprings rather than actually building the proper governance institutions at home needed for prosperity. Scholarly research suggests that countries that receive a lot of aid do not make the same effort to collect taxes from their citizens as do countries that receive little aid.[24]

Recipient Economic Problems

Aid is also characterized by several economic problems. Aid inflows can cause inflationary pressures in the receiving country if the money enters without a commensurate increase in imports, investment opportunities, or productivity. Most aid seems to increase consumption (and especially government consumption) but not investment, so this necessary commensurate increase is often absent.[25] A greater amount of money chasing the same amount of goods is the classic recipe for inflation. Furthermore, aid can also be harmful to long-run economic growth by disadvantaging manufacturers in the recipient nation. The entry of foreign funds appreciates the local currency, which makes the country's exports more expensive (and thus less competitive) in foreign markets.[26] Similarly, when donors send clothing and shoes to an LDC, they are undercutting its makers of clothing and shoes.

A final economic problem with development assistance, especially aid in the form of funds to foreign governments, is that it is **fungible**. This means that it can be applied across many uses, so upsurges in development assistance may not cause net increases in investment or in spending on the social realms it presumably targets. A recipient country government can neutralize aid revenues that are earmarked for social improvements by shifting existing funds in its own budget that were initially intended for these social improvements over to less humanitarian purposes. For example, a government receiving a foreign grant to build schools may see it as an opportunity to shift money away from its education budget to its defense budget. If so, the net effect of the aid donation was to actually boost funding for defense, not to provide more schools.

Critique: Defending Foreign Aid and Its Record

Development assistance to the world's poorest has numerous celebrity advocates, including pop culture icons such as Angelina Jolie and Bono Vox. The intellectual community also has its aid advocates who meet aid skepticism with fierce retorts. What are some of these defenses of foreign aid and its record?

Theoretical Defenses

Intellectual support for foreign aid has theoretical roots in 1950s and 1960s studies in development economics and modernization theory. Leading development economists such as Ragnar Nurkse, Paul Rosenstein-Rodan, and Walt Rostow argued that foreign aid was an important element of a **big push** that underdeveloped countries needed to progress.[27] To these thinkers, LDCs were caught in a poverty trap that was due in part to a financing gap. Because citizens of LDCs were poor, they needed to devote most of their income to consumption and so had little by way of savings. In turn, the lack of savings trapped LDCs in poverty because it meant they lacked the means to finance capital and technological accumulation. To grow an LDC economy, an external force, namely the country's domestic government with assistance from foreign funding, was needed to provide the big push—a massive infusion of finance that could break the vicious cycle of low savings and slow growth. The leading intellect behind the aid advocacy community today, economist Jeffrey Sachs, also espouses heightened aid flows on these theoretical grounds.[28] Figure 6.3 graphically depicts the nature of the poverty trap and the big push.

Similarly, many modernization theorists (a body of thought described in more detail in Chapter 7) working in political science and sociology in the 1950s and 1960s also espoused development assistance to the less developed world. Their reasoning was that aid brought growth-promoting Western influences to so-called traditional societies. Aid could promote adoption in these societies of Western ways of life, political institutions, and economic structures that were needed to lift them out of poverty.

Foreign Aid's Many Successes

Aside from these theoretical defenses of development assistance, Sachs and other advocates of more aid point to its numerous success stories. Aid's most impressive successes lie in the realm of health outcomes. (Even Easterly admits that "health is the area where foreign aid has enjoyed its most conspicuous successes."[29]) Examples are plentiful. In 1967, the WHO opened its Smallpox Eradication Unit to rid the world of a disease that had almost wiped out the Native American population and continued to strike 10 million people per year. By aggressively promoting vaccination worldwide, its efforts contributed to the near-complete eradication of smallpox in just thirteen years' time.[30] More recently, the attention and resources that U.S. presidents and the United Nations have put toward the HIV/AIDS epidemic have raised the number of people receiving proper drug treatment for HIV from nearly zero to over 5 million.

Aid has also seemingly contributed to some notable gains in economic growth and productivity. Aid funded the adoption of new seed types and fertilizers in Asia in the 1960s and 1970s, a process that dramatically boosted crop yields and all but ended India's and other countries' recurring bouts with famine. Aid advocates also hasten to point out growth success stories as well. Chile, Israel, and South Korea all used aid profitably in service of their dramatic economic growth spurts in the second half of the twentieth century.

The Aid Trickle

Proponents of development assistance also contend that aid is simply not plentiful enough to be the cause of all the ills that aid skeptics attribute to it. Many aid advocates criticize the modern aid regime (just like the skeptics), but they do so for its sins of omission rather than its sins of commission. According to this line of thought, a primary cause of global poverty is the stinginess of Western governments and publics: the aid that Western countries and donors send is a pittance, especially when seen as a portion of their total wealth, and the United States is one of the worst offenders.

Since the end of World War II, the West has given about US$2.5 trillion in foreign aid to the less developed world. This sounds like an enormous amount of money, but as a share of what the West could give, it is not. Western societies devote just 0.30 percent, or thirty cents of every US$100 they have, to ODA.[31] That comes out to less than US$30 in aid per year per LDC resident. Figure 6.4 lists the share of GNI that most of the world's wealthiest countries devote to official development assistance. Keeping in mind the 0.70 percent goal stated by the UN in 1970, a majority gives less than half a percent (.50) of their GNIs to LDCs as development assistance. The United States gives about .20 percent, which amounts to about US$40 per American per year. The few countries that do exceed 1 percent of GNI are all relatively small economies. In fact, the European Union, Japan, and the United States give four times more in subsidies each year to their own farmers than they do to the foreign poor.[32]

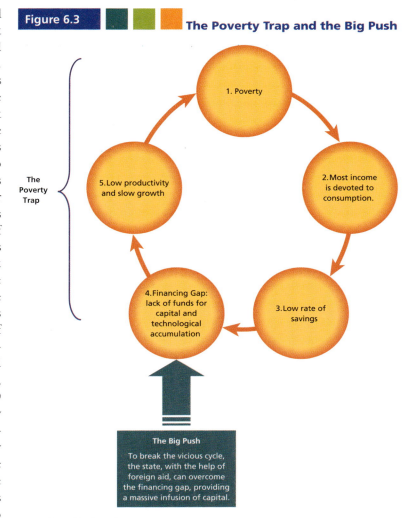

Figure 6.3

The Poverty Trap and the Big Push

The Poverty Trap

1. Poverty
2. Most income is devoted to consumption.
3. Low rate of savings
4. Financing Gap: lack of funds for capital and technological accumulation
5. Low productivity and slow growth

The Big Push

To break the vicious cycle, the state, with the help of foreign aid, can overcome the financing gap, providing a massive infusion of capital.

Source: Created by the author.

Learning from Past Mistakes

A final defense of the foreign aid regime is that, in recent years, aid agencies and donors have shown an impressive willingness to learn from their past mistakes and address many of their shortcomings, an indication that the effectiveness of aid may be on the upswing. A few recent innovations and examples point in this direction. The first example is that donors are taking program evaluation—that is, research and assessment of an aid project's effectiveness—much more seriously, allowing them to learn what works and does not work in aid. Perhaps the most visible example of this is the explosion in randomized control trials, an experimental technique in which aid benefits are disbursed only to a random selection of people or groups who are chosen from a larger population of study.[33] By choosing aid recipients at random from a larger population, donors and

Figure 6.4   Aid Outflows as a Percentage of Gross National Income (GNI), 2010

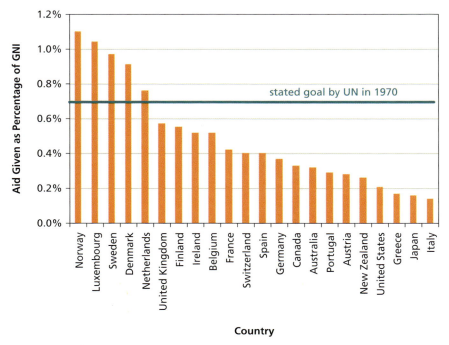

Source: Compiled from the Organisation for Economic Co-operation and Development, International Development Statistics, www.oecd.org/dac/stats/idsonline.

in the past to shovel money continually to corrupt or wasteful governments. Much aid now is channeled directly to NGOs, which are often more committed and more effective than developing world governments in addressing social problems. NGOs also cannot negate the effect of an aid inflow by simply shifting other funds to less humanitarian purposes. Moreover, when money is given directly to governments, donors now seek to privilege ostensibly clean and honest governments. For example, the Millennium Challenge Corporation (MCC), a U.S. aid agency created by George W. Bush to disburse aid from the Millennium Challenge Account, only gives money to countries that are deemed to be sufficiently democratic, transparent, and market oriented.

researchers ensure that those who receive the benefit are, on average, equivalent to those who did not receive it across all factors *except* for the benefit. Any subsequently observed differences in development outcomes between the beneficiaries (the treatment group) and the nonbeneficiaries (the control group) must be due to the aid itself. Administering aid in this way allows donors and researchers to calculate its precise impact on a variety of development outcomes. Randomized control trials thus provide valuable information about where aid can be most effectively deployed and about the piecemeal changes that it can and cannot achieve.

The second example is that the aid regime is increasingly sensitive to the problems of poor governance, low absorptive capacity, and fungibility. Western governments are less likely than they were

The Bretton Woods Institutions: The IMF and the World Bank

The first half of this chapter focused on the foreign aid regime as a whole. However, two multilateral organizations that redistribute funds internationally for development purposes deserve special focus. The **World Bank** and the **International Monetary Fund (IMF)** are two international financial institutions (IFIs) that are collectively known as the **Bretton Woods institutions**. To be sure, they are not always considered aid agencies, at least under some of the strictest definitions of development assistance. The primary reason is that both disburse loans, not grants, to recipient countries. Also, the IMF (unlike the World Bank) does not lend exclusively to underdeveloped countries. Regardless of these definitional issues, this chapter on foreign aid does discuss the two Bretton Woods institutions at length, especially given their importance to international redistribution and debates on the causes of global poverty. While they do offer only loans, the loans are highly concessional, meaning they are made at low interest rates to the borrower. Moreover, with respect to the IMF, *most* of its loans have been disbursed to LDCs.

A Brief History of the IMF and World Bank

The IMF and the World Bank are called the Bretton Woods institutions because they were jointly proposed in 1944 at a meeting of delegates from forty-four countries in Bretton Woods, New Hampshire. (They were officially founded in Washington, D.C., one year later.) Members of the allied nations of World War II met at Bretton Woods to develop new institutions that could govern the global economic system. Although much has changed since 1945, their defining missions remain an important part of what they do.

Shifting Goals. Two major concerns drove the thinking and goals of the Bretton Woods delegates. First, they wanted to avoid a replay of the Great Depression, which experts at the time agreed was a key trigger of the war and had itself been caused by a series of competitive currency devaluations among European countries. Delegates approved the establishment of the IMF to help countries maintain their currency exchange rates in a stable and desirable range. Specifically, the organization was to make loans to Western countries that were facing a balance-of-payments crisis, a situation in which a country is running out of the foreign currency it needs to purchase imports and to service foreign debt. An emergency loan would buy the borrowing country time to take the measures it needed (such as making its exports more competitive or attracting foreign investment) to maintain its exchange rate and avoid a rapid devaluation. Second, Bretton Woods delegates wanted to rebuild war-torn Europe. For this, they established the International Bank for Reconstruction and Development (IBRD). The IBRD was tasked with making loans in Europe to fund specific infrastructural projects, such as dams, bridges, and highways, that the private sector might not produce on its own. The IBRD was soon colloquially called the World Bank. In sum, the IMF was designed to make large loans to assist countries under macroeconomic strain, while the World Bank was designed to make smaller and more targeted loans for specific reconstruction and development projects. Roughly speaking, these differences in mission still distinguish the two organizations to this day.

That said, both institutions have undergone changes in how they carry out their missions since their founding. In the 1950s and 1960s, both shifted their efforts from lending to Europe to lending to mostly LDCs. Europe's rapid growth, decolonization in Asia and Africa, and the belief that development could provide a bulwark against communism all contributed to a shift toward more development-oriented lending. The World Bank expanded from focusing strictly on financing infrastructural projects to making loans for broader development issues such as agriculture, education, health, and the private sector. The IMF began making almost all of its loans to LDCs in crisis. Indeed, when wealthy countries moved to a system of flexible, market-based exchange rates in 1971, the original purpose of the IMF ceased to exist.[34]

The Rise of Conditional Lending. A more controversial shift occurred in the 1980s and 1990s when both organizations reenvisioned their lending as a means to promote fundamental institutional and policy change throughout the less developed world. Officials at both agencies grew increasingly concerned with the fact that the same countries kept experiencing economic crises and asking for loans. For example, between 1950 and 1980, virtually every country in Latin America had requested multiple IMF loans, yet in 1982 the region became the epicenter for the developing world debt crisis.

In an attempt to fix these recurring problems, World Bank and especially IMF officials began attaching strict **conditionalities** to the loans they made. Conditionalities can be thought of as strings attached to a loan that force the borrower to change certain behaviors in order to receive the loan in the first place. Prior to the 1980s, the IMF had always attached conditionalities to its loans (the World Bank less so), but these conditionalities tended to be relatively mild. For example, borrowing governments had to promise to do things such as reduce their budget deficits, raise their interest rates, or delay certain investments, all of which were stopgap measures meant to alleviate a balance-of-payments crisis. In the 1980s and 1990s, however, these conditionalities became more encompassing and stringent. IMF officials concluded that the conditionalities they had been attaching to loans were not fundamental enough to solve the recurring, and thus seemingly structural, problems of less developed economies. World Bank officials agreed.

Under the new conditionalities, LDCs accepting an IMF loan had to consent to implement **structural adjustment programs** that required the borrowing governments to transform their domestic economic policies in important ways. The required reforms could include privatization of state-owned enterprises, deregulation of labor markets, lowering of barriers to international trade, the relaxation of price subsidies, and the opening of the capital account to foreigners. For its part, the World Bank made numerous loans to support implementation of specific pro-market policy reforms. The areas targeted by the more traditional conditionalities also came under seemingly harsher focus, with state budgets being balanced by promises to cut spending on workers in the public sector and some social priorities. For example, in 2000, an IMF loan to Ecuador stipulated that it cut teachers' salaries and stop subsidizing fuel and electricity prices.[35]

The nature of the conditionalities and structural adjustment reforms were informed by IMF and World Bank officials' near-universal preference for market-oriented solutions to underdevelopment. Most of the professional staff at both institutions had doctorates in economics and were trained in the tenets of **neoclassical economics**, a body of thought that advocated free markets over state intervention and that dominated the economics profession in the United States at the time. Officials in the two institutions largely believed that their free-market prescriptions and a reversal of the state-oriented policies adopted by most LDCs at mid-century would set their borrowers on a path to rapid economic development. IMF and World Bank staff members were also active in playing an advisory role to government officials throughout the developing world, encouraging them to adopt market-friendly measures. Both organizations also produced mountains of professional research that tended to promote neoclassical thought.

Relaxing Conditionalities. Today, the two institutions continue to play out their respective roles, but not without further changes. The 2000s was a quiet decade for the IMF, as most LDCs grew and financial crises were relatively rare. When the IMF did make loans, it did so with fewer conditionalities attached, a partial response to the long-running criticism of the practice (discussed below). The World Bank expanded its remit further by promoting gender equity and clean government through its project lending, but it too became more humble in requiring structural adjustment as part of its lending procedures.

Causes of Underdevelopment: Imposing Market Fundamentalism

Despite their seemingly humanitarian purposes, the Bretton Woods institutions are two of the most controversial international organizations in the world. The IMF, because of its greater size and scope, is a particularly frequent target of criticism.[36] The number of LDCs that have never taken an IMF loan is less than twenty. The IMF is alleged by some to be "the single most powerful non-state institution in the world," whose policies, according to geographer Richard Peet, "directly affect the economies of 185 countries and influence, sometimes drastically and often disastrously, the lives of the vast majority of the world's people."[37] What are the allegations behind the claim that the IMF and World Bank are a (and to some *the*) primary cause of ongoing poverty in the developing world?

Foisting Capitalism on the Developing World

The most widely stated and serious criticism is that both organizations blindly espouse "market fundamentalism"[38] that, through the conditionality stipulations of their loans, they impose on borrowing countries to the detriment of the poor. The conditionalities that borrowers are forced to accept with their World Bank and (especially) IMF loans are, to critics, a set of capitalist policies that yield brutal short- and long-term consequences for LDCs. In this view, IMF and World Bank conditionalities are the means by which the wealthy West pries open the less developed economies to global competition. In doing so, they also expose the poor to the savages of the free-market system by stripping them of their state-provided social protections and jobs.

The ways in which structural adjustment programs do this are manifold. The privatization of state-owned enterprises often results in the dismissal of many workers as the newly private firms streamline to become more efficient. Trade liberalization can precipitate job losses, as heightened competition from international goods leads to a restructuring of industry. Opening to inflows of foreign capital can make less developed economies more volatile. The end of price subsidies makes food staples, electricity, fuel, and other necessities more expensive. Efforts to lower deficits in government budgets can result in cuts to crucial social services, sometimes those that serve the poor. In fact, agreements have been followed by what are called IMF riots, which are protests carried out by the groups (such as state employees or beneficiaries from price subsidies) who stand to become poorer from them. Finally, systematic research by political scientist James Vreeland shows that IMF programs tend to reduce growth and increase economic inequality.[39]

Nobel laureate economist Joseph Stiglitz raises yet another economic problem stemming from the Bretton Woods institutions' market fundamentalism.[40] He argues that IMF agreements push policy fixes that heap economic pain on top of pain. The IMF often imposes higher interest rates and fiscal austerity (government spending cuts and/or tax increases) as loan conditions to address the balance-of-payments problem. These measures lessen demand for imports and presumably attract foreign investors, but they have the by-product of slowing economic growth, effectively inflicting new hardship on a country in crisis. Stiglitz claims that the IMF should preach what most wealthy countries practice when they have their own economic crises: economic stimulus. Stimulus, which was implemented by most Western countries amidst the 2008 global financial crisis, is the opposite of fiscal austerity: increases in government spending and/or lower tax rates. These measures boost aggregate demand and economic growth, mitigating the severity of an impending downturn. In overlooking this,

Stiglitz argues that the Bretton Woods institutions make bad economic situations in poor countries worse.

Critics further add that, in imposing market-friendly policies, the IMF violates the borrowing country's national sovereignty, which is its ability to set its own economic course and make political decisions without foreign influence. The IMF and World Bank hold to a stated intention of being neutral with respect to a borrowing country's internal politics, yet this is violated by mere virtue of making a loan in the first place. After all, in making a loan, they are assisting or bailing out an incumbent government, a fact that may help the incumbent's chances of remaining in power. To worsen things, the government whose life is being prolonged by an IMF loan may be a bad one, since it got the country into a crisis scenario. By way of example, Haiti received twenty IMF loans during the nearly thirty years in which it was governed, both brutally and ineptly, by François (1957–1971) and Jean-Claude Duvalier (1971–1986).[41]

Other Criticisms

As if these impositions were not enough, the means by which the Bretton Woods institutions arrive at their decisions are widely criticized as undemocratic and disadvantageous to poor countries. While all of the nearly 200 dues-paying member states have voting rights in the IMF and World Bank, it is not a case of one country, one vote. Instead, each country's vote is weighted according to its quota—that is, the amount of dues it pays, and these are roughly based on economic size. In the IMF, the votes of the nine weightiest members comprise a majority share, with the United States alone receiving a 17 percent share. (See Figure 6.5.) This is the case despite the fact that the top three members (United States, Japan, and Germany) have never even received an IMF loan. In contrast, Brazil, which has received millions of dollars in IMF loans, has just a 1.7 percent share. Moreover, by tradition the director of the IMF is European and the head of the World Bank is American. In other words, wealthy, capitalist states dominate voting and decision making in the Bretton Woods organizations, so it is no wonder that, to many critics, they impose policies that serve the interests of Western investors.

Another argument contends that both the World Bank and the IMF increase debt in the developing world since they offer mostly loans, not grants. When considering the cost of interest on the loans, borrowing countries often end up

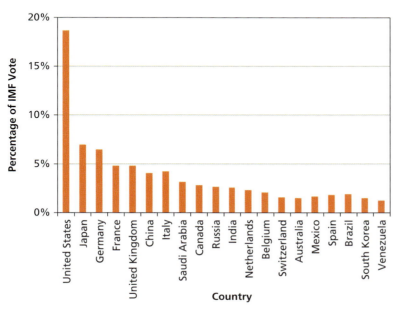

Figure 6.5 ▪ ▪ ▪ **Voting Shares of the Twenty Most Powerful Members of the IMF**

Source: International Monetary Fund, http://www.imf.org/external/np/sec/memdir/members.aspx.

repaying more than they ever received in the first place. Repayments by governments of the borrowing countries thus divert funds from more useful purposes such as social services or, at the very least, loan repayments to other types of lenders. (The IMF requires its borrowers to pay back IMF debt before servicing debts to other types of lenders.) Some critics also accuse the IMF of creating a vicious circle of ballooning debt through **defensive lending**, whereby it grants new loans to a troubled country with the sole purpose of keeping that country from missing a payment on a previous loan it took out from the IMF.

A final important criticism levied specifically at the IMF is that it creates a **moral hazard** problem that is often inherent to insurance arrangements. In general, moral hazard refers to the fact that persons or groups who are insured are more likely to engage in the risky behavior that might cause the costly or undesirable outcome for which they are insured. For example, people with car insurance might drive more recklessly, knowing that their insurance company will pay for any damage incurred from a car accident. The IMF can be thought of as an insurance provider: states pay dues to the IMF on the premise that they can get a soft loan from it in hard times. Because of this, member states might be more irresponsible with their domestic spending and stewardship of foreign currency reserves, knowing that the IMF will bail them out in the event that their behavior leads to crisis. In this way, the mere existence of the IMF and its insurance function actually increases the frequency with which balance-of-payments and other economic crises occur.

Critique: Defending the Bretton Woods Institutions

This case against the much-reviled Bretton Woods institutions is seemingly a strong one. Their proponents, however, have a number of defenses.

Loans and Conditionalities as a Choice

Proponents of the IMF and World Bank retort that the institutions do not impose austere capitalist policies on a hapless developing world. After all, IMF loan agreements are a two-way street, such that borrowing states *choose* to approach the IMF and request a loan. If the loans and their conditionalities are as harmful as critics claim, then a state is free to deal with its impending crisis on its own by seeking other lenders. The fact that so many do go to the IMF suggests that the organization plays an important role as a **lender of last resort**—that is, one that is willing to lend to states to which no one else wants to lend because of their precarious financial situations. Moreover, say IMF advocates, if states do not want to be involved with the IMF, then they are free to not engage in the irresponsible economic behaviors, such as deficit spending or inflationary monetary policy, that foment the domestic crises that lead so many to knock on its door. Similarly, the World Bank does not impose its project lending on LDC governments. Governments that do not like the conditionalities need not accept its project loans.

On top of this, the conditionalities themselves are largely a choice. Conditionalities are not a *fait accompli* once a borrowing country signs an IMF agreement or accepts World Bank financing. In actuality, the country's government must then choose to make the conditionalities part of domestic law, and history shows that many of them choose not to comply. Some studies find that IMF borrowers do not comply with more than half of all the conditions to which they agreed,[42] casting serious doubt on the standard portrayal of the organization as a violator of national sovereignty. When conditions are ignored, the organizations' only recourses are to discontinue the loan or not loan to the country in the future, but in practice they only rarely follow through on either potential threat.[43] For example, Zambia received multiple IMF loans throughout the 1980s and 1990s, each time consenting to be more upstanding with its fiscal position and even to privatize the country's vast copper reserves. However, these promises went repeatedly unfulfilled because Zambia's leaders had little commitment to implementing these reforms.[44]

Finally, when domestic leaders do choose to implement conditionalities, they are often policies that the leaders would have had to implement anyway. Faced with a budgetary or balance-of-payments crisis, states would have to implement some combination of budgets cuts, tax increases, interest rate cuts, and devaluation regardless of whether the IMF mandated them. If they did not, they would eventually run out of money to purchase imports, to pay public-sector employees, to pay for public services, and so on. According to Vreeland, having the IMF seemingly require the government to implement tough measures allows leaders in borrowing countries to blame the IFI for the promulgation of hardship-inducing policies that are nonetheless necessary.[45]

The Ethics of Conditionalities

Even if conditionalities were imposed, proponents claim that the philosophy behind them is not as troubling when viewed from a different ethical light. Again, governments that request an IMF loan are often there because they have engaged in unsustainable economic policies such as spending more than they can afford or borrowing more than they can repay. These behaviors create a short-term bubble of euphoria and growth, but eventually the bubble must burst, causing widespread hardship. Is it thus unreasonable for a lender, one who is concerned not just with the borrower's ability to repay but also with the well-being of the borrowing country's citizens, to require the borrowing government to avoid such behaviors in the future and to address the fundamental causes of the country's economic ills?

To its proponents, the IMF is like the well-heeled aunt of a profligate nephew who has a history of running up massive debts on his credit card. If the nephew asks his aunt for a personal loan to bail him out of debt, it is surely reasonable for her to expect the nephew to show signs that he will act better in the future by, say, getting a job and not overspending. Through this lens, one can interpret even the more stringent conditionalities (trade and capital account liberalization, privatization, and public sector and fiscal reform) as a means by the which the IMF is trying to combine short-term assistance with fundamental reforms that will promote long-term growth.

The Case for Market Policies

IMF and World Bank advocates also stand firmly behind the superiority of the free-market policies that were among the conditionalities they attached to loans. A fuller review of the debate and evidence regarding market-oriented reforms in the developing world appears in Chapter 8, so just a few points are in order here. The decade of the 1990s was admittedly a volatile one for many LDCs. International financial crises struck East Asia, Latin America, and the former communist bloc, and economic performance was particularly disappointing in Africa and Latin America. Not coincidentally, this decade saw the peak of international criticism of the Bretton Woods institutions.

In contrast, for much of the 2000s, the developing world has seemingly righted its ship. Most African and Latin American countries, as well as headliner states such as India and Russia, enjoyed their most successful economic decade in at least forty years and, in some cases, ever. All of these regions and countries were deeply involved with the IMF and World Bank in the recent past and implemented at least some of their market-oriented conditionalities, yet few critics attributed these recent economic successes to the Bretton Woods IFIs. In other words, critics are quick to heap blame on the IMF and World Bank when economies in the developing world sour, but few lend them praise when their free-market policies seem to yield beneficial results.

HAS FOREIGN AID MADE PAKISTAN POORER?

Pakistan, the world's sixth-largest country with a population of nearly 180 million people, has some of the worst social indicators in the world. In 2009, just 40 percent of Pakistani women were literate, and more than half had never attended school. Two-thirds of the population was below the global poverty line, with a quarter of the population living in extreme poverty. Almost half its children are malnourished.[46] On the Asian continent, Pakistan's child mortality rate is second only to Afghanistan's.[47] Twenty percent of its schools meet outside rather than in a building.[48] Given these dismal figures, it may be surprising to learn that Pakistan has been the third leading recipient of foreign aid since World War II.[49] Clearly, therefore, foreign aid is failing to develop Pakistan, and it may even be responsible for the country's ongoing economic and social underdevelopment. Table 6.1 compares some statistics on potential development causes and consequences for Pakistan with those of Sweden, one of the most generous (in terms of aid-giving as a percentage of GDP) countries in the world.

Table 6.1 **Development Comparison: Pakistan and Sweden**

Indicator	Pakistan	Sweden
GDP per capita at PPP	US$2,640	US$34,395
Human Development Index	.504	.908
Aid received/given since 1960	$29.7 billion (received)	$76.8 billion (given)
Number of political regimes since 1947	6	1
Cubic meters of freshwater per person	311	18,089

Sources: Data on GDP per capita at PPP compiled from Gapminder, www.gapminder.org; Human Development Index, http://hdr.undp.org/en/statistics/hdi/; aid received/given from Organization for Economic Co-operation and Development, International Development Statistics, *www.oecd.org/dac/stats/idsonline;* political regimes from Autocratic Regime Data, Pennsylvania State University, http://dictators.la.psu.edu/.

The West: The Failures of Aid and the IMF

If foreign aid and the Bretton Woods institutions were effective, then Pakistan would be rich today. It has received more than twenty IMF and major World Bank loans and some US$60 billion in development assistance. Why has so much money accomplished so little?

The Social Action Program Debacle. The Social Action Program (SAP) of the 1990s is a case study in foreign aid's failures. Conceived by the World Bank and assisted financially by the aid bureaucracies of Britain, the Netherlands, and the European Union, the SAP was meant to improve Pakistan's social indicators. With nearly a half billion dollars in hand, the World Bank partnered with Pakistan's provincial governments to, among other things, build health clinics and schools, provide new medical and educational materials, and train health and educational workers. The results were abysmal. Pakistan's poverty rate *grew*

HAS FOREIGN AID MADE PAKISTAN POORER?

over the ten years in which the program was active, and rates of enrollment in primary school declined.[50] In the end, the World Bank itself admitted that the project "did not achieve any of its stated key objectives."[51]

In retrospect, the SAP failed for several reasons. Adopting the misguided belief that more aid giving is inherently better, the donors were motivated merely to move money out the door and to achieve superficial and immediate objectives such as building x number of schools and training x number of workers.[52] The aid agencies involved were not incentivized to achieve more important goals such as actually teaching children some marketable skills or lowering infant mortality rates. For example, the World Bank budgeted for training health workers, but not for the salaries to employ them after training or for medical supplies to allow them to ply their newly learned skills. As if to prove how incapable it was of learning from its mistakes, in 1999 the World Bank approved another aid program to revamp Pakistan's social sector, this one of US$1 billion.

The recipients of aid were equally guilty. By having the Pakistani government shoulder an important part of the load in providing social services, the program inherited all of the shortcomings and dysfunctions of Pakistan's bureaucracy and political system. For example, using donor funds, the government "built" many health clinics and schools that existed on paper only. In 1998, the Pakistani army discovered 50,000 "ghost" schools that were funded by donors and the government but did not exist. Corrupt officials had pocketed the monies that were intended for construction and teachers' salaries.[53]

The IMF in Pakistan. Pakistan has also had deep involvement with the IMF, another potential cause of its disappointing economic performance. Since

independence, Pakistan has received more than US$10 billion in disbursement from the IMF.[54] It has had a prevailing arrangement with the IMF for more years of its existence than not, and it had one in almost every year between 1988 and 2012.[55] As one example, in 2008 the IMF agreed to give US$11 billion in loans, one of the largest agreements the IMF has ever made with an LDC, in return for the promise from Pakistan that it would implement a number of structural adjustment policies. These conditionalities, meant to lay the groundwork for sustained economic growth, included some potentially painful measures, such as a hike in interest rates, better tax collection, a new tax on agricultural incomes, and the termination of subsidies for energy and fertilizer.

All of the IMF agreements have failed to improve Pakistan's economy or to get it to change its corrupt and inefficient ways, yet they have managed to increase Pakistan's indebtedness. With each failed agreement, the IMF's response to Pakistan was to let some time pass and then to make a new loan, with many of the same hardship-provoking conditionalities, when Pakistan returned to request more money. In most instances, the impetus for the new request from Pakistan was fear that it would not be able to make a future repayment on the money it owed the IMF for previous loans. In other words, the IMF kept lending to Pakistan, even though it yielded no tangible results, simply so Pakistan could remain current on its loan repayments to . . . the IMF. Meanwhile, foreign debt mounted and social development continued to stagnate.

***

The international aid regime seems tone deaf to these failures, but is it a cause of Pakistan's poverty? Advocates of the World Bank and the IMF would retort that blaming these IFIs for Pakistani

Pakistanis protest their government's dealings with the International Monetary Fund. The IMF has been lending money to Pakistan for decades, but the loans and the reforms the IMF has urged Pakistan to adopt have produced disappointing social and economic results.

underdevelopment is like blaming doctors for illness. Sick people are more likely than healthy ones to be in the presence of a physician, just as these two IFIs are more likely to be lending to poor countries than to rich ones. This does not mean, however, that the doctors are causing illness, just as it does not mean that the World Bank and IMF are causing poverty in Pakistan or elsewhere. Pakistan often ignores the tough conditionalities attached to its loans and therefore opts not to adopt the capitalist policies it needs, according to neoclassical economists, to grow. The causes of Pakistan's poverty may thus lie within.

The South: The Worst of Continuity and Change

Economic and political institutions in Pakistan may be far more damaging to social progress than international organizations and aid. Its domestic institutions retard economic growth by exhibiting

the worst features of continuity and change. On the continuity side, local power relations, especially in rural areas, are dominated by retrograde landowners called feudals whose families' rights to plots of land date back decades (and sometimes centuries) and who inhibit economic redistribution, emergence of rule of law, and social development.[56] In some areas, feudals carry out roles typically reserved for the state. Many act as a court system, adjudicating disputes among members of their communities and sometimes even enforcing jail terms in their own personal prisons.[57] They often appoint relatives to serve as teachers and doctors without regard to merit. Some have been known to use public school buildings as their own personal possessions, utilizing them for storage or guest houses. Feudals are also notorious for opposing land redistribution and agricultural taxes (such as those required by the IMF) out of resistance not only to loss of wealth, but also to a state that would educate and modernize the indigent

HAS FOREIGN AID MADE PAKISTAN POORER?

rural populace. After all, an educated population, the feudals fear, might demand democracy and redistribution, thereby overturning the feudals' privileges.[58]

On the change side, Pakistan's national-level political system has been one of the most unstable in the world over the sixty-plus years since its independence in 1947. The instability severely dampens any efforts to advance economic productivity. Amidst a country with an extreme degree of cultural diversity—sixty different languages are spoken and dozens of ethnic groups exist—regimes often collapse in the face of factional conflict. In the first ten years of its existence, Pakistan had seven different prime ministers. This was followed by decades of see-sawing between military dictatorships and short-lived, highly corrupt civilian regimes. One government lasted for a mere thirty-nine days. The army has been in power for more than half of Pakistan's existence and still exercises considerable pull in the current civilian-led political system. This instability has had a stifling effect on investment and economic growth. Without certainty about the future, investors hesitate to be entrepreneurial, since "each change of government would throw countless private sector investment projects off course."[59]

The Natural World: The Paradox of Flooding amidst Dryness

Pakistan faces a number of natural constraints on its attempts to develop. Most importantly, it is one of the world's driest countries, and its large and rapidly growing population is making freshwater more scarce. Although tucked in the Indus River basin, Pakistan's rugged, mountainous terrain has relatively little rainfall. Just a quarter of its land is

cultivated, and this land requires major irrigation efforts to make it fertile. It draws much of the irrigation from underground, but doing so is exhausting Pakistan's groundwater. In some places, the surface of the groundwater is now 1,000 feet below ground and continuing to fall at ten feet per year. In the 1950s, Pakistan had 5,000 cubic meters of available freshwater per person. Today that number is down to 1,000, and two-fifths of Pakistanis lack safe drinking water. The problem is only going to get worse: global warming is melting the Himalayan glaciers that feed the Indus River, and this could reduce the water supply by another 30 to 40 percent.[60]

Paradoxically, dry Pakistan has recently struggled with massive floods that may have been caused by global warming. Although human-caused climate change is likely to make Pakistan even drier, it will make what rainfall it has more intense. In 2010, a fifth of the country's land area was flooded by overflow of the Indus River, killing 1,700 and affecting 20 million. A year later, one wet season's worth of rain fell in a single day, affecting about 5 million people, including many who were displaced from the previous flood. Aside from these human costs, the economic costs of each flood were vast.[61]

***

Good intentions have not been enough for Pakistan. The West has showered it with aid, but good news on the development front has been rare. Is it fair, however, to blame this benevolence for Pakistan's social and economic ills? Pakistan's own political leadership has been lackluster, and nature has not cooperated by sending natural disasters. In the end, Pakistan's future trajectory will surely depend on a combination of factors associated with the West, the South, and the natural world.

Thinking Critically about Development

- What measures, if any, could be taken to make aid and soft loans to Pakistan more effective? Or should all forms of aid be ceased entirely?

- If Pakistan had received no development assistance or IMF loans since independence, what would its economy and society look like today?

- Is Pakistan's political instability a cause or a result of its poverty?

 ## Key Terms

absorptive capacity, p. 140

aid agency, p. 132

aid dependency, p. 141

aid effectiveness, p. 137

big push, p. 142

bilateral aid, p. 132

Bretton Woods institutions, p. 144

conditionalities, p. 146

debt relief, p. 132

defensive lending, p. 149

donor fragmentation, p. 140

foreign aid, p. 132

fungible, p. 141

Heavily Indebted Poor Countries (HIPCs) initiative, p. 135

International Monetary Fund (IMF), p. 144

lender of last resort, p. 149

Millennium Development Goals (MDGs), p. 135

moral hazard, p. 149

multilateral aid, p.132

neoclassical economics, p. 146

soft loans, p. 132

structural adjustment program, p. 146

tied aid, p. 139

World Bank, p. 144

Suggested Readings

Easterly, William. *The Elusive Quest for Growth: Economists Adventures and Misadventures in the Tropics*. Cambridge: MIT Press, 2001.

———. *The White Man's Burden: Why the West's Efforts to Aid the Rest Have Done So Much Ill and So Little Good*. New York: Penguin, 2006.

Lancaster, Carol. *Foreign Aid: Diplomacy, Development, Domestic Politics*. Chicago: University of Chicago Press, 2006.

Moyo, Dambisa. *Dead Aid: Why Aid Is Not Working and How There Is a Better Way for Africa*. New York: Farrar, Straus and Giroux, 2009.

Sachs, Jeffrey. *The End of Poverty: Economic Possibilities for Our Time*. New York: Penguin, 2005.

Stiglitz, Joseph. *Globalization and its Discontents*. New York: W. W. Norton and Company, 2002.

@ | Web Resources

AidData, www.aiddata.org/content/index

International Monetary Fund, www.imf.org

Millennium Development Goals Indicators, http://mdgs.un.org/unsd/mdg/Default.aspx

Organisation for Economic Co-operation and Development, Aid Statistics, www.oecd.org/dac/aidstatistics/

US Aid, www.usaid.org

World Bank, www.worldbank.org

A Vietnamese couple gets married in a Confucian ceremony. Vietnam's economy, like those elsewhere in East Asia, has been booming in recent decades. The rise of so many East Asian economies has prompted some scholars to suggest that Confucian values promote economic growth.

Culture and Identity

Baghdad, the capital of Iraq, was once a proud and thriving city. For a few centuries around 900 CE, it was the world's largest city. As a trading and cultural hub for the Arab and Islamic worlds, it had a diverse population and the nickname "Center of Learning" because of its high-quality educational institutions. For centuries, Baghdad was central to Islam's Golden Age (roughly 750 to 1250), a period when Islamic peoples led the world in scientific and artistic advances while Europe languished in the Middle Ages. Yet Baghdad, much like the surrounding Arab world, has struggled since Europe began its Industrial Revolution. By 1900, the West had left it far behind in terms of human development and then piled on the humiliation during the subsequent century by colonizing and invading Baghdad on multiple occasions.

Is the culture of Baghdadis to blame for the city's inability to achieve sustainable human development? Baghdad is dotted with some of the world's most beautiful mosques, yet observers have argued that the adherence of Baghdadis to the conservative traditions of Islam leads them to reject the technological, scientific, and cultural advances that economic growth requires. Alternatively, perhaps it is the cultural divisions within the Baghdadi community that weigh so heavily on its economic advance. Baghdad, once a diverse and integrated place known as the "City of Peace," saw an outburst of interethnic violence between its Shia and Sunni populations in the wake of the 2003 U.S. invasion. A rapid process of segregation occurred through massive internal relocations, and today neighborhoods are almost exclusively Shia or Sunni. Lines of communication and exchange across the ethnic divide have broken down.

This chapter focuses on a body of thought—one with a long pedigree in social science—that claims that culture matters for prosperity. These arguments look at norms and behaviors among the masses, many of them influenced by religion, as the fundamental causes of social and economic development. The chapter also considers a newer body of thought that attributes underdevelopment to cultural divisions within a society.

Understanding Culture and Social Identity

Culture is the shared set of norms, beliefs, and recurring practices of people in a society. Culture largely refers to values and behaviors that exist among the masses, as opposed to the values and behaviors of rulers and other elites or the policies and institutions that elites create. Culture is learned, imbued into individuals through various agents of socialization such as family, friends, mass media, religious institutions, and other organizations. Most scholarly treatments of culture see it as a relatively stable phenomenon, changing only gradually over the course of decades or even centuries. A society's culture encompasses a wide variety of psychological and behavioral orientations—everything from food preferences to the status of children in the family. Given the breadth of this definition and the diversity of cultures in the developing world, this chapter could not possibly summarize the many non-Western cultural traditions. Instead, it will focus on a few aspects of culture that, according to numerous social scientists, are logically germane to notions of human development and economic growth.

Social Identity

A crucial element of culture is social or group identity. Social identity is the part of a person's self-understanding that stems from her or his membership in a group of people that is larger than the immediate family. Social identities

include things such as race, ethnicity, nationality, and religion. These types of social identity (defined in Table 7.1), along with two major scholarly perspectives on social identity, are described in this subsection.

Primordialism versus Constructivism. Two schools of thought exist on the nature of group identity. The primordial perspective sees group identities as being implanted into individuals through socialization in early childhood and, as a result, impervious to subsequent change throughout the life cycle. The identities that individuals develop through this process play to humanity's biological and largely subconscious need to belong to groups and, in belonging, to hold a certain distance from or even distaste for persons not in the same group.[1] Given the largely unconscious roots of identities and prejudice, primordialist scholars often see group attachments and intergroup conflict as revolving around immutable and genetically determined physical differences such as skin color. Centuries-old religious, linguistic, or territorial identities and mutual distastes, such as those that exist between Muslim Palestinians and Jewish Israelis, are also assumed to be imbued automatically into the individuals born into the groups that hold them.

Table 7.1	The Major Types of Social Identity
Social Identity Type	**Description**
Race	A group identity based on some biologically determined and easily observed physical traits that society has deemed to be of social significance.
Ethnicity	A group identity rooted in shared history, values, and practices.
Nationality	A group with a shared identity that also has or wishes to have specific political rights or even full political and territorial sovereignty for itself.
Religion	A set of beliefs, moral codes, rituals, symbols, and supporting organizations that relate humanity to spirituality.

How do I belong?

In contrast, a constructivist approach sees identities as more malleable, resulting from choices by individuals and socializing agents. All individuals have multiple potential group-identifying markers at their disposal: their nationality, skin color, religion, ethnicity, gender, language group, state of residence, place of origin, and so on. As a result, they may choose to emphasize different ones in different contexts or at different stages of their life cycle. To a constructivist, it is social agents such as politicians and other leaders rather than biological processes that play the primary role in determining which markers become the basis for group identity and conflict. **Stereotypes**, meaning the oversimplifying narratives about group members' characteristics, are also constructed by social agents. In sum, constructivists treat identities and perceptions of groups as socially crafted and therefore flexible. A constructivist take on the Israeli–Palestinian divide would note that there is nothing immutable about this conflict. Jews and Palestinians have lived side by side for centuries, and it was only in the twentieth century that political leaders and events shaped these group identities into their current lines of conflict.

types of identities

Race. One example of this distinction between the primordial and constructivist approaches lies in the concept of race. A **race** is a category of persons who share some biologically determined and easily observed physical traits (such as skin color, facial structure, and hair type) that society has deemed to be of social significance. In the nineteenth and early twentieth centuries, most scholarly conceptions of race were primordial, treating race as the major biological divisions of humankind. Scholars delineated humans into a fixed and finite number of genetically differentiated races or even subspecies of humanity, such as black, white, and yellow. Today, this taxonomic conceptualization has been largely abandoned for a constructivist notion that sees race as more fluid and subject to

human interpretation. For example, blonde- and brown-haired persons are physically distinct from one another, just as are white-skinned and black-skinned people. Yet societies such as the United States have tended to craft more binding identities and prejudices around the black and white skin-color markers, rather than the blonde and brown hair-color ones. In other words, blonde is not a race because the physical distinction is not of social significance. Black and white are races in the United States because of their long-running political, economic, and social import.

Ethnicity. Another commonly held social identity is **ethnicity**, which is a group identity rooted in shared history, values, and practices. Most frequently, the shared history of an ethnic group is based on a common ancestry and territorial origin, such as Irish American. In turn, ongoing practices (such as a distinct language, religion, or set of cultural traditions) serve to reinforce ethnic identity. Tibetan is an example of an ethnic identity. Tibetans recognize a shared ancestry and historical homeland in Tibet, practice the religion of Tibetan Buddhism, and speak the language of Tibetan. In China, where most Tibetans reside, these cultural markers distinguish Tibetans since members of other Chinese ethnic groups speak wholly different languages and pursue distinct religious traditions. For example, few Han Chinese, the world's largest ethnic group at 90 percent of the Chinese population, speak Tibetan. These lines of distinction, especially between Tibetans and the Han Chinese majority, create and reinforce Tibetan identity.

Some ethnic groups in the developing world are **indigenous** (also called first peoples). Although a difficult concept to define, indigenous ethnic groups typically have at least some of the following characteristics: their ancestors occupied a given territory before the ancestors of any other surviving groups in their country, they continue to live on or near these ancestral lands, and they carry on cultural traditions rooted in this ances-tral past. The cultural markers of indigenous peoples often include a language and spirituality that are distinct from those prevailing elsewhere in their country, and indigenous economies are often organized around local agricultural and hunter-gathering activities. The developing world contains hundreds of indigenous ethnic groups and hundreds of millions of indigenous persons, including the Yanomami in Brazil and Venezuela, the Vedda of Sri Lanka, and the Akha of Southeast Asia.

3 Nationalism. Ethnicity is distinct from a third type of social identity: nation or **nationality**. The ideas of nation, nationality, and nationalism combine group identity with claims to political institutions that correspond specifically to the group. When a group with a shared identity also has or wishes to have specific political rights or even full political and territorial sovereignty for itself, it is a nation or a nationality. Today, most nations and nationalities do have political and territorial sovereignty over themselves in the form of a modern state. Brazilian and Japanese are examples of nationalities for which a corresponding state exists. This illustrates why many social scientists see the term **nation-state** as a more descriptive and useful one than the term "country." Most modern countries combine a nation, a psychologically shared adherence among the citizenry, with a corresponding political structure or state. Not all nations, however, have their own territorially circumscribed state. A common example of a nation without a state is the Kurdish nationality, a group of 30 million people who live across northern Iraq, southeastern Turkey, northeastern Syria, and northwestern Iran. Kurds are an ethnicity based on their distinct language and ancestry. They are also a nation because most Kurds aspire to have a singular sovereign state just for the Kurdish people in the territory in which they currently reside.

Nationalism refers to a group's shared feelings and expressions of national identity. The term is often reserved for instances when these sentiments are particularly intense and even exclusive. To illustrate, American patriotism is a nationalist sentiment, since it invokes feelings of goodwill and belongingness not just to a group (the U.S. population), but also to an extant state and territory. Yet the term "nationalism" is heard most frequently in reference to more fervent national identities that include a defense of existing political rights or a claim to political rights that do not yet exist. Tibetans in China again provide an example. For the cultural reasons described above, Tibetan is an ethnicity. But Tibetans have for the past several decades also made political demands of the Chinese state that range from greater autonomy (self-rule) over themselves and their territory to secession from China through the formation of a new Tibetan nation-state. The sentiments that drive these claims are called Tibetan nationalism.

4 Religion. A final social identity type of major importance is religion. A **religion** is a set of beliefs, moral codes, rituals, symbols, and supporting organizations that relate humanity to spirituality and the supernatural. Religions are particularly important because, aside from being a source of social identity, they provide explicit guidance about proper behavior and goals for the current life. Table 7.2 reports the percentage of citizens in five world regions and China that adhere to various religions.

Broadly speaking, four major religions can be found in the developing world: Buddhism, Christianity, Hinduism, and Islam. Christianity, and in particular Roman Catholicism, is the leading religion in Latin America, and rates of adherence to Christianity have risen gradually in sub-Saharan Africa over the past century. Islam is dominant throughout North Africa, the Middle East, and the northern parts of sub-Saharan Africa. For example, the northern halves of Ghana and Nigeria have mostly Muslim populations. Some countries in South Asia (Bangladesh and Pakistan) and

Table 7.2  **Religious Affiliation in the Developing World (as a percentage of population)**

Country/Region	Largest Religion	Second-Largest Religion
China	Agnostic or atheist (40 percent)	Chinese folk religion (30 percent)
East Asia and Pacific (without China)	Islam (37 percent)	Buddhism (27 percent)
Latin America	Roman Catholic (80 percent)	Protestant (9 percent)
Middle East and North Africa	Islam (90 percent)	Christian (7 percent)
South Asia	Hindu (56 percent)	Islam (32 percent)
Sub-Saharan Africa	Christian (59 percent)	Islam (29 percent)

Source: Compiled from the Association of Religious Data Archives, www.thearda.com/Archive

Southeast Asia (Indonesia and Malaysia) have Muslim majorities. Hinduism is widely practiced in India and Nepal, and Buddhism predominates in the non-Muslim countries of Southeast Asia. China is the one major country where relatively few citizens practice any of these four religions. Most Chinese citizens are either secular, following the official atheistic stance of the ruling Chinese Communist Party, or they practice Chinese folk religions that overlap with Taoism.

Aside from these major religions, a number of important philosophical worldviews comprise important elements of culture and identity in the developing world. Most notable are animism and Confucianism, which are not formal religions because they do not have supporting organizations and institutions. Animism is the belief that a spiritual world imbues and controls the physical and human world. It is a central component of folk traditions in sub-Saharan Africa, and many Africans who are formally classified as Christian adhere more to traditional animist beliefs. Confucianism, a worldview grounded in the teachings of the ancient Chinese philosopher Confucius (551–479 BCE), is an important part of East Asian and especially Chinese culture. A few of these philosophical worldviews are described in greater detail later in the chapter.

Other Cultural Traits

National cultures can be characterized by the nature of their social identities, but social scientists have also pinpointed other important attitudinal or psychological orientations that constitute part of a country's culture. One is how religious or secular the people of a country are. Identifying a society as Catholic, Hindu, or Muslim is one thing, but specifying the extent to which religion and belief in the supernatural structure everyday behavior and outlooks about the current life is another. For this, scholars use the terms "secularity" and "religiosity" to refer to the extent to which persons adhere to religious practices and believe that supernatural forces influence daily life. In general, rates of secularity are lower (and religiosity higher) in less developed countries than in developed ones. For example, in a 2006–2007 survey, 85 percent of Indonesians and 90 percent of Zambians described themselves as "a religious person." In contrast, 41 percent of Norwegians and 43 percent of Germans did so.[2]

Another such cultural trait is the degree of trust among persons who are strangers or not of the same family. Formally defined, **interpersonal trust** exists when an individual has expectations about future actions from other individuals that move her or him to rely on them. As with religiosity, there is a strong relationship between economic prosperity and the degree of interpersonal trust in a society. Wealthy countries have more trusting citizens than do less developed ones. Figure 7.1 gives some evidence from public opinion surveys for this relationship.

Causes of Underdevelopment: The Culturalist School

An important line of scholarly thought known as the **culturalist school** locates the fundamental causes of a society's poverty or prosperity in the shared norms, beliefs, values, and attitudes of its common citizens. These cultural explanations for underdevelopment have come in a wide variety of forms.

Max Weber and the Protestant Ethic

The most well-known and first modern culturalist explanation is *The Protestant Ethic and the Spirit of Capitalism*, a book written by German sociologist Max Weber in 1904 and 1905. Weber pointed out that after the Protestant Reformation of the early 1500s, Protestant Northern Europe grew wealthier than Europe's Catholic regions. The reason for this divergence, he argued, was cultural. Catholics held to traditional attitudes that valued leisure and consumption, while Protestants were instilled with a work ethic and an ascetic ideal that motivated them to achieve unprecedented wealth accumulation under capitalism.

Weber located the source of these different cultural orientations in the contrasting theological teachings of the two denominations. The Roman Catholic Church guaranteed salvation to all of its parishioners so long as they respected priestly authority and received the sacraments. This lent a comforting degree of certainty to Catholics about their eternal fate. In contrast, Protestants had far greater doubts about their personal salvation status, which led them to work harder than Catholics. Inspired by Calvinist doctrine, many Protestant churches of the time preached predestination, which is the notion that humans play no role in determining their salvation since God long ago decided who will be damned and who will be saved. Protestant parishioners thus carried around a nagging fear of eternal damnation, even if they were morally upright, faithful churchgoers. As a result, they sought palpable signs from their daily lives to reassure themselves that they were among the ranks of the saved. One such sign was the successful pursuit of a vocational calling, hence the "Protestant work ethic." To Weber, Protestants carried out their

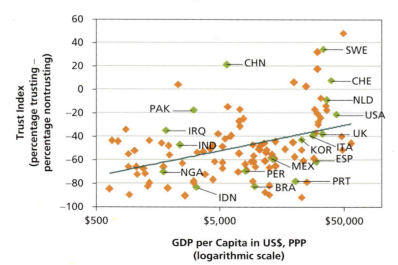

Figure 7.1 ■ ■ ■ **The Relationship between Interpersonal Trust and GDP per Capita**

Sources: World Values Survey, Latinobarómetro, Globalbarometer, East-Asian barometer, ASEP/JDS, http://www.jdsurvey.net/jds/jdsurveyMaps.jsp?Idioma=I&SeccionTexto=0404&NOID=104.

Note: The question wording was usually as follows: "Generally speaking, would you say that most people can be trusted or that you need to be very careful in dealing with people?"

The fear of eternal damnation
forced protestants to work harder.
difference in cultural theology

Culture and Identity   165

work with an underlying religious fervor to quell their fears of eternal damnation; leisure and financial failure were "symptomatic of a lack of grace."[3] Moreover, Puritanical ascetic teachings chastised Protestants for squandering their earnings on luxury goods and carnal experiences, so they were more likely to save and invest. To summarize, Weber saw Protestants' theological beliefs as driving them to carry out the hard work and investment that made Northern Europe wealthier than the Catholic parts of Europe.

Weber's writings on religion and capitalist success did not only look at Europe. Of greater relevance to the developing world were his claims about the nature of prosperity in Confucian, Hindu, and other societies. In *The Religion of China*, Weber argued that capitalist growth failed to thrive in China because Confucianism shuns active work for personal extravagance and enrichment.[4] Confucians thus did not engage in their work with the same intensity and sense of purpose as Protestants. In *The Religion of India*, he attributed India's underdevelopment to the Hindu caste system.[5] The caste system is one of strict social stratification based on hereditary groupings. In the strictest form of the caste system, one is born into not just an immutable social status, but also an occupational calling. This gives little hope of moving upward in caste, even with hard work and skill acquisition. Fulfillment of one's occupational caste obligations is pious, with hope of advancement saved for subsequent lives. To Weber, this imbued Hindus with a fatalistic traditionalism that prevented capitalist development. Confucian + Hindu
teachings also do

Modernization Theory   not encourage
tedious work.

Fifty years after Weber wrote *Protestant Ethic*, a body of thought that also emphasized cultural values as a cause of societal prosperity emerged within U.S. social science circles. **Modernization theory** ended up dominating academic thinking on underdevelopment for decades, peaking in influence in the 1950s, 1960s, and 1970s. During that time, it was the leading alternative to dependency theory (discussed in Chapter 5) among scholars writing on the developing world.

Modernization theory had numerous adherents and disciplinary strains, so it defies simple summary. Nonetheless, fundamental to all conceptions of modernization theory was the notion that societies fall somewhere on a continuum that runs (in the words of adherents to the theory) from "traditional" or "backwards" on one extreme to "modern" on the other. (See Figure 7.2.) Modernization intrinsic theorists held that traditional societies feature a differences number of cultural, institutional, and behavioral characteristics that are at the root of their poverty. For example, social status in traditional societies is ascriptive and assigned mostly through heredity, making for a strict hierarchy and a low degree of social mobility. To modernization theorists, traditional societies are also atomized into small and tightly knit familial groups that do little to communicate or empathize with one another. Power relations are arranged in a hierarchical way, meaning subordinate persons yield deferentially to authority and are inordinately prone to extremes in political ideology.[6] Binding political decisions are made by rulers in an arbitrary and ad hoc way. Religiosity is high and worldviews are ascientific, shaped by the irrationalities of folklore and ancient scriptures. Economies feature subsistence production and little division of labor, a problem reinforced by the lack of exchange among social groups. Education and labor-market skills are minimal, and individuals are suspicious of change.

In contrast, modernization theory viewed modern societies as possessing a wholly different palate of cultural and institutional forms. In modern societies, social status is meritocratic, determined by an individual's achievement and thus providing for a high degree of social mobility. The nuclear family is relevant but deeply embedded in societal structures, lending individuals an empathy and connection with a wider collective. Politics is pluralistic and participatory, and the rule of law prevails. The dominant worldview is secular and grounded in rational scientific thought. Economies feature high

Figure 7.2 ▪ ▪ ▪ The Modernization Theory Continuum

Traditional Society

- Social status determined arbitrarily
- Hierarchical governance
- Religious and superstitious worldview
- Limited interaction across families and tribes
- Little economic specialization

Modern Society

- Social status determined by merit
- Pluralistic governance
- Secular, scientific worldview
- Strong social connections among nonrelatives
- Sharp division of labor

rates of specialization, backed by an abundance of labor-market skills. The dominant group in society is the middle class, which has high rates of formal education and is politically moderate. Individuals are open to innovation and change.

To most modernization theorists, countries could evolve out of traditional society and poverty by rejecting the traditional worldview and adopting the cultural norms and social behaviors of modern societies. Stated differently and more controversially, LDCs were poor because they had the "wrong" culture, and they could overcome their backwardness by adopting the culture of the West. Modernization theorists thus interpreted development as movement on a path from tradition to modernity, with traditional societies needing to follow the same path previously followed by the West itself. As this modernization occurred in a country, all aspects of its society—politics, economics, social relations—would be jointly transformed, gradually converging toward institutions, values, and ways of life that resembled those prevailing in the modern Western societies. Western countries themselves could help along this transition to modernity by exposing traditional societies to their culture through channels such as foreign aid, study-abroad opportunities, trade, and investment.

To be sure, modernization theory as a collective body of thought differed from Weber in that it did not place sole emphasis on mass psychological orientations as the cause of economic underdevelopment. Some scholars within the tradition did,[7] but others saw cultural values as part of a broader suite of factors that included societal institutions and elite governance. To these thinkers, this suite of factors caused, was caused by, and was symptomatic of economic underdevelopment. Still, mass values and worldviews played a more central role in modernization theory than they did in most theories of economic underdevelopment.

Social Capital and Trust

Modernization theory had fallen out of favor in most academic disciplines by the 1980s, due in part to growing distaste with its underpinnings of Western cultural superiority. Cultural explanations for development, however, experienced a new lease on life in the 1990s with the emergence of two strains of research, one on social capital and the other (discussed in the next subsection) a return to Weberian arguments on religion and national culture.

Biggest problem of culturalist school

The first strain is research on interpersonal trust and social capital. **Social capital** is the benefit a group or society receives from the ability of its members to trust each other and cooperate with one another. Most scholars who study social capital claim that, for there to be prosperity, individuals in a society need a wide "radius of trust," or one that encompasses strangers and people across lines of difference.[8] Sociologist Mark Granovetter calls this the presence of "weak ties," meaning trusting relationships and contacts among people who are not close friends and family.[9]

The existence of trust among nonfamily members and strangers boosts prosperity because it dramatically lowers the costs of economic exchange, thereby expanding the scope of markets and the degree of specialization that can be realized. Trust applies an informal grease to the wheels of economic exchange. If two individuals do not trust one another, then their fears that the other will betray them will prevent them from exchanging with one another, even if the act is as simple as paying for a good or service. The one exception is if a third party such as a state or local strongman can effectively enforce terms to which the two individuals agree. However, if this is the only means by which exchange can take place, then it becomes extremely expensive for individuals in a society to do so on a recurring basis. In short, trust is needed to make markets work cheaply and effectively.

The claim that interpersonal trust is necessary for economic progress is widely accepted, but analysts in the culturalist school take this observation a step further. They claim that a society's level of trust and social capital is a largely fixed psychological and social orientation that determines how wealthy it is. As political scientist Frances Fukuyama puts it, "A nation's well-being . . . is conditioned by a single, pervasive cultural characteristic: the level of trust inherent in the society."[10] Fukuyama and Robert Putnam popularized this view in the 1990s.[11] Fukuyama sees societies as inherently high-trust ones or low-trust ones. For example, he claims that deeply

rooted in China's cultural history is a familism that makes it a low-trust, and thus relatively poor, society. The Chinese exhibit exceedingly high levels of trust among family members, but families are highly insular and do not extend their trust outside the family. One concrete cost of this is that China struggles to raise small, family-run businesses to a larger scale, since such businesses do not like hiring nonfamily members. Similarly, Putnam argues that northern Italians have higher incomes than southern Italians because northerners have deeper norms of trust and reciprocity. Putnam argues that the north's richer associational life was forged as much as 800 years ago and still explains its higher level of wealth today.

Religion and National Culture

The second strain of research that emerged in the 1990s draws on the Weberian tradition of finding traits in religious beliefs and national cultures that are more or less conducive to economic growth. Although different scholars within this tradition have varying emphases, the traits they collectively deem to be conducive to economic progress are reminiscent of those mentioned by Weber and modernization theory: hardworking, thrifty, willing to delay gratification, open to change, accepting of risk, admiring of achievement over ascription, empathic of the collective beyond the family, secular, and scientifically minded.[12]

Asian Values. One of the most important claims within this vein is the **Asian values** argument.[13] Its proponents argue that East Asians have a Confucianist cultural heritage that caused the various economic growth miracles in the region during the second half of the twentieth century. These miracles were Japan's; then those of the newly industrialized countries (Hong Kong, Singapore, South Korea, Taiwan); then the slightly less dramatic ones in Malaysia and Thailand; then most recently the one in China. According to the argument, the most relevant Confucianist value is the subordination of individual needs and welfare to those of the family and society. Order, social harmony, and deference to one's superiors are strongly preferred to individual extravagance, nonconformity, and attention-getting behavior. Personal sacrifice and effort to further the good of the broader collective are particularly praiseworthy, while personal failings or even complaining bring shame to oneself and one's family.

Advocates of the Asian values argument, who include the father of Singapore's economic boom, Prime Minister Lee Kuan Yew (1959–1990), link these cultural traits to successful economic performance through a number of channels.[14] Confucian values encourage thriftiness and high savings rates. The distaste for conspicuous spending on luxuries and the pride of striving for collective, not personal, welfare made it easy to mobilize East Asians to work hard and to save, which provided precious funds for capital investment.[15] For example, South Koreans saved 35 percent of the country's GDP in 1989, while the equivalent figure in Latin America was in the single digits. Even today, China is fueling its boom with one of the highest savings rates in the world. Moreover, the privileging of conformity and social harmony, as well as the respect for authority and social hierarchy, kept industrial strife to a minimum. During their takeoff periods, workers in South Korea and China were willing to accept relatively low wages and not strike since, according to the argument, they knew revenues were being plowed into investment for the welfare of the greater society.

New Claims about Religion and Prosperity. New arguments about the religious roots of underdevelopment in the Middle East, Latin America, India, and sub-Saharan Africa have also emerged in recent years. Islam has been particularly scrutinized by culturalists as a source of the Middle East's delayed development. Historian David Landes argues that, in contrast to Europe's centuries-long openness to scientific and technological innovation, Islamic culture has been resistant to change since the Industrial Revolution began.

Traditional social norms push Muslims to be skeptical of change and progress, he says, and their rivalry with and distaste for the West makes them hesitant to accept technological innovations that originate therein.[16] For example, starting in the fifteenth century, the largely Muslim Ottoman Empire rejected the printing press for three centuries. Moreover, Islam makes its followers fatalistic. After all, the meaning of the term "Islam" is "submission to God," so Landes sees Muslims as relatively indifferent to their earthly well-being. Islamic education also emphasizes rote learning and discourages critical thinking, severely limiting the availability of skills in the labor force.[17] Landes also claims that Islam's ongoing espousal of homebound roles for women limits half the population's potential contributions to human development. Finally, the charging of formal interest (usury or *riba*) is disallowed in much of the Islamic world due to its prohibition (according to some interpretations) in the Koran. This proscription discourages lending and thus capital accumulation.

For Latin America, recent arguments are similar to those of Weber's original thesis. Lawrence Harrison argues that, with the onset of colonization by the Portuguese and Spaniards 500 years ago, Latin America gradually became imbued with a quasifeudal Catholic Iberian culture that has been inimical to economic progress even to this day.[18] In particular, many of the religious values propagated by the Roman Catholic Church bleed over into citizens' orientations about work and material success. For example, the Catholic Church structure is hierarchical, so Latin American societies are also hierarchical. To Harrison, Latin Americans do not see merit, education, and achievement as the means to success; they instead fatalistically accept the economic status to which they are ascribed at birth. The strong sense of fatalism is reinforced by the Catholic Church's, and thus the Latin American population's, unscientific focus on the afterlife and relative indifference toward success in the current life. This keeps citizens in a conservative mindset, valuing the status quo rather than a future where risk, intelligence, and innovation are seen as a means to personal advancement. For this reason, Harrison adds, leisure is preferred over work, a fact that makes Latin Americans blow any income windfalls on lavish luxury items rather than saving it. As evidence, Latin American countries often have some of the lowest savings rates in the world.

A final culturalist viewpoint draws from the fact that sub-Saharan Africa's animist tradition has been surprisingly resilient in the face of modern Christian and Islamic proselytizing. According to economist Daniel Etounga-Manguelle, animism and widespread belief in the supernatural make Africans inherently fatalistic and submissive to events, not goal-oriented and committed to shaping their own lives and futures. Etounga-Manguelle says, "The world and [Africans'] behavior are an immutable given, bequeathed in a mythical past to our founding ancestors, whose wisdom continues to illuminate our life principles. The African remains enslaved by his environment. Nature is his master and sets his destiny."[19] This viewpoint holds that fatalism makes Africans hesitant to accept uncertainty, to take entrepreneurial risk, and to save. Animism also enables African leaders and elites to credibly claim divine authority or even magical powers, with citizens in turn doing little to demand better governance or a reshuffling of social standing and power relations. Finally, Etounga-Manguelle argues that Africans are community oriented and fail to value individual achievement and criticism of the collective will.

Critique of Culturalist Claims

Despite their reemergence in recent decades, culturalist explanations for underdevelopment are not widely adhered to by political scientists, economists, and sociologists. Their logic can often seem compelling: it is tempting to view the beliefs and habits of the poor population as the root cause of their poverty. Ultimately,

however, criticism of the approach comes from a wide variety of theoretical and political perspectives.

→ easy to blame poor people

Culture as Consequence, Not Cause

The vast majority of political scientists and economists see culturalist explanations for poverty as highly misguided. Most scholars of development in these fields believe that states that can erect the right policies and institutions can incentivize people, regardless of their culture, to pursue productive activities and, in doing so, increase societal prosperity. (Some of these arguments are the focus of chapters 8 through 10.) In this line of thought, cultural values that are alleged to be a brake on economic progress in the less developed world (poor work ethic, spendthrift outlook, mistrust, fatalism, reticence to accept risk and innovation) are a result of bad political leadership and suboptimal economic institutions and policies. In other words, culture is a result of economic and political context, not a cause of it. Figure 7.3 contrasts the

Figure 7.3 ■ ■ ■ **The Cause-and-Effect Relationship between Culture and Prosperity in Two Schools of Thought**

Culturalist View

Cultural Traits

Economic Prosperity

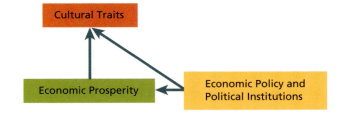

Mainstream View in Economics and Political Science

Cultural Traits

Economic Prosperity

Economic Policy and Political Institutions

different notions of cause and effect between the culturalist view and the mainstream economics and political science view.

A number of examples illustrate this critique of culturalist claims. First, if the poor in LDCs save less, it is surely because they must spend a higher share of their income on consumption to survive. Furthermore, most LDCs do not even offer the poor an opportunity to save in formal financial institutions, as banks do not want to provide deposit services to them. Second, if LDC citizens are less trusting of others, it is probably because they reside in places with higher rates of elite corruption, street crime, and political violence. On top of this, legal systems fail to protect their rights in the event of theft or a dispute, making them more hesitant to trust and engage in economic exchange with strangers.[20] The family unit is so much stronger than linkages among nonfamily members because the poor must rely more on extended family for economic sustenance. Third and finally, fatalism among the poor is probably less a result of particular religious worldviews and more a psychological mechanism for coping with a harsh reality.

Mischaracterizing Culture in LDCs

Many critics go a step further and claim that culturalists' depictions of culture in the developing world are themselves inaccurate. To critics, the notion that peoples in the developing world are poor because they lack a work ethic is highly dubious. Billions carry out back-breaking agricultural work or menial factory tasks, and most do it for longer hours than citizens in the developed world. For example, Latin American workers actually work more hours per year than do those in Western Europe and the United States.[21] (See Figure 7.4.) Moreover, for many tasks, those in the developing world must work much harder than people in the developed world to achieve the same ends. Contrast fetching water from a few

kilometers away with turning on a water faucet, or gathering fuel wood versus flipping a switch on the stove. According to dependency theorists and other critics on the political left, culturalist claims about poor work ethics in the global South are a case of blaming the victim since these scholars see workers in LDCs as having most of the fruits of their hard labor extracted via global exploitation.

Critics also question the prevalence of two other traits that culturalists allege to be widespread in LDCs. First, the notion that LDC citizens lack entrepreneurial spirit is belied by the sheer number of them who run their own businesses in the informal sector. The number of small-business owners as a share of the population is actually far greater in countries such as Brazil, Ecuador, Egypt, and India than in the United States.[22] Poor entrepreneurs actually must be more accepting of risk than rich-world ones because a failure of their business ventures can yield utter destitution and even death. Second, the notion that the poor in LDCs are less thrifty may also be false. Maintaining a steady level of consumption in the face of volatile income flows requires a certain degree of saving, which many do by stashing money around the home or harboring extra money with a friend. The poor also save in seemingly hidden ways such as harboring livestock instead of slaughtering them, or maintaining their home. According to Peruvian economist Hernando de Soto, "The value of savings among the poor is, in fact, immense—forty times all the foreign aid received throughout the world since 1945."[23] All told, these examples suggest that poverty is not a result of people not working hard or not saving, but rather a failure of their society to channel their hard work and savings into high productivity.

To illustrate this criticism further, it is worth revisiting the culturalist interpretation of the Muslim world's underdevelopment. Recall that Landes and other culturalists criticize Islamic teachings and culture for fomenting an inherently conservative worldview among the masses. This worldview allegedly causes Muslims to reject productivity-enhancing technologies and ideas, especially those originating in the West.[24] Some culturalists also cite the Muslim prohibition on the charging of interest as a reason why the Arab world struggles to accumulate capital. Problems with this argument about Islamic culture are multiple.[25] It often confuses the preferences of many Muslim leaders with those of the citizens they rule. For example, it is true that the Ottoman Empire rejected crucial technologies, as evidenced by Sultan Bayezid II's rejection in 1485 of the printing press. This was a choice, however, of the Ottoman authoritarian leadership, not of Ottoman citizens themselves. Once allowed to adopt printing technology in the late eighteenth century, Ottoman citizens did so with alacrity.[26] Today, the fact that most residents of the Middle East use cell phones and 30 percent use the Internet makes claims of an inherent technological conservativism to Islam implausible.[27] As for the prohibition on interest collection, Muslim financiers have long found creative ways around the proscription, such as the charging of borrowing fees, or they have ignored it all together.[28] A final problem with the Landes argument is that, for the last century, the Middle East's collective economies have grown as rapidly as those of the West.[29] Islamic culture clearly did not prevent economic growth in the twentieth century.

Mixed Evidence

Various critics also point out the fact that a culturalist approach leaves too many unexplained

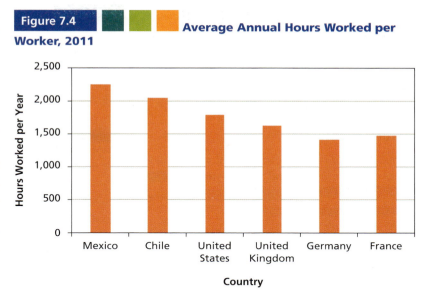

Figure 7.4 **Average Annual Hours Worked per Worker, 2011**

Source: Organisation for Economic Co-operation and Development, StatExtracts, http://stats.oecd.org/Index .aspx?DatasetCode=ANHRS.

empirical discrepancies. Cultural explanations fail to explain economic change—especially the myriad transformations of the twentieth century—with what is largely a static variable. At the time of Weber's writing, Catholic-majority France was already among the wealthiest countries in the world, but the second half of the twentieth century was particularly unkind to his argument. Catholic countries such as Ireland, Portugal, and Spain joined the high-income club, as did Confucian ones such as Japan and Singapore. China's economic takeoff began rather starkly in the late 1970s, yet this was not preceded by any fundamental change in Chinese culture.

Critics also point out the differences in prosperity levels among societies with nearly equivalent mass cultures. Most dramatic is the disparity in livelihoods between North and South Korea, two countries that, after centuries of political and cultural unification, have been separate from one another for only six decades. In that relatively short time span, the two have diverged to the point where South Koreans are seventeen times wealthier than North Koreans.[30] Comparisons of other pairs of societies with formerly integrated peoples and cultures but divergent living standards yield similar results. Wealthy Taiwan and middle-income China used to be part of the same country, as did prosperous Singapore and less developed Malaysia.

Cultural Relativism

A final body of criticism toward culturalist arguments comes from **cultural relativism**, adherents of which sometimes go so far as to call culturalist explanations ethnocentric or racist. A central tenet of cultural relativism is that each culture is distinct and equal in its inherent value and desirability. Thus, to speak of one culture as more conducive to wealth accumulation, or even to consider an economically prosperous society as more desirable than a poor one, is to provide a rank order of which cultures are better than others. Modernization theory is particularly well known for raising such hackles, given its belief that the adoption of Western culture would be universally beneficial. Even today, arguments that some cultures have the right work ethics, savings habits, and innovativeness for growth chafe with critics who see such statements as thinly veiled statements about the laziness of peoples and inferiority of values in the less developed regions of the world.

Causes of Underdevelopment: The Costs of Cultural Diversity

The culturalist claims discussed thus far tend to treat national and religious cultures as undifferentiated wholes, but few LDCs have a single culture or group identity. **Cultural diversity** (also cultural pluralism) exists when there are more social identities within a country than just the national affinity for the extant country. Few countries are culturally homogeneous, and some countries have greater cultural diversity than others.

On average, less developed countries have higher degrees of cultural pluralism than developed ones, meaning the former tend to have a larger number of distinct identity groups within their borders. There are numerous exceptions to this pattern, such as the diverse United States and the relatively homogeneous Haiti. Nonetheless, a loose negative correlation between GDP per capita and cultural diversity does exist. Map 7.1 illustrates this pattern by coloring each country according to its degree of cultural diversity, as measured by an **ethnic fragmentation** (or fractionalization) index. The index varies between 0 and 1, with higher scores indicative of more ethnic diversity. (See Understanding Indicators: Measuring the Degree of Cultural Diversity for a fuller description of the index.) As the map illustrates, African countries stand as the most ethnically diverse, on average, in the world.

A recent wave of research on underdevelopment focuses on cultural diversity as a constraint on economic growth. According to economists William Easterly and Ross Levine,[31] it is not (as Weber said) the cultural and religious attitudes of a country that ultimately determine its level of prosperity, but rather the number of different cultures within it. A high degree of cultural diversity in a country is detrimental to economic success, while homogeneity is more conducive to prosperity. Having a large number of social identities and, especially, mutually antagonistic groups can inhibit economic and human development in a number of ways.

Underprovision of Public Goods and Fragmented Markets

Culturally divided societies tend to underprovide the public goods (schools, roads, clinics, ports, water delivery systems, and so on) that are requisites for economic growth and human development. The existence of deep and multiple identity cleavages makes it difficult for people to cooperate in order to provide these kinds of amenities. Difficulties in communicating across group lines due to language barriers, geographical segregation, and differences of habit can complicate cooperation. For example, in highly diverse sub-Saharan Africa, ethnic groups

Map 7.1   **Ethnic Fractionalization Index**

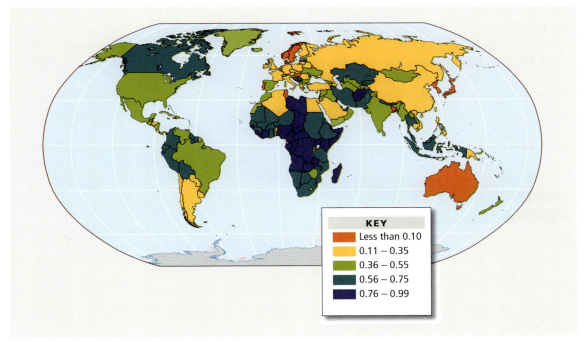

Source: Alberto Alesina et al., "Fractionalization," *Journal of Economic Growth* 8, no. 2 (2003): 155–194.

Note: A rank of 1 equates to a highly diverse ethnic population, while a lower ranking signifies greater ethnic homogeneity. No data was available for French Guiana, French Polynesia, Puerto Rico, the U.S. Virgin Islands, the West Bank, and Yemen.

are usually linguistically and territorially distinct, which limits contact across lines of ethnic difference, especially in rural areas. Disagreement among different groups about which public goods to prioritize can also retard cooperation. For example, if there is mutual distaste between group A and group B, then group A will not be enthusiastic about working toward provision of a public good that will largely benefit group B. Finally, stronger informal norms of trust and reciprocity make cooperation easier within homogenous communities.[32]

Along these lines, cultural diversity also lowers the radius of trust in society, fragmenting domestic markets and limiting the potential gains from exchange and specialization. Groups that do not like one another are less likely to employ one another, trade with one another, and provide investment opportunities for one another. This discrimination is reinforced

by stereotypes about deficiencies of another group's aptitude. All told, this market fragmentation yields all of the negative economic consequences of low-trust societies discussed above. For example, under the racist apartheid regime in South Africa (1948–1994), white business leaders faced severe restrictions on their ability to hire black workers. This limited the talent pool from which they could hire and slowed the country's economic growth in the 1970s and 1980s.

Poor Governance and Conflict

A mounting body of evidence suggests that another reason for underdevelopment in culturally diverse societies is that they have worse governments. Governments in culturally plural societies redistribute less and provide thinner social safety nets, seemingly drawing cues from their societies' inhospitable and uncharitable intergroup relations.[33] Politicians in plural societies are more likely to exercise favoritism toward one group at the expense of others. Political leaders tend to bestow more public goods on citizens of their own identity grouping, in part because of their natural affinity for their own group and in part because they may owe their political survival to that constituency. For example, evidence from Africa indicates that changes in the ethnicity of the president cause a boost in the educational resources provided to citizens of that president's ethnicity and a relative decline in those going to other ethnic groups.[34]

At the extreme, cultural diversity and divisions among groups can devolve into violent conflict and make a society completely ungovernable. When deep-seated identities are involved, the stakes of political and economic competition seem particularly high to the relevant players, making compromise more difficult and acts of violence more likely. Since independence, sub-Saharan Africa has had a relatively large number of violent societal conflicts, almost all of them internal civil wars because of the number and depth of its ethnic cleavages. Conflict in plural societies can be stoked and exacerbated by political leaders who play on ethnic and religious fears, fomenting historical myths of group betrayal to motivate followers to commit acts of violence. As one example, part of the motivation behind Rwanda's 1994 genocide was the widely held narrative of the Tutsi minority's historical wrongs committed against the Hutu majority. Propagated by Hutu elites, these myths contributed to the fervor that drove many Hutu citizens to participate in the massacre of the Tutsi minority. In the end, ethnic fragmentation and cleavages can be the raw materials for violence, which can have major human and economic costs.

Stereotype Threat

Finally, cultural heterogeneity may have pernicious psychological effects on the self-esteem and achievement motivation of disadvantaged groups. In recent decades, social psychologists have uncovered the existence of a phenomenon known as stereotype threat, which is the tendency of a negative stereotype about a social group to be internalized in a way that it becomes self-fulfilling.[35] In settings where one group is less affluent than others, stereotypes about the individual-level causes of this economic disadvantage (for instance, that one group is lazy or unintelligent) can be self-perpetuating. In one study of India, stereotype threat stemming from caste discrimination was found in student test scores. Lower-caste children performed far worse in completing mazes when reminded of their caste (achieved merely by asking them their full name) than when not reminded of their caste.[36] As another example, two-thirds of girls worldwide who drop out of primary school are ethnic minorities in their country, a fact that may be due in part to them and their parents playing out the low expectations that society holds for them. Given the ubiquity of negative stereotypes in contexts of cultural difference, it is possible that stereotype threat contributes to underachievement and underdevelopment in vast swathes of the developing world.

Critique: Diversity as Consequence, Not Cause

As with some of the critiques of culturalist arguments, the primary criticism of the claim that diversity is bad for prosperity questions this alleged direction of cause and effect. The cultural heterogeneity of many less developed countries may be more a symptom—or even a result—of poor political and economic performance than their ultimate cause. As emphasized by the constructivist school, identities are pliable and thus not fixed entities that unidirectionally shape economic outcomes and political institutions. Instead, they are subject to being reshaped by political elites and the institutions elites build. If this is true, then the fact that culturally unified countries are more prosperous results from the ways that wealth affords a society the ability to unify its peoples and not from the fact that societal homogeneity breeds wealth accumulation and growth.

Measuring the Degree of Cultural Diversity

Many social scientists have tried to come up with a single number for each country that captures its degree of cultural diversity. The standard approach is to calculate a number for each country that is one minus the probability that two randomly chosen individuals are from the same identity group. These fragmentation indices (also called fractionalization indices) thus vary between 0 and 1. High numbers close to 1 mean a high degree of cultural heterogeneity (that is, two randomly chosen people are likely from different groups), and low numbers close to zero indicate homogeneity or a low degree of diversity. For example, in a relatively homogenous country with, say, one large group that comprises 90 percent of the population and one small group that comprises 10 percent, the probability that two people are from the same group is .82, so the fragmentation score is $1 - .82 = .18$.

Developing fragmentation indices is fraught with difficulties. One problem is defining what the relevant cultural groups are, since, as emphasized by the constructivist school, people have multiple and malleable identities, each with varying relevance to society.[38] For the U.S. case,

identifying African Americans as an important and distinct ethnic and racial group is seemingly straightforward, but what about Americans of European descent? They might be a single group, but overt expressions of a unified "white" identity are rather rare and even considered by many to be racist. It might make more sense to focus on the individual ethnicities within the white racial group (such as Greek American or Irish American), yet the importance of these identities to economic, political, and social matters is rather limited. Alternatively, perhaps these racial and ethnic groupings are not the right focus and analysts should instead use a measure of religious diversity to gauge U.S. cultural diversity, tallying Catholics, Lutherans, Pentecostals, Baptists, Jews, atheists, and so on separately.

A second problem with the standard approach is that it ignores the extent of mutual distaste across lines of cultural difference. In making cross-national comparisons, two groups with little history of rancor are treated no differently than two groups with a violent past. For example, in many fragmentation indices the Hutu and Tutsi ethnic

groups of Rwanda, one of which orchestrated genocide against the other in 1994, are treated the same as the many groups, such as Irish American and Greek American, who have no mutual animosity. In fact, given the size of the Hutu majority (85 percent) relative to the Tutsi minority (14 percent), indices treat Rwanda as a place of relatively high ethnic homogeneity.

A final problem lies in the math. Technically speaking, there are an infinite number of group distributions associated with each fragmentation score. For example, a country with two equally sized groups (50 percent each) has a fragmentation index of .50, but so does a country with one large group of 66 percent and two small groups of 16 percent each. Even a casual observer can see that the nature of cultural pluralism is different between the two cases despite the equivalency of their fragmentation scores.

These problems notwithstanding, fragmentation indices are plentiful and widely used in a variety of social science circles. The table here reports three of them for three countries: the United States, Rwanda, and India. The indices shown are

(Continued)

(Continued)

Three Fractionalization Indices

	Linguistic	Religious	Ethnic
United States	.25	.82	.49
Rwanda	.00	.51	.32
India	.81	.33	.42

Source: Alberto Alesina et al., "Fractionalization," Working Paper 9411, National Bureau of Economic Research, December 2002, http://www.nber.org/papers/w9411.pdf?new_window=1.

based on underlying tallies that define groups according to three different criteria: language, religion, and ethnicity. For each country, the extent of cultural diversity jumps around depending on how one chooses to define cultural groups. The three look very different on linguistic and religious heterogeneity, but rather similar in terms of their ethnic fragmentation. In the end, because ethnicity is the broadest concept that can encompass linguistic, religious, racial, and other identity markers, scholars tend to prefer measures of ethnic fragmentation.

- What are the advantages and drawbacks of using fragmentation scores to gauge cultural diversity across countries?

- Which type of fragmentation—linguistic, religious, ethnic, racial, or some other type—is the most relevant for shaping economic and social development in a society?

In particular, countries with successful economies and effective political leadership can, with time, reduce the number of distinct and mutually antagonistic cultural identities through a variety of means. The establishment of a national system that provides universal mass education can construct a unified sense of national identity through the curriculum and also create linguistic unity by teaching in a common tongue.[39] Wealthy countries are more able to afford mass communication systems that contribute to common language usage and create a sense of national identity.[40] Well-heeled states can breed a singular nationalist identity by exerting effective state authority and power throughout their territories, something poor states struggle to do.[41] Moreover, subnational identities may be less politicized and salient where there is enough wealth to lower the stakes of ethnic cleavages.

The United States and the countries of sub-Saharan Africa provide contrasting examples. At the time of its independence, the United States was a loose collection of thirteen different former colonies, each with different governing institutions and religious cultures. The advent of an effective national government via the ratification of the U.S. Constitution in 1789 led, over the subsequent century, to the creation of national-level economic markets and the establishment of compulsory public schools. In turn, these developments laid the foundation for the gradual emergence of an American national identity. To this day, this identity provides a certain degree of cultural unity despite the presence of competing subnational identities based on race, ethnicity, language, and religion. By contrast, most of Africa's states have been too ineffective and lacking in cash to provide services that could unify their countries' linguistically and ethnically diverse populations.

Aside from this critique about the direction of causal influence, some scholars have argued that the alleged costs of cultural diversity can be overblown. In actuality, the vast majority of ethnic groups live peacefully with nearby groups and even frequently engage in economic and other forms of interpersonal exchange. The well-publicized cases of

Violence among groups is an exception?

ethnically based violence in recent years—Nigeria, Rwanda, Russia, former Yugoslavia—are exceptions to the rule] For example, Africa's hundreds of ethnic groups rarely fight one another, and Latin American countries have only rarely experienced ethnic conflict over the past century. Given the potential opportunities for interethnic conflict and violence, the number of realized incidents is extremely rare.[42] In short, the detrimental effects of diversity on economic and social development may be exaggerated.

STUDY

ARE IRAQIS POOR BECAUSE OF ISLAM AND ETHNIC CLEAVAGES?

Iraq has been a politically and economically troubled country for decades. Since 1980, it has fought three major interstate wars and a civil war. These included the longest conventional war of the twentieth century (the Iran-Iraq War of 1980–1988) and two others (the first and second Gulf wars) against history's most well-endowed military power: the United States. Iraq's economic collapse was also of historic proportions, with its GDP per capita falling from a First-World-sounding US$20,000 in 1979 to just US$3,000 in 1991. Much of this tragedy played out before an internationally attentive audience, given Iraq's vast oil reserves and its repeated wars with Western powers. Amidst this attention, the cultural practices and subnational identities of Iraqi citizens have come under particular scrutiny, with many observers blaming them for the country's ills. Table 7.3 compares Iraq and the United States on some major development indicators, as well as some other indicators that are discussed below.

The South: Islam and Sectarian Divisions

Two aspects of Iraqi culture may provide the roots of its underdevelopment. First, nearly all Iraqis are Muslim, a religion that, according to some culturalist scholars, is not amenable to modern economic growth. Second, Iraq's Muslims are divided among themselves, often violently so. In other words, it may suffer from the costs of cultural diversity.

Islam and Underdevelopment. The role of Islam in shaping Iraqis' values and behaviors has been the focus of particularly close inspection. Ninety-seven percent of Iraqis are self-identified Muslims. Under Ottoman rule for nearly 400 years (1534–1920), the peoples living in the region that is modern-day Iraq rejected much of the Scientific Revolution that took place in Europe and gradually fell behind economically during this time. Today, many scholars still see these basic signs of Islamic conservativism and rejection

of modern ideas in how Iraqi society treats women. Because of Islam's views on female societal roles, women are sidelined from the Iraqi economy, denying Iraq the gains from this huge pool of human talent. In 2005, only 15 percent of Iraqi women were in the labor force, the world's lowest rate.[43] According to this culturalist view, Islam also makes Iraqis passive players in shaping their own economic and political fates, as they instead defer to tribal sheiks, authoritarian politicians, and religious leaders.[44]

Moreover, Iraq is a low-trust society, once called a "social desert,"[45] in which social contacts hardly extend beyond the immediate family, a fact that fragments markets and provides a brake on economic growth. To one observer, "Family loyalty remains at the heart of the Iraqi culture, taking priority over other social relationships. For this reason, relatives tend to be preferred as business

ARE IRAQIS POOR BECAUSE OF ISLAM AND ETHNIC CLEAVAGES?

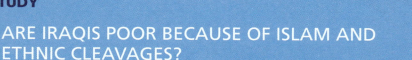

Table 7.3 ▪▪▪ **Development Comparison: Iraq and the United States**

Indicator	Iraq	United States
GDP per capita at PPP	US$3,708	US$41,728
Human Development Index	.573	.910
Armed ethnic conflicts since 1946	5	0
Invasions by Western powers since 1990	2	0
Oil income, 2000–2012 (percentage of GDP)	88.7 percent	.5 percent

Source: Data on GDP per capita at PPP and Human Development Index from Gapminder, www.gapminder.com; armed ethnic conflicts; Lars-Erik Cederman, Andreas Wimmer, and Brian Min, "What Makes Ethnic Groups Rebel? New Data and New Analysis," *World Politics* 62, no. 1 (2010): 87–119; oil income from World Bank, World Development Indicators, http://data.worldbank.org/sites/default/files/wdi-final.pdf.

partners since employing people one knows and trusts is of primary importance."[46] Iraqis allegedly lack a get-up-and-go attitude that is needed to lend them an entrepreneurial spirit and a work ethic needed for growth. They instead prefer the certainty and safety of the status quo: "Decisions [in Iraq] are made gradually, change is not eagerly accepted and risks are very rarely taken."[47] Deference to the status quo and to autocratic leaders provides a "brake on the development of ideas, such as personal responsibility and self-help."[48]

The Ethnic Divide. Beneath these widely shared cultural orientations lies another problem with dire consequences for the country's economy and governability: Iraq's infamous sectarian divisions. Most Iraqis are members of one of its three major ethnic groups: Arab Shiites (~65 percent), Arab Sunnis (~20 percent), and Kurds (~15 percent). These groups hold deep mutual animosities and self-identify less as Iraqis and more as Shiites, Sunnis, and Kurds, respectively. For example, Arab Shiites and Kurds suffered under the presidency of Arab Sunni Saddam Hussein (1979–2003). Hussein carried out well-planned deportations and massacres of Kurdish civilians, including the release of poisonous chemical agents over Kurdish villages in the late 1980s. He also systematically

excluded members of the Arab Shiite majority from his government and bureaucracy, and he committed indiscriminate violence in crackdowns against Shia mass uprisings in the 1990s. After Hussein's deposal at the hands of the U.S.-led coalition in 2003, sectarian violence actually worsened. Under U.S. occupation, the ethnic cleavages exploded into a civil war, with various Shia and Sunni militias carrying out ethnically targeted acts of terrorism against civilians and security personnel. The violence was the leading cause of the George W. Bush administration's primary foreign policy embarrassment, the failure to quickly pacify Iraq after it had declared "mission accomplished" and the end of major combat operations in Iraq on May 1, 2003.

Today, Iraq's ethnic divisions make the country largely ungovernable. Although multiple free and fair elections since 2003 have been held, the resulting governments have been highly fractious and ineffective. The political party system is oriented around ethnicities and religiosities rather than broad policy debates and issue positions. The largest parliamentary party bloc, the Iraqi National Movement, is largely a mouthpiece for secular Sunni interests, while the second- and third-largest blocs are almost strictly Shia-backed ones. The social identity basis behind political competition

Sunni Muslims in Iraq protest the Shia-dominated central government. The mutual distrust between Sunni and Shia ethnics exploded into civil war after the U.S.-led invasion of 2003. In response, some activists and experts espoused the breakup of Iraq along ethnic lines.

gives politics a zero-sum feel: groups do not wish to compromise since public goods and the spoils of office are hard to share across ethnic lines. In one telling example, Iraq went nine months without a government after the parliamentary election of 2010. Party and ethno-religious infighting delayed the formation of a majority-sized coalition, all while unemployment rose and service provision stagnated.[49]

***

Needless to say, these claims about the inherent problems of Iraqi culture are hotly contested. Evidence from Iraq itself shows that Islam and Iraq's ethnic divisions can be wholly compatible with modern economic growth. From 1900 to 1979, Iraq's GDP per capita at purchasing power parity increased tenfold. To be sure, these income gains were partly due to high prices for its main export, oil, but these

gains in income were also accompanied by important improvements in human development. For example, life expectancy at birth nearly doubled (from thirty-two to fifty-eight) in the thirty years leading up to 1979, and educational attainment, especially that for girls, also shot upward in the 1970s.[50]

The West: The British Mandate and War with the United States

Culturalist explanations for Iraq's economic and political struggles are particularly contentious when they come from Western mouths, since the West may have some responsibility for the country's underdevelopment. After all, it was Great Britain that forced the three ethnic groups to live under a single state. Through its invasion (1918) and then mandate over Iraq (1920–1932), Britain drew the country's borders to include three contiguous but otherwise

ARE IRAQIS POOR BECAUSE OF ISLAM AND ETHNIC CLEAVAGES?

unrelated former Ottoman provinces. It was also Britain that installed a subservient King Faisal during the mandate, entrenching a tradition of autocratic rule by the Sunni Arab minority that was not broken until 2003. Even after independence in 1932, Britain maintained a heavy military and advisory presence in Iraq. It orchestrated a large-scale invasion and coup in 1941, installing a government more to its liking.

After 1990, it was the United States that became Iraq's new Western archrival by invading twice, creating the conditions for the violent and low-trust society that has plagued Iraq's economy and politics. In 1990, Saddam Hussein invaded and occupied neighboring Kuwait. In the subsequent Gulf War (1990–1991), a U.S.-led coalition of military forces responded, pushing Iraq's forces out of Kuwait but leaving Hussein in power. Thereafter, the United States spearheaded a UN measure to impose economic sanctions on Iraq with the goal of keeping Hussein from acquiring biological, chemical, and nuclear weapons. Until 1996, Iraq was not allowed to export any of its vast oil reserves, and until 2003 it was only permitted to import medical equipment and food for direct humanitarian purposes. The result of the economic isolation was, according to some critics, heightened rates of malnutrition among children, the death of over 500,000 civilians, and a decade of deep economic stagnation.[51]

To top it all off, the United States, joined by old Iraqi nemesis Great Britain, invaded yet again in 2003, launching the Iraq War (2003–2011). This time it did so under the justification that, despite the sanctions, Saddam Hussein was harboring weapons of mass destruction that could be deployed against Israel or Europe in a matter of minutes. As it turns out, he was not. Meanwhile, 100,000 Iraqi civilians died in the conflict[52] and, while the invasion did topple Saddam Hussein, the subsequent occupation was poorly handled, unleashing widespread civil conflict, political chaos, and still more economic stagnation.

The Natural World: Oil and Sand

In addition to these problems with its culture and the West, Iraq is a leading example of yet another alleged cause of underdevelopment: the oil curse. Iraq ranks in the top five worldwide in proven oil reserves, and, for most of its independence, petroleum has accounted for over 90 percent of its export earnings. This concentration has kept Iraq from diversifying its economy into other productive pursuits in the industrial and services sectors. The demand for Iraq's oil drives up the price for its currency, making it difficult for Iraqi manufacturing firms to compete at home and abroad. Moreover, with so much of its economy riding on oil, Iraqi livelihoods are volatile and uncertain. As oil prices boomed in the 1970s, so did Iraq's economy. Average living standards doubled in that decade, vaulting its GDP per capita to almost US$20,000 per person. As oil prices collapsed in the 1980s, however, so did Iraq's economy, shrinking in size by over 80 percent.[53]

Nature also cursed Iraq with rather unproductive land. Thousands of years ago, the fertile territory between the Tigris and Euphrates rivers was host to perhaps the world's first major civilization, Sumer. Today, however, these arable lands comprise just 20 percent of Iraqi territory. The rest is mostly desert.[54] Even the existing arable land is of poor quality. Most farmers can only grow one crop a year, and even this annual yield is often threatened by drought and the highly salinized water table.

***

Iraq's troubles have been in the international spotlight for decades now. A brutal dictatorship, three major wars since 1980, stifling economic sanctions, interethnic violence, and a host of other problems are part of its all-too-visible tragedy. Compared to this past, its status as of 2011, when most U.S. forces departed, actually looks promising. Ethnic conflict had simmered down, oil revenues were flowing in again, and the trappings of a democracy, albeit a highly imperfect one, were in place. Perhaps an era of development success will see the world, mercifully, divert its attention from Iraq.

Thinking Critically about Development

- Why do Iraqis seem to exhibit a lack of trust toward one another? Is this a relatively fixed characteristic, as culturalists would argue, or is it the result of more immediate circumstances and contexts?

- Who or what bears the most responsibility for Iraqi underdevelopment: Saddam Hussein, the United Kingdom and United States, oil, or Iraqi citizens themselves for their unwillingness to put aside sectarian divisions?

- Saudi Arabia sits right next door to Iraq and the two countries share numerous features. Both are Muslim, oil-rich, arid, and historically nondemocratic, but Saudi Arabia is far wealthier. What accounts for the difference?

 ## Key Terms

Asian values, p. 167	ethnic fragmentation, p. 172	primordialism, p. 160
constructivism, p. 161	indigenous, p. 161	race, p. 161
culturalist school, p. 164	interpersonal trust, p. 163	religion, p. 162
cultural diversity, p. 172	modernization theory, p. 165	social capital, p. 167
cultural relativism, p. 172	nationalism, p. 162	social identity, p. 160
culture, p. 160	nationality, p. 162	stereotypes, p. 161
ethnicity, p. 161	nation-state, p. 162	

Suggested Readings

Easterly, William, and Ross Levine. "Africa's Growth Tragedy: Policies and Ethnic Divisions." *Quarterly Journal of Economics* 112, no. 4 (1997): 1203–1250.

Fukuyama, Francis. *Trust: The Social Virtues and the Creation of Prosperity*. New York: Free Press, 1995.

Landes, David S. *The Wealth and Poverty of Nations: Why Some Are So Rich and Some So Poor*. New York: W.W. Norton and Co, 1999.

Lerner, Daniel. *The Passing of Traditional Society: Modernizing the Middle East*. New York: Free Press, 1965.

Putnam, Robert, with Robert Leonardi and Raffaella Y. Nanetti. *Making Democracy Work: Civic Traditions in Modern Italy*. Princeton, NJ: Princeton University Press, 1994.

Weber, Max. *The Protestant Ethic and the Spirit of Capitalism*. New York: Penguin, 1905 (2002).

 ## Web Resources

Association of Religion Archives, www.thearda.com/

Fractionalization Data, www.nsd.uib.no/macrodataguide/set.html?id=16&sub=1

World Values Survey, www.worldvaluessurvey.org/

Agricultural workers harvest a field on a collective farm in North Korea. Most food in North Korea must be sold to a government agency that sets prices. The country has one of the few remaining socialist economies, a remnant of a previous era when state intervention in the economy was widely practiced.

States, Markets, and Development Models

"What took us so long?" chuckles Jairam to himself, reflecting on India's economic history as he closes his textile factory for the night. His business has had a banner year, something he attributes in part to India's relatively new development model. Born in the 1940s when India was still a British colony, Jairam came of age in the 1970s at the peak of his country's experiment with a state-led approach to economic growth. The government owned major enterprises and created a labyrinthine system of bureaucratic red tape to regulate investment. It also tried to create a self-sufficient India, walled off from the global economy. On multiple occasions during those years, Jairam tried to turn his small textile business, run out of his modest home with just a few family employees, into a larger enterprise, but state regulations blocked him every time. He could not secure the licenses—or, more accurately, afford the bribes to secure the licenses—to grow his business, to buy computers, to import supplies, and so on.

That all changed, however, when India shifted course in the early 1990s, dropping many of the extensive licensing requirements and barriers to international trade. Jairam was finally able to grow his business, and today he owns and manages a successful textile factory with nearly 600 employees and several clients in Japan. Jairam has also enjoyed the economic transformation taking place around him, as India's new economic model has produced an impressive boom. Why it took so long to get there, Jairam will never know.

India was not the only LDC to enact an economic strategy of heavy state involvement in the middle decades of the twentieth century. Most did, and many critics see this as a primary source of the ongoing poverty in today's non-Western world. This chapter looks at the various development models employed by countries outside the developed world throughout the twentieth and twenty-first centuries.

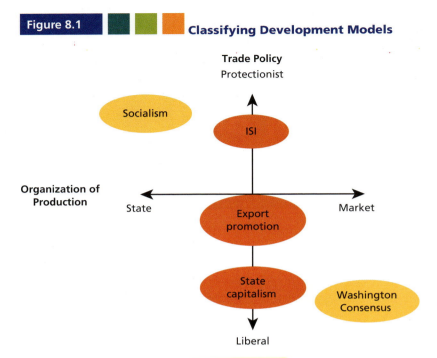

Figure 8.1 ▪ ▪ ▪ **Classifying Development Models**

A **development model** is the set of policies that a state chooses to shape economic activity within its borders. Figure 8.1 presents an overview of some of the major development models employed in LDCs and discussed in this chapter. Broadly speaking, development models can be defined by their orientation on two dimensions: the coordination of production and the degree of global engagement. The first dimension considers who organizes economic production. In some development models, the state coordinates a large share of production via direct ownership of major economic assets and through mechanisms such as bureaucratic planning and industrial policy. In others, private actors organize production through market-based transactions. Most development models fall in between these two extremes, containing a mixture of state and market organization, but each can be characterized as having more or less state involvement than others. The second dimension captures how integrated a domestic economy is with the global economy. Some development models establish a liberal policy of openness

to international trade and capital flows, while others hold to a more protectionist or inward-oriented position toward the global economy.

Figure 8.1 places five different development models on these two dimensions. The five are import substitution industrialization (ISI), export promotion, state capitalism, socialism, and the Washington Consensus. The first three, which are colored in red in the figure, are all variants of what is called state-led development. (ISI and export promotion were introduced in the Chapter 5 discussion on globalization, but this figure and current chapter put the two into a broader context.) Since state-led development models dominated economic policy in the developing world in the decades following World War II, this chapter discusses them first. It then moves to the socialist development model, which was adopted during the same decades but by far fewer LDCs. The chapter then describes the market-oriented Washington Consensus, which was adopted with varying degrees of enthusiasm by most LDCs in the 1980s and 1990s. In proceeding, the chapter describes some of the intellectual thought behind each model, how it worked in practice, and some of the strengths and weaknesses of how it performed.

State-Led Development

The middle decades of the twentieth century, ranging roughly from the 1930s to the 1980s, were a distinctive era in the economic development of LDCs. During these years, most LDCs pursued a development model known as **state-led development**.

Under state-led development, states were heavily involved in the economy, choosing to do things such as producing for markets, subsidizing or discouraging certain forms of private economic activity, and muting the competition that markets created. State-led development is thus not pure capitalism because the state intervenes heavily in the economy, but it is also distinct from socialism in that the state does not completely replace private-market activity. Within the broad definition of state-led development lie numerous variants and nuances, some of which are discussed below. A few synonyms for state-led development have received widespread usage, such as developmentalism, Arab socialism, and the East Asian developmental state.

State-Led Development in Thought

In the middle decades of the twentieth century, the notion that the state should take an active role in the economy was popular in many intellectual circles. Even numerous scholars that were repelled by socialist and communist approaches thought it necessary to inject various forms of statist involvement into a capitalist economy. Three schools of thought were particularly noteworthy.

Keynesianism. Writing his most important work in the wake of the Great Depression, British economist John Maynard Keynes developed the most profound and influential scholarly justification for the mixed economy. His body of thought, eventually called **Keynesianism**, would influence subsequent scholarly work on development in low-income societies, even though Keynes was himself largely silent on the topic.[1]

Before Keynes, most economists believed that freely functioning market economies would always produce full employment, a scenario in which virtually everyone who wanted a job could find one. Keynes disagreed, arguing that full employment was not a natural state of competitive markets and that the level of employment in an economy was a function of aggregate demand—the total quantity of goods and services demanded by a society. When aggregate demand was low, unemployment would be high, and the economy could get stuck in this low-growth and high-unemployment trap. To Keynes, the resolution to such a problem lay in fiscal policy, which refers to government taxation and expenditure measures. Government could stimulate aggregate demand via increased spending while holding the level of taxation steady. For example, state investment in things such as public works would create jobs, and the increased consumption by these newly employed workers would boost demand and create even more jobs. Keynes also wanted state-run central banks to stimulate aggregate demand when needed by lowering interest rates, a measure that made it cheaper to borrow and thus invest.

Early Development Economics. A decade after Keynes published his most important ideas, scholars working in the nascent field of development economics used some of his thought to argue that, if left to their own devices, markets and private economic actors would fail to produce development in the global South. Writing in the 1940s, Paul Rosenstein-Rodan argued that "international depressed areas" were stuck in a number of vicious cycles and poverty traps.[2] Wages in these areas were held low by the excess supply of unskilled laborers, most of them still toiling in subsistence agriculture and other rural work. With such low wages, people could barely save. In turn, with such little savings, society had no funds with which to invest and accumulate the capital needed to raise productivity. Moreover, Rosenstein-Rodan added that potential industrial entrepreneurs had no incentive to invest what little capital was available because there were no other industries or consumers to buy from them. To break out of this vicious cycle of poverty breeding poverty, Rosenstein-Rodan espoused a "big push" strategy of balanced growth to be coordinated by the state. In poor areas of the world, the state was the only entity of sufficient size to have large amounts of capital. The state should use this capital to invest simultaneously in a wide range of industrial firms that could in turn create demand for each other's outputs.

Albert Hirschman was another development economist who espoused heavy investment by the state.[3] Hirschman diagnosed the problem of underdevelopment as one of a lack of entrepreneurial and managerial knowledge. For this reason, he was skeptical of the Rosenstein-Rodan proposal to have the state invest across a large number of industries as the resources would be wasted on firms with poor leadership. Rather, Hirschman wanted the state to protect and invest in a small number of strategic sectors, defined as those that had a high capacity for creating supply to and demand for other sectors. For example, investment in the steel sector would create demand for the raw materials that go into steel making, something Hirschman called a backward linkage. In turn, a healthy steel sector could supply other firms (a forward linkage) that needed steel to produce their goods, such as automotive and construction firms. To Hirschman, it was the state's job to foster an unbalanced growth strategy by picking strategic sectors, rather than all of them, and provide those chosen sectors with investment funds.

Structuralism. Along with these arguments from European economists, a set of more homegrown ideas from developing world thinkers also laid an intellectual groundwork for the mixed economy. The most influential of these was the thought of Argentinean Raúl Prebisch and other Latin American structuralists in the 1940s and 1950s. (See Chapter 5 for more on Prebisch.) They provided a justification for inward-oriented development policy, a set of measures to block imports in the name of encouraging industrialization and self-sufficiency. Prebisch famously argued that less developed countries were experiencing steadily declining terms of trade (meaning the price of

exports relative to the price of imports) since they were exporting cheap primary products in exchange for ever more expensive manufactured imports from rich countries. Prebisch believed that this problem justified protection of domestic industries from competition with imports so that domestic firms could flourish in filling local consumer demand. Structuralists also argued that the state could boost investment through progressive taxation and the nationalization of certain industries. Many also argued for a state-led system of land redistribution, since Latin America's *latifundia* (large estates) owners left vast tracks of the region's land fallow merely as a symbol of prestige.

State-Led Development in Practice

The state-led development model, and in particular the ISI variant, was first implemented in Latin America and parts of the Middle East in the 1930s. Most South Asian and African countries embraced ISI soon after achieving independence in the 1940s, 1950s, and 1960s. East Asian countries adopted ISI as well in the mid-twentieth century, although they transitioned to export promotion, a distinct form of outward-oriented, state-led development around the 1960s. Governments pursuing the state-led development course used a variety of levers to advance development and, in particular, their countries' manufacturing sectors.

State-Owned Enterprises and Industrial Policy. Most prominent was the establishment of **state-owned enterprises** (SOEs, also called parastatals, public enterprises, or nationalized industries) in strategic sectors. Many firms in the heavy industries (such as steel and chemicals), mining and extraction (petroleum, natural gas, and copper), and utility provision (water, sanitation, electricity, and telecommunications) were either founded as SOEs or nationalized during this time. In some parts of the less developed world, especially Africa, state ownership even existed in some light industries (textiles and footwear). Through SOEs, states played a direct role in decisions about investment, production, and pricing in their economies. Figure 8.2 shows the significant extent of SOE involvement in total domestic investment by the late 1970s. Rates of SOE involvement in LDCs were triple those prevailing in high-income countries.

Political leaders in LDCs decided to let SOEs proliferate for a variety of reasons. The era was one of skepticism among political leaders, as was the case among scholars, about the ability of a freely operating private sector to generate industrialization and sustained growth. Because major firms required massive amounts in start-up funds and investment, private entrepreneurs did not have the capacity to establish firms in mining, steel, utilities, and other capital-intensive sectors. Politicians also did not want foreign investment and management of such firms because they viewed major firms in these sectors as being of military and geostrategic import. Politicians also believed that the lack of vulnerability to the whims of the market was a plus for SOEs. Absent the imperative of earning annual profits, SOEs could take a longer time horizon and absorb short-run losses in the name of facilitating long-run gains for society as a whole.

Furthermore, many leaders used SOEs to achieve what they saw as more collective goals than private profit seeking, such as creating large numbers of jobs and providing low-priced goods and services to poor consumers or strategic firms. For example, price controls on cement made by an SOE could subsidize construction. In the case of raw materials extraction, states often nationalized under the expressed rationale that a country's natural endowment belonged to the entire populace, and the only way for everyone to benefit from it was through state ownership. For example, when Brazil established its state-owned oil company in 1953, the

Figure 8.2 **Share of Domestic Investment by SOEs in Four World Regions, 1978**

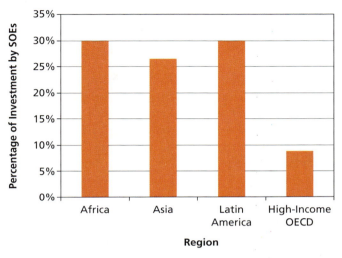

Source: The World Bank, *Bureaucrats in Business* (New York: Oxford University Press, 1995).

move was accompanied by the motto "the petroleum is ours!" Stated differently, states saw SOEs as revenue generators.

State ownership was typically just one element of a much broader **industrial policy**, which is a set of measures designed to grow the manufacturing base by the favoring of certain firms and sectors by the state. Direct ownership via SOEs was the most intrusive form of industrial policy, but other tools included tax credits, cheap finance with easy repayment terms, subsidized inputs, and direct payments, all targeted to benefit firms that the state deemed central to economic progress. For example, in the 1950s, Morocco created a state-owned development bank to channel investment funds to sectors that it feared were growing too slowly.[4] Industrial policies were often drawn up as part of grandiose state plans in which government bureaucrats laid out the specific means by which they would shape economic activity to achieve clearly specified performance goals. Countries such as Argentina, Egypt, and India periodically enacted five-year state plans to guide industrial policy and other economic measures. Although less enamored of five-year plans, the East Asian developmental states also pursued active industrial policies such as assisting firms in research and technological adoption and providing subsidies to those that exported.

Trade Policy. Throughout Latin America, the Middle East, and South Asia, states coupled their strategies of direct ownership and industrial policy with heavy doses of protectionism, meaning they sheltered their domestic economies from international competition. This was the import substitution industrialization strategy (described in detail in Chapter 5) of implementing high barriers to imports of light manufactured goods. The goal was to allow local firms to emerge that could replace imports in the domestic consumer market with their own products. States hoped this would improve prosperity by growing the local manufacturing sector. In many countries, ISI was accompanied by imports of capital machinery that could be used to produce these light manufactured goods. Some inflows of foreign capital were also allowed, although typically under strict regulation.

Much of Southeast and East Asia pursued a similar trade policy in the 1950s. However, starting in the 1960s and 1970s, several countries in these regions diverged from the triad of SOEs, industrial policy, and ISI. While still playing active economic roles via industrial policy and direct ownership of some industries, governments in countries such as Malaysia, the Philippines, Singapore, South Korea, and Thailand turned to a policy of export promotion, or export-oriented industrialization (EOI). The key difference between ISI and EOI was that, under EOI, governments sought to build up firms that could successfully compete with and export to foreign consumers, not just domestic ones. Backed by elements of industrial policy, many Southeast and East Asian firms dramatically increased their light manufactured exports to global markets. The strategy also entailed a lowering of protectionist barriers to trade. Whereas average tariffs (a tax levied on imported goods and services) for the major Latin American economies were above 100 percent in the 1960s, in these East Asian countries they were generally less than 30 percent.[5]

Two Regional Variations. In Latin America, countries also had leaders who engaged in **economic populism**. Economic populism is a policy approach that seeks to achieve redistribution toward lower- and middle-income groups via a mix of generous state spending, mandated wage increases for these popular classes, price controls, and expansive monetary policy. Urban labor unions were often the key targeted beneficiaries of such policies, and they in turn rewarded populist leaders by providing them with political support. The archetypical populist was Argentinean president Juan Perón (1946–1955, 1973–1974). Perón expanded social benefits such as social security for organized labor and built up the public health-care system. Under Perón and other populists, ISI was a natural complement to populism since it protected industrial workers' jobs from global competition.

In sub-Saharan Africa, agricultural marketing boards played a major role in efforts to industrialize. Farmers were legally required to sell their cash crops to a government agency known as the **marketing board**, which in turn sold the items on to domestic and foreign consumers. Marketing boards existed throughout the developing world, but they were particularly important in African economies where such a large share of the population engaged in rural work. The stated purpose of marketing boards in Africa was for the state to provide steady demand and price stability to farmers and to promote sales abroad. In their role as the mandated sole buyer, marketing boards often bought low and sold high, meaning they paid a low price to farmers and then sold the crops on to foreign consumers at a high one. The state pocketed the difference as a form of taxation on rural producers and invested it in urban industry and public-sector jobs. Marketing boards also sold some of the crops to urban consumers at discounted prices to subsidize the well-being of city dwellers.

Causes of Underdevelopment: Failures of the State-Led Model

During the 1980s and 1990s, the dominant line of thought in the economics profession as to why so many LDCs were still poor was that they had misguidedly pursued these state-led development policies. The rise of neoclassical economic thought, described in detail below, inclined economists to see most forms of state intervention as counterproductive and inferior to the operation of free markets.

To critics, many of the advantages that politicians initially saw when setting up SOEs eventually proved to be problems. Because they were both state-owned and (quite often) monopolies, SOEs did not need to achieve profits and market success to survive, so they had weak incentives to be efficient. SOEs had a soft budget constraint, meaning they could go into debt without consequence since most could borrow at low or no cost from the state. The soft budget constraint created a spiral of indebtedness for many SOEs in which inefficiency bred indebtedness and the ease of covering debts discouraged greater efficiency.

Inefficiencies were caused by a number of things. Politicians used SOEs as a source of **patronage**—that is, as a means to provide jobs to family, friends, and supporters rather than to meritorious workers. For this reason, SOEs were frequently labeled "employment mills" and often had "ghost workers" who were paid but never showed up to work. Indebtedness also came from their mandate of underpricing their products as a subsidy to buyers. SOE indebtedness meant

that taxpayers subsidized them, diverting precious state revenues from more pressing needs in education and health. Moreover, by the 1970s and 1980s, many states, especially those in Latin America, were themselves so indebted that they lacked funds to invest in SOEs, sapping one of the primary reasons for initially creating SOEs in strategic industries. Finally, inefficiency was present in the fact that SOEs had weak incentives to provide quality goods and services to consumers. For example, throughout many LDCs, state-owned utilities were associated with electricity blackouts and years-long waiting lists for installation of a residential telephone line.

The alleged shortcomings of industrial policy were typically along similar lines, with many critics viewing state benefits for selected private firms as suffering from a softer version of the problems surrounding SOEs. In Latin America, hundreds of inefficient private firms were kept afloat by the subsidized credit and supplies granted to them by the government, long after any compelling intellectual case for their strategic import had withered away. Many firms secured or maintained subsidies merely because of their lobbying skills or crony relations with politicians. In many LDCs, large companies also successfully lobbied for restrictions on entry of new firms, effectively limiting the internal competition they faced. As a result, consumers suffered under high rates of firm concentration (one or a few companies providing nearly all goods and services) in many product markets.

Economic populism in Latin America, according to its critics, also proved disappointing. Populist policies were seemingly implemented with good intentions: to redistribute wealth to popular classes and increase wages for organized labor. Populist governments, however, typically paid for increased state benefits with debt, and they mandated wage increases without corresponding increases in workers' productivity. Both are classic recipes for inflation and even shortages of consumer goods, since they increase aggregate demand without a commensurate boost in output. They are also fiscally unsustainable, thus raising the state's debt burden. Economists Rudiger Dornbusch and Sebastian Edwards speak of populist cycles in which the short-term euphoria from higher wages and benefits implodes into a spiral of unsustainable debt, high inflation, and recession.[6]

For Africa, political scientist Robert Bates[7] argues that marketing boards placed a particularly strong drag on economic growth because they favored an urban minority at the expense of the rural majority. Marketing boards kept farmers, who comprised the vast majority of African populations, mired in poverty because they were paid such a low price for their crops. Had they been able to sell directly to consumer and world markets, farmers would have received higher prices and thus had higher incomes.

Critique: Successes of State-Led Development

While these and other analysts were quick to blame state-led development for the underwhelming economic performance of the global South, proponents of state intervention had two central responses. First, some made the case that the period of state-led development produced superior outcomes to the free-market era that came before it.[8] Many countries experienced economic growth miracles under ISI. In Latin America, the average annual growth rate in GDP was a robust 5.5 percent in the 1960s and 1970s, and in the Middle East it was 6.6 percent. Largely agricultural societies with economies oriented around food or mineral exports grew into urbanized ones with expansive manufacturing sectors. Emerging from the colonial era, sub-Saharan Africa also grew at a decent average clip of 4.3 percent per year.[9] More importantly, improvements in human development were substantial in the state-led era, as nearly every country in the developing world enjoyed gains in life expectancy and enrollment rates for primary education.

In contrast, a more market-oriented model was pursued before the state-led development era in the developing world, and it largely failed. For example, the sovereign states of Latin America had few SOEs and relatively low tariffs in the nineteenth century, and they relied heavily on primary-product exports during this time. Not only did they fail to develop, but this was the century in which they fell behind the West economically. It was not until Latin America turned inward and expanded the role of the state in the middle decades of the twentieth century that its industrial base, economic growth rates, and human development outcomes improved.

Second, key observers interpreted the phenomenal economic successes of the East Asian Tigers as a vote for state intervention. The East Asian Tigers (Hong Kong, Singapore, South Korea, and Taiwan) were exceedingly poor in the early 1950s, but by the 1980s they had graduated to high-income status based on three decades of virtually unprecedented economic growth. Economists Alice Amsden and Robert Wade argued that these countries and territories grew so impressively because of the savvy involvement of their states.[10] Taking a cue from Hirschman, Amsden and Wade argued that the Tigers would not have developed strategic sectors in open markets because they would have faced crushing competition from the established firms of the developed world. To overcome this market failure, industrial policy measures targeted at companies in strategic sectors allowed a domestic manufacturing base to emerge. States further provided incentives such as subsidies to the winners of export contests for many firms to become efficient enough to compete in global markets. To be sure, not everyone agreed. Advocates of free markets use the comparison of the Tigers' success with Latin America's struggles (especially in the 1980s) under ISI as evidence of the superiority of the Tigers' more open trade policies. All told, however, advocates of state-led development argued that it was the government intervention in markets that industrialized the Tigers.

Socialism

Most LDCs practiced some variant of state-led development between the 1930s and 1980s, but some exceptions exist. The most important exceptions are those countries that practiced **socialism**, an economic system in which most economic assets are owned by the state and most major decisions about economic production and activity are made by state officials. To be sure, state-led development often contained elements of socialism, namely state ownership and state planning. However, the scope of state influence in socialist economies was far greater as they typically left only a minimal presence for private enterprise. In other words, state-led development was a mixed system while socialism had a much more encompassing state presence in the economy.

Since this book does not cover the countries of the former Soviet Union (a socialist economy), the treatment of socialism here will be briefer than that of state-led development. Nonetheless, many of the countries that are today considered developing ones did have socialist economies at some point in the twentieth century. The timeline in Figure 8.3 depicts some of these, reporting the years in which socialist economics was practiced. Most important is China, which practiced socialism roughly from 1949 to 1978. A few Southeast Asian states (Cambodia and Vietnam) also enacted socialism. In Latin America, it was Cuba and Nicaragua, and in Africa, Ethiopia, Tanzania, and a few other small states implemented forms of African socialism. It is also important to note that, even in LDCs that did not enact full-scale socialism, political parties and movements that espoused socialism often existed and played a crucial role in the political system, sometimes even as combatants in civil wars.

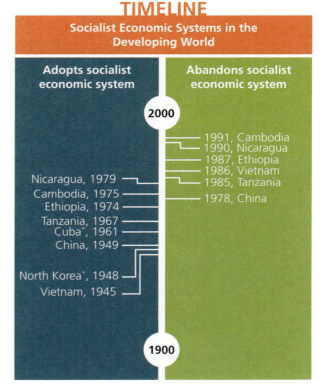

Source: Compiled by the author.

* Cuba and North Korea maintain their socialist economic systems today.

Marxist Thought

Much of the intellectual inspiration for socialism in the twentieth century came from the writings of German philosopher Karl Marx, who wrote his most important works in the mid-nineteenth century. Paradoxically, Marx wrote little about what a working socialist economic and political system would look like, instead devoting almost the entirety of his writings to a rigorously reasoned critique of capitalism.

The Nature of Capitalist Exploitation. In Marx's time, **capitalism** (a system distinguished by the existence of privately owned property) referred to the nascent system of industrial production in urban Europe. In this context, Marx saw capitalism as a struggle between two social classes. The capitalist class, which he called the *bourgeoisie*, was defined as those who owned the factories and machinery that comprised the inanimate means of economic production. The industrial working class, the proletariat, was comprised of those who provided the labor component in the means of production. The proletariat worked in return for wages paid by the *bourgeoisie*.

According to Marx, the *bourgeoisie* exploits the proletariat by extracting from it an economic surplus. Economic surplus is the difference between the value of a commodity and the necessary costs of producing it. If society values a pair of shoes at US$30, but the worker who made them only receives US$10 for his efforts, then the worker is being exploited by the capitalist who keeps much of the remaining US$20 as profit. (The actual surplus is this US$20 minus the non-labor costs of producing the shoes, such as the leather materials.)

Capitalism's Demise. Marx argued that capitalism would inevitably collapse, and, from its ruins, socialist systems would emerge. From a political standpoint, Marx believed that the proletariat would not stand for its exploitation indefinitely. Eventually, it would become aware of its collective enslavement by the *bourgeoisie* and form a revolutionary movement to overthrow the capitalist class. Moreover, Marx also saw capitalism as economically self-defeating. The fervent competition among firms would force the *bourgeoisie* to adopt more machinery to replace human labor. This would lower wages and consign increasing numbers of workers to joblessness, eventually evaporating the consumer demand for the fruits of capitalist production. The loss of human labor would also lower the rate of profit for the *bourgeoisie*, since Marx believed that only human labor could produce value and thus profit. As a result,

the capitalist class itself was also due for inevitable demise.

To Marx, once capitalism collapsed, a socialist system would emerge and then itself be supplanted eventually by a communist one. In the socialist system, the state would be led by a dictator governing on behalf of the workers (dictatorship of the proletariat) that would ban most private property, own and coordinate factories and other means of production, and be the sole provider of credit and finance. In doing so, the socialist state would eliminate the function of the capitalist class and end the private extraction of surplus. Once a classless society had been created under socialism, the state itself would be unnecessary and wither away, and a utopian **communist** society would emerge. Land and all other means of production would be collectively shared and owned. Laborers would work for the collective good and take only what they needed, losing their selfish propensities toward crime, war, and exclusionary nationalist and religious identities.

Socialism in Practice

A wide variety of economic rules and arrangements have been labeled "socialist." These range from systems comprised mostly of rural cooperative farms in poor societies to some in middle-income ones dominated by huge state-owned industrial conglomerates. Still, it is possible to point out some commonalities shared by most socialist systems.

Agricultural Collectives. In the countries under consideration, many socialist leaders chose to establish **agricultural collectives**, or communities in which land was jointly owned by residents or the state. Residents or state bureaucrats coordinated farming tasks on collectives and decided jointly how to distribute revenues from sales. Crops were typically sold to government agencies that set prices and quotas and in turn distributed food to urban and other consumers. Under some socialist economies, such as those in China and Cambodia, collectives were even scaled up into larger **communes**, which were intended to be self-reliant communities in which virtually all economic activities and services (including health and child care, education, and dining) were coordinated by and provided to residents.

Central Planning. Most socialist economies featured state ownership of all firms in the manufacturing and financial sectors. Decisions about production in these SOEs were made by **central planning** agencies comprised of government bureaucrats. These central planners decided how much each firm should produce, what prices it would charge, where its inputs came from, where it would sell its products, and so on. Stated differently, political officials operated a **command economy** in which resources were allocated by a relatively centralized executive agency rather than a market. Most decisions regarding production were expressed in the form of quantity targets or quotas: a firm was ordered to produce *x* units over a set time period. Central planners also produced forward-looking, multiyear plans based on longer-term visions. In doing so, planners tended to privilege the buildup of heavy industry (steel, capital machinery, infrastructure, defense, energy) and related grandiose projects at the expense of other economic sectors, such as handicraft services (blacksmithing, tailoring, shoemaking) and light industry (consumer goods such as textiles, food processing, and electronics). Planners also exacted a monopoly over international trade, allowing in imports only in cases of clear domestic shortages.

Achieving Equality. Most socialist systems attempted to provide comprehensive social safety nets to achieve high levels of income equality. Medical services were often provided by health professionals who were state funded or who provided services to their commune. With just a few exceptions, educational services were also provided by the state or commune. Moreover, in socialist systems wages were more equitable across different sectors and occupations than were wages in capitalist countries. Unemployment was typically nonexistent. Firms were often barred from firing their workers, and any worker who wanted to be in the labor force could secure a paying job. In China, workers with jobs in SOEs were said to be part of an "iron-rice bowl," receiving generous benefits and job security. Finally, the redistribution of land, often through state expropriation and collectivization, was often a part of socialism in practice.

Causes of Underdevelopment: Failures of Socialism

Nearly every socialist economy ever established has collapsed, and virtually all have been associated with political coercion and repression. A number of issues led to these seemingly recurring problems. Socialist policies toward the agricultural sector had consequences that ranged from the mildly discriminatory to the genocidal. Collectivization was almost always forced on unwilling peasants, a process that at times entailed violent repression and compelled migration. Moreover, as a means to promote industry, planners typically assigned lower prices to food than to manufactured goods, a policy that sapped resources and investment away from agriculture. During China's Great Leap Forward (1958–1961), leader Mao Zedong even diverted some peasant labor away from food production by having the peasants set up backyard steel mills in which they produced their own (highly flawed) farm tools. All told, collectivization and the socialist bias for industry redistributed wealth from rural to urban residents, and in some instances the underinvestment in agriculture contributed to chronic food shortages and a need to ration. In the most extreme circumstances, socialist policies resulted in famine. Between 1959 and 1961, an estimated 30 million deaths occurred from famine in Mao's China.[11]

Even in industry, where socialist leaders' efforts were more earnest, production was inefficient. Industrial workers were unmotivated, as the goals of wage equality ran up against the need to incentivize workers. Some official efforts to incentivize workers, such as rewarding them with piece rates (bonuses linked to the volume of physical output) and work points (bonuses based on others' perception of one's effort) had problems or internal contradictions and largely failed. SOEs in socialist systems also carried the problems of SOEs in mixed economies mentioned above: soft budget constraints led to overemployment and indebtedness. Finally, industrial firms produced at the behest of state planners, not consumers. Consumer options were extremely poor because planners gave simple quantity goals to firms, effectively encouraging them to produce easy-to-make units without regard to their durability, variety, or innovativeness. The apparent advances in industrial production that did occur in most socialist economies fail to reflect the unsuitability of their output for consumer satisfaction and demand.

Finally, the present and past socialist economies of the developing world were built in authoritarian political systems that featured heavy doses of coercion and human rights abuse. The formation of opposition political parties and criticism of incumbent leaders were banned and punished with kidnapping, torture, or execution. Mao notoriously repressed critical speech and artistic expression, and he conducted ruthless purges of opposition figures and disloyal co-partisans. Moreover, the collectivization of agriculture almost always occurred under duress and violent coercion, since rural landowners, even smallholding peasants, resisted out of opposition to loss of their privately held land. For example, through Tanzania's "villagization" campaign, some 11 million peasants were forced to resettle on collective farms, and the military

often destroyed their homes and villages so that they could not return to them.[12] State-sponsored class warfare was also widely practiced, and reached genocidal rates in some instances. In Cambodia, the Communist Khmer Rouge regime killed an estimated 2 million people, including "class enemies," who were members of the upper, urban middle, and landholding classes.

Critique: Socialism's Successes

These major problems notwithstanding, socialism did achieve some successes. Socialism in China did foster a certain degree of industrialization. By mobilizing citizens' savings and channeling it into the heavy industries, China was able to establish a nascent industrial base under Mao and grow average incomes by 90 percent. Socialism was also highly equitable, with most individuals earning relatively similar incomes. Policies to equilibrate wage levels and eliminate unemployment were successful toward this end. Citizens could also count on health care and education services from the state or commune, so human development gains were often impressive under socialism. Fidel Castro's Cuba has long had better health care and health outcomes than many other Latin American countries. Figure 8.4 shows how impressive Cuba's gains in life expectancy under Castro look alongside those of nonsocialist Jamaica, a country with a similar average income. Even in China, where Mao temporarily shut down the university system for ideological reasons, rates of primary education and literacy boomed as the government invested heavily in educating the rural poor.[13]

Despite these achievements, most socialist countries, as was the case with those trying state-led development models, reached a crisis and turning point in the 1980s. The market-oriented model that followed swept throughout the developing world, transforming its economies in dramatic ways.

The Market-Oriented Strategy

Figure 8.4 **Life Expectancy at Birth in Cuba and Jamaica, 1950–2010**

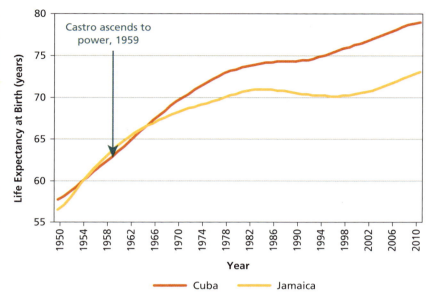

Source: Data compiled from Gapminder, www.gapminder.org.

In the 1970s, the loose consensus among economic thinkers and policymakers in favor of heavy state intervention in the economy began to unravel. The 1970s was a decade of economic stagnation in developed countries, and the Latin American debt crisis of 1982 convinced many leaders of the global South that state-led development was problematic. Throughout the 1980s and 1990s, most LDCs enacted a variety of measures to adjust their economic strategies in a more **market-oriented** or capitalist direction. They reversed their existing development models by privatizing SOEs, lowering barriers to international trade and foreign-capital inflows, tapering industrial policy measures, and closing marketing boards. This set of market-friendly policies was embraced with widely varying degrees of eagerness, but it was adopted at least to some extent in virtually every LDC. A variety of labels exists for both the intellectual thought backing the free-market shift and the development policies themselves: neoclassical economics, neoliberalism, economic orthodoxy, and the Washington Consensus.

Neoclassical Economic Thought

The intellectual foundation of the market-oriented approach lies in neoclassical economics. The "classical" reference in the term alludes to eighteenth- and nineteenth-century thinkers such as Adam Smith and David Ricardo who made their path-breaking arguments in favor of free trade and, more broadly, a hands-off (*laissez faire*) role for the state in the economy. With his famous invisible hand metaphor, Smith argued that the market harnessed self-interest for the public good: individuals produced for the market in pursuit of personal enrichment, yet the fruits of their labor provided consumer goods and services that benefited society as a whole. In the twentieth century, the neoclassical school emerged, sharing the classical school's taste for free markets and minimal state intervention. By the 1970s, it had grown to dominate the economics profession in most American universities. Economists trained in neoclassical thought also took over international financial institutions such as the International Monetary Fund (IMF) and the World Bank. By the 1980s, they even began holding important political posts in some LDCs.

Mises, Hayek, and Friedman. Two of the intellectual forefathers of the neoclassical school were Austrian economists Ludwig von Mises (1881–1973) and Friedrich Hayek (1899–1992). Mises and Hayek published their most influential work between 1910 and 1950, long before their neoclassical ideas were ascendant in the profession. Much of their thought was a reaction to the Keynesian and socialist intellectual environments in which they lived. Like Smith, Mises and Hayek saw markets and productive activities arising spontaneously as a natural consequence of humanity's self-interested behavior. Thus, incentives for production and a workable economic order did not require extensive construction or guidance by a central authority, and the incentives provided were even superior to those that any state-imposed order could provide.

Mises and Hayek argued that a capitalist order promotes efficiency by solving a crucial problem inherent to the human condition—that of limited information.[14] Individuals have relevant economic knowledge only about their immediate surroundings since information about a domestic economy is spread diffusely across large populations. Lacking in omniscience, no state planning agency could ever correctly have all the relevant information to organize and incentivize highly efficient forms of economic production. Mises and Hayek argued that markets solve this problem with the price mechanism. Under capitalism, economic agents set prices on labor, capital, and goods in response to a host of factors, such as supply, demand, the cost of production, and so on. Prices are thus a summary of the myriad elements that go into economic activity, so they send accurate signals to channel economic behavior into its most efficient uses. For example, if the price of a good drifts too high, entrepreneurs will take the risk to invest in innovations and technologies that could produce the good more cheaply.

Finally, Hayek was particularly vehement in his rejection of state intervention on philosophical grounds as well. States, he claimed, concentrate power, whereas markets spread it diffusely. Since humans have diverse purposes and goals, true freedom only exists when individuals are allowed to pursue these at their own discretion. Thus, state intervention in the economy is tantamount to coercively usurping humanity's goals and its right to pursue them. In other words, market systems offer greater freedom themselves and are more compatible with political systems that allow for personal freedoms.

A more recent progenitor of neoclassical economics and the minimalist state was Milton Friedman (1912–2006), whose most influential work was published in the 1950s and 1960s. Friedman's primary intellectual contribution was a sharp critique of Keynesianism. The use of fiscal policy and particularly deficit spending to boost aggregate demand was ineffective, he argued, since consumers would simply save more in anticipation of the needed future tax hikes.[15] If government must intervene to boost aggregate demand, it should only do so by influencing interest rates (expanding the money supply). Friedman was also a fierce critic of most welfare state provisions, saying they bred personal dependence on the state, as well as government monopolies in the provision of public goods.[16] Aside from his intellectual contributions, Friedman advised governments such as those of Chile, the United Kingdom, and the United States on their adoption of market-oriented approaches.

The Washington Consensus. In the 1970s and 1980s, the new neoclassical thought also revolutionized scholarship on economic development, reversing the statist consensus of development economics. Economists such as Peter Bauer, Deepak Lal, and Anne Krueger were instrumental in resetting the prevailing view. A central tenet was a rejection of the notion, first promoted by Hirschman, that economic agents in underdeveloped economies were lacking in entrepreneurial ability or were fundamentally different at all from those in developed ones. Instead, these scholars argued that poor and undereducated people in LDCs were just as entrepreneurial and driven by incentives as were those in developed countries. They diagnosed the causes of global poverty as a problem of government policy and particularly the developing world's taste for state-led development. This development model, they argued, stifled the productive instincts and efforts of citizens in the developing world. If governments in LDCs would just allow the invisible hand of the market to work, it would create prosperity in the developing world, just as it had in the developed.

Neoclassical advocates alleged that the state distorted the free and efficient functioning of markets in LDCs. For example, they criticized industrial policy, SOEs, and protectionism as sources of harmful **economic rents**, which are economic gains that persons or firms accrue by rigging a market to their own advantage rather than by producing.[17] States tended to favor politically powerful and often monopolistic businesses with their targeted credit, grants for research and development, and limitations on market entry. Bloated and indebted SOEs provided rents to their overpaid but underworked employees at the expense of taxpayers. The benefits of trade protection enjoyed by lackluster domestic enterprises were also rents, effectively paid for by consumers consigned to buy their expensive and shoddy products. To summarize, the logic of the rent-seeking argument holds that state-led development certainly benefited some people in LDCs, such as those working in SOEs and the private companies targeted by industrial policy. However, the rest of the population suffered by having to indirectly fund these beneficiaries through their tax dollars and by being subject to the resulting inefficiencies in consumer markets and elsewhere.

From this and other critiques, the neoclassical school forged a consensus on the need for economic policy reforms that ended the developing world's state-led model. The collection of policies it espoused became known as the **Washington Consensus**. It was named as such by economist John Williamson in 1989 to reflect the fact that the market-friendly orientation was now the dominant line of thought about development in various governmental agencies housed in the U.S. capital, namely the U.S. State and Treasury departments; the International Monetary Fund (IMF); the World Bank; and the Inter-American Development Bank.[18] Williamson listed the following ten elements of the new orthodoxy: (1) fiscal discipline, (2) reorientation of public expenditures toward strictly social and infrastructural concerns, (3) tax reform to raise revenues, (4) market-determined interest rates, (5) competitive and unified exchange rates, (6) trade liberalization, (7) openness to foreign direct investment, (8) privatization of state-owned enterprises, (9) deregulation of markets, and (10) secure property rights. In sum, the new neoclassical consensus advocated measures to reform the state, mostly by means of privatization, fiscal restructuring, and regulatory reform, and to open LDC economies to foreign trade and investment inflows.

The Market-Oriented Strategy in Practice

The three decades following 1980 were ones of economic reform in the less developed world. Countries in Latin America, the Middle East, Africa, and Asia all enacted a variety of reforms from Williamson's list, although individual countries did so with varying degrees of enthusiasm. Some, but surely not all, of these new policy adoptions occurred as part of agreements made with the IMF, whereby the governments borrowing from the IMF consented to enact structural adjustment programs that included a variety of market-oriented policies.

Reforming the State. A central tenet of this package was **privatization**, which is the transfer of ownership (typically by sale) of a public enterprise from the state to private investors. Privatizations were widespread in the heavy industry, utilities, and infrastructure sectors. The wave of sell-offs saw hundreds of steel mills, petrochemical businesses, telecommunications firms, electricity providers, railroad and toll road operators, and airlines sold to their new private owners. Privatizations of banks and extractive industries such as mining and petroleum companies were also common. Both state-led and socialist economies, such as China and Vietnam, where SOEs were even more ubiquitous, saw hundreds of sell-offs. Figure 8.5 depicts this wave of privatizations in the developing world. Although many SOEs still remain, the thousands of sell-offs that occurred did substantially reduce the role of the state in production.

Privatization contributed to a broader effort to liberalize prices so that they were set by free-market exchange and not by state policy. To neoclassical advocates, a crucial aspect of reform was "getting prices right," so that, as Mises and Hayek wrote, they would send the proper signals to consumers, workers, farmers, and investors about how to allocate scarce resources. For example, upon being privatized, Brazil's telecommunications firms were allowed to raise their rates for telephone subscriptions and calls, which until then had been among the lowest in the world. The elimination of state-mandated price controls, such as those that kept tortillas inexpensive in Mexico, was also an element of reform in many places. In Africa, most agricultural marketing boards were eliminated, freeing up farmers to sell their crops at market prices. The diminished role of state planning agencies, both in state-led and socialist countries, also freed up prices to be set by private agents.

Fiscal policy reforms were also important elements of the new thinking among economic policymakers. In particular, governments took newfound care to maintain budgetary discipline. In some instances, this resulted in **fiscal austerity**, meaning deep cuts in government spending. More commonly, states increased their tax revenues and were more careful about the unfunded spending increases that often triggered populist cycles. For most LDCs, government expenditure on social priorities such as health, education, and antipoverty programs actually increased, slightly countering the trend toward state shrinkage. However, these increases were typically carried out with more fiscal responsibility than they were under populism, meaning they were accompanied by state revenue increases.

Opening to the World. The other central element of the new development model, and one that was already elaborated on in Chapter 5, was a package of reforms that lowered barriers to inflows of foreign goods and capital. The protectionist barriers raised under ISI, export promotion, and socialist approaches to foreign

Figure 8.5   Number of Privatizations in the Developing World, 1988–2008

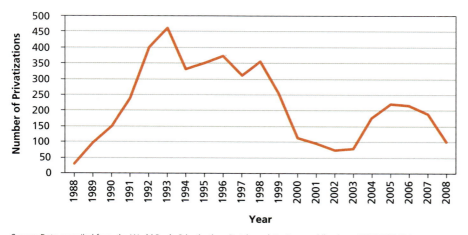

Source: Data compiled from the World Bank, Privatizations Database, http://go.worldbank.org/W1ET8RG1Q0.

trade were lowered, often dramatically. Countries that had average tariff rates in the range of 50 percent to 70 percent lowered them by half or more. For example, China's average tariff rate fell from 50 percent in 1980 to 10 percent in 2004, and India's fell from 75 percent to 28 percent over the same time period.[19] LDCs also banished thousands of nontariff barriers, such as caps on the number of imported goods and licensing requirements to import. Most decreases in protectionist barriers occurred through unilateral decision by country leaders, but international free-trade agreements among countries, such as NAFTA and ASEAN, also proliferated.

Governments also relaxed restrictions on foreign investment, a measure known as capital market liberalization. The new policies allowed multinational corporations (MNCs) to increase their direct investments into LDCs, at times expanding into sectors from which they had previously been disallowed, such as retail, information technologies, finance, and utilities. Ownership and managerial control of firms by foreigners boomed in quantity as investors, many of them based in wealthy Western countries, poured capital into LDCs. In China, foreign direct investment leapt from virtually nil under Mao to 6 percent of GDP in the 1990s.[20] Dozens of other LDCs, from Brazil to India to Nigeria, also became magnets for MNCs. Foreign lenders were also increasingly allowed to purchase locally issued stocks and bonds, known as foreign portfolio investment. These loans from foreigners flooded in and, in many instances, just as quickly flooded out.

Causes of Underdevelopment: Shortcomings of the Market-Oriented Strategy

Criticism of the Washington Consensus and the new market-oriented development model has been fierce. By some measures, its consequences

have been disappointing. Moreover, forms of heavy state involvement in systems labeled "state capitalist" linger and show signs of success.

Disappointing Results

To its critics, the new market-oriented model has not met the expectations advocates raised when it was implemented. African and Latin American leaders often undertook market reforms with promises that they would quickly become newly industrialized countries, like the East Asian Tiger success stories. For the most part, this did not transpire. Economic growth rates sputtered for years in both regions. In the 1990s, Latin America's average growth rate was just 2.9 percent, and sub-Saharan Africa's was 2.1 percent. Both of these were lower average rates than those that prevailed in the 1960s and 1970s.[21] Rather than exporting their way to prosperity with newly streamlined manufacturing firms, companies and workers in these regions struggled to compete in global markets. Many countries experienced a loss of industry because of the newfound competition from foreign firms and investors. The vast majority of Africans remain rural peasants, and, despite the eradication of most marketing board restrictions, agricultural productivity on the continent has hardly budged.

Moreover, the move to the market was accompanied by a host of human costs. Millions of public-sector workers lost their jobs after the companies for which they worked were privatized since the new owners sought to streamline and get rid of unnecessary employees. Fiscal austerity measures also resulted in layoffs of some state employees, such as teachers and health workers. Globalization also caused job losses as domestic firms closed in the face of competition from imports and newly arrived MNCs. Many of these laid-off workers only found subsequent work in the highly precarious informal sector. Critics also allege that the move to the market increased income inequality in many LDCs. In several Latin American countries in the

understanding INDICATORS

Gauging State Intervention in the Economy

Scholars studying economic policy often need quantitative measures that allow them to compare the extent of state intervention across countries and through time. To this end, two think tanks have developed indicators of economic freedom that annually score countries on the degree of state involvement in their economies. The Fraser Institute publishes the Economic Freedom of the World indicator, which is an index ranging from 0 to 10 that is an amalgamation of individual measures of government size, security of property rights, monetary policy, trade policy, and business and labor market regulations. The Heritage Foundation publishes the Index of Economic Freedom, an index ranging from 0 to 100 that summarizes a very similar set of factors. For both, higher values correspond to less state involvement. These indicators can be used to illustrate the trend toward a diminished role for the state in economies throughout the developing world. For example, the figure here shows the scores of the two indices for India for all available years, and both illustrate this pattern. The Freedom of the World indicator is particularly useful since it starts in 1970, although it did not begin

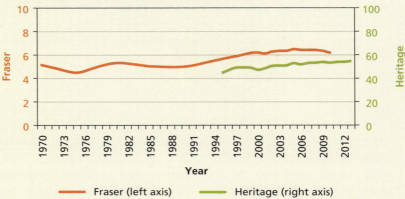

Trends in Economic Freedom in India, 1970–2012

Source: Compiled from the Fraser Institute, Economic Freedom Network, www.freetheworld.com/index.php, and the 2013 Index of Economic Freedom, www.heritage.org/index/.

producing scores on an annual basis until 2000.

Potential users of these indices should be aware that many scholars treat them with skepticism. Perhaps most importantly, the think tanks that produce them are themselves ideological advocates of a minimal state. This is partially evident in the indices' names, which equate a small state presence with economic freedom. Not everyone agrees that a market-oriented way of organizing economic activity—one that allegedly empowers large private corporations—is indicative of economic freedom. More consequentially, this ideological preference is evident in some of the measures that go into each group's index. For example, both include measures of the volume of government fiscal effort, tallying

low taxation and expenditure as more free. This decision is tantamount to assuming that the people in a rural African village without a primary school have more economic freedom than those in a village with a publicly funded school. Because of this, low-income countries, which are lacking in many public services because their states are too ineffective to raise sufficient revenue, score highly on this particular element of the broader indices.

- Is it possible for data and quantitative indicators to be free of ideological bias?

- What might be some better ways to capture the degree of state intervention in the economy?

1990s, globalization increased the average wages for educated workers while those for unskilled labor stagnated. This was due in part to the fact that educated workers could take better advantage of productivity-enhancing technologies such as computers.[22] In former socialist economies such as China, the previously unknown specter of unemployment and the introduction of market-determined wage rates dramatically boosted income disparities.

The permissive environment for foreign-capital inflows has also created an environment that is more conducive to roller coasters of economic volatility triggered by various financial crises. The peso crisis originating in Mexico (1995), the Asian financial crisis (Thailand 1997), the *rouble* crisis (Russia 1998), the samba crisis (Brazil 1999), and the Argentine crisis (2002) all struck when countries experienced a rapid outflow of foreign capital. These crises were contagious, spreading beyond their originating countries when international investors assumed the problems of the initial country were common to nearby ones. Each produced deep recessions for the LDCs involved, and the 1990s was a volatile decade for much of the developing world.

State Capitalism

Despite the wave of economic reform in the 1980s and 1990s, states in LDCs have not completely shed themselves of their roles in economic production. In particular, the privatization wave stopped in the early 2000s, leaving thousands of SOEs in existence. For example, nearly all of the developing world's large oil and gas firms are state owned. Also, states still frequently seek to guide decisions of large private corporations. This combination—state ownership or guidance of major firms that operate in capitalist and increasingly globalized markets—has been labeled **state capitalism**.[23] Some critics of the Washington Consensus hail state capitalism as a successful alternative to the free-market model,

especially since some of its leading practitioners, such as China, India, and Russia, have been growing so quickly. Advocates of state capitalism assert that it provides the best of two worlds. Major firms are large and backed by the state, so they can have the global presence and capital for large projects that smaller private firms lack. Yet they are relatively efficient because they must operate in competitive markets.

Despite enacting hundreds of privatizations in the 1990s, China is today the paradigmatic example of state capitalism. Major banks, steel mills, mobile phone companies, petroleum firms, and electricity distributors are still majority owned by the government. Unlike SOEs of the past, the Chinese state grooms those of today to be efficient and productive competitors in domestic and global markets. For example, the profits in state-owned Sinopec (petroleum) and China Mobile (telecommunications) are greater than those of the 500 largest private Chinese firms combined, and the majority of LDC-based companies listed in the global Fortune 500 are state owned.[24] The Chinese state also exercises control over private firms by favoring some large ones with a variety of industrial policy measures, one of which is seed money for research and development. Most large private corporations also have strict oversight by officials of the ruling Communist Party, who ensure that company leaders' decisions are in line with the party's economic and political goals. All told, despite decades of market reforms, China's economy remains a highly mixed one.

Critique: Successes of the Washington Consensus

Not surprisingly, neoclassical economists and other advocates of the Washington Consensus reach very different conclusions about the economic consequences of the new market policies and the merits of state capitalism than do its critics.

The successes, they claim, are more plentiful than the failures, and ongoing failures are due to lingering instances of state intervention and not to market reforms themselves.

Success Stories

The most visible success has been a general decrease in consumer price inflation. Inflation is the annual average change in the prices of consumer goods, and high inflation is often triggered by populist measures. In the 1980s and 1990s, several Latin American countries even struggled with hyperinflationary events in which prices increased at 50 percent or more per month. Hyperinflationary problems are now largely a thing of the past. In the 1970s and 1980s, average annual inflation in Latin America was 13 percent, but in the first decade of the 2000s it was just 5 percent.[25] The average inflation rate has also declined by more than half in sub-Saharan Africa and the Middle East. Budgetary discipline and the end of recurring populist cycles have played important roles in defeating inflation. Trade liberalization has also helped in quelling price inflation since the influx of imports has typically expanded the range and quality of consumer choice.[26]

Advocates also point out several beneficial aspects of privatization. States no longer need to provide budgetary support to so many indebted SOEs, thus unloading a major fiscal burden. Newly privatized businesses have become more efficient, which has boosted overall productivity. In many instances, privatization and the influx of new private capital improved the provision of consumer services. For example, in Argentina, newly privatized water companies were able to expand their potable water infrastructure faster than state-owned ones.

Moreover, whereas the 1990s was a disappointing decade for economic growth in the developing world, the 2000s were less so. Economic growth rebounded once the effects of the various financial crises ebbed in the early 2000s. The new liberal trade policies meant that many LDCs were able to take advantage of the increase in global prices for their commodity exports, a trend that emerged after 2007 with the boom in food and oil prices. Rather than succumbing to yet another financial crisis, most LDCs weathered the economic storm emanating from the United States in 2008 extremely well. Africa, often stereotyped as an economic basket case, has numerous countries that have experienced quiet and gradual success since reforming their economies in the 1990s. Nearly twenty of sub-Saharan Africa's forty-eight countries, ranging in size from tiny Lesotho to large Ethiopia, have strung together fifteen years of uninterrupted economic growth.[27] Similarly, Brazil and the rest of Latin America have been growing at a rapid clip since 2002, and Chile, the region's earliest reformer and most successful economy, experienced rapid growth long before then. Finally, since 2002, income distributions in most Latin American countries have been growing more, not less, equal.

Debating State Capitalism

Neoclassical thinkers interpret the rise of China, India, and other practitioners of state capitalism as a vote for more markets, not more state. In other words, these countries are growing because of their adoption of some market policies, especially trade liberalization, and not because of the lingering presence of their states. Moreover, the neoclassical interpretation of the economic disappointments in some LDCs in the 1990s is that they had not gone far enough in adopting Washington Consensus policies. Remaining SOEs, enduring protectionism, and ongoing regulations against firm entry and foreign investment are to blame when market reforms have seemingly produced unimpressive results.[28]

State capitalism, the argument goes on, will ultimately suffer some of the same problems of state-led development if left unreformed. The SOEs and coddled private firms of today are not necessarily better for the economy than were those of the past. A few enormous, globally competitive firms can invoke national pride, but they are not themselves indicators of a healthy and prosperous economy. In China, the presence of large firms with state backing typically means that smaller ones are being disadvantaged or completely shut out of the market. This can stifle innovation and hurt consumers by limiting competition. Moreover, evidence seems to suggest that, as in the past, today's SOEs are less productive than private firms, with their apparent success stemming largely from government largesse.[29]

CASE | STUDY

DID INDIA'S POSTCOLONIAL DEVELOPMENT MODEL DELAY ITS ECONOMIC RISE?

These days, the world's largest democracy is often in the news for its economic rise, but it was not always thus. India only recently emerged as an economic success story, as the start of its boom lagged behind that of its now-richer Chinese rival by more than a decade. Prior to that, Indian leaders pursued a state-led development model for some forty years, a model that is today much maligned for its inefficiencies and alleged failures to produce sustained economic growth. This case study considers the role of this development model, as well as colonialism and topography, in shaping India's underdevelopment. To aid in thinking about these different causes of underdevelopment, Table 8.1 compares them and their possible consequences in India and its former colonizer, the United Kingdom.

The South: India's State-Led Development Model

A leading interpretation of India's development failure is that its government created excessive state intervention in the economy following independence in 1947. This occurred largely under the leadership of the first prime minister, Jawaharlal Nehru (1947–1964), and his daughter, Prime Minister Indira Gandhi (1966–1977, 1980–1984). Although neither leader turned India into a full-scale socialist economy, both drew some inspiration from the apparent successes of the Soviet Union's industrialization drive under extensive state ownership.

Elements of the Model. The Indian model had three main elements: an expansion of state ownership, a wide-ranging set of licensing regulations for industrial activity, and economic self-sufficiency.[30] Under the guidance of its periodic five-year plans and other state initiatives, India created numerous state-owned enterprises in heavy industry and finance. Among them were steel firms, which Nehru created on the conviction that private investors lacked the funds to sufficiently build up and maintain the sector. State-produced steel was also sold on to other firms at subsidized prices to spur forward linkages. Nehru also declared state monopolies in areas such as railways and military equipment. For her part, Gandhi nationalized coal and oil firms, along with all major banks and insurance companies.

The Indian state further shaped industrial activity by establishing the License Raj, a set of bureaucratic agencies, rules, and procedures

DID INDIA'S POSTCOLONIAL DEVELOPMENT MODEL DELAY ITS ECONOMIC RISE?

Table 8.1 ▪ ▪ ▪ **Development Comparison: India and the United Kingdom**

Indicator	India	United Kingdom
GDP per capita at PPP	US$3,163	US$31,330
Human Development Index	.547	.863
Public sector's share of capital investment in 1970s (gross fixed capital formation)	48 percent	21 percent
Trade balance with specified partner as percentage of GDP, 1911–1915	+1.3 percent (with UK)	−1.2 percent (with India)
Percentage of population living within 100km of the coast	24 percent	90 percent

Sources: Data on GDP per capita at PPP and Human Development Index compiled from Gapminder, www.gapminder.org; capital investment, World Bank, World Development Indicators, http://data.worldbank.org/data-catalog/world-development-indicators and European Commission, Eurostat, http://epp.eurostat.ec.europa.eu/portal/page/portal/national_accounts/data/database; trade balance, Angus Maddison, *The World Economy: Volume 1, A Millennial Perspective* (Paris: Organisation for Economic Co-operation and Development, 2006); population living near coast, National Aggregates of Geospatial Data Collection, Population, Landscape, and Climate Estimates, http://sedac.ciesin.columbia.edu/data/set/nagdc-population-landscape-climate-estimates-v3.

that regulated private investment. Most forms of private investment, such as starting a small business or expanding an existing one, required the potential investor to secure a license from the state. Bureaucrats granted licenses based on the proposed investment's adherence to extensive legal limitations on private involvement in certain sectors, all largely meant to protect existing public and private businesses. For example, in the 1960s and 1970s, the License Raj enforced a prohibition against the involvement of medium or large businesses in the production of light manufactured goods such as clothing and shoes.

The License Raj was also instrumental in enforcing the Indian economy's inward orientation. Convinced that India's hard-won political independence also required economic self-sufficiency, Nehru raised barriers to trade and foreign investment. Imports in many sectors were banned or highly taxed, and firms wanting to import an item had to convince the

License Raj that it was essential and not produced in India. Bureaucrats of the License Raj were also stingy in granting licenses to foreign private investors, as rules against capital inflows were also tight.

Consequences. India's economy failed to flourish under this experiment, growing at an annual rate of just 3 percent to 4 percent on average. This was far too slow to make a substantial dent in the poverty rate, especially since population growth of 2 percent to 3 percent per year swallowed most of these meager economic gains. The sluggishness led analysts to quip that India was permanently consigned to this slow "Hindu rate of growth."

According to its critics, state-led development kept India's economy unproductive and inefficient for several reasons. Despite the high-minded rhetoric from leaders about the superiority of state-owned enterprises and self-sufficiency, the various forms of state intervention largely served to protect existing public and private businesses from unwanted competition. This ended up aiding them at the expense of consumers and potential entrepreneurs, a classic example of rent-seeking. For example, License Raj procedures for securing licenses to conduct business involved extensive paperwork, multiple visits to an agency office, and waiting times that often could be counted in years. Potential entrepreneurs could expect to receive a license after a long wait, or they could simply pay an expensive bribe to speed up the process. Many were too discouraged to even try to invest in the first place and either gave up entrepreneurial hopes or entered the inefficient informal sector. The rules and procedures also prevented technological acquisition for existing businesses, as obtaining a license to import a computer took, on some estimates, three years and fifty trips to a Delhi office.[31] In most product markets, consumers were at the mercy either of bloated monopolies or of small firms that were not even allowed to achieve the efficiency gains of size.

As if in proof of the model's futility, India's economy began to grow rather rapidly upon abandoning it. A reversal of many of the state-led policies was initially enacted through some gradual reforms in the 1980s and then a set of more encompassing and systematic ones in the early 1990s under Prime Minister Narasimha Rao (1991–1996). Many of the licensing restrictions were abandoned and protectionist barriers were lifted. Over the subsequent two decades, import and export volumes exploded, nearly tripling their share in India's GDP. Numerous privatizations also occurred in the 1990s and 2000s, and private businesses of all sizes proliferated and grew. As of 2013, the Hindu rate of growth was a distant memory. India had been averaging annual growth rates of 6 percent (with slower population growth) for over two decades, and gains in human development had been substantial.

***

To be sure, India did make numerous economic advances under state-led development. British colonial rule largely prevented the emergence of a vibrant manufacturing sector, so at independence in 1947 India had little industry of which to speak. Under Nehru's nurturing measures of state investment and protectionism, industry grew at a rate of 7.4 percent per year, somewhat faster than the rate of growth in the 1980s and 1990s.[32] Whether the private sector acting alone and in the face of global competition could have produced such industrial growth is in doubt. Gandhi's nationalization of the banks increased credit to entrepreneurs of small businesses and farmers of small plots. Private commercial banks were not lending to these sectors because they were not profitable, instead preferring to give loans to urban industrialists who, in some cases, actually owned the bank that lent to them.[33] State-led development enabled India to seemingly overcome some of these failings of the private sector. Even today, as India grows more rapidly, the state still plays a major role in the economy by continuing to own giant utility and steel firms and by regulating foreign investment in various sectors. In other words, India's current boom may be due to state capitalism, not to the turn to more unfettered capitalism.

The West: Exploiting the "Jewel in the British Crown"

The role of India's economic development model in its relatively disappointing postindependence economic performance can be debated, but it certainly cannot explain why it was so poor at the time of independence. According to many experts, that responsibility rests on the United Kingdom, which directly colonized the "Jewel in the British Crown" from 1857 to 1947 and indirectly colonized parts of it via the British East India Company (EIC) for a century before that.[34]

DID INDIA'S POSTCOLONIAL DEVELOPMENT MODEL DELAY ITS ECONOMIC RISE?

In its areas of control, the EIC levied high taxes on Indian peasants, effectively engaging them in forced labor. In doing so, the EIC empowered Indian *zamindars*, aristocrats who owned large tracts of land, as middlemen to use all necessary means to extract the imperial tribute. The EIC also enjoyed a monopoly on trade with the Indians it oversaw, meaning it was able to unilaterally set prices for the silks and other commodities it so desperately sought. These arrangements extracted precious resources from India while deepening its class inequalities.

The exploitation of India continued when the British metropole took control from the EIC in 1857. The British imposed a regime of free trade on India, exporting its manufactured goods (mostly textiles) to the colony in exchange for cotton and other raw materials. The imposition deindustrialized India.[35] The colony had been developing an export-oriented textiles sector in the mid-nineteenth century, but this disappeared in the face of competition from British imports. A capitalist class that could invest in and foster local industry thus never emerged.[36] British exploitation through this trading relationship is evident in the fact that India carried a trade surplus with Britain for most of the era, meanings its exports to Britain were of greater value than its imports from it.[37] Moreover, the British Empire also extracted wealth from India via home charges, which were remittances of funds from the Indian treasury to London on the grounds that colonial administration held costs for the metropole.

The Natural World: Topography and Transport Costs

The locational distribution of India's population on the subcontinent is largely unique among the world's major land masses, matched in part only by the one continent that is poorer: Africa. In particular, India has the world's highest interior population density, meaning a large number of its people live inland and not along its long ocean coastline. For example, only one (Mumbai) of India's five largest cities is on the coast, and 76 percent of its population lives more than 100 kilometers from the ocean. (In Africa the figure is 81 percent.)[38] This is so for two reasons. First, topographically, India's terrain begins rising within a few hundred miles of the coast, leveling out in a plateau that covers much of the country's interior. Many people have preferred to live on this plateau where the cooler temperatures are more

Prime ministers Jawaharlal Nehru (right, 1947-1964) and Indira Gandhi (left, 1966 – 1977 and 1980-1984), his daughter, dominated Indian politics for the first four decades of its independence. Both were convinced that development in a postcolonial state required economic self-sufficiency, strict state regulations on investment, and heavy doses of public ownership.

comfortable and lessen the prevalence of tropical diseases. Second, historically, another large share of the population has chosen to live in the plain surrounding the Ganges River in the subtropical north.

This fact is relevant to economic growth because residence in the hinterland, instead of on the coast, makes transport and transaction costs high. It is far cheaper to transport goods via water than land, yet human populations can only take advantage of this cost advantage when they live near a body of water. Living inland thus raises Indians' costs of exchanging among themselves and with the world. The Ganges River provides some relief from these high transport costs to inland dwellers, but even so it has historically served to attract Indians deeper into the interior and away from the coast. Moreover, India remains relatively distant from the two major epicenters of global economic activity, Europe and the United States. This distance would have complicated any efforts, if attempted, to pursue an export-oriented growth strategy.

* * *

After decades of spinning its postindependence wheels and centuries of ill treatment by the British, India's economy has finally started to grow in a sustained way. Whether India's current rise is because of a new market-oriented development model or because of the state's ongoing hand in the economy can still be debated, but the facts of

human development are undeniable. Its extreme poverty rate has been halved in just thirty years, and by virtually any indicators educational and health outcomes have improved dramatically. Many problems remain, but India in the twenty-first century looks better poised to develop than it did in the twentieth.

Thinking Critically about Development

- The debate over state capitalism and further economic reforms continues to rage for the Indian case. Should India privatize all of its SOEs and completely liberalize its markets to trade and capital inflows, or does continued growth depend on state involvement in production and protection?

- Historian David Landes says of India that "whatever nefarious deeds one may ascribe to imperialism, one can hardly argue that the states of the subcontinent were on their way to an industrial revolution before the Europeans interrupted."[39] Is this true, or would India be rich today if the West had left it alone?

- Despite its high interior population density, many aspects of India's geography are favorable to economic growth: lots of arable land (60 percent) and fertile soils, a high share of subtropical land with a relatively low malaria burden, and millennia of access to draft animals and other large mammals. Is India a poor fit for the geography hypothesis?

Key Terms

agricultural collective, p. 192

capitalism, p. 191

central planning, p. 193

command economy, p. 193

commune, p. 193

communism, p. 192

development model, p. 184

economic populism, p. 188

economic rents, p. 197

fiscal austerity, p. 198

industrial policy, p. 187

Keynesianism, p. 185

market-oriented strategy, p. 195

marketing board, p. 188

patronage, p. 189

privatization, p. 197

socialism, p. 191

state capitalism, p. 201

state-led development, p. 184

state-owned enterprises (SOEs), p. 186

Washington Consensus, p. 197

 Suggested Readings

Amsden, Alice H. *Asia's Next Giant: South Korea and Late Industrialization.* New York: Oxford University Press, 1992.

Chang, Ha-Joon. *Bad Samaritans: The Myth of Free Trade and the Secret History of Capitalism.* New York: Bloomsbury Press, 2008.

Edwards, Sebastian. *Left Behind: Latin America and the False Promise of Populism.* Chicago: University of Chicago Press, 2010.

Haggard, Stephan. *Pathways from the Periphery: The Politics of Growth in the Newly Industrializing Countries.* Ithaca, NY: Cornell University Press, 1990.

Panagariya, Arvind. *India: The Emerging Giant.* New York: Oxford University Press, 2008.

Williamson, John. "What Washington Means by Policy Reform." In John Williamson, *Latin American Adjustment: How Much Has Happened?,* chapter two. Washington, DC: Institute for International Economics, 1990.

 Web Resources

Commanding Heights Video, PBS, www.pbs.org/wgbh/commandingheights/

Fraser Institute, Economic Freedom of the World Index, www.freetheworld.com/

Heritage Foundation, Index of Economic Freedom, www.heritage.org/index/

World Bank, Privatization Database, http://data.worldbank.org/data-catalog/privatization-database

People move along a dirt road in an urban slum on the outskirts of Sanaa, Yemen's capital. Most urban slums in the developing world are informal settlements, meaning the residents have no government-secured rights of ownership to their homes or land. Without these formal protections, many slum dwellers are hesitant to make improvements on their homes.

Economic Institutions and Informality

Marianela reaches into her purse to pay for the aspirin she needs for her daughter's headaches, but, much to her embarrassment, she does not have enough money. She sheepishly asks the storekeeper to float her a loan on the spot. He begrudgingly consents since she has faithfully repaid him for a number of previous loans. But first she has to agree to pay him back almost double the price of the aspirin by the end of the week.

Economic life where Marianela lives—in a slum on the outskirts of Lima, Peru—is often precarious like this. Marianela lives in a ramshackle shanty made of wooden materials that she and her family collected in a piecemeal fashion. Her family does not technically own the home. No one in the neighborhood owns their home. In fact, her neighborhood's existence remains technically illegal, since it was founded two decades earlier by individuals who "invaded" a piece of state-owned land and set up housing literally overnight. The case has been languishing in the court system ever since, so Marianela does not know if she might have to one day leave. For income, Marianela sells artisan products in a street market, but this is her fifth attempt at successful self-employment in less than five years. She has never been able to save or borrow enough to invest in or grow the various businesses she has started. Instead, she simply moves from one business idea to another, hoping that one will catch hold. Since she is dependent on customer demand, some weeks are better than others—hence her need to occasionally borrow from the storeowner.

Marianela's story exemplifies how economic institutions shape material and social fortunes. According to scholars of development in a variety of social science disciplines, the ways in which finance, employment, business, and property usage are organized play a major role in determining whether a country thrives or fails economically. In Marianela's case, these various aspects of her economic context are organized informally, a common feature of the developing world. This chapter focuses on the nature of economic institutions, and particularly the distinguishing trait of informality, in the global South. It considers arguments for and against the case that bad economic institutions and informality lay at the root of underdevelopment. The subsequent chapter continues this focus on institutions by looking at the role of political institutions in development.

Institutions are organizations and rules that structure human interactions. Institutions have at least some resilience to and existence beyond the individual persons and personalities that are part of them. By way of example, marriage is an institution since it is a recurring pattern of social behavior grounded in laws and unwritten traditions. It thus has a certain degree of imperviousness to the millions of people who practice it. Similarly, a university is an institution since it is an organization constituted by relatively stable rules and occupational roles that outlive its occupants. In turn, an **economic institution** is a set of rules or an organization that structures human decisions about how to allocate material resources. A multinational corporation is one such institution, but this chapter focuses on four major economic institutions, each of which constitutes a major area of economic activity: property markets, labor markets, the structure of business firms, and financial services.

The nature of some of these institutions in LDCs was touched on in previous chapters. For example, Chapter 5 on globalization described countries as being more or less open to foreign capital, a feature of financial service markets. Chapter 8 contrasted state-owned and privately owned enterprises, two different types of firm structure. For the most part, these previous discussions have focused on institutions within the formal economic sector—that is, the portion of the economy that is legally recognized and regulated by the government. The current chapter will not give a full summary and review of formal-sector

economic institutions. Rather, it will focus on what is the most distinguishing feature of economic institutions in less developed economies: the presence of a large informal sector.

The **informal sector** (also called an irregular, gray, shadow, or unofficial economy) is comprised of the economic activity that occurs outside the monitoring and legal purview of the state. In other words, the informal sector is not formally recognized, regulated, or taxed by government. Informal economic activity can include illegal activities such as narcotics and sex trafficking, but the vast majority of informal activity is best characterized as extralegal. This means otherwise legal and ethical activities such as selling food, saving money, or owning a home that are done outside of the formal legal system. The greater presence of informally organized economic institutions in the developing world than in the developed is a possible cause of differences in prosperity levels.

Property Markets and Informal Ownership

A society's **property market** refers to how it organizes the ownership and exchange of major economic assets, most commonly housing, land, and business capital. In the developed world, governments recognize, regulate, and enforce **property rights**, which are the recognized legal rights to use, transfer, and earn income from an economic asset. Ownership rights over major assets are typically embodied in a title deed, a document that delineates an asset and its owner(s). In the event that someone encroaches upon the specified party's ownership, titles in the developed world carry the implicit guarantee of protection by a largely impartial judiciary and bureaucracy. In contrast, a large share of the property markets in LDCs tends to be organized informally. As a result, most residents of the developing world live in homes and on land over which they do not have government-guaranteed rights of ownership. By one estimate from 1997, 85 percent of urban land tracts in the less developed world were informally owned, and the corresponding figure in rural areas exceeded 40 percent.[1]

Urban Slums and Rural Land

The most visible manifestation of property market informality can be observed in the many urban slums of the developing world, the vast majority of which were founded as and remain **informal settlements**. An informal settlement is a neighborhood constructed on land and with houses to which the occupants have no or only a weak legal claim of ownership. Informal settlements often come about through squatting or (to its detractors) invasion, whereby residents, without legal permission, move onto a piece of land that is the property of the state, a private landowner, or no one in particular. The residents then construct homes and public services themselves. However, the lack of public planning and legality means that most homes are dilapidated, and public services such as garbage collection, modern sanitation, and potable water delivery are limited. For this reason, informal settlements, aside from the lack of property rights, are often in violation of official building, zoning, and environmental codes.

Urban informal settlements, most of which are slums, have become iconic features of the developing world, in part because they have exploded in size and frequency due to rapid urbanization over the past several decades. In fact, many of the local terms for urban slums are internationally known: "shanty towns" in South Africa, "*favelas*" in Brazil, and "*villas miserias*" in Argentina. The United Nations estimated that in 2010 over 1.1 billion people in LDCs lived in urban slums, defined as neighborhoods with nondurable housing and limited public services. Between 60 percent and 70 percent of urban residents in sub-Saharan Africa and South Asia are slum dwellers, while percentages in the other developing regions are in the thirties.[2] Table 9.1 reports the percentage

Table 9.1	Prevalence of Urban Slum Dwellers in Various LDCs, 2001
Country	**People Living in Slums (as a percentage of urban population)**
China	38 percent
Egypt	40 percent
Guatemala	62 percent
India	56 percent
Mozambique	94 percent
Philippines	44 percent

Source: United Nations Human Settlements Program Data, ww2. unhabitat.org/programmes/guo/statistics.asp.

of urban dwellers in a variety of LDCs that reside in slums.

Informal land use and a lack of property rights are also common in rural parts of the developing world. Most peasants lack title deeds to the land they cultivate and instead simply use and presume ownership over the plots their families have tilled for generations. For example, in much of rural sub-Saharan Africa, who uses what land is largely governed by **customary law**, or unwritten norms based on recognized tradition and enforced by tribal chiefs. Under customary law, the right to cultivate a piece of land is one that is passed from parents to their children by assumption, and no written contracts or wills formally establish the next generation's right. Disputes over land usage and ownership are usually adjudicated by tribal chiefs, although in some cases government courts also recognize and adjudicate customary tenure.

Causes of Property Informality

In LDCs, the causes of informality in land and home ownership are multiple. Excessive regulations can make it prohibitive for the poor to secure formal ownership rights to their assets. A study of Egypt found that acquiring and formally registering state land for personal ownership required the involvement of thirty-one bureaucratic agencies and the completion of seventy-seven procedures that could last up to fourteen years.[3] High taxes on land transactions can also exacerbate the problem, with countries such as Nigeria and Syria charging more than 20 percent of the property value in a one-off tax.

Ineffective government also contributes to informality since the recognition and protection of private land ownership requires an active state role. States must have the ability to survey tracts of land and keep registries that record contracts and titles. Most governments in LDCs can hardly afford to provide these services. For example, Haiti has a legal code that establishes private land ownership rights, but its bureaucracy is too small and inept to enforce it. It takes almost a year to go through the process of formally registering property in Haiti (compared to a month in most developed countries) and costs the owner almost 7 percent of the value of the property.[4] As a result, less than 5 percent of Haitian land is registered with public records.[5] Moreover, neutral and efficient courts and police forces are needed to enforce and protect private property rights, but these are also in rare supply in LDCs. In Guatemala, it takes nearly four years for the courts to adjudicate a contract dispute and for the bureaucracy to follow through on enforcing it. In many high-income countries, it takes less than a year.

Finally, many governments in the developing world simply do not have the will to reduce informality by providing property rights for the poor. Many municipal politicians want to prevent resident ownership of urban slum land so that they can later develop a new neighborhood with high-rises or shopping malls on the land, a prospect that requires the removal of many residents. Furthermore, when a settlement is established through invasion on land already owned by a private landowner, local officials are often reticent to aggrieve this wealthy citizen by transferring ownership to the squatters. Similarly,

most African politicians are unwilling to usurp the power of local tribal chiefs by overturning a customary system that has lasted for generations. Finally, formalization costs money and takes time, and many governments see other social needs as carrying a higher priority.

Causes of Underdevelopment: Informal Property Markets

In recent decades, a dramatic shift has occurred in scholarly work on the causes of economic and social underdevelopment. **New institutionalism** (also neoinstitutionalism), a body of thought that spans several social science disciplines, stresses the independent impact of rules and organizations on development outcomes. The school of thought views previously privileged explanations of economic prosperity, such as the rate of technological acquisition, as a consequence of the more stable organizational forms that are more fundamental or ultimate causes: "Development is no longer seen as a process of capital accumulation, but as a process of organizational change."[6] To new institutionalist scholars, institutions are so important because they shape the incentives that underlie elites' and common citizens' economic behaviors. Individuals will only engage in activities that lead to economic progress for society as a whole if institutions give them the incentives to pursue personally enriching behaviors that also have wider societal benefits. In this view, the developing world is poor because the laws, informal rules, and organizations that govern economic decision making discourage citizens from being as productive and innovative as they might otherwise be.

New Institutional Economics and Property Rights

In the economics discipline, the institutionalist turn has taken the form of **new institutional economics (NIE)**. For NIE scholars, and especially the school's pioneer, Douglass North, the most important institution for economic growth in a society is the property market.[7] In particular, North claims that the degree of property rights protection is a fundamental cause of long-run economic performance. The presence of strong property rights in a society protects citizens from having their assets expropriated by the state or by non-state actors such as common criminals or even friends and acquaintances. To North, the existence of such a system is a requisite for sustained economic progress since, if faced with the fear of having their property taken away, individuals will have little incentive to acquire new, more productive property or to make improvements to the property they already own.[8] Without property rights, productivity improvements are simply not on their agendas. For example, a farmer would not buy a tractor if he thought it possible that it or his land might be forcibly taken away. However, if assured that everyone will respect his ownership rights over his farm and his farm equipment, the farmer can safely buy the new tractor. This will enhance his crop yields and thus his income. It will also improve the productivity and prosperity of society as a whole.[9]

Property rights are not a naturally occurring phenomenon. Rather, they require a number of institutions to be in place. One is a legal code that is committed to protecting property ownership, another is an independent judiciary that can fairly apply the legal code, and yet another is a bureaucracy that will enforce the legal code. Systems that successfully uphold property rights have a judiciary that acts as a neutral third party in adjudicating contract disputes between two persons or entities. This means ruling against the state and powerful private citizens if either violates a contract that stipulates someone else's right to ownership. Moreover, the state needs to be present and effective throughout its entire territory so that it can maintain order and enforce contracts. A unified and centralized state presence is also beneficial since it expands the scope of market activity, allowing individuals to safely make exchanges

with strangers who live within the same state. To NIE scholars, the West was the first world region to develop because it was also the first to develop strong property rights protections under a centralized and effective state. In 1900, 75 percent of U.S. families in rural areas owned their land.[10] By contrast, in 2004 barely one African in ten lived in a house with a formal title deed.[11]

Dead Capital

According to Peruvian economist Hernando de Soto, the lack of property rights for the millions of poor people who only have informal ownership over their major assets creates yet another drag on economic prosperity in the less developed world. It keeps the possessions of the poor locked up as **dead capital**—that is, assets that have no value or use beyond their immediate purpose. Without legality, the owner of a physical asset such as a house or land has no ability to convert its potential value into productive uses outside those dictated by its material features. In de Soto's words, it remains "commercially and financially invisible."[12] Legality allows the owner to produce value beyond an asset's natural state by giving others the confidence that it exists and that the government will uphold its value if exchanged.[13]

How can assets produce value beyond their physical state? The most common example is the use of a home or land as collateral to secure a loan. A major cost of dead capital lies in the fact that individuals cannot use informally owned assets as collateral when requesting a loan. **Collateral** is a piece of the borrower's property that he or she promises to give the lender in case the borrower cannot repay the loan. Banks the world over deny or charge higher interest rates on loans that are not secured with collateral, since, without collateral, they are left empty handed if the borrower does not repay. Many poor people, despite their poverty, do have physical assets that could be offered as collateral. These might include a modest home on a plot of land, a small field that has been in the family for generations, or a few heads of cattle. If the poor possess these assets informally, however, they are unable to use them as collateral. That is, they cannot point to a title deed or government registry that proves ownership. The potential value of these assets for securing a loan thus remains locked up as dead capital, and the poor face prohibitive interest rates or no access to credit as a result. By contrast, in the United States, persons who own a home can take out a home equity loan, which effectively posts part of the home as collateral. This allows many Americans to engage in productive pursuits such as starting a business or funding their children's college education.

The existence of dead capital also impoverishes informal owners and the economy as a whole by raising **transaction costs**, which are the costs—other than the price of the good or service being exchanged—that are needed to make an exchange possible. In informal markets, the information that two people need in order to decide whether to trade a major asset is largely limited to that which can be gathered through personal relationships. Collecting this information—such as the current value of an asset, its future security, and the trustworthiness of the other transactor—is costly if one must do it through personal connections only. Given these costs, many people will simply not engage in the transaction, especially if it is with a stranger or involves an asset that is physically distant. The costly need to collect personal information thus keeps exchange in informal markets small and localized in scope.

In contrast, formal markets collect and store information about assets and individuals, making it available to people as they weigh the costs and benefits of potential major transactions. Prices, value, credit worthiness, and the safety of property rights can all be gathered through impersonal channels, a fact that integrates property markets across disparate places and persons. For example, a woman in Florida who must move to Seattle can easily check on the asking price and estimated value of Seattle homes from her computer in Florida, and the bank in New York from which she might borrow can easily check on her credit worthiness in public records. This relative ease of collecting information greases the wheels of economic exchange and, as a result, economic growth.

Finally, widespread informality in ownership of property makes it more difficult for societies to construct infrastructure and provide security. In many of the developing world's informal settlements, addresses are given as "the wooden shack with the rusty door three houses down from the bakery." This obviously makes mail delivery difficult, but it can also complicate the provision of public utilities as electricity and water companies have no formal address to link to or charge. Physical anonymity also makes it easier for people to evade their debts since bill collectors struggle to find them. Moreover, security personnel have a much harder time locating suspected criminals.

In his 2000 book *The Mystery of Capital*, de Soto tallied up the value of dead capital throughout the developing world in an attempt to estimate the deleterious effects of informality on LDC economies. His estimate was a staggering US$9.3 trillion, most of it tied up in the informally owned homes and land of the poor. At the time, this figure was forty times the amount of foreign aid that the less developed world had received from the West between 1945 and 2000. In other words, the global poor are sitting on a gold mine that awaits unlocking by their states. In response to de Soto's claims, numerous developing world governments have implemented programs, often under guidance by de Soto and his team of consultants, to grant title to poor people living in informal settlements. It is partly for this reason that former U.S. president Bill Clinton called him "probably the world's most important living economist."[14]

Critique: Is Formality Worth It?

Formal property rights are a highly valued institution by NIE scholars and critics of informality such as de Soto, but not all scholars agree with their assessments. Geographer Alan Gilbert points out that existing informal norms about property rights are often serving the same purpose as formalized ones.[15] Few of the global poor living in informal settlements face the real prospect of the government or thieves expropriating their homes. Wholesale removals of entire neighborhoods are the exception rather than the rule. As a result, evidence suggests that most people in these contexts feel comfortable and secure in making improvements to their home, in connecting them to utility services, and in buying and selling them.

Other critics allege that formal property rights are an imposition of Western notions of capitalism and individualism and are thus alien to local cultures in the developing world. For example, the granting of formalized property rights to Africans would seemingly overturn a generations-old system of land tenure that is more native to the local culture. Under customary law in Africa, informal property rights are widely respected by most community members, even in lieu of formal delineation and legal enforcement.[16] Norms around lineage and inheritance identify plot users and owners, and violations of these norms are met with swift sanctions from fellow community members in the form of social shaming or exclusion. Worries about eviction or expropriation are relatively rare, giving farmers sufficient security to invest in improvements if they wish to do so.

Finally, some critics question the effects of formal property rights on growth and prosperity. Several studies cast doubt on de Soto's main purported mechanism—that the poor are likelier to get loans when they have title deeds and thus collateral to offer.[17] In actuality, among the poor, the effect of holding a title on the ability to borrow appears to be minimal for a number of reasons. In the event of default, banks would still have to repossess the house and sell it in the real estate market. These are costly and risky propositions themselves, especially when property

is in dilapidated slums or distant rural outposts and no well-developed real estate market exists. Title deeds must also be backed by the right state institutions, meaning fair and efficient enforcement mechanisms provided by impersonal courts and security bureaucracies. Few LDC have these. Moreover, titling is expensive for governments and individuals, so the opportunity costs are high. One study of Bogota, Colombia, found that it cost an average of 102 percent of a poor person's annual consumption to get a home titled.[18] These efforts might be more profitably devoted to providing actual infrastructure to informal settlements or to other development purposes, especially if the benefits remain in question.

Informal Work, Firms, and Finance

The **labor market** is the economic institution that encompasses the pursuit of employment by individuals and the pursuit of employees by hirers. The organization of business refers to how a firm is structured—whether it is a joint-stock company, a sole proprietorship, a partnership, a state-owned firm, or something else. These two institutional realms are conceptually distinct, but in practice in the developing world, they are deeply intertwined. These two are discussed together in the next subsection. The subsequent subsection then describes the nature of informality in the financial services sector.

Labor and Business Informality

In most LDCs, a large share of the labor force earns its living in the informal sector, meaning these people do not have legal labor contracts or formally registered businesses. Figure 9.1 reports the percentage of people in the nonagricultural workforce who earn their living in the informal sector. The figure ranges from 40 percent to 80 percent across most LDCs.

Figure 9.1　　　　**Employment in the Informal Economy**

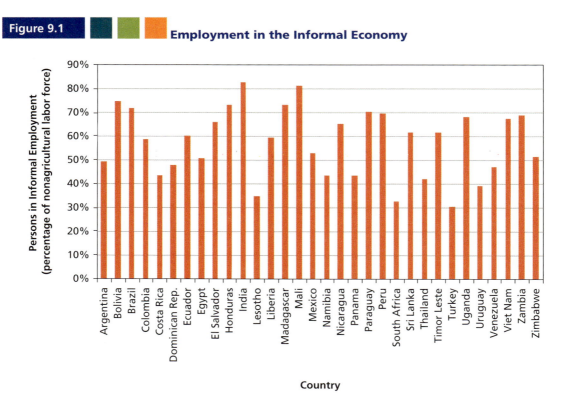

Source: International Labor Organization, Department of Statistics, "Statistical Update on Employment in the Informal Economy," June 2011, http:// laborsta.ilo.org/sti/DATA_FILES/20110610_Informal_Economy.pdf.

The allocation of workers in LDCs into formal and informal sector tiers is often referred to as labor market dualism.

Most commonly, informal-sector activity comes in the form of people owning and operating a small unregistered business by themselves, hence the close connection between informal employment and the structure of firms in LDCs. In other words, because so many informal-sector workers run their own firms, the vast majority of businesses in the developing world are sole, informal proprietorships. One study of eighteen LDCs found that an average of 50 percent of the urban poor had their own business, the vast majority of them informal.[19] Informal status also applies to individuals who are employed by unregistered firms or carry out work for others on an under-the-table basis. Many of these are casual workers who work seasonal or other kinds of temporary positions. In the eighteen-country study, 40 percent of all urban residents who worked for someone else were informal casual workers. All told, whether they are employees or business operators, the work and livelihoods of individuals who are in the informal sector are not subject to state regulations that provide for things such as a minimum wage, work safety standards, hiring and firing guidelines, payroll taxation, unemployment insurance, retirement pensions, and other state-sponsored benefits.

understanding INDICATORS

Measuring the Informal Economy

Measuring the size of a country's informal economy is notoriously difficult. By definition, informal activity is not registered with formal authorities, so there is no central location to tally which persons and firms are in it. Moreover, much informal activity is hidden from official view by people who are seeking to avoid taxes or legal sanctions. Finally, informality is a continuum and not an either/or condition for many firms and workers. For example, a firm may comply with some taxes and regulations but not all, or a worker may combine income from a formal-sector job with that from under-the-table activity performed on the side. Although they each have their drawbacks, scholars have derived a number of ways to estimate the size of a country's informal economy. Some of these

are shown for Bolivia in the table below.

One set of approaches is to administer survey questionnaires to firms or workers. The World Bank Enterprise Survey gives anonymous questionnaires to firm managers asking them to report the amounts by which they underreport their revenues and employees when making tax payments. Even if guaranteed anonymity, however, respondents may be nervous about reporting noncompliance with the tax code. This approach surely understates the amount of informality, especially since researchers tend to undersample completely unregistered firms.[20] Another survey approach is to administer questionnaires to a nationally representative sample of workers

and tally those who say they are self-employed as informal sector workers. The problem with this approach is that it would miss the many members of the informal sector who are working for others. A third approach is to ask workers if they are covered by state-mandated worker protections such as a retirement pension plan and classify those who are uncovered as informal. While this measure can tap informal salaried workers, it is less useful in the many countries where self-employed workers are not required to have pension plans.

A second set of approaches involves inferring the amount of informal activity from observed macroeconomic factors. One such technique is to use a country's total volume of electricity

Comparing Estimates of Bolivia's Informal Economic Activity, 2000

Measuring Technique	Estimated Informal Economic Activity (as a percentage of all economic activity)
Interview of firms for underreported revenues and employees	20 percent
Survey to determine self-employment	42 percent
Survey to determine those with no state-mandated worker protections (such as retirement plans)	73 percent
Analysis of increased demand for currency	68 percent

Source: Guillermo E. Perry et al., *Informality: Exit and Exclusion* (Washington D.C., World Bank, 2007), 29.

(Continued)

(Continued)

consumption as a proxy for its real amount of both formal and informal economic activity, based on the assumption that electricity consumption is closely associated with economic production. Since measures of the amount of formal activity do exist, they can be subtracted out from the amount of electricity consumption (converted to a monetary equivalent) to derive an estimate of informal activity. While creative, this technique has a number of

shortcomings, among them the assumption that the amount of economic output a society can produce with a given unit of electricity is constant through time. In fact, economic progress tends to yield increased output per unit of electricity. A second technique proxies total economic output with the amount of currency in circulation, since greater economic production yields an increased demand for currency. Unfortunately, this approach

assumes that transactions in the informal economy all occur in cash and thus underestimates its size.[21]

- Which type of approach, a survey or a macroeconomic analysis, is likely to yield more accurate estimates of informal-sector size?

- Why are the first two estimates of Bolivia's informal-sector size so much smaller than the last two estimates?

Causes of Labor Informality

The immediate cause of the high rates of informal-sector activity in LDCs is the relative lack of formal-sector jobs. The government and manufacturing posts that provide relatively stable jobs with state-provided benefits are only plentiful enough to employ a minority of the labor force, so the remainder must seek a living in the informal sector.

What accounts for this relative lack of formal businesses and jobs? A common answer is that governments set high **entry costs** to the formal economy in the form of bureaucratic red tape and corruption.[22] Procedures for registering businesses with the government are onerous and costly in most LDCs, thereby creating high obstacles to legality.[23] Table 9.2 shows some of these costs in time and money. In the average high-income country, the required five procedures to register a small firm with authorities can be completed in just twelve days at a cost of around one-twentieth of annual per-capita GDP. In the business-friendly United States, it takes only six days at a cost of one-seventieth of annual per-capita GDP. In contrast, in regions such as Latin America and sub-Saharan Africa, the average length of time is more than three times as long, and interested

parties must come up with 30 percent (in Latin America) to 80 percent (Africa) of annual per-capita GDP to cover fees. In Ecuador, it takes an average of thirteen procedures over two months, and in Niger it costs more than a year's average income to register a business.

Other factors also contribute to high informality in LDCs. For the relatively few firms that overcome the barriers to entry, remaining formal can be equally challenging. Staying in compliance with the long list of regulations requires putting forth effort to even be knowledgeable about business law in the first place, not to mention shouldering the costs of complying. Formalization also brings direct financial burdens such as paying taxes and minimum wages. In short, the long list of business regulations in LDCs means that maintaining formality can be just as daunting as getting there. Moreover, labor market regulations, meaning rules about hiring, firing, worker remuneration, and benefits, can be onerous enough to discourage existing formal firms from hiring workers, leaving most to languish in the informal sector.

Rhetorically, LDC governments tend to justify this thick web of permit requirements in the name of raising revenue to redistribute from business to

Table 9.2	Costs of Starting a Formal Business, 2012		
Region	**Number of Procedures**	**Time (days)**	**Fees (as percentage of income per capita)**
High-Income OECD	5	12	4.7 percent
East Asia and the Pacific	7	37	22.7 percent
Latin America and the Caribbean	9	54	37.3 percent
Middle East and North Africa	8	20	35.0 percent
South Asia	7	23	21.6 percent
Sub-Saharan Africa	8	37	81.2 percent

Source: Data compiled from the World Bank, Doing Business Data, http://www.doingbusiness.org/data.

workers and to regulate unfettered economic activity for zoning, safety, and environmental purposes. Critics, however, see it as little more than an opportunity to generate economic rents for government bureaucrats and existing firms. All of the licensing requirements provide a *raison d'être* for a relatively small number of state-sector jobs that are fundamentally unnecessary, and they create opportunities for these same bureaucrats to ask for bribes. As evidence, in Peru almost all of the regulations originated within the executive branch and its bureaucratic agencies, not within the legislature. Furthermore, the high costs to entry lower the competition faced by existing formal-sector firms. Many LDCs have product markets that are dominated by politically connected formal-sector monopolies and cartels that can pressure government to keep entry costs high so that they can maintain their privileged positions.[24]

Financial Services

Financial services are the instruments that societies provide their citizens for borrowing (such as obtaining credit) and for storing or investing their savings. These two topics are discussed in turn.

Borrowing. To get a loan, the poor use commercial banks and other formal credit institutions less than 5 percent of the time.[25] Formal-sector commercial banks in the developing world tend not to lend money to the poor for a variety of reasons. The administrative costs of a large number of small loans are much higher than those for making a small number of large loans. Also, the poor are often a higher risk than the rich to default on a loan because they do not have steady employment. The poor can also offer little by way of attractive collateral, as described earlier in the chapter. As a result, banks end up charging higher interest rates to the poor, if they choose to extend a loan at all.

The poor find ways to borrow nonetheless. One way they borrow informally is to get a loan from a friend or relative, sometimes with no interest charged. Often, however, they borrow from a local moneylender. Moneylenders are typically residents of the borrower's community—nearby shopkeepers are common—who make small loans to acquaintances for a one-off fee. Informal moneylenders are willing to lend where banks are not because they are embedded in a community and thus know their borrowers' and potential borrowers' ability to repay better than does a large, impersonal bank. They can also monitor repayment more closely by making periodic visits.

Many of the poor in LDCs also rely on informal self-help or savings club groups to generate capital. The two most common forms are rotating savings and credit associations (ROSCA) and accumulating savings and credit associations (ASCA). In a ROSCA, a small group of people pool some of their savings so that they can provide rotating payouts to each member. Each member pays a fixed amount to the fund on a recurring basis, with one member receiving all of the payments at each payment period. The recipient member is rotated so that each person gets the payout once before the group is disbanded or the rotation begins again. ROSCAs have the obvious advantage of providing interest-free capital to members. An ASCA differs in that the payouts do not rotate. They are instead managed by a person that group members have appointed. ASCA directors often charge interest for loans, but they also distribute profits from interest and the original funds back to all members when the group disbands.

In recent decades, the developing world has seen an explosion in microcredit loans made by **microfinance institutions (MFIs)** to try to address the huge unfulfilled demand for formal-sector lending. Most forms of microcredit work through solidarity lending. This means making loans to a group of borrowers who are either jointly liable for repayment of the entire group loan or who are individually liable for just their portion but meet regularly to monitor each others' repayment progress. Through solidarity lending, MFIs encourage each borrower to make sure that fellow group members are remaining current on repayments. A borrower can assist or cajole fellow members that may fall behind on repayment, and weekly group meetings are often held to collect payments. In farming out the costs of monitoring and enforcing repayment to the borrowers themselves, microcredit institutions can charge lower interest rates than those set by commercial banks and often local moneylenders. Borrowers are essentially offering what is called social collateral in lieu of the physical kind to keep interest rates lower. The decentralized, community-based nature of microcredit lending is deemed by many observers to be a primary reason why default rates on microcredit loans are so low: 2 percent to 5 percent for most MFIs. In other words, the social pressures applied by fellow group members are usually powerful enforcers.

Saving. As with lending to the poor, most commercial banks are largely uninterested in letting the poor save with them. Banks make little profit when opening accounts for individuals who will only deposit a small amount since the administrative costs for opening and maintaining small accounts can quickly become higher than the benefits the banks get from lending out the deposits. They thus charge high fees for savings accounts, checking accounts, and withdrawals that the poor can hardly afford, and they pay interest only to large depositors. In other words, the poor must pay to save, while the rich are paid to save. As a result, the poor in LDCs largely fail to use formal-sector banks to deposit and grow their savings. The percentage of the poor who keep savings in a formal bank is in the single digits.[26]

That said, poor people in LDCs do save, but (again) they mostly do so informally. In fact, the poor have to save to survive, since "the reality of living on two dollars a day is that you don't literally earn that sum each day; instead, your income fluctuates up and down."[27] They cannot spend money as soon as they get it or they would starve during periods of no income. The most common way the poor save is via a simple piggybank method, stashing money somewhere in their own home. Many choose to store their money elsewhere, often with a trusted friend or relative. Alternatively, the counterpart on the savings side of the ledger to the moneylender is the informal moneyguard, who is paid to harbor other people's savings.[28] For example, deposit collectors called *susus* in West Africa work in public markets and are often recognizable for wearing coats with many pockets. *Susus* take daily contributions from individuals and then, after a specific period of time, pay back the saver the entire deposit minus a fraction to compensate themselves.

Recently, some MFIs have also begun to fill the gap by diversifying into microsavings, providing formal savings options for the poor. Some MFIs have introduced savings plans where individuals are expected to make regular monthly deposits that can be withdrawn at any time. They also offer commitment savings schemes that disallow withdrawals until a goal or date is reached after periodic deposits. Mobile phone technology has offered another potential solution that dramatically lowers the administrative costs of savings accounts. For example, in Kenya, cellular device owners can deposit money into their phone account and transfer that money to another user such as a grocery store or moneylender with a few key taps.

Causes of Underdevelopment: Challenges of Informal Firms and Finance

These realities of informal labor and informal finance certainly make life difficult for millions of LDC residents. They may also lie at the root of their countries' social and economic underdevelopment.

The Drawbacks of Informal Work

Besides emphasizing the perils of informal property ownership, de Soto attributes economic impoverishment in the developing world to the size of the informal-labor sector. To de Soto, the legions of poor in LDCs are capable, thrifty, and full of productive energy, far from the culturalist arguments' implications that the poor are lacking in work ethic or economic savvy. For example, consider the following portrayal of Pakistan's second city:

> Lahore has so much vitality. It's really overwhelming. . . . There are donkey carts, bicycles with two or three people on each one,

pedestrians walking in the road, motor-scooters with two to five people on each one (often with a toddler clinging to the handlebars), cars, hand-pushed carts, trucks, motor rickshaws, taxis, tractors pulling overloaded wagons, as well as garishly painted buses packed with people clinging to their sides. People throng the markets in the old city, where the lanes are so narrow that the crowds almost swallow the cars. I see people buying, people selling, people eating, people cooking. Every street, every lane is crammed with shops, each shop with people. This is a private economy with a lot of dynamism.[29]

Because of this energy and activity, de Soto asserts that the global poor are just as entrepreneurial and capitalistic in behavior as are successful developed world businesspeople: "The cities of the Third World . . . are teeming with entrepreneurs."[30] The poor thus have the most to gain, he goes on, from a formal capitalist system: "The constituency of capitalism has always been poor people that are outside the system. Capitalism is essentially a tool for poor people to prosper."[31] What makes them unable to translate their efforts into sustained wealth creation is an overbearing and misguided state that keeps them on the outside of capitalism looking in. By establishing such high entry costs, the state keeps the poor in an informal economy that stifles the productivity growth that propelled the West to prosperity. To summarize, LDC economies underutilize the entrepreneurial energies of the poor, thereby remaining relatively poor as a whole.

Inefficiency and Risk. One way informality stifles economic growth and prosperity is to prevent small informal-firm operators from growing and from becoming more profitable. The cost to society as a whole is high inefficiency because of the proliferation of small unproductive firms. Informal-sector firms tend to remain small—operated by one individual or just a few family members—for several reasons. Poor entrepreneurs have a hard time growing their firms because they cannot access finance. Since they live just one or two slow business weeks away from economic disaster, informal business owners tend to save windfalls rather than invest them in expansion or the acquisition of new skills. Even if they could invest savings in new business assets such as an improved store location or a piece of machinery, informal entrepreneurs may not enjoy police protection and security of ownership over these assets since their firms exist outside the purview of the state. Finally, many informal business owners prefer to keep their operations small since growing larger might make their tax avoidance more detectable to state authorities.

Unfortunately, firm size matters. Small informal firms have low profitability and productivity because they do not achieve economies of scale, which are the efficiency gains from being large. All else equal, the cost of producing a single unit of a particular good or service declines with firm size, since large firms can do things such as buy supplies in bulk and invest in large machinery that speeds production. In the end, the many operators of small informal businesses face high unit costs of production and thus low productivity and profitability.[32]

Another problem with informal self-employment is that earning a living in this way makes for a precarious and risky economic existence. Even in developed economies, income flows from business ownership can be wavy, so businesses there tend to be started by people who can afford to take risks. In less developed countries, income flows can be even more volatile, as small entrepreneurs are exposed to the whims of local demand. Moreover, the informal sector is highly competitive, and most firms cannot differentiate themselves from one another other than by offering a low selling price. For example, millions of informal-sector entrepreneurs work as vendors in street markets selling food and other goods alongside other street vendors selling exactly the same products.[33]

For these and other reasons, many, if not most, small informal entrepreneurs would probably prefer to have stable employment from someone else rather than owning and operating their own businesses. Economists Abhijit Banerjee and Esther Duflo label the urban poor who run informal sector businesses the "reluctant entrepreneurs," stating that "the enterprises of the poor often seem more a way to buy a job when a more conventional employment opportunity is not available than a reflection of a particular entrepreneurial urge."[34] After all, in the developed world, most people do not own and operate a business, but rather work for the relatively few that do. In LDCs, however, the relative lack of formal-sector jobs makes stable employment a prospect that only a few can enjoy.

The other major kind of informal work, employment by an informal-sector firm, can be equally precarious. Informal-sector employers do not have to abide by minimum wage laws, rules against wrongful dismissal, and safety standards. Employees of informal firms do not have access to work-related benefits such as unemployment insurance or retirement pensions. Many such informal-sector jobs are short-lived. According to a study of workers in Delhi, India, half of those who had wage-paying jobs lost that job within a year and had to seek new work. This makes it hard for workers to develop specialized skills, and it also discourages saving and investments in the health and education of workers' children.[35]

Low State Revenue. A final problem associated with large informal sectors is that the states in which they are housed suffer from low revenues. By definition, informality means that economic activity is taking place without state taxation of it. This means that the state is missing out on precious revenues it could be collecting to fund social and infrastructural development. Figure 9.2 shows the negative cross-national relationship

Figure 9.2 Tax Revenue by the Degree of Informality in the Labor Market

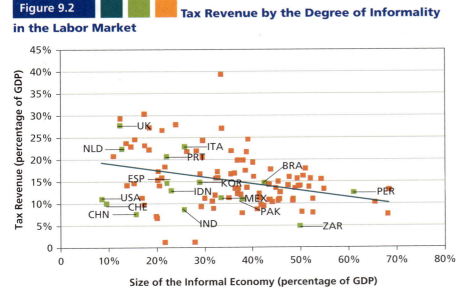

Source: Informality data from Friedrich Schneider, "Shadow Economies and Corruption All over the World: What Do We Really Know?," September 2006, http://ftp.iza.org/dp2315.pdf; Tax revenue data, the World Bank, World Development Indicators, http://data.worldbank.org/sites/default/files/wdi-final.pdf.

them. Customers often must hunt for loans from several sources before finding one.[36] Moreover, moneylenders are sometimes known to use violence, intimidation, social ostracism, and other forms of abuse against borrowers who do not repay or who are indebted to them. For their part, ROSCAs, despite the allure of interest-free credit, can unravel if even a single member is unable to keep up with the periodic payments. ROSCAs are particularly risky since members who

between a country's tax revenues and the degree of informality in its labor market.

Shortcomings of Informal Finance

The nature of financial services in LDCs is paradoxical: The poor, who need them most, face the highest costs to using them. Informal services are more accessible and convenient to the poor, but they feature several major drawbacks. Most importantly, informal borrowing has high costs. Most local moneylenders charge fees that are, by developed-world lending standards, extremely expensive. Moneylenders often charge fees that are equivalent to 5 percent to 10 percent interest per month. These equate to interest rates of 75 percent to 200 percent per year, in contrast to 10 percent to 20 percent annual interest for most unsecured loans in the developed world. In part because they are often relatively poor themselves, moneylenders can be unreliable in that they do not have monies to lend when customers need

received one of the first payouts in the rotation lose some incentive to continue paying in.

Informal savings instruments also have major shortcomings. Stashing money at home means the savings is not earning interest and is thus losing value with inflation. It also carries the risk that the monies will be lost or stolen. Its presence in the home also provides an ongoing temptation to the saver, who might plunder the piggybank in a moment of weakness to spend the savings on frivolous consumption. Moneyguards can help prevent this, but they carry obvious security risks. They are ripe targets for theft, and moneyguards themselves may run off with the funds. Moreover, depositors effectively earn a negative interest rate by paying the moneyguard to keep their money.

The lack of formal instruments for savings and credit exacerbates the problem of capital shortages in the developing world. An important role of commercial banks and other formal-sector financial institutions is to channel savings into productive uses. They take deposits and lend them out

DEVELOPMENT in the FIELD

Microfinance Institutions

The beginnings of modern microcredit lending are attributed to Grameen Bank of Bangladesh and its founder, Muhammad Yunus. Yunus and Grameen Bank began lending to groups of poor Bangladeshi peasants in the 1970s. Since then, microlending has exploded in popularity, riding the wave of a microfinance revolution that began in the 1980s. According to one set of experts, "Microcredit has generated more enthusiasm and support than perhaps any other development tool in history."[37] Worldwide, lending by thousands of microfinance institutions (MFIs) has reached some 200 million clients seeking to invest in their own small businesses, and Yunus and Grameen Bank won the Nobel Peace Prize in 2006.[38]

A primary reason for its popularity, especially among charitable donors, is an idea that appeals to observers from across the political spectrum: give the poor a proverbial fishing pole—a means to sustain themselves for the long-term—and not just a fish. Evidence shows microloans to have been instrumental in getting millions of small businesses in the developing world off the ground or to expand.[39] The vast majority

(more than 80 percent[40]) of microcredit borrowers worldwide are women, largely because MFIs see them as being more likely to repay the loans than men. MFIs are most active in South and East Asia, and they remain nascent and limited in Africa and Latin America.

MFIs come in a variety of forms. Most are, like Grameen, based in a developing country and are not-for-profit banks or NGOs that get their funding from a variety of sources. Grameen raises most of its funds from customer deposits and interest charges. Many MFIs also take contributions from donors, and local sources of capital (such as bond sales or central banks) are also common. MFIs can also be for-profit and even publically traded, as is, to some controversy, the largest one in Latin America, Mexico's Compartamos Bank. (For a list of leading MFIs, see Forbes Top 50 Microfinance Institutions.[41]) Finally, a number of aid agencies based in the West raise funds from rich-country donors and channel them to MFIs or affiliates in the developing world. FINCA International and Kiva are perhaps the two largest U.S.-based examples of this.[42]

Despite its popularity, microlending is not without criticism. Systematic research on the consequences of microloans shows them to yield the transformative effects touted by advocates in only a small minority of cases.[43] On average, they seem not to improve borrowers' health, increase their families' food consumption, or raise their children's school enrollment.[44] This may be so in part because interest rates on microloans are still quite high, averaging between 30 percent and 80 percent in most LDC markets.[45] Borrowers who do not experience a return on their loan-financed business investment that exceeds their interest rates are technically made poorer. This is particularly problematic since returns exceeding 30 percent to 80 percent in LDC business environments can be hard to come by.

Microloans are also criticized for their rigidity. They require borrowers to cobble together a group of interested and trustworthy persons, to have a concrete business proposal in place, to make multiple trips to an MFI branch, to attend periodic group meetings, and to start repayment almost immediately in weekly installments. In contrast, informal moneylenders can often make loans on the spot for unspecified purposes, allowing borrowers to meet the cash flow and consumption needs that are more widespread and recurrent in the lives of the poor than the needs to invest in a business.[46] Informal moneylenders can also offer longer repayment periods that allow investment-oriented borrowers to take more risks.

Finally, some observers have moral compunctions against microlending, criticizing the profiteering that occurs from collecting interest on loans to the poor. Some critics also see microfinance as a shirking of the state's role to provide social services for the poor, a "privatization of welfare" that keeps them exposed to brutal market competition.[47]

to borrowers who have a seemingly good use for the credit, such as a business investment or home purchase. When savings are simply stashed under a mattress or held by a moneylender or moneyguard, this reallocation to more efficient purposes does not occur.

Critique: Formalization as a False Solution

Life in the formal sector may not be as rosy as critics of informality claim. Many poor entrepreneurs choose to avoid formality altogether because it means paying taxes and following a host of new regulations once legalization has occurred. Whereas informal entrepreneurs have a hard time growing their businesses to the point where they can hire an employee or two, formal ones in many LDCs face other obstacles to hiring, such as high payroll taxes, minimum wage laws, working hours minimums, and rules against laying off employees. Managers of informal-sector firms are also able to skirt what they see as onerous environmental and worker safety standards, licensing requirements, zoning laws, and price controls. Merely being knowledgeable of and compliant with all of these regulations requires extra work and, for many small businesses, an extra employee. The low entry costs in the informal sector thus surely make entrepreneurs out of millions of people who would otherwise not be in business at all. In other words, informality is a choice for many entrepreneurs in LDCs because they do not see the alleged gains to formality as outweighing its hefty costs.

Moreover, even if they could afford it, formalization is surely not a panacea for many informal-sector entrepreneurs. Another reason why so many small firms remain informal is precisely because they are inefficient and poorly run, not the reverse. De Soto's romantic view of the developing world's many informal-sector entrepreneurs assumes that many, if not all, could run thriving businesses if only it were easier for them to formalize. In truth, many are surely not talented business operators, and many of those who are would still lack access to capital, low-cost supply networks, and other keys to successful business if legally registered with the state. In other words, formalization would not give them a new lease on life, but would rather drive them out of business.[48] Finally, even the incredibly popular microfinance movement, an oft-proposed solution to the problems of informal finance, has its critics, as discussed in Development in the Field: Microfinance Institutions.

DOES INFORMALITY EXPLAIN PERU'S DELAYED DEVELOPMENT?

Peru has millions of self-starting, hard-working business owners. By some measures, nearly 40 percent of its entire labor force is self-employed in this way.[49] However, this entrepreneurial energy does not translate into prosperity. Peru's average income is less than one-quarter that of the developed West, and that of these self-employed millions is even lower. A primary reason for this inability to reward entrepreneurial effort is that nearly all of these self-employed individuals toil in the informal sector, running small, precarious, and relatively inefficient businesses. Is Peru's widespread informality a cause of its underdevelopment, or is some other factor at work? Table 9.3 compares several possible causes and measures of Peru's underdevelopment with those of its former colonizer, Spain.

Table 9.3 ■ ■ ■ **Development Comparison: Peru and Spain**

Indicator	Peru	Spain
GDP per capita at PPP	US$8,865	US$26,767
Human Development Index	.725	.878
Size of the informal economy (percentage of GDP)	61 percent	22 percent
Number of years under colonial rule since 1500	288	0
Number of large land mammal species domesticated by people living on territory before 1500	1	5

Sources: Data on GDP per capita at PPP and Human Development Index compiled from Gapminder, www.gapminder.com; informality, Friedrich Schneider, "Shadow Economies and Corruption All over the World: What Do We Really Know?," September 2006, http://ftp.iza.org/dp2315.pdf; mammals, Jared Diamond, *Guns, Germs, and Steel* (New York: W. W. Norton, 1997).

The South: Informal Economic Activity

In his classic 1986 book *The Other Path*, Hernando de Soto reported on his efforts to formally register a one-worker garment workshop with state authorities in Lima, Peru.[50] As a researcher, his sincere interest was not in selling garments, but in seeing how long it would take and how much it would cost to follow all of the legal procedures. His findings were eye-opening.

De Soto's Findings. De Soto's research team set to work securing the required eleven permits from eleven different government agencies, spending six hours per day on the task. They gathered personal documents, rode buses to different government offices, waited in queues, and filled out paperwork. Along the way, team members paid almost US$200

in permit fees and were asked for a bribe ten times. They were ultimately able to register the firm—but only after 289 days! The total cost of compliance, including fees, bribes, and foregone wages, was thirty-two times the prevailing monthly minimum wage, well outside the reach of the vast majority of Lima residents. De Soto also reported that, at the time, it took an average of seven years of bureaucratic legwork for a group of poor families to have an otherwise unused plot of state land designated for their ownership and their private residential use with building permits.[51]

De Soto saw these high state barriers to legality as the cause of Lima's enormous informal sector. He found 83 percent of the street markets in Lima to be illegal, even as they teemed with entrepreneurial energy. He found 95 percent of public transport to

Peruvian women sell food and artisan crafts in a market. Marketplaces such as this one are typically informal, meaning they exist outside the purview of government protections and regulations. Because formal employment opportunities are limited, millions of Peruvians are small-time vendors in the informal sector to make ends meet.

be unregistered with the state, despite the fact that it kept the city moving. And he found that half of all Lima houses were informal and that only 30 percent of new dwellings constructed each year were formal. The people of Lima, he claimed, could not get loans, had little incentive to make their businesses more productive, and hesitated to improve their homes. In short, informality kept them trapped in poverty.

Informality Today. Since then, Peru has made only slow progress in decreasing informality. One study of Peru in the early 2000s found it to have one of the highest rates of informality in the world. Fully 60 percent of its economic production was carried out by informal sources, 40 percent of its labor force ran informal small firms, and 80 percent of its workers were not covered by a formal pension scheme. These figures were higher than the rates prevailing in regional peers Chile, Colombia, and Mexico, and much higher than those in high-income countries.[52] The reason may still lie in the country's onerous entry costs. Aspiring formal-sector business operators had to spend an average of twenty-six days and 12 percent of the country's average income to start a business. While this was certainly an improvement over de Soto's experience nearly thirty years earlier, it still ranked Peru as only fifty-fifth worldwide in ease of business entry.

The economic and social consequences of informality in Peru are, to de Soto and other critics, severe. On average, a worker in Peru's informal sector is 50 percent less productive than one in its formal sector, even if both work in the same type

DOES INFORMALITY EXPLAIN PERU'S DELAYED DEVELOPMENT?

of service or industry and in similarly sized firms. This 50 percent gap is the largest in Latin America, and it translates into vastly lower wages for the informal workers themselves and lost economic growth for Peru as a whole.[53] Moreover, because of their neighborhoods' informality, thousands of Peruvians live in urban slums (many of them on the outskirts of Lima) that have little by way of amenities and infrastructure.

***

To be sure, this explanation of Peru's underdevelopment is not airtight. By some measures, Peru actually has relatively low entry costs for business, yet it has a high rate of informality. Its bureaucratic red tape has been dramatically reduced in recent decades, some of which occurred at the very behest of de Soto's think tank, the Institute for Liberty and Democracy. Peru's overall ease of doing business ranks it second in Latin America, just behind much wealthier Chile, and it ranks higher than wealthier and more formalized countries such as Hungary, Luxembourg, and Spain. Easing entry to the formal sector does not seem to be expanding its size. Furthermore, informality prevails in Peru despite the fact that, according to one study, it has the best climate for microfinance of any developing country.[54] Finally, the Peruvian government has issued more than 1.5 million title deeds to individual homes since 1996, but the results have been mixed at best. The program has increased property values and investment in housing, but there are no indications that titling has granted the new homeowners increased access to credit. Collateral or no collateral, most Peruvian banks still do not want to lend to the poor.[55] Might the causes of Peruvian underdevelopment lie somewhere else?

The West: Spanish Colonialism and British Neocolonialism

Critics of colonialism and its legacy point out that 300 years of colonial rule by the Spanish left a disastrous economic, social, and political legacy that may be the ultimate cause of Peru's

widespread informality and underdevelopment today. In the 1530s, Spain conquered the Inca Empire, a civilization centered in territory that is today part of Peru. Soon thereafter, Spain established the Viceroyalty of Peru, commencing a period of colonial rule that lasted until independence in 1821. During this time, the absolutist, militaristic, feudal, and hierarchically organized Spain imposed these elements of Iberian culture on its subjects through colonial administration.[56] For example, the Spanish crown rewarded conquering Spanish military heroes in the New World with large land grants and the right to exploit the labor of the natives living on this land. The Spaniards also imposed their preference for strong corporate identities and rights—such as those based around organized bodies like the military or Catholic Church—over those of the individual. These impositions shaped Peruvian culture into one that, even long after independence, produced its own forms of class and racial hierarchy, authoritarian and militarized leadership, and strong corporate organizational forms that usurped individual rights. By contrast, democracy and prosperity flourished in the United States because it was colonized by Great Britain after Britain had seen the emergence of Enlightenment-inspired notions of individual liberty.

Other explanations for the Western roots of Peruvian underdevelopment look at the neocolonial relationship that emerged between Peru and Europe soon after independence. In particular, Peru became heavily involved in the global economy during the Guano Era (roughly 1845–1869) when British demand for Peruvian guano (the dried excrement of seabirds used as fertilizer) ballooned. The explosion in foreign trade spawned an economic boom for Peru, including the emergence of an urban upper class that could afford glittery European imports. But the long-term consequences of the guano boom were largely negative. Many of the revenues from guano were spent on luxuries by this new aristocracy, not reinvested into industry or other modernizing sectors so that a domestic business class could emerge.[57] Moreover, the Peruvian government became heavily dependent on British purchases of guano during the era. Around 75 percent of its revenues were from the trade, a fact that was devastating when the international price and demand for guano collapsed in the 1870s.[58]

The Nature World: Pizarro Wins the Lottery

These arguments about the role of colonialism and neocolonialism are compelling, but what about Peru made it possible for the Spanish to colonize it in the first place? In other words, what enabled Spaniards to travel to and conquer the Inca in the early 1500s instead of the reverse? One answer looks at the contrasting physical geographies of Peru and Spain. Prior to the arrival of the Spaniards, the Inca Empire was the most prosperous civilization of the Western Hemisphere. At its peak in 1532, the empire commanded 12 million subjects and 300,000 square miles of territory, most of which it had annexed through military conquest and diplomatic coercion.[59] In November of that year, Spanish explorer Francisco Pizarro, using just 170 soldiers and sixty horses, took on an empire with an 80,000-soldier army—and won. In this seemingly improbable victory, Pizarro's forces killed Incan emperor Atahualpa and initiated the process of South American colonization.

According to physiologist Jared Diamond, the Spaniards were able to accomplish this because they had been winners of a long-running geographical lottery. They and their ancestors were residents of a supercontinent (Eurasia) that housed large land mammals such as pigs, goats, cows, sheep, and horses that were extremely useful to human economic productivity. These land animals made high-protein foods available to their human domesticators. Some also provided draft labor to pull plows, thereby increasing agricultural productivity. In contrast, the only domesticable large land mammal in the Western Hemisphere

available to the Inca was the llama. Over millennia leading up to 1532, the Spaniards had harnessed the economic advantages proffered by their superior array of mammals to develop the ships, guns, steel armor, and iron swords that enabled them to travel to and conquer the Inca Empire, whose shields and weaponry were flimsy by comparison.

Moreover, use of these animals granted two other advantages to the Spaniards in their conquest. First, although there were only sixty of them, horse-mounted Spanish cavaliers had advantages in speed and height over the earthbound Inca soldiers in the heat of battle. Second, having lived in close quarters with land mammals for generations, Spaniards had immunity to crowd diseases such as smallpox and measles, to which the natives did not. These diseases eventually wiped out most of the Inca population.

***

For the past decade, Peru has been one of Latin America's fastest-growing economies. Whether this is due to its government's efforts to ease the formalization of work and property ownership remains a hotly debated issue, but it is certainly one sign that formalization may help. Either way, Peru's recent successes are evidence that institutions and development outcomes are always evolving.

Thinking Critically about Development

- Why might Peru's informal sector be so large despite its relatively low entry costs? Is de Soto wrong that these are the main causes of informality and causes of underdevelopment?

- Was trading with the British and other Westerners a good development strategy for Peru in the nineteenth century, or would the country have been better off remaining closed to the global economy?

- Was the conquest of the Inca and the colonization of Peruvian territory by Spaniards a geographical inevitability as Diamond says, or was it caused more by human decisions and institutions?

Key Terms

collateral, p. 215

customary law, p. 213

dead capital, p. 215

economic institution, p. 212

entry costs, p. 220

informal sector, p. 212

informal settlements, p. 213

institutions, p. 212

labor market, p. 217

microfinance institution (MFI), p. 222

new institutional economics (NIE), p. 214

new institutionalism, p. 214

property market, p. 212

property rights, p. 212

transaction costs, p. 216

 ## Suggested Readings

Banerjee, Abhijit V., and Esther Duflo. *Poor Economics: A Radical Rethinking of the Way to Fight Global Poverty.* New York: Public Affairs, 2011. Chapters 6–10.

Collins, Daryl, Jonathan Morduch, Stuart Rutherford, and Orlanda Ruthven. *Portfolios of the Poor: How the World's Poor Live on $2 a Day.* Princeton, NJ: Princeton University Press, 2009.

de Soto, Hernando. *The Mystery of Capital: Why Capitalism Triumphs in the West and Fails Everywhere Else.* New York: Basic Books, 2000.

———. *The Other Path: The Invisible Revolution in the Third World.* New York: Harper and Row, 1989.

Gilbert, Alan G. "On the Mystery of Capital and the Myths of Hernando de Soto: What Difference Does Legal Title Make?" *International Development Planning Review* 24, no. 1 (2002): 1–20.

North, Douglass C. *Institutions, Institutional Change and Economic Performance.* New York: Cambridge University Press, 1990.

 ## Web Resources

International Labor Organization Database of Labor Statistics, http://laborsta.ilo.org/

Microfinance Information Exchange (MIX) Database, www.mixmarket.org/

United Nations Human Settlements Program Data, ww2.unhabitat.org/programmes/guo/statistics.asp

World Bank, Doing Business Statistics, www.doingbusiness.org/

World Bank, Enterprise Survey, www.enterprisesurveys.org/

Political Institutions and Governance

n the 1930s and 1940s, Shugui was the farmer and owner of a thirty-acre plot of land and a large house in the province of Sichuan, China. He experienced a variety of life challenges, including indebtedness and a freeloading, opium-addicted brother. Nonetheless, Shugui was able to feed and house his immediate and extended family using revenues from farming and the rental of parts of his land. In 1949, however, Mao Zedong and the Communist Party ascended to power in China with an eye toward redistributing farmland from landowners to poor peasants. Shugui was labeled a rich landowner, and village officials soon revoked his title to his farm and granted it to strangers. Although Shugui stayed in his house, his misfit brother, who had taken to street-begging right before Mao's rise to power, was also allowed to live in the house, largely because he had (conveniently) become a member of the Community Party. Shugui considered himself among the lucky ones—many landowners were simply killed.

On command of the Communist Party, Shugui's former tract of farmland was merged into a much larger agricultural commune in 1958 as part of a nationwide campaign to rid the country of privately owned landholdings. On the commune, Shugui carried out menial farming tasks well below his skill and knowledge level. For this, he and his family received a weekly supply of grain and a meager income, neither of which encouraged Shugui to work very hard. In 1959, famine struck Sichuan, largely because Chinese agricultural production collapsed due to the new way of organizing farming. At the age of fifty-two, Shugui died in the famine, one of perhaps 40 million Chinese citizens to do so.[1]

Shugui's and China's tragedy was seemingly caused by the misguided land ownership policies and repressiveness of the country's authoritarian political leadership. In fact, Mao Zedong himself, upon reflecting on the famine that occurred on his watch, said,

"Without democracy, you have no understanding of what is happening down below."[2] An important line of scholarly thought called new institutional economics argues that the root of the developing world's poverty lies in its political leadership and political institutions. In other words, LDCs are ultimately poor because they have bad governance. This chapter describes the nature of governance and political institutions around the world. It then lays out and critiques the argument that these aspects of politics are the root of development and underdevelopment.

Governance refers to the manner in which authoritative decisions are made and executed in a society. This includes the process by which positions of authority are filled, the manner in which these authority figures make decisions, the fairness and effectiveness of these decisions, and the ability to implement the decisions. **Political institutions** are the most crucial part of governance. They are defined as the rules and organizations that dictate the exercise of power and authority in society. Political institutions can be legally codified rules such as the laws regulating criminal behavior, and/or they can be unwritten patterns of recurring behavior. They also include organizations such as legislatures, political parties, and regulatory agencies that are involved in the political process. In the countries of today's world, governance is carried out by the overarching political institution of the state. States vary dramatically in how they are structured and in the quality of their governance.

Political Regimes

An important aspect of governance is the kind of political regime a country has. **Political regime** refers to the set of rules that shape how a society is governed—that is, the rules that determine who governs and what they can do in office. A country's political regime can thus be thought of as its basic form of government. Since a political regime refers to fundamental rules and practices of governing, a change in the party or leader in power does not in and of itself mean a regime has changed. To be sure, regimes do change. Many countries have experienced regime change, and it entails something much more dramatic than just a simple switch in political officeholders.

Chile provides a useful example. In 1970, Salvador Allende (1970–1973) of the Chilean Socialist Party was elected president and succeeded outgoing president Eduardo Frei Montalva (1964–1970) of the Christian Democratic Party, who had been elected in 1964. This switch in administration and the ruling party was not a case of regime change, since both men were democratically elected six years apart under the same constitution and according to similar rules. However, in 1973, the Chilean armed forces launched an attack on the Allende administration that resulted in Allende's death and the inauguration of General Augusto Pinochet as the new president. This was an instance of regime change. The *coup d'etat*, or illegal change in the chief executive, instigated a seventeen-year, Pinochet-headed dictatorship that discarded the prevailing constitution, thereby changing the rules of governance entirely. For example, elections for president were no longer held, and many constitutionally guaranteed human rights disappeared.

Political scientists categorize the existing regimes of the modern world into two broad types: democracy and authoritarianism. Both feature rule by a few persons—democracies are not rule "by the people" or "by the majority"—but they differ in how leaders are selected and in the powers they exercise in office.

Democracy

A **democracy** is a political system that meets the following two criteria: the most important political leaders are chosen through periodic free and

fair elections, and there is observed legal protection of the population's basic human rights. The first criterion captures the notion that democratic rulers are accountable to the ruled. Free and fair elections for top positions are the most widely used and effective institutional mechanism for achieving this accountability. For elections to be free and fair, suffrage must be universal, meaning all adults are allowed to vote. Vote-counting must be free of fraud, and citizens' vote decisions must not be coerced. Rules must allow all interested persons to seek elected office, and elections must have more than one contestant. Some definitions of democracy also add in the stipulation that elections feature real competition among elites so that there are occasional changes in which persons or groups rule.[3]

The second criterion refers to human rights, meaning various legal and practical constraints on what rulers can do in office. To be a democracy, the state may not coerce (through means such as fines, imprisonment, torture, and death) citizens because of their expressed political views, their social organization memberships, or their group identity. The existence of these oft-recited political freedoms or civil liberties—of speech, assembly, association, press, religion—is as important for democracy as free and fair elections.[4] After all, if an elected leader exterminated the minority that did not vote for him or her at the wishes of his or her supporters, the regime would clearly not be democratic.

Democracies come in a variety of forms. Perhaps the most important way that political scientists differentiate among them lies in the nature of relations between the legislative branch (the branch in charge of making laws) and the executive branch (the branch in charge of administering and enforcing laws). In a **presidential system**, there is one chief executive post. This post is occupied by the president, who is chosen through a direct, nationwide election and serves a term of fixed length, such as six years in Mexico. Positions in the legislature (a body of anywhere from several dozen to several hundred lawmakers) are also determined by popular election.

In contrast, a **parliamentary system** differs from a presidential one in several ways. First, it has two chief executives: the head of government, known as the prime minister, and the head of state, often a president or monarch. The prime minister is the more important of the two, with the head of state being a ceremonial figurehead for the country with few real political powers. Second, the prime minister is not chosen to be the head of government through a direct nationwide election. Instead, prime ministers are designated by the parliament (the popularly elected legislature), which chooses one of its own to be the head of government. In other words, voters only indirectly choose the prime minister. They first elect the legislature, which in turn appoints a prime minister. Third, executive and legislative terms are not of fixed length in parliamentary systems. In actuality, elections can be called at any time by (depending on a country's specific rules) the prime minister or the parliament. The only constraint is typically a mandated maximum number of years between consecutive elections.

Most of the democracies of the developing world have presidential systems. With just a few exceptions, the democracies of Latin America and Africa are all presidential, and Indonesia and the Philippines are also presidential democracies. Parliamentary democracies are rarer in the developing world. India is the largest parliamentary democracy, with Bangladesh, Thailand, and Turkey also other notable examples. The developing world also has a few semipresidential systems, a third type that melds elements of both presidentialism and parliamentarism. Semipresidential systems divide executive powers between a president chosen by nationwide popular vote and a prime minister appointed by the legislature. Kenya and a few other African countries practice semipresidentialism.

Authoritarianism

An **authoritarian regime** (also called an autocracy) is one in which the most important leaders are chosen in a way that does not seek periodic input from a freely participating electorate and in which the state does not respect basic human rights. The first element of this definition captures the notion that authoritarian regimes do not have mechanisms in place to hold their rulers, known as dictators, accountable to the population. There are a variety of ways in which rulers in authoritarian systems can achieve this. Some dictators pronounce themselves president for life and never hold meaningful elections. Others come to power by winning a free and fair election but proceed to stay in power by rigging all subsequent ones. In some autocracies, leaders are periodically changed but never the party in power. The second element of the definition refers to the fact that authoritarian regimes tend to commit human rights violations, using the coercive power of the state against some members of their populations because of those members' political views or group affiliations. Rights to free speech, association, assembly, and press are not upheld in autocracies.

This definition of authoritarian regime is very broad and thus subsumes a huge variety of political arrangements. In actuality, various types of authoritarian regimes have been delineated by political scientists, of which six are described here.[5] These types are largely defined by which institutions or persons—the military, a political party, a dominating personality, the clergy, a monarch, a totalitarian government—hold power. Numerous countries feature regimes with a mixture of these types. Table 10.1 lists these six types, their definitions, the number of each that exists in the developing world, and an example of each.

Dominant Party Regimes. The first type of autocracy is a **dominant party regime** (also called a hegemonic or single-party system), in which one political party holds the major leadership positions and controls policymaking for an extended period of time. The presiding political force in such a regime is not a person or the military, but rather a political party organization with staying power. Members of the dominant party hold most or all major political offices, and party officials choose who will fill these leadership positions. Some single-party regimes do hold elections and allow opposition parties to exist, but the dominant party manages to win nearly all elections through a combination of means: fraud, control of the media, rigging election law in its favor, repression of opposition leaders, and/or the strategic use of state funds.[6] Others do not bother to hold elections or allow opposition parties to exist, and leaders are chosen by a small group of party leaders.

The most well-known dominant party system today is China. In China, the Communist Party holds all major political offices, and a small elite within the party makes decisions about who will fill national-level posts. Mexico also had a dominant party system for much of the twentieth century, although it differed from China's current one. From 1929 to 1994, Mexico had recurring elections that were contested by multiple parties. However, the Institutional Revolutionary Party (PRI) won every presidential and nearly every gubernatorial election during that time, based in part on its advantages in government spending and media control. Today, single-party systems are most common in sub-Saharan Africa.

Personalist Regimes. The next authoritarian regime type is a **personalist regime**, a system that concentrates most political power in a single person. In a personalist regime, the top leader rises to power through military might or skilled political maneuvering rather than an established rule of succession. Decisions about who holds subordinate political offices and who reaps the fruits of office are mostly made at the top leader's and his or her cronies'

Table 10.1   Types of Authoritarian Regimes

Type	Definition	Number in Developing World*	Examples*
Dominant party regime	A system in which one political party holds the major leadership positions and controls policymaking.	14	China
Personalist regime	A system that concentrates most political power in a single person.	18	Afghanistan
Military regime	A system in which a group of elite military officers determines who the leader or leaders are and exerts substantial or total control over policymaking.	2	Myanmar
Monarchy	Rule by a king or queen who received supreme power via heredity and who is succeeded in power only at death.	7	Jordan
Theocracy	Rule by religious clergy or other persons who rely largely on well-established religious law to govern.	1	Iran
Totalitarian communism	A system in which the government makes extensive attempts to shape the goals, behavior, and thought of its citizens so that they actively support a communist ideology.	1	North Korea

Source: Barbara Geddes, Joseph Wright and Erica Frantz, "New Data on Autocratic Breakdown and Regime Transitions," Penn State, September 8, 2012, http://dictators.la.psu.edu/pdf/pp10.pdf.

* As of 2010.

discretion. Without rules of succession in place, most personalist leaders intend to remain in power indefinitely, relying on their personal contacts and charisma to protect them from challenges to their post. Given their unbridled power, personalist leaders tend to be highly corrupt, using the state treasury for personal and other private purposes.

The prevailing regime in Afghanistan, installed soon after the U.S. invasion of 2001, is a personalist one. President Hamid Karzai oversees a poorly institutionalized political system in which political parties and the military are unstable and weak. Karzai's administration is also notoriously corrupt. Sub-Saharan Africa also has several personalist regimes, such as those in DR Congo and Uganda.

Military Regimes. The third type is a **military regime** (also military dictatorship). In military regimes, a group of elite military officers determines who the leader or leaders are—typically choosing people from their own ranks—and exerts substantial or total control over policymaking. Military regimes often come to power through a military coup, an event in which the military uses its control of the instruments of violence and coercion to illegally depose the existing government. Throughout history, militaries have decided to intervene in politics and govern for a variety of reasons: to overthrow a government that they see as ineffective and illegitimate, to impose stability and order on a society that is increasingly violent and chaotic, to strengthen their position in an ongoing domestic conflict, and/or to protect

their own perceived interests. In underdeveloped countries with weak states, the military has often been the most well-organized and powerful institution in society, so its temptation to govern when the status quo has seemed unworkable has been great.[7]

Today, military regimes are relatively rare. The two most notorious ones of recent years are those of Myanmar (1988–2011) and Pakistan (1999–2008). Prior to the 1990s, military regimes were much more common. Most Latin American countries had military dictatorships at some point between 1955 and 1980, as exemplified by the Pinochet regime in Chile (1973–1990). About half of sub-Saharan Africa's countries had military coups and regimes in the two to three decades after its wave of independence began in the late 1950s. Although less common, some Middle Eastern and other Asian countries also experienced military regimes during this time period.

Monarchies and Theocracies. The fourth type of authoritarian regime is a **monarchy**, which is rule by a king or queen who received supreme power via heredity and who is succeeded in power only at death. In concentrating power in the hands of a single person, absolute monarchical rule has many similarities with personalist dictatorship. However, its distinguishing feature from personalist rule is the presence of a clear plan for how the top leader is designated, with the rule of succession typically intending to keep leadership in the same family for generations. Today, true monarchical rule by kings exists in just a handful of less developed (and almost exclusively Middle Eastern) countries, such as Jordan, Kuwait, and Morocco.

Another type of authoritarian regime is a **theocracy**, which is rule by religious clergy or other persons who rely largely on well-established religious law to govern. In other words, to be labeled a theocracy, religious clergy either must hold the top leadership positions or exact ultimate control over who does. Alternatively, some scholars would give the label theocracy to any regime that adopts wholesale an existing body of religious precepts as its primary source of law. Theocracies are almost nonexistent in the modern world, but the Islamic Republic of Iran fits the definition most closely. While it does have a popularly elected president and parliament, these officials are subservient to the unelected supreme leader (currently Ali Khamenei since 1989) and the twelve-member Guardian Council that he appoints, all of whom are experts in Islamic law.

Totalitarian Regimes. Before concluding this discussion of different authoritarian regime types, it is important to mention totalitarian regimes. Scholars disagree as to whether totalitarian regimes are a subset of authoritarianism or a third type of political regime alongside democracy and autocracy. For the purposes of this chapter, the precise classification is unimportant, especially since totalitarian regimes are exceedingly rare in the twenty-first century. A **totalitarian regime** is one in which the government makes extensive attempts to shape the goals, behavior, and thought of its citizens so that they actively support the government and its ideology. Totalitarian regimes are like authoritarian ones in that they violate civil liberties and do not hold free and fair elections. They differ, however, in that they attempt not just to suppress opposition, but also to mobilize comprehensive support for the regime.

The totalitarian regimes of the twentieth century existed in one of two forms: fascist or communist. The defining feature of fascist regimes is the belief in national superiority, with a central expectation that citizens will submit their individual desires to the needs of national furtherance and success. Fascist regimes have economies with elements of both state and private ownership. Under fascism, the state tightly regulates economic activity to ensure minimal foreign influence, relative harmony among classes, and the production of goods that are crucial to the nation's development and strategic power.

Fascist totalitarian regimes existed in Europe before and during World War II—Adolph Hitler's Germany (1933–1945) and Benito Mussolini's Italy (1922–1943)—but have not emerged since then and have been uncommon in the less developed world. By contrast, communist regimes are distinguished by their Marxist-inspired economic features, which can include bans on private property, mandated collective or state ownership of the means of production, and bureaucratic planning of the economy. The Soviet Union (1922–1991) and China under Mao (1949–1976) were the largest and most notorious Communist totalitarian regimes. They also existed in some countries, such as Cambodia (1975–1979) and Vietnam (1976–1986), that are considered less developed ones today. By most classifications, communist North Korea is the world's only remaining totalitarian regime.

Hybrid Regimes

These definitions of democracy and authoritarianism describe two opposing extremes: free and fair elections versus no free and fair elections, or respect for human rights versus no respect for human rights. In reality, many regimes fall somewhere in between these two poles. To provide a means of classifying such regimes, political scientists have invented new labels that reflect the intermediate status of these regimes and implicitly conceptualize regime type as falling on a continuum rather than being an either/or prospect.[8]

Figure 10.1 depicts what it means for regime type to be on a continuum. At either extreme are regimes that fit the definition of democracy and authoritarianism almost perfectly. In between are regimes that have elements of both democracy and authoritarianism. Scholars have labeled these a variety of things, including **hybrid regimes**, semidemocracies, illiberal democracies, anocracies, and partly free regimes. For example, an illiberal democracy has some of the trappings of democracy. It holds elections with universal suffrage that feature contestation among multiple political parties, but it falls short of being at the democratic extreme because rulers overstep the constitutional bounds on their power. Leaders may do so by failing to uphold the political rights of their opponents, pressuring the media into subservience, or redrafting existing law to grant themselves greater powers.[9]

A recent example of a hybrid system was the regime headed by the late Hugo Chávez in Venezuela. Chávez was elected repeatedly (in 1998, 2000, 2006, and 2012), and public opinion surveys showed that he was indeed the most popular candidate in each contest. As president, however, Chávez chipped away at the legal constraints on his presidential power and political authority. After his initial election, he spearheaded a move to rewrite the country's thirty-eight-year-old constitution and included in it new provisions to heighten his ability to promulgate decrees without the approval of the legislature. Subsequently, he packed the judiciary with subservient judges that imprisoned some of his political opponents, successfully sought approval to

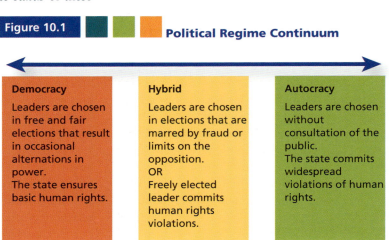

Figure 10.1 **Political Regime Continuum**

Democracy
Leaders are chosen in free and fair elections that result in occasional alternations in power.
The state ensures basic human rights.

Hybrid
Leaders are chosen in elections that are marred by fraud or limits on the opposition.
OR
Freely elected leader commits human rights violations.

Autocracy
Leaders are chosen without consultation of the public.
The state commits widespread violations of human rights.

lift all limits on the number of times he could run for reelection, and revoked the licenses of media companies that were known critics of his administration.

Political Instability and Regime Change

A related but conceptually distinct characteristic of political regimes is the degree of political instability a country experiences. Regimes in which political instability is absent and whose rules are widely accepted by virtually all important political actors are called **consolidated regimes**. In contrast, **political instability** exists when there is high uncertainty about the future existence of the current political regime. It is distinct from regime type since it refers to the sustainability of an extant regime, regardless of whether it is democratic or authoritarian. The existence in a society of widespread protest, political assassinations, terrorism, armed insurgencies, international conflict, frequent turnover of the chief executive, and coup attempts are all indicators that the existing regime is under threat and could fall at some point in the near future.

For example, Thailand experienced a spate of political instability after 2006 when yellow-shirted street protestors, many of them from the urban middle class, called for the ouster of two-term prime minister Thaksin Shinawatra. They lobbied for his ouster on the grounds that he was corrupt and insufficiently loyal to the monarch. With the protestors' backing, the military staged a coup in September of that year, exiling Thaksin and putting an interim caretaker prime minister in his place. In his absence, Thaksin's allies managed to win elections in 2008, but their government soon fell again in the face of more yellow-shirted protests and a court ruling that dissolved the ruling party. Enraged, thousands of Thaksin supporters, many of them poor rural workers, donned red shirts and took to the streets themselves. Among other things, they paralyzed the city's two major airports, occupied parliament, and burned a TV station's headquarters. In 2010, the protests culminated in violent clashes between the pro-Thaksin protestors and security forces that left almost 100 dead.

When a regime changes, a country has experienced a **regime transition**. Sometimes regime transitions involve the replacement of one authoritarian regime with another authoritarian one. For example, in 1974 Ethiopia experienced a transition from monarchical rule to a communist military dictatorship. Emperor Haile Selassie I, the last leader of a monarchical dynasty that claimed origins in the 1200s, was deposed through a coup and succeeded in leadership by the Derg, a military group that ultimately established a brutal Marxist-Leninist regime. Regime transitions can also entail movement in a more or less democratic direction. In the Chilean case, the military coup of 1973 invoked a transition from a democracy to an authoritarian system. When Pinochet stepped down in 1990, he was replaced by a system with recurring elections and much higher human rights standards. This shift from authoritarianism to democracy is an example of **democratization** or a democratic transition.

The Relationship between Political Regimes and Prosperity

One of the most enduring and important relationships in the political science literature is the relationship between economic development and regime type. Stated plainly, developing countries are less likely to be democratic than developed ones. In other words, there is a strong positive correlation between GDP per capita and the probability that a country has a democratic political regime. According to one set of estimates, the median GDP per capita (PPP) of all the world's democracies in 2011 was nearly US$14,000. In its hybrid and authoritarian regimes, it was just US$4,222.[10] Map 10.1 shows the geographical distribution of democracies and autocracies around the world. Virtually all autocracies are outside the developed world.

Map 10.1 ■ ■ ■ Political Regimes

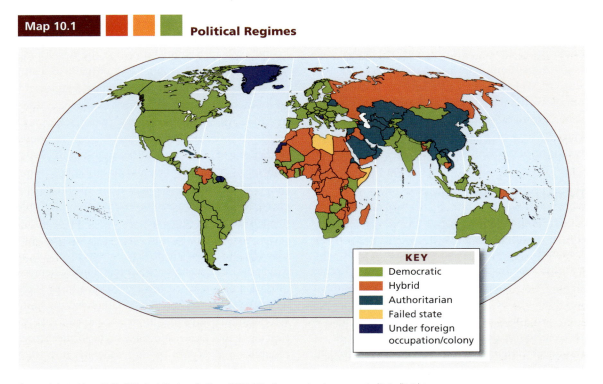

KEY
- Democratic
- Hybrid
- Authoritarian
- Failed state
- Under foreign occupation/colony

Source: Adapted from Polity IV Project: Regimes by Type, 2011, http://www.systemicpeace.org/polity/polity4.htm.

The developed countries (the United States, Japan, Australia, New Zealand, and those of Western Europe) are all democratic and have been so for at least half a century. As one moves down the global income scale, however, countries are more likely to have hybrid and authoritarian regimes. Moreover, even when a middle- or low-income country does have a regime that is classified as a democracy, it is likely to exhibit minor authoritarian elements that are mostly absent from the regimes of the developed world. For example, although middle-income Turkey has had recurrent elections and no military coups since the 1980s, human rights advocates have accused Turkey of politically motivated imprisonment, extrajudicial killings, and censorship of government critics.

The world's least democratic region is the Middle East. The Middle East has no democracies

(save Israel) and only a few hybrid regimes. It is dominated by monarchies and personalist regimes. Sub-Saharan Africa is a good deal more democratic on average than the Middle East. It features a handful of democracies in southern Africa and West Africa and a large number of hybrid regimes concentrated in East and West Africa. A significant number of Central and West African states, however, are fully authoritarian, most of which are dominant party or personalist regimes.

East Asia features the world's most diverse array of regime types. On one end of the spectrum is North Korea's totalitarian dictatorship, along with China's and Vietnam's dominant-party authoritarian regimes. On the other end it has the consolidated democracies of Mongolia and South Korea, the world's largest democracy (India), and

the nascent democracy of Indonesia. Hybrids include Pakistan's and Thailand's precarious semi-democracies, as well as the regime in Myanmar that began transitioning away from military dictatorship in 2011. Finally, Latin America is the developing world's most democratic region. Most of its states are democracies, with just a few hybrids (such as Venezuela) and Cuba as the last remaining authoritarian country.

Democracy's Third Wave

On average, there is less political freedom in the developing world than in the developed. However, a perspective that looks at regime type through time reveals an important democratizing trend. In particular, the developing world is much less likely to be authoritarian today than it was forty years ago. Recent decades have seen dramatic gains in democratic freedoms throughout the developing world. This trend is depicted in Figure 10.2.

Political scientist Samuel Huntington dubbed this trend the **third wave of democratization**, a wave that transformed political regimes in the developing world.[11] According to Huntington, the first wave of democratization occurred in the 1800s and early 1900s, when the West and Japan democratized. This first wave was followed by a reverse wave between World Wars I and II when Germany, Italy, and Japan turned to fascist dictatorships. The second wave occurred in the few years following World War II when these very same countries re-democratized. Several countries in Latin America, such as Argentina, Brazil, Chile, Costa Rica, and Venezuela, as well as some newly independent ones in Africa and Asia (most notably India) also held elections and became nascent democracies soon after the war. The 1960s and 1970s, however, witnessed the second reverse wave when most of these democratic regimes (with the exception of India) fell to military coups and dictatorships.

The third wave began in the mid-1970s with democratization in Portugal and Spain, but it quickly spread beyond Europe to the developing world. Between 1980 and 1990, virtually all Latin American countries shed their military regimes and established new democratic ones. Several countries in Asia, such as the Philippines, South Korea, and Turkey, also democratized in the 1980s. The winds of change reached parts of Africa in the early 1990s, as Benin, Ghana, Zambia, and several other countries held their first meaningful elections and experienced democratically driven alternations in their ruling parties. South Africa also shed its long-standing, racist *apartheid* regime and elected Nelson Mandela in 1994 in the first nationwide election in which the black majority could vote. Finally, democratization also reached the socialist world in 1989 when the collapse of the Soviet Union led the Eastern European states that it once occupied to set up thriving democracies, and some of the former Soviet republics moved in a more democratic direction. Overall, the third wave more than doubled (from about 30 percent to 60 percent) the percentage of the world's countries that are democracies.[12]

The one world region that was largely untouched by the third wave was the Middle East. Dictatorships that were in place before the third wave began, such as those of Muammar Kaddafi (1969–2011) in Libya, Hosni Mubarak (1981–2011) in Egypt, and Zine El Abidine Ben Ali (1987–2011) in Tunisia, were still in place as the third wave seemingly came to an end in the early 2000s. Beginning in late 2010, however, mass movements emerged in nearly every Middle Eastern country seeking overthrow of long-standing dictators, with some using peaceful protest and others armed insurgency as their primary tool. This Arab Spring led to regime change in several countries, most notably Egypt, Libya, and Tunisia. Here, dictators were deposed and new governments took their place, leading some observers to declare the advent of a fourth wave of democratization.[13] In actuality, it is not yet clear whether the Arab Spring has triggered a new wave of democratization. Not

only do the new regimes have questionable democratic credentials, but many of the old dictatorships, such as those in Jordan and Syria, remain in power, having successfully resisted the uprising.

The Judiciary and the Bureaucracy

Regime type is just one element of governance. Other important aspects of governance reside in the nature and quality of a country's judiciary, which is the branch of government that is in charge of interpreting the law for particular cases and disputes, and its public administration, which is the manner in which government policies are implemented. Most implementation is carried out by the bureaucracy (or civil service), the part of the executive branch that executes the tasks designated in public policy. Teachers, police officers, and foreign-service employees are all bureaucrats since they are tasked with providing the education, security, and diplomacy (respectively) that lawmakers have established as societal goals. Scholars have developed three central concepts to help observers characterize the nature and quality of judicial and bureaucratic governance.

Rule of Law

First, societies can operate according to the rule of law, the rule *by* law, or the rule of man. **Rule of law** exists when both state and society are bound by an impartial and neutrally enforced legal framework. In other words, the rule of law means that no one, including the highest-ranking political officeholder, is above the law.

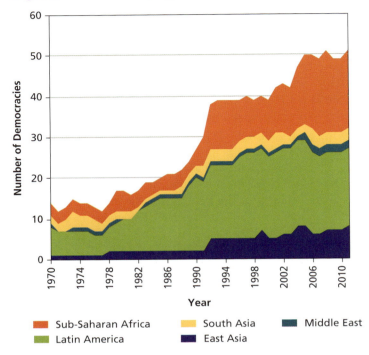

Figure 10.2   **The Third Wave of Democracy: Regimes in the Developing World since 1970**

Legend: Sub-Saharan Africa, South Asia, Middle East, Latin America, East Asia

Source: Polity IV Project, "Political Regime Characteristics and Transitions, 1800–2011," http://www.systemicpeace.org/polity/polity4.htm.

To achieve this goal, a judicial system must be independent of politicians in other branches and of societal pressures. There must also be an incorruptible bureaucracy (and especially police force) to implement judicial decisions. Moreover, rule of law requires that the law itself is unbiased in not unfairly disadvantaging any particular individuals or groups. Leaders who enact laws that stipulate their right to repress opponents or a minority group are engaging in rule by law, using the law as a tool to serve politically motivated and unfair ends. Finally, for rule of law to prevail, the law must have effectiveness, meaning that political authorities and the broader population largely respect its dictates. Countries where criminal behavior is rampant lack rule of law, even if a fair legal framework exists on paper.

Rule of law is the antonym of rule of man, in which binding legal decisions are made at the whims of powerful persons to further their own narrow interests. In such a context, the application of the law is arbitrary, based not on a fair and impersonal weighing of facts, but on the persons involved and on how the outcome affects the powerful. To invoke a classic metaphor, legal authority in a rule-of-man society is not blind to the parties involved. Examples of politically driven arrests by authoritarian regimes are plentiful and pepper coverage of international news. Just to cite one, in 2012, Cuban officials arrested Yaoni Sánchez, an internationally renowned blogger and government critic. The stated reason for her arrest was that she was about to disrupt the trial of another dissident. Given that her alleged crime had not yet even occurred, it was clear the government's motive was to prevent her from attending and blogging about the trial. Sánchez was released after thirty hours, but worldwide many arbitrary arrests result in permanent detention, torture, and even death.

Corruption

Second, societies vary in their degree of **political corruption**, which is the use of public authority to enrich or advantage oneself or a narrow group of persons. Political corruption can exist in any branch and at any level of government. When it involves high-level officials and large amounts of money, such as when a construction firm pays off the president in return for receiving a contract to build a state-funded highway, it is called grand corruption. When corruption involves small sums of money and lower-ranking officials, such as paying off a police officer to get out of a ticket, it is called petty corruption. When pervasive among judges or common bureaucrats, petty corruption undermines the quality of governance in the judicial and bureaucratic branches of government.

Many cases of political corruption are forms of bribery, whereby government officials sell for personal profit a public service or good to which they control access. Common examples include bribes to a desk worker in charge of filing paperwork to get a business registered or to a judge to secure a favorable court ruling. In sub-Saharan Africa, roadblocks set up by police, military personnel, or militias who extract bribes from drivers in exchange for passage have been a common occurrence, especially during wartime. In some instances, bribery can take the form of what is called agency capture (also regulatory capture), in which a particular branch of the bureaucracy shows recurring favoritism to a business or some other social actor who has paid it off. Finally, political corruption can take the form of outright theft of treasury funds, such as when officials use taxpayer dollars to procure a car or a home. In general, political corruption thrives under a lack of **transparency**. Transparency exists when government processes follow well-established regulations and are open to scrutiny by outside observers.

State Capacity

A final aspect of governance is a country's level of **state capacity**, which is the degree to which a state is able to successfully and efficiently carry out its designated responsibilities and provide high-quality public goods and services. State capacity rests on the bureaucracy's ability and willingness to follow through on the laws passed and interpreted by the legislative and judicial branches. For starters, to provide the services that political leaders intend and that populations expect, states must be able to generate revenue through taxation. However, many LDCs struggle to raise the revenue they need to fund their judicial and bureaucratic arms.

Another dimension of state capacity is the level of professionalism in the civil service. A bureaucracy is much more effective and fair when its members are guided strictly by established laws and procedures and carry them out in an impartial way.

For example, bureaucrats in charge of delivering publicly funded old-age pensions should determine monthly payment amounts to retirees based on the codified standards regarding age and work experience. If, however, one bureaucrat denies payments to people who voted for a candidate the bureaucrat does not like, then professionalism is absent. When politicized decisions like this are excessive, bureaucracies become dominated by **clientelism**. Clientelism occurs when government resources are distributed not according to impersonal rules, but at the discretion of individual politicians and bureaucrats who use the resources to attract or reward supporters. Clientelism is often involved in the process of appointments to public-sector jobs, as when politicians who control job appointments hire their supporters (patronage), close confidants (cronyism), or relatives (nepotism) over more competent persons. When civil servants are granted jobs for nonmeritorious reasons, they may also exhibit a lack of bureaucratic professionalism by not putting forth effort in or even attending their jobs. For example, (as documented in Chapter 2) absenteeism among public-sector educational and health workers is extremely common in South Asia.

Judicial and Bureaucratic Quality around the World

These three aspects of governance vary, just like regime type, according to a country's level of economic development. On average, LDCs are less likely to have the rule of law. They also have higher levels of political corruption and weaker state capacities. Figure 10.3

depicts some of these patterns by showing regional averages on the World Governance Indicators of rule of law, control of corruption, and state capacity (called "government effectiveness" in the figure). The regional averages are expressed as percentiles, meaning the region's average country ranking relative to all the other countries. (See Understanding Indicators: Measuring Regime Type and Governance for more details on how these scores are derived.) The high-income countries score the highest on all three, averaging around 85 percent. In contrast, the percentiles of sub-Saharan African countries average in the twenties, again for all three indicators. The remaining regions fall in between these two extremes.

Causes of Underdevelopment: Bad Political Institutions

In the 1980s, many political scientists and economists believed that all a country needed to achieve economic growth was to put the right development

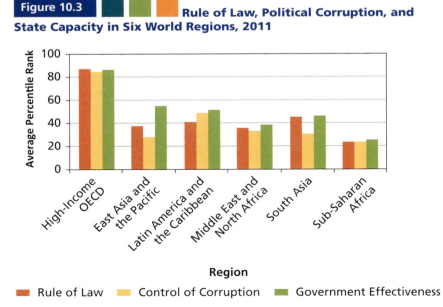

Figure 10.3 **Rule of Law, Political Corruption, and State Capacity in Six World Regions, 2011**

Source: The World Bank, World Governance Indicators, http://info.worldbank.org/governance/wgi/index.asp.

Measuring Regime Type and Governance

Social scientists have produced numerous indicators of the political institutions discussed in this chapter, but three are among the most widely used. (Each is exemplified for three countries in the table below.) The first is the Polity IV Project, which measures political regime characteristics in virtually every sovereign state in every year since 1800. (The classification of regimes in Figure 10.2 and Map 10.1 are based on Polity.) Polity rates each country on a 21-point scale, ranging from −10 to +10. A score of +10 is equivalent to a fully institutionalized democracy, and a score of −10 equal to a highly autocratic system. Polity arrives at this single number by summing up six component variables that score a country on things such as how its chief executive is chosen, the extent and competitiveness of its political participation, and the degree of constraint on executive power. Polity trains in-house coders to score each of these component variables based on knowledge gleaned from historical documents, media reports, and academic research on the individual countries.

The second indicator is the Freedom of the World scores assigned to nearly every sovereign country since 1972 by Freedom House. Like Polity, it builds up toward a broad label of regime type by scoring each country in each year on a relatively large number of subcomponents. Country and regional experts answer ten questions on political rights (such as the electoral process, political pluralism and participation, and the functioning of government) and fifteen on civil liberties (such as freedom of expression, associational rights, rule of law, and individual rights and autonomy) for each country. The answers to these questions are aggregated to produce a political rights score that ranges from 1 to 7 and a civil liberties score that also ranges from 1 to 7. In contrast to the Polity IV indicator, higher numbers equate to less freedom and democracy in the Freedom House index. The average of these two determines whether a country is labeled "free," "partly free," or "not free."

A final major data source on political institutions is the Worldwide Governance Indicators (WGI), some of which are presented in Figure 10.3. Since 1996, WGI has annually scored countries on each of six indicators: voice and accountability, political stability and absence of violence, government effectiveness, regulatory quality, rule of law, and control of corruption. Each of these six is a composite of numerous individual variables, many of which are scores from surveys of investors, mass publics, experts, public-sector organizations, and nongovernmental organizations that reside in or are familiar with the country. Each country receives a score between −2.5 and +2.5 for each of the six indicators, with higher scores equating to better governance.

These data collection efforts each produce hard quantitative measures of governance for a particular time and place. This should not disguise, however, what is clear from these descriptions, which is that a high degree of subjectivity and human interpretation underlies these numbers. For starters, subjectivity exists in the scoring process. For example, the coders for Polity and Freedom House necessarily make numerous judgment calls and assumptions in trying to distill a year's worth of political events in any given country into scores on six indicators or twenty-five questions, respectively. The investors responding to surveys for the WGI also probably allow their personal political biases to color their evaluations of bureaucratic quality and regulatory frameworks. By its very nature, corruption is difficult to measure and quantify, but the WGI codes it nonetheless, based in part on citizens' and investors' perceptions of a society's transparency.

Moreover, there is subjectivity in determining what goes into the indicators and thus how governance and regime types are defined. For example, Polity takes a narrow definition of democracy, overlooking the legal scope of political participation. As a result, it gives the United States high

Examples of Governance Measures for Three Countries, 2011

Country	Polity	Freedom House	Voice and Accountability (WGI)	Political Stability (WGI)	Government Effectiveness (WGI)	Regulatory Quality (WGI)	Rule of Law (WGI)	Control of Corruption (WGI)
China	−7	6.5 (not free)	−1.64	−0.70	0.12	−0.20	−0.43	−0.62
United States	10	1.0 (free)	1.13	0.54	1.41	1.49	1.60	1.23
Venezuela	1	5.0 (partly free)	−0.92	−1.30	−1.10	−1.49	−1.63	−1.22

Sources: Polity IV Project, "Political Regime Characteristics and Transitions, 1800–2011," http://www.systemicpeace.org/polity/polity4.htm; and The World Bank, World Governance Indicators, http://info.worldbank.org/governance/wgi/index.asp.

scores of 8, 9, and 10, even before women and African American slaves could vote. In contrast, Freedom House takes a broader approach, but it thereby includes among its twenty-five questions ones on property rights, economic exploitation, and the presence of war, things that are not part of standard definitions of democracy.

All that said, these indicators are highly correlated with one another, a sign that they are tapping something meaningful, and they remain the best available options for measuring democracy.

- Is it possible to quantify democracy and other aspects of governance, or are these efforts too riddled with subjectivity and error to make such measures worthwhile?
- What might be some better ways to measure the extent of corruption than asking investors and citizens their perceptions of it?

model into place. To scholars of the neoclassical persuasion, these policies, mostly found in the Washington Consensus list discussed in Chapter 8, included privatization, openness to foreign trade and investment, and sound fiscal and macroeconomic measures. However, when many countries in Africa, Latin America, and the Middle East implemented this market-friendly package in the 1980s and 1990s and experienced disappointing results, sentiments among many of these scholars shifted. They no longer saw changes to economic policy as sufficient to achieve growth. Instead, as part of the neoinstitutionalist turn discussed in the previous chapter, development scholars increasingly saw the crisis of economic underdevelopment as a problem of governance—that is, of politics and not just economics.

In particular, ideas from the new institutional economics (NIEs) school began to take a stronger hold on how scholars thought about the causes of and solutions to underdevelopment. To reiterate a point made in the previous chapter, NIE sees a society's political and economic institutions as the fundamental cause of economic performance since, according to Douglass North, they "shape the incentive structure of a society."[14] Scholars of development began arguing that authoritarian governments, corrupt officials, inefficient bureaucrats, and unfair judges were the ultimate cause of the developing world's failure to take off economically. Bad political leaders and the institutions they built established poor incentives for common citizens in their everyday lives, discouraging them from working, investing, and innovating to the extent they otherwise would. By the 2000s, economists at the World Bank were preaching reform of

less developed countries' state institutions to go along with the economic policy reforms they had long been promoting. At the UN, Kofi Annan in 2002 wrote that "good governance is perhaps the single most important factor in eradicating poverty and promoting development."[15] Good governance became the name of the development game.

Extractive Institutions

How, more precisely, does bad governance stunt social and economic development? Most of the rules, norms, and organizations that are relevant to economic performance are set up by political leaders, so a case of bad institutions in an LDC can also be thought of as a case of bad leadership: "Poor countries are poor because those who have power make choices that create poverty."[16] According to NIE scholars Daron Acemoglu and James Robinson, many leaders impoverish their populations by setting up **extractive institutions** that organize politics and economics so as to authoritatively redistribute major portions of society's wealth and potential wealth to a narrow group of powerful people that includes themselves.[17] In turn, extractive institutions remove many of the incentives that societal actors have to be productive and innovative, thereby keeping their countries poor.

How Extraction Occurs. In societies where elites have established extractive institutions, the extraction of resources mostly occurs through expropriation, petty corruption, and rent-seeking. Extraction occurs when a political leader engages in **expropriation**, seizing a citizen's private property and declaring it the property of the state, of the leader him or herself, or of someone else. This form of property rights violation can happen in a variety of ways. State officials may simply use the means of violence they have at their disposal to help themselves or their cronies to property they want. The state may also seize private property to redistribute it to others as part of a broad ideological project or to meet pressing fiscal needs. The state can also expropriate through excessive regulation or taxation. Grand corruption in the form of theft from the taxpayer- and donor-funded state treasury is also a form of expropriation.

Leaders can also build extractive institutions by allowing or promoting petty corruption. Giving state jobs on the basis of patronage or nepotistic ties is one example, while allowing legislators and low-level bureaucrats to work by accepting bribes and kickbacks is another. Finally, leaders can allow **rent-seeking** behaviors to proliferate. An economic rent is the income one gains by virtue of participating in a market that is not perfectly competitive. Groups and individuals pursuing rent-seeking activities typically try to enrich themselves by gaming political rules to their advantage rather than by engaging in genuinely productive activities. For example, a group of existing petroleum firms lobbying for government to subsidize the production of oil or to enact regulations that block new petroleum firms from entering the market is rent-seeking behavior.

Consequences of Extraction. To NIE scholars, extractive institutions have numerous negative effects on economic and social progress. Some consider expropriation of property to be the most harmful extractive behavior because it has a chilling effect on investment and technological advancement. Expropriation stokes fears of further property seizures, which scares off potential investors and discourages existing property owners from investing in improvements to their property. According to Acemoglu and Robinson, "A businessman who expects his output to be stolen, expropriated, or entirely taxed away will have little incentive to work, let alone any incentive to undertake investments and innovations."[18] Moreover, expropriation via theft of treasury funds diverts economic resources away from the health, educational, security, and transportation needs that are so pressing in LDCs. The overall quantity and quality of government-provided goods and services suffers.

Petty corruption yields a number of negative effects.[19] When widely practiced, patronage and nepotism mean that government jobs are not awarded on merit. These practices put people with suboptimal skills and weak performance incentives in charge of carrying out important tasks such as teaching children and keeping the peace. Similarly, the practice of firms providing kickbacks to the politicians that award them contracts for government projects means that many infrastructural projects are not constructed by the highest-quality and most competitive bidder. The bribery of low-level bureaucrats allows businesses and citizens to dodge regulations that are well-intentioned, such as antipollution rules, building safety regulations, or tests to obtain a driver's license. For example, after the Mexican earthquake of 1985, it was clear that many structures collapsed, including school buildings with children in them, because builders had not adhered to safety requirements. Petty corruption is also particularly hard on the poor since they are often more reliant on public services and are less able to afford bribes.

Finally, successful rent-seeking by the powerful makes markets less competitive, which harms consumers by keeping prices high and quality low. It also slows the process of creative destruction that is so fundamental to economic growth. Sustaining productivity gains requires that consumers and producers be able to freely adopt technological advances. The emergence of new technologies, however, creates economic losers out of producers who still use and sell older technologies. If powerful, these potentially losing producers can use political rules to block society from adopting new technologies, thereby harming consumers and overall economic productivity. Finally, successful rent-seeking creates perverse economic incentives by encouraging individuals to try to acquire wealth not through hard work, innovation, and investment, but by trying to change political rules to their favor, which is an inherently unproductive process.[20]

Extractive Institutions in Zimbabwe. Zimbabwe under the presidency of Robert Mugabe (1980–present) exemplifies the various extractive institutions and some of their negative consequences. Starting in 2000, Mugabe enacted the most notorious expropriations of the twenty-first century thus far, supporting violent thugs who chased white farmers off of their land and giving much of the seized property to cronies in his ZANU-PF ruling party. (To be sure, many of the white-owned farms were themselves extracted from native Africans during the colonial era.) Many scared whites left the country, taking their know-how with them, and the new landowners often had little interest or expertise in farming. Agricultural output collapsed, and food prices soared.

Mugabe's rule has also repeatedly distorted market competition so as to provide economic rents to his cronies. For example, the Zimbabwean government allowed the Posts and Telecommunications Corporation (PTC), the state-owned telecommunications company run by ZANU-PF elites, to maintain its monopoly over telecommunications until 1996. The problem for Zimbabweans was that the PTC only had the capacity to provide landline service. Private investors were already agitating to provide mobile phone services to millions of Zimbabweans who had no access to telephones of any kind, but the PTC monopoly effectively forestalled this option. Moreover, as if the PTC monopoly were not enough, Mugabe at one point banned private mobile phone operations in order to block the main source of competition to the PTC's landlines. In other words, to protect the potential victims of creative destruction (providers of landlines) from economic loss, he impeded the adoption of the new technology, mobile phones. In doing so, Mugabe effectively disallowed millions of Zimbabweans from using cellular technology and made them a captive audience of the PTC, which had a waiting list for residential landline installations that was ten years long.[21]

Grand corruption has also been rampant under Mugabe. For example, in 1995, senior government

officials used National Housing Fund monies, which were intended to be used to build housing for poor state workers, to build posh homes for themselves. Mugabe took no interest in prosecuting anyone for this theft. Most of the original intended recipients continued to live in substandard housing. All told, the consequences of these and other extractive measures by the Mugabe administration have been dire, as Zimbabwe has had perhaps the world's worst human and economic development trends since 1990.

Inclusive Institutions as the Solution

For NIE thinkers, the way to spark economic growth in LDCs is to replace the harmful extractive institutions with a package of more **inclusive institutions**, including democracy, rule of law, transparency, high state capacity, and property rights. These will provide the right incentives to societal actors, unleashing their inherent energies to produce, invest, and innovate.

Regime type is an important element of this package because, according to Acemoglu and Robinson, there is a synergistic relationship between political and economic institutions. When political institutions distribute power throughout the population, economic institutions are more likely to be equitable in nature and incentivize everyone to produce. Democracies empower citizens through elections to express a binding voice about who governs them. After all, when democratic leaders govern in an extractive way that enriches themselves at the expense of their societies, aggrieved citizens can simply vote them out of office at the next election and choose leaders who are keener to pursue the collective well-being. In other words, when common citizens have political power, they do not let extractive institutions last. In contrast, when political institutions concentrate power in the hands of a few, as in an autocracy, then dictators govern in the interest of the few. They set up extractive economic rules that enrich themselves and their cronies at the expense of everyone else, stifling the productive talents of their populations. Under autocracy, citizens

have no recourse to get rid of bad leaders, so extractive institutions remain in place.

Scholars have also pointed out other advantages of democracy for economic growth. Democracies have a freely operating media that can reveal the extractive abuses committed by political leadership when they occur. Living in a much more information-rich environment, democratic citizens can more easily monitor whether their countries' leaders are acting for the collective well-being. Also, democratic regimes tend to be more stable and long-lasting than authoritarian ones. This relative certainty about the political future encourages investment, both from foreign and domestic sources.[22] Most investors are hesitant to invest in contexts where the political and economic rules are prone to dramatic change.

NIE scholars point to various pieces of evidence to support these claims. The world's first developed countries, such as the United Kingdom, United States, and France, were also the world's first to develop inclusive political institutions. To them, it was the steady emergence of checks on executive power in Western Europe before the 1800s and then participatory democracy itself in the nineteenth century that chipped away at the extractive institutions that had previously existed under absolutist monarchs.[25] This enabled industrial revolutions and sustained economic productivity gains over two centuries to occur. In contrast, the world's authoritarian regimes, such as those in Latin America, failed to thrive economically as the democratic West took off in the nineteenth century.

More recently, evidence from the twentieth century shows that authoritarian regimes are more prone to economic disaster: 95 percent of the worst economic episodes of the last fifty years occurred under authoritarian regimes.[26] While growth can occur under authoritarian and extractive institutions, it seems to be not as sustainable as that which occurs under inclusive institutions. Economic progress in the democratic

DEVELOPMENT in the FIELD

Democracy Promotion

If NIE scholars are correct, democracy creates a win-win scenario. On the one hand, it is inherently desirable since it grants, among other things, freedoms and liberties that prevent governments from arresting or killing people for their political affiliation or ethnic status. On the other hand, it is instrumentally desirable since it creates the conditions for material prosperity.[23] As a result, one would expect that democracy promotion is an important focus of the international aid community, and this is indeed the case. But can democracy be created or promoted from the outside? Numerous aid agencies think so.

Democracy promotion can come in a number of forms. One is election monitoring, whereby an agency observes the logistics and administration of an election and reports on its level of fairness. The Carter Center, founded and run by former U.S. president Jimmy Carter, is one organization that engages in frequent election monitoring around the world. A second form of

democracy promotion is to foster a vibrant civil society. Among the organizations involved in this form of democracy promotion is the National Endowment for Democracy, which channels funds to civic groups in the developing world (such as independent labor unions, women's and student groups, and small business associations) that promote democracy awareness and lobby their governments for democratic reforms. Another means of democracy promotion is to promote rule of law. The American Bar Association sponsors the ABA Rule of Law Initiative, which provides technical assistance to judges, lawyers, and law students in nascent democracies with the goal of building effective and independent judiciaries. Finally, human rights organizations such as Amnesty International and Human Rights Watch can be thought of as democracy-promoting organizations. These are less focused on building sustained democratic institutions and more on individual cases in

which civil or political rights have been violated.

Despite their numbers and breadth, democracy-promotion agencies typically meet with highly mixed success. Changing political institutions from the outside—and often with meager funds to boot—can be a quixotic task, especially when leaders and powerful groups have entrenched interests to maintain the status quo. Many aid agencies have learned that democracy promotion is only worthwhile if there is a willing audience and leadership on the ground. Furthermore, the third wave of democratization that occurred in the 1980s and 1990s had little to do with pressure from democracy-promoting foreign aid agencies. More controversially, some democracy-promoting efforts can backfire, as authoritarian governments and even their citizens see it as a form of Western meddling in their internal affairs. In the Middle East, some U.S.-funded civic groups have been labeled traitors and have even become targets of repression themselves.[24]

West has been less subject to reversal and down-turn than that which occurred in many authoritarian societies, presumably because dictators prevent excessive economic and societal change

from occurring so as to hold on to power.[27] As a final point, economist Amartya Sen famously showed that famines have only ever occurred under authoritarian regimes, allegedly because

their leaders have less incentive to find a way to feed their populations in times of drought.[28]

Critique of NIE

Two of the central premises of NIE are that the direction of influence is from political institutions to economic performance and that inclusive political institutions and democracy cause sustained economic growth. Various schools of thought take issue with one or both of these premises.

Economic Development First

The first point is a controversy surrounding the direction of cause and effect. Many advocates of NIE take the strong correlation between political freedom and economic prosperity as evidence for their claim that democracy and other aspects of good government are the fundamental source of growth. The existence of this strong correlation, however, is just as indicative of the reverse cause-and-effect relationship, whereby economic prosperity leads to democracy and good governance. In fact, a number of logical reasons exist for thinking this might be the case, and, until quite recently, political scientists were far more likely to think the relationship worked in this direction.

This "economic development first" sentiment received its first systematic empirical and theoretical statement in the 1950s from modernization theorist Seymour Martin Lipset. Lipset argued that the observed correlation between a country's level of economic development and democracy, which existed in the 1950s just as today, was because democracy had certain social and economic requisites. Widespread mass education and a large middle class were chief among them, together creating a series of desirable traits among the masses that were amenable to democracy. To Lipset, formal education gave citizens the knowledge to "intelligently participate in politics" and make "rational electoral choices."[29] Education also

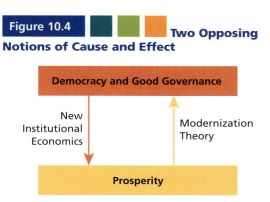

Figure 10.4 **Two Opposing Notions of Cause and Effect**

Democracy and Good Governance

New Institutional Economics

Modernization Theory

Prosperity

broadened citizens' outlooks, making them feel as if they were part of a unified national culture rather than a narrow, aggrieved group. Middle-class status made individuals politically moderate and imbued with the "self-restraint necessary to avoid succumbing to the appeals of irresponsible demagogues."[30] Societies with a large middle class were thus less polarized into competing ideological extremes. Absent poor people, who Lipset saw as more inclined to revolt and to want the state to redistribute large amounts of income away from the rich, the stakes of political contestation in wealthy societies were lower and democracy more sustainable.

Lipset's argument was highly influential, inclining a subsequent generation of scholars to largely agree that high income leads to democracy. As one example, the World Bank, IMF, and UN largely believed in the 1970s and 1980s that democracy was a luxury that would only take root and that should only be worried about after LDCs had grown wealthy enough to meet their citizenry's basic economic needs. As evidence, during this time some of the world's economic success stories, such as Chile, South Korea, and Taiwan, developed democracy after experiencing economic boom under dictatorship. Only recently did the NIE literature's claim that authoritarianism is the cause of these unmet economic needs gain some adherence in social science circles.

The direction of cause and effect has also been questioned in looking at other aspects of governance.[31] Having a professional bureaucracy and an independent judiciary are expensive propositions. Police officers, judges, teachers, health workers, customs officials, and other state workers are presumably more honest and effective if they are well compensated, yet states in poor countries cannot afford to pay decent wages to their employees. As a result, many state workers see bribes as a natural supplement to their meager state wages. For example, the average salary of a police officer in the Congo, where the taking of bribes is common, is US$30 per month.[32] Similarly, a high state capacity requires locating government workers (for example, police officers) and a supporting infrastructure (such as police headquarters, motor vehicles, and paved roads) throughout a country's territory, including in remote rural areas. This too is an expensive proposition that many less developed states cannot afford, making their weak state capacity more a consequence of their poverty than its cause. Similarly, it may appear to researchers that state capacity is weaker in underdeveloped societies because the challenges their states face are so much greater than those faced in developed societies.

The Authoritarian Advantage

The challenge to the second NIE premise comes from scholars who, while agreeing that regime type does cause economic performance, think that it is authoritarian regimes that have the upper hand over democracies in creating economic growth in LDCs. This authoritarian advantage argument has been raised by a number of scholarly traditions. It found a particularly explicit currency in a 1968 book by Huntington.[33] Huntington argued that, because of the pressing nature of their material needs, the poor prefer immediate consumption over investment. By binding leadership to this demand, democracy diverts resources toward consumption and away from the investment necessary to produce growth.

Subsequent to Huntington, some scholars argued that it was democracies that are more prone to the perils of rent-seeking behaviors than authoritarian regimes.[34] After all, democracies allow the self-interested, narrow groups that want to acquire rents to organize and lobby the government.[35] Democracy also empowers the poorer citizens, who demand soak-the-rich redistributive policies that may be bad for aggregate investment.[36] In contrast, a dictator is insulated from such demands and can thus govern to the benefit of society as a whole. Moreover, without needing to engage in shared decision making, authoritarian rulers can respond to problems more efficiently and quickly.

Scholars have also argued that a corrupt bureaucracy need not be the death knell for growth that NIE claims it to be. Huntington himself wrote that "in terms of economic growth, the only thing worse than a society with a rigid, over-centralized, dishonest bureaucracy is one with a rigid, overcentralized, honest bureaucracy."[37] His reasoning was that bribery enabled societal actors and especially businesses to grease the wheels, getting around the regulations and red tape that would stifle economic activity. Businesses in corrupt societies must often hire facilitators to successfully negotiate the bureaucracy, but those in less corrupt societies hire lawyers to accomplish the same. In many instances it is faster to simply pay the bribe so one can move on. Moreover, while NIE views bribery as a means to entrench powerful but undeserving businesses, the contrasting argument sees bribery as a means to reward businesses that are successful enough to pay bribes.[38]

Mixed Evidence

Aside from these two sets of theoretical challenges, the empirical support for the NIE claim that democracy and good governance are the

most crucial ingredients of growth is highly mixed. Although there has long been an obvious positive correlation worldwide between a society's wealth and its degree of democracy, many systematic statistical studies have found the impact of regime type to be minimal.[39] In actuality, dramatic improvements to economic livelihood have occurred under a wide variety of political institutions, including the totalitarian socialist regime of the Soviet Union (1917–1991), the dominant-party authoritarian regime of today's China (1978–present), the military dictatorship

of Park Chung-hee in South Korea (1963–1979), and the monarchy of Saudi Arabia (1932–present). Growth rates in all five cases far outpaced those in democratic India during its first forty years of independence. Moreover, growth has also occurred in countries that fall short in other ways of standard notions of good government. The Soviet Union industrialized despite a lack of private property, and Indonesia experienced an economic boom under the dictatorship of Suharto (1967–1998), who was once dubbed the world's most corrupt leader.[40]

CASE STUDY

DOES CHINA'S AUTHORITARIANISM EXPLAIN WHY IT IS POORER THAN THE WEST?

In the millennium following the collapse of the Roman Empire in 476, Chinese civilization was by some measures the world's wealthiest,[41] and it seemed more likely than Western Europe to experience an industrial revolution. After all, the Chinese had invented paper, gunpowder, the compass, movable type printing, and windmills before Europe did. Moreover, China had a highly centralized state staffed with the most meritocratic bureaucracy in the world. In the end, however, modern economic growth and industrialization began in the West, not the East. Western Europe and the United States left China far behind in the 1800s in what is called the Great Divergence,[42] and the civilization that Napoleon once (allegedly) called the "sleeping dragon" began to make up the lost ground in living standards only a few decades ago. Table 10.2 compares some development outcomes and causes in China with those in the United States.

The South: Serial Authoritarianism

To NIE thinkers, the reason for China's lost ground and fast turnaround lies in its history of authoritarian rule and extractive institutions.[43] This history of alleged poor governance is a long one, dating back to at least the 1400s. Although China has experienced various regime changes since then, it has merely shifted from one kind

of autocracy to another, a classic case of serial authoritarianism.

Missteps before the Industrial Revolution. In the middle of the fifteenth century, Europe was beginning its Age of Discovery through commercially minded seafaring explorations, and Great Britain was experimenting with new ways to protect property

Table 10.2 Development Comparison: China and the United States

Indicator	China	United States
GDP per capita at PPP	US$8,848	US$41,728
Human Development Index	.678	.910
Numbers of years as a democracy since 1800	0	203
Number of invasions by a foreign power (1839–1945)	5	0
Renewable internal freshwater resources per capita (cubic meters)	2,093	9,044

Source: Data on GDP and Human Development Index are from Gapminder, www.gapminder.com; number of years of democracy, Polity IV Project, "Political Regime Characteristics and Transitions, 1800–2011," http://www.systemicpeace.org/polity/polity4.htm; freshwater data, the World Bank, World Development Indicators, http://data.worldbank.org/sites/default/files/wdi-final.pdf.

ownership from royal expropriation through the courts.[44] Over the subsequent three centuries, European powers benefited from colonizing most of the world's territory. Revolutions to limit executive power occurred in Great Britain, France, and the United States, leading to nascent democracies and an emergent rule of law that entrenched the rights of citizens to securely own private property.

Meanwhile, Chinese leadership chose a different institutional route. In 1436, rather than encourage overseas exploration with its ship fleet—one that could have easily crossed the Pacific—Emperor Zhengtong banned it, denying his subjects access to valuable commodities and a chance for China to discover the New World. Zhengtong feared that trade would empower merchants, whom he saw as a threat to his regime and the Chinese monarchy. His successors agreed, and the ban on trade lasted almost 150 years. Moreover, as Europe later moved toward more inclusive institutions, China's government turned over from one monarchy to another. In 1644, a violent changeover in the ruling dynasty from Ming to Qing was accompanied by widespread looting of civilian property by warlords and soldiers.[45] Soon thereafter, Qing emperor Kangxi promulgated an effective expropriation through

the Great Clearance of 1661, ordering residents of China's southern coast to evacuate and move at least fifteen miles inland so that his troops could more easily patrol the area of dissidents.

Institutions during the Great Divergence. As late as 1800, China still had a chance to keep pace with the West, as the two had a similar average living standard and manufacturing capacity.[46] However, the subsequent two centuries were far less kind to China, perhaps because it pursued such an extractive institutional path. As democracies emerged in parts of Europe and the United States in the 1800s, China's monarchy dug in, growing increasingly distant from its subjects and making no overtures to grant them political rights. After a tumultuous century in which average living standards declined, the monarchy collapsed in 1911, and China underwent a rocky and prolonged regime transition. After more than a decade of political turmoil and division, a dominant-party authoritarian regime emerged under the leadership of the Nationalist Party in 1927. The nationalists expropriated much of China's industrial base so as to have direct control over the means of war.[47] By some estimates, China's already meager average income was lowered by half during this era.

DOES CHINA'S AUTHORITARIANISM EXPLAIN WHY IT IS POORER THAN THE WEST?

Little relief from authoritarian and extractive institutions came in 1949 when Mao Zedong overthrew the nationalists and declared the founding of the People's Republic of China under the leadership of his Chinese Communist Party. Mao set quickly to work building extractive institutions. He banned most private property, killed thousands of rural landowners, forced peasants onto collectively owned farms called people's communes, and brutalized millions for their independent thought and speech during the Cultural Revolution (1966–1976). His policies were also instrumental in causing perhaps world history's worst famine in 1962. Although some industrialization and

improvements to human health occurred under Mao, by 1976 China's GDP per capita was still below its 1800 level.

Institutional Change and the Current Boom.

Since Mao's death in that year, China's average incomes have grown by an order of magnitude.[48] According to NIE thought, the primary cause has been changes in China's political and economic institutions, many of them implemented by Deng Xiapoing after he ascended to de facto leadership in 1978.[49] Although not a democracy, China's political institutions have been less repressive than they were under Mao. They have evolved from a strict totalitarianism to a single-party authoritarianism in which the Communist Party is no longer considered the sole source of truth and in which elections for village leadership have been allowed. Moreover, economic institutions are far less extractive. Communes were disbanded, and farmers now lease individual plots of land from the state and keep earnings for themselves. Urban residents can own their own homes. Some state-owned enterprises have been privatized, and millions of small profit-seeking industrial firms have flourished. In sum, the standard NIE interpretation of China's success of the past thirty years is that it has moved in a more inclusive direction, even though it still falls far short of being a democracy.

***

Some critics of this explanation, most importantly the Chinese Communist Party, counter that it

A Chinese security official stands guard in front of the famous Mao Zedong portrait in Tiananmen Square (Beijing). China has been governed by the Communist Party that Mao founded since 1949, and before that it was ruled by military dictators or monarchs. It has never had a democratic regime.

is authoritarianism itself that created China's boom. Chinese history and culture put community and country before self, their argument goes, so China's society is not amenable to individual political rights. Democracy would foment social disunity and conflict. Moreover, it would unleash the selfish demands of thousands of interest groups and more than a billion people. This would distort and slow decision making to the detriment of the overriding goal of mobilizing massive amounts of investment for long-term growth. Some international observers speak of an emergent **Beijing Consensus** to countervail the Washington Consensus (described in Chapter 8). Rather than preaching free markets and democracy, the Beijing Consensus touts authoritarianism and state capitalist policies as the right formula for the developing world.

The West: A Century of Humiliation

Other critics of the claim that China's authoritarianism accounts for its underdevelopment assert that meddling by the West is the primary reason for China's delayed rise.[50] After all, until 1800 China largely kept pace with the West as a whole, and it was around the time that the West began invading and occupying parts of China that the Great Divergence began. Most notoriously, Great Britain launched the First Opium War (1839–1842) when it invaded China in 1839. This rudely thrust China into an international system it had long avoided and began what the Chinese call their "century of humiliation" at the hands of foreign superpowers.[51] Over the subsequent 100 years, wars with the British, French, and Japanese—all of which China lost—resulted in a series of "unequal treaties" that forced China to make major financial, territorial, and sovereignty concessions.

The First Opium War is a case in point. For decades, British traders had been selling opium grown in India to Chinese smugglers in defiance of a Chinese ban. Tired of the addictive toll it was taking on its population, as well as the drain on its reserves of precious metals, the Chinese government closed off all trade through Canton (the main port of opium entry) in 1839. It also seized a large amount of the British traders' opium. Britain sent troops and the world's most advanced war fleet, and its forces prevailed in a three-year war. Through the Treaty of Nanjing, Great Britain exacted a variety of humiliating concessions from the defeated Chinese Empire. These included financial compensation for the seized opium, reparations for war costs, the opening of Canton and several other ports to British imports, and the cession of the island of Hong Kong. Over the subsequent century, forced concessions to foreign superpowers were recurrent. China ceded more territory, eventually being "carved up like a melon." By the thousands, foreign administrators moved to and governed eighty different port cities. As the Western world experienced the Industrial Revolution, a once-leading civilization had to deal with semicolonial impositions.

The Natural World: Inhospitable Terrain

Although it is about the same size, shape, and latitudinal location of the continental United States, China's geography is far less conducive to economic growth. China is an extremely arid and mountainous country, making its terrain inhospitable to most forms of agriculture. Three-fourths of its territory is at least 500 meters above sea level, compared to just 40 percent in the United States and 20 percent in Europe. Also, it receives only about one-fourth of the annual precipitation amount that the United States does. As a result, just 15 percent of its land is farmable—and this in a country with 1.3 billion people. The amount of

DOES CHINA'S AUTHORITARIANISM EXPLAIN WHY IT IS POORER THAN THE WEST?

arable land per person is thus just one-sixth what it is in the United States.[52]

China's geography may also explain why its commercial engagement with the rest of the world was minimal before 1800. Its coastline is much smaller than those of Europe and the United States and more isolated from inland territory because of the land's ruggedness. China also lost the locational lottery by being situated much farther from the Americas than is Europe. Although both China and Europe had ocean-worthy shipping fleets, Europeans reached the New World first, allowing them to harness its resources to partly power Europe's industrialization drive.[53]

Finally, physiologist Jared Diamond argues that China's geography is the ultimate cause of its authoritarianism and resulting economic stagnation. A brief look at the map reveals Europe to be pocked with peninsulas and islands, while the Chinese landmass is largely a singular block with three major rivers connecting east and west. Diamond argues that China has been a politically centralized and unified civilization since 221 BCE (save a few ephemeral exceptions) due to this internal geographical connectedness. China's long line of emperors had little trouble imposing absolutist rule throughout a vast territorial expanse, and their decisions had to be taken by subjects as final. In contrast, Europe's more balkanized geography created a chronic but beneficial political disunity. Its islands and peninsulas provided natural barriers among states, allowing for multiple and competing centers of innovation to flourish. For example, when Christopher Columbus sought royal sponsorship for his explorations, he did not meet with success until approaching his fifth monarch. In China, all

seafaring exploration was shut down with a single decision in 1432.[54]

***

With its ongoing rise, China is making a bid to return to the position it once held of economic parity with the West. In growing so quickly, China is showing that human and economic development under authoritarianism are possible. But will the ongoing presence of extractive institutions eventually put a brake on China's efforts to grow, as some NIE scholars predict? Or will its rising economic prosperity soon trigger democratization, as modernization theory predicts? Alternatively, China may prove both wrong and simply continue on its current path of rapid economic growth under single-party authoritarianism, in confirmation of the Beijing Consensus. Regardless of who turns out to be right, the dragon is no longer asleep.

Thinking Critically about Development

- China was once the world's most advanced civilization. What caused it to be on the losing end of the Great Divergence?

- The Beijing Consensus asserts that one-party authoritarianism has facilitated China's boom since 1978, while the NIE school says that these kinds of political institutions are usually bad for growth. Which argument is more convincing?

- Is it right to attribute China's relative decline on nineteenth-century Western intervention when it was never fully colonized like Africa or Latin America?

Key Terms

authoritarian regime, p. 238

Beijing Consensus, p. 259

clientelism, p. 247

consolidated regime, p. 242

democracy, p. 236

democratization, p. 242

dominant party regime, p. 238

expropriation, p. 250

extractive institutions, p. 250

governance, p. 236

hybrid regime, p. 241

inclusive institutions, p. 252

military regime, p. 239

monarchy, p. 240

parliamentary system, p. 237

personalist regime, p. 238

political corruption, p. 246

political instability, p. 242

political institutions, p. 236

political regime, p. 236

presidential system, p. 237

regime transition, p. 242

rent-seeking, p. 250

rule of law, p. 245

state capacity, p. 246

theocracy, p. 240

third wave of democratization, p. 244

totalitarian regime, p. 240

transparency, p. 246

 ## Suggested Readings

Acemoglu, Daron, and James A. Robinson. *Why Nations Fail: The Origins of Power, Prosperity, and Poverty*. New York: Crown Business, 2012.

Huntington, Samuel Huntington. *The Third Wave: Democratization in the Late Twentieth Century*. Norman: University of Oklahoma Press, 1991.

Lipset, Seymour Martin. "Some Social Requisites of Democracy: Economic Development and Political Legitimacy." *American Political Science Review* 53, no. 1 (1959): 69–105.

Morris, Ian. *Why the West Rules—for Now: The Patterns of History, and What They Reveal about the Future*. New York: Farrar, Straus and Giroux, 2010.

Naughton, Barry. *The Chinese Economy: Transitions and Growth*. Cambridge: MIT Press, 2007.

North, Douglass C., John Joseph Wallis, and Barry R. Weingast. *Violence and Social Order: A Conceptual Framework for Interpreting Recorded Human History*. New York: Cambridge University Press, 2009.

Web Resources

Freedom House, www.freedomhouse.org/

International Society for New Institutional Economics, www.isnie.org/

Polity IV Project, www.systemicpeace.org/polity/polity4.htm

Transparency International Corruption Perceptions Index, http://www.transparency.org/country

Worldwide Governance Indicators, http://info.worldbank.org/governance/wgi/index.asp

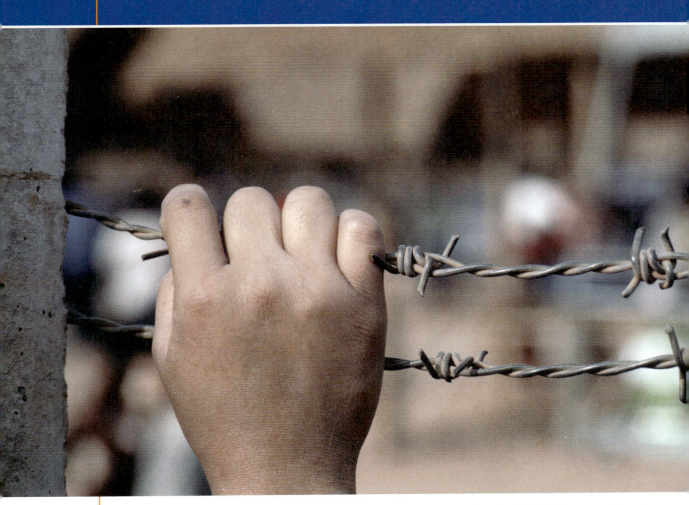

A child refugee stands behind barbed wire in Cambodia in 1990. The refugee camp housed civilians who had fled their homes out of fear of armed conflict. Cambodia was ravaged by international and civil war throughout the 1970s and 1980s.

Members of Chile's military junta stand at attention days before orchestrating a violent coup that overthrew democratically elected president Salvador Allende. General Augusto Pinochet (far left, 1973-1990) became the country's new president, heading a military regime that was notorious for the brutality and scope of its human rights abuses.

Violence and State Failure

Amina cannot bear the thought of eating oatmeal again. It is the only thing she has eaten all week, but she has little choice. The teenager lives in a refugee camp in Mogadishu, the capital city of Somalia. Just over a year ago, she and her family walked for fifteen days to settle in Mogadishu. They were fleeing a famine in the south that killed her youngest brother. Triggered by drought, the famine was worsened by the country's twenty-year-long civil war and lack of a functioning state. Local militias of the Islamist Al Shabab movement were preventing international development agencies from getting food aid to the starving, and the Somali central government was powerless to do anything to alleviate the starvation.

Amina's family practiced nomadic herding in the south, so they had no village or permanent home to abandon. Their most valuable possessions, several heads of livestock, were gradually slaughtered for food until they ran out, at which point the family fled. They thus would have little to return to—not to mention that Al Shabab still controls the area. That said, the options in Mogadishu are not much more attractive. There is little hope that Amina's father will secure a steady, decent-paying job, and the city has been called the world's most dangerous because of ongoing militia violence. In the end, they remain in the camp because it provides the certainty of food—albeit bland food—for now.

The human costs of war are well known, but Amina's plight also illustrates war's economic and social costs. Many of the poorest countries in the world are also plagued by war, other forms of political conflict, and criminal violence. Many of these same countries have central governments with limited to no governing authority. This chapter explores the impact of various forms of violence and state failure on development.

Political and Criminal Violence

This chapter focuses on two forms of social violence. **Political violence** is physically harmful or coercive organized behavior that is exercised to achieve a political end. Political violence can be carried out by states or non-state actors. Nonpolitical violence, classified as **criminal violence** in this chapter, is physically harmful or coercive behavior that does not have an explicitly political motive, such as robbery, assault, and homicide. Much criminal violence is carried out by individuals or small groups for personal motivations, but many LDCs also have violent organized criminal gangs and groups. Domestic and gender-based violence (such as rape and sex trafficking) are also a part of this category, but a full discussion of these is left for Chapter 12.

Political Violence

Scholars categorize episodes of political violence as either interstate or intrastate. **Interstate violence** occurs when multiple states use political violence against one another or when a state uses violence against non-state actors living in a different country. In **intrastate violence** (also civil violence), political violence occurs among state or non-state actors living within the same country. Civil violence encompasses a variety of things that include communal violence between ethnic groups, wars over territorial control and secession, and widespread repression of dissidents by a state. Some scholars use the terms "conflict" and "war" to make distinctions about the scope of an episode of political violence. When political violence is sustained and the number of casualties is relatively high, it is considered a war. Experts on political violence often treat 1,000 combat-related deaths as the cutoff between a war and a conflict.[1]

Figure 11.1 displays one estimate of the frequency of political violence in the developing world. The figure shows a count of the number of countries in the developing world that had episodes of political violence (defined here as any instance of political violence in which at least 500 deaths occurred) in each year between 1962 and 2008.[2] The totals distinguish between interstate or intrastate violence, and the latter category includes everything from sustained civil wars to episodes of interethnic conflict that surpass the casualty threshold. Three main patterns stand out. First, episodes of intrastate violence have been far more common than have those of the interstate variety. In other words, civil conflicts and wars occur much more frequently than wars and conflict between countries. In every year, fewer than ten LDCs were at war or in conflict with another country, and in some years none were. By contrast, the number of countries with intrastate violence was typically greater by a factor of at least two and often much more. Second, the number of countries with intrastate violence gradually rose during the observed time period. In fact, it tripled in the three decades before 1989, the year that corresponds to the end of the Cold War (1947–1989). In contrast, the incidence of interstate violence remained rather steady, even falling slightly after the mid-1980s. Third, the number of countries with intrastate violence fell dramatically after the end of the Cold War, more than halving in number by 2008. The remainder of this subsection elaborates on some of these trends.

Despite the fact that some of the most well-known and visible wars involving an LDC have been interstate ones, interstate wars are relatively rare. The Gulf War (1991), the Iraq War (2003–2011), and the War in Afghanistan (2001–present) were all wars between a U.S.-led coalition and a less developed country, but, in actuality, interstate wars like these that pit a Western power against an LDC are relatively rare. Moreover, wars between less developed countries are also relatively rare. Since the wave of independence that began in sub-Saharan Africa in the late 1950s, the continent has experienced just a handful of interstate wars. The same is true of Latin America, where interstate warfare has been nearly absent for over a century. Since World War II, interstate wars between LDCs have been most common on the Asian continent. For example, India has had multiple borders disputes with Pakistan and China, and Iran and Iraq fought the longest conventional interstate war of the twentieth century (1980–1988).

As a result of this relative absence of interstate war, civil conflict and war have been far more frequent occurrences in the developing world since World War II. In the mid-1990s, nearly a third of sub-Saharan African countries experienced intrastate conflict, and several civil conflicts and wars occurred in the Middle East (Egypt, Libya, Syria, and Yemen) as part of the Arab Spring that began in 2010.[3] Civil wars were also common in Asia and Latin America in the decades prior to 1989.

Many of these internal domestic conflicts were **governmental wars**, or struggles between an existing government and an insurgency group over control of the central state. During the Cold War, many civil wars with this profile were fought on ideological grounds. Numerous LDCs saw the emergence of Marxist and other leftist groups who took up arms to try to overthrow their governments and install communist states. These groups typically relied on **guerrilla warfare** tactics of surprise and mobility to exact damage on their foe while avoiding direct confrontation with the conventional (and usually superior) military force of the state. Guerrilla groups often use acts of **terrorism**, which are violent measures meant to achieve a political goal by provoking fear in a civilian population. Civil wars between governments and leftist groups were

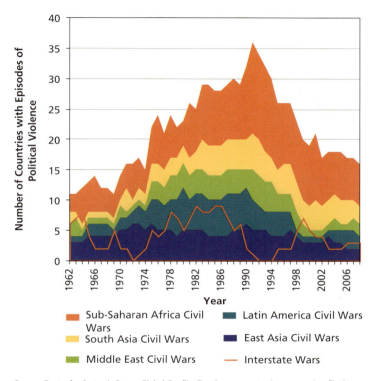

Figure 11.1 **Episodes of Political Violence in the Developing World by Region, 1962–2008**

Source: Center for Systemic Peace, Global Conflict Trends, www.systemicpeace.org/conflict.htm.

common in Latin America during the Cold War. In Argentina, Chile, El Salvador, and Guatemala, military governments waged particularly brutal campaigns against armed leftist movements, often brutalizing innocent civilians in the process. Aspects of the Vietnam War (1958–1975) had a similar logic, as the U.S.-supported anticommunist government of South Vietnam faced a guerrilla challenge from a Marxist group backed by North Vietnam and the Soviet Union. In some countries, however, the contestation was reversed: Marxist-inspired governments fought civil wars against anticommunist guerrilla insurgents (again, often backed by the United States). This was the nature of civil wars in places such as Angola and Nicaragua.

To be sure, many governmental wars have lacked this strong political and ideological orientation. In some instances, insurgencies are comprised of an aggrieved group that wishes to overthrow an existing leader or regime. The uprisings against Syrian leader Bashar Assad that began in March 2011 and escalated into a conflict that claimed at least 60,000 lives fit this description. In some of these cases, the lines of belligerence can correspond to cultural factors such as ethnicity, religion, or race. An ethnic group that has little say in government or a religious fundamentalist group that seeks to control the state may form an insurgency against the existing regime. In Syria, many of the militias fighting for Assad's overthrow are Sunni Muslim groups opposed to Assad for, among other things, his Alawite ethnic affiliation.

The other major form of civil conflict is secessionist wars. In a **secessionist war**, a separatist group fights against a central state over a territory that is a subset of the existing nation-state. The separatists generally seek to achieve greater self-rule and often a new breakaway nation-state. As the governments of most modern states prefer to keep their existing territories intact, they almost invariably resist secessionist calls, even peaceful ones. When secessionist movements turn violent, central states have typically responded in kind to maintain their existing borders and authority throughout their entire territory. Like governmental wars, secessionist wars can often occur along ethnic or other cultural lines. For example, the Kurdistan Workers' Party (PKK) has fought for an independent nation-state for the Kurdish ethnic minority residing in southeastern Turkey. Similarly, wars of secession between minority ethnic groups and central states have been common in sub-Saharan Africa in the independence era. For example, the Nigerian Civil War (1967–1970) ensued when the southeastern region of Biafra, comprised largely of members of the Igbo ethnic group, declared the independent Republic of Biafra. The war ended in Biafra's defeat and reunification with Nigeria. Elsewhere, the Eritrean War of Independence (1961–1991) is a rare modern case of a secessionist civil war that ended in actual partition. The nation-state of Eritrea became independent in 1991 upon driving out the military forces of the Ethiopian central state. A number of ethnic secessionist conflicts continue in sub-Saharan Africa to this day.

The distinction between intrastate and interstate wars is not just a technical one. Civil wars are not only more likely to occur, but they are also more intractable. The average civil war lasts seven years, more than ten times as long as the average length (six months) of an interstate war.[4] Moreover, civil wars are highly recurrent. Ninety percent of the conflicts that were initiated in the twenty-first century were in countries that had had a civil war within the previous three decades.[5] In the words of economist Paul Collier, countries can fall into a "conflict trap" from which it is hard to escape.[6] Finally, since World War II, poor countries with stagnant economies have been the most likely to see an outbreak of civil war.[7]

Criminal Violence

Criminal violence comes in two broad forms: organized and unorganized. Organized criminal violence is administered by or against gangs of at least moderate size who have an internal hierarchical structure and exist to profit from illegal activities. Unorganized violence captures most other forms of criminal violence, including things such as common street crime and crimes of passion.

Data on these forms of criminal violence are notoriously hard to collect and are often unreliable, but the United Nations Office on Drugs and Crime (UNODC) has made some rough estimates of homicide rates by country. A summary of these are presented in Figure 11.2. The figure shows the incidence of apolitical, non-conflict-oriented intentional murders of one person by another, expressed as the number of homicides per year per 100,000 people in six world regions. The numbers do show that homicide rates tend to be higher in LDCs than

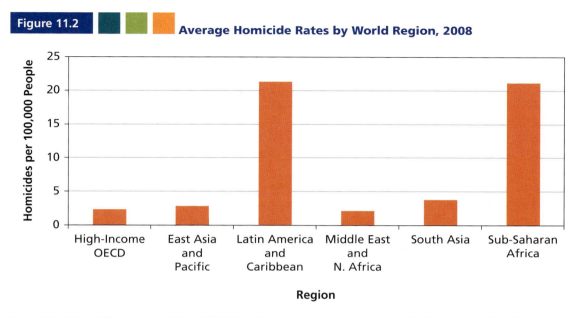

Figure 11.2 **Average Homicide Rates by World Region, 2008**

Source: United Nations Office on Drugs and Crime, UNODC Homicide Statistics, http://www.unodc.org/unodc/en/data-and-analysis/homicide.html.

in the developed world, but this relationship is driven almost entirely by the booming homicide rates of just two world regions. The incidence of homicide is quite low throughout the Middle East and much of Asia, but it is nearly ten times as high in sub-Saharan Africa and Latin America. All told, of the nearly half a million homicides that occurred worldwide in 2010, two-thirds of these occurred in Africa and the Americas.[8]

The nature and causes of homicide are different between these two regions. A large number of murders in Latin America occur through organized criminal violence, while most in Africa occur through unorganized violence. Within Latin America, the Central American isthmus and a few surrounding countries comprise what is, by some measures, the most violent zone on earth. Some of this region's homicide rates match or exceed those achieved by other countries in wartime, despite the near absence of political violence in the isthmus. In 2011, Honduras and El Salvador had the two highest homicide rates in the world at 91.6 and 69.2, respectively. Nearby countries such as

Venezuela (45.1), Jamaica (40.2), Guatemala (38.5), Colombia (31.4), and Mexico (23.7) were also among the world's most violent countries, at least according to the UNODC measures.

A large number of these homicides are related to the trafficking of illegal narcotics. Almost all of the world's coca leaf, the raw material for cocaine, is grown in the Andean foothills of Bolivia, Colombia, and Peru, and the largest consumer is the United States. Mexico also produces heroin and marijuana. As a result, vast quantities of illegal drugs are transported to the U.S. market through the Central American isthmus and Mexico by drug cartels and other organized criminal gangs. These gangs operate in a lawless underworld where profits are exceedingly high. With no formal or legal institutions to adjudicate disputes, many of the homicides are carried out as part of struggles between rival gangs for territorial and market control. Drug-related violence has escalated particularly dramatically in Mexico in recent years. Murders related to narcotics trafficking rose from 6,800 in 2008 to

15,000 by 2010, accounting for more than half of the country's homicides.[10]

In contrast, most homicides in sub-Saharan Africa are not carried out by organized criminal groups, but by individuals or small groups with personal and private motivations. Murders stemming from street crime and family or acquaintance disputes are the most common form of homicide in the region. South Africa is one of the world's most violent large countries, experiencing around fifty murders per day and annual homicide rates in the low thirties.[11] This number ballooned after the end of apartheid in 1994, although it began to show signs of decline in the late 2000s.

State Failure

State failure occurs when a state loses its monopoly on the popularly accepted use of violence within its territory. A failed state cannot successfully carry out most of the standard functions of governance within its formally designated territory and meet fundamental collective goals such as maintaining public order, extracting revenue from the population, or providing social services. Thought of differently, state failure is an extreme form of weak state capacity, a concept introduced in Chapter 10. Failed states do not provide education, maintain and expand roads, deliver utility services, arrest and imprison lawbreakers, and carry out other widely accepted practices of government. If such services are administered at all, they are done so by private persons and groups.

For example, it is often said that the central government of Afghanistan has little presence outside the capital city of Kabul, which is where its offices are located. Government police and military personnel are few in number or wholly absent from vast swathes of the country, and, where present, they are poorly trained and equipped. The government collects virtually no taxes in rural areas, but also provides to them no services such as electricity, schooling, or health care. The government can enforce few of its own laws, as evidenced by the fact that illegal opium is far and away its leading export. DR Congo, Iraq, Somalia, and Sudan are generally considered to be some of the world's other failed states, and some definitions of the concept even tally dozens of others.

To be designated as a failed state, a state authority must be absent in virtually all aspects of public service provision and throughout most of the country's territory. Mexico's inability to reign in the violence associated with drug gangs is an instance of state incapacity in the realm of public order, at least in the parts of the country where drug-related violence is common. Yet the Mexican government is not a failed state since it does successfully carry out a number of other standard functions of governance, such as negotiating international treaties, collecting taxes, and controlling the money supply. It has even been able to marshal a substantial counteroffensive against the traffickers, although with highly mixed success.

State failure tends to exist in countries experiencing widespread political violence and especially civil war, hence its inclusion in this chapter on violence.[12] The presence of hostile insurgencies, foreign troops, or criminal gangs within a country's borders is itself an indication of the state's inability to achieve a major collective goal of governance: what Max Weber called a monopoly on the legitimate use of violence throughout its entire territory. Moreover, the presence of ongoing violence tends to chip away at other forms of state authority. States cannot govern in territory under the control of hostile non-state actors, and because of this they may lack **legitimacy**, which is popular recognition and support for the idea that the state should be the sole source of political authority. In such instances, many civilians turn to the violent non-state actors themselves to provide the services their state is failing to deliver, such as physical protection, oversight of markets, and even social services.

The case of Afghanistan is again illustrative, demonstrating the role of political violence in state failure. Soon after a North Atlantic Treaty Organization (NATO) coalition led by the United States toppled Afghanistan's Islamic fundamentalist Taliban regime in December 2001, civil war broke out.

understanding INDICATORS

Measuring State Failure

Since the emergence of state failure as a scholarly concept in the 1990s, political scientists and other observers have generated a number of different measures that attempt to gauge it cross-nationally, but there remains no consensus on how to measure state failure. An early attempt was made in the early 1990s by the State Failure Taskforce (now renamed the Political Instability Task Force), which considered any of the following events to be an instance of state failure: revolutionary wars, ethnic wars, adverse regime changes, or genocides.[14] This definition, however, equates state failure with political violence and political instability, so the concept as measured has no meaning of its own outside these other ones. Standard definitions of state failure refer to a political factor—a state's capacity to govern—that is more encompassing than just the ability to keep the peace. For example, Colombia has had insurgent and paramilitary violence on its soil for decades, yet this violence has been largely confined to certain rural areas. It has not prevented the government from successfully carrying out

functions such as managing its macroeconomy and providing nearly universal primary education.

Map 11.1 shows a newer measure of state failure, the Failed State Index (FSI), which is far more encompassing. The FSI, generated for each country yearly by the Fund for Peace, is a composite of twelve different indicators, such as the country's degree of demographic pressures, poverty among societal groups, economic decline, political corruption, human rights violations, public service quality, and ethnic unity. Each indicator is scored on a 0 to 10 scale, with higher values indicating a more undesirable outcome. For example, in 2012 the Netherlands received a 1.3 for the human rights indicator and Afghanistan received an 8.5. The twelve scores are then totaled up to yield a single number for each country, ranging between 0 and 120. In 2012, Somalia received the dubious distinction of being the world's most failed state, with a score of 114.9, while Finland received the lowest score of 20.0. Based on a country's score, FSI assigns a label. These are shown in Map 11.1: "alert"

(90 or more), "warning" (60 to 90), "moderate" (30 to 60), and "sustainable" (below 30). Most of the alert states are located in what some analysts have described as the "arc of instability,"[15] which runs from West, Central, and East Africa through the Middle East and into parts of South Asia.

A common criticism of FSI is that, in comparison to the Political Instability Task Force measure, it goes too far in the other direction. The FSI index is too encompassing and includes many features that are potential causes and consequences of state failure rather than direct indicators of it. For example, one of the twelve indicators that is in the overall index is the presence or absence of economic decline. Another is whether society can provide enough life-sustaining resources to its population. These elements are aspects of social and economic development—possible causes and consequences of state failure—but not part of any standard definition of state failure. With their inclusion, the FSI risks becoming a general measure of underdevelopment rather than a specific measure

(Continued)

(Continued)

of state failure. Similarly, one of the other twelve indicators is the degree of state repression and human rights violation. Again, these things are certainly undesirable, but they are features of authoritarianism, not state failure. If anything, repression requires a good deal of state capacity since a formal security apparatus must be in place for it to occur.

- The Political Instability Task Force measure of state failure seemingly looks only at political violence, whereas the FSI looks at violence, human development, macroeconomic health, and other factors. Is there a happy medium to be had in measuring state failure?

- If the definition of state failure refers to a near-total collapse of state capacity, why do scholars not simply focus on this formal political factor when trying to measure the concept?

The Taliban and other groups formed insurgencies aimed at ousting NATO forces and overthrowing the new U.S.-backed regime. The Afghan government and allied NATO forces have little authority over the southern half of the country. Instead, throughout much of the south the Taliban operates its own political administration, complete with tax offices and Islamic religious schools (*madrassas*). They also

Map 11.1   **Failed States Index, 2012**

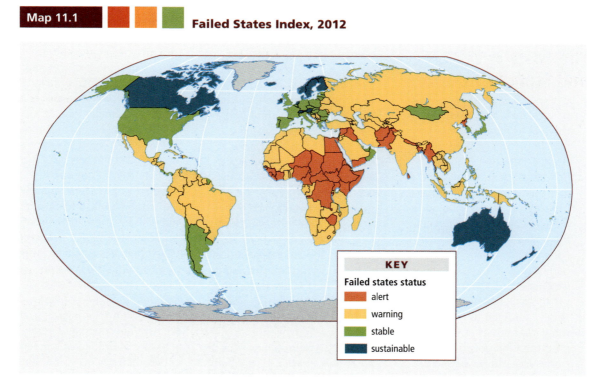

KEY

Failed states status
- alert
- warning
- stable
- sustainable

Source: Fund for Peace and Foreign Policy, Failed States Index, www.fundforpeace.org/global/?q=fsi-grid2012.

have a declared legal system of strict *sharia* (Islamic law) and courts and police to enforce it.

Although there are different interpretations of precisely which states are failed ones (see Understanding Indicators: Measuring State Failure), many experts believe their numbers to be on the rise. This may be due in part to the fact that many LDCs lost financial and military support from their Cold War patron (either the West or the Soviet Union) when the war ended. Former U.S. defense secretary Robert Gates called fractured or failing states "the main security challenge of our time."[13]

Causes of Underdevelopment: The Costs of Violence and State Failure

Violence has obvious immediate human costs since, by definition, it leads to disability and loss of life. It can also leave deep and lasting psychological wounds in individuals who experience trauma, causing permanent mental illness. Although these immediate human costs are important, this section focuses more on the less obvious consequences of violence (in both its political and criminal forms) and state failure. In particular, it describes the heavy toll these two take on social development and economic growth.

The Costs of Armed Conflict

Political violence can yield longer-term social development costs. Figure 11.3 illustrates a

Figure 11.3 **Comparing Social Development Outcomes in Peaceful and Conflict-Affected States, 2003–2008**

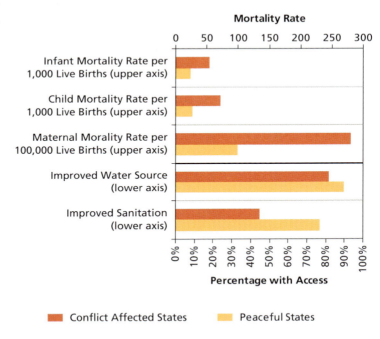

Mortality Rate

- Infant Mortality Rate per 1,000 Live Births (upper axis)
- Child Mortality Rate per 1,000 Live Births (upper axis)
- Maternal Morality Rate per 100,000 Live Births (upper axis)
- Improved Water Source (lower axis)
- Improved Sanitation (lower axis)

Percentage with Access

Conflict Affected States   Peaceful States

Source: The World Bank, World Development Indicators, http://data.worldbank.org/sites/default/files/wdi-final.pdf; and Scott Gates, Håvard Hegre, Håvard Mokleiv Nygård, and Håvard Strand, "Consequences of Civil Conflict," World Development Report 2011 Background Paper, October 26, 2012, https://openknowledge.worldbank.org/bitstream/handle/10986/9071/WDR2011_0012.pdf?sequence=1.

number of ways in which instrastate conflict is associated with poor social development outcomes. Conflict-affected states have higher child and maternal mortality rates, and they have worse water infrastructure. Evidence suggests that the effects of war on health last long past the cessation of hostility because of decimated health sectors and the spread of infectious diseases.[16]

Another social consequence is population displacement. In war-torn countries, many civilians flee their areas of residence out fear of potential violence. When people flee to another country, they are called **refugees**, and when they move elsewhere within their borders they are called **internally displaced persons** (IDPs). On average, 80 percent of refugees and IDPs are women and children. Many end up in camps established and administered by the United Nations High Commissioner for Refugees (UNHCR) and other international aid agencies. The camps are always intended to be temporary, with the hope that residents will move back to their homes or to other more permanent residences once it is safe to do so. According to a 2010 estimate, there were 42 million people worldwide who were victims of forcible displacement, and 15 million of these were refugees and another 27 million were IDPs.[18]

The economic losses from political violence occur through numerous channels. First, war has opportunity costs. In general, war focuses a country's attention on destruction and survival at the expense of economic production. As economist Mancur Olson puts it, "There is . . . little or no production in the absence of a peaceful order."[19] Second, wars can yield dramatic costs in terms of destroyed physical infrastructure and capital stocks. Roads, bridges, houses, factories, utilities, oil pipelines, and other physical assets are often targets of destruction in wars. Third, investors often forego investment or pull capital out of countries involved in conflict. Conflict breeds investor fears of expropriation or destruction of their assets. They also fear low returns due to the distraction of productive energies. Fourth, wars represent a destruction of human capital since part of the workforce is killed or disabled. Moreover, a disproportionate number of casualties are young adults at the beginning of their productive lives. Children in conflict-affected countries are twice as likely as children in more peaceful LDCs to be malnourished, a condition that typically creates permanent detriment in the children's physical and mental development. Fifth, war raises the costs of economic exchange. Aside from the destruction of physical infrastructure, individuals fear travel in war. Civil wars may harden identities and resentment between the combating

societal groups, further decreasing the scope of trust and potential exchange. Sixth, wars also have high fiscal costs. States boost military spending during wars, diverting funds from more profitable social purposes. Evidence also shows that they maintain high rates of military spending even after hostilities have ended. To exacerbate the problem, this shift in fiscal priorities occurs while the need for health-care spending booms.

When political violence is so widespread that state failure ensues, national economies become almost unable to function. State authority is a requisite for modern economic growth. In lieu of some degree of personal security and safe control of their property, individuals do not feel safe to produce, exchange, and invest in their own futures. According to economists Daron Acemoglu and James Robinson, "One must-have for successful economies is an effective centralized state. Without this, there is no hope of providing order, an effective system of laws, mechanisms for resolving disputes, or basic public goods."[20]

The economic toll of political violence is evident in the fact that most of the world's "bottom billion" countries—those that are the remaining laggards in the wave of development advances taking place throughout the developing world—have experienced some form of major conflict in the last three decades. Writing in 2007, Collier noted that 73 percent of people living in the bottom billion were living in a country with an ongoing or recently ended civil war. Moreover, the gap in economic indicators between conflict-ridden LDCs and more peaceful ones is growing, suggesting that violence may be the greatest current constraint on economic progress. For example, no reduction in poverty rates occurred in countries that experienced major violence between 1981 and 2005, while in all other LDCs poverty rates fell by more than 15 percentage points.[21] Given their prevalence, civil wars have been the most damaging form of political violence in the developing world for the past several decades. Civil wars are particularly damaging because they occur almost entirely on a country's domestic soil and because they are more enduring than interstate wars. Collier and Anke Hoeffler find the effects of civil war to be so dramatic that they call civil wars "development in reverse."[22] By their estimate, a civil war costs a low-income country an average of 250 percent of its GDP.

Mozambique's civil war (1975–1992) illustrates how economic consequences can be so dire.[23] In terms of physical capital, one-third of all retail shops, over half of all government buildings and post offices, and most water and electricity service providers were destroyed or rendered nonoperational. Cattle stocks, most of them owned by the poor, declined by 80 percent, due not just to destruction and looting by combatant forces, but also to starvation, forced abandonment, lack of veterinary care, a drying up of markets, and the immediate food needs of the poor. An estimated 60 percent of foreign investment inflows were cancelled. In terms of human capital, an astounding one-third of citizens (more than 5 million) were displaced either internally or to a foreign country. More than 3,000 schools were closed or destroyed, and nearly 80 percent of children in war-affected areas witnessed a killing. Indirect costs were also enormous. The cost of transporting Mozambique's main export commodities doubled. To pay for heightened military spending, the government raised taxation on an already poor population and increased foreign borrowing such that foreign debt reached 500 percent of GDP. (See Development in the Field: Violence Prevention and Post-Conflict Recovery.)

Other historical examples also seem to confirm the importance of peace for social and economic development. Western Europe, led by Great Britain, experienced its economic takeoff during the nineteenth century, which largely coincided with the Pax Britannica (1815–1914) when Europe, after centuries of warfare, experienced a peaceful interlude before World War I.[24] In contrast, the nineteenth century was an economic disaster for the newly independent states of Latin America, whose wars of independence became, in many countries, prolonged civil wars that lasted decades.[25] A third of South American countries had wars for most of the nineteenth century, and the remaining two-thirds had at least one major conflict. As a result, the continent, in sharp contrast to Europe, was barely wealthier in 1900 than it was at independence in the 1810s and 1820s.[26]

The Price of Criminal Violence

The effects of nonpolitical violence also go well beyond the obvious and immediate human costs, and in fact the economic and social consequences of criminal violence are akin to those of civil wars. Injuries and deaths caused by criminal violence can increase the burden on health systems. Rampant crime deteriorates the environment for investment. Theft is a form of property rights violation, making individuals and firms hesitant to invest. Organized crime rings can extort economic actors for money. Crime raises policing costs and leads many individuals and businesses to expend on hiring private security guards. One study conducted in 2000 estimated the costs of crime in El Salvador and Colombia to total 25 percent of annual GDP,[27] with much of this loss occurring through expenditures on the private security guards that outnumber police by a factor of four or five. Foreign investors and foreign tourists can also be deterred by the risk of criminal violence to their assets or themselves. Crime also deteriorates societal trust and social capital. To top it all off, the urban poor almost invariably bear a disproportionate burden of these costs.

Widespread violence can also undermine the institutions that are deemed favorable to development since it is often accompanied by violations of rule of law and property rights. In the Latin American states heavily affected by organized crime and drug-related violence, justice systems are infiltrated and compromised by criminal gangs. Organized crime groups fix judicial proceedings and legislative outcomes using bribes or threats to judges, prosecutors, and politicians. They also intimidate or kill witnesses. To make matters worse, law enforcement agencies often respond with excessive repression of their own, violating due process protections in ways that affect innocent civilians. In some countries, private citizens who are fed up with ineffective law enforcement have even formed their own vigilante groups and killed suspected criminals on the spot.

All told, rampant crime makes citizens' legal protections toothless, lending an air of insecurity to material assets. For example, in Guatemala, where less than 5 percent of murders result in a conviction, property extortion by gangs has become widespread. In Guatemala City, criminal gangs extort protection money from bus drivers who drive routes through neighborhoods under their control, and in recent years they have killed hundreds of drivers who could not or have refused to pay. Other drivers have simply quit, leaving thousands of urban residents with limited transportation options.

Critique: Reconsidering the Costs of Violence

As always, these arguments about the development costs of political and criminal violence are not universally accepted by social scientists. A first set of criticisms impugns the direction of causation. Political violence tends to occur in countries with low levels of economic development, but this may not be because conflict causes poverty. There are numerous reasons why the reverse—poverty causes conflict—may be the case. The opportunity costs of fighting are low for the poor, as they lack the well-paying jobs and comfortable amenities that might keep them tethered to civilian life. Stated differently, economic underdevelopment creates a large pool of individuals who have little to lose from taking up arms. It is particularly tempting for the poor to fight when doing so offers potential bounties from the looting of natural resources or rural villages.

One survey of youth rebels in several conflict-torn countries found a lack of job opportunities to be the most-cited reason for the soldiers' decision to fight. Forty percent mentioned this reason, in contrast to just 10 percent who cited belief in a cause as their motivating reason for joining rebellions.[28]

Moreover, violence prevention is costly. For example, well-staffed and well-equipped judicial branches and state security agencies are needed to build state capacity and provide an infrastructure for deterring and punishing violence, yet these are often luxuries that states in LDCs cannot afford. By a conservative estimate, Central America has 70,000 criminal gang members, a higher number than the region's military personnel. It is also the case that cash-strapped states lack the resources to create national unity through linguistically unified educational and mass media systems. The internal ethnic and class divisions that are the raw materials for some civil wars thus remain deep.

A second counterargument notes that a country's economy can rebound quickly from war, with some scholars arguing that war can even boost long-term growth. According to Collier and Hoeffler, after political hostilities subside, economies emerging from civil war grow (on average) by one percentage point *faster* than their normal annual growth rate, reaping a substantial peace dividend. Many economies in formerly war-torn countries thus rebound quickly and return to the level of prosperity they would have had without war in just twenty years time.[29] In other words, although it does cause a drop in living standards, major occurrences of political violence cannot provide a general explanation of underdevelopment since the downturn seems to be ephemeral. For instance, a study of postwar Vietnam found heavily bombed areas to be no poorer than lightly bombed ones, "leaving few visible economic legacies twenty-five years later."[30]

The evidence for these rebounds suggest that war may even be a catalyst for positive change in many societies. Destroyed physical capital can be rebuilt with newer materials and technologies.

DEVELOPMENT in the FIELD

Violence Prevention and Post-Conflict Recovery

Numerous aid agencies and development programs exist that seek to alleviate the human suffering that results from political violence and state failure. Some of their functions focus on prevention, others on alleviation of suffering amidst violence, and still others on post-conflict recovery.

With regard to prevention, the International Crisis Group (ICG) is a leading NGO in the field of conflict forecasting (also conflict early warning). The ICG deploys dozens of staff members in potentially troubled countries to gather information about the risk of future conflict. Reports in its monthly *Crisis Watch* bulletin and in other publications sound alarm bells when an outbreak of violence is expected. These are intended to provide governments, international organizations, and other relevant actors the information they need to prevent the outbreak.

One of the world's most well-known nongovernmental organizations, the International Committee of the Red Cross (ICRC), carries out humanitarian work to alleviate the human costs of ongoing conflict. The

ICRC has been providing health treatment to those wounded in war since 1863, and it famously commits to neutrality by treating victims regardless of their affiliation in a conflict. The ICRC also carries out a number of other services in conflict zones, such as aiding refugees, visiting detainees, and encouraging adherence to the 1949 Geneva Conventions on treatment of war victims. A number of other aid agencies, such as Doctors Without Borders (*Medecins Sans Frontieres* in the original French), the International Rescue Committee (IRC), and the United Nations High Commissioner for Refugees (UNHCR) also provide medical relief in conflict zones.

Finally, the provision of post-conflict services has become an important focus of development aid in recent years. In 2008, the World Bank inaugurated the US$100 million State and Peace-Building Fund to finance development projects in post-conflict societies. These projects range from rebuilding electricity networks to restoring property rights administration. Community-driven reconstruction programs

that establish local institutions to foster reconciliation among formerly warring peoples have also been tried in recent years. A number of organizations are also involved in rehabilitating former child soldiers, who often require intensive medical and psychological attention to facilitate reentry into their communities and civilian life. Child Soldier Relief works with a number of such grassroots organizations in places such as DR Congo, Sierra Leone, and Somalia.

Activism to alleviate conflict can be controversial. Preventing political violence on the basis of forecasts is difficult. Even highly knowledgeable individuals and well-specified forecasting models are wrong most of the time about when and where armed conflict will occur, especially given the relative rarity of such events. Also, neutrality in conflict prevention is often contentious. For example, the Red Cross has been criticized for providing medical treatment to members of the Taliban, Hamas, and other groups that U.S. leaders consider to be terrorist organizations.

Aid from the international community often flows in to reconstruct war-torn countries. The international attention provided by media coverage during war may even boost tourism after it. Finally, war can reshape economic institutions for the better. According to Olson, the fact that major World War II hostilities occurred on German, French, and Japanese soil helped to create these countries' economic booms in the postwar era. Rent-seeking groups (defined in Chapter 10) were disbanded amidst the chaos of war, so their economies ran unfettered by such groups for years after war's end. In contrast, the United Kingdom and United States, where the war's effect was less intense, grew more slowly because rent-seeking groups had continuity.[31]

A third and related criticism comes from **bellicist theory**, which argues that interstate war has been fundamental to successful state building and thus to modern economic growth. According to political scientist Charles Tilly, war drove the creation of the first modern nation-states in Western Europe and thus lies at the root of the continent's relative prosperity. European states evolved from geographically concentrated city-states into centralized units commanding authority over relatively large swathes of territory during the late medieval and early modern eras.[32] The driver of this process was warfare: "War made the state, and the state made war."[33] The prerogative of warfare led European leaders to consolidate power over their subjects and over increasing amounts of territory so that they could enlist soldiers, produce the instruments of warfare, and raise revenue. The fear of loss of territory to a competing neighbor also urged leaders to exact state power in remote rural territories that had hitherto been ignored. Moreover, the process of competitive warfare waged over centuries resulted in the disappearance of weak states and left only strong ones surviving. As a result of all of these factors, Europeans states were strong enough to provide the institutions and public services necessary for economic growth. In contrast, the nation-states of the world's poorest continent, Africa, have not faced external existential threats or waged interstate wars. (As mentioned above, nearly all of sub-Saharan Africa's wars since independence began in 1960 have been internal civil wars.) As a result, its states are weak, unable to extract revenues from their subjects and to broadcast other forms of authority throughout their territories.[34] State services are minimal, so economies stagnate.

case STUDY

IS SOMALIA POOR BECAUSE OF CIVIL WAR?

Somalia's capital, Mogadishu, was once known as the "Pearl of the Indian Ocean" because of its beautiful colonial architecture. In recent decades, however, Somalia has largely been known for its intractable civil war and its status as the paradigmatic failed state. Less flattering epithets—"the world's least governed state," "the world's most dangerous place," and "the outlaw state"—are now much more likely to be in the offing.[35] Somalia's political violence and weak governance settled into a country that could hardly afford them. Even before civil war broke out in 1991, it was relatively impoverished and had a low level of human development. This case study considers the degree to which Somalia would be more prosperous and developed today if war had never broken out. Table 11.1 compares some of Somalia's development-related statistics with those of one of its colonizers, Italy.

Table 11.1 🟫🟩🟨 **Development Comparison: Somalia and Italy**

Indicator	Somalia	Italy
GDP per capita at PPP	US$943	US$26,559
Life expectancy	51	82
Failed States Index ranking	1 of 177	145 of 177
Military interventions by the United States since 1990	1	0
Percentage of land that is arable	2 percent	23 percent

Source: Data on GDP from Gapminder, www.gapminder.com; Failed States Index, Foreign Policy, 2012, http://www.foreignpolicy.com/failed_states_index_2012_interactive; arable land, the World Bank, World Development Indicators, http://hdrstats.undp.org/en/indicators/68606.html.

The South: Civil War in the World's Least Governed State

Somalia has been at war with itself and largely ungoverned for more than twenty years. Its story is an all-too-vivid example of the various costs—human, social, economic—of political violence and state failure.

Civil War and State Failure. Between 1986 and 1991, a variety of rebel groups, operating independently and rooted in different clans and regions, took up arms in an effort to overthrow the long-standing military dictatorship of Siad Barre. In 1991, one of these groups, the United Somali Congress (USC), reached Mogadishu and deposed Barre, installing one of its leaders as the new president in the process. Few Somalis, however, recognized the new regime. The various rebel militias simply escalated hostilities against one another, and the Somali civil war was on. Several of these groups took effective control over their regional outposts, and in the northwest the region of Somaliland declared independence and became self-governing. State failure ensued as the Somali central government saw a complete collapse of its authority outside the immediate confines of Mogadishu.

Since 1991, the central government's writ has continued to be nonexistent outside Mogadishu, making most of Somalia a stateless society. It holds precarious authority in the capital city only with the assistance of a UN-mandated international force of African troops called AMISOM. Civil war has been ongoing, although its intensity has ebbed and flowed and the players have changed. The central government has turned over—more than a dozen times, in fact—and new rebel factions, independence movements, and subnational governments have emerged. For example, one of the newer rebel factions, Al Shabab, now controls major parts of the southern half of the country and governs it according to strict Islamic principles of *sharia*. Around 2006 and 2007, Al Shabab was on the verge of successfully overthrowing the recognized government in Mogadishu, although it has since been pushed out of the capital city. Moreover, in 1998 the region of Puntland declared itself a self-ruling state, and at times Ethiopian and Kenyan forces have controlled large swathes of southern Somalia. To make matters worse, Somali pirates, who plague international shipping lanes in the Indian Ocean and Gulf of Aden, are in control of part of Somalia's huge coastline. Despite the changing players in Somalia's tragedy, the theme has remained the same for more than two decades:

IS SOMALIA POOR BECAUSE OF CIVIL WAR?

ongoing civil war and severe state failure. FSI has ranked Somalia as the world's most failed state in every year since 2008.[36]

Human and Economic Consequences. The social and economic costs of civil war and state failure in Somalia have been deep. It has experienced multiple famines, including one in 2011 that killed tens of thousands. The conflict and anarchy were root causes of the 2011 famine, as Al Shabab disallowed Western food aid into its area of control in the south and prevented famine-stricken villagers from moving elsewhere. Millions of Somalis have fled to other countries as refugees, including 500,000 to neighboring Kenya.[37] The country has made few gains in education, as most state-run schools shut down at various points during the civil war. Its already meager health-care system is overburdened by war wounded, and few advances in curbing infant mortality have occurred. War has destroyed precious infrastructure. For example, government forces destroyed water pumping systems and poisoned wells with battery acid in the early days of civil war. At times, Mogadishu has been largely devoid of markets and public transport, as civilians were afraid to go outside: "Mogadishu is an empty moonscape of anarchy and destruction. There are precious few remnants of everyday life."[38] Many areas of the country produce little of their own food and are wholly dependent on international agencies to provide them with food and other services.

One way of measuring the concrete economic and social costs of civil war is to contrast the recent trajectories of Somalia and Ghana. In the early 1980s, Somalia was a good deal wealthier than Ghana, and Ghana was emerging from several tumultuous decades of political instability and authoritarianism. Over the subsequent decade, Somalia collapsed into war, while Ghana turned to peace. Somalia's ongoing civil war broke out in

1991, while Ghana adopted multiparty democracy. What has been the result? Living standards have fallen by a third in Somalia, while those in Ghana have more than doubled. Improvements in life expectancy slowed in Somalia, in part because half a million people have died in hostilities. In Ghana, life expectancies have grown by almost a decade since 1980. Ghana now experiences peaceful elections and alternations of the party in power, while Somali factions deal with their political differences through gunfire, creating the world's least governed state.

* * *

Yet one should be careful about attributing all of Somalia's economic and social problems to civil war and state failure. After all, Somalia was relatively impoverished and poorly governed even before 1991. Most Somali civilians have meager permanent possessions, so the possible gains from guerrilla rebellion or piracy are too great an allure for some. Moreover, long before civil war, Siad Barre implemented a series of misguided economic policies inspired by his belief in scientific socialism. He nationalized banks and collectivized farms, moves that drove up the foreign debt and triggered economic decline. In sum, war may be the consequence, not the cause, of Somalia's social and economic underdevelopment.

The West: The Legacy of Foreign Intervention

It is easy to heap blame for Somalia's implosion on its warring factions and absent leadership, but, like most other African countries, Somalia had a difficult birthright that laid a fertile groundwork for such problems. In particular, it was born with deep internal divisions, created in part through the imposition of an alien colonial state. Prior to European colonization in the 1880s, the Somali peninsula to the east of Ethiopia was

Government soldiers overlook a refugee camp in Somalia's capital city, Mogadishu. Often considered the paradigmatic failed state, Somalia's government has little presence outside the capital. The country has been torn by civil war for more than twenty years, and the violence has uprooted thousands of Somalis from their homes.

occupied largely by people of the Somali ethnic group. Despite their shared language, the Somali were subdivided into six major clan identities that tended to be stronger than the broader ethnic identity, largely because Somali clans had competed amongst themselves for scarce pastoral land for generations.[39] The drawing of colonial borders on the peninsula by European occupiers grouped together competing Somali clans within singular colonies. As the colonies of the peninsula became independent in the 1960s and 1970s, Somalia ended up with large shares of all six clans. Moreover, the fact that Somalia had been colonized by two different European powers—the British in the north (in today's Somaliland) and the Italians in the south—made its inheritance all the more fractured. Given this legacy of European colonialism, it is not surprising that Somalia

disintegrated into internal civil war just a few decades after independence.[40]

More recently, the West missed an opportunity to potentially derail civil war. The United States intervened militarily in Somalia in late 1992, soon after the outbreak of hostilities. The mission, Operation Restore Hope, was declared to be a humanitarian one to get food aid to starving civilians. Militia leaders were stealing existing supplies of food aid and diverting it from its intended recipients, using it instead to amass even more weaponry. Yet, in the interest of keeping its involvement a limited one, the United States declined the opportunity to attempt a disarmament of the militias, something that many Somalis expected them to do and that might have been accomplished through mutual agreement

IS SOMALIA POOR BECAUSE OF CIVIL WAR?

and enforcement. Moreover, the United States offered little in the form of development aid and expertise aside from the short-term solution of food dumps.[41] When the United States and the UN mission that followed it left Somalia in 1995, the country remained a war-torn and stateless place.

The Natural World: Climate and Nomadism

Somalia's problems may lie even deeper than these potential causes and consequences of violence. Its geography is rather inhospitable to modern economic growth. It has little rainfall and temperatures are hot year-round, and there are reasons to suspect that its poverty and state failure may have a lot to do with its dry climate. Its longest river, the Shabelle, dries up before reaching the ocean, and its periodic famines, while surely exacerbated by poor leadership, are due to recurring droughts. Because of the dryness, only about 10 percent of Somalia's land is suitable for agriculture. As a result, more than half of Somalis are pastoral nomads, a profession and way of life that has existed for generations. While observers bemoan Somalia's ongoing anarchy, in actuality the constant internal migration of nomadic families makes them hard to govern. Without a sedentary and settled population, it is difficult to develop the urban centers that foster modern economic growth.[42]

Besides giving it poor soil, nature endowed Somalia with two other problems. First, it has little that is demanded by the global economy. Somalia has a relative dearth of valuable mineral deposits. Despite the poor productivity of its agricultural sector, its main exports are food items, livestock, and bananas. Second, since it lies near the equator, Somalia has one of the highest tropical disease

burdens in East Africa. There are no good statistics on the incidence of malaria, snail fever, and dengue fever, but public health officials suggest that they are widespread and thus present a strong headwind against economic progress.

***

Given its tough geography, tribal divisions, and intractable civil war, Somalia seemingly has the cards stacked against it, but rays of hope have emerged in recent years. Political violence in Mogadishu has mostly subsided since the remaining insurgent group, Al Shabab, has little foothold in the capital city. As of 2013, Al Shabab was internally divided and on the defensive, losing grip over its remaining strongholds in the south. Somalia also inaugurated a new president in 2012 (Hassan Sheikh Mohamud) who inspired enough confidence internationally that diplomatic ties with United States were reopened, and internationally financed projects to rebuild Somalia were in the works. Hopefully, the world's least governed state will soon enter a postwar rebound.

Thinking Critically about Development

- Somalia was clearly underdeveloped before the outbreak of civil war in 1991, but, keeping in mind the argument that civil war is "development in reverse," what roles do war and state failure play in keeping it poor today?

- Would Somalia be better off if it had never been colonized by European powers, or would the area still have the same problems it has today?

- Is Somalia doomed to poverty because of its dry climate? Are there other countries with a similar geography that have better social and economic development outcomes than Somalia?

Key Terms

bellicist theory, p. 276

criminal violence, p. 264

governmental wars,
p. 265

guerrilla warfare, p. 265

internally displaced persons
(IDPs), p. 272

interstate violence, p. 264

intrastate violence, p. 264

legitimacy, p. 268

political violence, p. 264

refugees, p. 271

secessionist war, p. 266

state failure, p. 268

terrorism, p. 265

 ## Suggested Readings

Bates, Robert. *When Things Fell Apart: State Failure in Late-Century Africa*. New York: Cambridge University Press, 2008.

Collier, Paul. *The Bottom Billion: Why the Poorest Countries Are Failing and What We Can Do about It*. Oxford: Oxford University Press, 2007.

Herbst, Jeffrey. *States and Power in Africa: Comparative Lessons in Authority and Control*. Princeton, NJ: Princeton University Press, 2000.

Tilly, Charles. *Coercion, Capital, and European States, AD 990–1990*. Cambridge: Basil Blackwell, 1990.

World Bank. *World Development Report 2011: Conflict, Security, and Development*. Washington, D.C.: World Bank Publications, 2011.

@ Web Resources

Center for Global Policy, Political Instability Task Force, http://globalpolicy.gmu.edu/political-instability-task-force-home/

Center for Systemic Peace Armed Conflict Trends and War List, http://www.systemicpeace.org/

Correlates of War Project, www.correlatesofwar.org/

Fund for Peace Failed State Index, www.fundforpeace.org/global/

UNHCR Statistical Online Population Database, www.unhcr.org/statistics/populationdatabase

Uppsala Conflict Data Program and Peace Research Institute Oslo Armed Conflict Dataset, www.prio.no/CSCW/Datasets/

A young girl in Cameroon carries a bucket of water on her head. Girls are sometimes called the world's "water haulers," since they are more likely than boys to be made to carry freshwater over long distances when indoor plumbing is not available. In societies that provide little economic opportunities for girls, parents are more likely to keep their daughters out of school to perform household chores.

Gender Inequality

Fatima, a fifty-year-old Afghan mother, has led a difficult life. She never really went to school, at least not that she can remember. In early adolescence, she showed a talent for singing, but, since she was a girl, the thought of cultivating this talent never even occurred to her parents. Instead, they arranged for her to be married when she was fifteen. Fatima had no say in the matter, and the husband chosen for her ended up being violent, beating her sometimes just for burning dinner. At seventeen, she had a stillbirth and nearly died in the process. She survived, however, and birthed nine healthy children over the next eighteen years, stopping only when her husband passed away of an illness in his early forties.

Afghanistan, recently called "the world's hardest country [in which] to be a mother,"[1] will never enjoy hearing Fatima's beautiful singing voice. Its cultural norms regarding the role of girls and women in society consigned her to a homebound life of violence. At one point when Fatima was in her thirties, the Afghan government banned music altogether and even mandated public beatings of women who talked or laughed too loudly. A musical career was out of the question, and in fact the aspiration has not entered Fatima's mind in decades. The only role ever expected of her was to be a subservient housewife.

In the developing world, girls and women like Fatima face far greater life challenges than do those in the developed world. For starters, they live in relatively poor countries and thus confront the basic problems posed by income poverty and human underdevelopment. If this were not enough, inequality between men and women tends to be more severe in LDCs than in developed countries. (See Understanding Indicators: Measures of Gender Equity and Empowerment.) Women are less educated than men, they work longer hours for less pay, they are more likely to be victims of violence and catastrophic health outcomes, and they have less say in decisions made in their households and communities.

understanding INDICATORS

Measures of Gender Equity and Empowerment

The United Nations Development Programme (UNDP) has developed several measures that gauge cross-national differences in gender equity and empowerment. The Gender Inequality Index (GII), which is displayed in the accompanying map, is an indicator that combines five different concepts: (1) the gap between males and females in labor force participation, (2) the gap between males and females in educational attainment at the secondary level and above, (3) the share of parliament members who are women, (4) adolescent fertility, and (5) maternal mortality. The index is scaled to range between 0 and 1, and higher values indicate greater gender inequality. The creators of the index allege that it gauges strictly relative differences between men and women, since "none of the underlying measures pertains to a country's general level of development."[2] This assertion is questionable with regard to maternal mortality. Regardless, it is beyond refute that there is a strong relationship between economic prosperity and gender inequality. A look at the map gives a preliminary sense of this, as does a breakdown of the GII by human development levels. In 2011, countries with very high human development had an average GII of .224. By contrast, countries with medium human development averaged .475, and those with low human development averaged .606.[3]

Gender Inequality Index, 2011

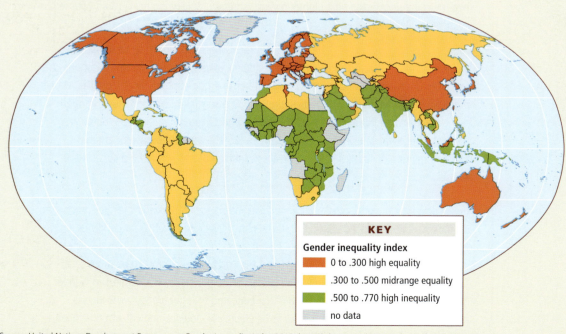

KEY

Gender inequality index
- 0 to .300 high equality
- .300 to .500 midrange equality
- .500 to .770 high inequality
- no data

Source: United Nations Development Programme, Gender Inequality Index 2012, http://hdrstats.undp.org/en/indicators/68606.html.

A related indicator is the Gender Empowerment Measure (GEM), which gauges the degree to which women have agency within their economic and political environments. The index combines four different concepts: (1) the share of members of parliament who are women, (2) the share of legislators, senior officials, and managers that are women, (3) the share of professional and other technical positions held by women, and (4) the ratio of the average male income to the average female income. The index is scaled to range between 0 and 1, and higher values indicate less female empowerment. In 2007, countries with very high or high human development averaged .659 on the GEM, while countries with medium or low human development had a score of .455.[4] Unfortunately, some of the indicators that go into the GEM are expensive and time-consuming to collect, so they are not always available. The GEM has not been updated since 2008, and even then it was only available for about ninety countries, few of which were of low-income status. The most recent report can be examined at http://hdr.undp.org/en/media/HDR_20072008_GEM.pdf.

- The GII is negatively correlated with human development. To what extent is this due to how researchers constructed the indicator versus how strong the relationship actually is between gender inequality and development?

- How good a measure of female equality and empowerment is the number of women in the national legislature? Does the gender of legislators matter for whether they represent women's interests?

These inequalities stem from **gender**, which refers to the attitudes, norms, expectations, and behaviors that societies construct around being male or female. Gender is distinct from sex, the strictly biological determination of male or female, in that it captures the cultural stereotypes and roles that humans create around being male or female. These give rise to **gender inequality**, which is the extent to which these societal creations around gender grant boys and men advantages in power, resources, and health. This chapter describes some of the special hardships that girls and women face in the developing world merely because of their gender, focusing first on female empowerment and then on female health issues. It also considers academic arguments that see the deep inequities between males and females as a cause of underdevelopment.

When females are barred from certain opportunities, such as schooling, political office, high-skill jobs, or a fair salary, merely because of their sex, then society is stripping them of control over their own fate. This section discusses forms of female disempowerment in the economic, educational, and political realms of the developing world.

The Gender Earnings Gap

Throughout the world, women are more likely to be poor than men, and they receive lower wages and other returns for the contributions they make to society. That is, there is a **gender earnings gap**, and the size of the gap tends to be wider in LDCs than in high-income countries. What are the sources of the gap?

The Gender Asset Gap. A **gender asset gap** contributes to the gender earnings gap. Men have easier access to economic assets and inputs, partially explaining why they are more productive than women even when they engage in similar economic

Female Empowerment

The extent of **female empowerment** in a society refers to the degree to which girls and women are active agents in shaping their own life chances.

pursuits. The gender asset gap exists for a number of reasons. Discriminatory institutions grounded in law and culture often pose a significant barrier to female acquisition and ownership of major assets such as land and houses. In many parts of the developing world, inheritance law, which dictates the distribution of a deceased person's assets in lieu of a recognized will, discriminates against daughters and widows of the newly deceased. For example, in many Islamic countries, daughters are entitled to inherit only half of what their brothers do. In some sub-Saharan African countries, most of the deceased husband's property is inherited not by his widow and children, but by his living siblings and parents.

Moreover, marriage laws and customs in many LDCs treat women as mere property of their husbands and even their husbands' extended families rather than as intrinsically valuable human beings. In countries such as DR Congo, wives may not enter into legal agreements and contracts without the consent of their husbands. Similarly, it is customary in much of sub-Saharan Africa for husbands to control all of the family income. Between 15 percent and 35 percent of women in the labor force on the continent say they are uninvolved in decisions about how to use the income they themselves generate.[5]

Women also face greater challenges than men in getting access to financial capital. Women are often discriminated against in credit markets, a problem exacerbated by the fact that they are less likely to have accumulated savings and collateral for loans. Female-owned firms in urban Africa have, on average, 2.5 times less capital at start-up than male-owned ones.[6] Research on African farms shows a similar problem: Female-owned farms are less technologically advanced, and women receive less than 10 percent of all agricultural credit even though they comprise a majority of the continent's agricultural workers.[7] As another result, the plots of land that women own and work are on average far smaller than those owned and worked by men. In Burkina Faso, male-worked farms are eight times the size of female-worked ones,[8] and in Latin American countries, the percentage of landowning farmers that are female ranges from just 6 percent to at most 24 percent.[9]

The Burden of Non-Market Activities. Another source of the gender earnings gap is that women perform much more uncompensated work than men. Women bear a disproportionate share of **non-market activities**, or work performed to upkeep a home and family (also called domestic work). Studies of time usage in developing countries show that the amount of housework and child care carried out by women is double or triple that done by men.[10] From one perspective, child care, food preparation, and cleaning are activities deserving of financial compensation since persons who perform them outside the home (such as nannies, chefs, and maids) receive it. Yet when done inside one's home, they are uncompensated. This can be particularly stinging in cases of divorce, as laws in much of the Middle East, sub-Saharan Africa, and South Asia do not allow divorced wives a share of marital assets in compensation for the non-market activities that contributed to their family's well-being.

The disproportionate weight of non-market activities not only disadvantages women in its own right, but it can also have negative consequences for earnings among those that also work outside the home. Many women in the labor market work what is called a double shift of full-time market activity and full-time non-market activities at home. In LDCs, the physical and emotional demands of domestic work, which are particularly high in the absence of laborsaving technologies such as dishwashers and laundry machines, can take a toll on women's productivity in labor outside the home. Moreover, women are more likely than men to seek shorter or more flexible work hours because they are so heavily burdened with non-market activities, giving them a disadvantage in competing for well-paying formal-sector jobs. Throughout much of the developing world, women are much more likely than men to work in the informal sector out of need for the scheduling flexibility. The result is less job stability, fewer benefits, and lower earnings.

Women in the Labor Market. Women also face discrimination within the labor market. Women are disproportionately part of the informal sector not just because of the demands of the double shift, but also because potential employers in the formal sector are more hesitant to hire women than men. Without strong antidiscrimination legal frameworks and family-leave policies in place, many businesses in LDCs see women as less desirable hires because they are more likely to request time away from a job due to pregnancy and rearing children. Moreover, occupational segregation, which is based on the sexual division of labor, runs particularly deep in LDCs. Women and men tend to have different occupations. Women are more likely to be employed in public services, retail, domestic work, agriculture, and light manufacturing. In contrast, women are far less prevalent in sectors such as heavy manufacturing, construction, and transport. For example, rare is the female cab or bus driver in Latin American cities. Research shows that the occupations that women tend to have pay less than those typically held by men.[11]

Female labor force participation rates (FLFPR), the percentage of women who perform work outside the home for monetary compensation, are not necessarily lower in less developed countries than in developed ones. Figure 12.1 depicts these rates by world region and contrasts the participation rates of females with those of males. The FLFPRs in sub-Saharan Africa, East Asia, and Latin America are near or even higher than those prevailing in high-income countries, and their gender gaps in labor force participation are similar in size to those in the developed world. In fact, many of the world's highest FLFPRs are in the world's poorest countries, such as Burundi (92 percent), Tanzania (89 percent), and Rwanda (88 percent), where most women enter the labor force as agricultural workers to make ends meet.[12] Systematic research shows the cross-national relationship between economic prosperity and FLFPR to be more of a U-shaped pattern than a linear one.[13]

FLFPRs are at their lowest in the Middle East and South Asia, and gender gaps in labor force participation are also yawning, averaging around 50 percentage points, in both. More than twenty countries with low rates, such as Iran, give husbands the legal right to prohibit their wives from

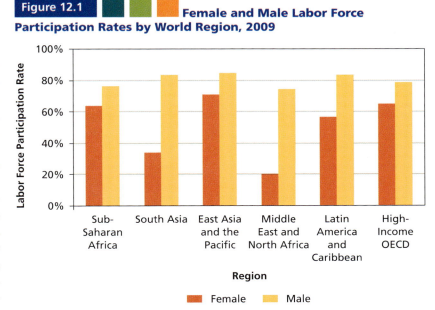

Figure 12.1 **Female and Male Labor Force Participation Rates by World Region, 2009**

Source: Data compiled from the World Bank, World Development Indicators, http://data.worldbank.org/data-catalog/world-development-indicators.

working outside the home, and many more grant husbands this right by custom.[14] In parts of Pakistan and northern India, the tradition of *purdah* prohibits women from working outside the home or even leaving their homes without permission from their husbands. Similar customs prevail in parts of the Middle East and West Africa, where women are not allowed outside the home without being accompanied by their husband or another male relative. In these places, women are clearly disadvantaged economically by being barred from deserved income and financial independence.

Trends and Improvements. A large gender earnings gap remains a stubborn reality for women in most LDCs, but a number of trends have served to shrink the gap in recent decades. The explosion of microfinance services (described in Chapter 9), almost all of which are used by women, has helped to narrow the gender asset gap and empowered millions as entrepreneurs. Legal barriers to asset ownership are also falling. For example, India has removed gender bias from its formal inheritance laws. Furthermore, women in LDCs are birthing fewer children over their lifetimes, which decreases the burden of non-market activities and allows adolescents and young women to stay in school.

A closely related development is that female labor force participation has increased in virtually all countries since 1980, including in the Middle East and South Asia. A partial cause is globalization, which has created millions of job opportunities for women, often in light manufacturing sectors. For example, women in Honduras and Cambodia comprise 65 percent and 90 percent of garment industry employees, respectively.[15]

The Gender Gap in Education

Another source of the gender earnings gap lies in gender differences in formal educational attainment, a topic that merits a detailed discussion in its own right. The formal education of girls and women is a crucial element of female empowerment as it increases job opportunities and wages and also makes women more efficacious participants in their communities. In most LDCs, women have less education than men. In sub-Saharan Africa, 38 percent of men have at least some secondary education, whereas the corresponding figure for women is just 24 percent. The gap is even greater in South Asia, where the figure is 50 percent for men and just 27 percent for women. A gender gap in education also exists in the Middle East (45 percent for men versus 32 percent for women) and East Asia (61 percent for men and 48 percent for women). In contrast, the gap in Latin America is a small one (53 percent for men versus 51 percent for women).[16] Because of these gender gaps in education, around two-thirds of the world's illiterate adults are women.[17]

This educational gap opens up in primary school, where girls drop out at younger ages than boys. According to 2010 statistics, 53 percent of the world's children who were not in primary school were girls. Dozens of LDCs do not have gender parity in primary enrollments, meaning boys are more likely to be enrolled in school than girls. For example, in sub-Saharan Africa in 2008, there were only ninety-one girls in school for every 100 boys, and in the most poorly performing countries, Chad, Mozambique, and Yemen, the ratios were below 80.[18]

Causes of the Gender Gap. A number of things explain the lack of gender parity in schooling. Often, girls drop out of school at younger ages than boys because of discriminatory attitudes by their parents—attitudes that are fed by societal norms. In societies where expectations are that women will not work outside the home and where good job opportunities for women are few, parents perceive little value to female education. In Pakistan, many parents do not want their girls to be well educated because it makes them less desirable to potential husbands. Many Pakistani men do not want to marry independent- and career-minded women, and marrying a better-educated woman is a cause for shame.

Moreover, the opportunity cost of female education can seem particularly high to parents. Girls are generally expected to do more housework (such as caring for siblings) than boys, so many parents choose to keep girls at home during the school day to provide valuable domestic help. A study of Malawi showed that primary-school-aged girls spent twenty-one hours per week on domestic work in comparison to thirteen hours for boys.[19] Perhaps the best example of this is the fact that women and girls are the world's "water haulers."[20] Since many villages and towns throughout the developing world lack immediate access to water and firewood, families often need someone to walk to the water source to collect it and haul it in a container on a daily or twice-daily basis. Families choose girls (such as Nathalie from Chapter 1) to perform this task more often than not. Studies show that reducing villagers' distance to a water source would boost girls' educational attainment at twice the rate at which it would boost that of boys.[21]

The parental devaluing of girls' education is not the only reason for the lack of gender parity in school enrollment. In rural societies where schools are distant from villages and homes, girls may drop out because they and their parents fear for their safety on their walk to school. Similarly, in some instances girls have withdrawn from school due to sexual harassment and assault by other students and even teachers. In South Africa, one study found that teachers were the perpetrators in a third of the rapes of girls under the age of fifteen.[22] Finally, adolescent girls can face tough decisions about school attendance upon reaching puberty. Many choose not to attend school during their menstrual periods for fear of embarrassment and discomfort. The inability to afford or access sanitary products, along with squalid bathroom facilities that offer no privacy, can contribute to periodic absences or even a decision to drop out.

Trends and Improvement. All that said, the developing world has made major strides in recent decades in narrowing the gender gap in education. Parents are leaving their girls in school longer and devaluing their education less than they did in the past. This wave of progress has brought a near majority of LDCs to gender parity in primary enrollments, and only a remaining few still have female-to-male enrollment ratios below ninety. Figure 12.2 summarizes some overall trends. Latin America and East Asia have now achieved virtual gender parity, catching up to the high-income countries in this regard. The other three regions have made dramatic advances, improving from ratios below seventy in 1970 (and thirty-five for sub-Saharan Africa in 1940)[23] to ratios around ninety-five by 2010. As a result, gender gaps in literacy are declining. In 1970, there were only sixty literate females for every 100 literate males in the developing world, but by 2000 that figure had reached eighty. As the young generations who enjoy parity or near-parity in primary enrollments replace the middle- and old-aged generations who did not, this gap in literacy will shrink even further.

The Gender Gap in Political Empowerment

A final element of empowerment that is unequal between men and women is political influence. Women have less of an impact on public policy and political institutions in the developing world. Again, while this is true in virtually every country, the gender gap in political empowerment tends to be larger in LDCs.

Descriptive Representation. Most importantly, women have less **descriptive representation** than men, meaning there tend to be far fewer

Figure 12.2 **Ratio of Female to Male Net Primary Enrollment by World Region, 1970–2010**

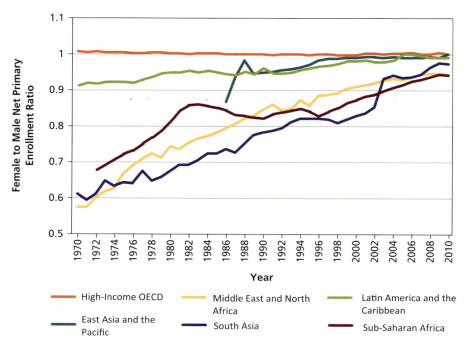

Source: Data compiled from the World Bank, World Development Indicators, http://data.worldbank.org/data-catalog/world-development-indicators.

women than men in positions of political power. On average, women made up less than 20 percent of national legislatures in the developing world in 2008. In the Middle East, just 9 percent of legislators are women, and in South Asia the figure is just 10 percent. These numbers are only slightly higher in sub-Saharan Africa (17 percent), Latin America (18 percent), and East Asia (20 percent). (That said, the average rate in high-income countries is only mildly higher at 21 percent.)[24] Moreover, female chief executives have been a rarity in the developing world. Just a smattering of LDCs—about thirty—have had a female head of government or head of state in their history.[25]

This gap in women's descriptive representation does not stem from unequal voting rights. Saudi Arabia is now the only country in the world that allows men to vote but not women. It is the case,

however, that women tend to be less likely to vote than men in LDCs, a gap that is nonexistent or even reversed in developed countries. Illiteracy and low education levels can make many women hesitant to vote. Women are also less likely to stand for political office because they lack the professional background and financial and time resources to do so. Finally, part of the problem lies in sexist beliefs held by both elites and masses. Public opinion surveys show that majorities of men and women in some democracies, such as India and Turkey, believe that men make better political leaders than women.[26]

Women's Movements. These barriers to formal political office notwithstanding, women throughout the developing world have formed women's social movements to pressure for policy and social change, and the number of these movements has exploded in recent decades.[27] A **social movement** is a group of people who share a common demand and who organize to seek social or political change favorable to that demand. Some women's movements are genuine feminist movements that seek to change discriminatory rules and norms. For example, Shanghai Women's Love in China stages small-scale protests against sexual harassment.[28] However, many social movements in LDCs feature groups of women who mobilize as women to press for a change that is not specific to gender. One of the most famous such movements was the Mothers of the Plaza de Mayo, a group of mothers in Argentina who formed in 1977 to protest the disappearance of their children by the military dictatorship. They met weekly in front of the military palace to silently mourn and draw attention to the regime's brutality and their kidnapped loved ones.

Trends and Improvements. Women's descriptive representation is on the rise in LDCs. Numerous countries have recently elected their first female president, including Argentina, Brazil, Chile, Costa Rica, Liberia, Nicaragua, Panama, and the Philippines. Women have also been chosen as prime ministers in countries such as Bangladesh, Jamaica, Pakistan, Thailand, and Ukraine. Additionally, women have been assigned an increasing share of government ministerial positions, and there has been some progress in increasing the number of women in national legislatures. Dozens of countries have adopted **gender quotas** that require a minimum number of party nominations or legislative seats to be occupied by women. In recent years, Rwanda has had the world's highest share of women in its national legislature, due in part to its quota system. In 2010, women held 56 percent of its seats.

More broadly, some observers have expressed optimism about steadily changing political attitudes worldwide on the issue of gender equality. The World Bank notes a "rising global consensus on the intrinsic importance of women's economic, social, and political empowerment."[29] As one example, in 1979 the UN General Assembly established the Convention on the Elimination of all Forms of Discrimination against Women (CEDAW). Over the subsequent three decades, nearly 190 states ratified or adopted the treaty, which requires countries to rid themselves of all forms of gender discrimination. Of course, merely adopting an international treaty does not make equality a reality, but the large number of countries willing to accept the ideal of nondiscrimination is one sign of changing beliefs among political leaders worldwide.

Causes of Underdevelopment: Disempowered Women and Girls

To many observers, gender discrimination and the relative lack of female empowerment are intrinsically immoral, but many scholars also see gender discrimination as an instrumental wrong. In this instrumentalist view, gender discrimination and maltreatment of women are not just symptoms or results of underdevelopment, but independent causes of it. In other words, according to a World Bank report, "gender equality is smart economics."[30] Improvements and investments in female welfare and empowerment yield greater economic benefits than do equivalent improvements and investments in males. This instrumentalist view is most associated with two lines of scholarly thought: the women in the development approach launched by economist Ester Boserup and the capabilities approach of Amartya Sen, which sees women as "agents of development."[31] Other bodies of thought are also critical of the effects of gender discrimination on economic and human development. Collectively, they reveal multiple mechanisms by which discrimination against women and girls can stifle prosperity.

Women in Development

When modernization theory dominated scholarly thought on development in the 1950s and 1960s, scholars and practitioners largely ignored the role of gender. They instead believed that economic growth in LDCs would benefit men and women in the same way. This was based on the assumption that women, who were largely left out of the non-agricultural workforce at the time, would simply enjoy the higher wages earned by their husbands. In a 1970 book, however, agricultural economist Ester Boserup famously took issue with modernization theory's presumption that economic growth automatically trickled down to women.[32] Boserup highlighted the sharp sexual division of rural labor in less developed societies, arguing that women performed most of the subsistence agricultural work in Africa while men performed most of it in Asia. In Africa, colonial and postcolonial states introduced new farming technologies and cash-crop markets almost strictly to male growers. This produced gains for men but not for women, who were left carrying out small-plot farming with traditional techniques.

Boserup's work helped launch a new line of thought known as **women in development (WID)**, which built on her point that poverty and growth affected men and women in different ways. WID enjoyed its ascendance in the 1970s and early 1980s, and it gained a foothold in how USAID and the World Bank implemented their projects. These practitioners reasoned that development policy and programs needed to think explicitly about ways to improve the lot of women, given their distinct economic roles. Of particular importance to the WID approach was that discrimination resulted in a lost opportunity for efficiency and productivity gains. For example, the failure to educate girls, to allow females into the modern labor force, and to provide females with equal access to economic assets is itself a massive waste of human talent. The mobilization of girls and women into modern economic activity through education and work is a relatively straightforward way to achieve economic growth, as it equates to the accumulation of more factors of production. For example, part of the economic growth miracles of East Asia and parts of Latin America in the 1960s and 1970s was the entrance of millions of women into the modern labor force. By leaving women's human capital and market labor dormant, societies with high gender inequities are foregoing massive economic benefits.

Although scholarly thinking has moved beyond the WID paradigm, its spirit lives on in development programs such as microfinance for female entrepreneurs that seek to mobilize women into productive market activities. Similarly, neoclassical economics sees gender discrimination as a problem in that it is a distortion of freely operating markets. When citizens use arbitrary traits to avoid economic exchange with someone, then markets are not allowed to operate efficiently. This produces suboptimal outcomes not just for the victims of discrimination but for society as a whole. For example, denying a talented woman credit solely because of her gender puts capital in the hands of a less talented man. The consequences reverberate to society through the lost gains from the woman's superior entrepreneurial acumen.

Women as Agents of Human Development

In his work in the 1990s, Sen stressed how the impoverishment and undereducation of women had detrimental human development consequences for future generations. Because mothers are usually the primary caregivers, their education feeds directly into the health of their children. Evidence from various LDCs shows that women who lack education are less likely to immunize their children,[33] to provide disease-free conditions in the home, and to seek adequate medical care in the event of acute illness. Sen notes that "the effect of female literacy on child mortality is extraordinarily large."[34]

Poorly educated women are also less likely to value education for their children. This often creates a vicious cycle in which an uneducated mother's own girls drop out of school early, marry young, birth many children, and get stuck performing strictly non-market activities in adulthood. Evidence of the beneficial effects of female education on whole communities further attests to the social and economic costs of gender discrimination. In Pakistan, the emergence of secondary education for girls after 1990 created a much larger pool of schoolteachers.[35]

Women as Decision-Makers

A final set of even more recent findings holds that men may actually make worse economic and political decisions than women, so societies that fail to give women a proper voice in these matters end up with bad outcomes. Mounting evidence suggests that, when women control financial decisions within households, they are more likely than men to use funds in a way that promotes health and human capital within the family. Women devote more income to purchases of food and educational materials, payments of school fees, pensions to their own parents or in-laws, contraception, and doctors visits. In contrast, when men make spending decisions, they are more likely to divert precious funds to luxury items that convey status and to leisure activities such as sporting events, cigarettes, and alcohol.[36] The effects are concrete: households throughout the developing world in which women control some financial resources have taller and better educated children.

Furthermore, some evidence suggests that women in politics are less corrupt than men. As in the household, female politicians seem to be more enthusiastic than men about promoting social welfare and less prone to squander public resources on unnecessary defense expenditures.[37] In short, a high rate of women's descriptive representation might be good for society as a whole.

Critiques of the Instrumentalist View

Scholarship that sees gender equity as smart economics is not the only school of thought on the role of gender and underdevelopment. Some alternatives take issue with this instrumentalist view. In response to the WID paradigm of the 1970s, a body of thought called gender and development (GAD) emerged in the 1980s that was grounded in socialist and other forms of leftist feminism. GAD critiques WID for being overly focused on women's productive roles and thereby ignoring the non-market (and typically reproductive) roles that make it difficult for women to even engage in market activities.[39] To GAD thinkers, the problem of underdevelopment is not just a failure to harness women's productivity in the market, but a far deeper problem of how unequal gender relations are constructed in society. Merely creating policies and programs to get women into the labor market is not enough, since this does not relinquish women from their subordinate roles as disproportionate bearers of non-market activities at home. As adherents of the political left, GAD advocates also critique the instrumentalist view for accepting as a given both the capitalist model of development and women's need to participate in it.

Another leading retort to the instrumentalist view is a methodological one. Gender inequality may be a symptom or result of income poverty, not a cause of it.[40] Female empowerment is certainly better in wealthier countries, but this does not mean that gender equity causes prosperity. Rather, it is possible that it was the increased wealth that improved gender equity. For example, economic resources allow governments to fund the social services that provide schooling for girls, and rising prosperity frees families from having to decide which children to send to school. It also opens up employment opportunities for women that encourage parents to invest more in their girls' education.

Finally, it is worth adding that not everyone agrees on the intrinsic value of gender equity, and not all of its detractors are patriarchic men. Many women of LDCs see calls for greater gender equity as a Westernizing cultural imperialism that would impose Eurocentric norms and practices on unwilling societies. For example, a majority of Afghan women support the use of the *burqa*,[41] a garment that covers their body from head to toe. Similarly, many female activists in the developing world reject Western notions of marriage, labor force participation, and modesty. This is done out of a concern that these practices breed divorce, illegitimate birth, emotional distance between mothers and their children, stress from work-life imbalance, and an unhealthy obsession with female sexuality and beauty.

Female Health, Physical Security, and Fertility

In addition to the relative lack of empowerment, women also face severe and ongoing challenges to their health and physical security in the developing world. Reproduction, gender-based violence, and fertility are gender-specific health issues that relate to the intrinsic well-being of women, as well as the instrumental welfare of society.

Excess Female Mortality and Missing Women

In 1990, Sen introduced the notion of missing women by writing a famous article stating in no uncertain terms that "more than 100 million women are missing."[42] Sen brought attention to the problem of **excess female mortality**, also known as gendercide, which refers to the death of females because of their sex. Worldwide, most instances of gendercide in females under the age of sixty occur in one of three ways. First, some girls go missing before birth due to sex-selective abortions (40 percent). Second, excess mortality in female children (20 percent) occurs, usually through parental neglect but also via infanticide. The third way is maternal mortality (35 percent).[43] All told, around

4 million women and girls under the age of sixty die every year either before or after birth because of their sex. In a few Asian countries an estimated 5 percent to 8 percent of all girls and women are missing simply because of their sex.[44] Estimates in 2010 put the number of missing women around 134 million, reflecting a probable increase since Sen's 1990 estimate.[45]

Sex-Selective Abortion. Sex-selective abortion of females by parents preferring a son is widely practiced in just a few LDCs, but the ones that do so happen to be among the most populated: China, India, Bangladesh, and Pakistan. The practice of aborting females is rooted in **son preference**, a norm that has existed in China and South Asia for generations. Son preference is a product of several cultural practices that have imbued parents with the belief that girls are a weightier economic burden than boys. For example, China and India have historically been patrilocal societies in which a woman is absorbed into her husband's family at marriage, stripping her parents of her assistance in their old age. Estates were willed to future generations through males, so keeping inheritance within the family required a son. Similarly, India and China are, by tradition, dowry-paying societies, whereby the family of the bride must produce an expensive payment in the form of cash and property at the time of marriage. In contrast, African societies, where son preference is virtually absent, are more likely to be bridewealth societies in which the man's family makes a payment to the bride's family at marriage.

Son preference has been nearly constant in China and India for centuries, but the incidence of sex-selective abortion and missing girls at birth has increased dramatically in recent decades for two reasons. First, technological advances have lowered the price and availability of ultrasounds and elective abortions, allowing even impoverished parents to affordably terminate pregnancies. Second, economic improvements and policy have lowered the number of children birthed per woman in China and India, raising the cultural need for a boy on the first or second try. In China, sex ratios (the ratio of the number of girls to the number of boys) among firstborns are at their natural rate of 950 girls for every 1,000 boys. Among second- and thirdborns, however, they are below 700. All told, in 2011 there were just 914 girls for every 1,000 boys in India.[46] China's sex ratio is even lower, numbering around 850 girls per 1,000 boys and, in some provinces, below 800 girls per 1,000 boys.[47]

Comparative Neglect of Daughters. Son preference does not only disadvantage girls when they are in the womb. At the time of Sen's writing in the late 1980s, the main culprit behind the world's 100 million missing women was not yet sex-selective abortion, but the comparative neglect of daughters by parents with a strong son preference. This can play out in several ways. Parents are not as quick to seek medical care for sick girls as they are for sick boys. They immunize their sons but not their daughters. When food and water are scarce, parents nourish their sons better than their daughters and reserve the cleaner water for sons. Because parents want to stop the contraceptive effect of breastfeeding early in the hopes of getting pregnant with a boy, girls are weaned at younger ages than boys. This denies them crucial health benefits and increases their likelihood of consuming unclean water.[48] Expert estimates suggest that, in 1990, as many as 1 million girls under the age of five, almost all of whom lived in China and South Asia, died for reasons of neglect.[49]

Mortality in Reproductive Years. The other time of their lives when women are at greatest risk of premature death is during their reproductive years (ages fifteen to forty-nine). **Maternal mortality** is the death of a woman due to complications from pregnancy or childbirth. The problem is at its worst in sub-Saharan Africa, where the maternal mortality ratio is 500 maternal deaths per 100,000 live births. Maternal mortality ratios are also much higher in South Asia (220), the Middle East (81), East Asia (83), and Latin America (81) than they are in the wealthy West (13).[50] Given that women in LDCs tend to have more births, the discrepancy between rich and poor countries in the risk of death per reproductive-age female is even higher than these ratios would indicate. Overall, the chance that a woman will suffer maternal death is one in thirty in sub-Saharan Africa, a rate that prevailed in Europe more than 100 years ago. Worldwide, one woman dies every two minutes[51] in childbirth. Half of these deaths occur in sub-Saharan Africa and another 45 percent in Asia.

Expectant mothers are most likely to suffer maternal death when their births are not attended by skilled health professionals such as obstetricians or midwives. Professionals save mothers' lives by performing Caesarean sections, stopping hemorrhaging, and administering anti-infectious drugs. The attention of skilled professionals to pregnant women is also crucial in the prenatal stage, as they can take measures to reduce mortality risk. In sub-Saharan Africa and South Asia, however, a skilled attendant is present at fewer than half of all births.[52] Moreover, unsafe abortions due to lack of medical services or legal restrictions are a contributor to maternal mortality, comprising more than 10 percent of all pregnancy-related deaths in LDCs.[53]

Another major health issue in the developing world that has a disproportionately negative effect on women of reproductive age is HIV/AIDS in Africa, where the epidemic is at its worst. In Africa, 60 percent of HIV-positive persons are female.[54] Biologically, women are at about a 20 percent higher risk to contract HIV since the virus is more likely to enter a woman's bloodstream than a man's during unprotected intercourse with an infected partner. The problem, however, also has roots in societal practices. Africa suffers from the notorious "sugar daddy" phenomenon that boosts HIV infection among young women. Teenage girls and young women in Africa often date much older men who provide gifts and financial support in an implicit exchange for sex and companionship. The problem is that older men are much more likely to be HIV-positive, and young women in this situation can find it hard to negotiate safe sex and peaceful breakups. Partly as a result, females in the fifteen- to twenty-four-year-old age bracket are nearly two-and-a-half times more likely to be HIV-positive than males in that age bracket.[55]

Trends and Improvements. These causes of excess female mortality notwithstanding, the health outcomes of women and girls have improved in LDCs in recent decades. Women and girls have benefited from the blanket improvements in health described in Chapter 2, but many gender-specific advances have also occurred. An overall indicator of this progress is that women's life expectancy has increased from fifty-four to seventy-one since 1960, a slightly faster improvement than that experienced by men (fifty-one to sixty-seven).[56] Most notably, maternal mortality is declining in frequency, due in part to more widely available medical attention during pregnancy and birth. Between 1990 and 2011, maternal deaths fell from around 543,000 to 274,000, a decline of 50 percent in just two decades.[57]

Furthermore, the fatal comparative neglect of girls appears to disappearing. In 1960, South Asian males had longer life expectancies than females, largely due to this problem. Today, however, females live a few years longer than males in the region, matching the pattern that holds almost everywhere else.[58] After its astonishing rise in Asia over the last three decades, even the practice of sex-selective abortion may have peaked in frequency due to improved economic opportunities for daughters and accompanying changes in social norms. A recent study found sex ratios to be returning to normalcy among India's middle class,[59] and in China's wealthiest city (Shanghai) sex ratios show no signs

of son preference. If all of these trends continue, the number of missing women worldwide will soon begin a rapid fall.

Gender-Based Violence

A related problem for women and girls in LDCs is gender-based violence, or violence in which the victim's femininity is a primary motive for the violence. This section considers just a few examples of gender-based violence, including domestic and ritual forms of violence such as female genital cutting. (Another example, sex trafficking, is discussed in Chapter 4.)

Domestic Violence and Rape. Statistics on the prevalence of domestic violence are notoriously hard to collect, but indications are that women in the developing world are frequently victimized by beatings and rapes committed by their intimate partners (mostly husbands or boyfriends). One study of several LDCs by the World Health Organization found that the percentage of women who, by self-report, had been victims of domestic violence ranged from 27 percent to 62 percent. High percentages, ranging from 10 percent in urban Brazil to 59 percent in rural Ethiopia, also self-reported as victims of intimate partner sexual violence.[60] Over 40 percent of Turkish women have suffered physical or sexual violence.[61] Other forms of evidence confirm these high percentages: 41 percent of Ugandan men admit to beating their partners, and more than a third of men in South Africa's Gauteng province admitted to having raped someone.[62]

Domestic violence and rape persist at such high rates in part because of the ineffectiveness of justice systems in LDCs. When victimized by gender-based violence, most women in the developing world lack access to justice. LDC court systems are politically compromised or pressed for resources as it is. When combined with sexist social norms that become entrenched within the justice system, it becomes difficult to punish perpetrators of gender-based violence and deter the practice. For example, one study showed that around half of all Indian judges believed that women were partly to blame when beaten by their spouses, and two-thirds agreed that sexually provocative attire on a woman was effectively an invitation of sex.[63] Given the low probabilities that women face of having their offenders punished, it is not surprising that few (estimated at less than 20 percent in most countries) ever even report gender-based violence to authorities.

Forced Marriage. A **forced marriage** is one in which at least one person marries under duress. In a majority of forced marriages, it is the female who is married against her will. Most Western experts consider sexual relations within such a marriage to be tantamount to rape, hence the classification of forced marriages as a form of gender-based violence. Forced marriages are common in West and East Africa, South Asia, and the Middle East. In many of Africa's bridewealth societies, marriages are often arranged by parents as the equivalent of a property exchange: daughter for economic assets. In South Asia's dowry-giving societies, marriages are also often arranged by parents, with parents of the bride keen on marrying their daughter into a family of higher social status.

Most forced marriages are actually child marriages. A child marriage is one in which one or both of the parties are children, although they typically entail the marriage of an adult male to a child female. Although opinions vary, many Western observers consider girls below the age of nineteen to be unable by definition to consent to marriage, a view that thus treats any marriage of a girl younger than nineteen to be a forced one. Throughout much of Africa, along with Bangladesh, India, and Yemen, between 40 percent and 75 percent of all females are married before the age of nineteen.[64] Many parents actually prefer their daughters to marry older men, who are often better placed than younger men to provide for their wife's financial needs. For their part, many

men prefer young girls because of the perception that they are likely to be virgins and the fact that, to maximize family size, procreation should start at a young age. Girls who marry as children rarely receive more education after they are married.

Female Genital Cutting. Gender-based violence can also take a ritual form, meaning it is carried out recurrently with traditional cultural meanings in mind. Perhaps the most widely performed instance of this is **female genital cutting** (FGC; also referred to as female genital mutilation or female circumcision). FGC is a common practice in Africa's northern half that involves partial or total removal of a girl's external genitalia. In Guinea, Egypt, Sierra Leone, Mali, Sudan, and the horn of Africa (Djibouti, Ethiopia, Eritrea, and Somalia), 90 percent or more of all women have undergone FGC at some point in their lives. In countries in the rest of Africa's northern half, the prevalence ranges from 5 percent to 80 percent. Worldwide, an estimated 130 million women have had their genitals cut, and an additional 3 million (one every ten seconds) undergo FGC every year.[65]

FGC is typically performed on girls between the ages of five and fifteen. The procedure is usually carried out by local women on girls who have no expectation of what is about to happen to them. The women who perform the procedure rarely have medical training, and they carry it out without anesthesia using any available sharp object, such as a razor blade, knife, tin can lid, scissors, glass, or sharp rock. Depending on a group's local and national tradition, the severity of the procedure ranges from (1) a clitoridectomy (removal of the clitoris and clitoral hood) to (2) clitoridectomy and removal of inner labia to (3) infibulation (removal of all outer genitalia and tying shut the vagina). Aside from the excruciation caused by the procedure, FGC carries risks that include infection or even death from excessive hemorrhaging. Down the line, many girls are permanently incontinent or develop scars that block urine or menstrual flow. Virtually all girls who undergo FGC will also have their ability to experience sexual pleasure permanently inhibited.

The cultural justifications for FGC are varied. Some cultures consider female genitalia to be unclean or the clitoris to be masculine. Most see it as part of an effort to discourage female promiscuity and keep a girl chaste by both inhibiting her sexual pleasure and, in cases of infibulation, literally tying her vagina shut until marriage. In cultures were FGC is widely practiced, women who never underwent the procedure are shunned as sexually licentious and have a hard time attracting a husband. As a result, the practice of FGC, while illegal in most of the countries where it occurs, has proved stubbornly difficult to combat. Mothers want their daughters to be cut because it is seen as a requisite for them to eventually get married, and men implicitly support the practice by not wanting spouses who have not been altered.

Reproduction and Fertility

A final important aspect of female health and physical security lies in women's reproductive role. Women in the developing world birth more children than those in the developed world. The **fertility rate**, or the average number of births per woman, is strongly and negatively correlated with GDP per capita, as depicted in Figure 12.3. In the developed West, the average fertility rate is 1.7 births per woman. By contrast, in sub-Saharan Africa, the fertility rate is 4.9 births per woman. Women average 2.7 births in South Asia, 2.6 in the Middle East, and 2.2 in Latin America. Only in East Asia (1.8) are fertility rates close to those of the developed countries.[66]

Causes of High Fertility. Westerners often assume that women in LDCs have so many children because they lack access to contraception. For the most part, this is far from the primary reason. In actuality, women and men in LDCs genuinely want more children than do Westerners. For example, surveys show that, on average, Kenyan women see four children as the ideal, Malagasy women say five, and Chadian women cite nine.[67]

Why do parents in LDCs have this high-fertility preference? The primary reason is economic. Poor rural parents often want many children so that their offspring can

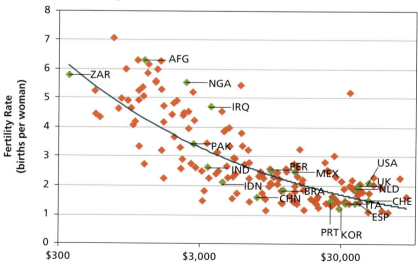

Figure 12.3 ▪ ▪ ▪ **The Relationship between GDP per Capita and Fertility Rates, 2010**

GDP per Capita in US$, PPP (logarithmic scale)

Source: Data compiled from the World Bank, World Development Indicators, http://data.worldbank.org/data-catalog/world-development-indicators.

work around the house and in the fields. Manual labor fills in where tractors and other modern equipment are not affordable. Poor parents also want many children who can then support them in old age and other times of need. Moreover, where child mortality is high, parents knowingly birth more children than they expect to survive in order to reach their ideal family size.

Cultural influences can also contribute to the preference for more children. Large families are signs of status, pride, and religious commitment in many parts of the world. Cultural attitudes, however, seem to take a back seat to economic concerns, for they are surprisingly pliant in the face of rising prosperity. Economic growth seems to lower fertility regardless of a nation's religiosity or cultural tradition. For example, conservative and Islamic Iran achieved a precipitous drop in its fertility rate from more than 6.9 children in 1965 to less than 2 in just forty years time.[68] Similarly, Roman Catholic Latin American now has fertility rates approaching those of high-income countries.

To be sure, lack of contraception is a contributing factor. Surveys show that some 120 million women would use contraception if they could get it.[69] Millions more do not use contraception because of a lack of knowledge about its use, as most developing world school systems provide abysmal training in contraceptive use. Rates of contraceptive use among married women are only in the teens in sub-Saharan Africa, and they are less than 50 percent in the Middle East and South Asia. Similarly, many women have a hard time getting their male partners to use contraceptive methods. Less than 15 percent of couples in the developing world use male-specific methods of contraception (such as condoms or vasectomies), often because men fear they will interfere with sexual pleasure. As a result of the shortfall in contraceptive use, 40 percent of all pregnancies worldwide are unwanted. Moreover, when

contraception is used, it is often the woman who bears its side effects. Female sterilization, which is based on an invasive surgery that causes permanent physiological changes to a woman, is probably the most common form of contraception in the world.[70]

Trends. In looking at a snapshot of the world, it is true that poorer countries have higher fertility rates. In shifting focus to the trend over the past few decades, however, it is clear that fertility rates have declined dramatically. Worldwide, fertility fell from 5.0 to 2.5 in the half-century after 1960, the fastest decline in human history.[71] Figure 12.4 depicts the trends since 1960 for each world region. Women are marrying later and are more likely to be in the workforce than in the past, giving them less time to procreate and less enthusiasm for large families. Contraception is also more affordable, widely available, and reliable.

Causes of Underdevelopment: High Fertility

Perhaps the most direct way in which these female health-related issues affect long-term economic development is through fertility. That high fertility and rapid population growth are bad for a society's economic well-being is one of the world's most firmly held beliefs, so much so that population control has often been state policy. China has its one-child policy, some Indian states enacted compulsory sterilization in the 1970s, and the Nigerian government today urges families to limit themselves to four children.

Scholars have given numerous reasons for why high fertility might slow economic growth. Rapid population growth means societies and states need ever-increasing numbers of schools, roads, housing, and food just to keep up with prevailing living standards. In other words, rather than increasing capital

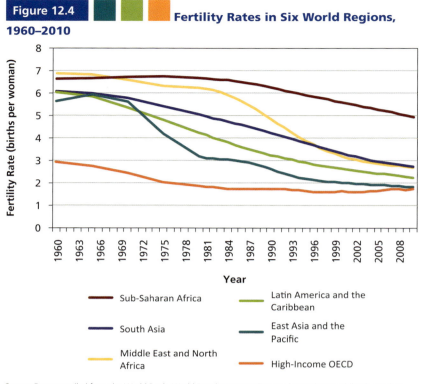

Figure 12.4 **Fertility Rates in Six World Regions, 1960–2010**

Legend:
- Sub-Saharan Africa
- South Asia
- Middle East and North Africa
- Latin America and the Caribbean
- East Asia and the Pacific
- High-Income OECD

Source: Data compiled from the World Bank, World Development Indicators, http://data.worldbank.org/data-catalog/world-development-indicators.

stock per person (a prerequisite for per-capita growth), additional capital is simply allocated to the extra persons.[72] Population growth also places ecological stress on a society, speeding up the depletion of natural assets such as mineral wealth and land and raising their cost. High fertility can also slow capital accumulation by discouraging parents from saving for their old age. They instead just expect to have the financial help of their many children down the line. Having a large number of children also makes it more difficult for a mother and her family to reap the income gains of her potential market work. Finally, negative consequences can result from what economist Gary Becker calls the quantity-quality tradeoff.[73] Impoverished families must give up some of the quality of their child rearing when the quantity of children is high. Some

children are less well fed than if they had fewer siblings, and poor parents often choose just one or two children to receive advanced education.

High fertility also delays the onset of a society's **demographic dividend**, which is the temporary economic boost a society receives from having nonworkers as a relatively small share of its population. First alluded to in the work of demographer Warren Thompson, the **demographic transition** is a process of shifting age distribution that societies go through as they move from premodern agri-

cultural societies to postindustrial ones.[74] The demographic transition has four stages, depicted in Figure 12.5. Stage one is the premodern, agricultural stage, in which fertility is high (depicted by the purple line) but population growth (depicted by the slope of the red line) is slow because death rates (green line) are high (that is, life expectancies are low). Stage two is an early modern stage and corresponds to the era of fastest population growth. In this stage, health technologies are adopted that dramatically raise life expectancies, but parents continue to have a large number of children. Societies in which women are disempowered and have high fertility can spend extended time in this stage of high population growth. Much of sub-Saharan Africa is currently in this stage. Most other LDCs passed through this stage between the 1940s and 1980s.

DEVELOPMENT in the FIELD

Aid for Female Empowerment

A large number of NGOs focus on female empowerment in LDCs, and many of them justify their cause with the instrumentalist argument. The most explicit use of the instrumental case is an aid agency called the Girl Effect, which holds that "girls are the most powerful force for change on the planet" and defines the "girl effect" as "the unique potential of 600 million adolescent girls to end poverty for themselves and the world."[38] The group invests in health and education programs for teenage girls in poverty. To raise donations, the NGO makes the case that investing in teenage girls is a highly effective way of growing the domestic economy and furthering the human development of future generations.

Other NGOs targeting female empowerment make a less explicit case for the instrumental rationale, instead relying on its intrinsic value. For example, Women for Women International provides financial and emotional support for women who are survivors of war and conflict. Numerous agencies ranging from the large (Bill and Melinda Gates Foundation) to the small (International Midwife Association) provide support for women's reproductive health, including the provision of contraception to limit fertility. A number of UN agencies, such as the United Nations Population Fund, also work against female genital cutting.

Opinion is mixed on whether these foreign-backed efforts are successful. No amount of Western money can change local cultural norms, so attempts to advance female empowerment with foreign money can run into roadblocks. For example, in a society where schools are of poor quality and eventual employers will only discriminate against them, keeping girls in school longer may not yield concrete benefits. Similarly, the promotion of low fertility often runs up against local preferences—often held by women themselves for economic reasons—in favor of large families and in opposition to birth control. Some people in LDCs even resent such efforts as a racially driven endeavor by the West to keep the world's nonwhite population from growing. International efforts against female genital cutting can also backfire, since they only heighten the resolve of people who want to differentiate themselves and their culture from the West.

In contrast, stage three is the era of the beneficial demographic dividend and slowing population growth. Parents finally realize that they can birth fewer children to have some around to support them in their old age. The decline in the number of children creates a low **age dependency ratio**, which is the ratio of the working-age (fifteen to sixty-four) population size to the nonworking-age (birth to fifteen, sixty-five and over) population size. This in turn boosts economic growth since active workers (parents) are financially supporting a smaller number of nonworkers (children and retirees) and since the lower fertility frees women to enter the workforce. Most countries throughout Latin America and Asia, which have lowered their fertility rates over the past few decades, are currently in this stage. Finally, stage four corresponds to the postindustrial societies of today's high-income countries, in which population sizes stabilize or even decline as fertility rates

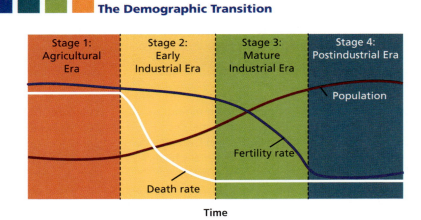

Figure 12.5 **The Demographic Transition**

Time

settle at or below the population replacement rate of 2.1. As Figure 12.4 shows, most LDCs outside of sub-Saharan Africa will probably settle into this stage within the next decade or two.

Critique: Doubting the Costs of High Fertility

Despite the compelling logic of the "high-fertility, slow-growth" argument, not to mention the hold it has had on governments in some of the world's largest countries, it may not be true. Most evidence suggests that high population density is good for economic growth. For most of human history, societies with more density and more rapidly growing populations have developed more quickly than sparsely populated ones.[75] Density brings people in close proximity to one another, which lowers the costs of economic exchange, creates economies of scale, and boosts the rate of innovation as people share ideas and collaborate. Recall that Chapter 4 presented

an argument that attributed Africa's underdevelopment to its relatively small population, which was thinned somewhat by the Atlantic slave trade. Africa remains a sparsely populated continent, especially in comparison to Europe, so its current baby boom may be beneficial to its long-term development prospects.

Moreover, whereas high fertility may delay the onset of the demographic dividend, it also delays the onset of stage four, in which population size stagnates or even declines. In this stage, economic growth can slow as age dependency ratios increase again. The share of elderly retirees in the population rises as these nonworkers enjoy longer life expectancies and are not fully replaced in the workforce due to low fertility and the relatively small number of young people. Because of its one-child policy, China will reach stage four at a lower level of development than practically anyone ever has, and concerns exist as to whether its state and workforce can sustain the coming boom in pensioners.

IS AFGHANISTAN'S TREATMENT OF WOMEN THE CAUSE OF ITS POVERTY?

Afghanistan has been in the global spotlight for decades and always for the wrong reasons. It was a battleground for global superpowers in the 1980s and 2000s, a fact that has put its catastrophic social and economic development failures in full view. Afghanistan has Asia's lowest average income and worst human development outcomes, a fact underscored by it also having the world's lowest life expectancy at birth. On the eve of the U.S. invasion in late 2001, the average income in Afghanistan was equivalent to what it was at independence some eighty years earlier.[76] One well-known feature of Afghanistan is the plight of its women and girls. The country has recently been called the "most dangerous country for women."[77] What is life like for Afghan women, and are their mistreatment and the country's deep gender inequalities the source of its underdevelopment? Table 12.1 gives some suggestive evidence by comparing Afghanistan with the Netherlands, the country that, in 2011, had the world's second-highest gender equality ranking.

Table 12.1 **Development Comparison: Afghanistan and the Netherlands**

Indicator	Afghanistan	The Netherlands
GDP per capita at PPP	US$1,139	US$42,772
Human Development Index	.398	.910
Gender Inequality Index	.707 (141st of 146)	.052 (2nd of 146)
Estimated battlefield deaths since 1978	~800,000	<50
Ratio of coastline to land area	0	13.30

Sources: Data on GDP per capita at PPP compiled from the World Bank, World Development Indicators, http://data.worldbank.org/data-catalog/world-development-indicators; Human Development Index, http://hdr.undp.org/en/statistics/hdi/; Gender Inequality Index, http://hdr.undp.org/en/statistics/gii/; battlefield deaths, Bethany Lacina and Nils Petter Gleditsch, "Monitoring Trends in Global Combat: A New Dataset of Battle Deaths," *European Journal of Population* 21, no. 2–3 (2005): 145–116 and Radio Netherlands Worldwide, "Another Dutch Soldier Killed in Afghanistan," http://www.rnw.nl/english/article/another-dutch-soldier-killed-afghanistan; ratio of coastline to land area, CIA World Factbook, https://www.cia.gov/library/publications/the-world-factbook.

The South: Mistreatment of Women and Girls

Many peoples of the developing world experience profound hardship, but, as a group, Afghan women may experience it worst of all. Afghan women have some of the worst health and education outcomes in the world. These harsh realities stem both from longstanding cultural traditions and government mandates.

Poor Female Health and Disempowerment.

In terms of female health outcomes, the list of unflattering superlatives for Afghanistan is long.

Women live just forty-four years on average, the world's lowest female life expectancy. In 2008, its maternal mortality ratio was 1,600 deaths per 100,000 live births, the world's highest. This, coupled with the world's second-highest fertility rate (6.6),[78] means that Afghan women are at extremely high risk of dying in pregnancy or from childbirth complications: one in eleven suffer maternal mortality.[79] There is also circumstantial evidence of medical neglect by parents of girls. The ratio of boys to girls in the birth-to-fourteen age range is unnaturally high in a country were sex-selective

IS AFGHANISTAN'S TREATMENT OF WOMEN THE CAUSE OF ITS POVERTY?

abortion is virtually nonexistent. All told, a 2003 study estimated there to be a million missing Afghan women, nearly 10 percent of the nation's female population and the world's highest percentage.[80]

Afghan women also lack empowerment outside the realm of health. They are probably the least educated and most illiterate female population in the world, a problem caused in part by the fact that Afghan girls were completely prohibited from attending school in the early 2000s. In 2009, only 38 percent of primary and secondary school children were girls, and 76 percent of women had never even been to school.[81] In family life, an estimated 70 to 80 percent of all marriages are forced, and the average age of first marriage for females (eighteen) is, yet again, the world's lowest.[82] Parents often promise a daughter to her cousin or to another adult male who can provide a lucrative payment in return. The cultural tradition of *baad*, which is reportedly widespread in rural areas, results in a girl being given to another family to settle a wrong committed against that family by one of her older relatives. Women and girls who resist their arranged marriages risk physical violence and even death at the hands of a family member.

In some periods of Afghanistan's history, hyper-conservative views on girls and women became government policy. Most famously, the Islamic fundamentalist Taliban regime (1996–2001) enacted a slew of draconian laws. The regime banned education for girls, shutting down hundreds of schools and turning them into religious seminaries. It disallowed women from being seen outside their homes unless accompanied by a male relative and regaled in a full-body *burqa* that blocked all flesh from strangers' view. Cosmetics, high-heeled shoes, bicycle-riding, loud laughing, and talking with males who were not relatives were prohibited for women. Violations of these regulations could result in immediate public beatings by roving police affiliates of the Department for the Preservation of Virtue and Prevention of Vice. Even in post-Taliban Afghanistan,

the country's justice system does little to protect women from gender-based violence.

The Instrumental Consequences. How might this mistreatment of women and girls cause Afghanistan's underdevelopment? For starters, in limiting educational and labor market opportunities for women, the country leaves the economic talents and productive energies of half of its population dormant. The undereducation of women also carries a heavy social toll on the young. Child mortality rates are among the world's highest (200 deaths per 1,000 live births), due in part to parental unfamiliarity with proper prevention of infectious diseases. The incredibly high fertility may also contribute to slow economic growth. It makes it difficult for women to get educated and enter the labor market, and active (mostly male) workers have a lot of mouths to feed. Finally, just three of Afghanistan's cabinet members are women. A stronger female presence in the notoriously corrupt government might result in a cleaner regime that is more focused on social development.

***

While overwhelming, the sheer scope of Afghanistan's mistreatment of women does not prove that its gender inequity causes its economic underdevelopment. Instead, the dire state of its female population may be a symptom of its income poverty. Despite the episode of Taliban rule and the list of egregious gender norms, a number of poor countries have equivalent or near-equivalent development outcomes for its women. Chad, DR Congo, Mali, and Niger all had worse gender inequality scores than Afghanistan in 2011 due to their high adolescent fertility rates, gender-based educational inequalities, and relative lack of women in positions of leadership. Moreover, the characterization of Afghanistan as a haven of gender discrimination may soon need updating. It has a higher share of female parliamentarians than does the United States (due in part to a quota that reserves

An Afghan woman pulls her burqa closely over her eyes so that she can see through it. Women in Afghanistan are no longer required to wear the full body covering, as they were under the Taliban regime (1996-2001). Many, however, still choose to do so out of modesty and habit.

25 percent of seats for women), and its fertility and maternal mortality rates are falling dramatically.

The West: Legacy of a Global Pawn

An alternative view sees the West, and not Afghanistan's own culture and government, as the source of Afghanistan's underdevelopment. Afghanistan has long been a pawn of the world's great powers. To be sure, many of these powers met with adversity in Afghanistan, as the country is sometimes called the "graveyard of empires." These foreign military interventions, however, left lasting impacts that may have been detrimental to Afghanistan's subsequent development.

The West's first major incursion occurred in the first half of the 1830s when the British Empire, already the colonizing power of neighboring India, sought to expand its influence over the Afghan region in the face of feared encroachments by the Russian Empire. Over the ensuing century, the British invaded and fought the three Anglo-Afghan wars, which often had brutal consequences for its troops. Although Afghanistan never fell to complete occupation and colonization by the British, it did not declare full independence until 1919. Sixty years later, a non-Western empire, the Soviet Union, invaded to prop up Afghanistan's Marxist-Leninist regime. It was struggling against the Islamist *mujahedeen* guerrilla movement that was itself backed by the United States and United Kingdom. The war ended in 1989 with Soviet defeat and humiliation. Finally, in 2001 the United States itself met with challenges upon entering Afghanistan while also precipitating great human costs. By the end of the 2000s, the United States was mired in a military quagmire while backing Afghanistan's new government, one of the world's most corrupt and inept political regimes.

IS AFGHANISTAN'S TREATMENT OF WOMEN THE CAUSE OF ITS POVERTY?

Although the British never got a full colonial foothold in Afghanistan during the nineteenth century, they did install puppet kings that governed more in the service of Britain than of Afghan subjects. These governments failed to establish inclusive economic and political institutions that could foment long-term industrial growth. The interstate conflicts of recent decades have also left damaging economic and social legacies. Nearly a million civilian deaths have occurred, most of them during the Soviet occupation. Rural and urban infrastructure has been destroyed, and millions of Afghan refugees, many of them well educated, have fled to neighboring countries. Today, a major share of Afghanistan's economy is either propped up by international assistance or oriented around illegal activities, namely opium production. The creation of a peacetime economy that can stand on its own could take decades.

The Natural World: Dry, Mountainous, and Landlocked

Long preceding these foreign interventions and its current gender norms, Afghan territory had its natural setting. While mountainous and beautiful, it does not lend itself to modern economic growth. Afghanistan is dry and thus has frequent droughts and degraded soils. This makes most of the land unsuitable for food production. Just 12 percent of the land is under cultivation, despite the fact that 80 percent of the population farms or herds for a living. Freshwater supplies, already in short supply, are threatened by poor management and contamination. One of Afghanistan's major rivers, the Helmand, has seen its water-flow volumes decline by 90 percent in just a decade.[83] Deforestation, caused both by the military conflicts and by household use of wood as a fuel, has contributed to the dryness and soil degradation.

Afghanistan's mountains have also proved troublesome for governance and growth. Building a state that can exercise its power uniformly throughout an entire territory is a linchpin of the modern nation-state and

a prerequisite for sustained economic progress. Yet ruggedness makes governing difficult.[84] In Afghanistan, building roads to unify the state presence is nearly prohibitive, and insurgents and splinter groups can often find protection from already meager state security forces behind natural mountainous barriers. As a result, much of Afghanistan is largely untouched by the central government in Kabul.

Finally, Afghanistan is landlocked and surrounded by mostly troubled, unstable neighbors.[85] Being landlocked makes trade with the outside world more expensive, since transporting over land is more costly than transporting over sea. The problem is compounded since the two countries that separate Afghanistan from the Indian Ocean, Iran and Pakistan, can effectively hold Afghanistan's commerce with the outside world hostage. At various points in history, these have been dysfunctional or unneighborly states.

* * *

Overall, Afghanistan's future is as uncertain as its past is tragic. In the decade since the U.S.-led invasion, women's rights have taken a step forward, and the new government, while corrupt and limited in its authority, does hold regular elections. Despite this, the economic, political, social, and geographical challenges are enormous, and only time will tell if this invasion will be the one when intervention by a foreign superpower pays off.

Thinking Critically about Development

- Soon after the U.S.-led invasion of 2001, the Taliban regime fell. Since that time, Afghan's average incomes have doubled, despite ongoing civil conflict. Is this economic growth merely the result of the infusion of foreign aid, or is it evidence of the instrumental benefits of improved gender equity? In other words, could this increase in growth be caused by the end of the Taliban's draconian laws restricting the rights of women and girls?

- Currently, 28 percent of Afghanistan's members of parliament are women, a figure that is higher than the international average. Will this female presence improve Afghanistan's social development, or do other factors make it not matter?

- Will Afghanistan's mountainous terrain make it impossible for the central state to ever govern the entire territory effectively, or can a well-meaning and well-equipped state eventually overcome these natural barriers?

 ## Key Terms

age dependency ratio, p. 301

demographic dividend, p. 300

demographic transition, p. 300

descriptive representation, p. 289

excess female mortality, p. 294

female empowerment, p. 285

female genital cutting, p. 297

female labor force participation rates (FLFPR), p. 287

fertility rate, p. 298

forced marriage, p. 297

gender, p. 285

gender asset gap, p. 285

gender earnings gap, p. 285

gender inequality, p. 285

gender quota, p. 291

maternal mortality, p. 295

non-market activities, p. 286

social movement, p. 291

son preference, p. 294

women in development (WID), p. 292

 ## Suggested Readings

Boserup, Esther. *Women's Role in Economic Development*. London: Allen and Unwin, 1970.

Kristof, Nicholas D., and Sheryl WuDunn. *Half the Sky: Turning Oppression into Opportunity for Women Worldwide*. New York: Random House, 2009.

Nussbaum, Martha. *Women and Human Development: The Capabilities Approach*. Cambridge: Cambridge University Press, 2000.

Seager, Joni. *The Penguin Atlas of Women in the World*. 4th ed. New York: Penguin Books, 2009.

Sen, Amartya. "More Than 100 Million Women Are Missing." *New York Review of Books* 37 (December 1990), 61–66.

World Bank. *Engendering Development*. New York: Oxford University Press, 2001.

———. *World Development Report 2012: Gender Equality and Development*. Washington D.C.: World Bank Publications, 2011.

@ ## Web Resources

Organisation for Economic Co-operation and Development, Gender Data Portal, www.oecd.org/gender/data/

United Nations Development Programme, Gender-Related Indices, http://hdr.undp.org/en/statistics/indices/gdi_gem/

World Bank, Gender Statistics, http://data.worldbank.org/data-catalog/gender-statistics

World Economic Forum, Global Gender Gap Index, www.weforum.org/issues/global-gender-gap

A Kenyan girl looks through the bednet hanging over her bed. The net is meant to prevent the mosquitoes that cause malaria from biting her while she sleeps. Malaria is one of the world's most deadly diseases, but it can only be contracted in warm climates. Advocates of geographical explanations of underdevelopment claim that malaria may be partially responsible for the relative poverty of the tropics.

Geography and Economic Prosperity

I n 1519, Spanish conquistador Hernán Cortés arrived in the New World with just 500 soldiers and thirty horses, landing his ships in what is today Mexico. With these meager resources, Cortés confronted the Aztecs, an advanced civilization with a population that numbered in the millions and a well-practiced army of tens of thousands. Despite these odds, Cortés deposed the Aztec leadership and took political control of its empire. This initiated 300 years of Spanish colonial rule over Mexican (and eventually most of Central and South American) territory. The effects still linger to this day, as contemporary Spaniards are, on average, more than twice as rich as Mexicans. What enabled a relatively small group of European men to defeat a skilled army that outnumbered it 100 to one and to carry out a process of conquest that would reverberate for centuries?

The two parts of the threefold framework that this book has covered thus far—the West and the South—do not provide satisfying answers to these questions. The claim that underdevelopment is due to the West because of enslavement, colonialism, globalization, and aid presumes that contact exists between West and South, yet the Cortés affair suggests that Europe had certain advantages over the Aztecs long before contact ever occurred. Also unconvincing is the claim that it is due to the policies, institutions, or cultural practices of the South. The Aztecs had in place an empire that featured commerce and economic specialization, a powerful war machine that had withstood all challenges up until the Spanish arrival, and some of the world's most advanced architectural and engineering feats. By comparison, Spain featured a rigid monarchical absolutism, and it would soon give way to the Netherlands and Great Britain as Europe's leading powers.

The inability of these two approaches to provide satisfactory answers justifies discussion of the third and final category of explanations for why some countries are rich and some poor: the natural world. This category attributes economic underdevelopment to disadvantages inherent to the physical settings of the developing world, such as climate, disease burdens, natural resource endowments, location, and availability of domesticable plants and animals. This list of variables differs dramatically from those considered under the South and the West categories in that it is comprised of factors that are either somewhat or entirely beyond human control. For example, two of the weapons that were indispensible to Cortés and the Spaniards in their conquest and colonization were immunity to smallpox and access to horses. A smallpox epidemic wiped out 90 percent of the New World's native population, and the height and speed of horses gave the Spaniards major advantages in the heat of battle. The Spaniards possessed both of these advantages not because of their superior cultures or institutions, but because of pure geographical luck. This chapter describes a number of geographical and physical features that LDCs share in common and then assesses these features as causal explanations for underdevelopment. It also considers arguments that geology, and in particular large endowments of natural resources, can have a paradoxically negative effect on development.

Geographical Commonalities of the Developing World

At first glance, a geographical explanation for world poverty seems counterintuitive. Underdevelopment comes in a huge variety of physical contexts. It exists in the rainforests of South America and Central Africa, the deserts of Central and Western Asia, the tropical islets of Southeast Asia, and the snowy mountains of Mongolia. Moreover, there are LDCs on every inhabited continent except

Australia. In short, finding geographical commonalities that could explain the generalized problem of underdevelopment seems nearly impossible. A closer look, however, does reveal some commonalities in geographies across the developing world, and some of these may even provide the key to understanding the roots of human poverty and underdevelopment.

The Tropics

Perhaps the easiest geographic feature to identify is that less developed countries are likely to be located in the tropics, which loosely corresponds to the area of the globe between the Tropic of Cancer and the Tropic of Capricorn. In contrast, wealthy countries are concentrated in temperate zones. Stated differently, as one moves further away from the equator, average incomes increase. Within the northern hemisphere, northward countries (such as those in Europe, as well as the United States, Canada, and Japan) are wealthier than more southward ones (such as those in Central America, South Asia, Southeast Asia, and North Africa). Even within Europe, the northwestern countries (United Kingdom, France, Germany) are wealthier than the southern ones (Italy, Portugal, and Spain). Within the southern hemisphere, the relationship flips, as it is the more southward countries (such as Australia and New Zealand) that are wealthier than the more northward ones (such as Angola and Papua New Guinea). This relationship even holds within continents: Argentina, Chile, and Uruguay have long been South America's wealthiest countries, and today Botswana, Namibia, and South Africa are among Africa's wealthiest.

In many instances, this relationship between development and distance from the equator even exists *within* countries. Historically, states in the southern United States have lagged economically behind those in other regions, and even today the poorest states are southern. An even starker north-south income gap characterizes Italy and Mexico.

In contrast, Brazil's southernmost states are its wealthiest. Most of Brazil's temperate states have the GDP per capita of Eastern Europe, while a few of its equatorial states have the per-capita GDP of Africa's lower-middle-income countries.

Figure 13.1 depicts this overall relationship with a scatterplot. It shows the relationship between a country's distance from the equator (in miles) and its GDP per capita. The trendline summarizes the overall relationship between the two. Since it slopes upward from lower left to upper right, it indicates a positive relationship between the two variables. Greater distance from the equator is associated with higher average incomes. Another way to summarize the relationship is to look at average incomes by latitude bands. In the tropics (countries lying between the Tropic of Cancer and Tropic of Capricorn), the median GDP per capita is US$3,700. Elsewhere, the median GDP per capita is nearly quintuple this amount at US$16,900. Is there a tropical disadvantage to development?

Other Commonalities

The Eurasian supercontinent, the enormous landmass comprised of Europe and Asia, seems to have had some historical advantages in development. Modern economic growth began in its westernmost portion (Northwestern Europe), but even prior to that the supercontinent housed many of the world's most advanced civilizations for their time: Mesopotamia, Greece, Rome, Han and Song China, the Gupta Empire (India), and the Soviet Union. By contrast, Africa, Central America, South America, and the Pacific Islands all contain less developed countries and *only* less developed countries (as classified by the map inside the front cover). Indeed, only four developed

countries exist outside of Eurasia: Australia, Canada, New Zealand, and the United States. Moreover, nearly all of the countries outside Eurasia, including these four developed ones, were colonized by Eurasian metropoles for extended periods of time. Within Eurasia, colonization by the Europeans, when it occurred in the era of Western imperialism, tended to be brief and more limited. In short, is there a "non-Eurasian" disadvantage to development?

A third geographical commonality shared by many LDCs is a relatively large distance from the world's major markets and trading centers. The world contains three major epicenters of economic activity and hubs for global trade: the United States, Europe, and East Asia. As these are all located in the northern hemisphere, countries in the southern hemisphere are far from the bulk of global economic exchange. Moreover, landlocked countries inside blocky continents, such as Bolivia, Uganda, and Uzbekistan, are particularly distant from these epicenters and must cross goods and people overland to reach them. Is there a curse of distance when it comes to development?

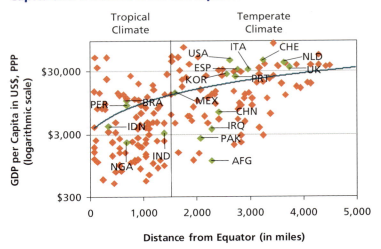

Figure 13.1 **Relationship between GDP per Capita and Distance from the Equator**

Sources: Data compiled from the World Bank, World Development Indicators 2009, http://data.worldbank.org/data-catalog/world-development-indicators, and Open Data by Socrata, https://opendata.socrata.com/.

Causes of Underdevelopment: Physical Geography and Climate

These three commonalities of the developing world loosely correspond to three sets of arguments about geography and underdevelopment. The tropical disadvantage argument claims a number of mechanisms by which tropical climates are detrimental to economic development. The arguments of Jared Diamond lay out a case for why parts of Eurasia, and especially Western Europe, developed before all non-Eurasian societies. The third set of claims looks at the impact of distance and transport costs on prosperity. These three are discussed in turn.

The Tropical Disadvantage

Even before the advent of modern economic growth, some thinkers invoked geography to explain the alleged gaps in societal progress between citizens of warmer climes and those of more temperate ones. Most such thinkers were Europeans who made self-serving arguments about why their own civilizations were allegedly superior. Most famously, French philosopher Montesquieu (1689–1755) made the claim that climate affected body chemistry, personal character and, as a result, the degree of prosperity. Heat, he claimed, slowed the flow of blood, breeding laziness and a "hot-tempered" capriciousness that worked against resolute and sustained action. In contrast, cooler temperatures increased blood flow, making people "more vigorous and bold" with regard to their work and more even-tempered in their behavior.[1]

A century later, the rise of physical anthropology in Victorian England and the misapplication of Charles Darwin's theory of natural selection saw the emergence of various theories of racial hierarchy, which attributed poverty in the tropics to the alleged biological inferiority of people of color. The association with these theories, today grouped under the label of scientific racism, turned the apparent link between tropics and underdevelopment into a taboo subject among scholars for several decades after World War II. However, the 1990s witnessed a resurgence of interest in the topic of geography and economic prosperity. Economist Jeffrey Sachs and other scholars developed cause-and-effect arguments about the tropical disadvantage that were not racially motivated and that carry more scientific credibility.

Tropical Disease. Human populations in the tropics face higher disease burdens than those in temperate climates. There is a long list of **tropical diseases** that are largely absent from temperate climates because the insect pests (mostly flies and mosquitoes) that carry and transmit dangerous parasites either hibernate or die during winter.[2] (Winter's beneficial effects led one author to call it "the great friend of humanity."[3]) Tropical diseases include malaria, dengue fever, sleeping sickness, Chagas disease, river blindness, and hookworm, each of which has varying degrees of severity and mortality. As one of the leading causes of premature death, **malaria** is considered the most harmful and costly tropical disease in the world today.

As Chapter 2 introduced, disease exacts economic costs in a variety of ways. Diseases can cause lost workdays, not just for the stricken but also for a family caregiver. They make children miss out on schooling. Sick workers and children that do manage to avoid absenteeism have their abilities and productivity impaired. Individuals and governments must devote precious funds to diagnosis, prevention, treatment, and care. A high incidence of disease can also cause an economically burdensome increase in human fertility, as parents procreate more to replace lost children or to insure against feared future loss. Diseases can impair fetal and child development, lowering cognitive abilities.[5] One study found that adults who spent their childhoods in malaria-free parts of Latin America earned 50 percent more per year than adults who

DEVELOPMENT in the FIELD

Tackling Malaria

Malaria is caused by a parasite carried by mosquitoes. The parasite enters the human bloodstream by mosquito bite, and in most instances (an estimated 225 million per year worldwide) it causes a seven-to-ten-day debilitating illness from which the human host recovers. Despite this recovery, when malaria occurs in pregnant mothers and children, it can stunt long-term brain and physical development. Moreover, in many cases (an estimated 650,000 per year), recovery never occurs and the infected person dies. Most of these deaths occur in children, and 90 percent of these are African children.[4] Given its severity, medical experts have tried for millennia to ease the disease's burden, but they have achieved only minimal success. The best known preventive methods

are draining the marshy areas where mosquitoes breed and sleeping under bed nets laced with insecticide. Some treatment drugs that shorten the illness are also available.

Malaria has been a focus of aid efforts for decades. In 1955, the World Health Organization began a major effort to eradicate malaria, but after a mere fourteen years it abandoned its efforts to pursue more tractable priorities. Interest in eradication was reinvigorated around the turn of the millennium, however, with the founding of several initiatives. The PATH Malaria Vaccine Initiative, funded in part by the Bill and Melinda Gates Foundation, conducts research on vaccines and treatment.

Although no completely effective vaccine exists, the group has developed some promising ones that reduce incidence by 30 to 60 percent. The United Nations' Global Fund to Fight AIDS, Tuberculosis and Malaria finances various preventive and treatment programs in LDCs, and the Roll Back Malaria Partnership coordinates efforts across a variety of aid agencies. Over the last decade, the number of deaths from malaria has declined. However, the development of a fully effective vaccine remains years away, and total eradication is decades away at best. Attainment of these goals is complicated by the fact that the parasites are constantly evolving resistances to humanity's preventive and treatment efforts.

did not.[6] Tropical diseases can also exacerbate the low agricultural productivity problem of the tropics, as they affect land mammals as well as humans. For example, cattle in Africa have long been susceptible to parasites carried by the tsetse fly, and a rinderpest plague wiped out 90 percent of the continent's cattle in the early 1900s.[7]

Overall, the detrimental economic effects of tropical diseases can be dramatic. John Gallup and Sachs argue that malaria alone lowers a country's GDP growth rate by 1.3 percentage points per year.[8] While 1.3 percentage points may seem

small, if accumulated over a long period of time it has an enormous effect on prosperity levels due to compounding. To show this, Figure 13.2 contrasts GDP per-capita levels in two hypothetical countries. The malaria-free country starts at the subsistence level (US$300) and grows at an annual pace of 5 percent, and the malaria-rife country starts at the same level but grows at a rate of 3.7 percent. After 100 years, the malaria-free country is more than three times as wealthy. It has the average living standard of Switzerland, while the malaria-rife country has that of Mexico.

Figure 13.2 — The Estimated Long-Term Effects of Malaria: Development Outcomes in Two Hypothetical Countries

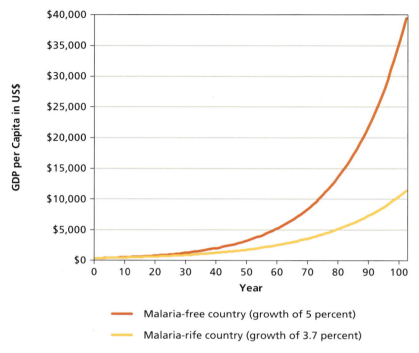

Malaria-free country (growth of 5 percent)

Malaria-rife country (growth of 3.7 percent)

Source: Calculations made by the author.

blocks sunlight to the floor, yet where humans knock down forests for food production, soils and their nutrients erode quickly due to rain and lack of protection from tree cover. Dry tropical climes only create different problems. In addition to causing nutrient decomposition, hot temperatures also speed up water evaporation and make drought more likely.[9] Sachs argues that, for all of these reasons, "Sustained agriculture-led development, whether in the United States, Australia, Denmark or Argentina, has always been a temperate-zone affair."[10]

Low Population Density. Sachs also argues that a long-term consequence of a high disease burden and low land productivity is that tropical Africa has for millennia been the most sparsely populated continent. Meager agricultural output, disease, and frequent famines prevented populations from growing quickly.[11] Since diseases thrive in areas of high population density, centralized states and cities only rarely emerged. As an exception that proves the rule, sub-Saharan Africa's first major civilization was Aksum, which is in the highlands (of modern-day Ethiopia) and thus cold enough to mitigate malaria's foothold. In fact, the entire human population remained quite small until a few early *homo sapiens* left Africa and settled elsewhere over 70,000 years ago. Moreover, low agricultural productivity has consequences for both rural and urban development in tropical Africa. It complicates small farmers' attempts to grow an **agricultural surplus** (meaning more food than they need for survival), which ties a large share of the population down to inefficient, small-scale agriculture.

Low Agricultural Productivity. Crop yields per square acre are 30 percent to 40 percent lower in the tropics than in temperate climates, and this is the case when comparing farms that use the same technological inputs to sow and harvest. This is so for several reasons. Many tropical soils are poor in nutrients. The organic matter that provides valuable nutrients decomposes quickly in high temperatures, whereas cold temperatures and winter freezes forestall the decomposition and mineralization.

Humid and dry tropical climates each present further, but distinct, problems. In humid tropical climates, heavy rains can leech soils of their nutrients, and recurrent floods can destroy months' worth of crop growth. Tropical rainforests are particularly detrimental to food cultivation. The forest canopy

Rural residents find it financially harder to leave the farm for urban areas and industrial jobs, so cities remain relatively small.

Without large cities and high population density, Africa has historically struggled to develop the economic specializations and low costs of communication and transport that are inherent to economic growth. By one estimate, a person living in a city of 10 million is 40 percent more productive than a person living in a city of 100,000. For this reason, it is said that "Africa needs more megacities."[12]

Guns, Germs, and Steel

As described in Chapter 4, the history of imperialism from 1500 to 1900 is largely one of Europe exploring and colonizing non-Eurasian territories. Almost the entirety of the Western Hemisphere, Australasia, and sub-Saharan Africa were colonized by Western Europeans at some point during these four centuries. To be sure, Western European entities also colonized much of the Middle East, South Asia, and Southeast Asia, but the largest chunks of the Eurasian landmass were either not colonized (Russia), only lightly colonized (China), or colonized briefly (much of the Middle East). What gave Western Europe such a huge advantage over non-Eurasian societies before the two entities made contact?

In a prize-winning book titled *Guns, Germs, and Steel*, physiologist Jared Diamond argues that Europe's advantage stemmed not from Europeans' superior intellects, cultures, or institutions, but from pure geographical luck.[13] To Diamond, Europeans were lucky enough to be on the Eurasian landmass, which featured the greatest supply and variety of consumable plants and large domesticable animals. This ample supply of domesticated plants and animals endowed Europe with large agricultural surpluses long before they were common outside Eurasia. This relatively high productivity enabled the rise of economic specialization, cities,

and political order. In turn, these factors contributed to the development of large standing armies and the adoption of the world's most advanced military technologies, such as steel swords, armor, and guns.

Moreover, Diamond adds that the simultaneous practices of urban living and animal domestication brought many Europeans into daily contact with one another, with their own human waste, and with their large mammals. This gradually endowed the European population with immunity to crowd and animal-borne diseases. In the end, two factors allowed the Europeans to colonize much of the world and gave them economic advantages that persist to this day: supremacy in military technology (guns and steel) and immunity to the diseases that wiped out most of the New World's native population (germs).

Understanding Europe's Geographical Advantage. To fully understand Diamond's argument, a few points should clarified. First, he notes that Eurasia had a more ample and nutritious supply of the very few plants that humans find worthy of domestication. This is somewhat surprising, since the New World and Africa have a rich and diverse flora. However, the vast majority of plants and trees in the world provide little to no nutritional value to humans. In fact, of the millions of wild plant species, only a few hundred have ever been domesticated, and a mere dozen (including staples such as wheat, rice, barley, and corn) comprise 80 percent of today's worldwide crop output. Of these nutritious crops, Eurasia had the wider variety.

Second, Diamond points out that Eurasia also had a luckier mix of land mammals from the (again) limited set of large animals that can be domesticated. Most large mammals, such as zebras and cheetahs, cannot be domesticated and are thus of limited use to humans. Some civilizations of the New World did domesticate dogs and guinea pigs, and parts of sub-Saharan Africa even domesticated rats. However, the usefulness of these small mammals pales in comparison to that of five large domesticable mammals that did not even exist in the Western Hemisphere and were only recent arrivals to sub-Saharan Africa at the time of European conquest: cows, horses, pigs, goats, and sheep. In Eurasia, these mammals provided high-protein meat and milk, fertilizer, wool and leather for clothing, and able bodies to haul cargo and pull plows. Horses are particularly valuable, as they provide rapid land transport and are a major asset in battles against horseless combatants. Europeans harnessed these Eurasian animals to build civilizations and increase their economic productivity before they set off to conquer the world. As a bonus, they unwittingly gained immunity from the deadly diseases that were instrumental in their military exploits of new lands.

Third, Diamond says that Europe had another locational advantage that gave it a head start over the rest of Eurasia and that explains why it gained the upper hand over the remaining 90 percent of the supercontinent. Europe lies near the fertile crescent (FC), the upside-down-U-shaped portion of land on the eastern Mediterranean coast where agriculture was invented some 9,000 years ago. The FC was a sweet spot for food production: rich forests and soils, a great climate, and a large number of domesticable plants and animals. The ancient civilizations of the FC eventually collapsed due in part to resource depletion, but not before their seed types, technologies, and ideas for cultivating food had spread to nearby Europe. This diffusion of agricultural practices was made possible by the fact that Europe lies on a similar latitude as the FC. Agricultural practices could spread much more easily in a westward or eastward pattern than in a northward or southward pattern. This is because territories on a similar latitude share the same day length and seasonal variation, and they also tend to share climate, disease, and vegetation types. By contrast, the innovations of the FC did not spread southward into sub-Saharan Africa because it would have

required crossing dramatically different climates zones, including the Sahara desert.

Finally, Diamond uses geography to explain why European settlers were able to develop some parts of the non-Eurasian world but not others. When Europeans settled the colonies that eventually became Argentina, Australia, Canada, South Africa, and the United States, most of the basic food production techniques that they had been using for millennia continued to work well. That is because each of these colonies was in a temperate zone, thus sharing basic climatic, seasonal, soil, and disease conditions with those the Europeans were used to back home. Each of these colonies is today either an upper-middle-income or developed country. In contrast, when explorers settled or tried to settle colonies in more tropical regions—Central America, the Caribbean, tropical sub-Saharan Africa, and northern South America—their seeds and cultivation techniques yielded far fewer crops, and they were plagued by tropical diseases. Most Europeans ultimately abandoned these settings, and subsequent economic development was slow.

Natural Barriers to Economic Exchange

For a society to experience the increases in productivity that are constitutive of economic growth, it needs its people to specialize. People produce more if they focus on a single vocation rather than trying to do many. This is because they can choose one at which they are talented and their skills improve with repetition. Specialization can only exist, however, if people are able to exchange the fruits of their labor with others. For example, it makes little sense for a man to specialize in manufacturing farm equipment if there are no farmers nearby to sell him food and buy his products. He would either starve or have to become a farmer himself, either of which would erase the gains that society enjoys from his expertise in producing farm equipment.

Nature can provide physical barriers to economic exchange, thereby discouraging specialization and economic growth. At best, natural barriers and sheer distance itself increase **transport costs**, making exchange expensive. At worst, the obstacles to exchange can be insurmountable, prohibiting it entirely. One set of scholarly arguments about geography and development asserts that less developed countries are poor because they face high natural barriers to exchange and thus prohibitive transport costs.

Adam Smith on Transport Costs. The first major thinker to make this case was eighteenth-century British philosopher Adam Smith. Smith pointed out that water transport was much cheaper and faster than land transport, a fact that remains true to this day despite the advent of railroads and automobiles. As a result, societies with easy access to water transport were and are more amenable to the rise of industry because firms prefer to locate along lakes, rivers, and seas so that they can have cheaper exchange with suppliers and customers. From this, Smith concluded that societies reliant on or limited to land transport would have less specialization, less industry, and, as a result, less prosperity.

A quick comparison of the silhouettes of the African and European continents vividly illustrates what Smith meant. (See the map inside the front cover.) Europe's coastline is jagged, with countless inlets and peninsulas. It contains numerous islands, two of considerable size. Its entire southern coast is bordered by the Black and Mediterranean seas, while its northern coast touches the North and Baltic seas. In contrast, Africa is blocky, containing no major inlets and just one large island. Europe's coastline is 50 percent longer than Africa's, even though its land area is a mere one-eighth of Africa's.[14] Furthermore, Africa's rivers provide little relief to the high costs of land transport. Most have impassable waterfalls some 50 to 200 miles inland since the land rises from the ocean to a central plateau. This blocks access to the sea for many Africans. To exacerbate the problem even more, African populations have historically lived in the inland highlands because it is cooler and disease burdens are lower, but this further isolates them from coasts and water transport. All told, just 21 percent of the sub-Saharan African population lives on an ocean coast or near a river that provides passage to the ocean. In Europe, this number is 89 percent.[15]

The remaining continents have a similar deficit in water transport capacity relative to Europe. Like Africa, South America lacks inlets, and its major passable river, the Amazon, is in a sparsely populated rainforest that can be impenetrable to humans. Asia also has an enormous inland territory that lacks water passage, although China and India do contain valuable river transport and Southeast Asia a high ratio of coastline to land area. To sum, to Smith and later scholars, the accidental fact of Europe's shape has given it a huge advantage historically in transport costs, enabling it to trade, specialize, and grow more quickly.

Human-Made Geographical Barriers to Exchange. Two other aspects of geography that increase transport costs for less developed countries were shaped by human activity and not handed down by nature. First, because most wealthy countries are in the middle latitudes of the northern hemisphere, LDCs in the tropics and in the southern hemisphere are distant from these hubs of economic activity.[16] Their distance from major foreign markets acts as a tax on international trade, increasing the cost of exporting and importing. This distance tax makes it expensive to import the capital equipment needed to produce manufactured goods, and foreign consumers are also expected to pay the distance tax if these goods are exported. These added costs can make it difficult for distant countries to employ export-oriented growth strategies, as the East Asian Tigers did. Trading with nearby LDCs provides little relief, since poor neighbors have limited buying power and low-tech exports themselves. Gains from exchange occur when people and countries swap products that are very different from one another, not similar.

Second, some LDCs are landlocked, which proves to be a severe geographical disadvantage. Africa has fifteen landlocked countries, South America has two, and Asia has twelve, half of which are clustered in Central Asia. Landlocked countries have no ports, so they must incur the costs of transporting goods overland before they can be shipped elsewhere. Building a land transport infrastructure of rail and highways is far more expensive than exploiting an existing lake, ocean, or river. Even when overland infrastructure exists, land transport remains more expensive than water transport. Furthermore, landlocked countries face added costs because they are at the mercy of a neighbor or neighbors in their need to gain access to the sea. Neighbors, even friendly ones, charge tariffs or fees just to allow goods to pass through their countries. Unfriendly neighbors can make passage expensive or prohibitive, as can neighbors engaged in civil or external wars.[17]

Critique of Geographical Determinism

Critics of geographical explanations for underdevelopment accuse scholars such as Diamond and Sachs of adhering to **geographical determinism**, or attributing development outcomes entirely to inanimate factors and physical contexts beyond human control. The problem with the geography-is-destiny outlook is that it overlooks humanity's impressive ability to control its natural surroundings and to overcome the constraints that nature poses to economic advancement. After all, development is by definition the reshaping and harnessing of one's physical surroundings to increase economic productivity. This is achieved through activities such as extracting and burning fossil fuels, prevailing over gravity to achieve flight, preventing

infectious disease to delay the inevitability of death, adjusting microclimates with indoor heat and air conditioning, and increasing nature's yield of edible plants and animals. To most critics of geographical explanations, underdevelopment exists where humans have made decisions that thwart these discovered capacities to overcome natural barriers.

Critique of Jeffrey Sachs

These alleged weaknesses in geographical arguments are evident in critiques of Sachs's claim regarding tropical diseases. To scholars as varied as Marxists, dependency theorists, culturalists, and new institutional economists, tropical diseases remain widespread in parts of the developing world because of failures of human action (such as capitalist exploitation, bad governments, unproductive cultural traditions, and unprioritized health systems), not because of geographical fiat. From these views, the observed negative correlation between malarial prevalence and the economic growth rate is not because disease causes poverty, but because poverty causes disease. After all, disease burdens, even from tropical ones, are not outside the control of human agency.

For example, smallpox, the very disease that nearly wiped out the native population of the Americas, was completely eradicated through an organized global effort to distribute a vaccine in the 1970s. The incidence of tropical diseases for which there is no known vaccine, such as sleeping sickness and river blindness, has declined in many parts of the world due to greater human knowledge and action around treatment and prevention. Even rates of infection from malaria have declined in many tropical countries, such as Brazil and India, through human effort. Singapore, an island nation rife with malaria as recently as 1960, is today free of malaria and one of the five richest countries in the world.

A similar critique is levied against Sachs's claim that tropical countries are poor because of their inherently unproductive soils. The knowledge and technology now exists to make tropical lands more productive through new irrigation systems, fertilizers, seed types, and pesticides. In recent decades, many of these innovations were adopted with highly beneficial effects on food yields in Asia and Latin America. (Chapter 14 discusses this Green Revolution in greater detail.) According to new institutional economics, the problem for farmers in the tropics (and especially in Africa) lies in the humanly devised economic and political institutions that shape farmers' decisions. Institutional rules governing things such as property rights, market pricing, and investment create little incentive for a farmer to adopt new technologies since the farmer would see little personal gain from increased food yields.[18] In sum, bad institutions, not bad geography, may be the primary source of low agricultural productivity in the developing world.

As a final general critique of Sachs's case for a tropical disadvantage, Daron Acemoglu and James Robinson point out that the relationship between distance from the equator and economic prosperity has not always been positive. In fact, peoples of colder climes were once poorer than those in tropical ones. Prior to the arrival of the Europeans in the Western Hemisphere, the most advanced civilizations were in the tropics. The Aztecs (living in modern-day Mexican territory), Incas (Peru), and Maya (Guatemala and southern Mexico) were far more advanced than the indigenous communities of the United States, Canada, and Argentina. Since 1500, a great "reversal of fortune" has occurred, whereby populations in colder climates are now more affluent.[19] Acemoglu and Robinson conclude that it is a stretch to speak of a tropical disadvantage when the apparent disadvantage has emerged relatively recently in human history, not to mention that it appeared to be an advantage at one point.

Critique of Jared Diamond

Diamond paints history with an impressively broad brushstroke, but in doing so his geographical explanation is open to the charge that he misses a lot of nuance. Most importantly, the geographical factors he pinpoints as the major causes of global inequalities,

such as climate and the availability of plants and animals, are exceedingly slow to change. This makes them an unlikely candidate to explain the constantly shifting economic and social realities of human existence.

For example, Diamond's model cannot explain the rises and falls of different civilizations within the Eurasian supercontinent, the very landmass that had presumably endowed all of its peoples with an advantageous geographical context. As the second millennium opened in 1000 CE, the Chinese and Muslim civilizations were more advanced than that of Western Europe. The two non-Western cultures featured systems of centralized political order and were developing innovations such as modern mathematics (Middle East) and gunpowder and printing (China). Meanwhile, Western Europe was mired in the Dark Ages, lacking in organized states and responsible for few lasting inventions. By the sixteenth and seventeenth centuries, however, it was Western Europe that was conquering the New World and even other parts of Eurasia, and by 1800 it began an unprecedented economic advance that left behind the other two Eurasian civilizations. Given the three civilizations' shared Eurasian geographical inheritance and their similar latitudinal placement, Diamond's thesis provides little guidance as to why the Industrial Revolution began in the westernmost outpost of Eurasia. Only theories that incorporate human agency can seemingly do so.

Examples of rapid economic change, including the twentieth-century rises of countries such as Botswana, China, Japan, and South Korea, are perhaps even more damning of geographical arguments. The North and South Korea comparison is useful (as it was in Chapter 7). The two countries share a peninsula and a very similar geography, yet today South Korea's average income is seventeen times that of North Korea. South Korea's transformation and divergence from North Korea can only be explained by the differences in human action between the two countries.[20]

Finally, whereas Diamond's thesis struggles to explain economic change, it also overpredicts change in the rare instances that rapid shifts in geographical endowments did occur. Geographic factors usually change slowly if at all, but in rare instances they have shifted dramatically. These historical cases provide a natural experiment to test whether economic and social development responded in kind. In particular, if things such as cows, horses, rice, and wheat are the trigger for development, then the New World should have caught up to Europe when it adopted these geographical gifts after the European conquest. While adoption did take place throughout the Western Hemisphere, sustained development did not.[21]

Overcoming Distance

History shows that being distant from global trading epicenters is not a kiss of death for development, largely because transport costs are rarely so high as to make trade prohibitively expensive. Distance certainly adds to costs, but these costs rarely outweigh the gains, even for the most remote of countries. For example, long before container ships, computers, and air flight dramatically lowered the costs of international exchange, Argentina was able to develop into one of the world's wealthiest countries by exporting wool, wheat, and beef to the leading epicenter of the late 1800s, Europe. Today, being separated by an ocean does not prevent China and the United States from exchanging half a trillion dollars' worth of merchandise each year.

Being landlocked is also not fatal to development, as evidenced by several wealthy European countries, such as Austria, Czech Republic, Hungary, Luxembourg, Slovakia, and Switzerland. Moreover, given that only a minority of LDCs are landlocked, this is far from a general explanation for underdevelopment.

The Resource Curse

Another argument in which nature, and in this case geology, plays a significant role in shaping development is the **resource curse** hypothesis. According to its advocates, there is a paradoxical relationship between the amount of minerals and fossil fuels with which nature has endowed a country and that country's prosperity. Resource-rich countries, it seems, are surprisingly poor. In using the term "resources," the literature on the resource curse uses an intentionally narrow definition of the term. Arguments typically revolve around a country's endowment of minerals such as diamonds and uranium and fossil fuels such as coal, natural gas, and petroleum. These are sometimes collectively called subsoil assets or nonagricultural commodities. Water, wind, trees, and crops are also natural resources, but scholars within the resource curse tradition see something unique about minerals and fossil fuels, with petroleum receiving a particularly large amount of attention.

Many less developed countries have an abundance of mineral wealth and fossil fuel reserves. The African continent has rich deposits of some of the world's most desired minerals, such as diamonds, gold, silver, iron ore, uranium, and coltan. South America contains large reserves of copper, tin, and nickel, and the continent was Portugal's and Spain's treasure trove of gold and silver during the three centuries of colonial rule. Collectively, the vast majority of the world's oil and natural gas reserves belong to countries in Africa, the Middle East, and the former Soviet Union. By contrast, many twentieth-century development success stories, such as Japan and South Korea, are rather resource poor. Of the top ten countries in proven oil reserves, none of them is a developed one,[22] and Western Europe and the developed countries of East Asia have meager petroleum and mineral reserves. In fact, part of the motivation for the emergence of the resource curse argument was to understand why parts of East Asia developed before more resource-rich LDCs in Africa, Latin America, and the Middle East.

In principle, LDCs that have won this natural lottery for subsoil assets could use their bounty to their economic advantage, exchanging these exports for imports of consumer goods and capital equipment to make their economies more productive. Strangely, however, this simple formula for economic

Figure 13.3 The Relationship between Natural Resource Wealth and Economic Growth, 1980–2009

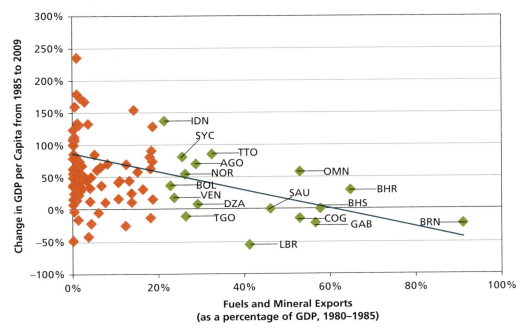

Source: Data compiled from the World Bank, World Development Indicators, http://data.worldbank.org/data-catalog/world-development-indicators.

Note: Resource rich countries are labeled.

growth and development rarely seems to work. Figure 13.3 shows a negative relationship between resource wealth (measured with mineral and fuel exports as a percentage of GDP in the early 1980s) and economic growth over the subsequent twenty-five years. On average, incomes in resource-rich countries increased by just a third during this time, while those in resource-poor ones increased by an average of 80 percent. Sachs and Andrew Warner have shown that this negative relationship existed in the two decades following 1970 as well.[23]

Causes of Underdevelopment: Natural Resources

According to the resource curse hypothesis, this counterintuitive negative relationship is more than just a coincidence. Scholars have produced a long list of reasons for why mineral and especially

oil wealth might be detrimental to long-term economic growth.

Dutch Disease and a Lack of Industry

Having large endowments of subsoil assets can make it difficult for economies to develop a manufacturing sector, a presumed necessity on the pathway to prosperity. **Dutch disease** is one way this can occur. A country with a valuable mineral or fuel export tends to have artificially high currency exchange rates because the international demand for its export drives up the cost of its currency. In turn, the overvalued currency disadvantages other domestic tradable goods sectors, many of which are manufacturing firms. Overvaluation makes their manufactured goods expensive to foreign buyers, and it makes competing imports cheap for domestic consumers. All told, the resource-rich country's industrial base faces a severe headwind—a lack of competitiveness in global markets—in building up its capacity.

Aside from this Dutch disease effect on exchange rates, a booming resource sector can attract investment and labor away from manufacturing firms. Investors flock to the sector because of its expected high returns, and workers seek out jobs in it because it offers relatively high wages. This incentive to grow the resource sector at the expense of industry can weigh on development in various ways. Extraction of certain kinds of resources, namely oil and gas, creates relatively few jobs. Once a pump and well are built, they operate with only minimal need for human oversight and maintenance. Moreover, what jobs are on offer in a resource sector tend to be less skill-intensive than those in industry, so citizens in a resource-rich economy have less incentive to become educated.[24]

Large endowments of nonagricultural commodities can also be detrimental to economies for the reasons that made structuralists and dependency theorists skeptical of the periphery's ability to achieve industrial growth through primary-product exports. (See Chapter 5.) Although hotly debated, natural resources may be subject to a declining terms of trade problem: steadily decreasing prices relative to those on manufactured goods. The international prices of mineral and fossil fuel exports also seem to be more volatile than those for manufactured luxury items.[25] Resource-rich countries thus have volatile economies since their fate is heavily contingent on the international supply and demand of one commodity. The instability discourages forward planning and thus investment throughout the economy. Moreover, dependency theorists have pointed out that resource sectors tend to exist as economic enclaves. In resource-rich LDCs, minerals and fossil fuels are extracted from underground and then almost immediately shipped abroad, producing little direct benefit or linkage to industry or the rest of the economy. For example, Iran and Nigeria have minimal capacity to transform crude oil into gasoline. When much of the extraction is carried out by foreign-owned firms,

as is often the case in poor LDCs, a good deal of the profits then accrue to foreigners.

Effects on Politics

Another element of the resource curse argument is that natural resource wealth creates perverse temptations for political leaders, resulting in poor governance in resource-rich countries. Revenues from natural resource sales are too tempting of an asset for politicians to ignore. In LDCs, the vast majority of petroleum and natural gas firms are state owned, having undergone a wave of nationalizations in the 1950s and 1960s. According to critics, this gives politicians the chance to enrich themselves by dipping into the revenue streams of the state-owned firms. In fact, governments in oil-rich countries may use their state-owned firms to keep oil contracts and revenues concealed from public view, fostering an atmosphere in which corruption thrives.[26]

A related argument holds that oil promotes authoritarian government. When a mining or petroleum firm is state owned, it creates a form of nontax revenue for the government that excuses politicians from being responsible leaders. Citizens can receive state benefits without having to pay taxes at a commensurate level, so they are more indifferent to or tolerant of government abuse and autocracy.[27] Dictators in oil-rich countries also have an added revenue stream with which to appease potentially discontent citizens, thus prolonging their time in office.

Finally, political scientist Michael Ross argues that resource wealth (and again petroleum in particular) disempowers women. In many middle-income countries, the burgeoning industrial sector pulls women into the workforce to take factory jobs. For example, most of the workers in textile, garment, and electronics factories worldwide are female. Since resource-rich countries do not have such jobs available (due to Dutch disease and other problems), many women stay out of the workforce entirely. This keeps them politically uninvolved, perpetuating traditional gender roles and discrimination in society and the law. Ross goes so far as to argue that it is oil, and not Islam, that makes gender inequalities so deep in the Middle East.

Critique: A Resource Blessing?

These theories and initial findings in support of the resource curse are suggestive, but evidence and theory to support the claim are highly mixed. It is important to point out that the resource curse is not a general theory of development, meaning that it does not provide an accurate answer in most cases to the question of why some countries are rich and others are poor. The vast majority of the world's poorest countries, such as Afghanistan, Bangladesh, Benin, Malawi, Nicaragua, and Tanzania, have little to no income from minerals or fuels extraction. Other factors have clearly caused their poverty. Most of the world's oil-rich countries, such as Iran, Libya, Russia, and Venezuela, are at middle to high levels of human development.

Moreover, the observation that wealthy and fast-growing countries have small resource endowments relative to GDP size is, as always, a correlation that does not prove cause and effect. Nonagricultural commodities may comprise a small share of these countries' economies because they have successfully developed large nonresource sectors for reasons (such as good institutions or the right culture) that have little to do with their lack of subsoil assets. Poor countries without well-developed industrial and service sectors have no choice but to rely heavily on whatever subsoil assets they have on hand, making the resource sector as a share of GDP large even if this is not indicative of huge resource endowments. Economist Paul Collier reports that the value of known subsoil assets in high-income countries is US$114,000 per square kilometer. In contrast, the value in Africa is only US$23,000, and in Asia and South America the average is only US$29,000. In other words, many LDCs only seem rich in subsoil assets because they are poor in other assets.[28] This gives the appearance of correlation between resource endowments and affluence, but the cause and effect relationship is far from that posited by scholars within the resource curse tradition.

These figures on subsoil assets suggest that resource endowments may even be a blessing. After all, the West tapped into fossil fuels, most of them domestically sourced, to power its industrialization drive in the 1800s rather than succumbing to some kind of resource curse. For example, Britain's status as the midwife of the Industrial Revolution is attributed by many to its voluminous and easily extractable coal reserves.[29] Similarly, the United States has been described as having "rich deposits of the key ingredients for ferrous metallurgy; plenty of wood and coal for fuel . . .; an abundance of petroleum . . .; copper ores in quantity."[30] Moreover, growth despite resource abundance is not the sole reserve of the West. Recent developers Botswana (diamonds) and Chile (copper) successfully harnessed their subsoil assets to partially fuel their status as two of the fastest-growing economies in the world over the last four decades.

The reasons for the mixed evidence could lie in a breakdown in the logical foundations of the resource curse argument. Dutch disease is not an inevitable by-product of resource-exporting booms. Evidence suggests that such booms draw in otherwise idle or underemployed labor rather than drawing labor away from industry. They also attract foreign capital, offsetting domestic-capital shortages of investment funds.[31] Moreover, countries can use their resource bounties to invest in industrial competitiveness, offsetting the effects of exchange rate appreciation.

Besides these problems with the Dutch disease claim, other logical underpinnings such as the declining terms of trade argument are empirically suspect (as described in Chapter 5). The assertion that a large petroleum sector is an enclave that has few effects on the domestic economy is hard to square with the argument that it simultaneously does everything from destroying industries to keeping women out of the labor force. Finally, claims about resource bounties and deteriorating governance are also questioned. Politicians have often dipped into state treasuries to illicitly enrich themselves and their supporters, so the reason why specifically resource-generated revenues heighten this temptation remains unclear.

IS GEOGRAPHY DESTINY IN MEXICO?

By 1500, the Aztec Empire, whose political capital was in today's Mexico City, was one of the two most advanced civilizations in the Western Hemisphere. (The Incan Empire of the Andes was the other.) Its economic achievements had far surpassed those of the native communities to its north in what is now the United States. The Aztecs' architectural and artistic achievements rivaled those of any contemporaneous world civilization in their sophistication, even wowing many of the European conquistadors. Their empire encompassed much of Mesoamerica and contained 25 million people on the eve of the Spanish arrival. Over the subsequent 500 years, however, the Mexican colony (known as New Spain, 1521–1821) and the independent state of Mexico (1821–present) lost ground. At the time of its independence, Mexico's average income was about half that of its colonizer Spain, and the ratio is about the same today. Why was Mexico so easily conquered and then left behind economically by Spain? Table 13.1 gives some points of comparison between Mexico and its former metropole.

Table 13.1 Development Comparison: Mexico and Spain		
Indicator	**Mexico**	**Spain**
GDP per capita at PPP	US$11,684	US$26,767
Human Development Index	.770	.878
Arable land (percentage of total land)	13 percent	25 percent
Exports to the United States (as percentage of all exports)	80 percent	4 percent
Number of years with a democracy since 1800	16	66

Source: Data on GDP per capita at PPP and Human Development Index compiled from Gapminder, www.gapminder.org; arable land from the World Bank, World Development Indicators, http://data.worldbank.org/data-catalog/world-development-indicators; exports to the United States from UN Comtrade, http://comtrade.un.org/; years with a democracy from Center for Systemic Peace, Polity IV, www.systemicpeace.org/polity/polity4.htm.

The Natural World: Mexico's Geographical Disadvantages

According to a variety of theories on geography and underdevelopment, Mexico has a difficult natural context that has slowed the pace of human development ever since the Spaniards arrived. In this sense, it provides a nice illustration of Diamond's and Sachs' arguments as well as the resource curse hypothesis.

Domesticable Animals and Plants. The Aztec civilization was a house of cards that was easily toppled when it was forced to face the advantages with which nature had endowed the Europeans. The only large domesticated mammal in the entire Western hemisphere was the llama. Llamas, however, resided only in the highlands of the Andes, more than 2,000 miles away from the Aztec capital. They were never transported northward to Mesoamerica because it would have required passage through a completely new climate zone: the humid, sea-level climate of Central America. As a result, the Aztecs were left to domesticate much smaller animals such as

A painting depicts captured Aztec king Montezuma (upper right) pleading with his subjects to surrender to his Spanish captors. Some scholars argue that it was certain geographical disadvantages of the European continent that enabled its conquistadors to overtake and colonize the indigenous populations of the New World.

dogs, turkeys, and ducks. Needless to say, none of these were useful in their battles against the horsebacked Spaniards.

Moreover, the lack of contact with large land mammals left the Aztecs highly vulnerable to animal-borne diseases, the root cause of their decimation from smallpox after the Spaniards arrived. The unavailability of large animals also made for a relatively protein-poor diet. This was exacerbated by the fact that the most commonly eaten food staples of Eurasia, wheat and barley, did not exist in Mesoamerica. In the end, the mighty Aztec army fell surprisingly easily to the small band of Spanish conquerors, and most of

the empire's achievements, not to mention its very population, withered away. The conquest initiated an oppressive colonization that stifled the territory's remaining people and economy for three centuries.

Climate. Even into the modern era, Mexico's geography may have slowed its economic and social development. Mexico has three major climate zones: a desert in the North, forested tropics in the south, and rugged mountains and plateaus in the center. The first two sit at opposite climatic extremes, yet both feature low agricultural productivity. Mexico's desert is too dry and its tropical forests too wet

IS GEOGRAPHY DESTINY IN MEXICO?

for high crop yields. Its central highlands are more temperate with more fertile soils, yet here economic growth can be hampered by high transport costs, as rugged terrain and a complete lack of major internal waterways make economic exchange over even moderate distances expensive. Mexico has also been host to numerous tropical diseases, including malaria, which was a threat throughout most of the country until the last few decades. Because its tropical lowland coasts have historically had a high disease burden, they have been sparsely populated, further distancing individuals from the sea and thus raising the costs of transport. Perhaps for these reasons, there is a strong correlation between distance from the equator and prosperity within Mexico. Its northern half is more affluent than its southern half.

The Oil Curse. Finally, Mexico may have succumbed to a resource curse when it struck oil in the early 1900s. Mexican president Lázaro Cárdenas famously nationalized all of the country's petroleum reserves and facilities in 1938, and Petróleos de Mexico (PEMEX) remains a state-owned monopoly to this day. Over those decades, PEMEX has provided an enormous revenue stream for politicians to tap. Between 1960 and 2006 Mexico ranked fourteenth worldwide in oil income per capita.[32] The Institutional Revolutionary Party (PRI) was particularly adept at using these revenues to its political advantage, sustaining an authoritarian system throughout most of the twentieth century. By showering voters with state benefits, the PRI was able to remain the country's ruling party for seventy-one years.

* * *

This geography-as-destiny argument has some obvious shortcomings. Spain's advantage in domesticable plants and animals before 1500 may explain why it so easily conquered the Aztecs, but it cannot account for subsequent economic

trajectories. In 1700, New Spain began its third century under colonial rule with a GDP per capita that was nearly equivalent to that of the thirteen British colonies to its north and about 70 percent of that in Western Europe.[33] A geographical argument could construe this near parity with Europe and the American colonies as resulting from the boost New Spain received from finally being able to benefit from wheat, cows, and horses. It cannot explain, however, why Mexico's average income today is less than one-third that in the United States and Western Europe. Calling forth Mexico's tropical disadvantage and rough terrain fails to account for why the parity ever existed in the first place, not to mention the fact that Mexico had the same GDP per capita as Spain as recently as 1960.[34] In short, the amount of economic change that has occurred undermines a geographical argument and suggests that other factors must be invoked to explain Mexico's underdevelopment. Besides, Mexico's proximity to the United States and the low costs of trade this entails could have just as easily made its geography a net advantage, rather than a disadvantage.

The West: Colonial and Postcolonial Exploitation

A large body of research on Mexico's political and economic institutions concludes that it was humans, not nature, that caused Mexico to fall behind Europe and the United States. The institutions established by Westerners during the colonial era are seen as being particularly pernicious. Spain conquered and colonized Mexico with the overriding goal of extracting resources (mainly gold and silver) from the land and taxes from its people. A small Spanish elite governed the colony and, with the blessing of the crown back home, established a variety of institutions that subjugated the native population. One was the *encomienda* system, whereby the crown granted to numerous conquistadores the right to extract tribute from all natives residing in a delineated tract of land. *Encomienda* rights were often granted to a Spaniard along with ownership of the tract, known as a *hacienda*, some of which were as large as modern-day Mexican states. Although natives could not be owned as slaves, the *encomienda* amounted to a system of forced labor since many natives had to spend the bulk of their working lives growing the crops demanded by their *encomendero*.

These economic and political institutions laid down by the Spanish colonizers amounted to much more than just theft from a native population already devastated by disease. They also had negative effects that long outlived colonialism, such as inequalities in land distribution, low wages for manual labor, racial and class hierarchy, authoritarian rule, and weak incentives to produce. For example, for centuries after the *encomienda* system and its legal successors were abolished in the 1600s, its spirit lived on through the practice of debt peonage. Wealthy landowners would force workers into their debt (through means such as giving them wage advances or by requiring them to pay off their ancestors' debt) and then require them to work indefinitely on the *hacienda* to pay it off. As another example, much of Mexico's rural population remained landless long after independence in 1821. In 1900, just 3 percent of rural Mexican families owned their land, as compared to 75 percent in the United States.[35] Both of these realities provided Mexico's rural majority with weak incentives to invest and be highly productive.

Moreover, the West was not done tormenting Mexico when the Spanish left. Far from posing an opportunity, Mexico's proximity to the United States may very well be the cause of its problems. Most notoriously, by the end of the Mexican-American War in 1848, the United States had annexed half of Mexico's territory, including most of what is today the southwestern United States. Soon thereafter, the United States invested heavily in Mexico, exploiting its mineral wealth and farmland under the autocratic regime of Porfirio Díaz (1876–1910). Today, due in part to the North American Free Trade Agreement (NAFTA), 80 percent of Mexico's exports go to the United States, a fact that caused the Mexican economy to also languish when the United States' one did after 2007. Mexico is even highly reliant on the United States for its jobs. Walmart is the biggest private-sector employer in Mexico,[36] and half of its foreign direct investment comes from the United States. Foreign investors seek to exploit the huge gap in manufacturing wages between the two. All told, Mexico's heavy dependence on the United States economy may be a source of its underdevelopment.

The South: Instability and Autocracy

Not all analysts focused on human agency attribute Mexico's long-running economic travails to the West. Plenty of blame could be placed on Mexico's own political leaders. In its first century of independence, Mexico was a picture of political instability and autocracy. After just forty years of independence, Mexico had had around fifty presidencies, including eleven different stints by one man, General Antonio López de Santa Anna. These were followed by various experiments in rule by regents, a foreign emperor, and (once again) presidents. After 1884, a twenty-seven-year tenure by Díaz provided a temporary reprieve from the instability but not from the autocracy. Díaz's reign ended in 1910 at the outbreak of the Mexican Revolution, at one point of which Mexico witnessed three different presidents in one day.

Clearly, legal codes on leadership succession were irrelevant: Virtually all of these turnovers in power occurred via force. Amidst the political chaos and

IS GEOGRAPHY DESTINY IN MEXICO?

rule by force, Mexican leaders had little authority or will to create competitive free markets and a unified national system of secure property rights for the masses. On the contrary, throughout the nineteenth century, it was common for government to seize land that was communally owned by indigenous peoples, and by 1910 a mere two banks held the majority of Mexico's banking assets.[37]

By the 1930s, once the dust settled from the revolution, a new political system emerged that was certainly more stable than its predecessors. Like clockwork, the president changed only once every six years for decades. The system, however, was authoritarian, ruled by a single party. The ruling PRI did little to create fairer economic institutions that would encourage the masses to invest and produce. For example, in the 1930s, the government grouped peasants into communal farms known as *ejidos*. While this was carried out in the name of land redistribution, the *ejido* system continued to deny peasants the right to own their plots. During that same decade, Cárdenas' nationalization of petroleum interests initiated a wave of increasing state ownership elsewhere in the Mexican economy. Similarly, through the 1970s, the government pursued a policy of import substitution industrialization that blocked its consumers' access to global markets. Eventually, the *ejido* program, the nationalizations, and the protectionist policies were reversed or disbanded in the 1980s and 1990s. Today, Mexico is a democracy, as the PRI finally lost a presidential election in 2000. Even so, Mexico still struggles to enforce rights and regulations in its huge informal sector, which, by some estimates, employs over 50 percent of the workforce.[38] Monopolies also remain in many sectors, a leftover from days when politicians granted favors to business cronies.

***

What does Mexico's future hold? Its political system is seemingly more stable and democratic than ever before. It continues to hold periodic elections and alternations in power are now commonplace. Geography, however, has thrown Mexico one more curveball: drug cartel violence. Lying to the immediate south of the world's largest consumer of illegal narcotics, Mexico is now the leading corridor for drug trafficking. Traffickers have infiltrated the country's political system, buying their impunity from politicians and judges. Innocent citizens are frequent victims of violence as they are caught in the crossfire of cartel disputes. The widespread insecurity also wreaks havoc on the economy. Whether the drug-related violence will cause permanent reversals of Mexico's recent institutional advances remains to be seen.

Thinking Critically about Development

- Is it fair to critique Diamond for his inability to explain Mexico's economic trajectory after 1500? Is Diamond's argument even meant to explain global inequalities so long after the Mexican conquest?

- If, as some critics say, development is entirely a product of human agency, then what explains the strong correlation between development and climate? In other words, why does human agency seem to produce better outcomes far from the equator than near the equator?

- One of the arguments in this case study attributes Mexico's relative poverty to its economic engagement with the United States, while the other attributes it to its lack of engagement from 1940 to 1980. Which has more merit, or can both be right?

Key Terms

agricultural surplus,
p. 314

Dutch disease, p. 321

geographical determinism,
p. 318

malaria, p. 312

resource curse, p. 320

transport costs, p. 317

tropical disease, p. 312

 # Suggested Readings

Acemoglu, Daron, Simon Johnson, and James A. Robinson. "Reversal of Fortune: Geography and Development in the Making of the Modern World Income Distribution." *Quarterly Journal of Economics* 117, no. 4 (2002): 1231–1294.

Bloom, David E., and Jeffrey Sachs. "Geography, Demography, and Economic Growth in Africa." *Brookings Papers on Economic Activity* 1998, no. 2 (1998) 207–295.

Diamond, Jared. *Guns, Germs, and Steel: The Fates of Human Societies*. New York: W. W. Norton, 1997.

Gallup, John L., Alejandro Gaviria, and Eduardo Lora. *Is Geography Destiny? Lessons from Latin America*. Stanford, CA: Stanford University Press, 2003.

Ross, Michael L. *The Oil Curse: How Petroleum Wealth Shapes the Development of Nations*. Princeton, NJ: Princeton University Press, 2012.

 # Web Resources

Climate Zone Climates of the World, www.climate-zone.com/

Food and Agricultural Organization of the United Nations Statistics, FAOSTAT, http://faostat3.fao.org/home/index.html

Socioeconomic Data and Applications Center, http://sedac.ciesin.columbia.edu/

World Health Organization, Tropical Disease, www.who.int/topics/tropical_diseases/en/

A woman in Tehran, Iran, wears a protective mask to protect her lungs from air pollution. Tehran has some of the dirtiest skies of any city in the world, and public officials have closed schools on days when going outside is particularly unsafe.

Environmental Change and Development

Kanang feels angry and hopeless. As a forty-five-year-old member of the Dayak indigenous ethnic group, which inhabits the interior of Borneo in Indonesia, he feels that his people's well-being and way of life are under threat. Located in the world's third-largest tropical rainforest, his village faces encroachment by two businesses that are seeking to log nearby land and establish palm oil plantations on the newly cleared sites. Palm oil cultivation has become a lucrative enterprise for Borneo, partially fueling Indonesia's economic rise, but it has human and environmental costs. Kanang and many other Dayaks depend on the surrounding forest for their livelihood, so they treat it in a sustainable way. The potential conversion of the land into plantations threatens this symbiotic relationship.

Kanang is now involved in an organized effort led by his tribal chief to stop the proposed land-use change, but he is pessimistic. The businesses' intentions are illegal, since the Indonesian government has not granted them a license for the change. In practice, however, many businesses simply proceed with deforestation anyway. They face little risk of prosecution because of the inefficient and corrupt judicial institutions. Many officials knowingly overlook illegal deforestation. Moreover, profits from the global demand for palm oil products are too tempting to pass up. Kanang attends protest meetings and has complained to local media, but in many ways he feels as if he is just going through the motions.

Often, one of the first things that Western visitors to a less developed country notice is the country's environmental problems. Tap water is not to be trusted. Many rivers and creeks are fetid, and open sewage can be a common sight. Automobile exhaust is darker, urban air noticeably greyer, and litter more visible. As exemplified by Kanang's story, ongoing deforestation may also be more common. This chapter takes up the topic of poor environmental quality in LDCs. **Environmental quality** is the ability of a natural context to continuously supply ecological services such as sufficient quantities of clean water and air, unspoiled places of natural beauty, natural resources for eventual human consumption, biodiversity, and favorable climatic, soil, and water conditions for productive agriculture and fishing.

Experts place the various instances of poor environmental quality into three categories: household, communal, and global. Household ones affect individuals in their homes and domestic life, and they generally result from economic scarcity. The most common are unclean water and improper sanitation. Since these were discussed at length in Chapter 2, they do not receive much attention in this chapter. Instead, the first half of this chapter discusses communal environmental problems, or ones that affect entire communities, such as the degradation of water sources, outdoor air, and land. The second half of the chapter examines an environmental issue of global import: anthropogenic climate change.

This chapter also considers how human-induced environmental change shapes development. In contrast to Chapter 13, which looked at how relatively immutable aspects of the natural environment shape development outcomes, this one focuses on instances where nature bends to human discretion. Human activities can have an enormous, and often detrimental, influence on nature, and this in turn can slow or even reverse development. Previous chapters have looked for causes of underdevelopment in the past and the present: colonialism, contemporary political institutions, and so on. This final chapter takes a different perspective by looking at how human-caused environmental damage may constrain development in the future.

Communal Environmental Problems

Environmental assets such as freshwater, trees, clean air, productive land, and minerals are called **natural capital** since they are crucial to

ecosystem functioning and have amenity value that comes from human enjoyment of their use. Many are also necessary inputs to economic production. Natural capital is more prone to depletion and exhaustion than human and physical capital because, in its natural state, it is typically in the form of a **common pool resource**. A common pool resource is one that all interested parties can benefit from because no one prevents them from using it. This makes it vulnerable to the **tragedy of the commons** problem: exhaustion because individuals who benefit from the resource have little incentive to use it sustainably.[1] A standard example is a lake in which anglers can fish at their own discretion. Any single angler benefits from catching as many fish as he or she can. However, since all nearby anglers act in this same way, a lake with no restrictions on fishing will eventually become emptied of its fish and all anglers will end up poorer.

In technical terms, the degradation of natural capital through economic activity is a **negative externality**, which is the cost incurred by third parties from economic exchange between a buyer and seller. For example, when a consumer buys a good from a factory, the air and water pollution the factory emitted in producing the good is a negative externality. That is, it is a cost absorbed by the entire community from the transaction between the consumer and the factory. This section discusses some communal externalities that are associated with the degradation of natural capital, and the next two subsections consider how they affect development.

Degradation of Natural Capital

Freshwater, air, and land are the three most important examples of natural capital. Humans have degraded these environmental assets in a variety of ways, creating negative externalities for their communities.

Freshwater Consumption and Pollution. Freshwater resources are not equally distributed around the world. By one estimate, around 700 million people in forty-three countries live in areas facing periodic or permanent water shortages.[2] Almost all are in the developing world (the Middle East; northern, eastern, and southern Africa; northern China; Central Asia; scattered parts of South America; and western India). These areas are naturally inclined to scarcity due to the dryness of their climates, yet human activities exacerbate this scarcity by contributing to water depletion, or the lowering of the supply of available water. Two main types of human activities cause water depletion: consumption and pollution.

The leading human-based cause of water depletion is water consumption, which is the permanent loss of water volume from a natural source due to human usage. Water consumption occurs when the amount of water withdrawn from a source exceeds the amount that is replenished by precipitation or human intervention. In the developing world, about 80 percent of all water withdrawal is for agricultural purposes, with 10 percent going to industry and another 10 percent to household use. Most water is withdrawn from **aquifers**, the underground basins that hold over 90 percent of the globe's available freshwater.[3] A borehole with a simple pump, now widely available in many LDCs, can be used to draw this groundwater up to the surface, and the practice occurs in many parts of the world at rates that are faster than nature's ability to refill the aquifers. Throughout places such as China, India, and Mexico City, groundwater, once plentiful just ten feet below ground, has receded to hundreds of feet down. Moreover, lakes and rivers have also seen diminished volumes due to water consumption. For example, China's Yellow River bed does not flow for several months out of the year due largely to human water consumption.

Water pollution is a second primary contributor to physical water scarcity. In most LDCs, the leading water contaminant is human waste due to the dumping of raw sewage into freshwater sources. Whereas developed countries tend to treat wastewater before returning it to a source, in most LDCs less than 20 percent of sewage is treated before being dumped into rivers, lakes, reservoirs, and oceans. A number of other water pollutants are common. Industrial effluent, which is the liquid waste created through many manufacturing processes, is often dumped into water sources, filling them with lead, mercury, and cadmium. Household garbage is also common. Runoff from farmland and waste dumps can also carry fertilizers, pesticides, cleaning detergents, and other chemicals into aquifers and other sources. Finally, as aquifers empty, their waters become saltier and more contaminated with harmful toxins such as arsenic. The most evident effects of pollution in highly contaminated rivers such as India's Ganges can be seen and smelled by passersby, but less visible is the proliferation of dangerous microbial pathogens or the demise of aquatic species due to lack of oxygen. For example, some rivers in Malaysia and Thailand contain between 30 to 100 times the number of pathogens that is deemed minimally unsafe for human health.[4]

Air Pollution. Unlike freshwater, air is not subject to withdrawal and consumption, but it is subject to degradation through pollution. In many middle-income countries, outdoor air pollution is a major problem. Suspended particulate matter such as sulfur dioxide and carbon monoxide and air toxins such as lead and diesel grey the urban skies in many countries that have a critical mass of vehicles and factories. The leading contributor to urban air pollution is typically motor vehicles, which tend to lack adequate emissions control devices in LDCs. Industry is the second-leading contributor to outdoor air pollution, and power plants are a top industrial polluter in countries that burn coal to generate much of their electricity. Outdoor air pollution is now a major problem throughout the developing world, as an estimated one-fifth of humanity resides in cities with air that is unsafe for human health. Cancer, lung infections, and asthma are common consequences, and lead from vehicular emissions can cause further woes such as stunted brain and physical development in children.

A major household environmental problem not mentioned in Chapter 2 is indoor air pollution, which is widespread in low-income countries and rural parts of middle-income ones. Poor families who lack access to gas or electricity typically collect nearby biomass such as wood or animal dung to heat their homes and cook. The burning of these fuels gives off smoke and particulate matter that is harmful to human health, weakening immune systems and causing such maladies as acute respiratory infections, lung cancer, and carbon monoxide poisoning. Worldwide, an estimated 2.6 billion people lack clean-burning cooking fuels,[5] and more than 5,000 deaths each day are linked to indoor air pollution.[6] At this rate, it is more deadly than malaria.

Land Degradation. Human activities are also contributing to the degradation of natural lands in LDCs. The most dramatic case is **deforestation**, which is the permanent removal of trees from wooded areas. Yearly, an estimated 1 percent of the globe's tropical forest area is felled, virtually all of it in the developing world. Deforestation occurs for two reasons: land-use changes (usually to convert forestland to pasture or cropland) and the harvesting of forest resources (often the trees themselves). In much of Africa and Asia, the removal of most trees occurs to provide household fuel and clear land for subsistence agriculture. In Latin America and Southeast Asia, most deforestation is carried out for market purposes such as cattle ranching, commercial agriculture, and logging. Because of the vastness and commercial potential of their rainforests, Brazil and Indonesia experience the greatest amount of deforestation each year.[7] Map 14.1 shows in red the parts of the world undergoing the most rapid rates of deforestation.

Deforestation has negative communal and global consequences. For the immediate community, it leads to soil erosion and a dryer ecosystem. Trees keep soils intact and rich in nutrients by providing a layer of protection from wind and water erosion, and they circulate water from underground into the atmosphere, increasing precipitation. For these reasons, crop yields on newly deforested land usually decline after just a few years. Deforestation also has negative consequences for the 400 million people, many of them indigenous ones like Kanang, that live in and around forests and rely on them for food, medicine, shelter, and other purposes. For example, many indigenous residents of Brazil's Amazon rainforest make their living extracting sap in a sustainable way from rubber trees, but their way of life is threatened by deforestation. As for global consequences, an estimated 20 percent of greenhouse gas emissions, the root cause of climate change, are from deforestation. This is far more than the world's entire vehicular fleet. Forests are known as carbon sinks because they extract carbon dioxide from the air and hold it. Burning them releases the carbon dioxide into the atmosphere.

Deforestation is not the only form of land degradation. The excessive irrigation of soils can cause waterlogging and salinization, and withdrawals of groundwater can dry them out. Livestock production can cause overgrazing. At its most extreme, overexploitation of land contributes to desertification, turning lush ecosystems into arid deserts (See Map 14.1.).

Why Communal Environmental Problems Are Worse in LDCs

Communal environmental problems tend to be most severe in the developing world and, more specifically, in middle-income countries. On average, the extent of these problems follow the environmental Kuznets curve (EKC) pattern introduced in Chapter 3. Their severity rises as economic

Map 14.1 ■ ■ ■ Deforestation Hot Spots

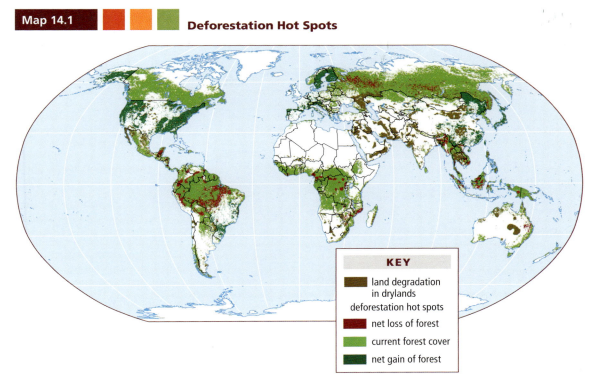

KEY

- land degradation in drylands
- deforestation hot spots
- net loss of forest
- current forest cover
- net gain of forest

Source: Millennium Ecosystem Assessment, "Locations Reported by Various Studies as Undergoing High Rates of Land Cover Change in the Past Few Decades," cartographer/designer: Philippe Rekacewicz, Emmanuelle Bournay, 2007, UNEP/GRID-Arendal, www.millenniumassessment.org/en/GraphicResources.aspx.

development occurs in low-income countries, and it peaks in middle-income countries before falling as development proceeds from middle- to high-income status. To illustrate, Table 14.1 lists eight of the cities with the world's worst air quality, as measured by their concentration of suspended particulate matter and sulfur dioxide. All of them are in middle-income countries. As a point of comparison, the table also shows figures for one city (Los Angeles) in a high-income country and one (Accra) in a low-income country.

It is straightforward to see why there needs to be a minimum level of development for communal environmental problems to exist: vehicles, industry, water pumps, and chainsaws all need to be on offer. Yet why are communities in LDCs less able to quell these problems than those in high-income countries?

Household and Government Priorities. For impoverished households, states, and societies, concerns about environmental quality often take a back seat to questions of cost and convenience. With many activities, the environmentally sustainable way to proceed is an expensive luxury or completely unavailable, so the poor become agents (as well as victims) of environmental degradation.[8] Examples are plentiful. Poor rural residents chop down nearby trees to cook meals since modern ovens are unaffordable or unavailable. Cash-strapped governments dump raw sewage into rivers because treating wastewater prior

Table 14.1 — Air Pollution in Ten Major Cities

City	Suspended Particulate Matter*	Sulfur Dioxide*
Cairo, Egypt	169	69
Delhi, India	150	24
Kolkata, India	129	49
Tianjin, China	125	82
Guiyang, China	70	424
Chongqing, China	123	340
Taiyuan, China	88	211
Tehran, Iran	58	209
Accra, Ghana	33	NA
Los Angeles, USA	34	9

Source: Data compiled from the World Bank, 2007 World Development Indicators, Table 3.13 Air Pollution, April 1, 2007, http://siteresources.worldbank .org/DATASTATISTICS/Resources/table3_13.pdf, 174–175.

* Micrograms per cubic meter.

in alternative energy sources. (Developed countries also have subsidies that are not environmentally sound, such as some of those offered to farmers and oil interests, but as a share of GDP they tend to be higher in developing countries.)

Policy Enforcement. Even when a government does have environmentalist intentions, it is less likely to have the capacity to enforce regulations. Underpaid security personnel, corrupt and inefficient court systems, understaffed tax collection agencies, and poor infrastructure are institutional realities of many LDCs. These can make it difficult for their governments to prevent firms from dumping effluent, citizens from littering, and ranchers from cutting down forests. In Brazil, an estimated 80 percent of deforestation activities in the Amazon rainforest are illegal, with many loggers using faked permits and cutting trees in remote areas where arms of the state are less likely to discover them.[9]

to dumping would divert resources from other fiscal priorities. Buyers and regulators choose dirty fuels and low-quality catalytic converters to make gasoline and automobiles less expensive.

Furthermore, many governments in LDCs take an intentional "grow first, clean up later" approach precisely because of the relative poverty of their citizens. Environmental standards are often more lax because leaders do not want tight regulations to slow gains in economic productivity. One notorious example of this is the **subsidies** that many governments offer on energy products and irrigation water in the name of boosting economic growth. For example, the governments of Iran, Nigeria, Venezuela, and other LDCs keep the consumer price of gasoline artificially low. Venezuelans pay the equivalent of about US$1.00 to fill up their gas tanks. Many other countries, including China and India, subsidize electricity in the name of development and consumer welfare. The underpricing encourages excessive consumption of fossil fuels and discourages investment

Furthermore, as a consequence of these governance and institutional problems, property rights over environmental assets in many LDCs are insecure. As a result, users are apt to treat the assets like a common pool resource, exhausting them through overuse. Many economists argue that a third party, often the state, needs to enforce property rights, quotas, or licensing to effectively exclude some potential users or limit current users from overexploiting a common pool resource. For example, locals living in a forest who have well-protected ownership rights to the land may treat it more sustainably since the rights effectively make them more forward thinking about their asset. In sum, advocates of property rights argue that, where such rights and other regulations against overuse are poorly enforced, environmental degradation and resource exhaustion are more likely to occur.

Globalization. Economic globalization is also often given as a reason why environmental quality is lower in LDCs than in high-income countries. Agriculture, mining, and manufacturing are more taxing for the environment than the service sector. Globalization has created an international economic system in which much of the activity in these dirtier sectors occurs in the developing world. Rich countries still consume products made in these sectors, but they are now able to import them from thousands of miles away and thus effectively offshore the negative environmental consequences. Critics of globalization argue that it is hypocritical for wealthy countries to tout their higher environmental standards when they continue to consume environmentally taxing products that are simply made elsewhere. Globalization may have turned some LDCs into what critics call "pollution havens" that use their relaxed environmental regulations as a carrot to attract foreign investors.

Fertility and Economic Development. Finally, developing countries tend to have greater fertility and population growth. Every year, the world adds an extra 70 million people, the vast majority of them in the developing world. This, coupled with the rapid economic growth in many LDCs, has dramatically increased demand for land, water, and the technologies that produce air pollutants. The heightened rate of water consumption is one example. Worldwide, water withdrawals have tripled in the last fifty years, with almost the entirety of this increase occurring in LDCs.[10] Population growth has been a partial driver of this trend, but economic growth in LDCs has increased per-person demand by giving individuals more water-intensive consumer tastes. Ever-richer citizens demand increasing quantities of meat and manufactured goods, both of which require more water to produce than the commodities that the indigent tend to consume.

Causes of Underdevelopment: A Malthusian Trap

Many observers see communal environmental problems and the loss of natural capital to be a threat to **sustainable development**. Sustainable development is "development that satisfies the needs of the present without compromising the ability of future generations to meet their own needs."[11] Thomas Malthus, a British minister and scholar writing in 1798 when the Industrial Revolution was in its infancy, believed that poverty and mass starvation were inescapable features of human existence because of environmental constraints. To Malthus, economic progress would always be short-lived because it would be accompanied by excessive population growth. Population size, he argued, increased geometrically (1, 2, 4, 8, 16 . . .), while the amount of food would increase only linearly (1, 2, 3, 4, 5 . . .) due to the finiteness of arable land. In other words, progress would always end in famines that reversed economic gains. Humanity's economic aspirations were doomed to be repeatedly swallowed up by hard environmental constraints.[12]

Are developing countries facing a new kind of **Malthusian trap**, where their unsustainable use of water, land, and air will eventually cannibalize economic progress and hamstring future generations? In modern times, a number of Neo-Malthusian thinkers have warned of impending environmental constraints and even catastrophe. Some point out that LDCs and their poor residents are particularly exposed to these economic consequences because they are more

understanding INDICATORS

The Environmental Performance Index

The environmental performance index (EPI) is a composite measure that ranges from 0 to 100 and is assigned to each country annually based on its overall environmental quality. Twenty-two individual indicators go into constructing the index. These twenty-two fall into two broad subcategories: environmental health issues that look at household environmental problems and ecosystem vitality issues that look at community and global ones. Indicators within the environmental health category include levels of indoor air pollution and the share of the population with access to sanitation and drinking water. The list of indicators under the ecosystem vitality category is more extensive, touching on air quality (such as sulfur dioxide emissions), climate change (carbon emissions per capita), freshwater availability (rate of water consumption), land use (rate of change in forest cover and pesticide usage), and sustainability of marine life (degree of fish stock overexploitation).

The accompanying figure gives a taste of the index by plotting 124 countries according to their EPI (*y*-axis) and their GDP per capita (*x*-axis) in 2010. The closer a country is to 100 on the EPI, the better its environmental performance. The figure shows that economic development is clearly associated with higher EPIs and better environmental quality.

Does the EPI, however, lump together too many disparate factors and thus disguise important trends? Relying strictly on the EPI composite score, one

Environmental Performance Index by GDP per Capita

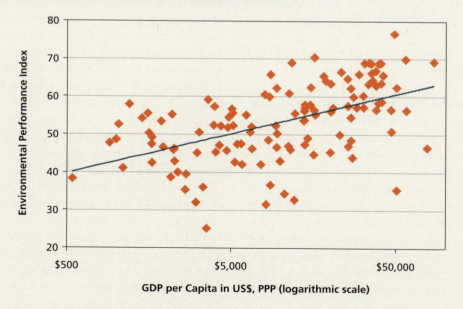

Source: Yale University, Environmental Performance Index, 2010, http://epi.yale.edu/.

would be unaware of the fact that wealthy countries have much higher carbon dioxide emissions than poor ones. All told, the index may be overly influenced by environmental issues that result from economic scarcity (such as household water and cooking fuel access) that have little to do with environmental sustainability.

In the end, researchers conducting in-depth research on environmental performance might be better advised to use the individual indicators rather than the composite index.

- Which of the individual indicators of environmental performance might follow the Kuznets curve pattern? Which might improve with higher incomes, and which might worsen with higher incomes?

- What other individual indicators of environmental performance might be useful in characterizing a country's environmental performance?

---

dependent on the environment for their livelihoods. For example, the poor are more reliant on agriculture and fishing for their incomes, leaving them economically vulnerable when environmental damage lowers crop yields and fish stocks. At the same time, the poor devote a high share of their income to food consumption, so the higher prices that would accompany food scarcity would have a disproportionate effect on them as well.

Environmental limits on economic growth may tighten in the future through a number of means. Like Malthus, biologist Paul Ehrlich believes that population growth will soon outrun nature's ability to feed humanity.[13] The number of people is expected to grow by 3 billion, or nearly 50 percent, over the next half-century, with almost the entirety of that growth occurring in the developing world. In fact, the fastest-growing population is on the poorest continent: Africa. Because of its high fertility rate, demographers expect there to be 2 billion Africans by 2045, moving it from half of Europe's population size in 1975 to nearly thrice that in just seventy years.[14] **Overpopulation** will thus further tax the already fragile stock of natural capital in places that can hardly afford to diminish it further.

Total agricultural output will need to grow by 60 percent to 100 percent to keep pace with population growth and the more environmentally taxing consumer tastes of LDCs. To worsen matters, this rise must take place in the face of the countervailing trend of increases in lost land due to urban sprawl and soil degradation as many cultivated lands lose their nutrient matter and dry out. Trends in lost land are already sapping about 0.5 percent of the developing world's agricultural land each year,[15] and many LDCs have little to no fertile land left that remains uncultivated. If the amount of land under cultivation is to rise, much of it will need to come from deforestation or the clearing of valuable wetlands. Boosts in agricultural yields on existing farmland may help, but the rate of such gains has been slowing in recent years, a worrisome trend that may be partially due to degraded soils and climate change.

The constraints on water resources may be even tighter since there are few freshwater reserves that remain untapped. To feed the growing population, farmers will need to increase water withdrawals by 50 percent in the next three decades alone, and this is even before considering the increased per-person demands of households and industry. Increased water consumption is expected to put half of humanity, up from 10 percent today, under water stress and dramatically raise the price of water.[16] All told, prices for the most basic commodities, food and water, may increase in the future, hurting many consumers in the developing world.

Health-care costs from environmental damage may also rise in LDCs. Diminishing supplies of clean freshwater could raise the incidence of diarrhea, which can be fatal in infants. Dirtier air means more respiratory problems. China devotes an estimated 3 percent of GDP per year to health costs associated with outdoor air pollution, and these costs could rise as the country continues to urbanize.[17] The higher price of food may boost rates of malnutrition and hunger among the poor. All of these undesirable trends in health could reverse recent gains in primary school enrollments as students succumb to more absences.

Critique: Recent History versus Neo-Malthusianism

Malthusian and neo-Malthusian concerns notwithstanding, for the past 200 years humans have exhibited an impressive capacity to repeatedly overcome environmental constraints on economic progress. It is a telling fact that the writers who tend to cite Malthus today are not his supporters but his detractors, who enjoy caricaturing how dreadfully wrong his gloomy predictions were. The Industrial Revolution did not end in mass starvation and a reversion to primitive economic ways, as he predicted, even though population growth boomed. How has humanity been able to avoid "ecocide," and how might the developing world elude it in the future?

What Malthus got so wrong was in failing to foresee that innovation and technology would boost agricultural productivity at a historically unprecedented rate. This enabled Great Britain and then the entire West to escape the Malthusian trap of food shortage and produce at a rate that far exceeded the geometrical growth of population. Technological advances in agricultural productivity later spread to much of the global South via the Green Revolution, which has been called "perhaps the twentieth century's greatest achievement."[18] The **Green Revolution** refers to the invention and dissemination of

irrigation systems, pesticides, fertilizers, and new seed types that enabled farmers around the world to extract increasingly more crop and meat volumes from virtually the same amount of farmland. Initially implemented in wealthy countries, the Green Revolution spread to Asia and Latin America during the three decades following World War II. It contributed to gains in productivity that have more than doubled farm output over the past half century, all while keeping the amount of land under cultivation largely the same.[19] Most of these gains occurred on farms in the less developed world. As one example, India used to be beset by periodic famines, yet, despite a doubling of its population size, it has not had one in decades.

Plenty of room for further improvements in agricultural productivity remains, suggesting that the Malthusian trap of food shortages is not an imminent threat. Most importantly, Africa has adopted few of the innovations of the Green Revolution. For example, Indian farmers use eighteen times the fertilizer per acre as do African farmers, so the potential for boosting agricultural productivity in the world's poorest continent is vast.[20] Moreover, many LDCs still cultivate livestock in a way that uses more land and yields less meat and dairy than do modern processes. Farmers in LDCs could meet the rising demand for animal products by adopting (admittedly controversial) factory farm techniques used throughout the developed world.

Several technologies that could alleviate water shortages are also ripe for adoption throughout the developing world. Drip-feed irrigation is a technique that delivers water directly to the plant's roots, avoiding evaporation and waterlogging. No-till agriculture, whereby a field is not plowed and part of the previous year's crop is left on it, lowers the need for irrigation by preserving water in the soil. **Desalinization** is the process of turning saltwater into freshwater, and it is already practiced in Israel and other dry parts of the world. Desalinization is expensive and emits carbon pollutants, but future advances could lower its cost and carbon intensity. If employed more broadly, it would dramatically lower water supply constraints since 97 percent of the world's water is in its oceans and seas. All told, critics of neo-Malthusianism see the current rhetoric about looming food and water shortages as alarmist and subject to the very error Malthus committed of assuming no future productivity improvements.

Critics of neo-Malthusian views also point to a favorable demographic trend. Although the human population continues to grow in size, it will not grow indefinitely. Due to worldwide declines in fertility (discussed in Chapter 12), the peak years of population growth are long past. World population growth peaked in the 1960s at just above 2 percent per year, and by early 2013 it was around half that amount. Today, 40 percent of humanity, including much of East Asia, lives in a country with a fertility rate at or below the replacement rate of 2.1. Another 40 percent, including most of Latin America, the Middle East, and South Asia, lives in a country with a rate that is only slightly above the replacement rate.

Because of this, the human population is expected to stop growing in 2050, leveling off at around 9 to 10 billion people.

Climate Change and Development

Anthropogenic climate change refers to changes in the global climate that are caused by humanity's emission into the atmosphere of greenhouse gases (GHGs), 80 percent of which are carbon dioxide. Through the burning of trees and fossil fuels such as coal and petroleum, humans are releasing carbon (which quickly joins with oxygen to form CO_2 molecules) into the atmosphere. Once in the atmosphere, emitted GHGs remain there for centuries, adding to the existing layer of GHGs that holds solar heat near the earth's surface. Deforestation contributes to their atmospheric concentration, since today there are fewer trees to remove carbon from the air and store it. As a result, average global temperatures have already risen about 1.5°F since 1880, as shown in Figure 14.1. If emitting behavior continues on its current trajectory, further increases could be in the range of 3°F to 10°F by 2100.

GHG emissions are different from household and community environmental problems in that they are more prevalent in developed countries than in less developed ones. Centuries before Brazil began destroying its rainforest in the twentieth century, many rich countries, such as Great Britain, had deforested

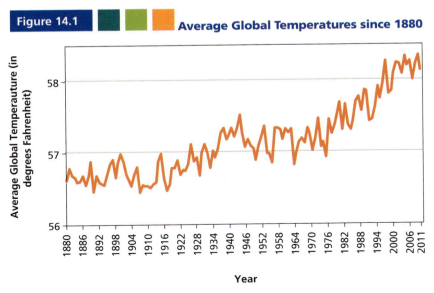

Figure 14.1 **Average Global Temperatures since 1880**

Source: NASA, Goddard Institute for Space Studies, GISS Surface Temperature Analysis (GISTEMP), http://data.giss.nasa.gov/gistemp/.

vast swathes of their land. Today, people in afflu-ent countries do more of the things—drive more cars, eat more meat, use more electricity, consume more paper—that result in carbon release than do LDCs. For example, there are nine cars for every ten people in the United States, while India only has one car for every ten people. Addition-ally, more than a billion people in the developing world do not even have electricity.[21] On average, an individual in a high-income country emits four times as much carbon dioxide as does the average person in a less developed country, and the ratio in per-person emissions between high-income and low-income countries is fifteen to one.[22] Of all the GHGs emitted by humans since 1850, the devel-oped world is responsible for two-thirds and the United States alone for nearly 30 percent.[23] Fig-ure 14.2 shows the extremely tight relationship

between per-capita carbon dioxide emissions and GDP per capita.

That said, LDCs in 2013 were responsible for half of annual GHG emissions, and they have been the leading drivers of growth in emissions in recent decades. By one estimate, such emissions from less developed countries have increased by 250 per-cent since 1970, in comparison to just a 40 percent increase in emissions by high-income countries over that same span.[24] Population growth and economic growth have contributed nearly equally to this increase. Particularly problematic is that coal, the major fossil fuel that releases the greatest amount of carbon per unit of energy generated, is driving much of that growth. For example, China gener-ates most of its electricity with coal and is today the world's leading carbon emitter, accounting for nearly 25 percent of global emissions.[25] Asia's other giant,

Figure 14.2 **The Relationship between Carbon Dioxide Emissions and GDP per Capita**

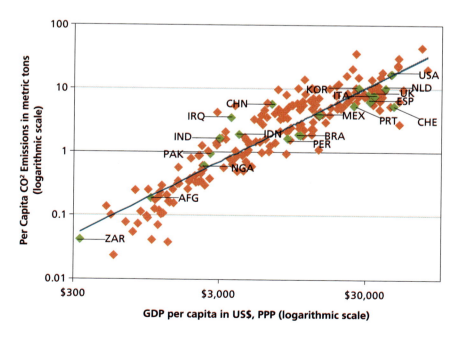

Source: Data compiled from the World Bank, World Development Indicators, 2009, http://data.worldbank.org/data-catalog/world-development-indicators.

India, has the fifth-largest coal reserves in the world, and it has relied heavily on them to drive its recent economic growth.[26]

Looking ahead, economic growth is expected to triple energy demand in developing countries over the next few decades, further increasing the developing world's share of global carbon emissions. For example, 80 percent of the 2.3 billion cars the world expects to add between 2005 and 2050 will be purchased in a less developed country.[27] Moreover, economic growth in many LDCs is locking them into the fossil fuel model of energy generation, making it more costly for them to transition away in the future. All told, estimates for 2050 show residents of today's less developed countries to be producing 70 percent of GHG emissions.[28]

The effects of climate change on the environment in LDCs cannot be known with certainty, but scientists have already made a number of predictions. In general, LDCs are expected to see more dramatic deteriorations in environmental quality than developed countries, in part because places with already high temperatures are most vulnerable to further warming. In many LDCs, freshwater will become scarcer as hotter temperatures speed up evaporation and prevent millions of tons of water from running off into rivers, lakes, and aquifers. The melting of mountain glaciers will also reduce freshwater availability in places such as China, South Asia, the Andes, and Central Asia. Anthropogenic climate change will also contribute to soil degradation as increased dryness in already arid and semiarid places boosts soil erosion. Many of the world's arid places, such as sub-Saharan African and the Middle East, will become even drier, with some estimates holding that the surface area of Africa's arid and semiarid lands will increase by 5 to 8 percent.[29] In wetter areas, heavier rains and flooding during wet seasons will increase waterlogging of soils. Finally, in parts of Southeast Asia, coastal land will experience greater flooding and, possibly, permanent inundation as sea levels rise due to melting polar ice caps.

Causes of Underdevelopment: The Economic Burden of Climate Change

As if the vulnerability of the developing world to community environmental problems were not enough, the looming effects of global problems, in the form of anthropogenic climate change, adds yet more potential for a Malthusian trap. The Intergovernmental Panel on Climate Change (IPCC), a UN-sanctioned international body of thousands of scientists that provides reports on the consensus within the climate science community, predicts that LDCs, and especially those in Africa, the Middle East, and South Asia, will endure 80 percent of the economic burden of climate change.[30] The economic costs of climate change can be divided into three categories: mitigation, adaptation, and lost productivity.

Mitigation costs are those needed to reduce the amount of GHGs that are accumulating in the atmosphere. Examples include the costs of switching to carbon-free energy sources and cleaner fuels. One approach to mitigating emissions would be for governments to tax fossil fuels according to their carbon content (a carbon tax), which would make fossil fuels more expensive and thereby discourage their use. A closely related idea (one currently in place in the European Union) is called emissions trading, whereby firms are required to hold permits that provide an allowance for how many tons of GHGs they can emit. Heavy emitters must purchase more permits, which they can buy from lower emitters, and government controls the total amount of emissions by placing a cap on available permits. In reality, LDC governments and residents, not to mention the United States and some other developed countries, have thus far had little stomach for mitigation costs like these. Attempts to encourage their adoption through international treaty and negotiations have largely failed. For example, the United States never adopted the UN Kyoto Protocol, which called for GHG emissions to go below their 1990s levels. The Copenhagen Accord of 2009, signed by the two leading emitters (China and the United States) plus Brazil, India, and South Africa, contains only vague statements about emissions reduction and is not even legally binding.

Given these minimal efforts to lessen emissions, LDCs are expected to face high costs in the form of lower productivity and adaptation. **Adaptation costs** are those needed to respond to or reduce vulnerability to climate change. Examples of both kinds of costs are discussed below. Perhaps the most important economic effect will be to lower agricultural yields by an estimated 5 percent to 30 percent by 2050 in most LDCs,[31] and this in a world with 2 to 3 billion more people. Such a trend would raise food prices by an estimated 30 percent to 50 percent, potentially reversing recent decreases in malnutrition rates.[32] The reasons for lower crop yields are manifold. Growing periods will shorten and the number of harvests per field may decline. Rainfall will be more variable, making crop failures more common. For example, sub-Saharan Africa faces the paradoxical prospect of both increased flooding and increased drought, a particularly damning combination in a continent that is highly dependent on agriculture and lacking in irrigation infrastructure. Unpredictable weather patterns also make it difficult for farmers to know when to plant and harvest. Furthermore, the increase in temperature itself will be costly since many crops do not grow on hot days. Finally, many of the prevailing seed types are not very adaptable to climate change.

A second result of climate change that will have negative economic consequences is an increase in the frequency of climate shocks (also known as extreme weather events or climate disasters) such as droughts, thunderstorms, floods, hurricanes, tropical storms, cyclones, wildfires, and heat waves. As it stands, virtually all (98 percent) of the people severely affected by climate disasters are residents of the developing world, so future trends could exact a steep toll on LDCs.[33] Greater variability in rainfall will increase the severity of storms and raise the frequency of flooding while at the same time lengthening the dry periods that cause drought and wildfire. Warmer temperatures may increase the frequency and severity of hurricanes, exacting steep costs in Central America and the Caribbean. Existing evidence suggests these trends in climate shocks have already begun. The proportion of LDC residents who were affected by extreme weather events rose by 75 percent from the 1970s to the 2000s.[34]

The immediate costs of climate disasters are visible in media portrayals: lives are lost, people are injured and displaced, and property is destroyed. However, they also yield less visible but longer-lasting deleterious effects on economic well-being. The poor are less likely than the wealthy to have deep savings or access to insurance. As a result, property losses have a greater finality for them, and treatment of injuries may require out-of-pocket payments. Families cope by eating fewer and less nutritious meals, selling assets, and increasing the number of income earners, many of which are children. Research from multiple regions in the developing world shows that children are more likely to drop out of school amidst a drought or severe flood. Families also grow poorer as they engage in distress sales, selling livestock, land, and household items just to survive. For example, as a result of Hurricane Mitch in 1998, the poorest quartile of Hondurans lost an average of a third of their wealth.[35]

Another economic and human consequence of climate change involves the changing geography of disease. As mentioned in Chapter 13, cold temperatures kill off many of the pests and parasites that cause tropical diseases in humans. As a result, warmer temperatures will expand the amount of territory that is habitable to these pests and parasites. The two most common fears on this front are increases in malaria and dengue fever. Millions of Africans live above the **malaria line**, which is the highest elevation at which malaria-bearing mosquitoes can survive. As average temperatures rise in these highlands, so will the malaria line, introducing millions of Africans to this daily threat. Some estimates hold that global warming will expose an extra 200 to 400 million people in Africa and elsewhere to the malarial threat. Dengue fever is another mosquito-borne tropical disease that is expected to rise in frequency with warmer temperatures. Latin America has already seen a boom in infection rates in recent years, and the share of humanity living in dengue-prone areas will double from 30 to 60 percent.[36]

The rise of ocean levels, a result of the melting of polar ice caps, is yet another looming consequence of climate change. In many coastal areas and islands, higher sea levels, which have risen twenty centimeters since 1870, are already causing problems as salty ocean water seeps into the groundwater. Low-lying territories could see increased flooding and, in some instances, permanent inundation. As many as 70 million people in Bangladesh, 6 million in Egypt, and 22 million in Vietnam now live in areas that will be permanently removed from the map if ocean levels continue to rise at their current rate.[37] Ten of the developing world's fifteen largest cities, including Mumbai and Shanghai, are in low-lying areas that could be affected.[38] The economic costs of asset loss and prevention could be vast.

Finally, the environmental stress of climate change could boost human migration and conflict. Climate migrants, people who seek to relocate within or across borders because their homes and communities have become environmentally inhospitable to human life, may proliferate. At the most extreme, island nations such as the Maldives may disappear underwater sometime in the next 100 years, forcing residents to seek permanent residence in an entirely different country. More commonly, millions of people may need to abandon areas that are excessively dry or that have flooded. Although it is only educated guesswork, one study expects 200 million people to be displaced, mostly due to desertification, by 2050.[39] Conflict among human groups could also increase as human groups compete over scarcer water and habitable land. Already, studies of Africa show that decreases in rainfall are associated with a greater likelihood of civil war.[40]

Critique: An Exaggerated Threat to Development?

Some thinkers, while accepting that climate change is being caused by human activities, argue that the threat that anthropogenic climate change poses to development and prosperity is quite minimal and often exaggerated.[41] Proponents of this view take particular umbrage at sentiments such as the following, which is a quote from officials at the United Nations Development Programme (UNDP): "Climate change is the defining human development issue of our generation. . . . Today, we are witnessing at first hand what could be the onset of major human development reversal in our lifetime."[42] The problem with this quote is that even the most pessimistic forecasting models about climate change's impact do not predict these major reversals. The most dire estimates posit a future world that is 20 percent poorer than it would have been without climate change, This 20 percent, however, is subtracted from a prosperity level for the developing world that is much higher than that prevailing today.[43] After all, estimates about future losses from climate change are predicated on continued economic growth in LDCs since this growth will produce increased GHG emissions. In one report, the IPCC laid out six possible scenarios for climate change effects by 2100. In its most pessimistic scenario, the GDP per capitas of most LDCs are assumed to be at least four times what they are today.[44]

Critics of what they see as climate change alarmism state that this increase in wealth will boost the developing world's ability to adapt to climate change, lowering in unforeseen ways its consequences. For example, even if agricultural productivity does decline in Africa, Africans will be better able to build infrastructure for food delivery and to afford imported food from the places where thawing will actually lift food yields, such as Canada, Northern Europe, and Russia. Similarly, higher incomes will provide greater protection against natural disasters. The main cause of death and economic loss from climate shocks is not their severity or frequency, but rather how well-protected and prepared people in the affected area are. Wealth brings sturdier housing and better warning systems. As evidence, the number of weather-related natural disasters and people affected by them has increased worldwide in recent decades, yet deaths from such disasters have declined.[45]

As with Malthus' predictions, critics allege that the most pessimistic forecasts about climate change effects underestimate the role of technological progress in addressing adaptation and mitigation problems. Regarding adaption, climate change itself could be slowed by technological interventions. **Geoengineering** refers to large-scale projects that are designed and implemented by humans to alter the climate. Ideas that are in early development stages among scientists and inventors include scrubbing carbon dioxide from the atmosphere and re-sequestering it underground, blowing cool ocean water into the air with giant misters, and placing giant disks in space to deflect sunlight. To be sure, all of these approaches are extremely expensive and would have known and unforeseen side effects, but subsequent research and breakthroughs could make them viable.

Similarly, many LDC governments are starting to take mitigation seriously. For example, a number of national incentive programs for renewable energy sources now exist, and around 25 percent of global investment in renewable energy sources occurs in LDCs. China was the first major developing country to systematically incentivize its renewable energy sector, and it now has the second-greatest wind-power capacity in the world. Renewable energy sources generate nearly 20 percent of its electricity.[51]

Although still lackluster, global and national policy efforts to limit GHG emissions through deforestation have been gradually improving. The rate of Amazon deforestation has fallen dramatically in recent years as the Brazilian government has stepped up efforts to monitor forest destruction and to enforce its own laws against logging.[52] The government and local organizations have also implemented schemes to pay landowners to leave trees standing on their land. A similar scheme is in its infancy on a global scale. Through Reducing Emissions from Deforestation and Forest Degradation (REDD), communities and people who live near forests are paid to ensure that trees are not destroyed. The funds mostly originate from rich-world taxpayers and are channeled to recipients via nongovernmental and international governmental organizations such as the UN and World Bank.

Finally, aside from the slowing of population growth discussed above, another favorable demographic trend is the ongoing **urbanization** of the human population. Popular portrayals of poor environmental quality often depict the poor waste disposal and water quality of the developing world's urban slums, where 810 million people live.[53] However, cities (defined as geographical areas with a high population density) offer a number of environmental improvements over rural life. They bring people in close proximity to one another, reducing transportation costs and thus their carbon footprint. Much less energy and materials are used to power and build fifty residences in an apartment high-rise than to do

DEVELOPMENT in the FIELD

Environmental Activism for Development

The number of activist groups focusing on the environment in LDCs is legion. A 1996 published directory of environmentalist organizations has 130 pages of listings in more than 200 countries.[46] Some groups focus on specialty issues such as overpopulation (World Population Awareness) and deforestation (The Rainforest Alliance). Others are more encompassing in their issue focus and geographical scope. For example, the well-known Greenpeace organization has offices in around fifty countries and engages in everything from lobbying to civil disobedience. An example of a small holistic group is the Green Belt Movement, which is based in Kenya and was founded by Wangari Maathai, the 2004 winner of the Nobel Peace Prize. This ecofeminist movement incorporates environmentalist efforts such as tree planting and opposition to environmentally damaging urban projects with promotion of female empowerment through the creation of ecologically oriented jobs for women. All of these groups' efforts dovetail with the objective of preventing further climate change, a goal that has also become a major focus of large international organizations such as the World Bank and various UN agencies. For example, the UNDP has said of climate change that "no issue merits more urgent attention—or more immediate action."[47]

A few observers concerned about development see some environmentalist efforts as misguided. According to political scientist Bjorn Lomborg, director of the Copenhagen Consensus Center think tank, many environmentalist claims are exaggerated and divert resources from more immediate and consequential problems.[48]

Every year, well over 15 million people in the developing world die prematurely of preventable causes such as malnutrition, diarrhea, respiratory infections, HIV/AIDS, poor maternal care, and malaria. In contrast, a 2002 estimate by the World Health Organization placed the number of deaths caused by climate change at 150,000 people, precisely 1 percent the number of preventable premature deaths.[49] The number of deaths from climate change may increase in the future, but it will take a long time (if ever) to reach even the 2 million that died in 2010 from indoor air pollution, a problem that could actually be reduced by increasing the use of fossil fuels.[50] To Lomborg, the concrete development problems of today can be addressed more cheaply and with more certainty than tomorrow's uncertain consequences from climate change.

---

the same for fifty equivalently sized free-standing houses. For example, New York City's per-capita GHG emissions are less than one-third the U.S. national average. Cities also reduce land usage: today's cities concentrate 50 percent of the world's population into just 3 percent of its land.[54] All told, 50 percent of humans live in cities, a figure that will rise to 70 percent over the next forty years. Nearly all of this urban growth will occur in the less developed world, providing a slight countertrend to other forces pushing toward increased GHG emissions.[55]

WILL MALTHUSIAN TRAPS END INDONESIA'S RISE?

The world's fourth most populous country (240 million) has been one of its unsung success stories of recent years. Between 1967 and 2011, the average income of Indonesian citizens increased more than fivefold.[56] Indonesia also has one of Asia's most robust democracies and is often "exhibit A" in arguments that Islam and democracy can be compatible. Its future seems so bright that some investors have made calls to convert the BRIC block of emerging market countries (Brazil, Russia, India, and China) into a new five-member BRIIC club. Yet Indonesia faces mounting environmental challenges that could squeeze its recent gains. This case study discusses these and other challenges to Indonesian development. Table 14.2 compares Indonesia to Switzerland, the country that received the world's top EPI ranking in 2012.

Table 14.2 **Development Comparison: Indonesia and Switzerland**

Indicator	Indonesia	Switzerland
GDP per capita at PPP	US$4,179	US$37,942
Human Development Index	.617	.903
Environmental Performance Index	52.29 (79th of 132)	76.69 (1st of 132)
Gender Inequality Index	.505 (100th of 145)	.067 (4th of 145)
Foreign direct investment inflows (percentage of GDP)	2.1 percent	0.1 percent

Sources: Data on GDP per capita at PPP and Human Development Index compiled from Gapminder, www.gapminder.org; Environmental Performance Index, http://epi.yale.edu/; Gender Inequality Index, United Nations Development Programme, "Human Development Report 2011," http://hdr.undp.org/en/media/HDR_2011_EN_Complete.pdf, 139–142; Foreign direct investment inflows, the World Bank, World Development Indicators, http://data.worldbank.org/data-catalog/world-development-indicators.

The Natural World: Indonesia's Malthusian Crisis?

Indonesia's reality exemplifies the role of all three kinds of environmental constraints (global, communal, and household) on human development. It is also central to the causes of anthropogenic climate change.

Climate Change. Indonesia is a central player in the unfolding climate change crisis. Through a combination of their population sizes and relative economic prosperity, China and the United States are the two leading emitters of GHGs in the world. It may thus come as a surprise that Indonesia, whose GDP is less than one-tenth the size of these two countries', sits in third place.[57] The reason for Indonesia's high ranking is straightforward: deforestation. Indonesia has the third-largest tropical forest in the world and some 20 percent of the world's total tropical forest land, yet it is burning and chopping down that forest at an unparalleled rate. From 1990 to 2008, its total forest area declined by 20 percent, twice the amount of decline for Brazil's Amazon rainforest, and the decline continues at a rate faster than 1 percentage point each year.[58] The main reason for Indonesia's deforestation is to convert forest land to plantations that grow palm trees for palm oil cultivation. Most of the destruction is technically illegal, but the laws against it are rarely enforced.

Indonesia stands to be a leading victim of the GHGs that it and the rest of the world are emitting. It is an archipelago of 17,000 islands, so some predictions hold that it could actually lose as many as 2,000 islands due to rising ocean levels.[59] Around 60 percent of Indonesians live in coastal or other low-lying areas that could face increased flooding or even permanent inundation. The capital and largest city, Jakarta, may lose 160 square kilometers of its coastal territory by 2050, and it already experienced severe flooding from a cyclone that displaced 400,000 people in 2007.[60] Moreover, as surrounding waters rise, groundwater in coastal areas will become increasingly contaminated by salty seawater.

Weather patterns will also change in ways to the detriment of food output and the 45 percent of the workforce employed in agriculture and fishing. Indonesia has a wet season and a dry season, and expectations are that the wet season will shorten by as much as thirty days, dramatically decreasing the number of growing days for crops.[61] At the same time, the wet season will be even wetter, and tropical cyclones are expected to rise in frequency and intensity. The greater precipitation will increase waterlogging and flooding of agricultural lands. Meanwhile, the dry season will be even drier, producing drought, wildfire, and falls in crop yields. According to one study, yields of Indonesia's corn crop could fall by 50 percent.[62] Moreover, ocean warming will diminish the stock of fish in the country with the world's second-longest coastline, increasing the scarcity of a major source of protein for consumers and straining the livelihood of millions of anglers.

Finally, global warming will also bring new health concerns to many Indonesians. Tropical illnesses such as malaria and dengue fever, which have been declining in frequency in recent decades, may experience a rebound as the pests that transmit these diseases thrive in the warmer temperatures. In recent years, dengue has already been found in new parts of Indonesia, and the number of cases is expected to quadruple by 2070.[63]

Household and Communal Problems. These problems from climate change will add to existing household and communal environmental challenges. Indoor air pollution is common for the rural poor. The use of felled trees and other biomass for cooking fuel causes an estimated 50,000 deaths through respiratory disease each year.[64] Outdoor air quality in Indonesia's cities is also poor. A 2004 study named Jakarta as one of the world's ten most air-polluted cities, and on most days the city is enveloped in a visible pall of thick smog. Some of the smog is from the city's 10 million vehicles, and some of it is from burning forests.[65] Respiratory infections from dirty outdoor air kill a further 35,000 Indonesians per year and substantially raise health-care costs.

Clean freshwater is also an increasingly scarce resource in Indonesia. In Jakarta, most of the freshwater needs are filled by groundwater, but this is becoming depleted through overuse and salinization. Its depletion is even making the city sink. Nationwide, tap water is to be avoided since it is contaminated by bacteria that cause diarrhea. Each year, waterborne parasites kill another 35,000 Indonesians, many of them children.[66]

* * *

These environmental problems are surely severe, but will they truly worsen and eventually reverse Indonesia's development gains? Reasons for optimism exist. For some aspects of environmental quality, Indonesia has probably reached the peak of

WILL MALTHUSIAN TRAPS END INDONESIA'S RISE?

the environmental Kuznets curve, meaning future economic gains will actually mitigate the problem. For example, Jakarta's air, while still badly polluted, is much cleaner today than it was in the early 1990s. This has occurred despite a nearly tenfold increase in the number of cars.[67] Stricter legal regulations on fuel efficiency and incremental advances in engine technology have been the main drivers of the cleaner air trend. Similarly, as in Brazil, the rate of deforestation has started to fall, in part because the issue has gradually become a government priority.[68] Finally, the increased tropical disease burden from climate change is easily exaggerated. The country's life expectancy has risen by ten years since 1980, a result of vastly improved preventative and palliative health care. Given these gains, the country appears well poised to respond to a slight upward blip in the number of tropical disease vectors.

The South: Poor Governance and Female Disempowerment

Instead of an alleged Malthusian trap, future threats to Indonesia's boom may come from elsewhere. Good governance is not always in ample supply. Corruption is widespread. Indonesia ranks as only the 100th cleanest country (of 183) in one authoritative ranking of societal graft.[69] For example, taxpayer dollars are wasted in public works projects all the time when funds are diverted to the pockets of public officials and political parties. In one high-profile case, a party leader accepted kickbacks from construction companies building the athletes' village for the 2011 Southeast Asian Games. Similarly, the overall infrastructure for doing business is also abysmal. In comparison to the prevailing average in high-income countries, starting a business in Indonesia takes four times as long and costs five times as much of an average person's income.[70] Indonesia ranks only 166th of 185 countries in terms of how easy it is to start a business. Overall, the country's corrupt bureaucracy and thick red tape will surely stifle vast amounts of entrepreneurial activity in the future.

Indonesia also ranks poorly in how it treats women and girls, a cultural choice that could slow economic progress in the future. It again ranks in the triple digits in international comparisons, this time in its level of gender inequality (100 of 145). The gap in labor force participation rates between women and men is 34 percentage points (52 percent for women, 86 percent for men), one of the largest such gaps outside the Middle East. Moreover, whereas almost a third of men have some secondary education, just a quarter of women do.[71] In other words, Indonesia is missing out on the productive talents of millions of women.

The West: Pathologies of Globalization

Alternatively, challenges to sustained growth in Indonesia may come from globalization and the West. The West has surely had a hand in creating Indonesia's underdeveloped status, as Indonesia was colonized by the Portuguese (in the 1500s) and then the Dutch (1603–1949) during the era of Western imperialism. In more recent times, Indonesia has been a victim of an alleged neocolonialism. In 1997, billions of Westerners' investment dollars were pulled out of the country almost overnight in a speculative attack. Critics of international capital flows note that the attack occurred through no fault of Indonesia's leadership or economic institutions but rather because of a contagion effect from the East Asian financial crisis. In other words, investors fled Indonesia merely because they expected other investors to also flee amidst the chaos. This created a self-fulfilling prophecy of capital flight in which the real losers were common Indonesians. Economic contraction of 15 percent occurred in just a year's time, and inflation reached 100 percent.

Since Indonesia righted its economic ship in the late 1990s, foreign investment from the West and elsewhere has poured back into the country, raising concerns among globalization's critics about a growing economic dependence. Many foreign

An Indonesian boy rests on a freshly cut tree stump in the Indonesian rainforest. In recent years, Indonesia's tropical forest, the third largest in the world, is being destroyed at a faster rate than that of the Amazon. This has had dire consequences for local communities as well as the global environment.

investors arrive to exploit Indonesia's relatively low wages, and the country is frequently cited in outcries against industrial sweatshops in the global supply chain. For example, some of the factories that make footwear for Adidas and Nike are located in Indonesia. They pay just a few dollars per day for long hours, and disfiguring accidents, often as a result of sleep deprivation, are commonplace.[72] Moreover, in one incident, the Taiwanese trade office pleaded with the Indonesian state to not allow Indonesian workers' wages to rise faster than inflation. If they did, the office added, Taiwanese-owned firms would leave. This moment of honesty revealed the exploitive hand of international capital, since the point was tantamount to saying that Indonesian workers should be disallowed from getting wealthier.[73]

***

All told, the challenges facing Indonesia as it seeks to continue its impressive streak of economic growth are immense and multiple. Problems with the environment, governance, and foreign economic interests may all pose some constraints on its ability to continue stringing together annual growth rates of 4 percent to 7 percent and reach upper-middle-income status in the foreseeable future. At the

same time, reason for optimism exists. Its human development outcomes have improved steadily for decades, and its economy, after bouncing back quickly from the East Asian financial crisis, also weathered the 2008 financial crisis well. The BRICs may become the BRIICs soon enough.

Thinking Critically about Development

- In May 2011, the Indonesian government declared a moratorium on the granting of new licenses for land-use changes in its tropical forest zones. Is this a sign of the environmental Kuznets curve at work—that a middle-income country can now afford the luxury of protecting its forests? Or will low state capacity keep the government from even being able to enforce rules against deforestation?

- Considering its problems of indoor air pollution and various nonenvironmental threats to human development, what priority should the Indonesian government give to climate change mitigation and adaptation?

- Are Indonesia's sweatshops evidence of exploitation by foreign markets, or are they evidence of export-oriented growth through the creation of labor-intensive jobs?

Key Terms

adaptation costs, p. 344

aquifer, p. 333

common pool resource, p. 332

deforestation, p. 334

desalinization, p. 340

environmental quality, p. 331

geoengineering, p. 346

Green Revolution, p. 340

malaria line, p. 345

Malthusian trap, p. 337

mitigation costs, p. 343

natural capital, p. 332

negative externality, p. 332

overpopulation, p. 339

subsidies, p. 336

sustainable development, p. 337

tragedy of the commons, p. 332

urbanization, p. 346

 ## Suggested Readings

Ehrlich, Paul. *The Population Bomb: Population Control or Race to Oblivion?* New York: Ballantine Books, 1968.

Lomborg, Bjorn, ed. *Global Crises, Global Solution.* New York: Cambridge University Press, 2004.

Ostrom, Elinor. *Governing the Commons: The Evolution of Institutions for Collective Action.* Cambridge: Cambridge University Press, 1990.

Stern, Nicholas. *The Economics of Climate Change: The Stern Review.* Cambridge: Cambridge University Press, 2007.

United Nations Development Programme. *Human Development Report 2011: Sustainability and Equity: A Better Future for All.* New York: Palgrave Macmillan, 2011.

World Bank. *World Development Report 2010: Development and Climate Change.* Washington, D.C.: World Bank Publications, 2010.

 ## Web Resources

Environmental Performance Index, http://epi.yale.edu/

Intergovernmental Panel on Climate Change Data Distribution Centre, www.ipcc-data.org/

World Bank Climate Change Knowledge Portal, http://sdwebx.worldbank.org/climateportal/index.cfm

World Health Organization, Public Health and Environment Health Topics, www.who.int/phe/health_topics/en/

Appendix: Country Codes

Country Name	Country Code
Afghanistan	AFG
Algeria	DZA
American Samoa	ASM
Angola	AGO
Antigua and Barbuda	ATG
Argentina	ARG
Bangladesh	BGD
Belize	BLZ
Benin	BEN
Bhutan	BTN
Bolivia	BOL
Botswana	BWA
Brazil	BRA
Burkina Faso	BFA
Burundi	BDI
Cambodia	KHM
Cameroon	CMR
Cape Verde	CPV
Central African Republic	CAF
Chad	TCD
Chile	CHL
China	CHN
Colombia	COL
Comoros	COM
Congo, Democratic Republic of	ZAR
Congo, Republic of	COG
Costa Rica	CRI

Country Name	Country Code
Cote d'Ivoire	CIV
Cuba	CUB
Djibouti	DJI
Dominica	DMA
Dominican Republic	DOM
Ecuador	ECU
Egypt	EGY
El Salvador	SLV
Equatorial Guinea	GNQ
Eritrea	ERI
Ethiopia	ETH
Fiji	FJI
Gabon	GAB
Gambia, The	GMB
Ghana	GHA
Grenada	GRD
Guatemala	GTM
Guinea	GIN
Guinea-Bissau	GNB
Guyana	GUY
Haiti	HTI
Honduras	HND
India	IND
Indonesia	IDN
Iran	IRN
Iraq	IRQ
Jamaica	JAM

Country Name	Country Code
Jordan	JOR
Kenya	KEN
Kiribati	KIR
Korea, South	PRK
Laos	LAO
Lebanon	LBN
Lesotho	LSO
Liberia	LBR
Libya	LBY
Madagascar	MDG
Malawi	MWI
Malaysia	MYS
Maldives	MDV
Mali	MLI
Marshall Islands	MHL
Mauritania	MRT
Mauritius	MUS
Mexico	MEX
Micronesia, Federated States of	FSM
Mongolia	MNG
Morocco	MAR
Mozambique	MOZ
Myanmar	MMR
Namibia	NAM
Nepal	NPL
Nicaragua	NIC
Niger	NER
Nigeria	NGA
Pakistan	PAK
Palau	PLW
Panama	PAN
Papua New Guinea	PNG
Paraguay	PRY
Peru	PER
Philippines	PHL

Country Name	Country Code
Rwanda	RWA
Samoa	WSM
Sao Tome and Principe	STP
Saudi Arabia	SAU
Senegal	SEN
Seychelles	SYC
Sierra Leone	SLE
Solomon Islands	SLB
Somalia	SOM
South Africa	ZAF
South Sudan	SSD
Sri Lanka	LKA
St. Lucia	LCA
St. Vincent and the Grenadines	VCT
Sudan	SDN
Suriname	SUR
Swaziland	SWZ
Syrian Arab Republic	SYR
Tanzania	TZA
Thailand	THA
Timor-Leste	TMP
Togo	TGO
Tonga	TON
Tunisia	TUN
Turkey	TUR
Tuvalu	TUV
Uganda	UGA
Uruguay	URY
Vanuatu	VUT
Venezuela	VEN
Vietnam	VNM
West Bank and Gaza	WBG
Yemen	YEM
Zambia	ZMB
Zimbabwe	ZWE

Notes

Chapter 1

1. The individuals described in these vignettes are fictional, although parts of their stories are compiled from nonfictional accounts.

2. All six of these regional categories are the designations used by the World Bank. The need to specify high income, instead of just OECD, is that the OECD now contains a few countries, such as Chile and Mexico, which are not strictly high income and are part of the traditionally defined developing world. The need for designating OECD, instead of just high income, in the category label is that there are a number of countries that only recently reached high-income status, such as Kuwait and Saudi Arabia, which are not part of the traditionally defined West or developed world. In the end, the "high-income OECD" category contains the following countries: Australia, Austria, Belgium, Canada, Czech Republic, Denmark, Estonia, Finland, France, Germany, Greece, Hungary, Iceland, Ireland, Italy, Israel, Japan, South Korea, Luxembourg, the Netherlands, New Zealand, Norway, Poland, Portugal, Slovak Republic, Slovenia, Spain, Sweden, Switzerland, United Kingdom, and United States.

3. Unless otherwise noted, regional averages are calculated using country population weights.

4. Matthew Ridley, *The Rational Optimist: How Prosperity Evolves* (New York: Harper, 2010), 22.

5. Branko Milanovic, *The Haves and the Have-Nots: A Brief and Idiosyncratic History of Global Inequality* (New York: Basic Books, 2011).

6. Statistics in this paragraph are from the World Bank's World Development Indicators, http://data.worldbank.org/data-catalog/world-development-indicators.

7. International Labour Organization, "Key Indicators of the Labour Market Dataset," October 16, 2011, www.ilo.org/empelm/what/WCMS_114240/lang--en/index.htm.

8. Abhijit V. Banerjee and Esther Duflo, *Poor Economics: A Radical Rethinking of the Way to Fight Global Poverty* (New York: Public Affairs, 2011), 160.

9. All data in this and the previous paragraph are from Gapminder, www.gapminder.org.

10. World Bank, *World Development Report 2008: Agriculture for Development*, 2007, http://siteresources.worldbank.org/INTWDR2008/Resources/WDR_00_book.pdf, 45.

11. William J. Bernstein, *The Birth of Plenty: How the Prosperity of the Modern World Was Created* (New York: McGraw-Hill, 2004), 193.

12. Angus Maddison, *Monitoring the World Economy, 1820–1992.* (Paris: OECD, 1995).

13. Gapminder, www.gapminder.org.

14. Milanovic, *The Haves and Have-Nots*, 102.

15. Benjamin M. Friedman, *The Moral Consequences of Economic Growth* (New York: Vintage Books, 2006), 354.

16. Charles Kenny, *Getting Better: Why Global Development is Succeeding—and How We Can Improve the World Even More* (New York: Basic Books, 2011), 19.

17. "The New Middle Classes Rise Up," *The Economist*, September 3, 2011, 23–24.

18. "Technology Quarterly: Making Data Dance," *The Economist*, December 11, 2010, 25.

19. Paul Collier, *The Bottom Billion: Why the Poorest Countries Are Failing and What Can Be Done About It* (Oxford: Oxford University Press, 2007).

20. Gapminder, www.gapminder.org.

21. Michela Wrong, *In the Footsteps of Mr. Kurtz: Living on the Brink of Disaster in Mobutu's Congo* (New York: Harper Collins, 2001), 99.

22. Ibid.

23. World Bank, World Development Indicators, http://data.worldbank.org/sites/default/files/wdi-final.pdf.

24. Jeffrey Herbst and Greg Mills, "There Is No Congo," *Foreign Policy*, March 18, 2009.

25. Joe Bavier, "Congo War-Driven Crisis Kills 45,000 a Month: Study," Reuters, January 22, 2008, www.reuters.com/article/2008/01/22/us-congo-democratic-death-idUSL2280201220080122.

26. Heidi Kriz, "When He Was King," Metroactive: News and Issues, May 22–28, 1997, http://www.metroactive.com/papers/metro/05.22.97/cover/mobutu-9721.html.

27. Thomas Pakenham, *The Scramble for Africa: White Man's Conquest of the Dark Continent from 1876 to 1912* (New York: Random House, 1991), 22.

28. Adam Hochschild, *King Leopold's Ghost: A Story of Greed, Terror, and Heroism in Colonial Africa* (Boston: Mariner Books, 1998), 271.

29. Ibid.

30. Nathan Nunn, "The Long-Term Effects of Africa's Slave Trades," *Quarterly Journal of Economics* 122, no. 1 (2008): 139–176.

31. World Lightning Map, Geology.com, http://geology.com/articles/lightning-map.shtml.

32. Miriam Mannak, "Malaria Remains Biggest Killer," Inter Press Service, October 27, 2008, http://www.ipsnews.net/2008/10/health-dr-congo-malaria-remains-biggest-killer/.

33. M. J. Morgan, "DR Congo's $24 Trillion Fortune," The Free Library, February 1, 2009, www.thefreelibrary.com/DR+Congo's+$24+trillion+fortune.-a0193800184.

Chapter 2

1. Amartya Sen, *Development as Freedom* (New York: Alfred Knopf, 1999), 4.
2. Martha Nussbaum, *Creating Capabilities: The Human Development Approach* (Cambridge: Harvard University Press, 2011), 152.
3. Sen, *Development as Freedom,* 33.
4. Charles Kenny, *Getting Better: Why Global Development Is Succeeding—and How We Can Improve the World Even More* (New York: Basic Books, 2011), 155.
5. United Nations Development Programme, *Human Development Report: The Real Wealth of Nations: Pathways to Human Development* (New York: Palgrave MacMillan, 2010); Kenny, *Getting Better.*
6. Kenny, *Getting Better.*
7. Greg Mortenson and David Oliver Relin. *Three Cups of Tea: One Man's Mission to Promote Peace … One School at a Time* (New York: Penguin, 2006).
8. William Easterly and Tobias Pfutze, "Where Does the Money Go? Best and Worst Practices in Foreign Aid," *Journal of Economic Perspectives* 22 (2008): 29–52.
9. John Krakauer, *Three Cups of Deceit: How Greg Mortenson, Humanitarian Hero, Lost His Way.* (San Francisco: Byliner, 2011).
10. All stats in this paragraph are from United Nations Development Programme, *Human Development Report: The Real Wealth of Nations,* 143–147.
11. World Bank. *Atlas of Global Development,* 2nd ed. (Glasgow: HarperCollins Publishers, 2009), 44–47.
12. Demographic and Health Survey, "Cambodia Demographic and Health Survey," 2010, http://www.measuredhs.com/pubs/pdf/GF22/GF22.pdf.
13. World Bank, *World Development Report 2006: Equity and Development* (Washington, D.C.: World Bank Publications, 2006), 30.
14. Abhijit V. Banerjee and Esther Duflo, *Poor Economics: A Radical Rethinking of the Way to Fight Poverty* (New York: Public Affairs, 2011), chapter 2. The Nutrition Puzzle," *The Economist,* February 18, 2012, 62–63.
15. Banerjee and Duflo, *Poor Economics,* chapter 2.
16. Jean Drèze and Amartya Sen, *Hunger and Public Action* (Oxford: Clarendon Press, 1989), 15.
17. "The Starvelings," *The Economist,* January 26, 2008, 58–59.
18. Dan Smith, *The Penguin State of the World Atlas,* 9th ed. (New York: Penguin 2012).
19. "The Nutrition Puzzle," *The Economist,* February 18, 2012, http://www.economist.com/node/21547771.
20. "Health: the Big Picture," United Nations Children's Fund, April 23, 2003, www.unicef.org/health/index_bigpicture.html. The fifth is malnutrition.

21. World Bank Health, Nutrition, and Population Statistics, http://data.worldbank.org/data-catalog/health-nutrition-population-statistics.
22. Ibid.; "Cholera and the Super-Loo," *The Economist,* July 30, 2011, 55.
23. Guy Howard and Jamie Bartram, "Domestic Water Quantity, Service Level and Health," 2003, http://www.who.int/water_sanitation_health/diseases/WSH03.02.pdf.
24. "Cholera and the Super-Loo," 55–56.
25. United Nations Development Programme, "Beyond Scarcity," 2006, http://hdr.undp.org/en/media/HDR06-complete.pdf, 112–113.
26. Banerjee and Duflo, *Poor Economics,* 46.
27. World Bank, *Atlas of Global Development,* 44.
28. United Nations Development Programme, *Human Development Report 2003: Millennium Development Goals: A Compact among Nations to End Human Poverty* (New York: Oxford University Press, 2003), 100.
29. World Bank, *Atlas of Global Development,* 52.
30. World Health Organization, "World Health Statistics 2010," *World Health Statistical Information System,* 2010, www.who.int/who-sis/whostat/2010/en/index.html.
31. Fernando Barros, J. Patrick Vaughan, and Cesar Victoria, "Why So Many Caesarian Sections? The Need for Further Policy Change in Brazil," *Health, Policy and Planning* 1, no. 1 (1986): 19–29.
32. World Bank, World Development Indicators, 2010 figures, http://data.worldbank.org/sites/default/files/wdi-final.pdf.
33. United Nations Development Programme, *Human Development Report 2003: Millennium Development Goals: A Compact among Nations to End Human Poverty* (New York: Oxford University Press, 2003), 99.
34. Nazmul Chaudhury, Jeffrey Hammer, Michael Kremer, Karthik Muralidharan, and F. Halsey Rogers, "Missing in Action: Teacher and Health Worker Absence in Developing Countries," *Journal of Economic Perspectives* 20 (2006): 91–116.
35. Quentin Wodon, *Access to Basic Facilities in Africa* (Washington, D.C.: World Bank, 2005).
36. Banerjee and Duflo, *Poor Economics,* Chapter 3.
37. "The Starvelings."
38. Ibid., 99.
39. Edward Miguel and Michael Kremer, "Worms: Identifying Impacts on Education and Health in the Presence of Treatment Externalities," *Econometrica* 72, no. 1 (2004): 159–217.
40. Dean Karlan and Jacob Appel, *More Than Good Intentions: Improving the Way the World's Poor Borrow, Save, Farm, Learn, and Stay Healthy* (New York: Dutton, 2011), 206.
41. Rodrigo R. Soares, "On the Determinants of Mortality Reductions in the Developing World," *Population and Development Review* 33, no. 2 (2007): 247–287.
42. Matthew Ridley, *The Rational Optimist: How Prosperity Evolves* (New York: Harper, 2010), 121.
43. Food and Agricultural Organization, "Food Security Statistics," 2010, http://faostat.fao.org/?lang=en.
44. Another commonly used and closely related measure is the gross enrollment ratio, which is the total number of people enrolled (regardless of age) expressed as a percentage of the total number of people in the relevant age group.

45. World Bank, *World Development Report 2006*, 37.

46. World Bank, World Development Indicators.

47. Paul Glewwe and Michael Kremer, "Schools, Teachers, and Education Outcomes in Developing Countries," in *Handbook of the Economics of Education*, ed. Eric A. Hanushek and Finis Welch (Amsterdam: Elsevier, 2006), chapter 16.

48. Ibid.

49. Raja Bentaouet Kattan and Nicholas Burnett, "User Fees in Primary Education," 2004, http://siteresources.worldbank.org/EDUCATION/Resources/278200-1099079877269/547664-1099079993288/EFAcase_userfees.pdf.

50. Glewwe and Kremer, "Schools, Teachers, and Education Outcomes in Developing Countries."

51. Ibid.

52. Ibid., 89.

53. World Bank, *Atlas of Global Development*, 34–37.

54. Ibid., 72.

55. United Nations Development Programme, *Human Development Report: The Real Wealth of Nations*, 28–38.

56. Ibid., 39.

57. The average is a geometric mean. See United Nations Development Programme, *Human Development Report: The Real Wealth of Nations*, 216 for details.

58. World Bank, World Development Indicators, 2010.

59. Statistics on human development scores and health are from United Nations Development Programme, *Human Development Report: The Real Wealth of Nations*, 143–147.

60. "Putting the Smallest First," *The Economist*, September 23, 2010, 35; "Global Targets, Local Ingenuity," *The Economist*, September 23, 2010, http://www.economist.com/node/17090934.

61. World Bank, World Development Indicators.

62. Ibid.

63. Banerjee and Duflo, *Poor Economics*, 55.

64. Jishnu Das, Jeffrey Hammer, and Kenneth Leonard, "The Quality of Medical Advice in Low-Income Countries," *Journal of Economic Perspectives* 22 (2008): 93–114.

65. Arvind Panagariya, *India: The Emerging Giant* (New York: Oxford University Press, 2008), 420.

66. United Nations Educational, Scientific, and Cultural Organization, *Correspondence on Education Indicators* (Montreal: 2010).

67. Statistics are from Gapminder.com and United Nations Development Programme, *Human Development Report: The Real Wealth of Nations*.

68. Panagariya, *India*, 435; "Annual Status of Education Report," Pratham USA, http://www.prathamusa.org/programs/aser.

69. Chaudhury et al., "Missing in Action"; Banerjee and Duflo, *Poor Economics*, 74.

70. Panagariya, *India*, 435–437.

71. Banerjee and Duflo, *Poor Economics*, 83.

72. United Nations Development Programme, *Human Development Report: The Real Wealth of Nations*.

73. World Bank, World Development Indicators.

74. United Nations Development Programme, *Human Development Report: The Real Wealth of Nations*.

75. Panagariya, *India*, 435.

Chapter 3

1. David Landes, *The Wealth and Poverty of Nations: Why Some Countries Are Rich and Some So Poor* (New York: W. W. Norton and Company, 1999), 435.

2. Arturo Escobar, *Encountering Development: The Making and Unmaking of the Third World* (Princeton, NJ: Princeton University Press, 1994).

3. Jeremy Tunstall, *The Media Are American* (New York: Colombia University Press, 1977).

4. Adam Smith, *An Inquiry Into the Nature and Causes of the Wealth of Nations* (London: W. Strahan and T. Cadell, 1776), 368.

5. Thorstein Veblen, *The Theory of the Leisure Class* (Mineola, NY: Dover Publications, 1994).

6. Marshall Sahlins, "The Original Affluent Society," http://www.eco-action.org/dt/affluent.html.

7. Ibid.

8. "Special Report: Mobile Marvels" *The Economist*, September 26, 2009, 1–20.

9. Tyler Cowen, *Creative Destruction: How Globalization Is Changing the World's Cultures* (Princeton, NJ: Princeton University Press, 2002), 146.

10. John Millar, *The Origin of the Distinction of Ranks* (London: J. Murray, 1779), 4.

11. Steven Pinker, *The Better Angels of Our Nature: Why Violence Has Declined* (New York: Penguin, 2011).

12. Benjamin M. Friedman, *The Moral Consequences of Economic Growth* (New York: Vintage Books, 2006), 306.

13. Charles Kenny, *Getting Better: Why Global Development Is Succeeding—and How We Can Improve the World Even More* (New York: Basic Books, 2011), 21.

14. United Nations Development Programme, *Human Development Report 2003: Millennium Development Goals: A Compact among Nations to End Human Poverty* (New York: Oxford University Press, 2003), 39.

15. Branko Milanovic, *The Haves and the Have-Nots: A Brief and Idiosyncratic History of Global Inequality* (New York: Basic Books, 2011).

16. Ibid., 115–116.

17. Ibid., 118.

18. World Bank, *World Development Report 2006: Equity and Development* (Washington, D.C.: World Bank Publications, 2005).

19. Nathan Ford and Els Torreele, letter to the editor, *Journal of the American Medical Association* 286, no. 23 (2001): 458–461.

20. Simon Kuznets, "Economic Growth and Income Inequality," *American Economic Review* 45, no. 1 (1955): 1–28.

21. Daron Acemoglu and James A. Robinson, "The Political Economy of the Kuznets Curve," *Review of Development Economics* 6, no. 2 (2002): 183–203.

22. World Bank, World Development Indicators, http://data.worldbank.org/sites/default/files/wdi-final.pdf.

23. Quoted in Amartya Sen, *Development as Freedom* (New York: Alfred Knopf, 1999), 73.

24. Daron Acemoglu and James A. Robinson, *Economic Origins of Dictatorship and Democracy* (Cambridge: Cambridge University Press, 2006).

25. Richard G. Wilkinson and Kate Pickett, *The Spirit Level* (New York: Bloomsbury Press, 2009).

26. David Dollar and Aart Kraay, "Growth Is Good for the Poor," *Journal of Economic Growth* 7, no. 3 (2002): 195–225.

27. Glenn Firebaugh, *The New Geography of Global Income Inequality* (Cambridge: Harvard University Press, 2003).

28. Kuznets, "Economic Growth and Income Inequality."

29. Jared Diamond, *Collapse: How Societies Choose to Fail or Succeed* (New York: Viking Press, 2005).

30. World Bank, *World Development Report 2010: Development and Climate Change* (Washington D.C.: The World Bank Group, 2010).

31. Global Humanitarian Forum, *Human Impact Report: Climate Change: The Anatomy of a Silent Crisis* (Geneva: Global Humanitarian Forum, 2009).

32. Bruce Yandle, Maya Vijayaraghavan, and Madhusudan Bhattarai, "The Environmental Kuznets Curve: A Primer," May 2002, http://perc.org/sites/default/files/Yandle_Kuznets02.pdf.

33. *The World's Most Polluted Places: The Top Ten (of the Dirty Thirty)* (New York: Blacksmith Institute, 2007).

34. "Environmental Performance Index: 2012 & Trend EPI: EPI Rankings," Yale University, http://epi.yale.edu/epi2012/rankings.

35. Matthew Ridley, *The Rational Optimist: How Prosperity Evolves* (New York: Harper, 2010).

36. Ibid., 143.

37. Sen, *Development as Freedom*, 215.

38. "How to Live with Climate Change," *The Economist*, November 27, 2010, 15.

39. Joseph A. Schumpeter, *Capitalism, Socialism, and Democracy* (New York: Harper & Brothers, 1942).

40. United States Department of Agriculture, "Growing a Nation: The Story of American Agriculture," http://www.agclassroom.org/gan/timeline/farmers_land.htm.

41. Sahlins, "The Original Affluent Society."

42. Barry Schwartz, *The Paradox of Choice: Why More Is Less* (New York: Ecco, 2004).

43. Easterlin, Richard A., "Does Economic Growth Improve the Human Lot? Some Empirical Evidence," in *Nations and Households in Economic Growth*, eds. Paul A. David and Melvin Reder (New York: Academic Press, 1974).

44. John Stuart Mill, "On Social Freedom," *Oxford and Cambridge Review* 69 (1907): 57–83.

45. Richard A Easterlin, "Does Money Buy Happiness?," *The Public Interest* 30 (1973): 3–10, 4.

46. Sen, *Development as Freedom*, 67.

47. Martha Nussbaum, *Creating Capabilities: The Human Development Approach* (Cambridge: Harvard University Press, 2011), 54.

48. Joni Seager, *Penguin Atlas of Women in the World* (New York: Penguin Books, 2009), 28.

49. Jonathan Watts, "Chinese Lesson in How to Put Food in the Mouths of Millions," *The Guardian*, May 27, 2004.

50. Data from Gapminder, www.gapminder.org.

51. World Bank, *World Development Indicators* (Washington D.C.: The World Bank Group, 2012).

52. Ibid.

53. Sam Dillon, "Top Test Scores from Shanghai Stun Educators," *The New York Times*, December 7, 2010.

54. Diamond, *Collapse*, 360.

55. Quoted in Barry Naughton, *The Chinese Economy: Transitions and Growth* (Cambridge: MIT Press, 2007) 108.

56. Naughton, *Chinese Economy*, 22.

57. World Bank, "China: Quick Facts," http://go.worldbank.org/4Q7SC8DU50.

58. Joseph Kahn and Jim Yardley, "As China Roars, Pollution Reaches Deadly Extremes," *The New York Times*, August 26, 2007.

59. Naughton, *Chinese Economy*, 492.

60. Kahn and Yardley, "As China Roars."

61. Naughton, *Chinese Economy*, 493.

62. Kahn and Yardley, "As China Roars."

63. United Nations Statistics Division, "Environmental Indicators: Greenhouse Gas Emissions: CO_2 Emissions Per Capita in 2007," http://unstats.un.org/unsd/environment/air_co2_emissions.htm.

64. Naughton, *Chinese Economy*, 217.

65. "The Mystery of the Chinese Consumer," *The Economist*, July 9, 2011, 59–60.

66. Naughton, *Chinese Economy*, 106.

67. Gallup World Poll, 2012, http://www.gallup.com/video/159179/gallup-world-poll.aspx.

Chapter 4

1. Abuja Pan-African Conference on Reparations for African Enslavement, Colonization, and Neo-Colonization, "The Abuja Declaration," 1993, http://www.ncobra.org/resources/pdf/TheAbujaProclamation.pdf.

2. John Reader, *Africa: A Biography of the Continent* (New York: Vintage Books, 1999), 380.

3. Ibid., 291.

4. Robert O. Collins and James M. Burns, *A History of Sub-Saharan Africa* (New York: Cambridge University Press, 2007), 229.

5. Stanley Engerman and Kenneth Sokoloff, "Factor Endowments, Institutions, and Differential Paths of Growth among New World Economies: A View from Economic Historians of the United States," in *How Latin America Fell Behind: Essays on the Economic Histories of Brazil and Mexico, 1800–1914*, ed. Stephen Haber (Stanford: Stanford University Press, 1997), 260–304; Hugh Thomas, *The Slave Trade: The Story of the Atlantic Slave Trade* (New York: Simon and Schuster, 1997).

6. Nathan Nunn, "The Long-Term Effects of Africa's Slave Trades," *Quarterly Journal of Economics* 123, no. 1 (2008): 139–176.

7. Patrick Manning, *Slavery and African Life,* (New York: Cambridge University Press, 1990).

8. Ibid.

9. Walter Rodney, *How Europe Underdeveloped Africa* (Washington: Howard University Press, 1972).

10. Reader, *Africa*, 395.

11. Ibid.

12. Ibid., 417.

13. Nathan Nunn and Leonard Wantchekon, "The Slave Trade and the Origins of Mistrust in Africa," *The American Economic Review* 101, no. 7 (2001): 3221–3252.

14. Joni Seagar, *Penguin Atlas of Women in the World* (New York: Penguin, 2009), 57.

15. Nicholas D. Kristof and Sheryl WuDunn, *Half the Sky: Turning Oppression into Opportunity for Women Worldwide* (New York: Vintage, 2010), chapters 1–3.

16. George L. Beckford, *Persistent Poverty: Underdevelopment in Plantation Economies of the Third World* (New York: Oxford University Press, 1972).

17. Engerman and Sokoloff, "Factor Endowments."

18. Reader, *Africa*, 408.

19. Jeffrey G. Williamson, "Five Centuries of Latin American Income Inequality," *Journal of Iberian and Latin American Economic History* 28, no. 2 (2010): 227–252.

20. Crawford Young, *The African Colonial State in Comparative Perspective* (New Haven, CT: Yale University Press, 1994), 63.

21. Angus Maddison, *The World Economy: Volume 1, A Millennial Perspective* (Paris: Organisation for Economic Co-operation and Development, 2006), 89.

22. Daron Acemoglu, Simon Johnson, and James A. Robinson, "The Colonial Origins of Comparative Development: An Empirical Investigation," *The American Economic Review* 91, no. 5 (2001): 1369–1401.

23. Ernest Mandel, *Marxist Economic Theory*, vol. 2 (New York: Monthly Review Press, 1968), 452.

24. Barrington Moore Jr., *Social Origins of Dictatorship and Democracy* (Boston: Beacon Press, 1966).

25. Acemoglu, Johnson, and Robinson, "The Colonial Origins of Comparative Development."

26. Young, *The African Colonial State in Comparative Perspective*, 283.

27. William Easterly, *The White Man's Burden: Why the West's Efforts to Aid the Rest Have Done So Much Ill and So Little Good* (New York: Penguin Group, 2006), 290.

28. Mahmood Mamdani, *When Victims Become Killers: Colonialism, Nativism, and the Genocide in Rwanda* (Princeton, NJ: Princeton University Press, 2002).

29. Mahmood Mamdani, *Citizen and Subject* (Princeton, NJ: Princeton University Press, 1996).

30. P. T. Bauer, *Reality and Rhetoric: Studies in Economic Development* (Cambridge: Harvard University Press, 1984), 90.

31. Peter Richens, "The Economic Legacies of the 'Thin White Line': Indirect Rule and the Comparative Development of Sub-Saharan Africa," *African Economic History* 37 (2009), 33–102.

32. Niall Ferguson, *Empire: The Rise and Demise of the British World Order and the Lessons of Global Power* (New York: Basic Books, 2003).

33. Timur Kuran, *The Long Divergence: How Islamic Law Held Back the Middle East* (Princeton, NJ: Princeton University Press, 2011), 37.

34. George B. N. Ayittey, *Africa Unchained: The Blueprint for Africa's Future* (New York: Palgrave Macmillan, 2005), 352.

35. Gapminder, www.gapminder.org.

36. Oladimeji Aborisade and Robert J. Mundt, *Politics in Nigeria*, 2nd ed. (New York: Longman Publishers, 2001).

37. Ibid., 158.

38. Nunn and Wantchekon, "The Slave Trade and the Origins of Mistrust in Africa."

39. Atul Kohli, *State-Directed Development: Political Power and Industrialization in the Global Periphery* (New York: Cambridge University Press, 2004), 324.

40. Ibid.

41. Transparency International, *Corruption Perceptions Index* (Berlin: Transparency International, 2010).

42. Richard Dowden, *Africa: Altered States, Ordinary Miracles* (London: Portobello Books, Ltd., 2008).

43. Elisabeth Rosenthal, "Nigeria Tested by Rapid Rise in Population," *The New York Times*, April 14, 2012, http://www.nytimes.com/2012/04/15/world/africa/in-nigeria-a-preview-of-an-overcrowded-planet.html?pagewanted=all&_r=0.

44. William J. Bernstein, *A Splendid Exchange: How Trade Shaped the World* (New York: Grove Press, 2008).

45. Aborisade and Mundt, *Politics in Nigeria*, 2nd ed.

46. Rhoda E. Howard-Hassmann, "Reparations to Africa and the Group of Eminent Persons," *Cahiers D'Etudes Africaines* 173 (2004), 81–97.

Chapter 5

1. Adam Smith, *An Inquiry into the Nature and Causes of the Wealth of Nations* (London: W. Strahan and T. Cadell, 1776).

2. David Ricardo, *On the Principles of Political Economy and Taxation* (London: John Murray, 1817).

3. Alan Richards and John Waterbury, *A Political Economy of the Middle East*, 3rd ed. (Boulder: Westview Press, 2007), 189.

4. Peter Kingstone, *The Political Economy of Latin America: Reflections on Neoliberalism and Development* (New York: Routledge, 2011), 36.

5. Raul Prebisch, *The Economic Development of Latin America and its Principal Problems* (New York: Economic Commission for Latin America, 1950).

6. Hans Singer, "The Distribution of Gains between Investing and Borrowing Countries," *The American Economic Review* 40, no. 2 (1950): 473–485.

7. Paul Baran, *The Political Economy of Growth* (New York: Monthly Review Press, 1957).

8. Theotonio Dos Santos, "The Structure of Dependence," *American Economic Review* 60, no. 2 (1970): 231–263, 231.

9. Arghiri Emmanuel, *Unequal Exchange: A Study of the Imperialism of Trade* (New York: Monthly Review Press, 1972); Samir Amin, *Unequal Development: An Essay on the Social Formations of Peripheral Capitalism* (New York: Monthly Review Press, 1976).

10. Andre Gunder Frank, *Lumpen-Bourgeoisie, Lumpen-Development: Dependence, Class, and Politics in Latin America* (New York: Monthly Review Press, 1972).

11. Stephen Schlesinger and Stephen Kinzer, *Bitter Fruit* (Cambridge: Harvard University, 1999).

12. Immannuel Wallerstein, *The Essential Wallerstein* (New York: The New Press, 2000).

13. Christopher Chase-Dunn, *Global Formation: Structures of the World Economy* (New York: Blackwell, 1989).

14. Jeffrey G. Williamson, *Trade and Poverty: When the Third World Fell Behind* (Cambridge: MIT Press, 2011).

15. Ibid., 183.

16. Norman V. Loayza, Romain Rancière, Luis Servén, and Jaume Ventura, "Macroeconomic Volatility and Welfare in Developing Countries: An Introduction," *World Bank Economic Review* 21, no. 3 (2007): 343–357.

17. Williamson, *Trade and Poverty*, chapter 10.

18. James M. Cypher and James L. Dietz, "Static and Dynamic Comparative Advantage: A Multi-Period Analysis with Declining Terms of Trade," *Journal of Economic Issues* 32, no. 2 (1998): 305–314.

19. Sebastian Edwards, *Left Behind: Latin America and the False Promise of Populism* (Chicago: University of Chicago Press, 2010), 47.

20. Thomas Oatley, *International Political Economy: Interests and Institutions in the Global Economy*, 2nd ed. (Boston: Longman, 2006), 318.

21. Edwards, *Left Behind*, 93.

22. Oatley, *International Political Economy*, 169.

23. World Bank, *Atlas of Global Development*, 2nd ed. (Glasgow: HarperCollins Publishers, 2009), 81; "Economic and Financial Indicators," *The Economist*, November 13, 2010, 113.

24. Thomas Friedman, *The World is Flat* (New York: Farrar, Straus and Giroux, 2005).

25. Charles Duhigg and Steven Greenhouse, "Electronic Giant Vowing Reforms in China Plant," *The New York Times*, March 29, 2012, http://www.nytimes.com/2012/03/30/business/apple-supplier-in-china-pledges-changes-in-working-conditions.html?pagewanted=all.

26. Quoted in Jeffrey A. Frieden, *Global Capitalism: Its Fall and Rise in the Twentieth Century* (New York: W. W. Norton and Company, 2006), 392–393.

27. William J. Carrington and Enrica Detragiache, "How Extensive Is the Brain Drain?," *Finance and Development: A Quarterly Magazine of the IMF* 36, no. 2 (1999), available online at http://www.imf.org/external/pubs/ft/fandd/1999/06/carringt.htm.

28. World Bank, *Atlas of Global Development*, 81.

29. Martin Wolf, *Why Globalization Works* (New Haven: Yale University Press, 2004); Jagdish Bhagwati, *In Defense of Globalization* (Oxford: Oxford University Press, 2004).

30. Andy Baker, *The Market and the Masses in Latin America: Policy Reform and Consumption in Liberalizing Economies* (New York: Cambridge University Press, 2009); Douglas A. Irwin, *Free Trade under Fire* (Princeton, NJ: Princeton University Press, 2009).

31. Bhagwati, *In Defense of Globalization*; Edward M. Graham, *Fighting the Wrong Enemy: Antiglobal Activities and Multinational Enterprises* (Washington, D.C.: Institute for International Economics, 2000).

32. Nathan M. Jensen, *Nation-States and the Multinational Corporation: A Political Economy of Foreign Direct Investment* (Princeton, NJ: Princeton University Press, 2008).

33. International Fund for Agriculture and Development, *Sending Money Home: Worldwide Remittance Flows to Developing and Transition Countries* (Rome: International Fund for Agriculture and Development, 2007).

34. Gapminder, www.gapminder.org.

35. Ibid.

36. Werner Baer, *The Brazilian Economy: Growth and Development* (Westport, CT: Praeger, 2001).

37. Williamson, *Trade and Poverty*, 174.

38. Celso Furtado, *The Economic Growth of Brazil: A Survey from Colonial to Modern Times* (Berkeley: University of California Press, 1963).

39. Frieden, *Global Capitalism*, 304.

40. Gapminder, www.gapminder.org.

41. Baer, *The Brazilian Economy*.

42. Lee Alston, Edwyna Harris, and Bernardo Mueller, "The Development of Property Rights on Frontiers," *Journal of Economic History* 72, no. 3 (September 2012): 741–770.

43. Stanley L. Engerman and Kenneth L. Sokoloff, *Economic Development in the Americas since 1500: Endowments and Institutions* (New York: Cambridge University Press, 2012).

44. Peter Evans, *Dependent Development* (Princeton, NJ: Princeton University Press, 1979).

45. Joseli Oliviera-Ferreira, et al., "Malaria in Brazil: An Overview," April 30, 2010, http://www.malariajournal.com/content/9/1/115.

Chapter 6

1. World Bank, World Development Indicators, http://data.worldbank.org/data-catalog/world-development-indicators.

2. Bono, foreward, in *The End of Poverty: Economic Possibilities for Our Time*, by Jeffrey Sachs (New York: Penguin, 2005), xv.

3. Carol Lancaster, *Foreign Aid: Diplomacy, Development, Domestic Politics* (Chicago: University of Chicago Press, 2006), 9–10.

4. Ibid.

5. Arjan de Haan, *How the Aid Industry Works: An Introduction to International Development* (Sterling, VA: Kumarian Press, 2009), 49.

6. Lancaster, *Foreign Aid*, 25.

7. Ibid., 95.

8. Organisation for Economic Co-operation and Development, http://www.oecd.org/dac/dacglossaryofkeytermsandconcepts.htm#ODA.

9. Lancaster, *Foreign Aid*, 57.

10. Louis Picard and Terry Buss, *A Fragile Balance: Re-examining the History of Foreign Aid, Security and Diplomacy* (Sterling, VA: Kumarian Press, 2009), 163.

11. Tony Blair, "Full Text: Tony Blair's Speech," *The Guardian*, October 2, 2001, http://www.guardian.co.uk/politics/2001/oct/02/labourconference.labour6.

12. Lancaster, *Foreign Aid*, 79.

13. Ibid, 358.

14. Roger C. Riddell, *Does Foreign Aid Really Work?* (New York: Oxford University Press, 2007), 358.

15. William Easterly, *The White Man's Burden: Why the West's Efforts to Aid the Rest Have Done So Much Ill and So Little Good* (New York: Penguin, 2006), 169.

16. William Easterly, *The Elusive Quest for Growth: Economists' Adventures and Misadventures in the Tropics* (Cambridge: MIT Press, 2001).

17. Robert Guest, *The Shackled Continent: Power, Corruption, and African Lives* (Washington D.C.: Smithsonian Books, 2004), 151.

18. Ibid.

19. P. T. Bauer, *Dissent on Development*, rev. ed. (Cambridge: Harvard University Press, 1976), 97–98.

20. Craig Burnside and David Dollar, "Aid, Policies, and Growth," *The American Economic Review* 90, no. 4 (2000): 847–868.

21. Riddell, *Does Foreign Aid Really Work?*, 344.

22. Dambisa Moyo, *Dead Aid: Why Aid Is Not Working and How There Is a Better Way for Africa* (New York: Farrar, Straus and Giroux, 2009), 66.

23. Ritva Reinikka, "Donors and Service Delivery," in *Reinventing Foreign Aid*, ed. William Easterly (Cambridge: MIT Press, 2008), 179–195.

24. Karen L. Remmer, "Does Foreign Aid Promote the Expansion of Government?," *American Journal of Political Science* 48, no. 1 (2004), 77–92.

25. Peter Boone, "Politics and Effectiveness of Foreign Aid," *European Economic Review* 40, no. 2 (February 1996): 289–329.

26. Raghuram Rajan, "Aid and Growth: The Policy Challenge," International Monetary Fund, December 2005, http://www.imf.org/external/pubs/ft/fandd/2005/12/straight.htm.

27. Walter Rostow, *The Stages of Economic Growth: A Non-Communist Manifesto* (Cambridge: Cambridge University Press, 1960).

28. Jeffrey Sachs, *The End of Poverty: Economic Possibilities for Our Time* (New York: Penguin, 2005).

29. Easterly, *The White Man's Burden*, 241.

30. Sachs, *The End of Poverty*, 260 and 263.

31. Jeffrey Sachs, *Common Wealth Economics for a Crowded Planet* (New York: Penguin, 2008), 48.

32. World Bank, *World Development Report 2006: Equity and Development* (New York: Oxford University Press, 2006), 220.

33. Dean Karlan and Jacob Appel, *More than Good Intentions* (New York: Penguin, 2011); Abhijit Banerjee and Esther Duflo, *Poor Economics: A Radical Rethinking of the Way to Fight Global Poverty* (New York: Public Affairs, 2011).

34. James Vreeland, *The International Monetary Fund: Politics of Conditional Lending* (London: Routledge, 2006), chapter 1.

35. Easterly, *White Man's Burden*, 217.

36. Vreeland, *The International Monetary Fund*, 28.

37. Richard Peet, *Unholy Trinity: The IMF, World Bank, and WTO*, 2nd ed. (New York: Zed Books, 2009), 66.

38. Joseph Stiglitz, *Globalization and its Discontents* (New York: W. W. Norton and Company, 2002).

39. James Vreeland, "The Effect of IMF Programs on Labor," *World Development* 30, no. 1 (2002): 121–139; James Vreeland, *The IMF and Economic Development* (Cambridge: Cambridge University Press, 2003).

40. Stiglitz, *Globalization and its Discontents*.

41. Easterly, *White Man's Burden*, 147.

42. James Vreeland, *The International Monetary Fund*, chapter 5.

43. Easterly, *White Man's Burden*, 230.

44. Guest, *The Shackled Continent: Power, Corruption, and African Lives* (Washington, D.C.: Smithsonian Books, 2004), 159.

45. James Vreeland, *The IMF and Economic Development*.

46. "Special Report: Pakistan," *The Economist*, February 11, 2012, p. 14.

47. Gapminder, www.gapminder.org.

48. William Easterly, "The Political Economy of Growth without Development: A Case Study of Pakistan," in *In Search of Prosperity: Analytical Narratives of Growth*, ed. Dani Rodrik (Princeton, NJ: Princeton University Press, 2003).

49. William Easterly, "The Political Economy of Growth without Development."

50. Nancy Birdsall and Molly Kinder, "The U.S. Aid 'Surge' to Pakistan," CGD Working Paper 205, Center for Global Development, Washington, D.C., March 2010.

51. Ibid., 29.

52. Samia Waheed Altaf, *So Much Aid, So Little Development* (Washington, D.C.: Woodrow Wilson Center Press, 2000), 9.

53. Ibid., 6.

54. The International Monetary Fund, "Pakistan: History of Lending Arrangements from May 01, 1984 to October 31, 2011," http://www.imf.org/external/np/fin/tad/extarr2.aspx?memberkey1=760&date1Key=2011-10-31.

55. Vreeland, *The International Monetary Fund*, 34.

56. Ishrat Husain, *Pakistan: The Economy of an Elitist State* (Karachi: Oxford University Press, 1999), chapter 2.

57. Owen Bennett Jones, *Pakistan: Eye of the Storm* (New Haven, CT: Yale University Press, 2003), 248–256.

58. Easterly, *Political Economy of Growth*.

59. Jones, *Pakistan*, 303.

60. "Special Report: Pakistan," 15–16.

61. Ibid., 14.

Chapter 7

1. Edward O. Wilson, *Sociobiology: The New Synthesis* (Cambridge: Harvard University Press, 1975).

2. World Values Survey, http://www.worldvaluessurvey.org/.

3. Max Weber, *The Protestant Ethic and the Spirit of Capitalism* (New York: Penguin, [1905] 2002), 105. Citation is from the 2002 version.

4. Max Weber, *The Religion of China: Confucianism and Taoism* (Glencoe, IL: Free Press, [1915] 1951).

5. Max Weber, *The Religion of India: The Sociology of Hinduism and Buddhism* (Glencoe, IL: Free Press, [1916] 1958).

6. Seymour Martin Lipset, *Political Man: The Social Bases of Politics* (Garden City, NY: Doubleday & Company, 1960).

7. Daniel Lerner, *The Passing of Traditional Society: Modernizing the Middle East* (Glencoe, IL: Macmillan Publishing Company, 1958); Edward Banfield, *The Moral Basis of a Backward Society* (Glencoe, IL: The Free Press, 1958); Gabriel A. Almond and Sidney Verba, *The Civic Culture: Political Attitudes and Democracy in Five Nations* (Princeton, NJ: Princeton University Press, 1963); Alex Inkeles and David Smith, *Becoming Modern: Individual Change in Six Developing Countries* (Cambridge: Harvard University Press, 1974).

8. Frances Fukuyama, *Trust: The Social Virtues and the Creation of Prosperity* (New York: Free Press, 1996), 205.

9. Mark S. Granovetter, "The Strength of Weak Ties," *American Journal of Sociology* 78, no. 6 (1973): 1360–1380.

10. Fukuyama, *Trust*, 7.

11. Robert Putnam, with Robert Leonardi and Raffaella Y. Nanetti, *Making Democracy Work: Civic Traditions in Modern Italy* (Princeton, NJ: Princeton University Press, 1994).

12. James Granato, Ronald Inglehart, and David Leblang, "The Effect of Cultural Values on Economic Development: Theory, Hypothesis, and Some Empirical Tests," *American Journal of Political Science* 40, no. 3 (1996): 607–631.

13. Fareed Zakaria, "A Conversation with Lee Kwan Yew," *Foreign Affairs*, March/April 1994, http://www.foreignaffairs.com/articles/49691/fareed-zakaria/a-conversation-with-lee-kuan-yew.

14. Joel Kotkin, *Tribes: How Race, Religion, and Identity Determine Success in The New Global Economy* (New York: Random House, 1993).

15. David S. Landes, *The Wealth and Poverty of Nations: Why Some Are So Rich and Some So Poor* (New York: W. W. Norton & Company, 1999), 371–391.

16. Ibid., 392–441.

17. Bernard Lewis, *The Muslim Discovery of Europe* (New York: W. W. Norton & Company, 1982).

18. Lawrence E. Harrison, *The Pan-American Dream: Do Latin America's Cultural Values Discourage True Partnership with the United States and Canada?* (New York: Basic Books, 1997).

19. Daniel Etounga-Manguelle, "Does Africa Need a Cultural Adjustment Program?," in *Culture Matters: How Values Shape Human Progress*, eds. Lawrence E. Harrison and Samuel P. Huntington (New York: Basic Books, 2000), 65–77, 69.

20. Daron Acemoglu and James Robinson, *Why Nations Fail: The Origins of Power, Prosperity, and Poverty* (New York: Crown Business, 2012), 56–63.

21. Organisation for Economic Co-operation and Development, Stat Extracts, http://stats.oecd.org/Index.aspx?Dataset Code=ANHRS.

22. Abhijit Banerjee and Esther Duflo, *Poor Economics: A Radical Rethinking of the Way to Fight Global Poverty* (New York: Public Affairs, 2011); Hernando de Soto, *The Other Path: The Invisible Revolution in the Third World* (New York: Harper and Row, 1989).

23. Hernando de Soto, *The Mystery of Capital: Why Capitalism Triumphs in the West and Fails Everywhere Else* (New York: Basic Books, 2000), 5.

24. Landes, *The Wealth and Poverty of Nations*, 410.

25. Timur Kuran, "Islam and Underdevelopment: An Old Puzzle Revisited," *Journal of Institutional and Theoretical Economics* 153, no 1 (1997): 41–71.

26. Acemoglu and Robinson, *Why Nations Fail*, 213–215.

27. International Telecommunication Union, *ICT Adoption and Prospects in the Arab Region* (Geneva: ITU, 2012), 1.

28. Timur Kuran, *The Long Divergence: How Islamic Law Held Back the Middle East* (Princeton, NJ: Princeton University Press, 2010).

29. Ibid., 3–4.

30. Acemoglu and Robinson, *Why Nations Fail*, chapters 2 and 3.

31. William Easterly and Ross Levine, "Africa's Growth Tragedy: Policies and Ethnic Divisions," *Quarterly Journal of Economics* 112, no. 4 (1997): 1203–1250.

32. James P. Habyarimana, Macartan Humphreys, Daniel N. Posner, and Jeremy M. Weinstein, *Coethnicity: Diversity and the Dilemmas of Collective Action* (New York: Russell Sage Foundation, 2009).

33. Alberto Alesina, Edward Glaeser, and Bruce Sacerdote, *Why Doesn't the U.S. Have a European-Style Welfare State?*, 2001, http://www.wcfia.harvard.edu/sites/default/files/423__0332-Alesina11.pdf.

34. Raphael Franck and Ilia Rainer, "Does the Leader's Ethnicity Matter? Ethnic Favoritism, Education, and Health in Sub-Saharan Africa," *American Political Science Review* 106, no. 102 (2012): 294–325.

35. Claude M. Steele and Joshua Aronson, "Stereotype Threat and the Intellectual Test Performance of African Americans," *Journal of Personality and Social Psychology* 69, no. 5 (1995): 797–811.

36. Karla Hoff and Priyank Pandey, "Belief Systems and Durable Inequalities: An Experimental Investigation of Indian Caste," World Bank Policy Research Working Paper No. 3351, 2004, http://elibrary.worldbank.org/docserver/download/3351.pdf?expires=1363799427&id=id&accname=guest&checksum=4F9AB5C0B864018CE44DD0A933D2B4E3.

37. World Bank, *World Development Report: Gender Equality and Development* (Washington D.C.: World Bank Publications, 2011), 75.

38. James D. Fearon, "Ethnic and Cultural Diversity by Country," *Journal of Economic Growth* 8 (June 2003): 197.

39. Ernest Gellner, *Nations and Nationalism* (Ithaca, NY: Cornell University Press, 1983).

40. Benedict Anderson, *Imagined Communities: Reflections on the Origin and Spread of Nationalism* (London: Verso, 2006).

41. Jeffery Herbst, *States and Power in Africa: Comparative Lessons in Authority and Control* (Princeton, NJ: Princeton University Press, 2000).

42. James D. Fearon and David D. Laitin, "Explaining Interethnic Cooperation," *American Political Science Review* 90, no. 4 (1996): 715–735.

43. Gapminder, www.gapminder.org.

44. Patrick Basham, "Can Iraq Be Democratic?" CATO Institute, January 5, 2004, http://www.cato.org/doc-download/sites/cato.org/files/pubs/pdf/pa505.pdf.

45. Charles Krauthammer, "Why Iraq Is Crumbling," *The Washington Post*, November 16, 2006, http://www.washingtonpost.com/wp-dyn/content/article/2006/11/16/AR2006111601359.html.

46. Jodie R. Gorrill, "Doing Business in Iraq: Iraqi Social and Business Culture," Communicaid, 2009, http://www.communicaid.com/access/pdf/library/culture/doing-business-in/Doing%20Business%20in%20Iraq.pdf, 1.

47. Ibid.

48. Basham, "Can Iraq Be Democratic?"

49. John Leland and Jack Healy, "After Months, Iraqi Lawmakers Approve a Government," *The New York Times*, December 21, 2010, http://www.nytimes.com/2010/12/22/world/middleeast/22iraq.html?_r=0.

50. Gapminder, www.gapminder.org.
51. Campaign Against Sanctions on Iraq, "UNICEF: Questions and Answers for the Iraq Child Mortality Survey," August 16, 1999, www.casi.org.uk/info/unicef/990816qa.html.
52. Iraq Body Count, www.iraqbodycount.org/.
53. Gapminder, www.gapminder.org.
54. Randy Schnepf, "Iraq's Agriculture: Background and Status," CRS Report for Congress, May 13, 2003, http://www.nationalag lawcenter.org/assets/crs/RS21516.pdf.

Chapter 8

1. John Maynard Keynes, *The General Theory of Employment, Interest, and Money* (London: Macmillan, 1936).
2. Paul Rosenstein-Rodan, "Problems of Industrialization of Eastern and South-Eastern Europe," *Economic Journal* 53, no. 210/211 (1943): 202–211.
3. Albert Hirschman, *The Strategy of Economic Development* (New York: Norton, 1958).
4. Mustapha K. Nabli, Jennifer Keller, Claudia Nassif, and Carlos Silva-Jáuregui, "The Political Economy of Industrial Policy in the Middle East and North Africa," The World Bank, March 2006, http: //siteresources.worldbank.org/INTMENA/422183-11316 56931098/20895775/ThePoliticalEconomyofIndustrial PolicyMarch302006.pdf.
5. Sebastian Edwards, *Left Behind: Latin America and the False Promise of Populism* (Chicago: University of Chicago Press, 2010), 56.
6. Rudiger Dornbusch and Sebastian Edwards, eds., *The Macroeconomics of Populism in Latin America* (Chicago: University of Chicago Press, 1992).
7. Robert Bates, *States and Markets in Tropical Africa: The Political Basis of Agricultural Policy* (Berkeley: University of California Press, 1981).
8. Ha-Joon Chang, *Bad Samaritans: The Myth of Free Trade and the Secret History of Capitalism* (New York: Bloomsbury Press, 2008).
9. World Bank, World Development Indicators, http://data.world-bank.org/data-catalog/world-development-indicators.
10. Alice H. Amsden, *Asia's Next Giant: South Korea and Late Industrialization* (New York: Oxford University Press, 1992); Robert Wade, *Governing the Market: Economic Theory and the Role of Government in East Asian Industrialization* (Princeton, NJ: Princeton University Press, 1990).
11. Barry Naughton, *The Chinese Economy: Transitions and Growth* (Cambridge: MIT Press, 2007), 72.
12. Martin Meredith, *The Fate of Africa* (New York: Public Affairs, 2005), 255.
13. Naughton, *The Chinese Economy*, 82.
14. Friedrich A. Hayek, *The Road to Serfdom.* (Chicago: University of Chicago Press, 1944).
15. Milton Friedman, *A Theory of the Consumption Function* (Princeton, NJ: Princeton University Press, 1956).
16. Milton Friedman, *Capitalism and Freedom* (Chicago: University of Chicago Press, 1962).
17. Anne Krueger, "The Political Economy of the Rent-Seeking Society," *American Economic Review* 64, no. 3 (1974): 291-303.
18. John Williamson, "What Washington Means by Policy Reform," in *Latin American Adjustment: How Much Has Happened?*, ed. John Williamson (Washington, D.C.: Institute for International Economics, 1990), chapter two.
19. Ming Wan, *The Political Economy of East Asia: Striving for Wealth and Power* (Washington, D.C.: Congressional Quarterly Press, 2008), 255.
20. World Bank, World Development Indicators.
21. Ibid.
22. Donald Robbins, *Trade, Trade Liberalization and Inequality in Latin America and East Asia: Synthesis of Seven Country Studies* (Cambridge: Harvard Institute for International Development, 1996).
23. Ian Bremmer, *The End of the Free Market: Who Wins the War between States and Corporations?* (New York: Portfolio, 2010).
24. "Special Report: State Capitalism," *The Economist,* January 21, 2012, 1–18.
25. World Bank, World Development Indicators.
26. Andy Baker, *The Market and the Masses in Latin America: Policy Reform and Consumption in Liberalizing Economies* (New York: Cambridge University Press, 2009).
27. Steven Radelet, *Emerging Africa: How 17 Countries Are Leading the Way* (Washington, D.C.: Center for Global Development, 2010).
28. Edwards, *Left Behind.*
29. "Special Report: State Capitalism."
30. Atul Kohli, *State-Directed Development: Political Power and Industrialization in the Global Periphery* (New York: Cambridge University Press, 2004); Arvind Panagariya, *India: The Emerging Giant* (New York: Oxford University Press, 2008).
31. "The Half-Finished Revolution," *The Economist,* July 23, 2011, 58–60.
32. Kohli, *State-Directed Development*, 258.
33. Panagariya, *India*, 69.
34. Ranajit Guha, *Dominance without Hegemony: History and Power in Colonial India* (Cambridge: Harvard University Press, 1997).
35. Ernest Mandel, *Marxist Economic Theory, Volume Two* (New York: Monthly Review Press, [1962] 1968), chapter 13.
36. Barrington Moore, Jr., *Social Origins of Dictatorship and Democracy* (Boston: Beacon Press, 1966).
37. Angus Maddison, *The World Economy: Volume 1, A Millennial Perspective* (Paris: Organisation for Economic Co-operation and Development, 2006), 89.
38. John Luke Gallup, Jeffrey D. Sachs, and Andrew Mellinger, "Geography and Economic Development," *International Regional Science Review,* 22, no. 2 (1999): 179–232, 183.
39. David Landes, *The Unbound Prometheus: Technological Change and Industrial Development in Western Europe from 1750 to the Present,* 2nd ed. (Cambridge: Cambridge University Press, 2003), 38.

Chapter 9

1. Hernando de Soto, *The Mystery of Capital: Why Capitalism Succeeds in the West and Fails Everywhere Else* (New York: Basic Books, 2000), 36.

2. UN-HABITAT, United Nations Human Settlements Programme, Statistics, 2003, http://ww2.unhabitat.org/programmes/guo/statistics.asp.

3. De Soto, *The Mystery of Capital*.

4. World Bank, "The Ease of Doing Business in: Haiti," 2012, www.doingbusiness.org/data/exploreeconomies/haiti#registering-property.

5. Anastasia Moloney, "Unclear Land Rights Hinder Haiti's Reconstruction," Alert Net, July 2010, http://reliefweb.int/report/haiti/unclear-land-rights-hinder-haitis-reconstruction.

6. Karla Hoff and Joseph Stiglitz, "Modern Economic Theory and Development," in *Frontiers of Development Economics*, ed. Gerald M. Meier and Joseph Stiglitz, 389–460 (New York: Oxford University Press, 2001), 389.

7. Douglass C. North, *Structure and Change in Economic History* (New York: W. W. Norton and Company, 1981).

8. Douglass C. North, *Institutions, Institutional Change and Economic Performance* (Cambridge: Cambridge University Press, 1990).

9. Lee J. Alston, Gary D. Libecap, and Robert Schneider, "Property Rights and the Preconditions for Markets: The Case of the Amazon Frontier," *Journal of Institutional and Theoretical Economics* 151, no. 1 (1995): 89–107.

10. Stanley L. Engerman and Kenneth L. Sokoloff, "Factor Endowments, Inequality, and Paths of Development among New World Economies," National Bureau of Economic Research, October 2002, http://www.nber.org/papers/w9259.pdf.

11. Robert Guest, *The Shackled Continent: Power, Corruption, and African Lives* (Washington, D.C.: Smithsonian Books, 2004).

12. De Soto, *The Mystery of Capital*. 32.

13. Ibid., 39–40.

14. John Gravois, "The De Soto Delusion," Slate, January 29, 2005, http://www.slate.com/articles/news_and_politics/hey_wait_a_minute/2005/01/the_de_soto_delusion.html.

15. Alan G. Gilbert, "On the Mystery of Capital and the Myths of Hernando de Soto: What Difference Does Legal Title Make?," *International Development Planning Review* 24, no. 1 (2002): 1–20.

16. Jean Ensminger, "Changing Property Rights: Reconciling Formal and Informal Rights to Land in Africa," in *The Frontiers of the New Institutional Economics*, ed. John N. Drobak and John V.C Nye (San Diego: Academic Press: 1997), 165–196.

17. Alan G. Gilbert, "On the Mystery of Capital."

18. Jean O. Lanjouw and Phillip I. Levy, "Untitled: A Study of Formal and Informal Property Rights in Urban Ecuador," Economic Growth Center, Yale University, April 1998, http://www.econ.yale.edu/growth_pdf/cdp788.pdf.

19. Abhijit V. Banerjee and Esther Duflo, *Poor Economics: A Radical Rethinking of the Way to Fight Global Poverty* (New York: Public Affairs, 2011), 135.

20. Enterprise Surveys: Methodology, www.enterprisesurveys.org/Methodology.

21. Guillermo E. Perry et al., *Informality: Exit and Exclusion* (Washington D.C., World Bank, 2007), chapter 1; Rafael La Porta and Andrei Shleifer, "The Unofficial Economy," National Bureau of Economic Research, December 2008, http://www.nber.org/papers/w14520.pdf?new_window=1.

22. World Bank, *World Development Report 2002: Building Institutions for Markets* (Washington, D.C., World Bank Publications, 2002), 139.

23. De Soto, *The Mystery of Capitalism*, 18.

24. World Bank, *World Development Report 2002*.

25. Banerjee and Duflo, *Poor Economics*, 159.

26. Ibid., 185.

27. Daryl Collins, Jonathan Morduch, Stuart Rutherford, and Orlanda Ruthven, *Portfolios of the Poor: How the World's Poor Live on $2 a Day* (Princeton, NJ: Princeton University Press, 2009), 17.

28. Ibid., chapter 5.

29. William Easterly, "Clueless in Pakistan," *The Globalist*, December 1, 2001, www.theglobalist.com/StoryId.aspx?StoryId=2229.

30. De Soto, *The Mystery of Capital*, 4.

31. "Commanding Heights: Episode 3: Rule of the Game," PBS, www.pbs.org/wgbh/commandingheights/shared/minitextlo/tr_show03.html.

32. La Porta and Shleifer, "The Unofficial Economy," 2008.

33. Banerjee and Duflo, *Poor Economics*, 205–234.

34. Ibid., 205 and 226.

35. Ibid., 228.

36. Collins et al., *Portfolios of the Poor*.

37. La Porta and Shleifer, "The Unofficial Economy and Economic Development."

38. Dean Karlan and Jacob Appel, *More than Good Intentions: How a New Economics Is Helping to Solve Global Poverty* (New York: Dutton Press, 2011), 19.

39. Banerjee and Duflo, *Poor Economics*, chapter 7.

40. Abhijit Banerjee, Esther Duflo, Rachel Glennerster, and Cynthia Kinnan, "The Miracle of Microfinance? Evidence from a Randomized Evaluation," Massachusetts Institute of Technology, May 30, 2009, economics.mit.edu/files/4162.

41. World Bank, *World Development Report 2012: Gender Equality and Development* (Washington D.C.: World Bank, 2011), 225.

42. Matthew Swibel, "The Top 50 Microfinance Institutions," Forbes, December 20, 2007, www.forbes.com/2007/12/20/microfinance-philanthropy-credit-biz-cz_ms_1220microfinance_table.html.

43. "Financial Institutions with a 'Double Bottom Line': Implications for the Future of Microfinance," Consultative Group to Assist the Poor, Occasional Paper, July 2004, www.cgap.org/sites/default/files/CGAP-Occasional-Paper-Financial-Institutions-with-a-Double-Bottom-Line-Implications-for-the-Future-of-Microfinance-Jul-2004.pdf.

44. Karlan and Appel, *More than Good Intentions*, chapter 4.

45. Banerjee et al., "The Miracle of Microfinance?"

46. Neil MacFarquhar, "Banks Making Big Profits from Tiny Loans," *The New York Times*, April 13, 2010, www.nytimes.com/2010/04/14/world/14microfinance.html?_r=1&pagewanted=all.

47. Collins et al., *Portfolios of the Poor*.

48. Gina Neff, "Microcredit, Microresults," Left Business Observer 74 (October 1996), available online at www.leftbusinessobserver.com/Micro.html.

49. Perry et al., *Informality*, 29.

50. Hernando de Soto, *The Other Path: The Economic Answer to Terrorism* (New York: Harper and Rowe, 1989).

51. Ibid.

52. Norman Loayza, "The Causes and Consequences of Informality in Peru," World Bank, November 2007, www.bcrp.gob.pe/docs/Publicaciones/Documentos-de-Trabajo/2007/Working-Paper-18-2007.pdf.

53. Perry et al., *Informality,* 173.

54. Economist Intelligence Unit, "Global Microscope on the Microfinance Business Environment, *The Economist,* 2010, http://idbdocs.iadb.org/wsdocs/getdocument.aspx?docnum=35379430.

55. Anthony Flint, "News Listing: Report Assesses Programs to Improve Latin America's Slums," Lincoln Institute of Land Policy, May 9, 2011, http://www.lincolninst.edu/news-events/news-listing/articletype/articleview/articleid/1597/report-assesses-programs-to-improve-latin-americas-slums.

56. Howard J. Wiarda, *The Soul of Latin America: The Culture and Political Tradition* (New Haven: Yale University 2001).

57. Heraclio Bonilla, *Guano y burguesía en el Perú* (Lima: Institute de Estudios Peruanos, 1974).

58. John Peter Olinger, "The Guano Age in Peru," *History Today* 30, no. 6 (1980), available online at http://www.historytoday.com/john-peter-olinger/guano-age-peru.

59. National Geographic, "Map: The Inca Empire," http://ngm.nationalgeographic.com/2011/04/inca-empire/interactive-map.

Chapter 10

1. Inspired by this story: Liao Yiwu and Wen Huang, "The Former Landowner," *Theme* 4 (Winter 2005), available online at http://www.thememagazine.com/stories/the-former-landowner/.

2. Amartya Sen, "Freedoms and Needs," *New Republic*, January 10, 1994, 34–35, 34.

3. Adam Przeworski, Michael E. Alvarez, Jose Antonio Cheibub, and Fernando Limongi, *Democracy and Development* (New York: Cambridge University Press, 2000).

4. Robert A. Dahl, *Polyarchy: Participation and Opposition* (New Haven, CT: Yale University Press, 1972).

5. Barbara Geddes, "What Do We Know about Democratization after Twenty Years?," *Annual Review of Political Science* 2 (June 1999): 115–144.

6. Kenneth F. Greene. *Why Dominant Parties Lose: Mexico's Democratization in Comparative Perspective* (New York: Cambridge University Press, 2007).

7. Samuel P. Huntington, *Political Order in Changing Societies* (New Haven, CT: Yale University Press, 2006).

8. Zachary Elkins, "Gradations of Democracy? Empirical Tests of Alternative Conceptualizations," *American Journal of Political Science* 44, no. 2 (2000): 193–200.

9. Fareed Zakaria, *The Future of Freedom: Illiberal Democracy at Home and Abroad* (New York: W. W. Norton, 2007).

10. Regimes are classified according to Polity IV (http://www.systemicpeace.org/polity/polity4.htm). GDP data are from the World Bank, World Development Indicators, http://data.world bank.org/sites/default/files/wdi-final.pdf.

11. Samuel Huntington, *The Third Wave: Democratization in the Late Twentieth Century* (Norman: University of Oklahoma Press, 1991).

12. United Nations Development Programme, "Beyond the Midpoint: Achieving the Millennium Development Goals," January 2010, http://content.undp.org/go/cms-service/stream/asset/?asset_id=2223855, 6.

13. Charles Hanley, "Fourth Wave of Democracy Breaks," *Daily Camera*, March 20, 2011, 9A.

14. Douglass C. North, "Economic Performance through Time," *American Economic Review* 84, no. 3. (1994), 359–368, 359.

15. United Nations Development Programme, *Human Development Report 2002: Deepening Democracy in a Fragmented World* (New York: Oxford University Press, 2002), 51.

16. Daron Acemoglu and James A. Robinson, *Why Nations Fail: The Origins of Power, Prosperity, and Poverty* (New York: Crown Business, 2012), 68.

17. Acemoglu and Robinson, *Why Nations Fail.*

18. Ibid., 75.

19. Pranab Bardhan, "Corruption and Development: A Review of Issues," *Journal of Economic Literature* 35, no. 3 (1997): 1320–1346.

20. Gordon Tullock, "The Welfare Costs of Tariffs, Monopolies, and Theft," *Economic Inquiry* 5, no. 3 (1967): 224–232; Anne O Krueger, *Foreign Trade Regimes and Economic Development: Turkey* (Cambridge: National Bureau of Economic Research, 1974), 271–339; Mancur Olson, *The Rise and Decline of Nations: Economic Growth, Stagflation, and Social Rigidities* (New Haven, CT: Yale University Press, 1982).

21. Robert Guest, *The Shackled Continent: Power, Corruption, and African Lives* (Washington, D.C.: Smithsonian Books, 2004).

22. Mancur Olson, "Dictatorship, Democracy, and Development," *American Political Science Review* 87 (September 1993): 567–576.

23. Amartya Sen, *Development as Freedom* (New York: Knopf, 1999).

24. Anna Khakee et al., "A Long-Lasting Controversy: Western Democracy Promotion in Jordan," EuroMeSCo, May 27, 2009, http://www.euromesco.net/euromesco/media/MEDAC-UJRC_Khakee.pdf.

25. Acemoglu and Robinson, *Why Nations Fail.*

26. Morton H. Halperin, Joseph T. Siegle, and Michael M. Weinstein, *The Democracy Advantage: How Democracies Promote Prosperity and Peace* (New York: Routledge, 2004), 14.

27. Acemoglu and Robinson, *Why Nations Fail*, 124–151; Douglass C. North, John Joseph Wallis, and Barry R. Weingast, *Violence and Social Orders: A Conceptual Framework for Interpreting Recorded Human History* (New York: Cambridge University Press, 2009).

28. Amartya Sen, *Development as Freedom* (New York: Alfred Knopf, 1999).

29. Seymour Martin Lipset, "Some Social Requisites of Democracy: Economic Development and Political Legitimacy, *American Political Science Review* 53, no. 1. (1959), 69–105, 75, 79.

30. Ibid., 75.

31. Marcus J. Kurtz and Andrew Schrank, "Growth and Governance: Models, Measures, and Mechanisms," *Journal of Politics* 69, no. 2 (2007): 538–554; Ha-Joon Chang, *Bad Samaritans: The Myth of Free Trade and the Secret History of Capitalism* (New York: Bloomsbury Press, 2007).

32. Tony Gambino, "Democratic Republic of the Congo," *World Development Report 2011*: Background Case Study, March 2011, http://reliefweb.int/sites/reliefweb.int/files/resources/Full_Report_985.pdf.

33. Samuel P. Huntington, *Political Order in Changing Societies* (New Haven, CT: Yale University Press, 1968).

34. Stephan Haggard, *Pathways from the Periphery: The Politics of Growth in the Newly Industrializing Countries* (Ithaca, NY: Cornell University Press, 1990).

35. Mancur Olson, *The Rise and Decline of Nations*.

36. Robert J. Barro, "Economic Growth in a Cross Section of Countries," *The Quarterly Journal of Economics* 106, no. 2 (1991): 407–443.

37. Huntington, *Political Order in Changing Societies*, 386.

38. Daniel Kaufmann and Shang-Jin Wei, "Does 'Grease Money' Speed Up the Wheels of Commerce?," Munich Personal RePEc Archive, 1999, http://mpra.ub.uni-muenchen.de/8209/1/Does_Grease_Money_Speed_Wheels_Commerce.pdf; Pranab Bardhan, "Corruption and Development."

39. Przeworski et al., *Democracy and Development*.

40. Transparency International, *Global Corruption Report 2004* (London: Pluto Press, 2004), 13.

41. Ian Morris, *Why the West Rules—for Now: The Patterns of History and What They Reveal about the Future* (New York: Farrar, Straus and Giroux, 2010), 385.

42. Kenneth Pomeranz, *The Great Divergence: China, Europe, and the Making of the Modern World Economy* (Princeton, NJ: Princeton University Press, 2000), 68.

43. Acemoglu and Robinson, *Why Nations Fail*, 231–234.

44. North et al., *Violence and Social Orders*, 84.

45. Morris, *Why the West Rules—for Now*.

46. Pomeranz, *The Great Divergence*.

47. Parks M. Coble, *The Shanghai Capitalists and the Nationalist Government, 1927–1937*, vol. 94 (Cambridge: Harvard University Asia Center, 1986).

48. Economic statistics in this section are from Gapminder, www.gapminder.org.

49. Acemoglu and Robinson, *Why Nations Fail*, 423–426; Yasheng Huang, *Capitalism with Chinese Characteristics: Entrepreneurship and the State* (New York: Cambridge University Press, 2008).

50. Robert A. Bickers, *The Scramble for China: Foreign Devils in the Qing Empire, 1832–1914* (London: Allen Lane, 2011).

51. Alison Adcock Kaufman, "The 'Century of Humiliation,' Then and Now: Chinese Perceptions of the International Order," *Pacific Focus* 25, no. 1 (2010): 1–33.

52. Barry Naughton, *The Chinese Economy: Transitions and Growth* (Cambridge: MIT Press Books, 2007).

53. Morris, *Why the West Rules*.

54. Jared M. Diamond, *Guns, Germs, and Steel* (New York: Norton, 1997), 411–417.

Chapter 11

1. Correlates of War, www.correlatesofwar.org/.

2. The year 1962 was chosen as the starting point for the following reason: The number of independent nation-states in the developing world has only increased slightly since 1962, as this was the year corresponding to the end of Africa's first major wave of independence. Therefore, any trends observed in the figure are not due to an increase in the number of LDCs.

3. Christopher Blattman and Edward Miguel, "Civil War," *Journal of Economic Literature* 48 (March 2010), 3–57.

4. Paul Collier, *The Bottom Billion: Why the Poorest Countries Are Failing and What We Can Do about It* (Oxford: Oxford University Press, 2007), 26-27.

5. World Bank, *World Development Report 2011: Conflict, Security, and Development* (Washington, D.C.: World Bank Publications, 2011), 57.

6. Paul Collier, *Breaking the Conflict Trap: Civil War and Development Policy* (Washington, D.C.: World Bank Publications, 2003).

7. Collier, *The Bottom Billion*, 18–26.

8. United Nations Office on Drugs and Crime, "Global Study on Homicide 2011: Trends, Contexts, Data," 2011, http://www.unodc.org/documents/data-and-analysis/statistics/Homicide/Globa_study_on_homicide_2011_web.pdf.

9. United Nations Office on Drugs and Crime, "Homicide Statistics," www.unodc.org/unodc/en/data-and-analysis/homicide.html.

10. "Drugs in Mexico: A Gruesome Paradox," *The Economist*, February 2, 2011, www.economist.com/blogs/dailychart/2011/02/daily_chart_drugs_mexico.

11. United Nations Office on Drugs and Crime, "Homicide Statistics."

12. Robert I. Rotberg, "The New Nature of Nation-State Failure," *Washington Quarterly* 25, no. 3 (2002): 83–96.

13. "Where Life Is Cheap and Talk Is Loose," *The Economist*, March 17, 2011, www.economist.com/node/18396240.

14. Jack A Goldstone et al., *State Failure Task Force Report: Phase III Findings*, September 30, 2000, www.cidcm.umd.edu/publications/papers/SFTF%20Phase%20III%20Report%20Final.pdf.

15. National Intelligence Council, *Global Trends 2025: A Transformed World* (Washington, D.C.: Government Printing Office, 2008), 61.

16. Hazem A. Ghobarah, Paul Huth, and Bruce Russett, "Civil Wars Kill and Maim People – Long after the Shooting Stops," *American Political Science Review* 97, no. 2, (2003): 189–202.

17. United Nations Office on Drugs and Crime, "Homicide Statistics."

18. United Nations High Commissioner for Refugees, *UNHCR Statistical Yearbook 2010: Trends in Displacement, Protection and Solutions* (Geneva: UNHCR, 2011).

19. Mancur Olson, "Dictatorship, Democracy, and Development," *American Political Science Review* 87, no. 3 (1993): 567–576.

20. Daron Acemoglu and James A. Robinson, "10 Reasons Countries Fall Apart," Foreign Policy, July/August 2012, www.foreignpolicy.com/articles/2012/06/18/10_reasons_countries_fall_apart?page=0, 7.

21. World Bank, *World Development Report 2011*, 60.
22. Paul Collier and Anke Hoeffler, "Civil War," in *Handbook of Defense Economics*, vol. 2, ed. Todd Sandler and Keith Hartley (Amsterdam: North-Holland, 2007), 711–739, 725.
23. Tilman Brück, "Macroeconomic Effects of the War in Mozambique," 1997, http://papers.ssrn.com/sol3/papers.cfm?abstract_id=259490.
24. David S. Landes, *The Wealth and Poverty of Nations: Why Some Are So Rich and Some So Poor* (New York: W. W. Norton & Company, 1999): 34, 53.
25. Adam Przeworski with Carolina Curvale, "Does Politics Explain the Economic Gap between the United States and Latin America?," in *Falling Behind: Explaining the Development Gap between Latin America and the United States*, ed. Frances Fukuyama (New York: Oxford University Press, 2008), 99–133.
26. Miguel Angel Centeno, *Blood and Debt: War and the Nation-State in Latin America* (University Park: Pennsylvania State University Press, 2002).
27. Juan Luis Londoño and Rodrigo Guerrero, "Violencia en América Latina: epidemiología y costos," August 1999, http://www.iadb.org/res/publications/pubfiles/pubr-375.pdf.
28. "The Economics of Violence," *The Economist*, April 16, 2011, 65.
29. Collier and Hoeffler, "Civil War," 726.
30. Edward Miguel and Gerard Roland, "The Long Run Impact of Bombing Vietnam," National Bureau of Economic Research, January 2006, http://www.nber.org/papers/w11954.pdf?new_window=1; Quote from Blattman and Miguel, "Civil War," 41.
31. Mancur Olson, *The Rise and Decline of Nations: Economic Growth, Stagflation, and Social Rigidities* (New Haven: Yale University Press, 1982).
32. Charles Tilly, *Coercion, Capital, and European States, AD 990–1990* (Cambridge: Basil Blackwell, 1990).
33. Charles Tilly, "Reflections on the History of European State-Making," in *The Formation of National States in Western Europe*, ed. Charles Tilly (Princeton, NJ: Princeton University Press, 1975), 3–83, 42.
34. Jeffrey Herbst, *States and Power in Africa: Comparative Lessons in Authority and Control* (Princeton, NJ: Princeton University Press, 2000).
35. James Fergusson, *The World's Most Dangerous Place: Inside the Outlaw State of Somalia* (London: Bantam Press, 2013).
36. Bridget Coggins, "The Pirate Den," *Foreign Policy in Focus* 180 (July/August 2010): 86–87.
37. Ken Menkhaus, "Somalia at the Tipping Point?," *Current History*, May 2012, www.currenthistory.com/pdf_org_files/111_745_169.pdf.
38. Alex Strick van Linschoten and Felix Kuehn, "Mogadishu Was a Blast," Foreign Policy, July/August 2010, http://www.foreignpolicy.com/articles/2010/06/21/mogadishu_was_a_blast.
39. Acemoglu, Daron, and James A. Robinson, *Why Nations Fail: The Origins of Power, Prosperity, and Poverty* (New York: Crown Business, 2012), 239.
40. Herbst, *States and Power in Africa*.
41. Walter Clarke and Jeffrey Herbst, "Somalia and the Future of Humanitarian Intervention," *Foreign Affairs* 75, no. 2 (1996): 70–85.
42. R. Lee Hadden, *The Geology of Somalia: A Selected Bibliography of Somalian Geology, Geography and Earth Science* (Alexandria, VA: Army Topographic Engineering Center, 2007), available online at www.dtic.mil/cgi-bin/GetTRDoc?AD=ADA464006&Location=U2&doc=GetTRDoc.pdf.

Chapter 12

1. Save the Children, *State of the World's Mothers 2011: Champions for Children* (Westport, CT: Save the Children, 2011), 5.
2. United Nations Development Programme, *Human Development Report 2010: The Real Wealth of Nations: Pathways to Development* (New York: Palgrave Macmillan, 2010), 90.
3. Gender Inequality Index, Human Development Reports, http://hdr.undp.org/en/statistics/gii/.
4. United Nations Development Programme, *Human Development Report 2007/2008: Fighting Climate Change: Human Solidarity in a Divided World* (New York: Palgrave Macmillan, 2007), 330.
5. World Bank, *World Development Report 2012: Gender Equality and Development* (Washington D.C.: World Bank, 2011), 163, 82.
6. Ousman Gajigo and Mary Hallward-Driemeier, *Constraints and Opportunities for New Entrepreneurs in Africa* (Washington D.C.: World Bank, 2011).
7. World Bank, *World Development Report 2012*, 234.
8. Christopher Udry, "Gender, Agricultural Production and the Theory of the Household," *Journal of Political Economy* 104, no. 4 (1996): 1010–1046.
9. Carmen Diana Deere and Magdalena Leon, "The Gender Asset Gap: Land in Latin America," *World Development* 31, no. 6 (2003): 925–947.
10. María Inés Berniell and Carolina Sánchez-Páramo, "Overview of Time Use Data Used for the Analysis of Gender Differences in Time Use Patterns," background paper for the World Development Report (Washington D.C.: World Bank, 2012).
11. World Bank, *World Development Report 2012*, chapter 5.
12. International Labor Organization (ILO), *Key Indicators of the Labour Market* (Geneva: ILO, 2010).
13. Ibid., 165.
14. Oxfam International, *Trading away Our Rights: Women Working in Global Supply Chains* (Oxford: Oxfam International, 2004), 17.
15. Robert J. Barro and Jong-Wha Lee, "A New Data Set of Educational Attainment in the World, 1950–2010," National Bureau of Economic Research, Working Paper No. 15902, 2010.
16. World Bank, *Atlas of Global Development* (Washington, D.C.: World Bank Publications, 2009), 38.
17. World Bank, *World Development Report 2012*, 107.
18. Flora J. Nankhuni and Jill L. Findeis, "Natural Resource-Collection Work and Children's Schooling in Malawi," *Agricultural Economics* 31, no. 2-3 (2004): 123–134.
19. Joni Seagar, *Penguin Atlas of Women in the World*, 4ed. (New York: Penguin, 2009), 76.

20. Jane Kabubo-Mariara and Domisiano K. Mwabu, "Determinants of School Enrollment and Education Attainment: Empirical Evidence from Kenya," *South African Journal of Economics* 75, no. 3 (2007): 572–593.

21. Rachel Jewkes, Jonathan Levin, Nolwazi Mbananga, and Debbie Bradshaw, "Rape of Girls in South Africa," *Lancet* 359 (January 2002): 319–320.

22. World Bank, *World Development Report 2012*, 112.

23. United Nations Development Programme, *Human Development Report 2010*, 160.

24. Seagar, *Penguin Atlas of Women in the World*, 99.

25. World Values Survey, "Official Aggregate 1981–2008," Madrid, 2009, www.worldvaluessurvey.org.

26. Arturo Escobar and Sonia E. Alvarez, eds., *The Making of Social Movements in Latin America: Identity, Strategy, and Democracy* (Boulder: Westview Press, 1992).

27. "Self-Dignified Indeed," *The Economist*, June 29, 2012, http://www.economist.com/blogs/analects/2012/06/new-fangled-feminism.

28. World Bank, *World Development Report 2012*, 22.

29. Ibid., 3.

30. United Nations Development Programme, *Human Development Report 2003* (New York: Oxford University Press, 2003), 7. Amartya Sen, *Development as Freedom* (Oxford: Oxford University Press, 1998), chapter 8.

31. Esther Boserup, *Women's Role in Economic Development* (London: Allen and Unwin, 1970).

32. World Bank, *Engendering Development* (New York: Oxford University Press, 2001), 9.

33. Sen, *Development as Freedom*, 197.

34. Tahir Andrabi, Jishnu Das, and Asim Khwaja, "Students Today, Teachers Tomorrow? Identifying Constraints on the Provision of Education," World Bank Policy Research Working Paper No. 5674, June 2011.

35. Lincoln C. Chen, Emdadul Huq, and Stan D'Souza, "Sex Bias in the Family Allocation of Food and Health Care in Rural Bangladesh," *Population and Development Review* 7, no. 1 (1981): 55–70; Esther Duflo, "Grandmothers and Granddaughters: Old Age Pensions and Intra-household Allocation in South Africa," *World Bank Economic Review* 17, no. 1 (2003): 1–25.

36. World Bank, *Engendering Development*, 96; United Nations Development Programme, *Human Development Report 2011*, 63–64.

37. The Girl Effect, www.girleffect.org/.

38. Caroline Moser, Gender Planning and Development: Theory, Practice, and Training (New York: Routledge, 1993).

39. Robert Barro and Jong-Wha Lee, "International Measures of Schooling Years and Schooling Quality," *American Economic Review* 86, no. 2 (1996): 218–223.

40. Nicholas D. Kristof and Sheryl WuDunn, *Half the Sky: Turning Oppression into Opportunity for Women Worldwide* (New York: Random House, 2009).

41. Amartya Sen, "More Than 100 Million Women Are Missing," *New York Review of Books* 37 (December 1990), 61–66.

42. World Bank, *World Development Report 2012*, 77.

43. Ibid., 121.

44. United Nations Development Programme, *Human Development Report 2010*, 76; Stephan Klasen and Claudia Wink, "Missing Women: Revisiting the Debate," *Feminist Economics* 9, no. 2–3 (2003): 263–299.

45. "India's Skewed Sex Ratio: Seven Brothers," *The Economist*, April 9, 2011, 45–46.

46. Joni Seager, *Penguin Atlas of Women in the World* (New York: Penguin Books, 2009).

47. Abhijit V. Banerjee and Esther Duflo, *Poor Economics: A Radical Rethinking of the Way to Fight Global Poverty* (New York: Public Affairs, 2011), 122.

48. World Bank, *World Development Report 2012*, 121.

49. World Bank, World Development Indicators.

50. Donald G. McNeil Jr., "Maternal Deaths Plunged over 2 Decades, to about 287,000 in 2010, U.N. Reports," *New York Times*, May 16, 2012, http://www.nytimes.com/2012/05/16/health/maternal-deaths-plunged-over-2-decades-un-reports.html?_r=0.

51. World Health Organization, "World Health Statistics 2010," http://www.who.int/whosis/whostat/EN_WHS10_Full.pdf.

52. United Nations Development Programme, *Human Development Report 2003*, 99.

53. World Bank, *Atlas of Global Development*, 52.

54. UNAIDS (United Nations Programme on HIV/AIDS), *UNAIDS Report on the Global AIDS Epidemic 2010* (Geneva: UNAIDS, 2010).

55. World Bank, *World Development Report 2012*, 62.

56. Donald G. McNeil Jr., "Maternal Deaths."

57. World Bank, *World Development Report 2012*, 65.

58. Surjit S. Bhalla and Ravinder Kaur, "The Girl Child's Future," *The Indian Express*, November 5, 2011, http://www.indianexpress.com/news/the-girl-child-s-future/870989.

59. World Bank, *World Development Report 2006*, 54; World Health Organization, *Preventing Intimate Partner and Sexual Violence against Women: Taking Action and Generating Advice* (Geneva: WHO, 2010).

60. "Women in Turkey: Behind the Veil," *The Economist*, May 14, 2011, 68.

61. David Smith, "One in Three South African Men Admit to Rape, Survey Finds," *The Guardian*, November 25, 2010, http://www.guardian.co.uk/world/2010/nov/25/south-african-rape-survey.

62. Naina Kapur, *Gender and Judges: A Judicial Point of View* (New Delhi: Sakshi, 1996); M. E. Khan, Aruna Bhattacharya, Ismat Bhuiya, and Aditi Aeron, "A Situation Analysis of Care and Support for Rape Survivors at First Point of Contact in India and Bangladesh," *Injury Prevention* 16 (September 2010): A160–161.

63. International Center for Research for Women, "Child Marriage Facts and Figures," http://www.icrw.org/child-marriage-facts-and-figures.

64. Seagar, *Penguin Atlas of Women in the World*, 55.

65. World Bank, World Development Indicators, 2010.

66. Seagar, *Penguin Atlas of Women in the World*, 35.

67. World Bank, World Development Indicators.

68. Kristof and WuDunn, *Half the Sky*, 134.

69. Seagar, Penguin Atlas of Women in the World, 36.

70. World Bank, *World Development Report 2012*, 62.

71. Oded Galor and David N. Weil, "The Gender Gap, Fertility, and Growth," *American Economic Review* 86, no. 3 (1996): 374–387.

72. Gary Becker, "An Economic Analysis of Fertility," *Demographic and Economic Change in Developed Countries* (Princeton, NJ: National Bureau of Economic Research, 1960).

73. Warren S. Thompson, "Population," *American Journal of Sociology* 34, no. 6 (1929): 959–975.

74. Michael Kremer, "Population Growth and Technological Change: One Million B.C. to 1990," *The Quarterly Journal of Economics,* 108, no. 3 (1993): 681–716; Douglass North and Robert Paul Thomas, *The Rise of the Western World: A New Economic History* (Cambridge: Cambridge University Press, 1976).

75. Gapminder, www.gapminder.org.

76. Lisa Anderson, "TRUSTLAW POLL—Afghanistan is Most Dangerous Country for Women," Trust Law, June 15, 2011, http://www.trust.org/trustlaw/news/trustlaw-poll-afghanistan-is-most-dangerous-country-for-women.

77. Gapminder, www.gapminder.org.

78. "The World's Five Most Dangerous Countries for Women," Trust Law, 2012, http://www.trust.org/trustlaw/womens-rights/dangerpoll/.

79. Stephan Klasen and Claudia Wink, "Missing Women: Revisiting the Debate," *Feminist Economics* 9, no. 2–3, (2003): 263–299.

80. World Bank, *World Development Report 2012,* 396; "What's Pashto for the Pill?," *The Economist,* June 18, 2012, www.economist.com/blogs/feastandfamine/2012/06/demography.

81. Gapminder, www.gapminder.org.

82. United Nations Environment Programme, *Afghanistan: Post-Conflict Environmental Assessment* (Nairobi: United Nations Environment Programme, 2003), 14.

83. Robert D. Kaplan, *The Revenge of Geography* (New York: Random House, 2012).

84. Paul Collier, *The Bottom Billion* (New York: Oxford University Press, 2006).

Chapter 13

1. Charles de Secondat Montesquieu, *The Spirit of Laws*, 1789, available for download from http://archive.org/details/spiritoflaws01montuoft.

2. Jeffrey Sachs, *The End of Poverty: Economic Possibilities for Our Time* (New York: Penguin Press, 2006).

3. David Landes, *The Wealth and Poverty of Nations: Why Some Are So Rich and Others So Poor* (New York: W. W. Norton, 1998), 7.

4. World Health Organization, *World Malaria Report 2010,* http://www.who.int/malaria/world_malaria_report_2010/malaria2010_summary_keypoints_en.pdf.

5. "Mens sana in corpore sano," *The Economist,* July 1, 2010, 75.

6. Hoyt Bleakley, "Malaria Eradication in the Americas: A Retrospective Analysis of Childhood Exposure," *American Economic Journal: Applied Economics* 2, no. 2 (2010): 1–45.

7. John Reader, *Africa: A Biography of the Continent* (New York: Vintage, 1999), 589.

8. John L. Gallup and Jeffery Sachs, "The Economic Burden of Malaria," *The American Journal of Tropical Medicine and Hygiene* 64, no. 1 suppl. (2001): 85–96.

9. John L. Gallup, Jeffrey D. Sachs, and Andrew D. Mellinger, "Geography and Economic Development," *International Regional Science Review* 22, no. 2 (1999): 179–232; David E. Bloom and Jeffrey Sachs, "Geography, Demography, and Economic Growth in Africa," *Brookings Papers on Economic Activity* 1998, no. 2 (1998): 207–295.

10. Jeffrey Sachs, "Nature, Nurture, and Growth," *The Economist* June 12, 1997, http://www.economist.com/node/91003.

11. Ibid.

12. Paul Collier, *The Plundered Planet: Why We Must—and How We Can—Manage Nature of Global Prosperity* (New York, Oxford University Press, 2010), 139.

13. Jared Diamond, *Guns, Germs, and Steel: The Fates of Human Societies* (New York: W. W. Norton, 1997).

14. Bloom and Sachs, "Geography, Demography, and Economic Growth in Africa."

15. Ibid.

16. John L. Gallup, Alejandro Gaviria, and Eduardo Lora, *Is Geography Destiny? Lessons from Latin America* (Stanford, CA: Stanford University Press, 2003).

17. Paul Collier, *The Bottom Billion: Why the Poorest Countries Are Failing and What We Can Do about It* (New York: Oxford University Press, 2007).

18. Daron Acemoglu and James A. Robinson, *Why Nations Fail: The Origins of Power, Prosperity, and Poverty* (New York: Crown Business, 2012).

19. Daron Acemoglu, Simon Johnson, and James A. Robinson, "Reversal of Fortune: Geography and Development in the Making of the Modern World Income Distribution," *Quarterly Journal of Economics* 117, no. 4 (2002): 1231–1294.

20. Daron Acemoglu, Simon Johnson, James A. Robinson. "Institutions as a Fundamental Cause of Long-Run Growth," in *Handbook of Economic Growth,* ed. Phillipe Aghion and Steven Durlauf (Amsterdam: North-Holland, 2005), 386–472.

21. Acemoglu and Robinson, *Why Nations Fail,* 52.

22. Michael L. Ross, *The Oil Curse: How Petroleum Wealth Shapes the Development of Nations* (Princeton, NJ: Princeton University Press, 2012), 55.

23. Jeffrey D. Sachs and Andrew M. Warner, "The Big Rush, Natural Resource Booms And Growth," *Journal of Development Economics* 59 (June 1999): 43–76.

24. Sachs and Warner, "The Big Rush."

25. Ross, *The Oil Curse,* 50–59.

26. Ross, *The Oil Curse.*

27. Collier, *The Bottom Billion.*

28. Paul Collier, *The Plundered Planet,* 66.

29. Kenneth Pomeranz, *The Great Divergence: China, Europe, and the Making of the World Economy* (Princeton, NJ: Princeton University Press, 2000).

30. Landes, *The Wealth and Poverty of Nations,* 295.

31. Michael L. Ross, "The Political Economy of the Resource Curse," *World Politics* 51 (January 1999): 306.

32. Ross, *The Oil Curse,* 73.

33. James A. Robinson, "The Latin American Equilibrium," in *Falling Behind: Explaining the Development Gap between Latin America and the United States,* ed. Francis Fukuyama (Oxford: Oxford University Press, 2008), 161–193.

34. Gapminder, www.gapminder.org.
35. Stanley L. Engerman and Kenneth L. Sokoloff, "Factor Endowments, Inequality, and Paths of Development among New World Economies," (Cambridge, MA: National Bureau of Economic Research, 2002).
36. "Walmart Is Latin America's Single Largest Employer, Says Latin Business," *Merco Press,* August 5, 2010, http://en.mercopress.com/2010/08/05/walmart-is-latin-america-s-single-largest-employer-says-latin-business.
37. Acemoglu and Robinson, *Why Nations Fail,* 34.
38. World Bank, *Informality: Exit and Exclusion* (Washington, D.C.: World Bank Publications, 2007), 29.

Chapter 14

1. Garrett Hardin, "The Tragedy of the Common," *Science* 162 (December 1968): 1243–1248.
2. United Nations Development Programme, *Human Development Report 2006: Beyond Scarcity: Power, Poverty and the Global Water Crisis* (New York: Palgrave MacMillan, 2006), 14.
3. Ibid., 138.
4. Don Hinrichsen, B. Robey, and Ushma D. Upadhyay, "Solutions for a Water-Short World," Population Reports, series M, no. 14. Johns Hopkins School of Public Health, Population Information Program (Baltimore: 1997).
5. World Bank, *World Development Report 2010: Development and Climate Change* (Washington D.C.: World Bank Publications, 2010), 191.
6. United Nations Development Programme, *Human Development Report 2011: Sustainability and Equity: A Better Future for All* (New York: Palgrave MacMillan, 2011), 51.
7. "Special Report: Forests," *The Economist,* September 23, 2010, 7.
8. World Bank, *World Development Report 1992: Development and the Environment* (New York: World Bank Publications, 1992), 30.
9. Wynet Smith, "The Global Problem of Illegal Logging," *Tropical Forest Update,* 12, no. 1 (2006): 3–6.
10. World Water Assessment Programme, *The United Nations World Water Development Report 3: Water in a Changing World* (Paris: United Nations Educational, Scientific and Cultural Organization, 2009).
11. United Nations World Commission on Environment and Development, *Our Common Future* (Oxford: Oxford University Press, 1987), 57–59.
12. Thomas Malthus, "An Essay on the Principle of Population as It Affects the Future Improvement of Society, with Remarks on the Speculations of Mr. Godwin, M. Condorcet, and Other Writers" (London: J. Johnson, 1798), chapter 1.
13. Paul Ehrlich, *The Population Bomb: Population Control or Race to Oblivion?* (New York: Ballantine Books, 1968).
14. "Demography: A Tale of Three Islands," *The Economist,* October 22, 2011, 30.
15. World Bank, *World Development Report 2003: Sustainable Development in a Dynamic World: Transforming Institutions, Growth, and Quality of Life* (Washington D.C.: World Bank Publications, 2003), 86.
16. World Water Council, "A Water Secure World: Vision for Water, Life, and the Environment," 2000, http://www.worldwatercouncil.org/fileadmin/wwc/Library/Publications_and_reports/Visions/CommissionReport.pdf.
17. United Nations Development Programme, *Human Development Report 2011,* 52.
18. Ian Morris, *Why the West Rules—for Now: The Patterns of History, and What They Reveal About the Future* (New York: Farrar, Straus and Giroux, 2010), 600.
19. Matthew Ridley, *The Rational Optimist: How Prosperity Evolves* (New York: Harper, 2010), 121.
20. "No Easy Fix," *The Economist,* February 26, 2011, 10.
21. United Nations Development Programme, *Human Development Report 2011,* 27.
22. United Nations Development Programme, *Human Development Report 2007/2008,* 69.
23. "Developing Countries and Global Warming: A Bad Climate for Development," *The Economist,* September 17, 2009, http://www.economist.com/node/14447171.
24. United Nations Development Programme, *Human Development Report 2011,* 32.
25. Gapminder, www.gapminder.org
26. "Energy in India: The Future is Black," *The Economist,* January 21, 2012, 77–79.
27. Marcos Chamon, Paolo Mauro, and Yohei Okawa, "Cars: Mass Car Ownership in the Emerging Market Giants," *Economic Policy* 23, no. 45 (2008): 243–296.
28. World Bank, *World Development Report 2010,* 203.
29. United Nations Development Programme, *Human Development Report 2007/2008: Fighting Climate Change: Human Solidarity in a Divided World* (New York: Palgrave MacMillan, 2007).
30. "Developing Countries and Global Warming."
31. International Food Policy Research Institute, "Food Security, Farming, and Climate Change to 2050: Scenarios, Results, Policy Options," Washington D.C., 2010, http://www.ifpri.org/sites/default/files/publications/rr172.pdf.
32. Christian Nellemann et al., eds, *The Environmental Food Crisis: The Environment's Role in Averting Future Food Crises* (Norway, United Nations Environment Programme, 2009), available online at http://www.grida.no/publications/rr/food-crisis/.
33. United Nations Development Programme, *Human Development Report 2007/2008,* 75–77.
34. World Bank, *World Development Report 2010,* 98.
35. United Nations Development Programme, *Human Development Report 2007/2008,* 74–87.
36. Pan American Health Organization, "Dengue," 2009, http://new.paho.org/hq/index.php?option=com_contnet&task=view&id=264&itemid=363.
37. United Nations Development Programme, *Human Development Report 2007/2008,* 9.
38. "Developing Countries and Global Warming."
39. Nicholas Stern, *The Economics of Climate Change: The Stern Review* (Cambridge: Cambridge University Press, 2007).
40. Edward Miguel, Shanker Satyanath, and Ernest Sergenti, "Economic Shocks and Civil Conflict: An Instrumental Variables Approach, *Journal of Political Economy* 112, no. 4 (2004): 725–753.

41. Claims that refute the existence of human-caused global warming are well outside the scientific mainstream, so they are not considered here.

42. United Nations Development Programme, *Human Development Report 2007/2008,* 1.

43. Stern, *The Economics of Climate Change.*

44. Intergovernmental Panel on Climate Change, "Emissions Scenarios," www.ipcc.ch/ipccreports/sres/emission/014.htm.

45. World Bank, *World Development Report 2010,* 98; Ridley, *The Rational Optimist,* 335.

46. Thaddeus C. Trzyna, Elizabeth Margold, and Julia K. Osborn, eds., *World Directory of Environmental Organizations,* 5th ed. (Sacramento: International Center for the Environment and Public Policy, 1996).

47. United Nations Development Programme, *Human Development Report 2007/2008,* 1.

48. Bjorn Lomborg, ed., *Global Crises, Global Solution* (New York: Cambridge University Press, 2004).

49. World Health Organization, *The World Health Report 2002: Reducing Risks, Promoting Healthy Life* (Geneva: World Health Organization, 2002), 72.

50. Ridley, *The Rational Optimist,* 333–338.

51. REN 21, "Renewables 2007 Global Status Report," Worldwatch Institute, 2007, http://www.worldwatch.org/files/pdf/renewables2007.pdf.

52. Rhett A. Butler, "Deforestation in the Amazon," Mongabay.com, May 20, 2012, http://www.mongabay.com/brazil.html.

53. United Nations, *State of the World's Cities 2008/9, Harmonious Cities* (London: Earthscan, 2008).

54. Ridley, *The Rational Optimist,* 190.

55. United Nations, *State of the World's Cities 2008/9, Harmonious Cities.*

56. Gapminder, www.gapminder.org.

57. PEACE, "Indonesia and Climate Change: Current Status and Policies," World Bank and DFID (Department for International Development, Indonesia), 2007, http://siteresources.world bank.org/INTINDONESIA/Resources/Environment/ClimateChange_Full_EN.pdf

58. United Nations Development Programme, *Human Development Report 2011,* 148.

59. PEACE, "Indonesia and Climate Change," 49.

60. PEACE, "Indonesia and Climate Change."

61. Michael Case, Fitrian Ardiansyah, and Emily Spector, "Climate Change in Indonesia: Implications for Humans and Nature," World Wildlife Fund, http://assets.wwf.org.uk/downloads/indonesian_climate_ch.pdf.

62. PEACE, "Indonesia and Climate Change," 4.

63. PEACE, "Indonesia and Climate Change."

64. United Nations Development Programme, *Human Development Report 2011,* 152.

65. World Bank, World Development Indicators, http://siteresources.worldbank.org/DATASTATISTICS/Resources/table3_13.pdf.

66. United Nations Development Programme, *Human Development Report 2011,* 152.

67. David E. Parry, "Jakarta Air Pollution: Not All Doom, Gloom and Catastrophe," *Jakarta Expat,* November 25, 2011, http://jakarta expat.biz/health/jakarta-air-pollution-not-all-doom-gloom-catastrophe/.

68. Erik J. Lindquist, et al., "Global Forest Land-Use Change: 1990–2005," Food and Agriculture Organization of the United Nations, 2012, http://www.fao.org/docrep/017/i3110e/i3110e.pdf.

69. Transparency International, "Corruption by Country/Territory," http://www.transparency.org/country#IDN.

70. World Bank, Doing Business Indicators, http://www.doing business.org/.

71. United Nations Development Programme, *Human Development Report 2011,* 141.

72. Richard Galpin, "Spotlight on Indonesian 'Sweat Shops,'" BBC, March 7, 2002, http://news.bbc.co.uk/2/hi/asia-pacific/1860217.stm.

73. "The Komodo Economy," *The Economist,* February 18, 2012, 44.

Glossary

absolute poverty: the inability to meet basic material needs.

absorptive capacity: the degree to which an aid-receiving country's economic, social, and political systems allow it to use aid effectively.

adaptation costs: the expense needed to respond to or reduce vulnerability to climate change.

adaptive preferences: the psychological tendency in human beings facing deprivation to fatalistically accept their situations and lower expectations about what they can achieve.

age dependency ratio: the ratio of the working-age (fifteen to sixty-four) population size to the nonworking-age (birth to fifteen, sixty-five and over) population size.

agricultural collective: a community in which land is jointly owned by residents or the state and farmed jointly by residents.

agricultural revolution: the invention and dissemination of farming, which occurred about 10,000 years ago.

agricultural surplus: the food that a farming family cultivates beyond that which it needs to survive.

aid agency: any organization that administers and distributes development assistance.

aid dependency: a situation in which a poor country becomes so reliant on foreign aid for providing its own public services that it fails to establish the proper policies and institutions needed to create prosperity.

aid effectiveness: the degree to which foreign aid delivers concrete improvements in development outcomes.

alienation: a term Karl Marx used to refer to any kind of disruption that occurs in the naturally harmonious relationships between humans and their surroundings.

anthropogenic climate change: changes in the global climate that are caused by humanity's emission into the atmosphere of greenhouse gases (GHGs).

aquifer: the underground basins that hold over 90 percent of the globe's available freshwater.

Asian values: an argument that East Asians share a Confucianist cultural heritage that has made their economies grow rapidly in recent decades.

Atlantic slave trade: a system of international trade flows that prevailed from the mid-fifteenth to the mid-nineteenth century in which African slaves were forcibly transported to the Western Hemisphere. As part of the trade, plantation goods such as sugar and tobacco were exported from the Western Hemisphere to Europe, and items such as guns, textiles, and sea shells were exported from Europe to Africa.

autarky: the largely hypothetical scenario in which a country is completely closed to trade with foreigners.

authoritarian regime: a political system in which the most important leaders are chosen in a way that does not seek periodic input from a freely participating electorate and in which the state does not respect basic human rights; also known as autocracy.

Beijing Consensus: a school of thought that puts forth authoritarianism and state capitalist policies as the right formula for the developing world.

bellicist theory: a theory that argues that interstate war has been fundamental to successful state-building and thus to modern economic growth.

big push: the scholarly idea that LDCs are stuck in a poverty trap and that the only way to break out of the trap is with large infusions of investment from the state and foreign aid.

bilateral aid: aid that a donor government gives directly to a foreign government, to an NGO, or to private citizens in an LDC without channeling it through any international organization.

brain drain: the migration of skilled citizens away from a country; also known as human capital flight.

Bretton Woods institutions: term referring to the World Bank and the International Monetary Fund (IMF), two international financial institutions (IFIs) established in 1944 to rebuild Europe and avoid a recurrence of the Great Depression.

capabilities: a set of opportunities that persons can choose that allows them to be who they want to be and do what they want to do; also known as substantive freedoms.

capability deprivation: a lack of freedom to pursue fundamental opportunities and, thus, to live the kind of life one has reason to value.

capital flight: the movement of savings and potential investment funds out of a country.

capital mobility: the movement of savings and investments across borders.

capitalism: an economic system in which property is privately owned and resources are allocated via exchange in competitive markets.

central planning: an aspect of socialist economic systems in which firms are owned by the state and state bureaucrats make most major decisions about economic production.

chartered trading corporations: companies (dominant in global trade during the seventeenth and eighteenth centuries) that were endowed by their European government sponsors with often state-like powers to secure valuable imports from throughout the world.

child labor: when a child under the age of fifteen provides sustained work, rather than just occasional household chores, either full- or part-time.

child mortality: the death of a child before his or her fifth birthday.

clientelism: a situation in which government resources are distributed not according to impersonal rules, but at the discretion of individual politicians and bureaucrats who use the resources to attract or reward supporters.

collateral: a piece of a borrower's property that he or she promises to give a lender in case the borrower cannot repay the loan.

colonial drain: the wealth transferred from colonies to their metropoles.

colonialism: the governing of a territory by individuals and institutions from outside the territory.

colony: territory claimed and governed by individuals and institutions from outside the territory.

command economy: an economic system in which resources are allocated and production decisions are made by a centralized government agency.

common pool resource: an asset that all interested parties can benefit from because no one prevents them from using it

commune: an economic unit with joint ownership of most assets that is intended to be a self-reliant community.

communism: in Marxist thought, an economic and political system in which there is no state, all means of production are collectively shared, and workers take for compensation only what they need.

comparative advantage: a term used to describe the good that a society produces at the lowest opportunity cost.

conditionalities: strings attached to an International Monetary Fund loan that force the borrowing government to promise it will adopt certain policies in order to receive the loan.

consolidated regime: a regime in which political instability is absent and whose rules are widely accepted by virtually all important political actors.

constructivism: an approach to understanding cultural identities that sees them as malleable characteristics that result from individuals' choices and from social construction.

consumerism: the insatiable obsession with acquiring goods and services.

criminal violence: physically harmful or coercive behavior that does not have an explicitly political motive, such as robbery, assault, or homicide.

creative destruction: the process created by economic growth in which innovation leads to the adoption of new technologies that replace older, less productive ones.

cultural diversity: a situation in which multiple social identities exist within a country rather than just the national affinity for the extant country; also known as cultural pluralism.

cultural relativism: the idea that each culture is distinct and equal in its inherent value and desirability.

culturalist school: a line of scholarly thought that believes the fundamental causes of a society's poverty or prosperity lie in the shared norms, beliefs, values, and attitudes of its common citizens.

culture: the commonly shared set of norms, beliefs, and recurring practices of a society.

customary law: an unwritten legal code that is based on recognized tradition and enforced by local authority figures.

dead capital: assets that have no value or use beyond their immediate purpose.

debt relief: aid in the form of forgiveness of part of an LDC's debt to foreign investors.

decolonization: the restoration of sovereignty and autonomy (self-rule) to the peoples of a colony.

defensive lending: a situation in which the International Monetary Fund (IMF) grants new loans to a troubled country with the sole purpose of keeping that country from missing a payment on previous loans from the IMF.

deforestation: the permanent removal of trees from wooded areas.

democracy: a political system in which the most important political leaders are chosen through periodic free and fair elections and in which there is observed legal protection of the population's basic human rights.

democratization: a political regime shift from authoritarianism to democracy; also called a democratic transition.

demographic dividend: the temporary economic boost a society receives from having nonworkers as a relatively small share of its population.

demographic transition: a process of shifting age distribution that societies go through as they move from premodern agricultural societies to postindustrial ones.

dependency theory: a body of neo-Marxist thought dominant in the 1960s and 1970s that held that economies in the global periphery are heavily conditioned and ultimately exploited by the decisions and development prerogatives of the core.

desalinization: the process of turning saltwater into freshwater.

description: the narration of a piece of reality to create an image and understanding of it in the reader's or listener's mind.

descriptive representation: the notion that a society's political officeholders should have the same distribution of politically relevant traits (such as ethnicity, race, place of origin, and gender) as the collectivity of people they represent.

development models: the set of policies that a state chooses to shape economic activity within its borders.

domestic inequality: the degree to which a country's total income is concentrated in the hands of a few people; also called within-country inequality.

dominant party regime: a type of authoritarian system in which one political party holds the major leadership positions and controls policymaking for an extended period of time; also called a hegemonic or single-party system.

donor fragmentation: the lack of coordination among aid donors in their development project efforts.

Dutch disease: a situation in which the foreign demand for a country's subsoil assets drives up the price of its currency and, in doing so, damages its manufacturing sector's international competitiveness.

Easterlin paradox: a finding from a 1974 study by Richard Easterlin in which there was no relationship between a country's GDP per capita and its average level of happiness, even though there was a positive relationship between wealth and happiness within countries.

economic globalization: the cross-border movement of goods, services, capital, and people.

economic institution: a set of rules or an organization that structures human decisions about how to allocate material resources..

economic populism: a policy approach that seeks to achieve redistribution toward lower- and middle-income groups via a mix of generous state spending, mandated wage increases for these popular classes, price controls, and expansive monetary policy.

economic rents: economic gains that persons or firms accrue by rigging a market to their own advantage rather than by producing.

entry costs: the costs in time and money that a firm must go through to become registered as part of the formal sector.

environmental Kuznets curve (EKC): a summary of the cross-national relationship between the degree of environmental degradation and GDP per capita that states that middle-income countries have the worst environmental degradation while low- and high-income countries have the least.

environmental quality: the ability of a natural context to continuously supply ecological services such as sufficient quantities of clean water and air, unspoiled places of natural beauty, natural resources for eventual human consumption, biodiversity, and favorable climatic, soil, and water conditions for productive agriculture and fishing.

ethnic fragmentation: the extent to which a society is divided into a large number of relatively small identity groups.

ethnicity: a group identity rooted in shared history, values, and practices.

excess female mortality: the death of females because of their sex; also called gendercide.

exchange rates: the value at which one currency can be converted for another.

explanation: argumentation about how one factor causes or influences another one.

export promotion: a development model meant to promote light manufacturing enterprises that could successfully produce for foreign markets; also called exported-oriented industrialization.

expropriation: the seizure by a political figure of a citizen's private property and the declaration that it is now the property of the state, of the leader him or herself, or of someone else.

extractive institutions: rules that organize politics and economics so as to authoritatively redistribute major portions of society's wealth and potential wealth to a narrow group of powerful people, often the rule-makers themselves.

female empowerment: the degree to which girls and women are active agents in shaping their own life chances.

female genital cutting: a traditional and common practice in Africa's northern half that involves partial or total removal of a girl's external genitalia; also known as female genital mutilation or female circumcision.

female labor force participation rates (FLFPRs): the percentage of women in a society who perform work outside the home for monetary compensation.

fertility rate: the average number of births per woman in a society.

fiscal austerity: deep cuts in government spending, sometimes accompanied by tax increases.

forced marriage: a marriage in which at least one person marries under duress.

foreign aid: public (state-controlled) resources that are loaned at lenient terms or given by a government to another government, a nongovernmental organization, or an international organization, and whose ultimate purpose is to enhance development within the developing world; also known as official development assistance (ODA).

foreign debt: the money a country owes to its foreign creditors.

foreign direct investment (FDI): the ownership and managerial control of a productive asset by a foreigner (and typically a multinational corporation).

free trade: the unfettered (meaning without protectionist barriers) exchange of goods and services among countries; also known as liberal trade.

fungible: the idea that aid inflows can be applied by their recipients across many uses.

gender: the attitudes, norms, expectations, and behaviors that societies construct around being male or female.

gender asset gap: the average difference between men and women in the amount of owned valuable economic resources such as savings, human capital, and property.

gender earnings gap: the average difference in income between men and women, typically grounded in the fact that women receive lower wages and other returns for the contributions they make to society.

gender inequality: the extent to which societal creations around gender grant boys and men advantages in power, resources, and health.

gender quota: a legal requirement that a minimum number of party nominations or legislative seats be occupied by women.

geoengineering: large-scale projects that are designed and implemented by humans to alter the climate.

geographical determinism: the line of scholarly thought that attributes development outcomes entirely to inanimate factors and physical contexts beyond human control.

Gini coefficient: an index that ranges between 0 and 1 and conveys greater degrees of inequality with higher values.

global income distribution: a concept that captures how evenly spread world income is across its 7 billion citizens.

governance: the manner in which authoritative decisions are made and executed in a society, including the process by which positions of authority are filled, the manner in which these authority figures make decisions, the fairness and effectiveness of these decisions, and the ability of government to implement the decisions.

governmental wars: armed conflicts between an existing government and an insurgency group over control of the central state

Green Revolution: the invention and dissemination of irrigation systems, pesticides, fertilizers, and new seed types that enabled farmers around the world, mostly in the twentieth century, to extract increasingly more crop and meat volumes from virtually the same amount of farmland.

gross domestic product: the value of all goods and services produced by a country within a specified timeframe.

guerrilla warfare: fighting that involves tactics of surprise and mobility to exact damage against a foe while avoiding direct confrontation with its conventional (and usually superior) military force.

Heavily Indebted Poor Countries (HIPC) initiative: a set of measures enacted by the World Bank in the 1990s to extend debt relief to poor countries that had demonstrated a commitment to implementing poverty reducing policies.

HIV/AIDS epidemic: a deadly health epidemic of the late twentieth century caused by spread of the Human Immunodeficiency Virus (HIV), the virus that causes Acquired Immunodeficiency Syndrome (AIDS).

human capital: the skill, knowledge, and health of a labor force.

human development: the process of removing substantive unfreedoms such as the inability to eat healthy foods or obtain an education in a society.

Human Development Index (HDI): an indicator varying between 0 and 1 that is a composite of a society's overall health, educational attainment, and income.

hybrid regime: political systems that have elements of both democracy and authoritarianism.

Iberian expansion: the period in the early 1500s when Portugal and Spain acquired colonial possessions, most of them in the Western Hemisphere.

import substitution industrialization (ISI): a development model in which states erect barriers to imports of finished consumer goods so that homegrown industries can outcompete them in the domestic market.

inclusive institutions: a package of rules and organizations that includes democracy, rule of law, transparency, high state capacity, and property rights.

indigenous: an ethnic group whose members have some or all of the following characteristics: their ancestors occupied a given territory before the ancestors of any other surviving groups in their national community, they continue to live on or near these ancestral lands, and they carry on cultural traditions rooted in this ancestral past; also known as first peoples.

industrial policy: a set of measures designed to grow the manufacturing base through the state favoring certain firms and sectors.

Industrial Revolution: the period beginning in the late eighteenth century in which Western Europe and the United States gradually replaced animal- and

human-based production processes with mechanical ones, dramatically boosting economic productivity.

infant mortality: the death of a child before her or his first birthday.

infectious disease: a contagious sickness resulting from the presence in the body of a harmful microorganism; also referred to as a communicable disease.

informal sector: the portion of an economy that is comprised of activity that occurs outside the monitoring and legal purview of the state; also called the irregular, gray, shadow, or unofficial economy.

informal settlement: a neighborhood constructed on land and with houses to which the occupants have no or only a weak legal claim of ownership.

infrastructure: the facilities that make economic activity and economic exchange possible, including systems that provide transportation, communications, energy, and water.

institutions: organizations and rules that structure human interactions.

intercountry inequality: the degree of difference across all countries' average incomes; also known as between-country inequality.

internally displaced persons (IDPs): people who leave their place of residence to move somewhere else within their country to flee a threat of armed conflict.

international migration: the changing of a person's residence from one country to another.

International Monetary Fund: a major international financial institution whose primary function is to make loans to governments that are under economic and financial strain.

international trade: the cross-border exchange of goods and services.

interpersonal trust: a sentiment toward others that exists when an individual has expectations about future actions from other individuals that move her or him to rely on them.

interstate violence: the use of political violence by multiple states against one another or against non-state actors living in a different country.

intrastate violence: political violence that occurs among state or non-state actors living within the same country; also known as civil conflict.

Keynesianism: a body of economic theory developed by John Maynard Keynes that argued that, in a capitalist economy, government could use monetary and fiscal policies to stimulate businesses and promote growth.

Kuznets curve: a summary of the cross-national relationship between the degree of domestic inequality and GDP per capita that states that middle-income countries have the highest degree of inequality while low- and high-income countries are the most equal.

labor market: the economic institution that encompasses the pursuit of employment by individuals and the pursuit of employees by hirers.

Latin American structuralism: a school of thought pioneered by Raúl Prebisch in the 1940s and 1950s that stressed the importance of rigidities, class roles, and organizational forces in keeping LDCs poor; most famous for developing the notions of core and peripheral economies, as well as the declining terms of trade argument.

legitimacy: popular recognition and support for the idea that the existing state is the sole source of political authority.

less developed country (LDC): a country in which a large share of the population cannot meet or experiences great difficulties in meeting basic material needs such as housing, food, water, health care, education, electricity, transport, communications, and physical security; also known as a developing country.

life expectancy at birth: the average number of years that newborns are expected to live if current mortality patterns prevail for their entire lives.

malaria: a tropical disease in humans and animals caused by a plasmodium, a microbial parasite that is carried by mosquitoes.

malaria line: the highest elevation at which malaria-bearing mosquitoes can survive.

malnutrition: a condition in which the body does not receive enough nutrients.

Malthusian trap: a situation in which a society's unsustainable use and destruction of water, land, and air cannibalizes economic progress.

market-oriented strategy: a development model based on private ownership, liberal trade, and free-market competition.

marketing board: a government agency that existed in many postindependence African countries that bought most or all of the country's cash crops and in turn sold them to domestic and foreign consumers.

maternal mortality: the death of a woman due to complications from pregnancy or childbirth.

mercantilism: a philosophy of governance and foreign affairs, particularly dominant in Europe in the sixteenth, seventeenth, and eighteenth centuries, that defined a country's strength in terms of its ability to stockpile precious metals such as gold and silver.

metropole: the governing country or entity in a colonial relationship.

microfinance institutions (MFIs): a financial institution that exists to provide financial services to the poor.

military regime: a type of authoritarian system in which a group of elite military officers determines who the leader or leaders are—typically choosing people from their own ranks—and exerts substantial or total control over policymaking; also called a military dictatorship.

Millennium Development Goals (MDGs): a declaration with a list of development goals (most of them to be achieved by 2015) that was signed by nearly 150 heads of government at a United Nations conference in 2000.

mitigation costs: the costs needed to reduce the amount of greenhouse gases that are accumulating in the atmosphere.

modernization theory: a major line of scholarly thought on development (particularly important in U.S. social science circles in the 1950s, 1960s, and 1970s) that saw societies as having a set of traits that placed them on a continuum between traditional and modern.

monarchy: a type of authoritarian system in which rule is carried out by a king or queen who received supreme power via heredity and who is succeeded in power only at death.

moral hazard: a situation in which an economic agent takes unwise risks because the agent would not personally absorb the costs if the risk goes badly.

multilateral aid: monies that a government gives to an international organization that in turn is distributed to recipient governments, nongovernment organizations, or private citizens for development purposes.

multinational corporation (MNC): a company with assets and operations in two or more countries.

nation-state: a sovereign political unit in which inhabitants share a cultural identity around the existing territory and polity.

nationalism: a group's shared feelings and expressions of national identity.

nationality: a social identity in which a group has or wishes to have specific political rights or even full political and territorial sovereignty for itself.

natural capital: Environmental assets that are crucial to ecosystem functioning and have amenity value that comes from human enjoyment of their use.

negative externality: the cost incurred by third parties from economic exchange between a buyer and seller.

neoclassical economics: a body of thought that advocated free markets over state intervention and that dominated the economics profession in the United States roughly starting in the 1970s.

neocolonialism: the notion that Western and other global powers still exploit and abuse LDCs even in an era of independence for the latter.

net enrollment ratio: the percentage of people of the relevant age group (ages six to eleven/twelve for primary, eleven/twelve to seventeen/eighteen for secondary) that are enrolled in school.

new institutional economics (NIE): a body of scholarly thought that sees institutions (rules and organizations) as the primary causes of economic growth rates and prosperity.

new institutionalism: a body of scholarly thought that spans several social science disciplines and stresses the independent impact of rules and organizations on development and other important outcomes.

non-market activities: work performed to upkeep a home and family that is not compensated by wages; also called domestic work.

noncommunicable diseases: diseases that are not contagious, meaning they are not transmissible from one person to another.

nonsettler colonies: colonies in which the individuals from the metropole and other foreign lands who are living therein are mostly government officials and do not intend to permanently settle in the colony.

overpopulation: the condition of having more humans than a habitat can support.

parliamentary system: a type of democratic system in which there are two chief executives: the head of government (known as the prime minister), who is designated by an elected parliament, and the head of state (often a president or monarch). In this system executive and legislative terms are not of fixed length.

personalist regime: an authoritarian system that concentrates most political power in a single person.

physical capital: the machines and factories that can be used to produce goods and services.

political corruption: the use of public authority to enrich or advantage oneself or a narrow group of persons.

political instability: the condition in which there is high uncertainty about the future existence of the current political regime.

political institutions: the rules and organizations that dictate the exercise of power and authority in society.

political regime: the set of fundamental rules and practices that shape how a society is governed, most importantly those that determine who governs and what they can do in office.

political violence: physically harmful or coercive organized behavior that is exercised by state or non-state actors to achieve a political end.

post-development theory: a body of scholarly thought that arose in the 1980s and that sees prevailing conceptualizations of development as Western inventions and impositions on the global South.

presidential system: a type of democratic system in which there is one chief executive post, the president, who is chosen through a direct, nationwide election and serves a term of fixed length; positions in the legislature are also determined by popular election.

primordialism: a scholarly perspective that sees group identities as being implanted into individuals through socialization in early childhood and as being impervious to subsequent change through the life cycle.

privatization: the transfer of ownership, typically by sale, of a public enterprise from the state to private investors.

property market: how a society organizes the ownership and exchange of major economic assets, most commonly housing, land, and business capital.

property rights: the recognized legal rights to use, transfer, and earn income from an economic asset.

protectionism: measures designed to block the entry of imports into the domestic market.

race: a group identity based on some biologically determined and easily observed physical traits that society has deemed to be of social significance.

race to the bottom: the notion that governments of LDCs are allegedly lowering their societies' wages, environmental standards, worker benefits, and public services to compete amongst themselves for foreign capital inflows.

refugee: a person who has fled her or his permanent residence to another country out of fear of violent conflict.

regime transition: a shift from one political regime to another.

relative poverty: deprivation in comparison to others in a community of which one is a part.

religion: a set of beliefs, moral codes, rituals, symbols, and supporting organizations that relate humanity to spirituality.

remittance: transfers of money made by expatriates to their family and friends in their country of origin.

rent-seeking: the practice of pursuing economic rents, which are economic gains that persons or firms accrue not by producing, but by rigging a market to their own advantage.

resource curse: a scholarly argument that states that large endowments of minerals and fossil fuels are paradoxically bad for economic growth.

rule of law: a condition that exists when both state and society are bound by an impartial and neutrally enforced legal framework such that no one is above the law.

Scramble for Africa: the era (roughly 1880 to 1914) in which various European states formally colonized almost the entirety of the African continent.

secessionist war: an armed conflict in which a separatist group fights against a central state over a territory that is a subset of the existing nation-state.

settler colonies: colonies in which individuals from the metropole and other foreign lands establish permanent settlements with no intention of returning home.

slavery: a system of labor in which a person is both owned by and forced to work for another person.

social capital: the benefit that a group or society receives from the ability of its members to trust each other and cooperate with one another.

social identity: the part of a person's self-understanding that stems from her or his membership in a group of people that is larger than that person's immediate family.

social movement: a group of people who share a common demand and who organize to seek social or political change favorable to that demand.

socialism: an economic system in which most economic assets are owned by the state and most major decisions about economic production and activity are made by state officials.

soft loans: aid given to a recipient with the expectation that it will be repaid but with terms for the loan that are lenient to the borrower; also known as concessional loans.

son preference: the norm held by many adults in China and South Asia to prefer having sons over daughters, in part because girls are seen as a weightier economic burden than boys.

state capacity: the degree to which a state is able to successfully and efficiently carry out its designated responsibilities and provide high-quality public goods and services.

state capitalism: a development model that combines state ownership or guidance of major firms with operation by these firms in a capitalist and globalized market.

state failure: a condition in which a state cannot successfully carry out most of the standard functions of governance within its formally designated territory and meet fundamental collective goals.

state-led development: a development model that is a mixture of capitalism and state intervention with the intent to encourage a country's industrialization.

state-owned enterprises (SOEs): firms that are owned by the state and operated by public employees; also referred to as parastatals, public enterprises, and nationalized industries.

stereotypes: oversimplifying narratives about group members' characteristics.

structural adjustment program: a set of economic policies (often market-oriented ones) that the International Monetary Fund (IMF) required borrowing governments to agree to implement before receiving an IMF loan.

subsidies: government-provided financial assistance to a firm or entire sector.

sudden stop: a situation in which foreign lenders quickly withdraw their assets from an LDC in response to something that evoked fear for the profitability of their investments.

sustainable development: development that satisfies the needs of the present without compromising the ability of future generations to meet their own needs.

tariff: a tax that local buyers are required to pay when purchasing a foreign-made good.

terms of trade: the value a country gets in imports for what it exports; more technically, the ratio of the average world price of a country's exports to the average world price of its imports.

terrorism: violent measures meant to achieve a political goal by provoking fear in a civilian population.

theocracy: a type of authoritarian system in which rule is exercised by religious clergy or other persons who rely largely on well-established religious law to govern.

theory: any well-reasoned argument about how a particular factor causes another one.

tied aid: aid granted to an LDC on the condition that the recipient uses it to purchase goods or services produced by the donor country.

totalitarian regime: a type of political regime in which the government makes extensive attempts to shape the goals, behavior, and thought of its citizens so that they actively support the government and its ideology.

trade liberalization: the lowering of a country's tariff and nontariff barriers to goods and services.

tragedy of the commons: exhaustion of a common resource because individuals who benefit from the resource have little incentive to use it sustainably.

transaction costs: the costs—other than the price of the good or service being exchanged—that are needed to make an exchange possible.

transparency: a condition that describes government processes when they follow well-established regulations and are open to scrutiny by outside observers.

transport costs: the price of moving goods and services to be exchanged over distances.

tropical disease: diseases that only exist in warm climates because the insect pests that carry them cannot survive or must hibernate during winter.

underdevelopment: for a society, the state of experiencing deprivations of basic material needs such as housing, food, water, health care, and education.

urbanization: the growth of areas of high population density via migration from rural areas to cities.

vaccine: treatments that make one immune to a certain disease.

Washington Consensus: nickname for the market-oriented policy agenda that neoclassical economists, the World Bank, and the International Monetary Fund recommended to developing world policymakers throughout the 1980s and 1990s.

welfare state: the part of government that seeks to promote or protect the well-being of its citizens by providing social services such as education, housing, water, and retirement pensions.

Westernization: the alleged convergence toward Western culture that occurs when a country becomes more economically prosperous.

women in development (WID): a body of thought among development scholars and practitioners (particularly ascendant in the 1970s and 1980s) that held that underdevelopment and development policy affect women differently than men and thus that women's issues need to be treated explicitly and separately in thinking about development.

World Bank: a major international financial institution whose primary function is to make soft loans to developing countries to fund development-related projects.

world systems theory (WST): a school of thought pioneered by Immanuel Wallerstein that views the world economy as a monolithic capitalist world system with a fully integrated division of labor and commodity chain that exploits individuals living in peripheral economies.

Image Credits

Index

About the Author

Andy Baker is an associate professor and former associate chair in the political science department at the University of Colorado at Boulder. He conducts research on Latin American politics, mass political behavior, and international political economy. His articles have appeared in a number of journals, including the *American Journal of Political Science*, the *Latin American Research Review,* and *World Politics.* His first book, *The Market and the Masses in Latin America,* published by Cambridge University Press in 2009, is about the nature and causes of citizens' attitudes toward free-market policies in eighteen Latin American nations. He lives with his wife and daughter in Boulder, Colorado.

SAGE researchmethods

The essential online tool for researchers from the world's leading methods publisher

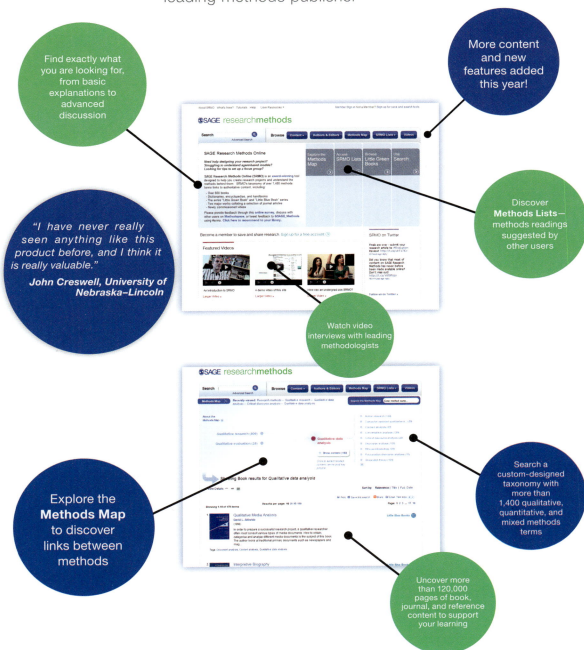

Find exactly what you are looking for, from basic explanations to advanced discussion

More content and new features added this year!

"I have never really seen anything like this product before, and I think it is really valuable."

John Creswell, University of Nebraska–Lincoln

Discover **Methods Lists**— methods readings suggested by other users

Watch video interviews with leading methodologists

Explore the **Methods Map** to discover links between methods

Search a custom-designed taxonomy with more than 1,400 qualitative, quantitative, and mixed methods terms

Uncover more than 120,000 pages of book, journal, and reference content to support your learning

Find out more at
www.sageresearchmethods.com